FORMAL SYNTAX

ACADEMIC PRESS RAPID MANUSCRIPT REPRODUCTION

Proceedings of the 1976 MSSB Irvine Conference on the Formal Syntax of Natural Language, June 9–11, 1976, Newport Beach, California

FORMAL SYNTAX

EDITED BY
PETER W. CULICOVER

School of Social Sciences
University of California
Irvine, California

THOMAS WASOW

Department of Linguistics
Stanford University
Stanford, California

ADRIAN AKMAJIAN

Committee on Linguistics
University of Arizona
Tucson, Arizona

ACADEMIC PRESS, INC.

New York   San Francisco   London   1977

A Subsidiary of Harcourt Brace Jovanovich, Publishers

ACADEMIC PRESS, INC.
111 Fifth Avenue, New York, New York 10003

United Kingdom Edition published by
ACADEMIC PRESS, INC. (LONDON) LTD.
24/28 Oval Road, London NW1

Library of Congress Cataloging in Publication Data

MSSB-UC Irvine Conference on the Formal Syntax of
        Natural Language, Newport Beach, Calif., 1976.
        Formal syntax.

        "Proceedings of the 1976 MSSB-UC Irvine Confer-
ence on the Formal Syntax of Natural Language,
June 9–11, 1976, Newport Beach, California."
        Bibliography: p.
        Includes index.
        1. Linguistics—Congresses.   2. Grammar, Com-
parative and general—Syntax—Congresses.   I. Culi-
cover, Peter W.   II. Wasow, Thomas.   III. Akmajian,
Adrian.   IV. Mathematical Social Science Board.
V. California. University, Irvine,   VI. Title.
P23.M25   1976   410   76-58854
ISBN 0-12-199240-3

CONTENTS

LIST OF PARTICIPANTS

Numbers in parentheses indicate the pages on which the authors' contributions begin.

ADRIAN AKMAJIAN (1, 427), Committee on Linguistics, University of Arizona, Tucson, Arizona

STEPHEN R. ANDERSON (361), Department of Linguistics, UCLA, Los Angeles, California

EMMON BACH (133), Department of Linguistics, University of Massachusetts, Amherst, Massachusetts

C. L. BAKER (61), Department of Linguistics, University of Texas, Austin, Texas

MICHAEL BRAME, Department of Linguistics, University of Washington, Seattle, Washington

JOAN BRESNAN (157), Department of Linguistics, M.I.T., Cambridge, Massachusetts

NOAM CHOMSKY (71), Department of Linguistics, M.I.T., Cambridge, Massachusetts

PETER W. CULICOVER (1, 7), School of Social Sciences, University of California, Irvine, California

JOSEPH EMONDS (239), Department of Linguistics, UCLA, Los Angeles, California

JAMES PAUL GEE (461), Department of Linguistics, Stanford University, Stanford, California

ALEX GROSU, Department of Linguistics, UCLA, Los Angeles, California

KENNETH HALE (379), Department of Linguistics, M.I.T., Cambridge, Massachusetts

HENRY HAMBURGER, School of Social Sciences, University of California, Irvine, California

ROBERT M. HARNISH, Department of Philosophy, University of Arizona, Tucson, Arizona

RAY JACKENDOFF (249), Department of English, Brandeis University, Waltham, Massachusetts

LAVERNE MASAYESVA JEANNE (379), Department of Linguistics, M.I.T., Cambridge, Massachusetts

RONALD KAPLAN, Xerox Corporation, White Plains, New York

ELLEN KAUFMAN, Department of Linguistics, University of New Mexico, Albuquerque, New Mexico

EDWARD KLIMA, Department of Linguistics, University of California, San Diego, California

WILL LEBEN, Department of Linguistics, Stanford University, Stanford, California

DAVID LIGHTFOOT (207), Department of Linguistics, McGill University, Toronto, Canada

JULIUS MORAVCSIK, Department of Philosophy, Stanford University, Stanford, California

JERRY MORGAN, Department of Linguistics, University of Illinois, Urbana, Illinois

RICHARD T. OEHRLE (317), Department of Linguistics, Stanford University, Stanford, California

BARBARA HALL PARTEE (197), Department of Linguistics, University of Massachusetts, Amherst, Massachusetts

STANLEY PETERS, Department of Linguistics, University of Texas, Austin, Texas

PAUL PLATERO (379), Department of Linguistics, M.I.T., Cambridge, Massachusetts

PAUL SCHACHTER, Department of Linguistics, UCLA, Los Angeles, California

ELISABETH SELKIRK (285), Department of Linguistics, University of Massachusetts, Amherst, Massachusetts

SUSAN STEELE (417), Committee on Linguistics, University of Arizona, Tucson, Arizona

JEAN-ROGER VERGNAUD, Department of Linguistics, University of Massachusetts, Amherst, Massachusetts

THOMAS WASOW (1, 327), Department of Linguistics, Stanford University, Stanford, California

KENNETH WEXLER (7), School of Social Sciences, University of California, Irvine, California

PREFACE

This volume presents the papers and formal comments prepared for the MSSB Irvine Conference on the Formal Syntax of Natural Language, held on June 9-11, 1976, at Newport Beach, California. Each paper was prepared in advance of the conference, and circulated to all of the participants. For each of the papers, one of the participants was invited to prepare a formal discussion, to be presented during the conference itself. After a short presentation by the author, his or her paper was discussed first by the commentator, and then by the participants in open discussion.

For various reasons it was decided that only the papers and the formal discussions prepared for the conference would appear in this volume, and no attempt to provide a summary of the open discussion has been made. Unfortunately, no written version of Edward Klima's discussion of Ray Jackendoff's paper could be prepared in time for inclusion in this volume. In some cases, questions that were raised in the discussions have since been answered in personal communications. We have encouraged discussants to leave those questions in their written versions, in order to encourage the authors to make their answers public.

ACKNOWLEDGMENTS

The material that appears here was prepared with the support of the National Science Foundation under grant No. SOC70-02316 AO4. The grant also provided Funding for the conference itself, for which the papers in this volume were prepared. We would like to express our gratitude to the National Science Foundation and the Mathematical Social Science Board for enabling us to bring together such a distinguished group.

Thanks are also due to Stan Peters and Duncan Luce for their sage advice; to Dean Christian Werner of the School of Social Sciences, University of California at Irvine, for making the resources of the School freely available to us; to Vivian Wayne for her assistance in organizing the conference and in preparing this manuscript; to Steven Weisler for doing the index; to Patrina Roman of the Newporter Inn in Newport Beach for providing us with facilities for the conference, and for attending to many of the logistical details.

Our deep thanks go also to the participants in the conference, whose good will and devotion to scientific inquiry made the event a very special one. We would like to thank particularly the contributors of the papers to the conference, who cheerfully and efficiently made their work available to the participants well before the conference began.

A NOTE ON FORMAL NOTATION

The reader will notice that no attempt has been made to regularize or standardize the formal notation used in the papers in this volume. As with current papers appearing in the standard journals, each paper in this volume specifies a formal notation and defines it as it is introduced. Thus, for example, in this volume certain authors will use the so-called "X-bar" notation with bars above symbols (e.g., $\overline{X}$), while others, for convenience, will have primes following symbols (e.g., X'). We have made no attempt to adopt any one particular usage, on the grounds that in current linguistics work a variety of notations are being used concurrently, and there is not yet any widespread or general agreement on what exactly constitutes the correct, or even the most convenient, formal notation for grammatical description.

INTRODUCTION

Peter W. Culicover
Thomas Wasow
Adrian Akmajian

Perhaps the most fundamental problem facing linguistic theory is that of accounting for the possibility of language acquisition. Chomsky (1972a) characterizes the problem as follows:

> A person who knows a language has mastered a system of rules that assigns sound and meaning in a definite way for an infinite class of possible sentences [p. 103] ... The child is presented with data, and he must inspect hypotheses (grammars) of a fairly restricted class to determine compatability with this data. Having selected a grammar of the predetermined class, he will then have a command of the language generated by this grammar [footnote omitted]. Thus he will know a great deal about phenomena to which he has never been exposed, and which are not "similar" or "analogous" in any well-defined sense to those to which he has been exposed ... This disparity between knowledge and experience is perhaps the most striking fact about human language. To account for it is the central problem of linguistic theory. [pp. 159-60]

Chomsky proposes that we approach this problem by seeking to limit the ways in which linguistic knowledge may in principle be affected by experience. That is, he suggests that "we must postulate a sufficiently rich internal structure . . .that constitutes [the child's] contribution to language acquisition" (1972a, pp. 158-9). The problem for linguistic theory, in other words, is to characterize as explicitly and precisely as possible the internal structure that makes language acquisition possible.

Over the past twenty years, transformational generative grammarians have attacked this problem in two stages. First, they have attempted to write detailed formal grammars for substantial fragments of natural languages. Second, they have tried to formulate general principles governing the form and organization of such grammars. The goal of this activity has been "to characterize a fairly narrow class of grammars that are available to the language learner; . . . in other words, . . to specify the notion 'human language' in a narrow and restrictive fashion" (Chomsky, 1972b, p. 67). In short, this line of research has been concerned with providing formal characterization of actual and—more importantly—possible human languages. Its central goal has therefore been to discover limits on the expressive power of the descriptive devices used in writing grammars, i.e., to provide formal constraints on linguistic theory. The work of Ross (1967), Chomsky (1973), and Emonds (1976) typifies this line of research.

The papers in this volume represent a number of approaches in this general domain that have developed over the past several years, and that promise to serve as central foci for research on linguistic theory in the next few years. Common to these approaches is what Hale et al. in this volume label "the autonomous systems view." According to this view, the grammar of a language is formulated in terms of the interaction of a number of distinct components, each formally characterizable as an independent system, subject to its own constraints and principles of organization. Several of the papers are explicitly concerned with identifying distinct classes of rules and formulating constraints on the form and functions of each class. All of the papers proceed from the premise that some such division into autonomous systems is both possible and desirable, though there is by no means agreement regarding where the boundaries between systems should be drawn.

The first four papers (Culicover and Wexler, Chomsky, Bresnan, and Lightfoot) are concerned with the problem of formulating appropriately restrictive constraints on the possible relations between elements of a phrase marker that are "involved" in rules of grammar. The next group of papers, (Jackendoff, Selkirk, and Wasow) investigate the sorts of constraints that can be imposed on the form of the components of grammar that provide the input to the transformational component, namely the base and the lexicon. The last two papers (Akmajian, and Hale et al.) concern themselves directly with the problem of autonomy: given complex data, how does one formulate a descriptively adequate grammar that nevertheless allows the autonomous system to be simple? This last question has been the source of much controversy in linguistics in recent years, and we will return to it below.

Culicover and Wexler seek to apply seriously the notion that the constraints on grammars delimit the class of grammars in such a way as to permit language learning to occur. They argue that through considering the problem of language learnability in abstract mathematical terms one can gain insight into the means by which the class of grammars available to the language learner may be sufficiently narrowed.

It is of some interest that there is empirical evidence in the grammar of English for the constraints that emerge from the learnability studies. While the learnability studies are suggestive and not predictive, the correspondence shown in the Culicover and Wexler paper points to the importance of formal language learnability theory as a step towards greater understanding of the organizing principles underlying the structure of human language.

Much the same point is made by Chomsky. He emphasizes that by restricting the class of grammars available to the language learner we can approach a solution to the fundamental problem of the possibility of language acquisition. One way such restriction might be achieved, he suggests, would be to cut down drastically on the possible transformations that a grammar might contain. More specifically, he proposes that the "core grammar" of English contains two transformations, *Wh*-movement and NP-movement. Both rules operate quite independently of context, the former moving a *Wh*-phrase into COMP, and the second, an NP into an unfilled NP node (as specified by Emonds' [1976] Structure-Preserving Hypothesis).

Chomsky then proceeds to investigate the consequences of this proposal, dealing in detail with two central problems. First, these rules will operate incorrectly in many cases, leading to massive "overgeneration," given that they operate free of context. Chomsky proposes that cases of overgeneration can be ruled out by rather general constraints on rules of "construal," provided that all movement transformations leave behind a "trace" of the sort proposed in Chomsky (1973, 1975b,c). Such a trace must be anaphorically bound by the moved constituent. There are independently motivated constraints on anaphora sensitive to the positions of the anaphoric element and its antecedents in derived structure. Chomsky suggests that movement of an NP (for example) to a position in the structure that yields ungrammaticality may be accounted for as a consequence of the fact that the NP is in a position such that it cannot be construed as anaphorically binding its trace.

The second problem is that there appear to be transformations that do not conform to the restrictive characterization proposed by Chomsky. In particular, it appears at first glance that there are more than two movement transformations, and that there are transformations that *delete* constituents over a variable. Chomsky attempts to show that this variety of transformation types is only apparent, and that all movement transformations (except NP-movement) and deletion transformations are in fact special cases of the very general rule of *Wh*-movement. The virtues of this sort of generalization are clear, since it would permit a severe restriction on the form of particular grammars. It would also provide a principled explanation for the fact that the derivation of the comparative construction, discussed in a number of papers by Bresnan (including the one in this volume) seems to display those characteristics that have usually been associated with movement transformations.

Bresnan's paper attacks this problem in a different way. In the first part of her paper she claims that it is in fact possible to have rules of grammar that perform deletion over a variable of unbounded length and offers a variety of arguments in support of this position and against Chomsky's proposal that comparatives are derived by a movement transformation.

In the second part of her paper Bresnan proposes a constraint on variables of unbounded length, which has the effect of blocking deletion or movement of a subject NP immediately to the right of a filled COMP. This constraint cannot be formulated as a constraint on variables if transformations that make crucial use of unbounded variables are ruled out by the theory. But, she argues, there does not appear to be an alternative account of the same phenomena in other terms; hence transformations must in fact be able to apply over unbounded variables. The question of whether or not a surface filter could be formulated that would account for the same phenomena engendered considerable debate during the discussion of Bresnan's paper at the conference, with no clear resolution of the issue. The third part of Bresnan's paper answers a number of objections raised by Chomsky to Bresnan's general approach.

Lightfoot's paper pursues in some detail the consequences of making various assumptions about the nature of the "inaudibilia" that appear in the literature of transformational grammar, including traces, dummies, PRO, and actual gaps. He also brings diachronic evidence to bear on some aspects of Chomsky's recent work, particularly the rule of NP-movement.

Jackendoff introduces a number of proposals concerning the proper form of the base component of a grammar, suggesting how the phrase structure rules for the English base can be formulated in such a way as to be consistent with these general principles. This serves as an introduction to Selkirk's paper, which tries to work out in detail a particular instantiation of the $\overline{X}$-notation in a way that is consistent with the principle proposed by Jackendoff, that grammatical relations generalize across categories and can be formulated in terms of various levels in the $\overline{X}$-notation.

Wasow's paper suggests a number of criteria for distinguishing structure-preserving transformations from relations among lexical entries. In a number of cases these criteria lead to the conclusion that a lexical relation and not a transformation relation is involved. A particularly interesting case is the passive construction, which, Wasow argues, is variously derived by a structure-preserving transformation, and by means of a relation in the lexicon.

Hale et al., and Akmajian concern themselves with the question of isolating the phenomena to be dealt with by an antonomous syntax. Akmajian is concerned with the question of what constitutes an "independent" syntactic analysis: that is, what does it mean to say that one can arrive at a "purely syntactic" (i.e., "formal") analysis of some grammatical construction without recourse to semantic evidence? Hale et al., arguing from facts from Hopi, Papago, and Navajo, show that apparent complexities of data can be dealt with in an interesting and revealing fashion if one restricts severely the sorts of conditions permitted on transformations, and relegates phenomena that might seem to require such conditions to other components of the linguistic description, e.g., pragmatics and phonology.

The common assumption of these papers, namely the autonomous systems view, has not gone unquestioned in recent years. For example, according to G. Lakoff (1974),

> Recent results indicate that the syntactic form sentences take is not independent of the meanings that they convey in context. In trying to account even for the distribution of morphemes, one must take into account not only the literal meaning of the sentence but also what you are communicating indirectly and how you are doing it; the function of the utterance in terms of communicative interaction cannot be ignored. One must consider both the expressive and communicative functions of language at the same time. (p. 178)

More generally, Postal (1972c) asserts that:

> ... given the same empirical base, on general grounds one must choose that theory which has the most restricted theoretical makeup. With respect to all competitors, such a theory must be held to be privileged, only to be abandoned in favor of some conceptually more complex alternative in the face of direct empirical evidence showing the need for such additions. (p. 137)

The crucial phrase here is "in the face of direct empirical evidence." Postal believes that any division of the grammar into components has to be directly observable in the data. On the contrary, the autonomous systems view holds that the character of the systems must be inferred in complex and indirect ways from the rather confusing data of natural language.

Nobody claims that it is clear pretheoretically where the boundaries should be drawn. Rather, the autonomous systems view constitutes a research strategy, and it can be justified and motivated to the extent that the research results that are derived under this guiding principle make interesting and correct predictions about the nature of language.

Any science is founded on certain idealizations. The legitimacy of such idealizations is measured by the fruitfulness of the theories they lead to. Insofar as an idealization contributes to advancing our understanding, it is a reasonable working hypothesis. The autonomous systems view is an idealization; thus, the question is not whether there are autonomous systems in some absolute sense, but rather whether the assumption that there are leads to significant insights into the nature of language.

It should be noted that the autonomous systems view is not universally accepted even on these terms. Indeed, G. Lakoff (1974) goes so far as to state:

> Perhaps the most interesting result to come out of transformational grammar is that . . . a limitation of the discipline is impossible—no coherent linguistic theory results from narrowing one's sights . . . This is an interesting result because it is not *a priori* true. In chemistry, for instance, there is a useful theory of ideal gases. It was thought that one might have been able to come up with a coherent theory of such a very limited domain in linguistics—"ideal grammar." The fact that the study of grammar ultimately had to take into account the study of meaning and use makes me wary of any artificial limitations of the domain of linguistics. (p. 151)

Not coincidentally, Lakoff also calls for less formal analyses: "At this time in history, a description of a language that adheres to some formal theory will not describe most of what is in the language . . . I think the time has come for a return to the tradition of informal description . . ." (Lakoff, 1974, p. 153).

The critical opinion of formal grammar expressed in this passage and the one quoted earlier is interesting, inasmuch as it harks back to a question which was posed from the very beginnings of transformational grammar. Chomsky (1957) put it this way:

> A great deal of effort has been expended in attempting to answer the question: "How can you construct a grammar with no appeal to meaning?" The question itself, however, is wrongly put, since the implication that obviously one can construct a grammar with appeal to meaning is totally unsupported . . . The question that should be raised is: "How can you construct a grammar?" (p. 93)

In his earlier work Chomsky tried to answer the second question raised here, offering a detailed set of formalisms for stating syntactic rules explicitly and precisely. He responded to critics who insisted that syntactic analysis must be based on semantics by pointing to the impressive collection of results his methods had achieved. "It is surely premature," he concluded, "to insist that the basis of linguistic theory be extended to include obscure and intuition-bound concepts, on the grounds that the clear notions of formal analysis are too weak and restricted to lead to interesting and illuminating results" (1955, p. 752).

As we approach the twentieth year following the publication of *Syntactic Structures*, critics of formal grammar are still questioning the legitimacy of the sorts of abstractions and idealizations that the autonomous systems view requires. The best response today, as it was then, is to exhibit the fruits of the research carried out within this framework. If analyses based on the autonomous systems view add significantly to our understanding of human language, then the research strategy which adopts that view is vindicated. We are convinced that it does, and that ours remains a viable approach to the study of language. We present these papers as evidence in support of this conviction.

SOME SYNTACTIC IMPLICATIONS OF A
THEORY OF LANGUAGE LEARNABILITY *

Peter W. Culicover
Kenneth Wexler

School of Social Sciences
University of California
Irvine, California

The Learnability Criterion

The question of how to choose a grammar for a language is, of course, an empirical one. Thus, the linguistic data would ideally determine the grammar (theory) that we choose. However, as has often been pointed out, it almost never happens in a serious science that the data uniquely determine a theory. Thus, in linguistics we are often faced with the question of which theory to choose when more than one is compatible with the available data. In this regard, Chomsky (1972b, p. 67) writes:

> The fundamental problem of linguistic theory, as I see it at least, is to account for the choice of a particular grammar, given the data available to the language learner. To account for this inductive leap, linguistic theory must try to characterize a fairly narrow class of grammars that are available to the language learner; it must, in other words, specify the notion "human language" in a narrow and restrictive fashion. A "better theory," then, is one that specifies the class of possible grammars so narrowly that some procedure of choice or evaluation can select a descriptively adequate grammar for each language from this class, within reasonable conditions of time and access to data. Given alternative linguistic theories that meet this condition, we might compare them in terms of general "simplicity" or other metatheoretic notions, but it is unlikely that such considerations will have any more significance within linguistics than they do in any other field. For the moment, the problem is to construct a general theory of language that is so richly structured and so restrictive in the conditions it imposes that, while meeting the conditon of descriptive adequacy, it can sufficiently narrow the class of possible grammars so that the problem of choice of grammar (and explanation, in some serious sense) can be approached.

Chomsky goes on to show how this problem (of achieving "explanatory adequacy") can be related to specific issues in linguistic theory. He shows, for example, that "complicating" linguistic theory by assuming that there are, say, two kinds of rules, phonological and transformational, is a step forward from a theory which "simply" assumes that there are rules. It is a step forward because it restricts the possible class of "sets of derivations" (that is, of languages), and thus, assuming that the condition of descriptive adequacy is met, it helps in the selection of a choice of grammar.

In this and a number of other cases that Chomsky discusses, the structure of the argument is that we are comparing two linguistic theories A and B, that is, two sets of definitions of kinds of rules and conditions for their application. If the class of sets of derivations allowed by B is a subset of the class of sets of derivations allowed by A, then we can say that B is a better theory than A (once again assuming that the condition of descriptive adequacy is met in both cases), since we have to reduce the class of sets of derivations until it is so small that it is learnable.

We will adopt the following terminology. A *language* is a set of derivations. Thus a class of languages is a class of sets of derivations. A linguistic theory defines a class of (possible) languages. If A is a linguistic theory, then let $K(A)$ be the class of languages it defines. To rephrase the structure of the argument that we are considering, we can say that for two linguistic theories A and B, if $K(A) \subseteq K(B)$, then A is preferable to B.

We must distinguish here between the general theoretical and methodological approach given in the quote cited above and the particular applications that have the argument structure that we have just given. We may interpret the general approach in the following way: we must ultimately find a theory that specifies a class of languages small enough such that each language is learnable. The particular argument, on the other hand, compares two theories to see which allows a smaller class of languages.

Obviously, the specific arguments do represent a step forward in the general problem since a class of languages cannot be easier to learn than any of its proper subsets. There are, however, two considerations that suggest that we might add other kinds of specific arguments in pursuit of the general goal. First, we want to be able to show at some point that we *do* have a learnable class of languages. Second, the form of argument given above is not universally applicable. In particular, it does not apply to cases where theory A and theory B both allow a descriptively adequate grammar of language L, but the subset criterion cannot be applied to A and B. That is, $L \in K(A)$ and $L \in K(B)$, but neither $K(A) \subseteq K(B)$ nor $K(B) \subseteq K(A)$.

Suppose that we had a definition of "learnable class of languages" explicit enough for us to determine for a given characterization of grammatical theory whether or not the class of languages that it allowed was learnable. Then we would have an approach to the first problem mentioned above (that of ultimately deciding whether or not a given class of languages was learnable). In some cases we might have an approach to the second problem as well: the question of how to choose between two descriptively adequate classes of languages that do not exhibit the subset relation. If it turned out that, say, theory A provided a learnable class of languages, and theory B did not, then, given that the condition of descriptive adequacy is met in both cases, clearly we would want to choose theory A.

In other words, the criterion of "learnability" can be useful in choosing between theories. Note that we are not suggesting that learnability is important to the linguist because we want to study the important psychological problem of the *course* of language acquisition, that is, ontogeny (although insight into this problem might result from learnability studies). Rather, we are suggesting that learnability can potentially play an important role in the linguistic problem of choosing the best grammatical theory.

In order to make this suggestion more concrete, we can consider an artificial example in which the criterion of learnability can be made to play the role suggested above. But first we need to define learnability. There are many issues of an empirical nature involved in this definition,[1] but for our purposes we can idealize away from many of these issues.[2] We can even ignore the sequential, input-by-input aspects of learning and return to the version of learnability presented in Chomsky's (1965) idealization of the problem.

Let us assume that $G = \{G_1, G_2 \ldots\}$ is a class of possible grammars. That is, the grammatical theory G can be looked upon as specifying what grammars can be grammars of natural languages. We imagine that the language learner is presented with a set D of "primary data" from exactly one of the languages $L(G_i)$, of one of the grammars G_i. Let $*L(G_i)$ be the set of sentences of $L(G_i)$. We will take the set D to be a finite set of grammatical sentences from $*L(G_i)$, that is $D \subseteq *L(G_i)$.[3] The problem that the language learner faces is to extrapolate from D to $*L(G_i)$. In general, we do not know how large D has to be, but we do know that it has to be finite, since no learner can have an infinite number of grammatical strings available as input.

The learner can be regarded as a function f from the class of sets of primary data into the class of grammars G. That is, for each set of primary data, the learner selects exactly one grammar out of the class of possible grammars. Since we do not know how large D must be, we say that f *learns* G_i if there exists *some* finite set of primary data D from G_i such that $f(D) = G_i$, and for every set of primary data D′ from G_i that includes D, that is $D \subseteq D′$, it is also the case that $f(D′) = G_i$. More simply, f learns G_i if there exists a finite $D \subseteq *L(G_i)$ such that for all finite $D′ \supseteq D$, $f(D′) = G_i$. In other words, not only does the learner pick the correct grammar based upon a particular set of primary data, but additional data will not change the choice.

We have defined the notion, the function f learns grammar G_i. Now we extend this notion in the natural way by saying that the function f learns the *class* of grammars G if f learns G_i for every $G_i \in G$. If a function exists that learns G, then we say that G is *learnable*.[4]

For an artificial illustration of the notion of learnability, consider grammars defined in the following way. Let S be the usual initial symbol of a context-free grammar, let other capital letters be nonterminal symbols and let small letters be terminal symbols or words. Let G_1 contain the rules $S \rightarrow aA$, $A \rightarrow aA$, and $A \rightarrow a$. G_2 contains the rules $S \rightarrow aaA$, $A \rightarrow aA$, and $A \rightarrow a$. In general, G_i contains the rules $S \rightarrow a^i A$, $A \rightarrow aA$, and $A \rightarrow a$. It is easy to see that $*L(G_i) = \{a^{i+1}, a^{i+2}, a^{i+3}, \ldots\}$. In other words $*L(G_i)$ contains all sequences of a's of length at least $i + 1$. We can also add to the set the grammar G_0 which contains the rules $S \rightarrow aA$, $A \rightarrow a$ and $S \rightarrow a$, so that $*L(G_0) = \{a, aa, aaa, \ldots\}$. The class of grammars is $G = \{G_0, G_1, G_2, \ldots\}$.

We can show that G is a learnable class of grammars. The function f that learns G simply selects the grammar that generates the smallest set of strings compatible with the data D. It does this by finding the shortest string in D and mapping D into the grammar that generates the language with that string as the shortest string. In other words, if a^{i+1} is the shortest string in D, then $f(D) = G_i$. Thus, if data from *$L(G_i)$ is being presented, any D which includes a^{i+1} will be such that $f(D) = G_i$ and for any $D' \supseteq D$, $f(D') = G_i$. Therefore G_i is learnable by f for any G_i. Thus G is learnable.

For an artificial class of grammars H that is not learnable, we will construct grammars H_i that generate the following languages *$L(H_i)$.

$$*L(H_1) = \left\{ a \right\}$$
$$*L(H_2) = \left\{ a, aa \right\}$$
$$*L(H_3) = \left\{ a, aa, aaa \right\}$$
$$\vdots$$

That is, *$L(H_i)$ includes the i shortest strings on the word a. We also include *$L(H_0) = \left\{ a, aa, aaa, ... \right\}$, the set of all strings on a. There are many ways, of course, of choosing the grammars of *$L(H_i)$. Let us choose the rules $S \rightarrow a, S \rightarrow aa, ..., S \rightarrow a^i$ for H_i, $i > 0$, and for H_0, the rules $S \rightarrow aS$ and $S \rightarrow a$.

The class H = $\left\{ H_0, H_1, ... \right\}$ is unlearnable. The intuition behind the proof is that for any finite set of data D (a set of strings on a), the function could choose either one of infinitely many finite languages, or it could choose H_0, which generates the infinite language. If the function always chooses finite languages, then when data from *$L(H_0)$ is presented, the function will never choose H_0 as it must if H were learnable. If, on the other hand, the function f consistently chooses the grammar for the infinite language H_0, then it will never be correct when data from one of the other, finite languages is presented. There is no way of rectifying this situation.[5] Note that it is incorrect to say that selecting H_0 causes no harm because its set of strings includes all the others. We would not accept a grammar for English that generated a superset of English.

It is not the "infiniteness" of H_0 that is the problem here, for the class G is learnable, although it contains an infinite number of infinite languages (or rather, grammars that generate infinite languages). Rather, it has to do with the particular spread of these grammars, the question of how their languages relate to one another.[6]

We will now construct an artificial example which will show how learnability considerations can discriminate between theories, both of which allow a descriptively adequate grammar for a language, but which are not bound by the subset relation. Suppose that a linguistic theory T says that all grammars are of the following form. Each grammar has exactly one rule of the form $S \rightarrow a^n A$, for some $n = 0, 1, 2, ...$. That is, a grammar might contain $S \rightarrow aA$, or it might contain $S \rightarrow aaA$ or $S \rightarrow aaaA$, and so on. Each grammar also contains the rules $A \rightarrow aA$ and $A \rightarrow a$. Thus a grammar containing the rule $S \rightarrow a^n A$ will generate all strings of a's of length $n+1$ or greater. In addition, a grammar may contain any finite number of rules of the form

$S \to a^i$, $i = 1, 2, \ldots$. In order to rule out ambiguous strings in a grammar, we could assume that if a grammar contains the rule $S \to a^n A$, then it contains no rule of the form $S \to a^i$ where $i \geq n+1$. For simplicity, we will make this assumption, although it is not crucial to the argument.

The set of languages generated by the linguistic theory T includes just those languages that for some integer n have all strings of length n or greater, plus possibly some strings of length less than n. This class is not learnable.[7]

Suppose now that we are studying a particular language L in order to determine its grammar. We note that for the most part the pattern is explainable by T. In particular, all strings of a's of length greater than or equal to three are in L. Also the string *aa is not grammatical, so that the grammar must contain the rule $S \to a^i A$, for some i 2. However, there is one anomaly. Whereas, according to the theory T, the language could have the string a or not (i.e., a or *a is possible), instead, the language contains the string ba. There are no other strings in the language, that is, the linguist decides that L = { $ba, aaa, aaaa, aaaaa, \ldots$ } .[8]

Since L is not allowed by T, clearly a change has to be made in T. But what change is to be made? We can consider two alternatives. In the first alternative, A, we decide that the grammar G for L contains the rules $S \to aA$, $A \to aA$, and $A \to a$, but none of the other rules allowed by T. However, we add a universal constraint to T, namely that, in any structure of the form

b must substitute for A and move to the front of the phrase marker to yield

(Note that this "constraint" will apply to exactly one phrase marker of each language.) Thus in this language

$$\begin{array}{c} S \\ /\backslash \\ a \quad A \\ | \\ a \end{array} \quad \text{becomes} \quad \begin{array}{c} S \\ /\backslash \\ b \quad a \end{array} \quad . \text{Thus}$$

the string aa in L becomes ba, and the universal constraint allows L to be generated. Notice that in every language there will now be exactly one string which conatins b, and we can interpret this situation as if this element had not been noticed before and thus not incorporated into linguistic theory.[9]

In adopting Alternative B we take a different approach. We also postulate the addition of a universal principle, but the principle is different. In every language there is a rule that obligatorily places b before the shortest string. Then for L we assume that the phrase structure rules are $S \to a$, $S \to aaA$, $A \to aA$, and $A \to a$. This set meets the conditions of theory T and the universal principle changes the string a into ba, thus generating language L.

Thus we are faced with two conflicting theories T_A and T_B, both of which allow language L.[10] How are we to choose between them? Note that the class of languages which T_A allows is not a subset of the class which T_B allows. Nor does T_B allow a subset of the class that T_A allows. That is, the theories are incommensurate according to the subset criterion. It thus appears that the only way to proceed is to appeal only to descriptive adequacy by looking at languages other than L.

But closer examination shows that this is not the case. Namely, we can show that T_A is to be preferred to T_B. The reason for this is that T_A is learnable, whereas T_B is not learnable. The artificial examples, of course, have been constructed so as to allow just this result. In T_A, the item b can be used to "code" the n such that the grammar contains the rule $S \rightarrow a^n A$. Thus when the learner is presented with a set of primary data D, which includes the string ba^n, he can assume that the rule $A \rightarrow a^n A$ is part of the grammar. The only other rules that have to be added are some rules of the form $S \rightarrow a^i$, for $i \leq n$. Since there are a finite number of such strings, they can be learned by memorization. Thus T_A specifies a learnable class of grammars. T_B, on the other hand, does not specify a learnable class of grammars. This result follows from the application of Theorem 1 in Wexler and Hamburger (1973) to the class of grammars generated by T_B.

Thus, short of further descriptive evidence, we have one theory that is learnable and one that is not. That is, although the classes of grammars are not commensurate by the inclusion relation, nevertheless, one provides a sufficient "scattering" of values of grammars compatible with fixed data, while the other does not.[11] Thus we would choose Theory T_A (once again, assuming no further descriptive evidence).[12]

Note that there are many languages that are allowed by both T_A and T_B. An interpretation of this situation would be that both theories allowed all existing natural languages. Thus the learnability criterion would tell us to prefer T_A to T_B even though no descriptive evidence (or the subset criterion) could distinguish the theories.

The Role of Constraints in a Theory of Learnability

We turn now from artificial grammars to see how these conceptual possibilities can be made to play a role in the analysis of natural language. In particular a set of constraints allowing us to prove that the class of transformational components is learnable will be discussed. The class T of transformational components satisfying these constraints is not necessarily a subset of other classes of components that have been proposed. Thus T would not receive any support from the subset criterion. Nevertheless, it seems reasonable to us, in accordance with our preceding argument, that, assuming descriptive adequacy, T should be preferred for reasons of explanatory adequacy over any class of components that cannot be shown to be learnable.[13]

In order to be able to describe how these particular constraints can be made to restrict transformational components in such a way that they can be learned, a very brief sketch of the assumptions will be necessary. We idealize the "learner" L as an abstract device that discretely takes in data about the language (that is, one datum is presented at each time $t = 1, 2, 3, \ldots$). At each time the learner L produces a "guess" or "hypothesis" as to which grammar is the source of the data. The data, of course, all come from one language. This language is generated by a grammar that is a member of the allowed class of grammars. We make the clearly falsifiable assumption that there is a universal syntactic context-free base component and that all grammars in the allowed class are definable by a finite set of grammatical transformations on the universal base. For a suggestion of how to weaken this universal base hypothesis and yet still retain learnability, see Wexler and Culicover (1974).[14]

What is the nature of the data presented to L? We assume that each datum is of the form (b,s) where b is a syntactic deep structure, that is, a phrase marker generated by the base rules, and s is the corresponding surface string derived from b by the transformational component. The rationale for this form of data presentation is a linguistic theory that incorporates a form of the Katz-Postal hypothesis that semantic interpretation is definable on deep structures. The assumption is that the learner L is presented with sentences in well-defined situations, where his cognitive theory (or theory of use) will allow him to derive the meaning of the sentence and from the meaning the deep structure.[15] Each datum is a (b,s) pair of this form. The data are presented in no particular order, but no pair may be systematically excluded. In particular, each pair has a nonzero probability of appearing at any given time.

Thus the task for the learner L will be to construct a finite set of transformations T, which account for all of the infinitely many possible (b,s) pairs. We assume a particular procedure P that L uses to construct his hypotheses. The procedure P makes hypotheses about the grammar, adding or discarding at most one transformation at each time, based on the grammar hypothesized at the last time and the new datum. We have proved (Hamburger and Wexler, 1975) that this procedure P succeeds in the sense of convergence with probability one. That is, for any number n between 0 and 1, there is a time t such that the probability is greater than n (and less than or equal to 1, of course) that the grammar that procedure P guesses at time t will generate the correct language. That is, this grammar will be either the correct grammar (that is, the grammar from which the data has been chosen) or another grammar that generates exactly the same—infinitely many—(b,s) pairs).

The proof consists essentially of two parts.[16] The first part is the demonstration that if the learner L's transformational component is not absolutely correct, that is if L's component maps some base phrase marker b into the wrong surface string s, then there is another phrase marker b' which is small (that is, b' is of degree less than some predetermined finite bound U) such that L's component also makes a mistake on b'. (The "degree" of a phrase marker is its depth of S-embedding.) In other words, if L's transformational component is not yet correct, then the smallest phrase marker on which it makes a mistake cannot be arbitrarily large. We will call this result BDE (for "boundedness of degree of error"). The second part of the proof demonstrates that at any time, and for any hypothesized transformational component, the learner L always has a chance, with probability greater than a bound greater than zero, of hypothesizing the correct component on the next appropriate sequence of data. The second part of the proof depends on the first, since we have to prove that if L's transformational component is not correct, then the probability of making an error is greater than a positive nonzero bound. This result follows from the first part.

It is the first part of the proof that is relevant here, because it is that part that depends crucially (and only) on the grammatical framework, whereas the second part depends on the learning procedure and on the result of the first part. What is important for the concept of explanatory adequacy, as we have described it here, is that in order to prove the first result (BDE), it is necessary to make special assumptions about the class of grammars, in particular to assume specific constraints on transformations. The Binary Principle and the Freezing Principle are two crucial constraints. In the next section we will offer linguistic evidence for these principles. Here we will try to offer an expository account of the role they play in the proof of BDE.

The Binary Principle says that when a transformation T applies at a cyclic node, the structural description of T may not apply (except for variables), to any node in the phrase marker not in the cycle at which T is applying or a cycle immediately below that one. It is called the "Binary" Principle because transformations may analyze only to a depth of two cycles. The Binary Principle is identical to Chomsky's (1973) Subjacency Condition.[17] What is important to notice is that the principles were proposed independently and for different reasons. The Binary Principle was proposed in order for BDE to be provable, and not for reasons of descriptive adequacy of grammars. That is, no syntactic data was used in its justification, except of course, for the not very strong fact that it seemed compatible with many transformations. In fact, it was proposed for learnability reasons against what seemed to be the syntactic evidence, because it was obvious that the transformation of *Wh* Fronting could apply more than two cycles down, as in (1).

(1) *Who did John think that Bill wanted Sylvia to suggest that Julia marry?*

At the time, the successive-cyclic analysis of *Wh* Fronting was unknown (at least to the developers of the Binary Principle). The Subjacency Principle, on the other hand, was justified by Chomsky (1973) in terms of syntactic data. Of course, at the same time, it contributed to explanatory adequacy in the subset sense, that is, the sense in which the class of languages with the Binary Principle is a subset of the class of languages with or without the Binary Principle. On the other hand, if another theory is proposed in which the Binary Principle is not assumed (and, of course, the relevant data explained in some other way) then, as explained before, the subset criterion may not be able to distinguish the two theories.

The Binary Principle is necessary for the proof of BDE in a straightforward way. Suppose that the Binary Principle were not true of the class of grammars. Then there is no bound on the minimal degree of phrase marker to which a given transformation T is applicable. Thus it is always possible for the learner L not to have learned the grammar. In other words, L can make a mistake on a datum and map a base phrase marker *b* into the wrong surface string *s*. This follows because L has not learned T, that is, T is not part of L's transformational component. But, assuming that the rest of L's transformational component is identical with the rest of the correct transformational component, the minimal phrase marker on which L makes a mistake is at least of degree equal to the minimal phrase marker to which T applies. But since the phrase marker of minimal degree to which T applies is of arbitrary (i.e., unbounded) degree, the minimal phrase marker on which L makes a mistake is of arbitrary degree. Thus we cannot derive BDE.

As an artificial example, suppose S is the only cyclic node and let S→AB and B→S be rules of the grammar. For any integer n, define a transformation T_n (obligatory) as follows:

T_n: Structural Description: A - A - ... - A - X - B
                              1   2 n $n+1$ $n+2$
       Structural Change: $n+2$ 2 ... n $n+1$ ϕ .

In other words, T_n moves B to the beginning of the phrase marker, provided that there are at least n As in the phrase marker. Consider the class of transformational components on this context-free base. For simplicity assume that all transformations apply only at the root.[18] There is no finite bound U over components such that if a component is not the correct one it must make a mistake on a datum of degree less than U. That is BDE is false of this class of components since if T_n is the only transformation in the correct component and the learner has assumed so far that there are no transformations in the correct component, then the smallest degree phrase marker on which the learner makes a mistake is the smallest phrase marker to which T_n applies. This phrase marker is of degree n, since if T_n applies to a phrase marker P, P must contain at least n As. This can only happen for this grammar if there are at least n Ss, that is if P is of degree n. But since the correct component may consist of a single T_n for any n, it may be that for any n the smallest phrase marker on which a component makes an error is n. Thus BDE does not hold.

If, on the other hand, the Binary Principle was assumed to apply to this grammar, then for any n larger than 2, T_n could never apply to any phrase marker. Thus the learner will never have to hypothesize any T_n except T_1 or T_2. Thus if the learner has a mistaken component, there must be some phrase marker of degree at most 2 on which the component is mistaken. Thus BDE holds. Note that an essential contribution of the Binary Principle is to make many potential transformations impossible, in the sense that there is no phrase marker to which they will ever apply. Thus there is no datum for which it would ever be reasonable for the learner to hypothesize such impossible transformations.

One might think that the Binary Principle would be *sufficient* to allow BDE to be derived. That is, since no transformation may analyze more deeply than two Ss down, there should be an error on a phrase marker of degree 2 or less, if there is any error at all. But this argument is mistaken, since it ignores the possibility that transformations may themselves create new structures that may be analyzed by transformations. Thus a transformation may not apply to any base phrase marker (or none of sufficiently low degree) but may apply to some phrase-marker that has been derived from a base phrase marker of (possibly arbitrarily) high degree. Thus BDE can be false, even with the Binary Principle. In particular, raising transformations may create new structures to which transformations may apply, which could not have applied had the raising transformations not applied.

Suppose, for an artificial example, that the base grammar consists of the rules $S \rightarrow AC$, $A \rightarrow B$, and $C \rightarrow \left\{ {S \atop D} \right\}$. Then we can derive a base phrase marker like P in (2).

(2)   P:

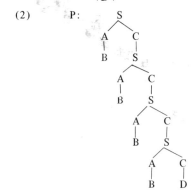

Now suppose that the transformational component can contain a transformation like

T: Structural Description: B A C
                                  1 2 3
        Structural Change: 2+1 ϕ 3

(where "+" indicates sister adjunction). In this example, we assume that transformations are cyclic.

What T does is to raise an A and sister-adjoin it to a B. Since the sister adjunction takes place under an A, when the operation repeats itself on the next cycle, raising the higher A, an extra B goes with it.[19] Thus after T has applied cyclically to P, we obtain the derived phrase marker P', in (3),[20]

(3)   P':

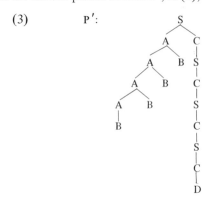

Notice that in P' there are four Bs at the beginning of the phrase marker. Thus a transformation T_4 whose structural description was B B B B X C could apply to P' (perhaps moving C to the front). Notice that the four Bs are all in the top S cycle of P', so that even the Binary Principle cannot prevent T from applying. If the learner's component does not contain T_4, then the component may make a mistake on the phrase marker P, which is of degree 4, but it may not make a mistake on any phrase marker of lower degree. The important point is that the raising transformation T may keep applying to larger phrase markers, thus bringing an arbitrarily long string of Bs to the front of the phrase marker, all of them in the matrix cycle of the derived phrase marker. Thus a correct component can have, for any n, a transformation T_n which applies only to phrase markers with a string of n (or more) Bs at the beginning of the phrase marker. But these phrase markers will be of degree at least n. Thus if a learner's transformational component has all the correct transformations except T_n, the smallest phrase marker on which it makes an error will be of degree n. But since n is arbitrarily large, the smallest phrase marker on which L's component makes an error will be arbitrarily large, and thus BDE will not hold.

The crucial point here is that transformations have created new structures that allow other transformations to apply that otherwise could never apply. This can be ruled out by assumption. The Freezing Principle states that no transformation may apply to any node under a frozen node, where a frozen node is one which does not immediately dominate a base structure. More formally, we can take the following definition from Wexler, Culicover, and Hamburger (1975):

> For nodes A and B in a phrase marker we have the notion A *dominates* B, where the root (i.e., the highest S-node) dominates all other nodes. We mean *strictly* dominate, so that A does not dominate A. If A dominates B and there is no node C so that A dominates C and C dominates B, then we say A *immediately* dominates B. The *immediate structure* of A is the sub-phrase marker consisting of A, the nodes $A_1 \ldots A_n$ that A immediately dominates, in order, and the connecting branches. The immediate structure of A is a *base immediate structure* if $A \rightarrow A_1 \ldots A_n$ is a base rule: otherwise it is non-base.

> **Definition:**

> If the immediate structure of a node in a derived phrase marker is non-base then that node is *frozen*.

We can then state the

> **Freezing Principle:**

> If a node X of a phrase marker is *frozen*, then no node which X dominates may be analyzed by a transformation.

> Note that no node which X dominates may be analyzed, not just the nodes which X immediately dominates. Also note that by this definition, since X does not dominate X, if X is frozen, it may itself be analyzed by a transformation (unless some Y which dominates X is also frozen).

> **Notation:**

> A box around a node X in a phrase marker P, i.e., $\boxed{X}$, indicates that X is frozen.

Notice how the Freezing Principle applies to the last example. First, since A→A B is not a base rule, after the transformation T applies at the most deeply embedded S at which it can apply, the higher node A is frozen. The three lower Ss are shown in (4), after T has applied.

(4)

Nevertheless, since no node dominating this A is frozen, T can again apply. In fact, P' can be derived in (3). However, the highest A in (3) will be frozen, again since A→A B is not a base rule. Thus when we try to apply T_n (for example T_4) at the top of (3) we will not be able to, since we cannot analyze under the top A to see if there are four Bs there. Thus the Freezing Principle, by allowing only base structures to be fit by transformations, together with the Binary Principle, will help to insure that BDE holds.[21] Once again, note that the effect of the constraint is to make many transformations impossible, namely those which never apply to a base structure.[22]

These examples have been intended to show how the Binary Principle and Freezing Principle play a crucial role in the theory of learnability. Thus we hypothesize that they are part of the innate capacity for language learning that the child brings to his task. The next step is to provide descriptive linguistic evidence that these constraints are correct, a task to which we now turn. While the basic notions behind these constraints appear fairly well-established by their role in the learnability proofs, their precise formulation is open to continued investigation and refinement, as is their application to the analysis of natural language phenomena.

The Freezing Principle

Let us consider first the rule of Complex NP Shift, stated approximately below.[23]

Complex NP Shift: X   V   NP   Y
                     1   2   3   4 ⇒ 1 2 ϕ 4 + 3
                     Condition: 3 is "complex."

This familiar transformation derives the (b) sentences below from the underlying structures corresponding to the (a) sentences.

(5)   a.   *Fred sent a box filled with chocolates to the chef.*
        b.   *Fred sent to the chef a box filled with chocolates.*

(6)   a.   *The government trades commodities which are of great value to*
                us to the competition.
        b.   *The government trades to the competition commodities which*
                are of great value to us. .

(7)   a.   *Frodo sold the painting which he had found for a nickel.*
        b.   *Frodo sold for a nickel the painting which he had found.*

We postulate that the position into which the NP is moved by Complex NP Shift is not one which it could occupy in the base, that is, only rule A is assumed to be a rule of the base component of English.[24]

$$A: \quad VP \rightarrow V \quad NP \quad PP$$
$$B: \quad VP \rightarrow V \quad PP \quad NP$$

This assumption is consistent with the formulation of the rule of Complex NP Shift as a transformation in the first place. Complex NP Shift captures the generalization that a complex NP can move to the end of the VP regardless of what follows it in underlying structure.[25]

The output of Complex NP Shift is a frozen structure. We illustrate this in (8) by placing a box around the frozen node.

(8)

Thus, by the Freezing Principle, VP is not analyzable by later transformations. The following examples, which involve Tough Movement, *Wh* Fronting, and Topicalization show that this is correct.[26]

(9)   a.   *It is easy to sell* $\left\{ \begin{array}{l} \textit{pictures stolen in Europe to Bill.} \\ \textit{to Bill pictures stolen in Europe.} \end{array} \right\}$

        b.   *Bill is easy to sell* $\left\{ \begin{array}{l} \textit{pictures stolen in Europe to } \phi . \\ \textit{*to } \phi \textit{ pictures stolen in Europe.} \end{array} \right\}$

(10)   a.   *We accused* $\left\{ \begin{array}{l} \textit{the man recently elected President of high crimes.} \\ \textit{of high crimes the man recently elected President.} \end{array} \right\}$

        b.   *Which crimes did you accuse* $\left\{ \begin{array}{l} \textit{the man recently elected} \\ \quad \textit{President of } \phi. \\ \textit{*of } \phi \textit{ the man recently elected} \\ \quad \textit{President.} \end{array} \right\}$

(11)   a.   *Susan bought* $\left\{ \begin{array}{l} \textit{a coat made of rabbit fur for Fido.} \\ \textit{for Fido a coat made of rabbit fur.} \end{array} \right\}$

        b.   *Fido, Susan bought* $\left\{ \begin{array}{l} \textit{a coat made of rabbit fur for } \phi. \\ \textit{*for } \phi \textit{ a coat made of rabbit fur.} \end{array} \right\}$

The frozenness of the VP obtains even if the complex NP has been moved over a constituent other than a PP, as the following examples illustrate.[27]

(12) a. *I discouraged* $\left\{ \begin{array}{l} \textit{the young soldier who had a short leave} \\ \textit{from visiting Sylvia.} \\ \textit{from visiting Sylvia the young soldier who} \\ \textit{had a short leave.}[28] \end{array} \right\}$

      b. *Which place did you discourage* $\left\{ \begin{array}{l} \textit{the young soldier who had a} \\ \textit{short leave from visiting} \; \phi. \\ \textit{*from visiting} \; \phi \; \textit{the young} \\ \textit{soldier who had a short leave?} \end{array} \right\}$

(13) a. *John believes* $\left\{ \begin{array}{l} \textit{the man in the gray suit to have stolen a fortune.} \\ \textit{to have stolen a fortune the man in the gray suit.} \end{array} \right\}$

      b. *How much does John believe* $\left\{ \begin{array}{l} \textit{the man in the gray suit to have} \\ \textit{stolen} \; \phi? \\ \textit{*to have stolen} \; \phi \; \textit{the man in} \\ \textit{the gray suit?} \end{array} \right\}$

(14) a. *Susan finds* $\left\{ \begin{array}{l} \textit{the students who are failing to be very eager for} \\ \textit{more homework.} \\ \textit{to be very eager for more homework the students} \\ \textit{who are failing.} \end{array} \right\}$

      b. *How eager does Susan find* $\left\{ \begin{array}{l} \textit{?the students who are failing to} \\ \textit{be} \; \phi \; \textit{for more homework?} \\ \textit{*to be} \; \phi \; \textit{for more homework the} \\ \textit{students who are failing?} \end{array} \right\}$

      c. *How much more homework* $\left\{ \begin{array}{l} \textit{the students who are failing to be} \\ \textit{eager for} \; \phi? \\ \textit{*to be eager for} \; \phi \; \textit{the students} \\ \textit{who are failing?} \end{array} \right\}$
          does Susan find

The frozenness of the VP correctly predicts the impossibility of applying Gapping after Complex NP Shift has applied. Example (15a), in which Complex NP Shift has not applied, is given for purposes of comparison.

(15) a. *John gave the book which he bought to Susan, and Fred gave the magazine which he stole to Sam.*

      b. *John gave to Susan the book which he bought, and Fred gave to Sam the magazine which he stole.*

      c. *John gave the book which he bought to Susan, and Fred, the magazine which he stole to Sam.*

      d. **John gave to Susan the book which he bought, and Fred, to Sam, the magazine which he stole.*

While it has been claimed (cf. Stillings, 1975) that Gapping cannot apply when there is more than one constituent following the gapped verb, we find examples like (15c) acceptable, even when they are shortened by removal of the relative clause.

(16)   *John gave the book to Susan, and Fred, the magazine to Sam.*

Example (16) is certainly far better than the corresponding example when Dative has applied—

(17)   **John gave Susan the book, and Fred, Sam the magazine.*

—a point to which we will return in our discussion of the Dative below.

As a final observation about the frozenness of VPs to which Complex NP Shift has applied, we note that it is also impossible to extract a constituent of the moved NP.[29]

(18)   a.   **What did you sell to Fred a beautiful and expensive painting of ϕ?*
        b.   **Who did you tell to the members of the club strange stories about ϕ ?*
        c.   **How many of the children did Fred send to the School Board accurate reports on ϕ ?*
        d.   **Who was there hanging on the wall a beautiful picture of ϕ ?*

This is predicted by our analysis, since the complex NP is dominated by a frozen node after application of Complex NP Shift.

Interestingly, examples which are similar to those in (18), but which are derived not by Complex NP Shift but by Dative, are far more acceptable.

(19)   a.   *What did you sell Fred a beautiful and expenisve painting of ϕ ?*
        b.   *Who did you tell the members of the club strange stories about ϕ ?*
        c.   *How many of the children did Fred send the School Board accurate reports on ϕ ?*

This may account for the fact that some speakers judge certain examples of the sort given in (18) acceptable. We find the difference fairly sharp, however; the following analysis of the Dative appears to account for the difference quite nicely.

To begin, we note that Complex NP Shift cannot move the indirect object after Dative has applied, as first noted by Ross (1967).

(20)   a.   *I gave the man at the desk ten dollars.*
        b.   **I gave ten dollars the man at the desk.*

(21)   a.   *The IRS sent the recently elected President an invitation to an audit.*
        b.   **The IRS sent an invitation to an audit the recently elected President.*

In contrast, the *direct* object may be moved by Complex NP Shift after Dative has applied.

(22)   a.   *I gave my brother $\left\{ \begin{array}{l} \textit{yesterday for his birthday} \\ \textit{for safekeeping} \end{array} \right\}$ the ten dollars which I owed him.*
        b.   *The IRS sent the recently elected President last week an invitation to an audit.*

Let us suppose that the impossibility of moving the indirect object after Dative has applied is due to the Freezing Principle: the indirect object is dominated by a frozen node in derived structure (while the direct object is not). Such a state of affairs would arise if Dative applied as illustrated in (23).

(23)

```
      V P                          V P
     /  \                         /  \
   / |    \                      /    \
  V  NP    PP         ⇒         V      NP
          /  \                 / \
         P    NP              V   NP
```

The indirect object, NP_2, is Chomsky-adjoined to V_0. The node V_* is therefore a frozen node, given the absence of a base rule of the form V V NP. The direct object, NP_1, is not dominated by a frozen node, and hence it is subject to later transformations. The examples in (22) show that Complex NP Shift may apply to this NP, while the examples cited earlier in (19) and those that follow illustrate that the direct object may be analyzed by *Wh* Fronting after Dative has applied.

(24) a. *What did you sell Fred?*
    b. *These figures are important to show the President.*
    c. *These books are the only things I would give Mary.*

The differentiation of NP_1 and NP_2 with respect to freezing is reflected in all other movement transformations except Passive. Examples such as the following were noted by Kuroda (1969) and have also been discussed by Fillmore (1965), and Jackendoff and Culicover (1971).

(25) a. **Who did you sell a dozen shovels?*
    b. **This is the woman who Mary gave the last copy of the book.*
    c. **Susan is tough to loan expensive jewels.*

(26) a. *How many shovels did you sell Mary?*
    b. *This is the book that Mary gave that woman.*
    c. *Expensive jewels are tough to loan Susan.*

In each case the NP dominated by the frozen node does not move, as predicted.[30, 31]

We turn now to consider the proper interpretation of the role of the Freezing Principle at a node from which an immediate constituent has been removed. The strongest form of the definition of a frozen node does not distinguish between ways in which non-base-structures may arise; a weaker form that might have some plausibility states that only non-base-structures which arise by attachment are frozen. It may in fact be possible to prove learnability with this weaker definition, given that the learnability proof sketched in the introduction to this paper relies heavily on restricting analyzability after attachment.[32]

Let us bring to bear some empirical considerations. We would like to investigate what happens in terms of the Freezing Principle when a constituent of a node is moved away from it. Some common movement rules of English are Tough Movement and *Wh* Fronting. If Tough Movement gives rise to a frozen node at the point of extraction, nothing else will be moveable from beneath that node.

This state of affairs appears to be reflected exactly by some data cited by Kuno and Robinson (1972), which they attribute to Berman: It is far preferable to move the *wh*-word from the PP–position in the VP, than to move the *wh*-word from the direct object position, when Tough Movement also applies.

(27)   a.   *Which violin is this sonata easy to play φ on φ?*
       b.   **What is this violin easy to play φ on φ?*

(28)   a.   *This is the knife that the salami is easy to cut φ with φ.*
       b.   **This is the salami that the knife is easy to cut φ with φ.*

(29)   a.   *Which closet is Fred easy to push φ into φ?*
       b.   **Who is the closet easy to push φ into?*

and so on.

A look at the structure shown in (30) will reveal that the ungrammatical examples above arise when Tough Movement applies to NP$_2$ in the PP. We know that Tough Movement must precede *Wh* Fronting because of the cyclic principle and the specifications of S and S' as cyclic nodes. This leads to the hypothesis that Tough Movement freezes the VP that dominates NP$_1$ and PP, so that later *Wh* Fronting of NP$_1$ is impossible.

(30)

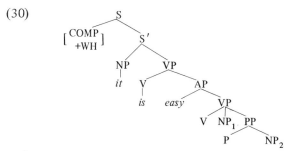

On the other hand, Tough Movement of the direct object does not freeze the VP, since *Wh* Fronting can later apply to the PP, as the (a) examples above illustrate. Hence in order to apply the Freezing Principle here we will have to show that movement of the object of the prepositional phrase is non-structure-preserving up to the VP.

A solution suggested in Culicover and Wexler (1973b) is that the movement of NP$_2$ by Tough Movement results in a nonbranching PP, which prunes, yielding the frozen structure of (31).

(31)

$$\boxed{VP}$$
$$V \quad NP \quad P$$

In order to make this analysis work we need a theory of pruning that will tell us when a nonbranching node should and should not be pruned. It is clear that a non-branching node should not be pruned if it is generated in the base, since all structures containing intransitive verbs would be frozen, as shown in (32).

(32)

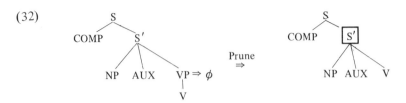

By the same token, pruning should not apply when the nonbranching node could have been nonbranching in deep structure; otherwise the derivation in (32) would occur when *Wh* Fronting applies to a direct object. This is impossible, since Inversion must analyze the S' after *Wh* Fronting and could not if the S' were frozen.[33]

Note that the difference cannot be attributed to *Wh* Fronting, since Tough Movement also does not cause freezing when the direct object is moved.

(33)   a.   *How easy will John be to please?*

        b.

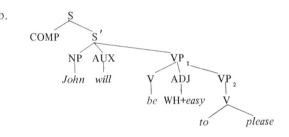

If VP$_2$ were to prune, VP$_1$ would be frozen, and the WH+*easy* would not be moveable on the S–cycle.

What this leads to is the principle that only frozen nodes are pruned when they fail to branch. That is, if A dominates only B, and if A
|
B

cannot be a deep structure configuration, then A prunes. It also entails that Tough Movement does not leave a syntactically significant dummy behind (or that dummies are ignored where pruning is concerned). And it must be shown independently, of course, that PP →P is not a rule of the base.

We cannot investigate the principle of pruning in detail here, and merely adopt it provisionally in order to permit the rest of the analysis to be presented and abandoned. We will later also abandon pruning. As far as the existence in the base of a rule PP → P is concerned, Emonds (1972a) has argued that there is in fact such a rule. We will summarize his arguments below, but first we will give another illustration of why we might wish to freeze the VP by Tough Movement.

Recall from our discussion of the interaction of Complex NP Shift and *Wh* Fronting that the former freezes the VP, so that the latter cannot apply. A typical example is (34).

(34)   *Who did John give to φ the beer which we found in the yard?

Complex NP Shift will also block Tough Movement, as the following examples show.

(35)   a.   *Mary is easy to give to φ the beer which we found in the yard.

       b.   *Harry is tough to shell with φ peanuts that we buy in New York.

       c.   *Oscar is nice to play on φ tricks that we learned in France.

It was unnecessary for us to consider the case where Wh Fronting precedes Complex NP Shift, because of the cycle and the assumption that S and S' are both cyclic nodes. However, this will not work in the case of Complex NP Shift and Tough Movement, since the two rules apparently apply at the same cycle.[34]

If Tough Movement freezes the VP, it will block Complex NP Shift.

(36)

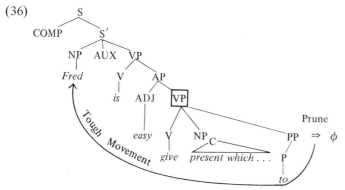

This is automatically predicted by the analysis we are entertaining, and requires no assumptions about pruning freezing or PPs beyond those we have already adopted.

Let us return to the question of whether there is a base rule of the form PP→ P. Emonds (1972a) has presented a number of arguments that particles are in fact intransitive prepositions. Since this is a crucial point, we will summarize his arguments briefly. Most of the examples are Emonds' or are based on his.

1)   Verbs such as put, sneak requires PP-complements or particles.

(37)
John put the books { *φ. / away. / in the closet. }

George was sneaking the salami { *φ. / in. / out. / into the room. }

2)   Only prepositional phrases and particles may be modified by right.

(38) John came right $\left\{\begin{array}{l} \textit{in.} \\ \textit{into the room.} \end{array}\right\}$

      Bill put the spices right $\left\{\begin{array}{l} \textit{on.} \\ \textit{on the meat.} \end{array}\right\}$

      *Fred is right angry.
      *We right left.
      *I fell right hard.
      *Mary left right early.

   3) Prepositional phrases and particles participate in the construction of the type illustrated below.

(39) *Off with his head!*
      Down with the leadership!
      Away with them!

      Into the dungeon with that traitor!
      To the river with those sandbags!
      Out the door with it!

   4) Prepositional phrases and particles can be preposed, and after having been preposed they constitute the environment for postponing a nonpronominal subject NP.

(40) $\left\{\begin{array}{l} \textit{Into the house} \\ \textit{In} \end{array}\right\}$ $\left\{\begin{array}{l} \textit{he ran.} \\ \textit{*ran he.} \end{array}\right\}$

      $\left\{\begin{array}{l} \textit{Down the stairs} \\ \textit{Down} \end{array}\right\}$ $\left\{\begin{array}{l} \textit{walked the commander.} \\ \textit{the commander walked.} \end{array}\right\}$

   Emonds cites only one exception to the generalization between PPs and particles, which is that the latter may not appear in focus position in cleft sentences.

(41) $\text{It was} \left\{ \begin{array}{l} \left\{\begin{array}{l} \textit{*up} \\ \textit{up the tree} \end{array}\right\} \textit{that she climbed.} \\[2ex] \left\{\begin{array}{l} \textit{*in} \\ \textit{into the house} \end{array}\right\} \textit{that Mary ran.} \\[2ex] \left\{\begin{array}{l} \textit{*out} \\ \textit{out of the house} \end{array}\right\} \textit{that I tossed the food.} \end{array} \right\}$

Since it is not certain what determines whether a given constituent may appear in this position, this exception does not in itself constitute a refutation of the generalization noted by Emonds.[35]
   What we have, now, is a choice between competing interpretations of the original data cited by Kuno and Robinson (1972). If the data are to be explained by the Freezing Principle, it is also necessary to freeze nodes from which extraction has occurred, and a general pruning convention will be required also. Then PP→P cannot be a base rule. If, on the other hand, we wish to attribute the data to some

other source, then *Wh* Fronting and Tough Movement *cannot* freeze the VP, assuming that the Freezing Principle is correct. Hence we will need another explanation for why Complex NP Shift cannot apply after Tough Movement.

Note now that the Freezing Principle analysis predicts that, in cases where the VP immediately dominates two or more prepositional phrases, extraction from either one would block extraction from the other. This follows if extraction from a PP freezes the node immediately dominating it.

(42)   a.

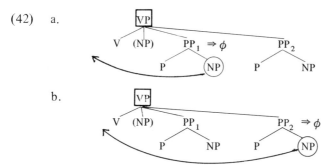

       b.

However, data corresponding to this situation do not support the prediction. The examples given below seem to follow the Kuno and Robinson (1972) account, in that the crucial variable is whether the extracted constituents line up in the opposite order to their original order in the VP.

(43)   a.   *It is tough to drive to Chicago with Susan.*

Susan is tough to drive $\left\{ \begin{matrix} to\ Chicago\ with\ \phi\ . \\ with\ \phi\ to\ Chicago. \end{matrix} \right\}$

Which city is Susan tough to drive $\left\{ \begin{matrix} with\ \phi\ to\ \phi\ ? \\ *to\ \phi\ with\ \phi\ ? \end{matrix} \right\}$

Chicago is tough to drive $\left\{ \begin{matrix} to\ \phi\ with\ Susan. \\ with\ Susan\ to\ \phi\ . \end{matrix} \right\}$

Who is Chicago tough to drive $\left\{ \begin{matrix} to\ \phi\ with\ \phi\ ? \\ *with\ \phi\ to\ \phi? \end{matrix} \right\}$

(44)   a.   *It is pleasant to talk to George about linguistics.*

Linguistics is pleasant to talk $\left\{ \begin{matrix} to\ George\ about\ \phi. \\ about\ \phi\ to\ George. \end{matrix} \right\}$

Who is linguistics pleasant to talk $\left\{ \begin{matrix} *to\ \phi\ about\ \phi\ ? \\ about\ \phi\ to\ \phi\ ? \end{matrix} \right\}$

George is pleasant to talk $\left\{ \begin{matrix} *to\ \phi\ about\ \phi? \\ about\ \phi\ to\ \phi? \end{matrix} \right\}$

What is George pleasant to talk $\left\{ \begin{matrix} to\ \phi\ about\ linguistics. \\ about\ linguistics\ to\ \phi. \end{matrix} \right\}$

Examples in which the PPs are separated from the verb also might display the difference, but somewhat less radically (perhaps because of their greater complexity).

(45)   a.   *It is easy to push Fred into the closet with a broom.*
        b.   *Which broom is the closet easy to push Fred into with?*
        c.   **Which closet is the broom easy to push Fred into with?*

The evidence suggests, then, that Tough Movement does not freeze the VP, for if it did, none of the examples in (43)–(45) in which Tough Movement has applied should be grammatical. [36]

This leads us to conclude that the Freezing Principle is not the proper account of the Kuno and Robinson data. Thus we abandon pruning. To maintain both pruning and the Freezing Principle would commit us to counterfactual predictions.

However, it should be noted that there is a plausible alternative that will allow us to keep pruning and the Freezing Principle together. This alternative involves leaving behind syntactically real, dummy nodes by those deletion or extraction transformations for which pruning is not appropriate for empirical reasons. This would guarantee that the node at which the deletion or extraction transformation had applied would have the same structure before and after application of the transformation, making the transformation structure-preserving. The empirical difference between this proposal and the one above is that in the case where the constituent is actually removed, the node can be frozen in principle. When a dummy is left behind, it is not. This is illustrated in (46).

(46)   Removal:

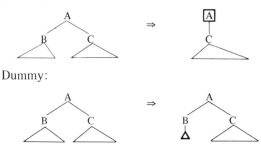

        Dummy:

There is some evidence that suggests that the correct position is that pruning does not apply to a frozen nonbranching node. We will show that there is a transformation that deletes one constituent of a binary branching structure with the consequence that the resulting structure is frozen. No freezing would be predicted if pruning applied.

The transformation in question is the one which deletes the preposition *on* before temporal NPs, sometimes obligatorily. [37]

(47)   a.   *I intend to fly to Europe (on) Tuesday.*
        b.   *We all go to basketball games (on) Tuesday evenings.*
        c.   *George caught a cold (*on) yesterday.*
        d.   *Things are getting tough (*on) these days.*
        e.   *Mary plans to retire (*on) next year.*
        etc.

For those cases where *on* is impossible it does not appear that there is any other acceptable preposition.

One might suppose that there is no rule deleting the preposition in these cases, but rather that there is an expansion of ADV as NP_{TEMP}. While this might appear plausible at first, the behavior of this NP with respect to transformations that move NP cannot be accounted for easily if it is adopted. The data point towards a deletion analysis in which the Freezing Principle plays an important role.

Consider first the rule of Tough Movement. While it is not always absolutely felicitous to apply Tough Movement to a temporal NP, there is clearly a difference in acceptability when the preposition is not present.

(48)   a.   *It is tough to find a handball court (on) Tuesday afternoon.*

     b.   *Tuesday afternoon is tough to find a handball court* $\left\{ \begin{array}{l} {}^*\phi \ . \\ on. \end{array} \right\}$

(49)   a.   *It is fun to go to the beach (on) weekdays.*

     b.   *Weekdays are fun to go to the beach* $\left\{ \begin{array}{l} {}^*\phi \ . \\ on. \end{array} \right\}$

We can block the ungrammatical (b) sentences by the Freezing Principle, given that the absence of the preposition is due to a non-structure-preserving deletion transformation.

(50)

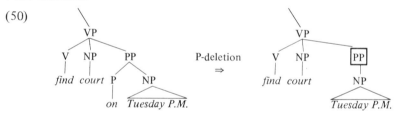

The frozen PP cannot be analyzed by Tough Movement.

There are two ways to block Tough Movement from applying *before* preposition deletion and deriving the ungrammatical examples in (48)–(49). If we assume that all nodes are cyclic (see notes 26 and 34) then preposition deletion will always precede Tough Movement. Or it may be that the structural description of preposition deletion requires that there be an NP following the preposition.

This analysis gives exactly the right results with respect to Passive as well. It is well known that Passive cannot apply in case a verb without a complement is followed by a temporal NP.

(51)   a.   *Our cat doesn't eat Tuesdays.*
     b.   **Tuesdays isn't eaten by our cat.*

(52)   a.   *Fred never woke up yesterday morning.*
     b.   **Yesterday morning was never woken up by Fred.*

(53)   a.   *Susan and Bill are marrying next week.*
     b.   **Next week is being married by Susan and Bill.*

Yet there is no natural way of blocking Passive in these cases, since the sequence
...V NP... of the (a) sentences here satisfies the structural description. This is
quite parallel, in fact, to the state of affairs noted by Chomsky (1973) in regard to
Raising. Chomsky shows that Passive will automatically apply to the subject of a
complement S, and in fact it would be a complication of the rule to restrict it to
direct objects only. The Raising data suggest that such a complication should be
avoided on empirical grounds.

In this case, restricting Passive to only sequential information appears to give the
wrong results. However, if the temporal NP is dominated by a frozen PP, as we
propose, then Passive cannot apply even though the sequence of constituents
apprears to satisfy the rule.

It is important to point out that this analysis will not work if we employ the
pruning convention. The output structure of the VP after pruning in a sentence like
(52a) would be that of a transitive verb; hence the VP would not be frozen; and
both Passive and Tough Movement could apply, contrary to the evidence we have
presented. This is illustrated below.

(54)

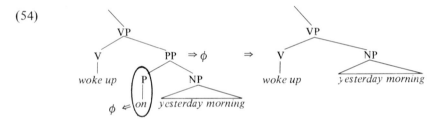

There are at least two potential problems that we can see with this analysis. First,
it turns out that the deletion of P does not block *Wh* Fronting or Topicalization.

(55)   a.   *Tuesday I intend to fly to Europe.*
       b.   *What day do you expect to visit Rome?*
       c.   *Tuesday evenings we all go to basketball games.*
       d.   *Next year I'm going to quit this business for good.*
       e.   *These days things are getting quite tough.*
       f.   *How many weekends did you visit Capri?*

This is not really a problem, however, because neither rule actually has to analyze
the PP. Topicalization involves movement of the topic constituent, and by definition
frozen constituents may be moved. *Wh* Fronting is somewhat more complicated,
since it applies to a constituent that has the feature [+WH]. However, it has often
been claimed that a PP that dominates a [+WH]-marked constituent automatically
receives the feature [+WH] also, and this device will account for the fact that *Wh*
Fronting applies after the preposition has been deleted from the temporal PP.
Topicalization, on the other hand, will just need to analyze the PP-node, but not
the structure it dominates.

The second problem is that there is an analysis of NPs of the form *yesterday's decision* that derives them from underlying *the decision P yesterday*. If it is shown that the derivation relies on prior deletion of *on*, then of course the Freezing Principle will incorrectly block it. If, on the other hand, an alternative source can be found, then deletion of *on* in such cases will have no effect on the derivation of the possessive.

While it is difficult to make clear judgements, it does appear to us that NPs such as those given in (56) are paraphrased by those in (57).

(56)   *yesterday's activities*
         each day's failures
         several day's journey
         next week's show
         last year's weather

(57)   *the activities of yesterday*
         the failures of each day
         the journey of several days
         the show of next week
         the weather of last year

In fact, some of the NPs in (56) do not have a source with *on* in place of *of*. While in some cases this may be idiomatic, in some it appears to be ruled out on semantic grounds.

(58)   **the activities on yesterday*
         **the failures on each day*
         **the journey on several days*
         **the show on next week.*
         **the weather on last year.*

We conclude, therefore, that this is not a true problem with the analysis.

Finally, to reiterate a point made earlier, this analysis presumes that it is in principle possible to actually delete a constituent. We make crucial use here of the strong version of freezing, which operates as a condition on phrase markers and not as a function of certain types of transformations.

The Binary Principle

Let us turn now to a different domain of syntax that bears equally crucially on the correctness of the form of the constraints arrived at in the learnability studies. We will investigate the consequences of applying the Binary Principle somewhat more extensively than was orginally proposed by Chomsky (1973) in his discussion of the Subjacency Condition. (As we noted in the introductory portion of this paper, the original Binary Principle is formally equivalent to the Subjacency

Condition. However, we will reformulate the Binary Principle in such a way that there are some differences between it and the Subjacency Condition.)

At the risk of ignoring a number of important problems we will begin by limiting ourselves to what we believe are the central issues that are addressed by Chomsky's (1973) analysis or that emerge from it. We ignore here, too, the criticism of the Subjacency Condition in Bresnan (1975; 1976a), where it is shown that if Comparative Deletion is a deletion transformation, something other than the Subjacency Condition is required. We believe that there might be a way out of Bresnan's argument, but the question is too involved to enter into here.[39]

In the original formulation of the Binary Principle, it was assumed that only S-nodes were cyclic. The Principle stated that in the structure

with transformations applying at S_0, no transformation could analyze (i.e., involve) any node dominated by S_2. However, Jackendoff (1972), Chomsky (1973), and Akmajian (1975) have argued that NP is also a cyclic node. We can generalize the Binary Principle to apply to all cyclic nodes if we assume that in a structure

where each B_i is a cyclic node, and with transformations applying at B_0, then no transformation may apply to a node dominated by B_2.

Note that in this sense cyclic nodes have two properties. First, they define the properties of the transformational cycle, since transformations "apply at" cyclic nodes. Second, they count in the Binary Principle.[40]

Since we have assumed that there is no extrinsic ordering of transformations, the data force us to assume that transformations can apply not only at S and NP, but also at S′ (for examples, see notes 26 and 34). Thus if we were to maintain the requirement that both properties were determined by the same set of nodes we would also have to count S′ in the Binary Principle. An alternative is to follow the suggestion of note 34 and to allow all nodes to be cyclic with respect to the properties of the transformational cycle, but to have a specified subset of nodes count in the application of the Binary Principle. A third alternative is to have two different subsets of nodes, one to count for each of the two properties. We will not pursue the differences between these analyses, but will simply assume that all transformations cycle on S′.

We may formulate the basic problem as follows: given that the domain of a transformation does not extend beyond the next "cycle" down, how does one define "cycle" so that the greatest number of restrictions on extractability are accounted for? We will call a node that counts in the application of the Binary Principle a "B-cyclic" node.

S' As a B-cyclic Node

We will begin with an argument that S' is a B-cyclic node. First notice that Extraposition of a sentential subject may apply at the S'-level of the phrase marker.

(59)

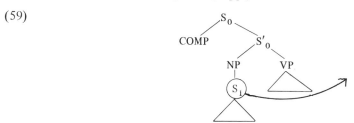

Assume that S' is *not* a B-cyclic node. Since NP and S are B-cyclic nodes, we must formulate the Binary Principle so that a transformation applying at S'_0 may analyze at least as far down into the phrase marker as the node S_1. More generally a transformation applying at S' must be able to "count down" to the second cyclic node dominated by S'.

But, as Chomsky (1973) observes, Passive must be constrained from moving the subject of a tensed S. E.g.,

(60)   a.   *Fred believed (that) Mary was rich.*
       b.   **Mary was believed that ϕ was rich by Fred.*

As is clear from the following tree, Passive applies at S'_0. The moved NP_1 in (61) is dominated by the cyclic node S_1, and no other cyclic nodes which S'_0 dominates.

(61)

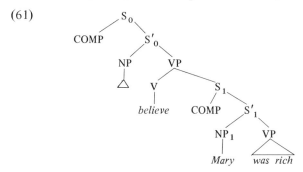

Thus, according to the Binary Principle as we have just formulated it, the ungrammatical (60b) will not be ruled out.

We can apply the Binary Principle correctly, however, if we assume that S' is a B-cyclic node. Given this, the Passive transformation applying at S'_0 can count down through the B-cyclic node S_1 to the B-cyclic node S'_1, but no further. Thus (60b) will be ungrammatical.

In contrast, suppose we analyze infinitives of a certain kind not as S-constituents, but only as S'-constituents, following Bresnan (1972). The sentence (62a) below would then have the structure illustrated in (63).

(62) a. *Fred believed Mary to be rich.*
      b. *Mary was believed to be rich by Fred.*

(63)

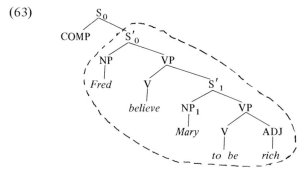

The dotted line indicates the scope of a transformation applying at S'_0 as restricted by the Binary Principle. Note that now Passive applying at S'_0 can count down through the B-cyclic node S'_1 to the B-cyclic node NP_1. This accounts for the fact noted by Chomsky (1973) that (62b) is grammatical, while (60b) is not. This lets us do without the Tensed S Condition of Chomsky (1973) for the cases involving the Passive. In the following discussion we will provisionally assume that S, S', and NP are B-cyclic nodes.

Another phenomenon that has often been pointed out is that it is impossible to extract a constituent of a subject. This restriction follows from our formulation of the Binary Principle when the subject is nominal, as the following shows.

(64)   **Who did a story about amaze you?*

(65)

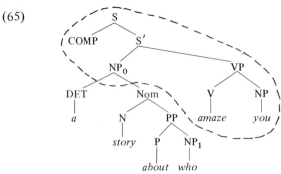

Since COMP is part of the structural description of *Wh* Fronting, the transformation must apply at the S-cycle. Therefore, the domain of *Wh* Fronting cannot extend beyond NP_0, according to the Binary Principle. Counting down two cyclic nodes from S takes us through S' to NP_0, but no further. Thus *Wh* Fronting may not apply to NP_1, and (64) is ungrammatical.[41]

It is also well known that it is possible to extract constitutents of object NPs in certain cases. E.g.,

(66)   *Who did John buy a picture of?*

As (67) shows, the grammatical (66) will be ruled out in precisely the same way that the ungrammatical (64) is ruled out.

(67)

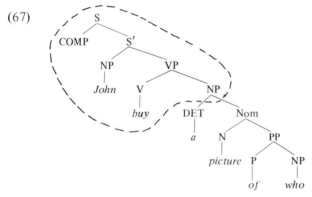

One possibility available to us here is that the rule of Extraposition of PP applies at the S'-cycle to restructure the phrase marker without altering the order of constituents. Note that in the output structure in (68), the extraposed PP is within the domain of *Wh* Fronting on the S-cycle.

(68)

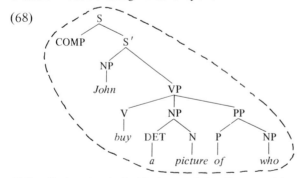

(66) will then be derivable by applying Extraposition of PP and then *Wh* Fronting. It is not unreasonable to suppose that the derived structure in (68) is a possible base structure. Thus the Freezing Principle will not prevent *Wh* Fronting from applying to (68).[42]

The Binary Principle as we have formulated it will block extraction from a sentential subject in exactly the same way as it blocks extraction from a nominal

subject. Examples such as those given in (69) were used by Ross (1967) as evidence
for the Sentential Subject Constraint, and by Chomsky (1964) as evidence for the
A-over-A Principle.

(69)   *Who would for Mary to marry φ bother Sam?
            *Who is that Fred is dating φ obvious?

(70)   Who would it bother Sam for Mary to marry φ ?
            Who is it obvious that Fred is dating φ ?

(71)

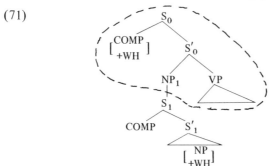

Of course, *Wh* Fronting can apply indefinitely far down into a phrase marker,
yielding examples of the following sort.

(72)   *Who did John believe that Mary claimed that Fred has seen φ ?*

If *Wh* Fronting could only apply at the root, such examples would be ruled out by
the Binary Principle. But we can adopt here Chomsky's (1973) successive cyclic
analysis of *Wh* Fronting, in which the *wh*-constituent is moved into the COMP of
the lowest S that dominates it, and is moved into the COMPs of higher cycles at
successive applications of the transformational cycle.

Thus, in order to derive (73)–

(73)   *Who does John believe that Mary married φ ?*

–*who* moves into $COMP_1$ on the S_1 cycle, and into $COMP_0$ on the S_0 cycle.

(74)

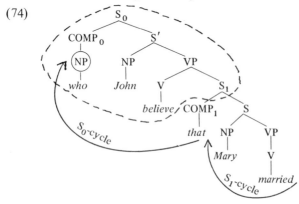

There is a problem, however: on the S_0-cycle, the domain of *Wh* Fronting includes S_1, but not $COMP_1$. Thus the Binary Principle would prevent (73) from being derived. To avoid this problem we will make the assumption that when an S-node is within the domain of a transformation (as specified by the Binary Principle), the COMP immediately dominated by that S is also within the domain of the transformation.[43] Notice that this convention does *not* permit extraction out of sentential subjects if sentential subjects are dominated by NP, as in (69).

The one serious problem that we can see with this analysis is that it does not allow us to extract constituents of deeply embedded infinitives. If we maintain the assumptions that S' is a B-cyclic node and that the infinitival structure lacks a COMP, then the Binary Principle as we have formulated it will block derivation of examples like that given in (75).

(75)   *Who did Mary believe Fred to have expected George to have*
         believed Sam to have visited ϕ?

Recall our motivation for assuming that there is no COMP in these infinitives: it accounts for the difference between tensed Ss and infinitives with respect to the Passive transformation.

One possible solution is obvious, but unacceptable if one adopts the position of Chomsky (1973) that there is no rule of Raising. If we raised each subject NP and pruned each nonbranching S' we would arrive at a structure that would contain only two B-cyclic nodes, all of the rest having been pruned.

(76)

It does not appear that there is any independent evidence for a rule of Raising[44] and, we have argued, pruning will give us the wrong results in a theory that employs the Freezing Principle.

Another possibility would be to assume a COMP in every infinitive. This would permit a successive cyclic analysis of *Wh* Fronting, but would rule out use of the Binary Principle to account for the difference between tensed S and infinitives.[45]

A third possibility is that the output structure in (76) is actually an underlying structure. This is something that we cannot seriously investigate here, due to the enormous problems it would raise elsewhere in the grammar: it would be necessary either to complicate cyclic rules like Passive, Tough Movement, and Raising to Subject, or to derive the outputs of these rules in the base as well. To the extent that either of these can be accomplished we might be able to abandon the underlying S'-infinitive.

The least disruptive solution, but one which at the same time gives the appearance of being ad hoc, is to define a string of successive S'-nodes as a single B-cyclic domain. We will demonstrate that this can be accomplished indirectly by a slight reformulation of the Binary Principle. Furthermore, this new version of the Binary Principle appears to account for a wider range of phenomena than the version we have been entertaining up to now.

The issue that faces us in deciding how to formulate the Binary Principle is the question of what to count. We saw this in our decision to count S', and the subsequent problem this raises. Intuitively, we would wish not to count S', because of the apparent accessibility of constituents of deeply embedded infinitives. Our reformulation takes us back to the earlier definition (and that of Chomsky, 1973) of S and NP as B-cyclic nodes. What we must also change, as a consequence, is the method of counting.

Suppose the transformational cycle is operating at a given node. Starting from this node, we move down a path in the phrase marker. Any transition to a B-cyclic node or from a B-cyclic node counts for the Binary Principle. The principle is that we may move along a path just as long as the count is less than two. When the count becomes two, the node just reached is the lowest node in that path to which a transformation may apply. Recall that S and NP are now the only B-cyclic nodes.

Let us consider an example.

(77)

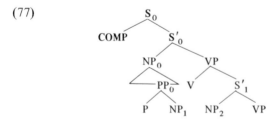

Suppose we are cycling on S'_0. A transformation applying at this level may apply to PP_0 (e.g., Extraposition of PP) since the path from S'_0 to NP_0 counts as one transition, and from NP_0 to PP_0 counts as the second. A transformation applying at this level may also apply to NP_2 (e.g., Tough Movement or Passive), or to an immediate constituent of NP_2.

At S_0, we may apply transformations to NP_0, since counting down from S_0 to S'_0 counts as one transition, and counting down to NP_0 counts as the second. Note that we cannot apply a transformation to a constituent of NP_0 at this level. We may apply a transformation at this level to NP_2, however, since the path through S'_0 to S'_1 does not contain any transitions from or to a B-cyclic node.

To take another example, consider (78).

(78)

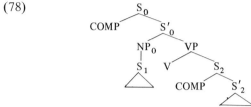

Again, at S'_0 we may apply a transformation to a constituent of NP_0, e.g., Extraposition of S_1. However, we may not apply a transformation at this level to a constituent of S'_2, since the transitions to and from S_2 will restrict transformations from going below this node. This will account for the failure of, e.g., Passive to apply to the subject of a tensed S or any other S with a complementizer.

This reformulation of the Binary Principle will capture all of the data that we have considered thus far. As we have already indicated, Passive will be applicable to the subject of an infinitive, but not to the subject of a tensed S. (See example (60).) At the S'-cycle, transformations such as Extraposition of PP and Extraposition may apply to constituents of a subject NP.[46] At the S-cycle, extraction transformations such as *Wh* Fronting will not be applicable to constituents of either nominal or sentential subjects. (See examples (64), (69).) As previously, in order to apply *Wh* Fronting successive cyclically out of *that*-complements, it will be necessary to specify that when an S is the lowest node in a path that may be analyzed, the COMP attached to this S may also be analyzed.[47] Finally, this reformulation of the Binary Principle permits extraction of constituents from indefinitely far down in a sequence of S'-infinitives, as the tree in (79) illustrates. Note that the first transition is from S_0 to S'_0, and the second transition is from VP_2 to NP_3.

(79)

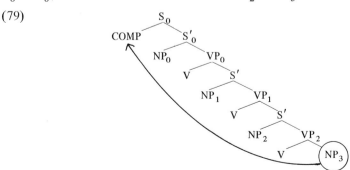

Our reformulation of the Binary Principle will also permit us to capture the Left Branch Condition which was adopted by Ross (1967) to block application of *Wh* Fronting to interrogative possessives and adjectival phrases that were constituents of noun phrases. E.g.,

(80)   a.   *Whose books do you want to buy ϕ ?*
            *Whose do you want to buy [ϕ books] ?

       b.   *How nice a person is Fred?*
            *How nice is Fred [ϕ a person] ?

and so on. As the following tree shows, our original formulation of the Binary Principle will block these incorrect applications of *Wh* Fronting, since *Wh* Fronting applies only on the S-cycle.

(81)

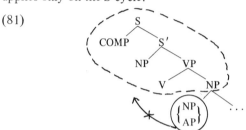

However, as has been pointed out to us by several people, a rule which applies at S', such as Passive or Tough Movement, will not be blocked by this version of the constraint. Some examples that illustrate this are given in (82).

(82)   a.   *John intimidated Fred's brother.*
            Fred's brother was intimidated by John.
            *Fred('s) was intimidated [ϕ brother] by John.

       b.   *It is tough to please Mary's mother.*
            Mary's mother is tough to please.
            *Mary('s) is tough to please [ϕ mother].

(83)

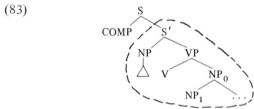

(83) illustrates the fact that NP_1 falls within the scope of a transformation applying at S', given the earlier formulation of the Binary Principle.

In our new formulation of the Binary Principle, NP_1 will not be accessible to a transformation applying at S' provided that it is dominated by a node other than NP_0. A candidate for such a node is not difficult to find, since it has long been assumed in the literature that the possessive NP is dominated by a determiner node DET, as shown in (84).

(84)

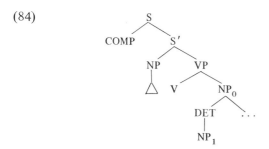

Transition from VP to NP_0 counts as one, and from NP_0 to DET counts as the second. Hence NP_1 could not undergo a transformation applying at S', by this formulation of the Binary Principle.

We turn now to further substantiation of the fact that S' cannot count as a B-cyclic node when there is a string of infinitives in the phrase marker. Our argument involves once again the rule of Tough Movement.

It appears, first of all, that Tough Movement contains a variable between each pair of terms in the structural description. Between *it* and the element governing the rule there may be an AUX, perhaps negation and adverbs, or nothing at all.

(85)
$$\textit{Cabernet Sauvignon} \begin{Bmatrix} \textit{may not be} \\ \textit{has been} \\ \textit{will definitely be} \\ \textit{used to be} \end{Bmatrix} \textit{difficult to find for under \$4.00.}$$

(86)   *I expect Cabernet Sauvignon (not) to be difficult to find for under $4.00 this year.*

This may be most simply expressed by a structural description of the form below:

$$\begin{array}{cccc} \text{Tough Movement:} & \textit{it} & \text{X} & [\text{+TM}] & \ldots \\ & 1 & 2 & 3 \end{array}$$

This immediately raises the question of what happens when the *it* and the element marked [+TM] are not constituents of the same simple S, as in (87).

(87)   *It is obvious to everyone that it is easy to please John.*

As (88) shows, Tough Movement cannot apply unless the *it* is in the same simple S as the [+TM] element.

(88)   a.   *It is obvious that John is easy to please φ.*
        b.   **John is obvious that it is easy to please φ.*

But (88) cannot be derived because the Binary Principle will prevent the structural description of Tough Movement from being satisfied by *it* and [+TM] in distinct B-cycles.

(89)

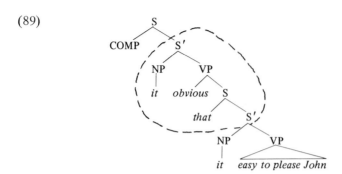

The structural description of Tough Movement must indicate the main verb, since only post verbal NPs may be moved.

(90) a. *It is easy for Fred to see the ocean from my room.*
      b. *The ocean is easy for Fred to see from my room.*
      c. *My room is easy for Fred to see the ocean from.*
      d. **Fred is easy for to see the ocean from my room.*

Between the [+TM] element and the verb there may a *for*-phrase. We can avoid stating the *for*-phrase in the rule if we introduce another variable.

Tough Movement: *it*   X   [+TM]   Y   V   . . .
                     1   2   3   4   5

This variable must be constrained also, since it is impossible to extract a constituent of a *that*-complement by Tough Movement.

(91) a. *It is easy for Mary to prove that she saw Fred.*
      b. **Fred is easy for Mary to prove that she saw φ.*

(92) a. *It is tough for us to admit Sam was here.*
      b. **Sam is tough for us to admit φ was here.*

(93) a. *It was pleasant to argue that Ivan had sold the Maserati to George.*
      b. **George was pleasant to argue that Ivan had sold the Maserati to φ .*
      c. **The Maserati was pleasant to argue that Ivan had sold φ to George.*

This is also ruled out by the Binary Principle.

(94)

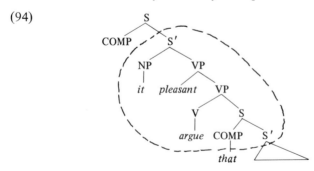

Finally, the fact that it is possible to move any one of a sequence of NPs that follow the verb suggests that there should be a variable in the structural description between V and NP.

$$\text{Tough Movement:} \quad \begin{array}{ccccccccc} it & X & [+TM] & Y & V & Z & NP & W^{48} \\ 1 & 2 & 3 & & 4 & 5 & 6 & 7 & 8 \end{array}$$

Without the constraint imposed by the Binary Principle, the ungrammatical examples in (91)–(93) could be derived by taking V to be the verb closest to the [+TM] element, and NP to be a constituent of the following *that*-complement.

In summary, it appears that the simplest statement of Tough Movement is possible only if the Binary Principle is adopted.

By adopting the Binary Principle we have an explanation for another phenomenon noted by Chomsky (1973): he notes the difference in acceptability between the following pair of sentences.

(95)   a.   *The hard work is pleasant for the poor to do.*
       b.   **The hard work is pleasant for the rich for the poor to do.*

Chomsky argues that there is an analysis of (95) in which the subject of the infinitive *to do* is the unspecified NP PRO, and *for the poor* is a constituent of the adjective phrase *pleasant for the poor*. A parallel structure is the only available one for (95), but in this case the subject is a specified NP *the poor*. Chomsky proposes the Specified Subject Condition, which blocks extraction over a specified subject.

Notice that the Binary Principle, as we have formulated it, will also block (95), given that the *for* is a complementizer and therefore signals the presence of an S-node.

(96)

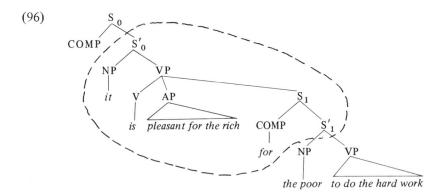

In order to derive (95) we need only hypothesize an S′-structure for the infinitive, although the derivation will also go through if the infinitive is simply a VP.

(97)

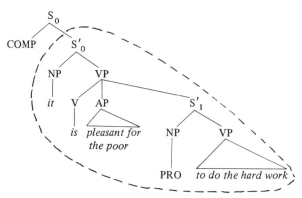

The difference noted by Chomsky is explicable in terms of the Binary Principle, and does not require an additional constraint such as the Specified Subject Condition.

In fact, the Specified Subject Condition is too strong, since it will block examples such as the following.

(98)   a.   *Fred is easy for John to persuade Mary to visit ϕ.*
       b.   *Fred is easy for John to believe Mary to have visited ϕ.*
       c.   *Fred is easy for John to expect Mary to believe Susan*
            to have visited ϕ.
       d.   *Fred is easy for John to expect Mary to believe Susan to*
            have proven George to have claimed to have visited ϕ.

It is impossible to derive these sentences by a successive cyclic analysis in the framework proposed by Chomsky (1973), even if we assumed that every infinitive contained a COMP. For *Wh* Fronting out of infinitives the *wh*-constituent may move up from COMP-to-COMP, but this is ruled out for Tough Movement by the constraint that a constituent that has been moved into COMP can only be moved into another COMP. Tough Movement would violate this constraint because it requires that the moved constituent end up in subject position.

Another illustration of the Binary Principle has to do with the rule of Gapping. Note first of all the difference in the structures corresponding to the two sentences in (99).

(99)   a.   *John believes that Mary won the footrace and that Susan*
            won the pole vault.
       b.   *John believes that Mary won the footrace and Susan won*
            the pole vault.

Adopting as before, Bresnan's (1972) analysis of the complementizer, we find that (99) has conjoined S-nodes, while (99b) has conjoined S'-nodes.[49]

(100) a.

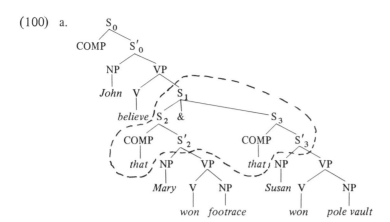

b.

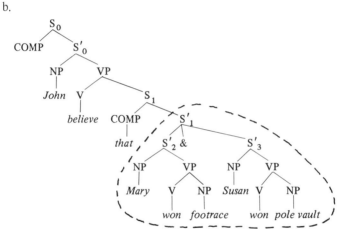

Consider now a transformation that applies to conjoined S-nodes, like Gapping. In the case of (99a) Gapping cannot apply until the conjoined S is reached, but at this point the Binary Principle will block the rule from looking at the verbs of the two conjuncts. This is shown in (100a). By comparison, in the case of (99b) Gapping applies at the level of the conjoined S', and it is not blocked from applying to the verbs by the Binary Principle. This difference in the structures predicts exactly the difference in grammaticality that we get by trying to apply Gapping to the examples in (101).[50]

(101) a. *John believes that Mary won the footrace and that Susan
            the polevault.
       b. John believes that Mary won the footrace and Susan, the pole vault.

(102) a. *Have you seen the pictures which John sent to Fred and which
            Susan, to Mary?
       b. Have you seen the pictures which John sent to Fred and
            Susan, to Mary?

To continue, we consider one further phenomenon that falls within the domain of the Binary Principle. Note first that the Binary Principle blocks access to any part of a relative clause from outside of the relative clause because the NP and the S that dominate it are both B-cyclic.

(103)   a.

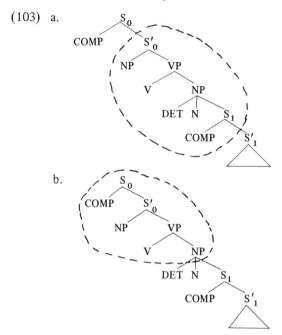

      b.

On the S'_0-cycle the only constituents of the relative clause that can be involved in a transformation are S_1 and any constituent of COMP of S_1. But constituents of COMP can only be moved into higher COMPs, and this is ruled out at the S'-level. So the only remaining possibility is that a transformation may apply to S_1, and in fact Extraposition from NP is such a rule.

(104)   *I gave [a book ϕ] to John **that I bought from Mary**.*

On the S_0-cycle no constituent of the relative clause may be involved in a transformation. This captures the generalization behind Ross's (1967) Complex NP Constraint and Chomsky's A-over-A Principle (1964; 1968).

The problem with this analysis is that it does not explain why the relative clause is unanalyzable even after it has been extraposed.

(105)   a.   *Who did you give a book that you bought from ϕ to John?*
             (no extraposition)
        b.   *Who did you give a book to John that you bought from ϕ ?*
             (extraposition)

The solution proposed by Ross (1967), who originally noted the problem, was to make Extraposition from NP a postcyclic transformation. Such a transformation would not apply at the topmost S, however, but could apply to any level of the phrase marker. It is worth investigating whether a device of such power can be avoided.

The Binary Principle does provide a natural solution if we adopt an analysis of the relative clause along the lines suggested by Chomsky (1973) and Emonds (1970). The crucial feature of this analysis for us is that there is a single position in the COMP into which an NP may be moved by *Wh* Fronting.[51] Once something has been moved into this position it is necessary to reach into the S' in order to extract any other constituent of the relative clause. However, as illustrated in (106), it is impossible to reach any further into the S' than S' itself because of the Binary Principle, even on the S'_0-cycle.

(106)

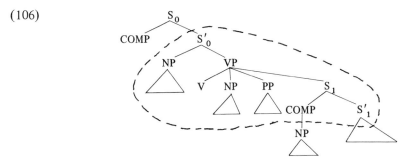

This explains not only the fact that *Wh* Fronting cannot apply to an extraposed relative, but also that Tough Movement cannot.

(107) a. *It should be easy to find a book for John that was written by Shakespeare.*
       b. **Shakespeare should be easy to find a book for John that was written by.*

Finally, a similar analysis of indirect questions will explain the observation of Kuno and Robinson (1972) that a constituent of an indirect question cannot be extracted from it. E.g.,

(108) a. **Who do you wonder what Bill gave φ to φ ?*
       b. **What do you wonder who Bill gave φ to φ ?*

(109)

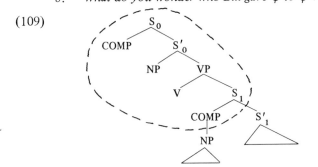

An analysis along similar lines may well account for the well-known fact that it is impossible to extract constituents of extraposed complements of nominals, e.g.,

(110) a.   *John put forth the claim to Bill that Sam had been buying wine.*
        b.   **What kind of wine did John put forth the claim to Bill that Sam had been buying?*

Emonds (1976) points out that it is possible to question out of such extraposed complements just in those cases where it is independently demonstrable that the *that*-complementizer is optional. Thus it may be the case that where the *that*-complementizer is underlying it blocks extraction even after extraposition, but where the *that*-complementizer is inserted, extraction from an extraposed clause is not blocked.

Bounding

It also follows from the Binary Principle that Extraposition will be "bounded" in the sense of Ross (1967, Ch. 5). Ross noted that it is impossible to extrapose a sentential subject beyond the VP of the lowest S which dominates it. Examples such as the following illustrate this fact.

(111) a. S_1 *[that S_2[that the world is round] is obvious] bothers me.*
        b. S_1 *[that it is obvious S_2 [that the world is round]] bothers me.*
        c.   *It bothers me S_1[that S_2[that the world is round] is obvious.]*
        d.   *It bothers me S_1 [that it is obvious S_2 [that the world is round]].*
        e.   **S_1 [that it is obvious] bothers me S_2 [that the world is round.]*

The crucial case is (111e), where the lowest S, S_2, has been extraposed to the right of the VP of the highest S rather than to the right of S_1, which is the S immediately above S_2. The tree in (112) shows that at S'_0 it is impossible to derive (111e) if the Binary Principle applies.

(112)

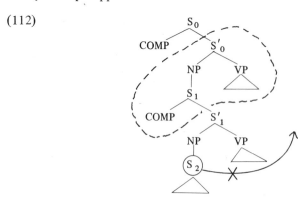

A similar observation is made by Akmajian (1975) with respect to Extraposition of PP. He points out that if NP is taken to be a cyclic (i.e., B-cyclic) node, then at an S it will be possible to move only the highest PP in a subject NP by Extraposition of PP. Examples are given in (113).

(113) a. *A review of a book by Fred appeared in the journal.*
       b. *A review appeared in the journal of a book by Fred.*
       c. **A review of a book appeared in the journal by Fred.*

It is of some interest to note that there are other instances in which we would expect Extraposition of PP and Extraposition to apply, but they do not. These cases involve reduced relatives, as the following show.

(114) a. *The man running to the store was my brother.*
       b. **The man running ϕ was my brother to the store.*

(115) a. *A book written by Fred has just appeared.*
       b. **A book written ϕ has just appeared by Fred.*
           (compare: *A book has just appeared by Fred.*)

(116) a. *The man claiming that the world is flat is crazy.*
       b. **The man claiming ϕ is crazy that the world is flat.*

It is clear first of all that the reduced relatives in these cases are at least VPs. It follows that the lowest node in the NP which contains the relative clause that could extrapose would have to be higher than the PP- or S-constituent of the reduced relative. This is shown in (117).

(117)

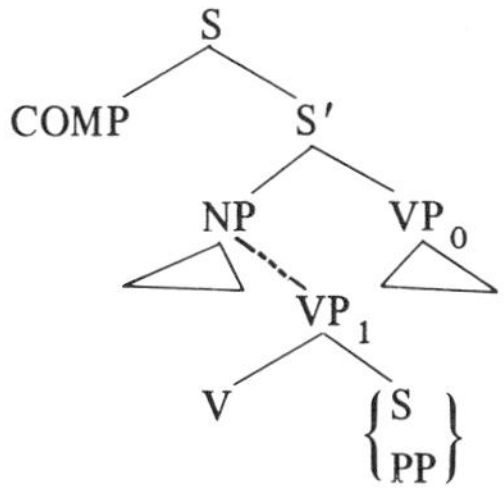

We can independently motivate a structure for the reduced relative like that in (118).

(118)

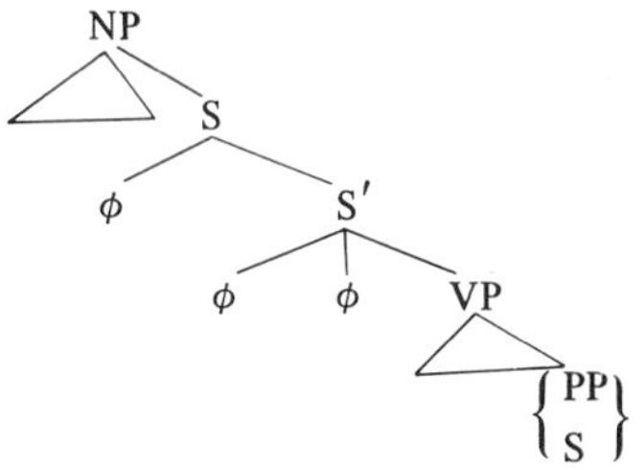

If the structure of the reduced relative were simply that of a VP, then we would expect that after extraposition of the reduced relative it would be possible to extract from it. That such extraction is impossible is shown by the following examples.

(119) a. *A man came in singing the Marseillaise.*
       b. **Which song did a man come in singing?*

(120) a. *A new book appeared written by Fred.*
       b. **Who did a new book appear written by.*

(121) a. *A man appeared claiming that Susan stole the money.*
       b. **What did a man appear claiming (that) Susan stole?*

This would be ruled out, however, by the Binary Principle, if the reduced relative was in fact an S, as in (118).

An analysis along these lines offers a potential solution to a puzzling problem: it is possible to question out of PP-complements of certain NPs, but not of others. E.g.,

(122) a. *Which countries do you put up with the weather in* ϕ *?*
       b. **Which wall did you steal a picture (hanging) on* ϕ *?*

(123) a. *Who did you try to meet a brother of* ϕ *?*
       b. **Which town did you try to meet a friend from* ϕ *?*

While we have not investigated this systematically, it may be that the only PPs from which extraction may take place are those that are true NP-complements. Those where extraction is impossible are, on the contrary, reduced relatives. As noted earlier, extraposition of a complement PP will put it into a position where it can be later analyzed, while extraposition of a reduced relative will make it no more analyzable.

(124) a.

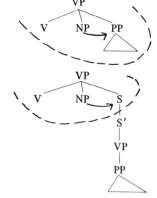

       b.

At least for the examples in (122)–(123) and those which are very similar, this analysis appears to have some virtue, since those cases permitting extraction are just those that lack full relative paraphrases.

(125)   a.   *I put up with the weather which is in France.
                   *I met a brother who was of Mary.

             b.   I found a picture which was on that wall.
                   I met a friend who was from Philadelphia.

Some additional examples which support this analysis are given in (126-129).

(126)   a.   We repaired the roof (*which was) of the house.
             b.   The sheriff was sitting in the back (*which was) of the room.
             c.   It would be impossible for John to have any advantage
                   (*which is) over Sam.
             d.   Mary is the author (*who is) of this book.
             e.   Susan proposed mercy (*that was) towards the victims.
             f.   Horatio measured the length (*which was) of the bridge.
             g.   Sam proposed a solution (*which was) of your problem.

(127)   a.   Whose house did you repair the roof of?
             b.   Which room was the sheriff sitting in the back of?
             c.   Who would it be impossible for John to have any
                   advantage over?
             d.   Which book is Mary the author of?
             e.   Who did Susan propose mercy towards?
             f.   What did Horatio measure the length of?
             g.   Which problem did Sam propose a solution of?

(128)   a.   I found a box (which was) of pine.
             b.   We cooked the meat (which was) in the refrigerator.
             c.   John met a woman (who was) under serious investigation.
             d.   Sam proposed a solution (which was) of little interest.

(129)   a.   *Which kind of wood did you find a box of?
             b.   *Whose refrigerator did you cook the meat in?
             c.   *How serious an investigation did John meet a woman under?
             d.   *How much interest did Sam propose a solution of?
                   (compare with (127g))

A final point, mentioned in note 23, is the fact noted by Postal that subjects of
that-complements cannot undergo Complex NP Shift. This follows from the Binary
Principle since on the higher S' the subject of the complement is outside of the
domain of Complex NP Shift.[52]

(130)

An Alternative Binary Principle

Another alternative formulation of the Binary Principle that yields substantially the same predictions is the following. Consider a node A on which a transformation T is cycling. T may apply no further down in the phrase marker than immediate constituents of the highest B-cyclic node dominated by A. Thus, if a transformation is applying to S in (131), its domain of application is that shown by the dotted lines.

(131)

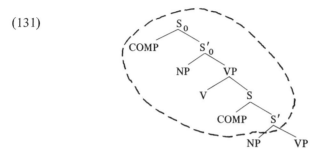

The interesting advantage that this formulation has over the one we have just been discussing is that in this case it is not necessary to specify that COMP-to-COMP movement is possible: such movement is automatically permitted by this formulation of the Binary Principle as long as it is formulated as a movement of the entire node COMP, as (131) shows. Without working out the details of this proposal, it seems to us that it might capture the range of data we have been considering.[53]

In conclusion, we have been able to find some support for the notion that the Freezing Principle and the Binary Principle, besides contributing in an important way to a proof of the learnability of a class of transformational grammars, are involved generally in the syntax of English. In some cases these two principles can be seen as stronger replacements for other principles, (e.g., the Tensed S Condition) and in other cases the two principles conflict with other principles, (e.g., the Specified Subject Condition) and we have been able to find some evidence to support the two principles. Of course, many problems remain,[54] both from the standpoint of learnability and of descriptive syntax. But in our view it is worth studying learning and syntax together, in the hope of achieving some insight into the fundamental problem of linguistic theory.

Notes

*   This paper is a joint effort and the listing of authors is purely alphabetical. This research was supported by the National Science Foundation under Grant NSF SOC 74-23469. We would like to thank Henry Hamburger for many useful comments.
 1. For some discussion see Wexler, Culicover, and Hamburger (1975).

2. But note that the more constraints of an empirical character that we can impose on the language learner (e.g., memory and computational load limits) then the stronger and more useful will learnability be as a criterion for choosing between theories, because fewer theories will provide learnable classes of languages.

3. Whether this is an adequate characterization of the set of "primary data" is an empirical question. See Wexler, Culicover, and Hamburger (1975) for discussion.

4. It is important to note that this definition is different from the one used in Hamburger and Wexler (1973, 1975). It is similar to the one given in Wexler and Hamburger (1973) but eliminates the time parameter and does not require effectivity. Also, we have slightly simplified the appropriate definition. We have to provide for the case where there is more than one grammar in G that generates $*L(G_i)$, that is, where there exists $j \neq i$ such that $*L(G_i) = *L(G_j)$. In this case we would only require that when D is chosen from $*L(G_i)$, there exist a D such that for all $D' \supseteq D$, $*L(f(D')) = *L(G_i)$.

5. For a formal proof, apply the superset lemma of Gold (1967) or Theorem 1 of Wexler and Hamburger (1973). In both of these references, effective procedures were demanded, but the same proof works with noneffective functions.

6. Or as Chomsky (1965, p. 62) puts it, "It is important to keep the requirements of explanatory adequacy and feasibility in mind when weak and strong generative capacities of theories are studied as mathematical questions. Thus one can construct hierarchies of grammatical theories in terms of weak and strong generative capacity, but it is important to bear in mind that these hierarchies do *not* necessarily correspond to what is probably the empirically most significant dimension of increasing power of linguistic theory. This dimension is presumably to be defined in terms of the scattering in value of grammars compatible with fixed data."

7. For a proof, apply Theorem 1 in Wexler and Hamburger (1973), with the superset language $L = \{a, aa, aaa, \dots \}$.

8. Of course, we cannot observe the infinite number of sentences. But we can make the usual generalization from a finite number of cases, as linguists do for natural languages.

9. Perhaps it would be more plausible if the string that contained *b* were not so short, or if the anomaly were the ungrammaticality of a particular sentence, rather than its grammaticality. Such examples could be constructed. Nothing crucial to our argument hinges on this choice.

10. Of course there are other possible theories. For illustrative purposes we limit ourselves here to two.

11. See note 6.

12. We do not know whether it is an accident that the learnable theory postulates a structure-dependent transformation of the kind familiar from grammars of natural languages, whereas the nonlearnable theory assumes a "word counting" transformation of a kind that is not found in natural language, to our knowledge. In general it is conceivable that the requirement that human language be learnable might provide an explanation for the fact that syntactic transformations in natural language are not arbitrary mappings from phrase markers to phrase markers, but rather are particular kinds of structure-dependent transformations. For discussion of related ideas see Wexler, Culicover and Hamburger (1975), and for discussion of the structure-dependent nature of transformations see Chomsky (1971, 1975b).

13. And of course T would be preferred even more strongly over any component that can be shown to be not learnable.

14. Our suggestion is that *semantic* structure is universal, and that there is a learnable class of possible mappings from semantic representations to deep structures. A number of predictions about syntactic universals follow from this hypothesis, which are discussed in Culicover and Wexler (1974).

15. Of course there will be many instances in which it will be impossible for the learner to recover the meaning from the situational context. However, it is conceivable that in these

cases the learner could ignore these sentences and learnability would be unaffected. Of course the learning procedure could be greatly ramified: partial learning of structure on a complicated input is plausible. The concept of a learner used here is a first step. Much remains to be done.

16. For details see Hamburger and Wexler (1975).

17. In the formal development of learnability theory in Hamburger and Wexler (1973, 1975), and Wexler and Hamburger (1973) it was assumed that the only cyclic node was S. In Chomsky (1973) the definition of Subjacency is given for *any* cyclic node. We mean that the Binary Principle (in its original version) and the Subjacency Condition are equivalent given that they apply to the same set of cyclic nodes. Also, the Binary Principle states that the structural description of a transformation may not apply to certain nodes. The Subjacency Condition in Chomsky (1973) is stated so that no transformation may "involve" two nodes X and Y, if X and Y are not in the same or adjacent cycles. (We take the statement "a transformation involves a node X" to mean "a transformation applies to a node X.")

18. If we assume that transformations operate cyclically and not just at the root, we could achieve the same demonstration as the following, but the exposition would be more complex.

19. The A-over-A Principle (cf. Chomsky, 1964, 1968, 1973) is not needed to insure that the higher A is raised, since we have built this requirement into the structural description of the transformation. In fact, we could have allowed either A to be raised without affecting the force of this example.

20. We ignore questions of pruning (cf. Ross, 1969c), which are irrelevant to the example.

21. Note that the Freezing Principle does not imply that no transformation may apply to a sub-phrase-marker of a phrase marker if the sub-phrase-marker was not in the base. If a transformation creates new structure in a phrase marker, the new structure itself being base structure, then this new structure is not frozen, and a further transformation may apply. For example, if an NP is raised to a position where an NP could be, then this NP will not be frozen, even though it was not in that position in this particular phrase marker.

22. In the original learnability results (Hamburger and Wexler, 1973, 1975), the Freezing Principle was not assumed. Rather we made other assumptions that had somewhat the same learnability effects as the Freezing Principle. For discussion, see Wexler, Culicover, and Hamburger (1975).

23. Our statement of this transformation differs from that of Ross (1967), Postal (1974a) and Bresnan (1975), all of whom adopt essentially the following statement.

Complex NP Shift: X   NP   Y
                    1   2   3   ⇒   1 ϕ 3 + 2
                    Condition: 2 is "complex."

Naturally this creates problems of overgeneration, since not just any complex NP can be shifted to the right. E.g.,

(i)   *I climbed into ϕ on a ladder the room that had been pointed out to me by the sergeant.*

Ross (1967, p. 226) blocks rightward movement out of PP by a specific constraint; Bresnan (1975) argues that this can be accomplished by the Relativized A-over-A Principle if the second term is allowed to range over PP and NP. In case the complex NP is immediately dominated by PP, the latter will be maximal with respect to the proper factorization of the tree according to the structural description of the rule, and thus will be the constituent to undergo the rule.

Postal (1974a) notes that the rule as stated will apply incorrectly to subjects of *that*-complements.

(ii)   *I believe ϕ is a millionaire the man that Mary married.*

Postal proposes that there is a constraint that prevents Complex NP Shift from applying to subject.

The problem noted by Ross and Bresnan can be avoided by restating the rule as we have done in the text. This means, of course, that Complex NP Shift will not be applicable to PPs internal to the VP that do not immediately follow the verb. However, it does not appear that the movement of PPs is due to the same rule, in view of the fact that a PP need not be "complex" in order to move to VP-final position. E.g.,

(iii)   *We spoke yesterday to Fred.*

As we will show later, the problem raised by Postal can be accounted for by the Binary Principle.

24. We have entertained elsewhere (cf. Culicover and Wexler, 1973a) the notion that the indirect object is a constituent of a higher VP, i.e.,

(i)

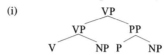

The arguments which led us to adopt this structure involved crucial use of pruning of non-branching nodes, a device we no longer believe is required. In this paper we will assume that the structure generated by rule A is the correct one, and in fact most of the analyses we constructed in terms of (i) will not be significantly altered if we abandon (i) in favor of the structure introduced by A. A further consideration, which we will take up again somewhat later in this paper, is that the structure in (i) completely invalidates the generalizations about anaphora argued for in Culicover (1976) and Reinhart (1974), which rely crucially on the notion *in construction with*. It is clear that the indirect object, for example, is not in construction with the verb in (i), but would be in the analysis which we are adopting here, which is assumed in the two works just mentioned. While (i) might actually be correct, we do not feel that it is possible to investigate its consequences in adequate detail here, given the sorts of complex problems that loom on the horizon.

25. This is not quite correct. It does not appear to be possible to move a complex NP over an S, as noted by Ross (1967).

(i)   a.   *It bothers φ that the world is flat the man who invented the first telescope.*
It surprised φ that you were staying the musical group that had been playing raucous noise all evening.
We informed φ that they had been hired the workers who submitted their applications on time.
I told φ that the world was flat the man I met in Chicago.

This may be accounted for if these Ss are not constituents of the VP that dominates the complex NP, but attached higher in the tree. We suggest later that the cycle operates on all nodes of the tree; if this is correct, Complex NP Shift will automatically move an NP to the end of the VP, thus leaving it to the left of the higher S-nodes.

26. We are adopting here the hypothesis that all appearance of rule ordering is due to intrinsic ordering. In the case of Complex NP Shift and *Wh* Fronting, for example, we assume that both S and S' are cyclic nodes, so that all transformations applicable on the lower cycle will apply prior to those applying on the higher cycle. Hence it is not necessary to demonstrate that application of *Wh* Fronting blocks application of Complex NP Shift.

However, since Tough Movement and Complex NP Shift apply within the same S' we must either show that Tough Movement blocks Complex NP Shift, or explain in some other way the fact that the two rules cannot apply to the same VP. We will argue that Tough Movement is structure-preserving in the VP, and this will lead us to extend the class of nodes on which the cycle operates to all nodes of the tree.

27. It may appear that the ungrammaticality of some of the examples below can be accounted
     for by Kuno's (1973) Clause Nonfinal Incomplete Constituent Constraint: it is not possible
     to move any element of phrase/clause A in the clause nonfinal position out of A, if what is
     left over in A constitutes an incomplete phrase/clause. Kuno suggests that a clause cannot
     be considered "nonfinal" if it is followed only by optional constituents. As Bresnan (1975,
     p. 52) notes, there are problems involved in formulating the notion "incomplete constit-
     uent" with sufficient precision. Also, it is not clear how this constraint will handle the
     ungrammaticality of examples in which all constituents of the verb phrase (except the
     verb) are clearly optional. E.g.,

     (i)   *Which city did you drive to φ the car which you bought in Duluth?

     (ii)   I drove the car.

     (iii) I drove to New York.

28. This example is taken from Postal (1974a, p. 87).

29. Examples such as these were pointed out to us by J. D. Fodor (personal communication),
     who might not agree with our judgments.

30. Apparently there is a dialect in which none of the examples of (25)–(26) are grammatical.
     For this dialect we would suggest that the structure derived by Dative is (i), so that NP it-
     self is frozen.

     (i)

     For further discussion, see Wexler, Culicover, and Hamburger (1975). We argue that this is
     precisely the sort of dialect difference one would expect, given the lack of clear evidence
     for the learner as to precisely what the output structure must be.

31. The original version of this paper that was presented to the conference contained at this
     point a digression dealing with Emonds' (1972a) argument based on Particle Movement
     that Dative is a structure-preserving transformation. We concluded tentatively that a non-
     structure-preserving analysis such as the one we propose is workable. However, the data is
     complex and unclear, and we have deleted the discussion to eliminate what we believe to
     be a distraction from the main thrust of the paper.

32. The issue is complicated, since the interplay of many assumptions is used in a learnability
     proof. In fact if a version of the Freezing Principle that only freezes after non-structure-
     preserving attachments replaces the principle which is listed as Restriction on the Use of
     Transformations Number 5 in Hamburger and Wexler (1975, p. 147), and if we maintain
     all the other assumptions (constraints on the operations of transformations) then the learn-
     ability theorem proved in Hamburger and Wexler (1975) is still provable. On the other
     hand, our current work is aimed at proving far stronger versions of the learnability theorem
     (for example, placing a severe bound on the complexity of "primary data" needed by the
     learner). Although we suspect that the "attachment" version of the Freezing Principle will
     be sufficient for these results, this has not been proved.

33. Perhaps certain kinds of obligatory root transformations do not follow the Freezing Princi-
     ple. One can imagine that learnability will not be affected by what happens at roots, since
     the kinds of problems created by transformations unconstrained by the Freezing Principle
     (cf. our earlier discussion) depend on creating new structures that undergo further raising.

34. We say "apparently," since it has been suggested by E. Williams that all nodes are cyclic
     domains for the purpose of rule application (cf. Chomsky, 1975b, p. 239, note 13). If this
     proves correct, then Complex NP Shift will always precede Tough Movement. This ordering
     must be maintained in any case, we will argue below, because it appears that Tough Move-
     ment does not freeze the VP.

35. A plausible alternative to Emonds' analysis of particles is that they are *adverbs*. In such
     an analysis, some prepositions would actually be adverbs that take NP complements. This
     would not affect the way the Freezing Principle applies, however. The advantage would be

that it would not be necessary to state in the grammar that prepositional phrases are adverbs, e.g., by a rule of the form ADV → PP.

36. In note 24 we noted that slight changes in the branching structure of certain nodes could have radical consequences both for the grammar and the theory if the Freezing Principle is adopted. An illustration of this involves Tough Movement. Suppose that each PP was introduced into the base structure by the rule VP → VP PP. If there were two PPs, the structure would be (i).

(i)

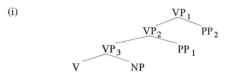

Let us consider the effect of pruning here. If PP_1 were frozen and did not branch, pruning it would freeze VP_2. Consequently the direct object could not be moved by a later transformation. However, VP_1 would not be frozen, and PP_2 could be analyzed. This would accomplish precisely what is desired in terms of the interaction between Tough Movement and *Wh* Fronting, since prior extraction from a PP would block movement of or from all constituents to the left, and would have no effect on constituents to the right.

As we observed in note 24, to adopt this structure we would have also to reconcile it with the constraint on anaphora proposed by Culicover (1976) and Reinhart (1974). We will not follow up this line of inquiry here.

37. It is possible that the rule applies as well to *at*. E.g.,

   (i)   *I plan to visit my folks (at) Christmas time.*

Emonds (1976, p. 79) notes that *for* may also be deleted in certain contexts.

   (ii)   *I have been sick (for) three days.*

However, *for* can be deleted only when it is used to indicate the duration of an event or a state, and not when it is used in negative contexts. While (iiia) is ambiguous, (iiib) is not.

   (iii)   a.   *I haven't been sick for three days.*
           b.   *I haven't been sick three days.*

We will ignore these complexities in our discussion.

38. A number of solutions come to mind. We could put features [+TRANS] and [−TRANS] on verbs to indicate whether they can undergo Passive (notice that +[__NP] will not do here), or we could state Passive in terms of the grammatical relations of subject and object. But these solutions entail an increase in the power of the theory, while the solution we propose does not. In fact, it entails a reduction in the power of the theory, through the Freezing Principle, of just the right sort. Of course, it is possible that other phenomena might require similar additions.

   Notice also that it will not be sufficient to assume that there is a dummy proposition in these adverbials. For one thing, if Jackendoff's (1974a) Empty Node Convention is correct, Passive will ignore the dummy preposition anyway. For another, Tough Movement is not sensitive to the presence or absence of prepositions at all, and so would not be blocked if we adopted such an analysis.

39. The structure of the alternative is the following: Bresnan shows that Comparative Deletion obeys all of the constraints on movement transformations which anyone has ever proposed. We will demonstrate below that the Binary Principle accomplishes bounding of extraposition transformations (along the lines pointed out by Akmajian, 1975). If we abandon the Binary Principle we can handle the comparative, but we are in trouble when it comes to bounding. Rather than give up the useful Binary Principle, which, it should be stressed, is instrumental in the learnability proof as well, we must show that Comparative Deletion is actually a movement transformation, along the lines of Relative Clause Formation. See

Culicover (forthcoming) where the details of the analysis are filled in, and where comparisons with Bresnan's analysis are noted.

40. Such a correlation is suggested by Chomsky (1975, p. 239, note 13).

41. Notice that this formulation of the Binary Principle will also block movement of the PP dominating NP_1 into the COMP of the S. This predicts that the following example will be ungrammatical.

    (i)   *About whom did a story amaze you?*

We tend to think that this sentence is ungrammatical, but our judgments are not firm.

    If (i) in fact is grammatical, it may be derived by first extraposing the PP to the right of the VP at the S'-cycle, and then applying *Wh* Fronting at S. An analysis along these lines would depend on the prior demonstration that the rule that extraposed the PP is structure-preserving at the node of attachment.

42. There are a number of aspects of this analysis of which we are not certain. First it is not clear to us precisely what the output structure of Extraposition of PP must be. Second, it is not obvious what convention will assign the correct output structure, given the statement of the transformations. And finally, the precise form of the base rules is open to question. These issues are worth investigating further, but are too complicated for us to deal with here.

43. The cases that motivate this convention are those that require Chomsky (1973) to formulate the Tensed S Condition so that it does not apply when a constituent of COMP is to be moved out of a tensed S.

44. Cf. Lightfoot (1976a) for discussion.

45. Unless infinitives had COMP in the following configuration:

    (i)

$$S'$$

COMP NP VP

However, we will argue below that even the presence of a COMP in every infinitive will not explain other cases in which a constituent of a deeply embedded infinitive may be extracted from it.

    For a proposal that *wh*-questions have essentially the structure of (i) see Grosu (1975).

46. When the cycle applies at S', in order for an extraposition transformation to apply to PP (or S) in the subject, PP (or S) must be an immediate constituent of NP. Thus extraposition could apply if the structure were as in (ia), but not if it were as in (ib).

    (i)   a.

NP

DET N {PP / S}

        b.

NP

DET Nom

N {PP / S}

    If (b) is independently shown to be the correct structure, then we may have to distinguish between "major" and "nonmajor" categories, where only "major" categories count for the Binary Principle. Assuming that Nom was not a major category, a transformation of extraposition could apply appropriately to (b). Cf. Selkirk (this volume) and Jackendoff (this volume, forthcoming) for proposals for NP structure.

47. Note that this formulation of the Binary Principle permits us to do without the restriction of Chomsky (1973), his condition (123 (iii)), which prevents raising of a constituent of COMP into a non-COMP position in the higher cycle. This will prevent, e.g., application of Passive to a fronted *wh*-constituent in an embedded S.

(i) *Fred forgot who John likes.*
   *Who was forgotten φ John likes by Fred.

(ii)

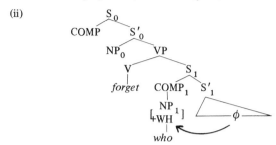

As can be seen in (ii), a transformation such as Passive applying at S'_0 may apply to $COMP_1$, but not to NP_1. The first transition is from VP to S_1, and the second is from S_1 to $COMP_1$. Thus we will not derive the ungrammatical (i).

48. The apparent complexity of this structural description can be avoided somewhat if there is always assumed to be a variable between any two category terms mentioned in a structural description, as Wendy Wilkins has proposed. While there are numerous problems with such a convention as it stands, a number of them can be handled by use of the Binary Principle, and others may be ruled out by some general constraints being investigated by Wilkins.

49. An alternative analysis of (99b) would treat the presence of a single *that* as due to the deletion of the second *that* by *that*-Deletion. This is implausible on prima facie grounds because of the Coordinate Structure Constraint of Ross (1967). In addition, if *that*-Deletion could occur in one conjunct we would expect it to occur only in the first, also, but this does not appear to be acceptable.

   (i) **John believes Mary won the footrace and that Susan won the pole vault.*

50. A possible alternative explanation for the ungrammaticality of (101a) is that the presence of the second complementizer before the NP *Susan* prevents the sentence from meeting the structural description of Gapping. In particular, Stillings (1975) proposes that Gapping cannot apply unless the structure can be factored as NP V* C $\left\{ \begin{matrix} and \\ or \end{matrix} \right\}$ NP V* C where V* is a string of Vs, and C a constituent variable.

   Both our analysis and Stillings' will account for the failure of Gapping to apply between main clause and subordinate clauses, e.g.,

   (i) a. **I saw Bill after Sam, Fred.*
        b. **Harold expects Susan (to), Mary to leave.*
        c. **After I saw Bill, Sam, Fred.*

and so on. It would be especially interesting if we could use the Binary Principle (and the Freezing Principle to account for facts that would otherwise require a complex structural description of a particular transformation. We have not investigated this possibility in detail, however.

51. This will account for the observation of Katz and Postal (1964) that at most one *wh*-constituent may be fronted in any simple S, e.g.,

   (i) **Who when where did you meet?*

52. This fact would also follow from the Tensed S Condition, on the assumption that the structural description of Complex NP Shift includes a V before the moved NP (as we argued earlier in the paper that it does). That is, we interpret the notion "involve" in Chomsky's statement of the Tensed S Condition as "be fit by a non-variable element of a structural description." On the assumption that tensed Ss contain S and S', then the Tensed S

Condition follows from the formulation of the Binary Principle presented here, but the converse does not hold. Thus, if this formulation of the Binary Principle can be supported, the Tensed S Condition can be eliminated.

Postal (1974a, p. 87n) notes an empirical consideration that is relevant here. There is no evidence that a subjunctive complement is a "tensed S"; in fact, the available evidence argues against the notion that subjunctives contain TENSE. However, it is not possible to extract a constituent of a subjunctive by, for example, Passive.

   (i) a. *Mary demands (that) Fred leave immediately.*
      b. **Fred is demanded (that) ϕ leave immediately (by Mary).*

(ib) is not ruled out by the Tensed S Condition, but it is ruled out by the Binary Principle, given that a subjunctive is an S.

53. The issue is not clear, because the precise application of this formulation of the Binary Principle depends crucially on the details of constituent structure independently arrived at. So, if AP is an immediate constituent of NP, this formulation will not rule out *Wh* Fronting of AP in (i), as illustrated in (ii).

   (i) **How nice did you meet ϕ a man?*

   (ii)

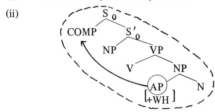

However, if there were another node between AP and NP, *Wh* Fronting could not apply to derive (i).

54. One problem involves the relation between the learning theory and the syntactic theory. The formulation of the Binary Principle that we have arrived at is based on the syntactic data. However, recall that we originally postulated the Binary Principle on learnability grounds. Namely, it played an important role in allowing us to prove BDE (boundedness of the degree of error). Although, as pointed out in note 17, the proof assumed that S was the only cyclic node, the result can be generalized to more than one cyclic node. However, it is crucial to the result that any category that can dominate itself with no cyclic node intervening be a B-cyclic category. However, the category S' in our final formulation of the Binary Priinciple is not B-cyclic and yet it can dominate itself. Thus BDE cannot be proved using the final formulation of the Binary Principle. We *could* of course prove BDE if we were only counting the depth of B-cyclic nodes. That is, a chain of S'-nodes would still only count as a depth of one. But then there could be an infinite number of base phrase markers of fixed degree, and the learnability theorem could not be proved.

It is not clear how to solve this problem. It may be possible that the particular learning-theoretic motivation that we gave for the Binary Principle (role in proving BDE) is wrong, and that BDE should be derivable from another constraint. It could be that when the range of grammatical rules and structures is expanded the Binary Principle can be seen to play a different role. For example, optional transformations yield particularly difficult learnability problems. Another possibility is that the Binary Principle is needed to allow the proof of BDE for transformations that operate *across* B-cycles, but that another constraint operates *within* B-cycles. To speculate even further, a hypothetical constraint that would work is the following: when the structural description of a transformation T applies to a phrase marker P, it may apply to at most one node of a given category within each B-cycle.

COMMENTS ON THE PAPER
BY CULICOVER AND WEXLER

C. L. Baker

Department of Linguistics
University of Texas
Austin, Texas

The paper by Culicover and Wexler raises many interesting issues, both of general approach and of technical detail. In order to give some structure to my discussion of their paper, I will concentrate on one central contention, namely, that the line of research being carried out by Culicover, Hamburger, and Wexler would profit from greater attention to the possibilities of imposing fairly severe restrictions on the form of transformational rules, as well as restrictions such as the Freezing Principle and the Binary Principle, which are restrictions on functioning.

Let me begin with a brief review of the learnability theorem proved in Hamburger and Wexler (1975). They define a procedure that is designed to "learn" a transformational component A on the basis of a random sequential presentation of ordered pairs (b, s), where b is a base phrase marker and s is a surface string associated with b by the set of transformations A. What the theorem states is that one can make the probability of a successful outcome for this procedure arbitrarily close to 1 by presenting a sufficiently large number of ordered pairs. A preliminary result that is essential in the proof of this theorem is that for the set of base phrase markers generated by an arbitrary context-free base component B, there is an upper bound U (a function of B) on the degree of the minimal phrase marker on which two transformational components C_1 and C_2 may disagree. Put more informally, if we suspect that two transformational components C_1 and C_2 do not give the same results when applied to the set of base phrase markers generated by B, we can satisfy ourselves one way or the other merely by comparing the effects of C_1 and C_2 on base phrase markers of degree less than or equal to U. As Culicover and Wexler note in the present paper, it is in the proof of this preliminary result (the "Boundedness of the Degree of Error," BDE for short) that the Freezing Principle and the original Binary Principle play essential roles.

In the first part of this discussion, I will raise some questions about the desirability of using the Binary Principle and the Freezing Principle as cornerstones of the theorem, and I will mention some simple constraints that have been suggested in recent papers that I believe might prove to have the same effectiveness in yielding a learnability theorem.

In the case of the Binary Principle, Culicover and Wexler themselves observe (in note 54) that their final version of this principle does not do the same work in the BDE proof that the original Binary Principle did. With the Freezing Principle, the basic problems seem to me to be descriptive. In at least one instance, the principle appears to yield incorrect results; in addition, the arguments given in support of it by Culicover and Wexler do not seem to me to be compelling.

The possible counterexample to the Freezing Principle is provided by the type of Subject-Auxiliary Inversion exemplified in (1): [1]

(1)   *Not one taco has Fred offered to the guest of honor.*

On most transformational analyses, (1) would be derived by first applying a transformational rule that preposes negative constituents and then applying Subject-Auxiliary Inversion. The structure serving as input to Subject-Auxiliary Inversion would thus presumably be something like (2):

(2)

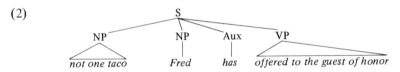

By Culicover and Wexler's definition of *frozen node*, one would expect the S-node in (2) to be frozen, since it is difficult to justify the rule in (3) as a base rule of English:

(3)   S → NP NP Aux VP

But freezing the S-node would block the application of Subject–Auxiliary Inversion, and sentence (1) would not be generated.

Let me turn now to the arguments that Culicover and Wexler offer in support of the Freezing Principle. Many of their most interesting examples can be explained by a simple pair of processing principles concerning the relation between the surface position of constituents and their "understood" position. It will be convenient to introduce these principles by showing how they apply to the sentences in (4), Culicover and Wexler's (43c):

(4)   a.   *Which city is Susan tough to drive with ϕ_1 to ϕ_2?*
       b.   **Which city is Susan tough to drive to ϕ_1 with ϕ_2?*

Each of these sentences involves two extractions, one by Tough Movement and one by *Wh* movement. As Culicover and Wexler note, there seems to be little possibility of making the Freezing Principle yield this particular distinction in acceptability. Instead, the distinction seems to fall under the rule of thumb given in Kuno and Robinson (1972) to the effect that sentences exhibiting dual extractions to the left are more acceptable to the extent that the surface structure order is the mirror image of the deep structure order. Sentence (4a) clearly satisfies this condition, whereas (4b) does not.

For the purposes of developing a general treatment of cases like this, let me introduce some informal terms. NPs like *which city* and *Susan* can be thought of as "prospective tenants," and the deletion sites in the VP can be thought of as "addresses." A prospective tenant is *eligible* to be assigned a certain address just in case there is a transformational rule in the language that could have the effect of extracting that NP from that address. Thus, both *which city* and *Susan* are eligible to occupy either of the addresses in the VP *to drive with ϕ_1 to ϕ_2*. The critical principles that make reference to these notions are those stated in (5):

(5) a.   As a sentence is processed from left to right, a prospective tenant *y* is *more current* than a prospective tenant *x* if *y* occurs to the right of *x*.

  b.   A prospective tenant is assigned to the first unoccupied address for which it is the most current of the eligible prospective tenants.[2]

The application of these principles to (4a) and (4b) is straightforward. In the former instance, the most current prospective tenant at the point at which the empty address after *with* is reached is the NP *Susan*. Consequently, *Susan* is correctly assigned this address. In the latter instance, by contrast, an incorrect association is made: *Susan* is the most current prospective tenant at the point at which the empty address after *to* is reached, and thus is incorrectly assigned to this address. In cases where these principles lead to the recovery of a bizarre underlying structure, lowered acceptability is predicted.

In addition to accounting for the Kuno–Robinson examples of dual extractions, the principles in (5) extend automatically to cases in which one extraction has been to the left and the other to the right. They thus predict the unacceptability of sentences like (6) (Culicover and Wexler's (9b)), in which a constituent is extracted to the left from a VP which also undergoes Complex NP Shift:

(6)   **Bill is easy to sell ϕ_1 to ϕ_2 pictures stolen in Europe.*

On the intended interpretation, *Bill* should be associated with the empty address after the preposition *to*, but the principles in (5) dictate an association with the empty address after *sell*, since this is the first empty address for which *Bill* is eligible. In similar fashion, the principles appear to provide an explanation for the impossibility of extracting a subpart of an NP that has undergone Complex NP Shift. An example of this sort is given in (7) (Culicover and Wexler's (18a)):

(7)   **What did you sell ϕ_1 to Fred a beautiful and expensive painting of ϕ_2?*

The interrogative word *what* is the current prospective tenant at the point at which ϕ_1 is reached, so that *what* is assigned the address ϕ_1 by principle (5b). This is of course at variance with the intended assignment.

The principles in (5) thus provide an alternative explanation for several of the cases of unacceptability that Culicover and Wexler offer in support of the Freezing Principle. Moreover, as I indicated in connection with examples (4a–b), these new principles also account for distinctions in acceptability that cannot be explained by the Freezing Principle. To the extent, then, that the principles in (5) can be sustained and provided with additional support, they diminish the force of the arguments based on structures showing the effects of Complex NP Shift. [3]

The other arguments that Culicover and Wexler offer for the Freezing Principle seem to me to be less clear than the ones discussed above. One argument is based on the unacceptability that results when an immediately postverbal indirect object is extracted by *wh*-movement or Tough Movement, as in the following examples (Culicover and Wexler's (25)):

(8) a. *Who did you sell a dozen shovels?*
     b. *This is the woman who Mary gave the last copy of the book.*
     c. *Susan is tough to loan expensive jewels.*

The use of the Freezing Principle to explain these judgments requires an otherwise unmotivated derived constituent structure (the right-hand side of Culicover and Wexler's (23)):

(9)

Furthermore, the freezing of V_*, while blocking the sentences in (8), would incorrectly interfere with the generation of the well-formed passives in (10):

(10) *John was $\left\{ \begin{array}{c} given \\ sent \end{array} \right\}$ a book about poker.*

A final weakness in this argument is that there are instances in English of double-NP VPs that do not appear to be naturally derivable from underlying prepositional constructions. Oehrle (1976) gives a great many examples. For our present purposes, just one will suffice:

(11) *The last hand cost someone a steak dinner.* (Oehrle, 1976, p. 240)

As Oehrle notes, the double-NP constructions that do not have corresponding well-formed prepositional paraphrases show exactly the same resistance to *wh*-extraction of the postverbal NP as do those that do have such paraphrases:

(12) *Who did the last hand cost a steak dinner?*

Returning, then, to the ill-formedness of the sentences in (8), we have reason to be skeptical of any explanation which, like Culicover and Wexler's, relies on the assumption that a transformational rule of Dative Movement has yielded a certain derived constituent structure.

Culicover and Wexler's final argument for the Freezing Principle is based on the behavior of time adverbs such as *Tuesday, yesterday*, and *next year*. These time adverbs share many of the characteristics of NPs, without, however, being able to undergo many of the transformational rules that extract NPs. Essential to Culicover and Wexler's explanation for these failures of extractability is the supposition that all of these time adverbs are to be derived by a transformational rule of *On* Deletion from underlying structures in which they are all preceded by a preposition. This rule would be optional for some lexical items ([*on*] *Tuesday*), but obligatory for others ([*on] *yesterday*). The application of this rule yields a derived structure PrepP node that dominates only an NP. Since the base component of English presumably does not contain a rule expanding PrepP as NP, the PrepP node in such cases would be frozen, and extraction of this NP by subsequent rules would be blocked by the Freezing Principle.

The strength of this argument for the Freezing Principle is clearly a function of the strength of the arguments that can be given for a transformational rule of *On*-Deletion. Culicover and Wexler give no arguments for this rule that are independent of the Freezing Principle. Moreover, the postulation of a transformational rule that is optional for some lexical items but obligatory for others is a descriptive maneuver that is highly questionable, given Culicover and Wexler's general commitment to solving the central problem of language acquisition. This is a point that I will amplify later in this discussion.

If the Freezing Principle and the original Binary Principle are not assumed, then some alternative assumptions will be required as a basis for a proof of the learnability theorem. Once interesting possibility would be to adopt the restrictions on form stated in (13), restrictions that are in the spirit of those suggested in Chomsky (1975c):

(13)   a.   Each transformational rule may "involve" at most two terms.
        b.   In addition to variable terms, the involved terms may be preceded
             or followed by single "contextual" terms.
        c.   Both involved terms and contextual terms must be specified as
             single constituents or as single terminal elements.

In effect, the constraints in (13) restrict structural descriptions to the format given in (14):

(14) $X-(\text{Context}_1)-\text{Involved Term}_1-(\text{Context}_2)-Y-(\text{Context}_3)-$
        $\text{Involved Term}_2-(\text{Context}_4)-Z$

If the descriptive evidence appeared to warrant it, these restrictions could be amended to allow for limited use of analyzability conditions on *sequences* of terms. Conditions of this latter sort are allowed in the transformational frameworks developed in Peters and Ritchie (1973) and in Bresnan (1976a); they are encountered in many current descriptive studies in the form of labeled bracketings of terms in structural descriptions. Judging by the use of these conditions in recent syntactic studies, it would appear to be possible to restrict such bracketings in structural descriptions to a depth of two or possibly three. Such a restriction would be in effect a "binary" or "ternary" principle governing structural descriptions.

Given a specific base component, these restrictions on form clearly yield a set of possible structural descriptions that is finite rather than infinite. Moveover, they appear to exclude in advance the two sorts of undesirable transformational rules that Culicover and Wexler offer to illustrate the role of the Freezing Principle and the original Binary Principle in the learnability theorem.

In the first place, the set of transformations represented by the schema in (15) is offered as an example of an infinite set of undesirable guesses that the Binary Principle would make unavailable for phrase markers of the form given in (16):

(15)   A - A - ... - A   -   X   -   B
             1   2   ...   n   n+1   n+2
            n+2   2   ...   n   n+1 ϕ

(16)

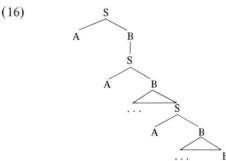

The involved terms in (15) are term 1 and term $n+2$, so that for any n greater than 2, a structural description of this form would violate the restrictions given in (13), by virtue of the extra contextual terms 3 through n. Thus the adoption of these restrictions would have the beneficial effect of excluding in advance all of the rules represented in (15) for which n was greater than two.

In the second place, the hypothetical transformational rule stated in (17) is offered as an illustration of the independent necessity of the Freezing Principle. A highly complicated derived phrase marker to which it could apply is given in (18).

(17)   B - B - B - X - C
             1   2   3   4   5
            5+1   2   3   4 ϕ

(18)

Here again, a transformational rule with this many contextual terms would be excluded in advance by the restrictions in (13). Although nothing in this more restricted framework would block the formation of a complicated derived phrase marker like (18), the framework would make it impossible to construct transformational rules that depended for their application on arbitrarily high degrees of derived structure complexity.

At the present time, I do not have a proof of the BDE result that rests on the restrictions in (13) rather than on the Freezing Principle and the original Binary Principle. However, in view of the fact that the new restrictions block at least some of the undesirable situations that would arise without the Freezing Principle and the Binary Principle, it seems to me that the possibility of obtaining a proof of the BDE result from these alternative assumptions would be well worth exploring. I should note that the general strategy employed in the original proof of the BDE result (Hamburger and Wexler, 1975) could not be adopted in a proof from the assumptions in (13). The reason is that the earlier assumptions made it possible to prove that, for a given base component, the set of "eligible structures" (phrase marker substructures available for analysis by transformational rules) was a finite set. The restrictions in (13), by contrast, allow infinite sets of eligible structures.[4]

Let me turn now to a second area in which tighter restrictions on possible transformational rules might have beneficial consequences for learnability. The Hamburger-Wexler learnability theorem assumed transformational components all of whose rules were obligatory. As Culicover and Wexler themselves observe (note 54), "optional transformations yield particularly difficult learnability problems." The central difficulty posed by optional rules is that no amount of data of the sort that is provided to the Hamburger-Wexler learning procedure would correct a tentative transformational component that contained an overly general optional rule. To take a simple example, suppose for the sake of illustration that the "correct" adult grammar for English contained an optional transformational rule of Dative Movement, with many verbs marked as negative exceptions to it. (This is the analysis that is assumed in Culicover and Wexler's paper.) Suppose, furthermore, that their learning procedure somehow arrived at a grammar that was identical to the "correct" one, except for lacking any negative rule features in the lexicon. In this situation, no amount of additional data of the sort that the procedure accepts would suffice to force the addition of the required lexical specifications. The only kind of data that would force a change would be data about sentences that were *not* grammatical. For instance, on this analysis, the feature specification [–Dative] in the lexical entry of a verb like *say* or *report* would not be motivated without some indication that the double-NP dative was ungrammatical with these verbs. The learning procedure assumed in Culicover and Wexler's paper and in earlier papers is not provided with negative data of this sort. The decision not to allow such data is justified very convincingly in Wexler, Culicover, and Hamburger (1975). The rationale rests on the fact that negative data of this sort do not appear to be routinely available to real human children. Consequently, an analysis of English that relies on a lexically governed rule of Dative Movement could apparently never be learned on the basis of the primary linguistic data with which English-speaking children are provided.

A similar problem exists with regard to rules like the putative rule of *On*-Deletion, which I discussed earlier. Here the problem is that the data that indicate the necessity of marking items like *yesterday* and *tomorrow* as "positive" exceptions are nonprimary in character rather than primary. Specifically, there is no evidence that children acquiring English are provided with the information that sentences like **John left on yesterday* are ungrammatical.

I might note here that obligatory rules do not create the same sort of problems of overgenerality. For any tentative obligatory rule that happens to be overly general, there will always be positive data that will provide motivation for restricting the domain of the rule. A simple example is provided by the general English rule of Subject-Auxiliary Inversion in direct questions. The unanalyzed interrogative phrase *how come* is an exception to this rule. Positive evidence for the exceptional nature of this form is provided every time a child encounters a normal adult utterance such as *How come you left the water running?*[5]

What strategy might be adopted, then, in order to bring facts like those concerning English datives into the realm of the learnable? One radical approach (actually the one that seems most promising to me) is to assume that English does not have transformational rules of Dative Movement or *On*-Deletion. The next step is to find a way of revising the transformational framework so that such rules are excluded in advance. Such a move has the effect of forcing an analysis for these English alternants that relies on multiple subcategorization; in such an analysis, problems of overgenerality like those discussed above do not arise.

There are a wide variety of possibilities for designing such a more highly restricted framework. One possible approach would be to develop a very restricted list of possible transformation types, perhaps along the lines suggested by Emmon Bach (1965, 1971). Another approach would be to try to find more purely formal characteristics that could be used to exclude unwanted rules. In the case of Dative Movement, for instance, a recent suggestion by Bresnan (1976a) might prove useful, a suggestion to the effect that individual transformational rules should be allowed to carry out only a single structural change. This restrictive hypothesis would allow rules that involve only movement or only deletion, while disallowing a rule like Dative Movement, which involves movement of an NP and concomitant deletion of a preposition. Such a restriction would of course entail a re-evaluation of the status of a great many other transformational rules that have been proposed. In at least some of the cases that I have looked at, it appears that the justification for a transformational treatment is much weaker than it was originally thought to be.

I hope that it has been clear that my disagreement with Culicover and Wexler concerning their adoption of Dative Movement and *On*-Deletion does not extend to their general approach to linguistic theory. I am essentially in agreement with the latter; indeed, my criticism of the particular analysis of English that they propose has been based on the learnability criterion that they suggest in the first section of their paper. Translated into their terminology, my arguments against Dative Movement and *On*-Deletion can be summarized as follows:

(19) a. If we assume that a language learner has no reliable access to negative data, then a descriptive framework that relies on standard definitions of *transformational rule* and allows a broad range of optional rules defines an unlearnable class of grammars.

  b. A more restricted framework, one in which many currently permitted optional transformational rules are excluded in advance, defines a class of grammars that is closer to being learnable.

  c. It is possible to construct an alternative analysis for English that stays within this more restricted framework without any loss of descriptive adequacy.

  d. Therefore, this alternative analysis, one that relies on multiple subcategorization, is to be preferred to an analysis that includes rules of Dative Movement and *On* Deletion.

What I have done in (19), then, is to offer one particular application of Culicover and Wexler's learnability criterion to an issue that arises in the study of English. It seems to me that the value of future work in generative syntax will depend in large part on the degree to which this criterion comes to be more widely understood, and more widely applied in the resolution of specific theoretical and descriptive issues.

Notes

1. I list this as a "possible" counterexample because of the variety of possibilities that exist for constructing a structure-preserving analysis for sentences of this sort. One suggestion, for instance, might be that the phrase *not one taco* has been moved into a complementizer node, so that sentences with preposed negative constituents are treated in exactly the same way as sentences with preposed interrogative constituents. An analysis along these lines seems questionable to me, in view of the fact that the complementizer *that* can generally precede preposed negatives, but can never precede preposed interrogatives:

  (i) *I am ashamed to tell you that not one taco has Fred offered to the guest of honor.*

  (ii) *I am ashamed to tell you what Fred said to the guest of honor.*

  (iii) **I am ashamed to tell you that what Fred said to the guest of honor.*

2. The reference to eligibility in (5b) makes it possible to avoid an incorrect prediction of unacceptability for a sentence like (i):

  (i) *For how many of the men is John easy ϕ_1 to get along with ϕ_2 ?*

  Although the NP *John* is the most current prospective tenant when ϕ_1 is reached, associating *John* with ϕ_1 would give an incorrect result. However, on the assumption that Tough Movement is stated so as to allow extraction only from a subordinate VP, *John* is not eligible to fill ϕ_1, so that the sentence-initial interrogative phrase is associated with ϕ_1.

3. One of Culicover and Wexler's arguments involving Complex NP Shift is not affected by the proposal I have suggested above. This is the argument based on unacceptable sentences such as (i) (their (15d)), a sentence that has undergone both Complex NP Shift and Gapping:

  (i) **John gave to Susan the book which be bought, and Fred, to Sam, the magazine which he stole.*

Since the hypothesis in (5) does not provide an alternative explanation for the unacceptability of (i), I would rate this particular argument for the Freezing Principle as the strongest
that Culicover and Wexler offer.

4. As Stan Peters has pointed out to me, the adoption of restrictions like those suggested in
(13) would necessitate changes in the learning procedure outlined in Hamburger and Wexler
(1975). The problem is that cases can arise in which a tentative transformational component
may fail to include two transformations that are necessary in the derivation of a certain sentence s from a base phrase marker b. If hypothesized transformational rules are drawn only
from the set defined by the more restricted framework, then the transformational component in the following trivial grammar is unattainable by the Hamburger–Wexler procedure:

(i)   a.   *Base component:*
           S → *abccd*
           Transformational Component:
           (1) a - b - X - d
                 1   2   3   4 $\Rightarrow \phi,\ 2,\ 3,\ 4+1$
           (2) b - X - d - a
                 1   2   3   4 $\Rightarrow 3+1,\ 2,\ \phi,\ 4$

This grammar generates the language consisting of the single string *dbcca*. The Hamburger–
Wexler procedure could not "learn" this transformational component, since the procedure
requires that only one transformational rule be added at a time. Given the initial tentative
transformational component (the empty one), the presentation of the datum ($_S$[*abccd*]$_S$,
dbcca) would not lead to any change in the component, since there is no single rule of the
form given in (14) that would suffice to carry out the necessary permutation of the terminal
elements. Several possibilities exist for modifying the procedure to avoid this problem.

5. This is not to say that obligatory rules create no serious learnability problems. Given a descriptive framework that allows both optional and obligatory rules without any restrictions,
the most serious problem is precisely that of learning whether a given rule is obligatory or
optional. Positive evidence would be of no avail here, since ungrammatical sentences characteristically provide the crucial evidence in favor of assigning obligatory status to a rule. This
is thus another area in which the possibilities for greater restrictiveness deserve to be investigated.

ON WH-MOVEMENT

Noam Chomsky

Department of Linguistics
Massachusetts Institute of Technology
Cambridge, Massachusetts

I will presuppose, in this paper, the general framework of the extended standard theory (EST), as outlined, for example, in Chomsky (1972, 1975b) and references cited there; and more specifically, the assumptions explored in Chomsky (1971, 1973, 1974, 1975b, c) and related work cited in these references. I want to examine some proposals put forth tentatively in the work cited and in so doing, to revise and extend some of the particular analyses and principles investigated. I will first review and somewhat reformulate some of the background assumptions drawn from earlier work and then apply them to several questions in English syntax.

I assume that a grammar is a theory of competence and that universal grammar (UG) is in essence a system of principles specifying the nature of linguistic representations and the rules that apply to them, and the manner in which these rules apply. A grammar (strongly) generates a set of structural descriptions and (weakly) generates a language, assigning one or more structural descriptions to each sentence of the language (and, in principle, to all potential sentences). A structural description of a sentence consists of a representation of the sentence on each linguistic level (cf. Chomsky, 1955). I assume that two of these levels are the levels of phonetic representation (PR) and what I will call "logical form" (LF), meaning by the latter the level that expresses whatever aspects of semantic representation are determined by properties of sentence-grammar. Cf. Chomsky (1975a,b,c) for discussion. Thus a grammar assigns to each sentence, in particular, a pair of representations (pr, lf), where pr is drawn from PR and lf from LF.

In accordance with EST, I assume here that a grammar consists of base rules, transformational rules, phonological rules and (semantic) interpretive rules. The base consists of a categorical component and a lexicon, the former satisfying the principles of some version of the X-bar theory (for recent discussion see Hornstein, 1975, Selkirk, 1975; Halitsky (1975); Emonds (1976); Bresnan, 1976a; Jackendoff, forthcoming), and the latter of the general character developed in Aronoff (1976). The base generates an infinite class of deep structures (initial phrase markers). I assume that thematic relations in the sense of Jackendoff (1972) and related work are determined by interaction of lexical properties and configurations of deep structures. The transformational component of the grammar generates derivations $D = (K_1, \ldots, K_n)$, where K_1 is a base-generated deep structure, K_{i+1} is formed from K_i by a transformation, and no obligatory transformation is applicable to K_n.

The derivation D must be related to PR and LF. I will have little to say here about the relation to PR. As for LF, I assume that it is determined by interpretive rules applying to K_n. Under this assumption, it must be that thematic relations are properly expressed in K_n, though determined at K_1. I will assume that this is the case, in accordance with trace theory, as outlined in the references cited above. If so, then interpretive rules extend the derivation D, carrying K_n to a representation in LF. These interpretive rules are the rules SI-1 of Chomsky (1975b,c). It is in fact misleading to call these "rules of semantic interpretation," as in these references and elsewhere; they are more properly described as rules concerned with the syntax of LF. Note that K_n will not be surface structure in the familiar sense. It is more "abstract," by virtue of trace theory, and may be subject to nontransformational rules (e.g., "scrambling"). Some crucial aspects of PR may be determined by the extended derivation from K_n to LF. Thus, as noted first by Lees (1960), deletion seems sensitive to some aspect of semantic representation, and under the present theory that means that the possibilities of deletion are in part fixed by properties of representations at LF or between K_n and LF. Cf. Sag (forthcoming, 1976) for an analysis of such rules as VP-deletion and gapping along these lines.

This outline is extremely sketchy, and the analyses cited are not even mutually compatible in detail. I present it only so as to locate the following discussion within a familiar general framework.

I will be concerned now with a kind of "core grammar" for English consisting of a few general rules and some general conditions governing the operation of these rules. The rules in question include two transformational rules (1) and three interpretive rules (2):

(1)   a.   Move NP
        b.   Move *wh*-phrase

(2)   a.   Reciprocal rule: assign to *each other* the feature [+anaphoric to i] in a structure containing NP_i
        b.   Bound anaphora: assign to a pronoun the feature [+anaphoric to i] in a structure containing NP , in the context [$_{NP}$—Possessive—N_x]
        c.   Disjoint reference: assign to a pronoun the feature [−anaphoric to i] in a structure containing NP_i

The rules of (2) are among those that Kenneth Hale has called "rules of construal" (cf. Hale, 1976). An informal explanation of their meaning will do for now. Let us assume that there is some standard method for indexing nonterminal symbols in deep structures, in particular, NPs; transformations will preserve the property that all nonterminals are indexed, in ways to be discussed. If *each other* is assigned the feature [+anaphoric to i], then the structure . . . NP_i . . . *each other* . . . (or . . .*each other* . . . NP_i . . .) is assigned the appropriate reciprocal interpretation, whatever this may be (for discussion, see Fiengo and Lasnik, 1973; Dougherty, 1974). A pronoun marked [+anaphoric to i] will be interpreted in LF as anaphoric to NP_i; the relevant choice of N_x will be essentially as discussed in Helke (1970), including, for English, *self*, so that English (nonemphatic) reflexive is understood as bound anaphora. A pronoun marked [-anaphoric to i] will be understood as disjoint in reference to NP_i; cf. Chomsky (1973); Lasnik (forthcoming). I assume that this rule falls under a more general rule of disjoint reference applying (in somewhat different ways) to all NPs. To make these vague remarks explicit, it is necessary to explain what is meant by the term "anaphoric." I assume that there is a procedure for introducing variables for NPs in LF, including pronouns, and that the notions "anaphoric," "nonanaphoric" will be understood as determining the choice of variables as the same or different. For present purposes, nothing much depends on how rules (2) are implemented, so I will not pursue the matter; as far as I can see, nontrivial questions arise in the case of (2a) and plural pronouns, the latter, a special case of problems concerning the semantics of plurality. I will assume that the rules (2) and others ultimately give representations in LF in a rather conventional form, with quantifiers and variables, for some empirical arguments, cf. Chomsky (1975c).

I assume that the rules (1) and (2) meet the following conditions:

(3)   Cycle: transformational rules, e.g., (1), meet the condition of the (strict) cycle; the subjacency condition is a property of cyclic rules, i.e., part of the definition of the cycle.

(4)   Propositional–island condition (PIC)

(5)   Specified subject condition (SSC)

I understand the notion of the cycle here in the sense of Chomsky (1973, (51)), with the qualifications given there. Assuming that transformational rules are either cyclic or postcyclic, it follows from this formulation that the rules (1), specifically (1b), are cyclic, since they apply in embedded structures.[1] I will understand the subjacency condition as holding that a cyclic rule cannot move a phrase from position Y to position X (or conversely) in (6):

(6) $\ldots X \ldots [_\alpha \ldots [_\beta \ldots Y \ldots] \ldots] \ldots X \ldots$, where α and β are cyclic nodes

For the present, I will take the cyclic nodes to be $\bar{S}$ and NP; on the effect of other choices, see below.

The subjacency condition applies to cyclic rules only; hence to cyclic transformational rules but not to interpretive rules or to postcyclic transformational rules. Thus for many people (myself included), such examples as (7) and (8) are fully acceptable:

(7)   *we want very much* [$_{\bar{S}}$ *for* [$_{NP}$ *pictures of each other*] *to be on sale*]

(8)   *the men expected* [$_{\bar{S}}$ *that* [$_{NP}$ *pictures of each other*] *would be on sale*]

Similarly, a postcyclic rule such as the major case of French clitic movement (cf. Kayne, 1975) need not, on these assumptions, meet the condition of subjacency.

It follows that rightward-movement rules are "upward bounded" (cf. Ross, 1967; Akmajian, 1975). But I am assuming that the same is true of "lowering rules" such as quantifier movement, and leftward-movement "raising" rules. It is easy enough to find phenomena that appear to violate the subjacency condition. Consider, e.g., the sentences (9), (10), where there is a relation between the phrase in bold face and the position marked by t, "violating" subjacency under the assumption that the rule in question is a movement rule:

(9)   *John* seems [$_{\bar{S}}$ *to be certain* [$_{\bar{S}}$ *t to win*]]

(10)   *who did Mary hope* [$_{\bar{S}}$ *that Tom would tell Bill* [$_{\bar{S}}$ *that he should visit t*]]

Putting the matter more carefully, a proposed condition on rules, such as subjacency, cannot be confirmed or refuted directly by phenomena of this (or any other) sort. A condition on rules can be confirmed or refuted only by rules, which observe or violate it, respectively. If the rule of NP-movement that yields (9) applies successive cyclically, as often assumed, then the rule will observe subjacency. If, as I have argued in the references cited, the rule of *wh*-movement applies successive cyclically, then it too will observe subjacency, giving (10). To find evidence to support or to refute a proposed condition on rules, it does not suffice to list unexplained phenomena; rather, it is necessary to present rules, i.e., to present a fragment of a grammar. The confirmation or refutation will be as convincing as the fragment of grammar presented. This is a simple point of logic, occasionally overlooked in the literature. The status of conditions on rules is empirical, but evidence can only be indirect and the argument, one way or another, is necessarily rather abstract and "theory bound."

The conditions (4) and (5) (PIC and SSC) refer to structures of the form (11), where α is a cyclic node:

(11) $\ldots X \ldots [_{\alpha} \ldots Y \ldots] \ldots X \ldots$

As in the case of subjacency, I will take $\bar{S}$ and NP to be the cyclic nodes, delaying the discussion of other choices until later. PIC (the "tensed-S condition" of the references cited) asserts that no rule can "involve" X and Y where α is a finite clause (tensed-S). SSC asserts that no rule can "involve" X and Y where α contains a specified subject, i.e., a subject not containing Y and not controlled by X (I modify an earlier formulation here; I assume that Y contains Y). If α contains a subject, then only the subject is accessible to rule, if the subject is specified in the defined sense.

The term "involved in" was left deliberately vague in the exploratory studies cited above, as was the category of rules to which the conditions are relevant. We may sharpen the formulation somewhat to include the desired cases and exclude unwanted ones. Let us restrict attention to rules specified in terms of a structural condition and a structural change, in the usual sense of transformational grammar (cf. Chomsky, 1955, 1961; Chomsky and Miller, 1963; Peters and Ritchie, 1973). We furthermore restrict attention to structural conditions of the elementary form (12), where α_i is a constant or $\alpha_i = vbl$, and each constant may be either a single element of the X-bar system or a terminal string (perhaps only a single symbol):

(12) $(\alpha_1, \ldots, \alpha_n)$

A terminal string with the successive factors $x_1, \ldots, x_n$ and the phrase marker K is subject to the structural change, with these factors, just in case $(x_1, \ldots, x_n)$ is analyzable as (12) with respect to K; i.e., x_i is an α_i with respect to K, where an arbitrary string is a *vbl*. Cf. references cited, and Chomsky (1975c).

We now say that a transformational rule *involves* X and Y when it moves a phrase from position X to position Y and a rule of construal *involves* X and Y when it assigns Y the feature [±anaphoric to *i*], where X has the index *i* (or conversely, in both cases). The two cases will be unified below.

Following a suggestion of Jean-Roger Vergnaud, we modify the definition of PIC, stipulating that α is the cyclic node immediately dominating the category of Y. Then rule (2b), giving (8), will not violate PIC. For discussion of the effect of PIC and SSC on postulated rules of grammar, see Chomsky (1971, 1973, 1974, 1975b,c); Lasnik and Fiengo (1974); Kayne (1975); Fiengo and Lasnik (1976); Quicoli (forthcoming a, b, c); Pollock (1976).

Plainly, rules can vary from language to language within the constraints imposed by UG, but it is often assumed that conditions on rules must be invariant. This assumption is somewhat arbitrary; cf. Ross (1967); Bresnan (1972); Chomsky (1973). There is no a priori reason not to assume the opposite, and in fact, a very high level of explanatory adequacy might well be attained by a theory of UG that permitted either rules or conditions to vary, within fixed limits. To consider a case in point, Kim (1976) observes that rules of anaphora in Korean meet a condition rather like PIC, but with a somewhat different condition on α of (11). There is no formal distinction in Korean between tensed and nontensed clauses, but there is a category of embedded clauses that are not islands, much like the infinitival clauses of English and the Romance languages: namely, the complements of a certain class of "assertive" verbs. It is interesting that these verbs are very close in meaning to the verbs that in English take infinitives. Thus we can formulate a variant of PIC for Korean, with the condition on α modified, and we can suggest a somewhat more abstract formulation of PIC of which English and Korean are special cases. In the absence of more extensive work on rule systems in other languages, I am reluctant to suggest anything further. Note again that evidence bearing on questions of this degree of abstractness requires a fairly credible grammatical analysis, since only rules, not phenomena, have bearing on the validity of conditions on rules.

Similarly, application of SSC in a language depends on the characterization of the notion "subject" in this language. The work cited on English and Romance seems to require a formal definition of "subject" in much the sence of Chomsky (1955, 1965). For some case languages, one might want to characterize "subject" in terms of such notions as ergative, absolutive, or nonoblique. Hale (1976) proposes certain conditions on what can be taken as subject in the syntactically "unmarked" situation; in accordance with his approach, a language might characterize the notion "subject" differently, but at a cost in the grammar, in accordance with the logic of markedness. One would expect that current work in "relational grammar" will shed much light on these questions. For the moment, I would prefer to think of the conditions cited as instances of condition-schemata, part of the core grammar of English, pending further relevant work on rule systems that may provide evidence bearing on their viability and the more general formulation of the relevant schemata.

In Chomsky (1973), two approaches to interpretation of conditions on rules are contrasted, an absolute and a relative interpretation; and the relative interpretation is proposed for conditions of the sort discussed there, including (4) and (5). Under this interpretation, a condition does not impose an absolute restriction against rules of a certain type (e.g., in the case of (4), rules not subject to PIC); rather a rule must be interpreted in accordance with the condition unless otherwise specified. Thus, one might construct a rule to "violate" the A-over-A condition, but only at a cost: the rule would have to make explicit the relevant structures so that it can apply without failing under the condition. "The logic of this approach," as noted, "is essentially that of the theory of markedness." That is, the conditions become an integral part of an evaluation measure, rather than imposing absolute prohibitions. I will continue to pursue this assumption here.

Let me now state the point somewhat more exactly. Assuming transformations and rules of construal to be defined as indicated above, in terms of (12), let us say that α_i, α_{i+j} are *adjacent* in (12) if each is constant (i.e., $\neq vbl$) and any term intervening between them is $=vbl$ (i.e., $j=1$, or $j=2$ and $\alpha_{i+1} = vbl$; these are the only cases we need consider in this rudimentary, but perhaps adequate theory of rules of transformation and construal).

Suppose now that we limit attention to rules of construal. Each such rule relates two categories of the phrase marker, assigning to one (the anaphor) the feature [+anaphoric to i], where i is the index of the other (the antecedent). Let us say that the antecedent and the anaphor are *involved in* the rule if they are adjacent; otherwise not. Specification of constant terms intervening between antecedent and anaphor will then make the conditions inapplicable, at a cost, in accordance with the logic of markedness.

Consider now transformational rules, specifically, movement rules, which we assume leave trace. It is natural to regard the relation between a moved phrase and its trace as essentially bound anaphora. Furthermore, by pursuing this suggestion we can derive, in an interesting class of cases, a principled explanation for the fact that certain rules and rule sequences are permissible while others are not; cf. Fiengo (1974), Chomsky (1974, 1975b). But now observe that we can extend the notion "involved in" defined for rules of construal to movement rules by permitting the latter to apply freely, then applying the conditions to the moved phrase (the antecedent) and its trace (the anaphor). We can then formulate a somewhat stronger condition of autonomy of syntax (cf. Lightfoot, 1976c); namely, the semantic conditions that enter into SSC are restricted to the interpretive rules. Taking this approach, the movement rule reflected in the surface structure (13a) is blocked for the same reason that the cases of bound anaphora in (13b), (13c) are blocked:

(13) a. *Bill seems [John to like t]   (t = trace of Bill)
      b. *Bill expected [Mary to like himself]
      c. *Bill expected [Mary to find his way home]

Restricting conditions (4) and (5), now, to rules of construal, we interpret them as applying to transformational rules as filters, in effect; the result of applying a transformational movement rule may or may not yield an appropriate case of "bound anaphora." It might be appropriate to give a similar interpretation to the subjacency condition for movement rules.

Under this interpretation of the application of conditions, we have the relative interpretation referred to earlier. That is, just as a language can have a rule that does not observe the A-over-A condition—at a cost, under the "logic of markedness"—so it can have a rule that does not observe, e.g., PIC—again at a cost, following the same logic. As an example, consider the "peripheral *Tous*-Movement phenomena" of Kayne (1975, pp. 63-64). Kayne argues for a general rule L-*Tous* moving quantifiers to the left; generally speaking, it observes the conditions on rules cited (cf. Quicoli, Pollock, for recent discussion). Unexplained in this or any other analysis is the appearance of the quantifier in such sentences as (14), accepted by many but not all speakers:

(14)   a.   *il faut toutes* [*qu'elles s'en aillent*]
       b.   *il faut tous* [*qu'on se tire*]

In (14), the quantifier is construed with a pronoun that is within a tensed sentence. Kayne does not formulate a rule for these examples. He notes that it is doubtful that the L-*Tous* rule can be modified to apply, for one reason, because L-*Tous* applies only when the quantifier is not part of a larger NP, which would be false in these cases, and for another, because *tous* does not appear with *on*.[2] It seems that the phenomena can be described by a rule such as (15):

(15) $(vbl, V^*, Q, que, \alpha, PRO, vbl)$

construing Q with PRO, where V^* is a certain class of verbs including *falloir, vouloir*, Q is a quantifier, and α is either null or is a "sufficiently short" NP; apparently, informant judgments, which are at best conflicting, strongly prefer pronouns or simply proper nouns, with acceptability rapidly declining as α becomes more complex. Suppose that (15) is the rule, more or less. Then, we do not have a violation of PIC, under the relative interpretation of conditions just outlined, the cost being the complexity of the rule (which does not strictly fall within the framework (12), incidentally). That is, PRO (or trace, if we regard the rule in question as a movement rule) is assigned the feature [+anaphoric to Q], but Q and PRO are not adjacent. As to whether this approach is general enough to deal with all such cases and no more, I would not hazard a guess, at this point. Note again that the question only arises when we can make a fair guess as to the relevant rule. Phenomena may be suggestive, but strictly speaking, they tell us nothing.

As formulated, conditions will apply to a construal rule when antecedent and anaphor are either (a) separated by *vbl* or (b) separated by nothing, i.e., successive. Case (a) is the general one; it is the familiar case of rules applying "over a variable." An example is *wh*-movement within a clause. Examples of (b) are few, and perhaps this case should be eliminated. One possible example is quantifier movement (or construal; it is irrelevant for present purposes whether the quantifier is moved or generated in place and interpreted), as described in Fiengo and Lasnik (1976), with the structural description (16) for the associated surface filter.

(16) $(vbl, \; t \;, NP, \; Q, \; X^n, \; vbl)$

where we take X^n to be an element of the X-bar system standing for the categories NP, VP, AP, and t to be the trace left by movement of the quantifier Q. The rule will permit (17) but not (18):

(17)   a.   *I gave the men all presents*
       b.   *I persuaded the men all to leave*
       c.   *I painted the houses all reddish-yellow*

(18)   *I saw the men all*

But as noted by Postal (1976), although (17b) is acceptable, (19) is not:

(19)   *I promised the men all to leave*

Assuming these judgments, Fiengo and Lasnik observe that we can explain the facts on the basis of a version of SSC that they formulate. Making slightly different assumptions than they do, suppose we assume the structures of (17b) and (19) to be essentially (20), where v is either *persuade* or *promise*:

(20)   *I - v - t - the men - all -* [PRO - *to leave*]

Suppose we take PRO in (20) to be nonterminal—in effect, a feature on the subject NP; reasons will be given below. Then (20) is subject to the analysis (16), and the rule relating *all* and t should apply. Suppose now we were to extend our notion of "involvement" to relate also adjacent constant terms, one of which is either antecedent or anaphor and the other a constant category of the X-bar system. Then the pair (*all, to leave*) is involved in the rule. Suppose that we modify the notion "specified subject," in a not unnatural way, revising SSC so that given (11), no rule can apply if X and Y are involved in the rule and α contains a subject not containing Y and not controlled by the category containing X or its trace (a slightly different formulation is needed if we take the rule to be one of construal). This modification leaves other cases unchanged, but now we will derive (17b) and not (19) by virtue of familiar properties of control. The case is interesting in that the constant terms "involved" are Q and VP, although the application of the rule related NP and Q. Judgments are unfortunately somewhat variable in the relevant cases and there are other possible analyses, but perhaps we can take this example at least as an illustration of the logic of the problem, and perhaps an actual illustration of the operative principles, though I am rather skeptical.

Assuming this framework, with or without the modification just discussed, we have such examples of application of conditions as the following:

(21)   *Reciprocal rule:*

       a.   PIC: (i)   **they** *want* [**each other** *to win*]
                  (ii) *they prefer [*that each other win*] [3]

b. SSC: (i) ***they** seem to me* [*t to like each other*]
       (ii) ****I** seem to them* [*t to like each other*]
      (iii) ***what books** do they expect* [*to read **t** to each other*]
      (iv) ****what books** do they expect* [*t to be read to each other*]
      (v) ****what books** do they expect* [*Bill to read to each other*]

Disjoint reference:

a. PIC: (i) *they want* [*them to win*]   (*they ≠ them*)
      (ii) *they prefer* [*that they win*]⁴

b. SSC: (i) ***they** seem to me* [*t to like them*]   (*they ≠ them*)
      (ii) *I seem to them* [*t to like them*]
      (iii) ***what books** do they expect* [*to read **t** to them*] (*they ≠ them*)
      (iv) ***what books** do they expect* [*t to be read to them*]
      (v) ***what books** do they expect* [*Bill to read **t** to them*]⁵

NP-movement

a. PIC: (i) ***Bill** is believed* [*t to be a fool*]
      (ii) ****Bill** is believed* [*t is a fool*]

b. SSC: (i) ***John** seems* [*t to like Bill*]
      (ii) ****Bill** seems* [*John to like **t***]⁶

Clitic movement :⁷

a. PIC: From infinitives, but not tensed clauses, by PIC⁸

b. SSC: (i) *cela **le** [fera téléphoner **t** à ses parents*]
          (compare *ce garçon* in place of *le* in base position)
      (ii) **cela **leur** fera* [*téléphoner ce garçon **t***] (compare *à ses parents*
                                          in place of *leur* in
                                          base position)
      (iii) *elle **lui** fera* [*boire du vin **t***] (compare *à son enfant* in place
                                          of *lui* in base position)
      (iv) **qui cette nouvelle m'a-t-elle fait* [*téléphoner t(**qui**) t(**me**)*]
              (compare *à Jean* in place of *moi* in base position)

Quantifier movement ⁹

a. PIC: (i) *J'ai **tout** voulu lui laisser* [*manger t(**tout**) t(**lui**)*]
      (ii) **J'ai **tout** voulu* [*que Marie mange **t***]

b. SSC: (i) *J'ai **tout** laissé* [*manger t a Jean*]
         j'ai **tout laisse* [*Jean manger t*]
        Pierre m'a tous semblé* [*t (Pierre**) les avoir t(**tous**) lus*]
        I ordered the boys [*to have each finished the work by noon*]
        **I promised the boys* [*to have each finished the work by noon*]

Extraposition from NP

SSC: (i)   [*a review of John's book*] *came out yesterday*

      (ii)   *a review came out yesterday of John's book*

      (iii)   [*Bill's review of John's book*] *came out yesterday*

      (iv)   **Bill's review came out yesterday of John's book*

These are typical illustrative examples.

Note that the subjacency condition implies the complex noun phrase constraint (CNPC) and also the *wh*-island constraints, when taken in conjunction with SSC and an independently motivated condition to block *"I remember what who saw" while permitting "I remember who saw what"; cf. Chomsky (1973, 1975b), for discussion. Thus any rule subject to subjacency must meet the CNPC and the *wh*-island constraint, which are independent (cf., e.g., *"what do you wonder who saw"; cf. Chomsky, 1973, for discussion of some problematic cases).[10] On the other hand, interpretive rules, which do not observe subjacency, do not, on these assumptions observe these constraints. Thus on these assumptions we should have such sentences as (22):

(22)   a.   *they heard* [*some funny stories about* [*pictures of each other*]][11]

       b.   *they developed* [*some strange attitudes about* [*each other's books*]]

We return to some examples involving rules of construal and *wh*-islands below.

When we consider interpretive rules that do not, I believe, fall within the range of rules of construal as considered here, the situation seems reasonably clear. For example, in languages where relativization involves no movement rule at all but simply interprets a base-generated pronoun in the relative clause,[12] relativization can violate the usual constraints fairly freely, as noted by Ross (1967) and many others since. In Hebrew, for example, there are two processes of relativization, one involving a movement rule (with optional deletion of the moved pronoun if it is a direct object, and, I assume, obligatory deletion if it is the subject) and the other involving just interpretation of a base-generated pronoun in the relative clause. The movement rule observes the usual constraints; the interpretive rule violates them fairly freely. For example, we have (23):

(23)   i.   *ze   ha-iš   še   (oto) ra'iti etmol*]

          (this-is the-man [that (him) I-saw yesterday])

      ii.   *ra'iti et ha-iš* [*še   natata   li   et   ha-sefer* [*še*   *hu*   *katav*   **oto**]]

          (I saw the-man [that you gave me the-book [that he wrote *it*]])

The same is true in the (rather artificial) English *such that* construction, which, though not part of normal English, can be used readily by English speakers without instruction, suggesting that they are drawing from resources of UG. Similarly, left-dislocation in English (using the term in a sense extended beyond Ross, 1967) allows such structures as (24):

(24)   *as far as John is concerned, I will never believe the claims that have been made about **him***

In (24), *him* is understood to refer to John, "violating" CNPC, the *wh*-island constraint, and subjacency. If our approach is correct, then, no movement rule applies in this case. Nor can a rule of construal apply, on the assumption that these rules are subject to PIC and SSC. A natural approach, I think, is to assume that pronouns are base-generated and permitted to refer freely (Dougherty's "anaporn relation"; cf. note 12). Thus, the base rules could have introduced arbitrary NPs in the italicized positions of (23ii), (24). In some cases, rules of bound anaphora (e.g., (2b)) limit the choice of NP to bound pronouns, in effect. In the present case, however, it is not a rule of construal that is involved but rather a rule of a different category that we may call "rules of predication" (cf. Faraci, 1974). The rule of interpretation for relatives requires that the relative be taken as an open sentence satisfied by the entity referred to by the NP in which it appears; hence there must be an NP in the relative that in interpreted as having no independent reference–i.e., a pronoun with the appropriate inflections that can be given the "anaphoric" interpretation. The requirement is met automatically where relativization is by a movement rule, under the trace-theoretic assumptions of the references cited. Left-dislocation might be assumed to have a similar rule. The proposition must be "about" the item focused in the left-dislocated phrase. How close the relation of "aboutness" must be is unclear; some speakers seem to permit a rather loose connection, roughly as in the somewhat comparable Japanese *wa*- constructions that are said to permit, e.g., (25):

(25)   *as for the circus (circus-wa), elephants are funny*

In the narrower case, where the left-dislocated phrase is an NP, the situation is comparable to relatives. So interpreted, the rules in question fall completely outside the framework I have so far discussed and are not subject to any of the conditions cited, as seems to be the case. The same is true of rules that are not rules of sentence grammar at all, e.g., VP-deletion, which, as observed by Sag and Hankamer (1976), can apply across speakers in discourses and, correspondingly, is not subject to principles or sentence grammar; cf. (26):

(26)   a.   Speaker 1: *John didn't hit a home run*
              Speaker 2: *I know a woman who did*
        b.   *John didn't hit a home run, but I know [a woman who did–]*
        c.   *that John didn't hit a home run is not surprising, but that Bill knows
              that John didn't–is a real shock.*

Cf. Sag (1976, forthcoming).

Before turning to *wh*-movement, I want to say a word about "trace theory."

Let us continue to assume, as before, that categories introduced in a base derivation are indexed. Thus rules of construal can be given in the form described and derivations can simply be extended to LF; the properties of deep structure relevant to LF, and only these, are represented in surface (or shallow) structure. The question then arises, what happens to the indexing of phrases under a movement rule? For sake of illustration, suppose that English contains a rule of NP-postposing, one component of the passive rule, as often assumed. What does the theory of transformations tell us about the derived constituent structure given by application of this rule?

Suppose that the structure to which the rule applies is (27):

(27) $[_S [_{NP_i} \textit{John}]\ [_{VP}\ \textit{be+en kill}\ [_{NP_j}\ \textit{Bill}]\ \textit{by}\ [_{NP_k}\ e]]]$

The rule of NP postposing moves NP_i, replacing the terminal identity element e, in NP_k. It is natural to assume that the moved NP, *John*, retains its index, so that in place of NP_k, we have NP_i of (27). It is generally assumed—and if we accept the framework of Emonds (1976), must be assumed— that the NP subject position remains after application of the rule, but that it is not filled by a terminal string. The position will later be filled by a structure-preserving rule of NP-preposing. Thus we do not assume that after NP-postposing (27) is just a VP. Following these assumptions, the output of NP-postposing is (28):

(28) $[_S [_{NP_i} e]\ [_{VP} \textit{be+en kill}\ [_{NP_j}\ \textit{Bill}]\ \textit{by}\ [_{NP_i}\ \textit{John}]]]$

On the same assumptions, after NP-preposing we will have (29):

(29) $[_S [_{NP_j}\ \textit{Bill}]\ [_{VP}\ \textit{be+en kill}\ [_{NP_j}\ e]\ \textit{by}\ [_{NP_i}\ \textit{John}]]]$

We may now define the substructure $[_{NP_i}\ e]$ of (28) as the "trace" of NP_i (= $[_{NP_i}\ \textit{John}]$), and represent it by convention as $t(i)$ (read: "trace of NP_i"). Similarly, the substructure $[_{NP_j}\ e]$ of (29) is the trace of NP_j, represented as $t(j)$.[14] We may think of "trace," then, as an indexed NP, with null terminal. The notion "trace," taken (as it must be) as a function, falls naturally out of some reasonable assumptions about derived constituent structure.

Consider now the status of the item often written as PRO, which appears in such structures as (20). We may take PRO to be just base-generated $t(x)$, x a variable; i.e., as base generated NP_x, an NP without a fixed index. The index is then assigned by a rule of control. E.g., in (20), if $v = \textit{persuade}$ and *the man* is NP_i, then PRO will become NP_i; and if $v = \textit{promise}$ and I is NP_j, then PRO will become NP_j. In the former case, PRO = $t(i)$; in the latter, PRO = $t(j)$.

It follows, then, that trace and PRO are the same element; they differ only in the way the index is assigned—as a residue of a movement rule in one case, and by a rule of control in the other. We would expect, then, that trace and PRO have the same effect on rule application. This seems to be the case; cf. Chomsky (1975c) for some discussion, following Quicoli (forthcoming, a). Note also that PRO is nonterminal, as required in the discussion of (16)–(20).

So conceived, trace theory (incorporating the theory of PRO), is a trivial modification of the conventional theory of transformations, making explicit assumptions about derived constituent structure that are fairly conventional, taken together with a theory of indexing that is rather natural within the framework of EST. But there are substantial empirical consequences that result from making explicit these assumptions.

This completes the review and restatement of the general framework I want to assume. Let us now turn to the rule of *wh*-movement. In this section too I will reformulate some assumptions of the work already cited.

According to the conceptions just outlined, *wh*-movement leaves a nonterminal trace, just as all movement rules do. That is, the position from which the *wh*-phrase moved remains in the derived constituent structure with its index, identical to the index of the *wh*-phrase, now in COMP. It seems clear that words such as *who, what*, etc., should be regarded (at least in questions) as quantifiers of some sort. Thus at the level LF, the sentence (30) will be represented essentially as (31):

(30)   *who did John see?*

(31)   *for which x, x a person, John saw x* [15]

There is good reason to suppose that the rules extending a derivation to LF form such expressions as (31), and that variables are introduced in other ways as well, in particular, by the expansion of NP quantifiers such as *every* and by a rule of FOCUS. Cf. Chomsky (1975b,c), where it is shown that a variety of "cross-over phenomena" can be explained on this assumption, modifying an approach proposed by Culicover and developed by Wasow (1972) to a set of problems discussed first by Postal (1971). The variable introduced by the rules giving the meaning of quantifiers (*who, every*, etc) is a terminal symbol of LF. Therefore, although the structure resulting directly from *wh*-movement does not have a terminal symbol in the position of trace, the structure resulting from the interpretive rule expanding the quantifier does have a terminal symbol in this position.

In Chomsky (1975c), I referred to trace as a terminal symbol. That was an error. It is not trace that is a terminal symbol but rather the variable introduced in the position of trace by the rules giving the meaning of such quantifiers as *every* and *who* (and also by the rule of FOCUS). Difficulties in the assumption that trace is terminal were shown by Lightfoot (1976a) and Pollock (1976). Furthermore, the assumption is incompatible with the analysis of quantifier-movement (or interpretation) given above, following (essentially) Fiengo and Lasnik. The error of identifying trace itself as the variable within the scope of the *wh*-quantifier, which is overcome in the much more natural theory just outlined, resulted from concentration on too narrow a class of *wh*-phrases. Thus when we consider only such sentences as (32), the trace can be virtually identified with the variable:

(32)   *who did Mary say that John kissed t*

But the distinction becomes obvious when we consider more complex cases, such as (33), (34):

(33)   *whose book did Mary read t*

(34)   *pictures of whom did Mary see t*

Here, trace marks the position from which the *wh*-phrase was moved, but the rule expanding the quantifier *wh* will have to yield the LFs (35), (36), respectively:

(35)   *for which x, x a person, Mary read* [*x's book*]

(36)   *for which x, x a person, Mary saw* [*pictures of x*]

Correspondingly, the correct LF for (32) should be (37):

(37)   *for which x, x a person, Mary said that John kissed* [*x*]

The LF (37) has a terminal symbol, x, in the position of the NP source of *who*, but (32) has only a trace, i.e., only the structure $[_{NP_i}$ e$]$, where i is the index of *who*.

The rule of interpretation for *wh*-phrases must introduce the expressions given in brackets in (35)–(37) in the position of trace. We may take the rule to be essentially as follows:[16]

(38)   Given an $\bar{S}$ of the form:
        $[_{COMP} \text{--}[wh\text{-}\bar{N}]\text{--}[+\text{WH}]] \quad [_S \ldots t \ldots]$
        where t is the trace of $[wh\text{-}\bar{N}]$, rewrite it as:
        $[_{COMP}$ for which x, x an $\bar{N}]$, $[_S \ldots [\text{--}x\text{--}] \ldots]$

The framework assumed here is that of Chomsky (1973), and the analysis can be extended to the other cases discussed there; cf. Vergnaud (1974), for extension to relatives.

Note that on this theory, the phonetic consequences of presence of trace are limited to the terminal symbols (variables) introduced by the rule (38). We can then maintain the analysis of such examples as (39) as outlined in Chomksy (1975c), but without the complications noted by Lightfoot (1976c):

(39)   *who do you wanna see Bill*

Similarly, consider the case of French liaison discussed by Selkirk (1972). She observes that in one style, there is no liaison across the site of *wh*-movement, though there is liaison acress the site of raising of NP to subject (and, it seems, clitic movement, though she states that the facts are obscure in this case). According to the present theory, NP-raising and clitic movement cannot have phonetic effects, but *wh*-movement may, depending on the ordering of the rule (38) and the rule of liaison. In fact, it seems that speakers of French agree that there is liaison across the raising site, but there is much variation and uncertainty about the *wh*-movement cases. Perhaps this means that the ordering of rules is rather uncertain in this (somewhat artificial) style. Unfortunately, the relevant data are much less clear than one might hope, and since the style in question is not conversational but rather taught, it is not so clear how seriously one can take the facts. Some educated speakers regard them as quite dubious.

To summarize, we assume that when a phrase moves by a transformation, its category remains as an "unfilled node," and that the moved phrase and the original position have the same index. The unfilled node labelled i is $t(i)$, the trace of P_i, the phrase moved from position i. The trace will invoke SSC and is available for assignment of thematic relations. PRO and trace are identified; they differ only with respect to the origin of the index. The position of trace may be filled by a phrase containing a variable, by expansion of a quantifier. There may be phonetic effects of trace in the latter case.

The rules and conditions given so far permit *wh*-movement within a clause, giving such sentences as (40), but not extraction of *wh*-phrases from a clause,[17] as in (41):

(40)   *who did Mary meet t*

(41)   *who did you tell Mary that she should meet t*

The two cases are in fact quite different in character. Many languages permit the first but not the second (e.g., Russian, German). Furthermore, whereas *wh*-movement within a clause is unconstrained, extraction from a clause is lexically governed, as has frequently been remarked. Thus we have such examples as (42):[18]

(42) a. **what did John complain that he had to do this evening*
      b. **what did John quip that Mary wore*
      c. *?who did he murmur that John saw*

Just what property of the matrix VP permits it to be a "bridge" (in the sense of Erteschik, 1973), permitting escape of the *wh*-phrase from the $\overline{S}$ "island," is unclear, Some proviso is necessary, however.

Suppose that we formulate the basic rule of *wh*-movement essentially as (43):

(43) move *wh*-phrase into COMP

The rule will apply freely clause-internally, but will not yet move the *wh*-phrase over a bridge. We may then formulate a language-specific COMP–COMP movement rule (44):

(44) move *wh*-phrase from COMP to a higher COMP over a bridge

The structural description of this rule (subject to modifications about placement in COMP to be discussed) will be approximately (45):

(45) (COMP, X, *wh*-phrase, *vbl*), where X contains a VP with certain special properties

If we incorporate the "bridge" properties in (45), then the rule will not fall strictly within the format we have proposed for transformational rules. Moreover, under the relative interpretation of conditions discussed before, it might be argued that the conditions are inapplicable; more precisely, it is easy to see how "involved in" can be sharpened so as to make them inapplicable, along the lines discussed earlier. Suppose, alternatively, that we dispense with (45) and interpret the "bridge" conditions as conditions on rules of interpretation. Then COMP–COMP movement by (43) will be blocked by the conditions. We must therefore introduce a language-specific proviso in (11), for English, namely, (46):

(46) where Y is not in COMP

Which of these approaches is preferable is unclear. I will assume the latter, without much reason. Thus we add the language-specific proviso (46) to (11), permitting COMP–COMP movement, and we assume that the "bridge" conditions fall within the interpretive rules, either SI-1 or SI-2 (cf. Chomsky, 1975b, c; Erteschik, 1973).

Sentence (41) will be formed, as in the references cited, by successive-cyclic application of *wh*-movement, now understood to be reapplication of (43). The rule is subject to all of the conditions on movement rules, so that we have the consequences already noted.[19]

Continuing to adopt the framework of the references cited, as modified above, I will assume that the rule (43) places a *wh*-phrase within the COMP node to the left of [±WH], which is realized phonetically as *that, for*, or null. There are a number of apparently rather idiosyncratic rules that determine the phonetic realization of the items in COMP. A formulation given in Chomsky (1973) can be considerably improved and extended, but I will not go into the matter here. One general rule for Modern English is that sequences of the form *wh*-phrase +complementizer are not permitted, as they were in earlier stages of the language. Thus we will have rules such as (47), (48):

(47)   *wh*-phrase becomes null

(48)   a.   *that* becomes null
        b.   *for* becomes null

One of the three must apply, By general conditions on recoverability of deletion, which we may assume to exist though they are not understood in detail, (47) will be inapplicable when the *wh*-phrase contains actual lexical content (e.g., prepositions, possessives, etc.). The rules (48) apply more broadly; e.g., *that* can be deleted under certain circumstances in nonrelatives, *for* is deleted immediately following verbs of the *want* category and under certain circumstances before *to*, etc.

I will assume that the *wh*-phrase moved by the rule is as determined by Bresnan's relativized A-over-A principle (cf. Bresnan, 1976a; Woisetschläger, 1976, Sag, 1976, for somewhat different versions).

The rule of *wh*-movement has the following general characteristics:

(49)   a.   it leaves a gap
        b.   where there is a bridge, there is an apparent violation of subjacency, PIC, and SSC
        c.   it observes CNPC
        d.   it observes *wh*-island constraints

The properties (49) follow, on the theory outlined, from the assumption that *wh*-movement moves a phrase (implying (a)), observes SSC, PIC, and subjacency (implying (c) and (d)[20]), and is permitted from COMP-to-COMP under "bridge" conditions (implying (b)).

So far, I have been recapitulating and somewhat revising earlier work. Now I want to turn to the main question of this paper, namely, (50):

(50)   Where we find the configuration (49) in some system of data, can we explain it on the assumption that the configuration results from *wh*-movement?

In other words, does the configuration (49) serve as a kind of "diagnostic" for *wh*-movement. That it may has been suggested, quite tentatively and without elaboration, in earlier work. I now want to investigate the plausibility of the contention. The following remarks, then, have a narrower and a broader aim. The narrower aim is to provide evidence that certain examples with the configuration (49) may in fact plausibly be understood as cases of *wh*-movement. The stronger aim is to suggest that this may be true in general. By the logic of the question, the stronger proposal cannot be demonstrated but only suggested.

I will assume, following the analysis in the references cited, that *wh*-movement is what underlies restrictive and nonrestrictive relatives and direct and indirect questions. There are, of course, some distinctions among these cases. Some of them can be accounted for by considering the contexts in which the *wh*-movement rule applies. E.g., questions but not relatives can have *wh*-movement of adjective phrases, but this distinction will obviously follow from the rule of relativization, whether it is a raising rule (cf. Vergnaud, 1974) or an interpretive rule. In other cases, stipulation may be necessary to distinguish some types from others (though this is not obvious), but if so, there seems no compelling reason to suppose that the stipulation is a condition on the *wh*-movement rule itself, though even if it were, it would not materially affect the point at issue.

Apart from these cases, the best-studied relevant example is the case of comparatives. It has been frequently noted (first, I believe, by David Vetter) that comparatives essentially have the properties (49), and it was therefore proposed in Chomsky (1973) and Vergnaud (1974) that "comparative deletion" is in reality a case of *wh*-movement. The contrary position is argued by Bresnan in an important article (Bresnan, 1975), which, together with Bresnan (1972, 1973), constitutes the most extensive and illuminating study of comparatives available. The issue is complex. Let me try to sort it out.

First, is there evidence for a *wh*-movement rule underlying comparatives? For some dialects of English, there is direct evidence for such a rule, as noted in Bresnan (1972). Thus many dialects of American English normally have such comparatives as (51):

(51) a. *John is taller than what Mary is*
      b. *John is taller than what Mary told us that Bill is*

For such dialects, the comparative rule is virtually identical to the general rule of *wh*-movement. Subject to the qualifications given above, it seems that the rule postulated for relatives and questions can simply extend to comparatives, with essentially no change. The properties (49) will then follow directly.

But there is evidence (Richard Kayne, personal communication) in support of a *wh*-movement analysis for other dialects of English as well. Consider the sentence (52), where brackets bound internal cyclic nodes:

(52) a. *Mary isn't the same as [she was five years ago]*
      b. *Mary isn't the same as [John believes [that Bill claimed [that she was five years ago]]]*
      c. **Mary isn't the same as [John believes [Bill's claim [that she was five years ago]]]*
      d. **Mary isn't the same as [I wonder [whether she was five years ago]]*

This construction has the properties (49). The "gap" is an adjective phrase, just as in comparatives; we can replace "the same as" by "taller than" throughout. There are similar constructions in which even the phrase *the same* does not appear, as in (53), etc.:

(53) a. *Mary is (more or less) as she was five years ago*
      b. *Mary is rather like John thought she was* [in colloquial English]
      c. *Mary isn't as John believes that Bill claimed that she was five years ago*

In these cases, a deletion analysis, if possible at all, seems rather artificial, since in contrast with comparatives, there is no overt matrix phrase that can trigger and control the deletion. We can easily account for (52-3) by a *wh*-movement rule of the sort postulated for the dialects that permit (51). The rule will give (54a), just as it gives (54b) in the dialects that have an overt *wh*-form in comparatives:

(54) a. *Mary isn't (the same) as* [*what she was five years ago*]
      b. *Mary isn't taller than* [*what she was five years ago*]

Sentence (54b), for dialects that do not permit it, can be regarded as the structure underlying (55) by a rule of *wh*-phrase deletion, falling under (47):

(55) *Mary isn't taller than she was five years ago.*

The same rule will give (52-3). The dialects differ, then, in obligatoriness of *wh*-phrase deletion; as noted, this and related rules are subject to a variety of apparently rather idiosyncratic conditions.

According to this analysis, the sentences of (52)-(53) are regarded as analogous to those of (56):

(56) a. *Mary isn't different than* [*what she was five years ago*]
      b. *Mary isn't different than* [*what John believes* [*that Bill claimed* [*that she was five years ago*]]]
      c. **Mary isn't different than* [*what John believes* [*Bill's claim* [*that she was five years ago*]]]
      d. **Mary isn't different than* [*what I wonder* [*whether she was five years ago*]]

Examples (56c,d) are ruled out by subjacency, PIC, and SSC. Under the analysis that presupposes (54a) underlying (52a), (53a), the same is true of (52c, d), etc.

Proceeding, we may treat *as, than* as prepositions, analogous to *than* in (56). This seems reasonable anyway; it means that such sentences as (57) will be analyzed as having final prepositional phrases of the form P NP, rather than being derived by deletion of *be* from (58):

(57) *John is taller than Bill*

(58) *John is taller than Bill is*

Cf. Hankamer (1973) for arguments supporting this analysis of (57).

The analysis of (52-3) along these lines seems natural and perhaps compelling. If it is correct, then all dialects that permit (52-3) have a rule of *wh*-movement forming comparatives. Therefore, there is no need for a new rule of comparative deletion.

If this is correct, we might propose further that there do not exist rules of "deletion over a variable." Thus the category of permissible rules is reduced, always a welcome step. Furthermore, we have some support for a positive answer to the question (50). Correspondingly, we have some evidence that the island constraints of (50iii, iv) can be explained in terms of general and quite reasonable "computational" properties of formal grammar (i.e., subjacency, a property of cyclic rules that states, in effect, that transformational rules have a restricted domain of potential application; SSC, which states that only the most "prominent" phrase in an embedded structure is accessible to rules relating it to phrases outside; PIC, which stipulates that clauses are islands, subject to the language specific "escape hatch" (46)[21]). If this conclusion can be sustained, it will be a significant result, since such conditions as CNPC and the independent wh-island constraint seem very curious and difficult to explain on other grounds.[22] Whether or not these further consequences prove tenable, it seems clear that a strong argument would be required to show that English has a second rule of comparative deletion that gives exactly the same forms as the independently motivated and quite general wh-movement rule (subject, again, to the qualification on p. 87). It would be rather paradoxical for a language to contain a general rule of wh-movement forming all comparatives (and much else), along with a second rule (comparative deletion) that is extensionally identical (as a mapping) with the first over the subdomain of structures such as (58).

Bresnan (1975) argues that the rule of comparative formation falls together with her rule of comparative subdeletion, which gives such sentences as (59):

(59)   *they have many more enemies than we have—friends*

She argues further that comparative subdeletion is a rule of deletion over a variable. Let us put aside the second contention for the moment and ask whether there is strong evidence that comparatives fall under a rule that gives comparative subdeletion as a special case. I am not convinced. In fact, Bresnan cites differences that seem to me significant (cf. pp. 58-9, particularly note 10), and that raise a serious question as to whether these rules are subcases of a single process. A rule to provide the cases of comparative subdeletion is no doubt needed, in some form, but I see no compelling reason to suppose that a rule of comparative deletion will fall out as a special case. If not, then there is no reason on these grounds for postulating a rule of comparative deletion, essentially duplicating the effects of the rule of wh-movement and wh-phrase deletion (independently motivated for (51), (52), and far more general in extension) over the subdomain of comparatives. I will tentatively conclude, then, that English does not have a rule of comparative deletion.

It remains to discuss Bresnan's argument that comparative subdeletion is a rule of deletion over a variable meeting such conditions as (50iii, iv), and other arguments that she puts forth to show that island constraints cannot be explained in the terms suggested here. I will return to these questions below. Note that these considerations relate to the query (50) and the broader aim sketched above, but they do not bear on the question as to whether English has a rule of comparative deletion in addition to wh-movement and wh-phrase deletion.

Bresnan notes that comparatives have the cross-over properties discussed by Postal, Wasow and others. She then argues that cross-over properties are not a diagnostic for movement rules, on her assumption that comparatives are formed by a deletion rule. If she is correct, it would follow that the explanation for cross-over suggested in Wasow (1972) and in another form in Chomsky (1975b,c) is incorrect or at least incomplete, since it would seem that this explanation could not be extended to deletion rules. But if comparatives are formed by *wh*-movement, as suggested above, it follows at once that they should have exactly the cross-over properties of relatives and questions; the proposed explanations would directly cover the cases that Bresnan cites, with no changes. It seems to me fair to take this as an indirect but significant additional argument in favor of the hypothesis that comparatives are formed by *wh*-movement. The argument is, in this case, that under this hypothesis we retain a fairly general, and, I believe, rather convincing explanation for cross-over phenomena.

The cross-over cases that Bresnan cites are (essentially) the following:

(60)   a.   *more students flunked than—thought they would (flunk)*
        b.   *more students flunked than they thought—would (flunk)*

Students is the understood subject of *think* in (a) and *flunk* in (b). But in (a), *they* can refer to the students, whereas in (b) it cannot.

According to a *wh*-movement analysis, the structure of (a) and (b) after *wh*-movement will be approximately (61a), (61b), respectively:

(61)   a.   *more students flunked than* [[*wh-many* (*students*)] [*t thought* [*they would flunk*]]]
        b.   *more students flunked than* [[**wh-many** (*students*)] [*they thought* [*t would flunk*]]]

The structures of (61) are analogous in relevant respects to the direct questions (62a), (62b):

(62)   a.   *how many (students)* [*t thought* [*they would flunk*]]
        b.   *how many (students)* [*they thought (did they think) [t would flunk*]]

The analysis proposed in the references cited accounts for all of these cases, in what seems to me a very natural way, on the basis of fairly general principles. It remains to be determined whether all cases of cross-over in comparatives fall so readily under the analysis developed for *wh*-movement.

I am not arguing that a language might not have two rules yielding a single structure such as comparatives, but rather that a substantial argument must be given to motivate a second rule, particularly, when it is extensionally equivalent to the first over a subdomain of the first. Cases of "double rules" exist, it seems. Recall the case of Hebrew relatives discussed above (cf. (23)). Here, however, the two processes do not cover the same domain for principled reasons, as noted.

Let us turn now to another example of a grammatical process that gives the configuration (49), namely, topicalization.   To begin with, topicalization does yield this configuration. Thus we have (63):

(63) a.   *this book, I really like*
      b.   *this book, I asked Bill to get his students to read*
      c.   **this book, I accept the argument that John should read*
      d.   **this book, I wonder who read*

Before proposing an analysis of topicalization, let us consider again left-dislocation as in (64) (cf. (24)):

(64) *as for this book, I think you should read it*

Plainly in this case, there can be no transformational analysis in our terms since no transformation can "create" the structure "as for this book" or even more complicated phrases that can appear in this position. Suppose, then, that we postulate the base rule R1 in addition to Bresnan's R2, already assumed:

(65) R1: $\bar{\bar{S}} \rightarrow \text{TOP } \bar{S}$

      R2: $\bar{S} \rightarrow \text{COMP } S$

In addition, we assume the semantic rule of predication already discussed informally in connection with (24).

As Sag observes, structures such as (64) can be embedded, with varying degrees of acceptability, as in (66):

(66) *I informed the students that as far as this book is concerned, they would definitely have to read it*

To accommodate such cases, let us revise rule R2 to (67):

(67) R2: $\bar{S} \rightarrow \text{COMP} \left\{ \begin{matrix} \bar{\bar{S}} \\ S \end{matrix} \right\}$

These rules will allow recursions, giving such sentences as (68):

(68) *as for John, as far as this book is concerned, he will definitely have to read it*

If such structures are to be permitted, the rule of predication will have to be extended in an obvious way.

Let us now return to topicalization. Suppose that the analysis is just like left-dislocation, except that in the TOP $\bar{S}$ structure, $\bar{S}$ is a *wh*-clause—in effect, a kind of free relative, as in comparatives. Thus (63b) will derive from (69), which in turn derives from (70):

(69) $[_{\bar{\bar{S}}} [_{\text{TOP}}$ *this book*$]$ $[_{\bar{S}} [_{\text{COMP}}$ *what*$]$ $[$ *I asked Bill to get his students to read t*$]]]$

(70) *this book, I asked Bill to get his students to read what*

To form (63b) from (69) we use the obligatory rule of *wh*-phrase deletion already motivated for comparatives.

On these assumptions, (63b) is analogous to such sentences as (71):

(71)   a.   *this book is what I asked Bill to read*
        b.   *it is this book that I asked Bill to read*

From the point of view of the semantics as well as the syntax, the analogy seems appropriate.

In (69) the rules already discussed introduce a bound variable, giving (72):

(72)   [$_{\bar{\bar{S}}}$ [$_{TOP}$ *this book*] [$_{\bar{S}}$ [$_{COMP}$ *what x*] [*I asked Bill to get his students to read x*]]]

Deletion of the *wh*-phrase leaves an open sentence,[25] which we may assume to be interpreted by the predication rule that applies in the case of left-dislocation and relatives.

It follows from these assumptions that topicalizations, like left-dislocation, should be possible with varying acceptability within embedded clauses, as in (73):

(73)   *I informed the students that this book, they would definitely have to read*

I seems to me that (73) is about on a par with the formally analogous (66).

It also follows that topicalization should have the properties of (49), as was illustrated in (63).

Before we leave this topic, let us consider some further consequences of the analysis. Notice that although topicalization is possible within *that*-clauses, as in (73), it is impossible within relatives or questions. Thus we cannot have (75) corresponding to (74):

(74)   *John gave away the books to some friends*

(75)   a.   **to whom the books did John give away* (*to whom did the books John give away*)
        b.   **whom the books did John give away to*
        c.   **the boy to whom the books John gave away*
        d.   **the boy whom the books John gave away to*

The structure underlying, e.g., (75c,d) would on our assumptions be (76):

(76)   *the boy* [$_{\bar{S}}$ COMP [$_{\bar{\bar{S}}}$ [$_{TOP}$ *the books*] [$_{\bar{S}}$ COMP *John gave away which to whom*]

The structure (76) is generable by the base rules. Furthermore, *wh*-movement can apply to *which* in the embedded sentence, placing it in the internal COMP position and leaving a trace. If the dominating $\bar{S}$ were within a *that*-clause instead of a relativized NP, we would then derive (77):

(77)   *I believe that the books, John gave away to some friends*

While (77) is not very elegant, it is surely far better than (75c,d), which would derive from (76) by still another application of *wh*-movement, namely to (*to*) *whom*, placing it in the position of the higher COMP.

The problem with (75) does not seem to be just a surface difficulty; compare the sentences (78), which seem much better than (75) and more or less on a par with (77):

(78) a. *I believe that this book, you should read*
      b. *I believe that this book, you should give away*
      c. *I believe that his friends, John gave some books away to*

We can explain the impossibility of the sentences (75) by essentially the same line of argument that accounts for the *wh*-island constraint. Movement of *(to) whom* to the internal COMP is blocked, because the internal COMP is already filled by *which* under the *wh*-movement analysis of topicalization. Movement of *(to) whom* to the higher COMP node is impossible because it would violate SSC and PIC (and, if S is a cyclic node, subjacency). Even if the already moved *which* could move by COMP–COMP movement to the higher COMP, freeing the lower one, subsequent movement of *(to) whom* to the lower COMP would be excluded by strict cyclicity. Since the trace left by movement of *which* is (when replaced by a variable) taken to be satisfied by *the books* under the predication rule, there is no possible interpretation of (76) or of any of the sentences of (75). Thus there are a number of reasons why (75) are ungrammatical, on the *wh*-movement analysis of topicalization. In effect, we can form (75) only by extraction from a *wh*-island.

There is some reason to suppose that $\bar{\bar{S}}$ is indeed a cyclic node. Thus consider the sentence (79):

(79) *it is believed* [$_{\bar{S}}$ *that* [$_{\bar{\bar{S}}}$ [$_{TOP}$ *this book*] [$_{\bar{S}}$ *you should read*]]]

As it stands, (79) is on a par with (78). But NP-movement cannot apply to (79) to yield (80):

(80) **this book is believed you should read*

The explanation for this fact could be that $\bar{\bar{S}}$ is a cyclic node, so that the application of NP-movement to (79) would violate subjacency. Note that we cannot appeal to PIC in this case, because TOP is outside of the finite clause, presumably.

On the assumption that $\bar{\bar{S}}$ is cyclic, it follows that left-dislocation should also be impossible in relatives, just as topicalization is. Thus (81) should be as bad as (75):

(81) *the boy to whom, as far as this book is concerned, John gave it away*

My intuitions collapse at this point. Some instances of these structures seem to me perhaps acceptable, e.g., (82):

(82) *I want to find a corporation to which, (as far as) my new invention (is concerned), I can offer (it) with a feeling of security that it will be exploited for the good of mankind.*

Compare (82) with the parenthesized phrases deleted. If, indeed, these two sentences are significantly different in status, this may show that $\bar{\bar{S}}$ is not a cyclic node, since on the assumption that it is not, (82) should be grammatical but the corresponding topicalized form (with parenthesized phrases deleted) should not be. However, I do not think that any conclusion can rest on such data.

There is, I think, a clear difference between topicalization and left-dislocation in direct questions. Compare (83), (84) (and (75)):

(83)   a.   *_to whom, this book, should we give_
       b.   *_this book, to whom should we give_
       c.   *_John, who do you think saw_

(84)   a.   *_to whom, as for this book, should we give it_
       b.   _as for this book, to whom should we give it_
       c.   (_as for_) _John, who do you think saw him_

The sentences (83a,c) are ruled out by SSC and PIC (i.e., extraction from _wh_-island), as before. (83b) is ruled out because it has a doubly filled COMP node under the _wh_-movement analysis of topicalization. There is no barrier against (84b,c) however, since there is no _wh_-movement in left-dislocation, just as I assume that there is none in relativization where a pronoun appears in the open sentence. To block (84a) we must assume either that $\bar{\bar{S}}$ is cyclic or that TOP is not a bridge for COMP–COMP movement.

Indirect questions are apparently like relatives, requiring no special comment.

Over a considerable range, then, analysis of topicalization as _wh_-movement seems quite reasonable. The proposal is that in the TOPIC position there is a base-generated structure and that the associated proposition, which is an open sentence except for some cases of left-dislocation, says something about it. There are in principle two ways to derive an open sentence: by _wh_-movement (and _wh_-phrase deletion; but cf. note 25) or with an uninterpreted pronoun. Both of the available ways are used. The first gives topicalization; the second, left-dislocation.

I do not want to suggest that there are no remaining problems. There are—quite a few. Unfortunately, crucial examples seem often to involve ambiguous judgments. I will simply leave the matter here. As far as I can see, the _wh_-movement analysis of topicalization is reasonably successful, has some explanatory power, and does not, to my knowledge, face difficulties that do not arise in a comparable form on other approaches. It also has the advantage of extending the framework outlined to yet another class of cases, thus offering some further evidence in support of a positive answer to (50).

Consider next cleft sentences. In Chomsky (1974) I suggested that these be derived from a structure in which the focussed phrase is base-generated in the predicate position of the matrix sentence rather than by a movement rule. We can then take the associated proposition to be formed by _wh_-movement, in conformity with the analysis that we are now considering. As has often been noted, topicalization and cleft seem to share striking properties. The suggested analysis exploits this fact.

Actually, we can draw an even closer connection between topicalization and clefts by pursuing a slightly different path. Suppose that we take the underlying structure of cleft sentences to be as in (85):

(85)   _it – is_ – $\bar{\bar{S}}$

Then any topicalized sentence can appear in (85) in the position of $\bar{\bar{S}}$. Thus alongside of (63) we have (86):

(86) a.   *it is this book that I really like*
      b.   *it is this book that I asked Bill to get his students to read*
      c.   **it is this book that I accept the argument that John should read*
      d.   **it is this book that I wonder who read*

Two provisos are necessary. First, we must stipulate that left-dislocations cannot appear in (85); the $\overline{S}$ within $\overline{\overline{S}}$ must be subject to *wh*-movement. Second, as in a number of other constructions, the COMP node cannot become terminally null under rules (47), (48).[26] As far as *that* is concerned, deletion in topicalization and left-dislocation is presumably a special case of the process that applies uniformly in matrix sentences.[27] Perhaps one can extend to (86) the restriction against deleting *that* in subjects and extraposed *that*-clauses.

Let us assume that these matters can be properly worked out. Then we should expect to find such sets as the following:

(87) a.   *the book is what I read; the book, I read; it was the book that I read*
      b.   *this book is what I asked Bill to read; this book, I asked Bill to read; it was this book that I asked Bill to read*
      c.   *John is who I want Bill to tell Mary to meet*[28]*; John, I want Bill to tell Mary to meet; it is John that (who) I want Bill to tell Mary to meet*
      d.   *in England is where I told Bill that I want to live; in England, I told Bill that I want to live; it was in England that I told Bill that I want to live*
      e.   *where he went to school is what I wish you would ask him to emphasize in his application; where he went to school, I wish you would ask him to emphasize in his application; it is where he went to school that I wish you would ask him to emphasize in his application*
      f.   *pea green is what he painted his boat; pea green, he painted his boat; it is pea green that he painted his boat.*[29]

The structures, in each case, are as in (88), respectively:

(88)   NP *is* $\overline{S}$; [$_{\overline{\overline{S}}}$ TOP $\overline{S}$] ; *it is* [$_{\overline{\overline{S}}}$ TOP $\overline{S}$]

In each case, *wh*-movement must take place within S. Once would not expect the parallelism to be exact, since the surface rules of interpretation for the three structures, though similar, seem to be somewhat different. It seems to me a reasonable hypothesis, however, that it is just the interpretive rules that account for whatever differences there may be among the three structures. Of course, this hypothesis suggests a direction for research rather than a confirmed result.

There are other examples of clefts that cannot be analyzed in this way, however; e.g., the following, from Pinkham and Hankamer (1975):

(89) a.   *it's only when it rains that we have to sweep the court*
      b.   *it was (purely) out of spite that he assigned it that number*
      c.   *it was only reluctantly that he agreed to swim at all*

Note that in these cases we do not have parallel structures of the sort illustrated in (87). We do, however, have parallels with adverb preposing:

(90)   a.   *only when it rains we have to sweep the court* 30
        b.   *(purely) out of spite, he assigned it that number*
        c.   *only reluctantly he agreed to swim at all* 30

Suppose we postulate that adverb preposing, in some cases at least, places the adverb in the position TOPIC. Then rule (85) already accommodates (89). If this is correct, we have in effect two sources for clefts but no separate rules; furthermore, we need not postulate a "structure-building" rule, adding the "it—be—Predicate" structure by transformation. The latter is a much-to-be-desired consequence for two reasons. Most importantly, it is a vast and otherwise (to my knowledge) unmotivated extension of the power of transformations to permit them to be "structure-building" in the required sense.[31] Furthermore, it would simply be an unexplained accident that the "structure-building" rule would yield an already existing structure, derived from another source under the two-rule analysis. This point is similar to Dougherty's observation with regard to the anaporn relation. Cf. note 12.

Following this analysis, we would expect clefts that derive from preposing to TOPIC to have the same sources as the noncleft analogues. Thus, just as in (91) the preposed constituent is naturally construed with the matrix rather than either embedded clause and presumably is extracted from the matrix clause, so in (92) we have the same interpretations:

(91)   a.   *out of spite, I asked the students to refuse to hand in their assignments*
        b.   *only reluctantly did I order the students to refuse to hand in their assignments*
        c.   *only under highly unusual circumstances do I ask students to refuse to hand in assignments*

(92)   a.   *it was out of spite that I asked the students to refuse to hand in their assignments*
        b.   *it was only reluctantly that I ordered the students to refuse to hand in their assignments*
        c.   *it is only under highly unusual circumstances that I ask students to refuse to hand in assignments*

In contrast, clefts that derive from topicalization, hence ultimately from *wh*-movement, permit construal with the embedded sentences, as in (87b–e). This difference of behavior is a consequence of the proposed analysis, and provides another reason to suppose that there is no independent rule (or rules) of cleft-formation.

A direct prediction of this analysis is that such pairs as (93a,b) should have the same interpretations:

(93)   a.   *only rarely are the students believed to have handed in their assignments on time*
        b.   *it is only rarely that the students are believed to have handed in their assignments on time*

I am not sure that this is correct. It seems to me that (b) may permit construal with the most deeply embedded clause more readily than (a), but my judgments are quite insecure. If there is a systematic distinction, contrary to the data of (91), (92), then either the analysis is incorrect or there is still another source for clefts or (more plausibly, in my opinion) such distinctions as there may be are to be attributed to the rules of interpretation for cleft and preposing.

Again there are unsolved problems, but it seems to me that it is reasonable to explain the class of cleft sentences that have the properties (49) (e.g., (87) but not (89); cf. (92)) in terms of a rule of *wh*-movement. If the proposal proves tenable, we have still further evidence in support of a positive answer to (50).

Consider next indirect questions. These have the general properties (49), and it seems that a rule of *wh*-movement is involved, analogous to direct questions. I will assume here the general analysis of Chomksy (1973). Thus we have (94):

(94) a. *I wonder [who John saw]*
      b. *I wonder [who John believed [that Mary would claim [that Bill would visit]]]*
      c. **I wonder [who John believed [the claim [that Bill would visit]]]*
      d. **who$_2$ did you wonder [who$_1$ t$_1$ saw t$_2$]*

As is well known, in the contexts of (95) there can be no lexical NP:

(95) a. *I wonder [who – to visit]*
      b. *I wonder [where – to put the book]*
      c. *I wonder [how – to get to Chicago]*
      d. *it is unclear [what – to do]*

We might stipulate that in the base rules, NP is required to be $t(x)$ (i.e., to be NP with variable index, not further specified lexically), our element PRO, in the context (96):

(96) $[[_{COMP} +WH] [- to VP]$

In this context, the value of x of $t(x)$ is determined by a rule of control or NP_x is given the sense: unspecified NP. Presence of PRO invokes the *wh*-constraint, under SSC; in contrast, SSC is inapplicable in the complement of *want*-type verbs (cf. note 4). Perhaps the base condition (96) falls together with other similar rules for "bare" infinitivals, e.g., the *promise-persuade* cases.

Given the stipulation (96), we can add infinitival indirect questions to our list of constructions based on *wh*-movement, with the properties (49), as illustrated in (97), analogous to (94):

(97) a.   *I wonder [who to see]*
      b1. *I wonder [who to order [32] Mary [to promise [to visit]]]*
      b2. *I wonder [who to persuade Mary [that she should promise [to visit]]] [33]*
      c.   **I wonder [who to insist on [the principle [that Bill should visit]]]*
      d.   **who$_2$ do you wonder [what$_1$ to give t$_1$ to t$_2$]; *what$_2$ do you wonder [[to whom]$_1$ to give t$_2$ t$_1$]* (cf.: *I wonder (don't remember) [what to give t to whom]; I wonder [to whom to give what t]*)

Correspondingly, we have infinitival relatives alongside of the finite relatives, as in (98).[34]

(98)   a.   *I found a book* [[*which for*] *you to read t*] – *I found a book for you to read*
        b.   *I found a man* [[*to whom for*] PRO *to give the book t*] – *I found a man to whom to give the book*

Infinitival relatives, under this analysis, differ from finite relatives in the rules specifying the surface form of the elements in COMP. Thus in a finite relative corresponding to (98a) we may delete either *which* or the complementizer *that*, giving either (99a) or (99b); or we can delete both, obtaining (99a):

(99)   a.   *I found a book which you can read*
        b.   *I found a book that you can read*
        c.   *I found a book you can read*

But in the infinitival relative, the rule (47) deleting *wh-* is obligatory, as in other cases already discussed. Recoverability of deletion prevents it from applying in (98b), just as it cannot apply in (100):

(100)   *I found a man to whom you can give the book* (**I found a man that you can give the book*)

Thus in (98b) the complementizer *for* must delete, as *that* must delete in (100); we have already remarked that there are rules deleting *for* before *to* (recall that PRO is not terminal).

A further difference between finite and infinitival relatives is that the latter cannot have a lexical NP subject when the complementizer is deleted. Thus we have (98b) but not (101):

(101)   *I found a man* [[*to whom*] *you to give the book*]

This observation recalls the property of indirect questions captured in (96). Perhaps in place of the base rule (96) we should impose a surface condition excluding phrases of the form (102):

(102)   [$_{COMP}$ *wh*-phrase] NP to VP, where NP is lexical or trace ($\neq$ PRO)

This will cover the cases excluded by (96) and will also block (101), while permitting (98). It also eliminates the need to make *wh*-phrase deletion obligatory in infinitival relatives (cf. (98), (99)). One might try to generalize (102) to include other phenomena, e.g., the obligatory PRO in infinitival complements of *persuade–promise* type verbs and the heavy restrictions on null complementizers in infinitives at the surface, the surface filters that exclude *for–to* structures, and the rules governing *that*-deletion. I will not pursue these questions here, however. Cf. Chomsky and Lasnik, forthcoming.

The suggested analysis for infinitival relatives seems to me reasonably satisfactory, though the status of (102) remains open along with other questions. Under this analysis, the rule of *wh*-movement extends to all relatives and to both direct and indirect questions, finite or infinitival.

Consider now the sentences (103):

(103)   a.   *John found* [$_{NP}$ *a book* [$_{\bar{S}}$ *which for*] *him to read t*]]
        b.   *we found* [$_{NP}$ *books* [$_{\bar{S}}$[*which for*] *each other to read t*]]
        c.   **who*$_2$ *did he find* [$_{NP}$ *a book* [$_{\bar{S}}$ [*which*$_1$ *for*] *t*$_2$ *to read t*$_1$]]

In all three cases, *which* must delete, by the processes just discussed; in (103c), *for will delete* as well, before *to*.

Case (c) is excluded by our conditions, which make the relative clause an island.

But the position marked by t$_2$ in (c) should, on our assumptions, be accessible to interpretive rules, for which the subjacency principle does not hold. Thus in (103a), the rule of disjoint reference (2c) applies, compelling *him* to be distinct in reference from *John*; Similarly, (103b) should be subject to reciprocal interpretation under (2a).[35] On the assumptions we are investigating, bound anaphora (rule (2b)) may also apply in the position of the anaphor (*him, each other,* t$_2$) in (103), giving, e.g., (104), which becomes (105) by EQUI (cf. note 4 and references cited there):

(104) *John found* [$_{NP}$ *a book* [$_{\bar{S}}$ [*which for*] *himself to read t*]]
(105) *John found a book to read*

The examples (103)–(105), then, illustrate one primary difference between transformational rules and rules of construal, turning on cyclic application and subjacency. Cf. (7), (8), (22), and the discussion in Chomsky (1973).

Infinitival relatives, under this analysis, should have the properties (49). Thus we should find the arrangement of data in (106):

(106)   a.   *I found a book for you to read t*
        b.   *I found a book for you to arrange for Mary to tell Bill to give t to Tom*
        c.   *I found a book for you to insist that Bill should read t*
        d.   *I found a book for you to insist that Bill tell Mary that Tom should read t*
        e.   **I found a book for you to insist on the principle that Tom should read t*
        f.   **who did he find a book t to read* (=(103c)).[36]

Cases (106c,d) seem to me less acceptable than the comparable examples in the applications of *wh*-movement cited in finite clauses. If this judgment is correct, then the special COMP–COMP movement rule, which permits certain apparent violations of PIC,[37] is less readily available in the case of infinitival relatives.[38] I do not know why this should be so, and am unsure of the judgements. But if (106d) is not acceptable then we really have no argument that the CNPC is in force in (106e), since a demonstration that CNPC is operative requires that analogous cases of comparable complexity with S in place of NP be grammatical. The same question seems to me to arise in other cases of infinitival complements, including (97b2).

Again, it seems to me plausible to extend the rule of *wh*-movement to infinitival relatives as well.

Let us now turn to infinitival complements within the category of adjective phrases.[39] Consider first structures of the form (107), where I assume that $\bar{S}$ is a complement of the adjective qualifier *enough*.

(107)   *John is tall* [*enough* [$_{\bar{S}}$ *for us to see him*]]

Note that although we would normally take *him* in (107) to refer to John, it is not clear that this is necessary, and, in fact, we have such sentences as (108) in which, with the parenthesized material deleted, the complement of *enough* contains no term referring to John:

(108)   a.   *John is tall enough for us to be able to see Bill (by standing on his*
             (= John's) shoulders)
        b.   *John is slow enough for us to win the race(against him(= John))*
        c.   *the car is fast enough for us to win the race(driving it (= the car))*

It seems that (107) can be interpreted as analogous to (108), with the reference of *him* free. If so, then structures such as (107) have essentially the properties of left-dislocation, as described above; that is, we have a focused NP and a proposition that we would normally take to be about this NP, the natural (though not necessary) method being to apply the rule of predication that takes the complement to contain an open proposition satisfied by the referent of the NP, the pronoun taken as a free variable. Assuming that this is the right tack, we may conclude that the base rules generate $\bar{S}$ freely in such structures as (107).

Alongside of (107) we also have (109), which I assume to derive from (110):

(109)   *John is tall* [*enough* [$_{\bar{S}}$ *for us to see*]]

(110)   *John is tall* [*enough* [$_{\bar{S}}$[*who for us to see t*]]]

The *wh*-phrase in (110) deletes obligatorily, as in comparatives and topicalization. Thus we can have (111) but not (112):

(111)   *John is poor enough for us to give present to*

(112)   **John is poor enough to whom to give presents*

Examples (111) and (112) are analogous, respectively, to (113), (114):

(113)   *I found a person for us to give presents to*

(114)   *I found a person to whom to give presents*

Note that (114) (derived by EQUI, cf. (105)) is grammatical but not (112), the difference being that *wh*-phrase deletion is not obligatory in the headed relatives; cf. (100).

There examples suggest that the complement of *enough* has a structure analogous to the TOPIC and relative structures described earlier. The complement in this case is infinitival, but, as in the case of TOPIC (and in some languages, relative), it may be either a full sentence with a preference for interpretation as an open sentence, or a *wh*-derived sentence with a free variable in the position marked by trace, which must be interpreted as an open sentence. If so, we would expect to find that alongside of such structures as (107) (analogous to left-dislocation), we also have *wh*-infinitivals with the properties of (49), except for the obligatory deletion of the *wh*-phrase, already noted; these structures, then, combine the properties of topicalization and those of infinitival relativization. Thus we have (115) analogous to (106):

(115) a. (i) *John is tall enough for you to see t*
         (ii) *the job is prestigious enough for us to offer t to John*
         (iii) *the job is prestigious enough for us to advertise t*

       b. (i) *John is tall enough for us to arrange for Bill to see t*
         (ii) *John is famous enough for us to arrange for the committee to offer the job to t*
         (iii) *the job is prestigious enough for us to arrange for the committee to offer t to John*
         (iv) *the job is prestigious enough for us to arrange for the committee to advertise t*

       c. (i) *John is tall enough for us to insist that John (should) pick t for the team*
         (ii) *John is famous enough for us to insist that you (should) visit t*
         (iii) *the job is important enough for us to insist that they (should) advertise t*
         (iv) *the job is important enough for us to insist that they (should) offer t to John*

       d. (i) *the job is important enough for us to order them to insist that the committee (should) advertise t*
         (ii) *the job is important enough for us to order them to insist that the committee (should) offer t to John*

       e. (i) **the job is important enough for us to insist on the principle that the committee should advertise t*
         (ii) **the job is important enough for us to insist on the principle that they should offer t to John*

       f.   **who$_2$ was the job good enough for us to offer t$_1$ to t$_2$* (etc. as in note 36).

There is no question that (e) and (f) are excluded, as in (106). Note that in all cases, there is an alternative form, with a pronoun in place of *t* (the analogue of left-dislocation). This alternative form is highly preferred for the (c), (d) cases. We have discussed the analogous observation in connection with infinitival relatives. That is, (106c,d) are also dubious or starred. The (c and d) cases of (115) seem to me still worse than those of (106), which may perhaps be attributed to the fact that in the case of (115), but not (106), there is an alternative form, namely, with a pronoun in place of *t*.

With these provisos, the case of infinitival complements seems to me to be essentially as predicted under the *wh*-movement analysis, namely, as having essentially the intersection of properties of infinitival relatives (since *wh*-movement is involved) and topicalization (since there is a parallel form without *wh*-movement).

Before we leave this topic, let us consider further the relevant cases of the *wh*-island constraint. Consider the sentences (116), (117):

(116) a. *the job was good enough [for us to offer it to John]*
       b. *who was the job good enough [for us to offer it to t]*
       c. *to whom was the job good enough [for us to offer it t]*

(117) a. *the job was good enough [(which) for us to offer t to John]*
       b. *who$_2$ was the job good enough [(which$_1$) for us to offer t$_1$ to t$_2$]*
       c. *[to whom$_2$] was the job good enough [(which$_1$) for us to offer t$_1$ t$_2$]*

On the assumptions of our analysis, the examples of (116) should all be grammatical (subject to dialect differences with regard to preposition stranding). Similarly, (117a). But (117b,c) should be ruled out by the *wh*-island constraint (ultimately, subjacency and SSC). I think that these conclusions are correct. Problems arise, however, when we try to question the direct rather than the indirect object in such cases as (116). Compare (118), (119):

(118) a. *John was famous enough [for us to offer the job to him]*
       b. *what job was John famous enough [for us to offer t to him]*

(119) a. *John was famous enough [(who) for us to offer the job to t]*
       b. *what$_2$ job was John famous enough [(who$_1$) for us to offer t$_1$ to t$_2$]*

As expected, (119b) is ungrammatical. But (118b) ought to be grammatical, under our assumptions. It does not seem to be, however. The status of (116b,c) is also unclear. One can imagine a formulation of bridge conditions that would rule out all of these examples, or assign them a marginal status, analogous to (42).

Summarizing, it seems to me that the *wh*-movement analysis gives a reasonably good first approximation in this case, though some problems concerning infinitval clauses remain. I know of no problems specific to this analysis.

Other complements of adjective qualifiers, as in (120), have about the same properties as the complements of *enough*, so far as I can see, so I will have nothing to say about these:

(120) *Muhammad Ali is too good [(who) for Bill to arrange for John to fight t]*

The final case I would like to consider is that of the infinitival complements of *easy*, etc. The analysis proposed in Chomsky (1973) was unsatisfactory, as pointed out by Sterba (1972), Lasnik and Fiengo (1974), and Bach and Horn (1976). With regard to such structures as (121) there have been two widely studied proposals:

(121) *John is easy (for us) [to please]*

One proposal assumes that the subject, *John*, is moved from the object position in the embedded complement phrase by a transformational movement rule. The other assumes that the subject is generated in place and that a rule of object-deletion (or interpretation) guarantees that John is interpreted as the object of *please* in (121).

I will not try to survey the arguments here. Rather, let us take a fresh look within the present framework.

I will assume that the phrase *for us* in (121) is, as indicated, generated in the matrix sentence. Cf. Bresnan (1971), Chomsky (1973), Lasnik and Fiengo (1974), and Brame (1975). If so, then according to our present assumptions, the underlying structure must contain an embedded S̄ as complement to *easy*, with an obligatory PRO subject, as in the case of the infinitival complements already mentioned.[40] In some similar structures the *for-phrase* appears in both the matrix and embedded sentence, as in (122):

(122) a. *it is a waste of time for us [for them to teach us Latin]*
       b. *it is pleasant for the rich [for the poor to do the hard work]*

And there are, of course, adjectival complements of various sorts that exhibit the full infinitival construction, e.g., (123):[41]

(123) a. *John is eager [for Bill to leave]*
       b. *John would be happy [for Bill to win]*
       c. *the house is ready [for John to buy (it)]*

On the assumption that the complement clause in (121) is essentially the same as those in (122), (123), we may take the underlying structure for (121) to be essentially (124), though nothing much depends on the choice of complementizer, it seems:

(124) *X is easy (for us) [$_{\bar{S}}$ for PRO to please Y]*

The complementizer *for* will then delete before *to*, as in cases discussed above, e.g., (125):[42]

(125) a. *who does John want very much (for) to win*
       b. *he is the man who John wants most of all (for) to win*

Assuming this much, we now face the question: what are *X* and *Y* in (124)?

Our assumptions lead us to suppose that each of the competing familiar analyses is in part correct: that is, *X* = John—the subject is generated in place—but there is a movement rule applying to *Y*, namely, *wh*-movement.[43] Thus we may take the structure directly underlying (121) to be (126):

(126) *John is easy (for us) [$_{\bar{S}}$ [who for] PRO to please t]*

In (126), *wh*-movement has applied on the inner cycle and we have obligatory deletion of the *wh*-phrase, as in other cases already discussed. We are left, then, with an open embedded proposition; the now familiar predication rule will correctly interpret it as being about the subject John.

We then expect to have, again, the properties (49), as in the infinitival relatives and related constructions. Thus we have (127) corresponding to (106):

(127) a.   *John is easy (for us) to please t*

       b. (i) *John is easy (for us) to convince Bill to do business with t*
           (ii) *John is easy (for us) to convince Bill to arrange for Mary to meet t*

c.   *John is easy (for us) to convince Bill that he should meet t*

d.   *John is easy (for us) to convince Bill to tell Mary that Tom should meet t*

e. (i)   **John is easy (for us) to convince Bill of the need for him to meet*

   (ii) **John is easy (for us) to describe to Bill a plan to assassinate t*

f. (i)   **what$_2$ is John fun (for us) [(who$_1$) to give t$_2$ to t$_1$]* (from a source like: *John is fun (for us) to give presents to*

   (ii) **who$_2$ are the presents fun (for us) [(which$_1$) to give t$_1$ to t$_2$]* (compare: *the presents are fun (for us) to give to him*

   (iii) **[to whom]$_2$ are the presents fun (for us) [(which$_1$) to give t$_1$ t$_2$]* (compare: *the presents are fun (for us) to give to him*)

As in other cases discussed, cases (c) and (d) are marginal.

In short, the basic properties of *easy-to-please* constructions follow directly from the assumptions we have already made, assuming that here too *wh*-movement is crucially involved. The latter assumption is particularly natural in this case, since we have analogous forms in which the *wh*-phrase may directly appear. Thus following our analysis, (121) is analogous to (128), and in such cases, we may have the full *wh*-phrase, as in (129) [44]:

(128) *John is an easy person to please*

(129) a.   *this is an easy violin on which to play sonatas*
      b.   *this is a pleasant room in which to work*

Whatever the correct analysis of these strucutres may be, it seems clear that they involve, at some level, a phrase such as (130), as an adjectival modifier:

(130) a.   *easy – on which to play sonatas (violin)*
      b.   *pleasant – in which to work (room)*

Our analysis simply assumes that the same is true quite generally of *easy*-complements. In the case of (130), the structures are embedded (presumably, in some manner, as relatives) within an NP with a head; in the case of (121), there is no NP antecedent and the structure must be interpreted as an open sentence, as in topicalization and other examples discussed above. Thus *wh*-deletion is obligatory, as in the other cases discussed, and forms analogous to (130) do not appear in the *easy-to-please* structures, just as we do not have (112), etc.

It should follow that in general, *easy-to-please* constructions have the relevant properties of *wh*-movement. Parallels have been observed in the literature. E.g., Lasnik and Fiengo (1974) note such parallels as (131)[45]

(131) a.   *what did you give to John*
      b.   **who did you give a book*
      c.   *who did you give a book to*
      d.   *John is dumb enough to sell the Brooklyn Bridge to*
      e.   **John is dumb enough to sell the Brooklyn Bridge*
      f.   *John is easy (for us) to sell the Brooklyn Bridge to*
      g.   **John is easy (for us) to sell the Brooklyn Bridge*

Notice that the cases (127f) are exactly analogous to other examples of wh-island constraints, on this analysis, e.g., as in (132) and many examples already cited:

(132) a.   *who$_2$ do you wonder [what$_1$ t_2 saw t_1]
       b.   *I wonder [who$_2$, this book, [(which$_1$) t_2 really likes t_1]]
       c.   *who$_2$ is John more friendly to Mary than [(what$_1$) he is t_1 to t_2]

In all of these cases, the sentences are ruled out on the assumption that wh-movement has taken place, by the wh-island constraint, which, as noted, follows from the conditions postulated. In the form immediately underlying case (132a) there is a residual wh-phrase indicating that wh-movement has taken place; in the case of (127f), (132b,c), and many others discussed above, there is no such residual phrase, but the effects of wh-movement are still evident.

There is a well-known puzzle concerning application of wh-movement to the sentences (133):

(133) a.   the sonata is easy to play on this violin
       b.   the violin is easy to play sonatas on

Consider first (b). The phrase sonatas appears to be in a position susceptible to wh-movement; compare (134):

(134) a.   John was told to play sonatas on his violin
       b.   what was John told to play on his violin

But in (133b), wh-movement is impossible. We cannot have (135):

(135) a.   *what sonatas is this violin easy to play on
       b.   *the sonatas that this violin is easy to play on—are in your book

We now have an explanation for this fact. In terms of our analysis, sonatas in (133b) is within a wh-island, just as t_2 is within a wh-island in the topicalization and comparatives of (132). The structure to which wh-movement must apply to give (135) is (136):

(136) this violin is easy [$_{\overline{S}}$ (which) for PRO to play sonatas on t]

But sonatas in (136) is not subject to wh-movement because of SSC, as in the cases discussed earlier. Consequently, the examples of (135) are ruled out. While superficially (133b) is analogous to (134a), in the mental computation underlying (133b) there is, we now assume, a wh-phrase blocking the application of wh-movement.

Consider now (133a). Suppose that we apply wh-movement to this violin. The result is (137):

(137) a.   what violin is the sonata easy to play on
       b.   the violins that the sonatas are easy to play on—are being repaired

Many speakers find these acceptable, in contrast to (135), which are universally rejected. By our analysis, the underlying structure for (133a) is (138), which should be immune to wh-movement just as (136) is:

(138) the sonata is easy [$_{\overline{S}}$ (which) for PRO to play t on this violin]

why, then, should the examples (137) have a different status, for some speakers, than those of (135)?

Notice that in other contexts, the embedded $\bar{\bar{S}}$s of (136), (138) are, as expected, both immune to *wh*-movement. Consider (139a,b), with the same embedded sentences as (136), (138), respectively:

(139) a.   *you found a violin* [$_{\bar{S}}$ *(which) for* PRO *to play sonatas on t*]
       b.   *you found a sonata* [$_{\bar{S}}$ *(which) for* PRO *to play t on this violin*]

Application of *wh*-movement gives (140), impossible in both cases:

(140) a.   **what sonata did you find a violin to play on*
       b.   **what violin did you find a sonata to play on*

Example (140a) is analogous to (135); example (140b) is analogous to (137). Comparing these cases, we see that it is the acceptability of (137) (for some speakers) that is the exceptional case, somehow to be explained.

A possible explanation is that there is another structure underlying (133a), namely, (141), where the PP *on this violin* is associated with the VP rather than the adjective phrase:

(141)   *the sonata is* [$_{AP}$ *easy* [$_{\bar{S}}$ *(which) for* PRO *to play t*]] *on this violin*

If (141) is taken to underlie (133a), under one option, then (137) will be derivable by *wh*-movement. No such alternative analysis is possible in the case of (133b), (139). Therefore, no *wh*-movement is possible in these cases.

If this is the correct explanation, then we should find that in forms analogous to (133a) but where the PP is not separable from the embedded verb, forms analogous to (137) should be on a par with (135) rather than (137).[46] Compare (142), (143):

(142)   *the book is easy* [$_{\bar{S}}$ *for* PRO *to put t on the table*]

(143) a.   *what table is the book easy to put on*
       b.   *the table that the book is easy to put on*

It seems to me that the prediction holds; that is, the examples (143) are excluded, in contrast to (137). The question deserves fuller investigation, but in a large class of rather puzzling cases it seems that we have an explanation for the facts in terms of a *wh*-movement analysis, given the framework of conditions and rules outlined earlier.

Consider next the examples (144):

(144) a.   *it is a waste of time for us* [*for them to teach us Latin*]   (=(122a))
       b.   **Latin is a waste of time for us* [*for them to teach us*]

In Chomsky (1973) the distinction was explained in terms of conditions on rule application, but that approach is ruled out in the present analysis. The correct explanation for the ungrammaticality of (144b), I think, lies in a base condition. In the underlying structure (145), the subject of the embedded infinitival must be PRO, as in the *persuade–promise* cases and others that we have discussed:

(145) NP *is* Predicate (*for us*) [$_{\bar{S}}$ *for – to* VP]

The conditions on NP and Predicate in (145) must be specified in the base. Note that where NP is a dummy element *it* (however this is introduced), there is no constraint on −; cf. (122). The restriction to PRO applies only when the matrix NP subject is lexically specified. Furthermore, in such examples as (123a,b), where *wh*-movement is excluded in the embedded clause, there is also no constraint on − in (145). Thus we seem to have either the base condition (146a) or (146b):

(146) a.   in (145), − is PRO if $\overline{\text{S}}$ is subject to *wh*-movement
       b.   in (145), − is PRO if $\overline{\text{S}}$ is obligatorily subject to *wh*-movement.

Of these two conditions, (146a) is preferable, if it is tenable; it is more general and can, I believe, be reformulated so as to fall together with other cases with obligatory PRO subject under generalizations relating *it* and choice of complementizer. It seems to cover all cases except for (123c).

The argument that the *for*-phrase in (123c) is within the complement offered by Bach and Horn (1976) does not seem to me entirely compelling. They note that the *for*-phrase is not preposable in (147), though it normally is when part of the matrix. Thus we have (148) but not (149):

(147)   *the house is ready for John to buy*

(148)   *for the rich, it is pleasant for the poor to do the hard work*

(148)   **for John, the house is ready to buy*

But this argument seems inconclusive, since even in the case of (149), where *for John* is surely a PP of the matrix, it is not preposable, for some reason:

(149)   *the house is ready for John*

(150)   **for John, the house is ready* (cf. *for John, the problem was easy*)

They give supplementary arguments in terms of right node raising and gapping, arguing that (151), (152) are acceptable:

(151)   *the moussaka is ready and Mike says that the egg–lemon soup is almost ready − for us to eat*

(152)   *the kidney pie is ready for us to put in the oven, and the salad − for you to put on the table*

Assuming that the *for*-phrases in *easy*-structures are in the matrix, a point that they do not contest, the strength of these arguments depends on the distinction between (151), (152) and (153), (154):

(153)   *young children are quite difficult, and Bill says that older children are still more difficult − for untrained teachers to control*

(154)   *the young children are difficult for Bill to control, and the older children − for Mary to teach*

I am not convinced that there is any relevant difference. Consequently, it is possible that the *for*-phrase associated with *ready* is also in the matrix sentence where the complement is subject to *wh*-movement, contrary to (123c). If so, then (146a) may be the correct principle.

Whichever case of (146) holds, (144b) is ruled ungrammatical on the grounds that it requires a base form not generated by base rules (or a corresponding surface condition).

Notice that if the subject NP of the complement in (145) is PRO, then it can never be assigned *wh*- or moved by *wh*-movement. Thus it follows that the rule applying to *easy-to-please* structures is limited to an NP in the embedded predicate.

Consider again the form (126), repeated here as (155), underlying (121):

(155)   *John is easy (for us)* [$_{\overline{S}}$[*who for*] PRO *to please t*]

Suppose that *wh*-movement were to apply to (155), as in the COMP–COMP case of *wh*-movement, giving (156):

(156)   *who is John easy (for us) to please*

Plainly (156) is ungrammatical. We might account for this fact by rule-ordering, i.e., requiring that the obligatory deletion of *who* preced *wh*-movement on the matrix cycle. But there is in fact a simpler approach that requires no such stipulation. Thus note that the resulting structure corresponding to (156) is (157), after interpretation of the *wh*-quantifier, in contrast to (158), underlying (121):

(157)   *for which x, x a person, John is easy (for us)* [*for* PRO *to please x*]

(158)   *John is easy (for us)* [*for* PRO *to please x*]

We have assumed that (158) is interpreted by the general rule of predication described for topicalization and other forms, with an open proposition taken to be satisfied by the referent of the focused NP, in this case, the matrix subject. But the rule of predication is inapplicable to (157), since there is no open proposition: the variable x is bound in (157) by the quantifier "for which x." Thus the sentence is uninterpretable, just as "John is easy to please Bill" is uninterpretable. This seems a natural way to account for the ungrammaticality of (156).

Some might object that (156) must be excluded as ungrammatical on syntactic grounds rather than on grounds of uninterpretability. I have argued elsewhere that, whereas speakers can make judgments of acceptability, they have no direct access to the grounds of these judgments. Thus I have no intuitive insight into the source of the unacceptability of (156). Only if these acceptability judgments come marked as "syntactic," "semantic," etc., can the objection be sustained. It seems to me that there is no merit to the contention.

Suppose that in fact convincing arguments can be given that in (123c) the *for*-phrase is embedded even where *wh*-movement takes place in the embedded clause, so that we have the underlying structure (159), where either subject or object of the embedded clause is accessible to *wh*-movement:

(159)   *the house is ready* [*for* NP *to buy* NP]

Applying *wh*-movement to the object, we derive (160):

(160)   *the house is ready* [*(which) for John to buy*]

Application of subsequent *wh*-movement to an NP in the position of *John* is impossible for familiar reasons.

Suppose that we apply *wh*-movement to the embedded subject of a structure like (159), obtaining (161):

(161)   *the house is ready* [[*which for*] *t to fall down*]

With obligatory deletion of *which* followed by *for*-deletion before *to*, we derive (162):

(162)   *the house is ready to fall down*

If, in contrast, applicability of *wh*-movement to the embedded clause is taken to correlate with PRO subject, as in (146a), then (162) would derive only from (163) by EQUI, just as (165) derives from (164):

(163)   *the house is ready* [*for itself to fall down*]

(164)   *John is eager* [*for himself to please*]

(165)   *John is eager to please*

Assuming that we do derive (161), consider the effect of applying the COMP–COMP rule of *wh*-movement to give (166):

(166)   **what is the house ready to fall down*

But this is ungrammatical on the same grounds that rule out (156). Thus nothing much seems to depend on where the *for*-phrase appears in (123c), apart from the generality of the base principle or corresponding surface filter.

Other structures similar to (121) are much more restricted in scope, e.g., (167):

(167)   *Mary is pretty to look at*

In this case, we do not have the full range of properties (49). Thus there is no form (168), analogous to (127b):

(168)   *Mary is pretty to tell Bill to look at*

Furthermore, in such structures as (167) there are very narrow restrictions on the choice of the matrix adjective and embedded verb. We may propose the same analysis as in the *easy-to-please* cases, but with idiom interpretation rules associated with the adjectives in question. Note that there are structures such as (169), but in this case the embedded complement is not associated with the adjective but with the adjective qualifier, *too*:

(169)   *Mary is too pretty to expect anyone to look at (her)*

As has long been known, structures of the *easy-to-please* type do not appear as nominals, in contrast to the superficially similar forms with *eager*: compare (170):

(170)   a.   *John's eagerness to please – surprised me*
        b.   **John's difficulty to please – surprised me*

Various explanations have been proposed, relying on particular analyses of movement or deletion in the *easy* cases. Under the assumptions of EST, including the lexicalist hypothesis, the distinction between (170a) and (170b) must be formulable without reference to ordering of transformations and the like, on the assumption that *eagerness, difficulty*, etc., are drawn from the lexicon.[47] On our assumptions, the NPs of (170) have the underlying structures (171a,b), respectively:

(171) a. $[_{NP}$ *John's* $[_{\bar{N}}$ *eagerness* $[_{\bar{S}}$ *for himself to please* $]]]$
       b. $[_{NP}$ *John's* $[_{\bar{N}}$ *difficulty* $[_{\bar{S}}$ *(who) for* PRO *to please t* $]]]$

The form (171a) is analogous in structure to nouns with sentential complements, as in (172):

(172) a.   *John's certainty that Bill will leave*
       b.   *John's desire for Bill to leave*
       c.   *the fact that Bill left*

In contrast, (171b) has the formal structure of a relative, as in (173):

(173) a.   *the certainty that you feel*
       b.   *the desire (for Bill to leave) that you expressed*
       c.   *the fact that Bill cited*

But the rule of interpretation for relatives plainly cannot apply in (171b), any more than it can in (174):

(174) a.   *the eagerness* $[$ *(who) (for Bill) to visit t* $]$
       b.   *the certainty* $[$ *(who) that Bill will visit t* $]$
       c.   *the desire* $[$ *(who) for Bill to visit t* $]$
       d.   *the fact* $[$ *(who) that Bill visited t* $]$

More precisely, if the rule of relative interpretation were to apply in these cases, it would take the relative to hold of the head, as in (175):

(175) a.   *a book* $[$ *(which) for you to read* $]$
       b.   *the book* $[$ *(which) that you read* $]$

Cf. the discussion of relativization above. This interpretation is senseless in (171b); furthermore, infinitival relatives (or relatives altogether) do not occur in general with such determiners. Thus expressions such as (171b) are ungrammatical. Perhaps this is the explanation for the absence of derived nominals corresponding to the forms of (170b). We might proceed further, in terms of the X-bar system, to assign sentential complements of nouns, which are immune to *wh*-movement (or, perhaps, to relative interpretation), a different position in the hierarchy than relatives. Cf. Jackendoff (forthcoming) for some suggestions.[48]

   To summarize, I have suggested that we can eliminate from the grammar rules of comparative deletion, topicalization, clefting, object-deletion and "tough movement," rules for adjective and adjective-qualifier complements, and others, in favor of the general rule of *wh*-movement that also yields direct and indirect questions (finite and infinitival) and finite and infinitival relative clauses, several rather general rules of interpretation, and some language-specific properties of base and surface structures. If this analysis proves tenable, we can drastically reduce the grammatical apparatus for the description of English; but more important, we can drastically limit the class of possible rules. Some curious and otherwise unexplained phenomena fall into place quite naturally, under this simplification of grammatical theory and the description of English. The properties (49), which appear (with the provisos noted) in a wide range of cases, fall together naturally, as a consequence of independent and, I think, rather natural conditions on rules: the subjacency condition, which in effect limits the "memory" available to transformational rules; SSC, which selects a most prominent NP in an embedded cyclic category that is alone accessible to rules if it is present; and PIC, which immunizes a certain category of propositions from rule application, subject to the language-specific proviso that permits COMP–COMP movement over a "bridge." Each of these conditions may be thought of as a limitation on the scope of the processes of mental computation that ultimately determine phonetic and logical form.

This discussion provides evidence in support of a positive answer to the query (50), and specifically, to the thesis that the phenomena that fall under CNPC and the wh-island constraints are to be explained in terms of more general properties of rules. But the evidence does not (and could not) suffice to establish the thesis, even if everything suggested here proves to be correct. This is, it remains an open possibility that some of the phenomena that fall under these constraints must be explained in other terms. Before turning to this question, I want to consider the effects of some modifications of the conditions discussed at the outset.

In our formulation of the basic conditions on rules, the notion "cyclic node" plays a crucial role. The cyclic nodes were taken to be NP and $\bar{S}$ (and perhaps $\bar{\bar{S}}$) in the foregoing discussion. Suppose that we were to add S to the category of cyclic nodes. A slight reformulation of PIC is then required, but it is otherwise unaffected. There are interesting consequences in the case of SSC and subjacency, however.

Consider the effect on SSC. Given a structure of the form (176), no rule can now involve X and Y if S contains a subject not containing Y and not controlled by X:

(176) $\ldots X \ldots [\,_S \ldots Y \ldots\,] \ldots X \ldots$

Suppose in particular that Y is NP. Then a rule such as wh-movement, extracting an NP to the COMP position X outside of S, can apply to Y only if Y is the subject of S. In general, only subjects are accessible to movement rules involving an element outside of S, on this interpretation of SSC. It is well known that in many languages only subjects are accessible to many rules. Cf. Ross (1972); Keenan and Comrie (1973). Perhaps this fact can be explained by a modification of SSC for such languages in the manner just suggested. Note that if such a language also has COMP-to-COMP movement, the effect will be that only the subject of a subject sentence will be accessible to rules. For an apparent example, see Bell (1976).

The effect of incorporating S among the cyclic nodes is more far-reaching in the case of subjacency. It now follows that in a structure of the form (177), wh-movement cannot extract Y to COMP:

(177) $[_{\bar{S}}COMP [_{S} \ldots [_{NP} \ldots Y \ldots] \ldots]]$

In particular, it follows that *wh*-movement cannot extract anything from the subject of a sentence. Since the earliest work on transformational grammar, it has been clear that *wh*-movement must somehow be restricted in this fashion. E.g., it is noted in Chomsky (1955) that the rule of *wh*-movement must be prevented from applying to (178), to give (179):

(178)   [*your interest in him*] *seemed to me rather strange*

(179)   **whom did* [*your interest in*] *seem to me rather strange*

In the earliest work, it was assumed that the structural description of the rule must be designed to exclude this possibility. Later, general conditions were proposed on the functioning of rules, e.g., the Subject Condition of Chomsky (1973)[50] The Subject Condition follows at once from subjacency, when S is taken to be a cyclic node.

Of course, it follows as well that *wh*-movement cannot extract a phrase from a nonsubject NP, as in (180):

(180)   *who did you see* [*a picture of t*]

But the sentence (180) is grammatical. It was for this reason that subjacency was not extended to include S in Chomsky (1973). We return to this problem directly. Let us assume that it can be overcome and that subjacency is correctly formulated with S as one of the cyclic nodes.

As a consequence of this decision, we now have the general property (181):

(181)   In the structure (177), *Y* cannot be extracted from S; in particular, *wh*-movement cannot move *Y* to COMP.

If the general approach sketched earlier proves tenable, then perhaps the special case of (180) is the only case.

Notice that nothing prevents extraction of *Y* outside of NP within S, in (177). Thus there is now no barrier against the rules indicated in (182):

(182)   a. $[_{\bar{S}} COMP [_{S} [_{NP} $ *a review* $ t_1] $ *was published* $ [$ *of Bill's book*$]_1]]$
        b. $[_{\bar{S}} COMP [_{S} [$ *of the students in the class*$]_1 [_{NP} $ *several* $ t_1] $ *failed the exam*$]]$

Whether (182b) is the correct surface structure may be questioned. Note that extraction of PP as in (182b) is incompatible with *wh*-movement:

(183)   a.   **of the students in the class, which exam did several fail*
             **which exam, of the students in the class, did several fail*
             **I don't know which exam, of the students in the class, several failed* [51]

The impossibility of (183a) follows directly from the suggested analysis, but not that of (183b,c). These examples suggest that the PP is extraposed to COMP, contradicting our assumption, or perhaps that the PP is adjoined to S, creating a new S-category in the usual way, so that subjacency blocks *wh*-movement. In support of the latter alternative (or 182b)) are such structures as (184):

(184)   *I told Mary that of the students in the class, several will fail*

Let us suppose tentatively that (182b) is correct in essence, assuming that the problem posed by (183b,c) can be overcome as suggested. Note that extraction of phrases from the subject, as in (182), contradicts the Subject Condition of Chomsky (1973), as noted by Postal (1974a). But it is compatible with the reformulation of this condition in terms of subjacency, which of course has the added advantage of eliminating a rather ad hoc condition. Let us tentatively assume, then, that the Subject Condition is dropped in favor of subjacency as just amended. Cf. note 50.

A different approach to these questions is suggested by Bach and Horn (forthcoming). They propose a general constraint that they formulate as follows:

(185)   The NP Constraint.   No constituent which is dominated by NP can be moved or deleted from that NP by a transformational rule [apart from free deletions, if such exist].

The NP Constraint differs in its empirical consequences from the modified subjacency condition in that it excludes all movement from NP, whereas the subjacency condition excludes only those movement rules that extract an element from S as well as NP; just *wh*-movement, if the foregoing analysis is correct.

The NP Constraint is immediately falsified by such examples as (182).[52] In fact, if the foregoing analysis is correct, the apparent generality of (185) is illusory: the only rule subject to it is *wh*-movement, which is also the only rule extracting a constituent dominated by NP from S as well as NP. All other extraction rules, it seems without exception, apply freely to subparts of NPs, as do all interpretive rules (subject to SSC, of course, as in *"we read [Bill's stories about each other]," "they read [Bill's stories about them]" with coreference of *they, them*).[53] The unique status of *wh*-movement from NPs is exactly what is captured by the analysis in terms of subjacency, since only this rule extracts a phrase not only from NP but also from S (on the assumptions of the foregoing analysis).

Let us now turn to the remaining problem, namely, *wh*-movement from nonsubject NPs, as in (180). Bach and Horn argue, very plausibly I believe, that the interrogative (186) derives from (187), with the structure as indicated, rather than from (188) (see also Cattell, 1976):

(186)   *who did John write a book about*

(187)   *John wrote [$_{NP}$ a book] [about who]*

(188)   *John wrote [$_{NP}$ a book about who]*

They argue further that (187) is base-generated alongside (188), as shown by the fact that we can have such sentences as (189) and by the unambiguous interpretation of (190a) as compared with the ambiguity of (190b,c):

(189)   a.   *John wrote it about Nixon*
        b.   *a book was written about Nixon by John* [54]

(190)   a.   *John destroyed [his first 5 books about Nixon], in 1965*
        b.   *John wrote [his first 5 books about Nixon], in 1965*
        c.   *John wrote [his first 5 books] about Nixon, in 1965*

Correspondingly, on their assumptions, we can question "a book" in (187), obtaining (191), but we cannot form (193) from (192):

(191)   *what did John write about Nixon*

(192)   *John destroyed a book about Nixon*

(193)   a.   **who did John destroy a book about*   (cf. (186))
        b.   **a book was destroyed about Nixon by John*   (cf. (189b))
        c.   **what did John destroy about Nixon*   (cf. (191))

Suppose that we follow Bach and Horn in assuming that when *wh*-movement has taken place in nonsubject position, it has not extracted from inside an NP but rather from a PP that is not dominated by NP, but directly by VP, as in (187). This eliminates the remaining problem in the formulation of subjacency suggested above.

It remains to determine how structures of the form (194), which are subject to *wh*-movement of each NP, are derived:

(194)   COMP NP [$_{VP}$ V NP [P NP]]

Bach and Horn assume that all of these are base-generated. The contention is plausible in the special case of (187), where we have the corresponding pronominal form (189a), but not, I believe, in many other cases, e.g., (180) or many such cases as (195):

(195)   a.   *who did he find a picture of t*
        b.   *what books did he write reviews of t*

In these cases we cannot have forms corresponding to (189). Thus:

(196)   a.   **he saw it of John*
        b.   **he found it of John*
        c.   **he wrote them of three novels*

But in these cases we can question the NP in the PP. Thus the properties that Bach and Horn consider do not correlate, contrary to what they assume. Base-generability seems to me plausible only in such cases as (187), where "write a book" is treated virtually as a verb, and in fact possessive determiners are impossible; see below; also (vi), (vii) of note 10.

Departing now from Bach and Horn's analysis, suppose that we postulate a rule of extraposition from NP to give (198) from (197), perhaps related to the familiar rule (cf. (21)), though more likely, a kind of "readjustment rule."

(197)   *he saw* [$_{NP}$ *a picture* [$_{PP}$ *of John*]]

(198)   *he saw* [$_{NP}$ *a picture t*] [$_{PP}$ *of John*]

The conditions on the choice of the matrix verb are obscure; thus the rule can apply to *see, find*, but not *destroy*; There appears to be some vacillation and disagreement in informant judgment on this matter, as one might expect in the case of a marginal rule such as this.

The extraposition rule forming (198) produces a structure just like the base-generated structures, apart from the trace t in (198). We can at one explain the impossibility of pronouns in the NP position of (198), (196); these are not base-generated structures. For the same reason, we cannot have (199):

(199) *what did he see of John*

Application of *wh*-movement and passive to (198) gives the forms (200):

(200) a. *who did he see a picture of t*
       b. [*what picture t*] *did he see* [*of John*]
       c. [*a picture t*] *was seen* [*of John*]

The status of (b) and (c) is obscure; cf. note 54. Pending further investigation, I will put them aside.

We now have the following three cases, with the deep structures indicated:

(201) *he took* [$_{NP}$ *a picture*] [$_{PP}$ *of John*]

(202) *he destroyed* [$_{NP}$ *a picture of John*]

(203) *He saw* [$_{NP}$ *a picture of John*]

The lexically governed extraposition rule gives (204) from (203), but does not apply to (202):

(204) *he saw* [$_{NP}$ *a picture t*] [$_{PP}$ *of John*]

The cases are differentiated in the following way:

(205) a. Possibility of pronoun in place of *a picture*: (201) but not (202), (203-4)
       b. Applicability of *wh*-movement to *John*: (201), (204) but not (202)
       c. Possibility of a possessive NP in place of *a*: (202), (203-4) but not (201)

Notice that we cannot have (206):

(206) **who did he see Bill's picture of t*

The reason is that extraposition from NP is impossible in (207) because of SSC (cf. (21)).

(207) *he saw* [*Bill's picture of John*]

Since extraposition from NP is impossible in this case, subjacency (and also SSC) will prevent *wh*-movement; hence (206).

Since possessives are in any event impossible in the quasi-idiomatic case (201), we do not have (208):

(208) a. **who did he take Bill's picture of*
       b. **who did he write Bill's book about*

Bach and Horn argue that the forms underlying (208) are blocked by base rules. But their analysis does not extend to case (203) (*see, find*, etc.), where *wh*-movement is possible from the PP, but we do have possessive forms, as in (207). They note the problem for their analysis in the special case of (190b,c), leaving it unsolved, but in fact the problem is considerably more general, as we have seen. The problems all seem to be overcome in a natural way along the lines just sketched, with essential reliance on SSC and the modified version of subjacency.

There seems to be some reason, then, to take S to be a cyclic node for the definition of subjacency (and for some languages, perhaps, SSC as well). The basic insight of Bach and Horn makes it possible to overcome what seemed to be a fundamental objection to this approach, and when incorporated within the framework outlined earlier, provides a natural explanation for an interesting class of phenomena.

There are further consequences that should be investigated. Thus, it is no longer clear that $\bar{S}$ must be taken as a cyclic node for subjacency. The question has consequences with regard to preposing rules and other matters. Furthermore, the standard argument for the relative rather than absolute interpretation of the A/A principle—namely, that NP can be extracted from NP by *wh*-movement—disappears, leaving open the possibility that this principle can be interpreted differently. Cf. Kayne (1975) for some ramifications. Cf. also note 54. I will have to leave these interesting questions open.

I will conclude this discussion with some remarks about the adequacy of the general thesis (50): specifically, can we appeal to *wh*-movement and the conditions assumed for a general explanation of CNPC and *wh*-island constraints? Do these and similar phenomena appear outside of the domain of rules of construal in the sense suggested (including movement rules, under the trace theory)? I cannot hope to review the substantial literature on this question here, but will consider a few cases.

Some examples in the literature allegedly illustrating conditions on rules may have been wrongly analyzed. For example, I have just been arguing that the analysis of (209) in Chomsky (1973) was incorrect:

(209)   *who did you see John's picture of*

To take another example, it is argued in Chomsky (1973) that (210b) is blocked by SSC applying to the rule associating *not, many*, giving essentially the meaning "few":

(210)   a.   *we didn't see pictures of many of the children*
        b.   *we didn't see John's pictures of many of the children*   (* on the relevant interpretation)

But consider (211):

(211)   *we didn't believe that Bill had seen pictures of many of the children*

It seems that in this case *not* can be associated with *many*, violating SSC and PIC if the rule is a rule of construal. In our present framework, there is no reason to suppose that it is. Thus we are left without an explanation for (210).

Perhaps what blocks (210) is not SSC but rather a prohibition against associating *not* and *many* when the latter is within a "specific" NP, whether definite or specific indefinite. Consider (212):

(212)   a.   *we didn't see the pictures of many of the children*
        b.   *we didn't see certain pictures of many of the children*

In all such cases, association of *not, many* seems difficult or impossible. Perhaps, then, the problem with (210b) is simply that the possessive NP *John's* is definite.[55] Thus what appeared to be a case of SSC fails under a different principle.

Analogous questions arise in the case of the quantifier *any*, often held to be subject to island conditions on scope determination. Fauconnier (1975) argues that (213b) is prevented by CNPC from having scope outside of NP, as compared with (213a):[56]

(213) a. *I didn't see **anyone's** husband at the meeting*
        b. **I didn't see the man **anyone** is married to at the meeting*

However, a further look suggests that specificity of the NP, not CNPC, may be what is involved. Consider (214):[57]

(214) a. *we can't find books that have **any** missing pages*
        b. **we can't find the books that have **any** missing pages*
        c. **we can't find certain books that have **any** missing pages*

The cases differ just as (210)–(212) do. One may interpret (214a) with wide scope for *any*, as for example, in despair after a search for certain missing pages has failed, even though *any* is within a complex NP.

Some discussions purporting to show that island constraints hold without movement seem to me to be based on rather questionable data. For example, Bresnan (1975) argues that CNPC applies in nonmovement rules on the grounds of such examples as (215):

(215) a. *who was planning to buy what*
        b. *who was arguing about a plan to buy what*

As she notes, we must exclude the interpretation as echo questions. We can do this, for example, by embedding (215), as in (216):

(216) *I wonder (don't remember)*   a. *who was planning to buy what*
                                      b. *who was arguing about a plan to buy what*

To demonstrate that CNPC holds in these cases, where there is plainly no movement rule applying, we must argue that (216b) is starred but not (216a).

I do not myself perceive any significant difference in acceptability between (216a) and (216b). But even if there is such a difference, it does not suffice to show that CNPC holds in this case. To establish that CNPC holds it is necessary to show that structures of equivalent complexity with a cyclic node $\bar{S}$ in place of NP are acceptable, while the structures with NP are not. Thus to establish that CNPC holds of direct questions does not suffice to compare (217) with (218), where brackets bound cyclic categories:

(217) *who do you believe [that John saw]*

(218) **who do you believe [the claim [that John saw]]*

These examples suffice only to establish the weaker "complex phrase condition."

To show that the relevant condition is, rather, CNPC, it is necessary to contrast (218) with (219):

(219) *who do you believe [that Bill claimed [that John saw]]*

Noting that (219) is grammatical while (218) is not, we establish that the "complex phrase condition" does not suffice and that in fact CNPC is operative. This is the course we have followed in the foregoing discussion.

Returning now to (216), to establish that CNPC holds we must consider such cases as (220):

(220) *I wonder (don't remember)*   (a) *who was arguing [that Bill planned [to buy what]]*
                                       (b) *who was arguing about [a plan [to buy what]]*

Only if (a) and (b) differ crucially in grammaticalness is there an argument for CNPC from these cases. But I see no difference, certainly nothing comparable to the distinction between (219), (218), which is the relevant analogue. It seems to me that double-*wh* structures are fairly free, in violation even of such constraints as the coordinate structure condition (cf. (221), subject to some qualifications about increasing complexity and its effect on naturalness, which may very well hold quite generally (e.g., in such cases as (219)), and therefore belong to an independent component of the full system of language and language use.

(221) *I wonder (don't remember) who went to the store to buy wine and what*

(222) *I don't remember who wondered how to do what to whom*

Similarly, Bresnan argues on the basis of (223) that the rule in question observes CNPC, but a satisfactory argument would require a basic difference between (223b) and (224):

(223) a. *who saw pictures of whom*
       b. *who heard claims about pictures of whom*

(224)   *who heard that Bill saw pictures of whom*

I am not at all convinced that there is a relevant difference. My judgments on these examples are not at all firm, but I would tend to take them as evidence that non-movement rules do not observe the constraints in question.

Bresnan's most interesting and important argument, however, deals with another matter, namely the rule she calls "comparative subdeletion" (C-Sub), which yields such sentences as (225), from Bresnan (1975):

(225) a. *they have many more enemies than we have **friends***
       b. *she seems as happy now as she seemed **sad** before*
       c. *my sister drives as carelessly as I drive **carefully***

Elimination of the boldfaced word in (225) gives the coresponding comparatives, which Bresnan takes to be derived by a deletion rule falling together under a single generalization with C-Sub.

Bresnan argues further that C-Sub observes CNPC, as illustrated in (226)–(228):

(226) a.   *this policy has been as harmful to our interests as people believed
            it would be beneficial*
       b.   **this policy has been as harmful to our interests as people believed
            the claim that it would be beneficial*

(227) a.   *I'll have to give as many Fs as you've proposed to give As*
       b.   **I'll have to give as many Fs as you've dicussed a proposal to give As*

(228) a.   *it has done no less harm than you say it has done good*
       b.   **it has done no less harm than you have the opinion that it has
            done good*

To show that CNPC is involved, rather than just a "complex phrase constraint," we must compare not the (a) and (b) cases of (226)–(228), but rather the (b) cases and such examples as (229)–(231):

(229)   *this policy has been as harmful to our interests as people believed that
        Tom claimed that it would be **beneficial***

(230)   *I'll have to give as many Fs as you've mentioned that Bill proposed to
        give As*

(231)   *it has done no less harm than you informed me that it has **done good***

Certainly (229)–(231) are much less acceptable than the corresponding comparatives, with the boldface phrases removed. This is characteristic. To take another, simpler case, consider (232):

(232) a.   *the desk is as high as it is wide*
       b.   **the desk is as high as they believe the claim that it is wide*
       c.   *?the desk is as high as they believe that Bill claims that it is wide*
       d.   *the desk is as high as they believe that Bill claims that it is*

In (232), the basic judgments seem to me to be that (a) and (d) are fully acceptable, whereas (b) and (c) are not. Case (232a) is C-Sub; case (232d) is comparative formation, which I have argued is *wh*-movement. If there is no further difference between (232b) and (232c), then we may simply say that a "complex phrase constraint" applies to C-Sub. If we take the difference to be significant, with (232c) considerably more acceptable than (232b) (and comparably in the examples (226)–(231), then we might decide to accept (232c) as grammatical, explaining its relative unacceptability in some other terms, say, in terms of some performance factor—though why such a factor should apply in C-Sub but not in comparatives is unclear.

Bresnan notes that "acceptability of sentences involving Subdeletion seems to decay more rapidly as length and complexity increase than with [Comparative Deletion]." She also notes that "natural contrasts" or "foci" are required in C-Sub to a much greater extent than in comparatives, citing Akmajian. But these considerations raise some doubt as to whether in fact C-Sub observes CNPC and whether it can be coalesced with comparative deletion or regarded as a rule operating over a variable. The "variable" in question must be subject to some condition indicating that it is not too complex, in some sense, and that the appropriate parallelism holds. This notion of "complexity" is qualitatively different, it seems, than the performance factors that may apply in cases of *wh*-movement (comparatives in particular). It may well be that the conditions of complexity and parallelism, when properly formulated, will simply rule out such cases as the (b) examples of (226)–(228) and (232) as being particularly bad. If so, we do not have a case of CNPC, just as (210) does not illustrate SSC, though superficially it appears to do so.

It seems, in fact, that very slight modifications suffice to cause decay of acceptability of C-Sub. Consider such cases as the following:

(233) a. *the desk is wider than it is high*
       b. *the desk is wider than it used to be **high***
       c. *the desk was wider than it seems to me to be **high** now*

(234) a. *she seems as happy now as she seemed sad before*
           (=(225b); Bresnan's (83))
       b. *she seems as happy now as she* $\left\{ \begin{array}{l} \textit{was } \textbf{sad} \textit{ before} \\ \textit{has ever been } \textbf{sad} \\ \textit{will ever be } \textbf{sad} \end{array} \right\}$

(235) a. *John is happier today than be usually is **sad***
       b. *John is happier than he looks **healthy***
       c. *John looks more satisfied than he is **happy***
       d. *John is more healthy now than he has been **happy** for many years*

It seems to me that (233b,c), (234b), and (235) are very low in acceptability, hardly better than (232b) (if at all), although the comparatives formed by removing the italicized word in these examples are perfectly acceptable and the modification that gives the unacceptable C-Sub forms is rather slight. Thus it seems to me difficult to establish that C–Sub meets CNPC, that it falls under the same generalization as comparative formation, or that it is a rule operating over a variable.

To summarize so far, I have argued that comparatives are formed by *wh*-movement, and that there seems no reason to postulate a second rule of comparative deletion that is extensionally identical (as a function) to *wh*-movement over a subdomain of the latter. I see no reason to believe that C-Sub constructions challenge that conclusion. However, it remains to determine how C-Sub relates to the general thesis (50). Specifically, is C-Sub a rule of deletion over a variable meeting the conditions (49)? If the answer is positive, we must permit a new category of rules, deletion over a variable, thus expanding the class of permitted grammars. Furthermore, we must abandon the thesis (50) and with it the explanation for CNPC, *wh*-island constraints, and cross-over.[58] But the crucial data seem to me relatively unconvincing. Until some formulation of the relevant notion of "complexity" or "parallelism" is advanced, we really have no way of knowing whether the restrictions on C-Sub bear on the thesis (50) at all.

But in fact further analysis shows, I think, that little hinges on the question of whether C-Sub is taken to observe the conditions (49). We can see why by considering more carefully the applicability of Bresnan's relativized A-over-A condition (RAOAC) to the case of C-Sub.

Recall that RAOAC guarantees that application of *wh*-movement to (236) will give (237), not (238):

(236) a. *John read* [[*how many*] *books*]
       b. *John is* [[*how (much)*] *tall*]

(237) a. *how many books did John read*
       b. *how tall is John*

(238) a. **how many did John read books*
       b. **how (much) is John tall*

The condition guarantees that the larger bracketed phrase of (236) is extracted, in these cases. Bresnan argues that the same condition is applicable in the case of C-Sub. Given (239) we form (240) by C-Sub, deleting X:

(239) *the desk is as high as it is* [[X] *wide*]

(240) *the desk is as high as it is wide*

Bresnan takes X to be a QP, say, *that much*. Why doesn't RAOAC apply, deleting (241a), as it moves (241b) in (236b) or (according to Bresnan's analysis) as it deletes (241a) in (242):

(241) a. [[X] *wide*]
       b. [[*how (much)*] *tall*]

(242) a. *this desk is as wide as that one is* [[X] *wide*]
       b. *this desk as as wide as that one is*

The reason, Bresnan argues, lies in the principle of recoverability of deletion. Thus RAOAC requires that we apply the rule to the maximal appropriate phrase that is not distinct from its antecedent; (241a) is distinct from its antecedent in (239) but not (242a); therefore only X is deleted in (239). It is this assumption that permits Bresnan to take comparative deletion and C-Sub to be the same rule.

But the assumption seems to me questionable. Notice in the first place that on this approach, we must take (243) to be analogous to (244) rather than (245).[59]

(243) a. *John is taller than Bill is* **tall**
       b. *John is taller than he is* **tall** (take *he* to refer to John)

(244)   how is John tall (=(238b))

(245) a. *John's height exceeds Bill's* **height**
       b. *John's height exceeds his* **height** (take *he* to refer to John)

The reason is that under this analysis, (243a,b) derive by the same violation of RAOAC that gives (244). But this conclusion seems to me highly counterintuitive. Rather, it seems to me that (243a,b) are quite analogous to (245a,b) and very different from (244); specifically, (243b) seems to be simply a logical contradiction, like (245b).

But in fact there is additional evidence that Bresnan's analysis of C-Sub is defective. A crucial requirement of this analysis is that (243) must be marked ungrammatical, as a violation of RAOAC. But in fact, neither (243a) or (245a) (nor, for that matter, (243b) and (245b), which I take to be just contradictory) is ungrammatical, as we can see readily by constructing an appropriate context. If this is correct, then we can understand why (243) seem analogous to (245) rather than (244), which really is ungrammatical. As relevant contexts, consider the following:[60]

(246) Speaker A: *John is more courageous than Bill is **intelligent***
        Speaker B: *No, you've got it all wrong; John is more courageous than Bill is **courageous***

(247) Speaker A: *this desk is higher than that one is **wide***
        Speaker B: *What is more, this desk is higher than that one is **high***

(248) Speaker A: *this desk's height exceeds that desk's **width***
        Speaker B: *In fact, this desk's height exceeds that desk's **height**, too*

Similar examples can be constructed for (243), (245), apart from the difficulty of finding a natural contrast to "tall":

(249) Speaker A: *John is taller than Bill is **heavy***
        Speaker B: *What is more,* (243a)

(250) Speaker A: *John's height exceeds Bill's weight*
        Speaker B: *Furthermore,* (245a)

In short, when context supplies an adequate reason for placement of the required stress on the compared form in C-Sub constructions, examples such as (243), (245) (but never (244)) are quite all right. The simplest explanation for this fact, avoiding any elaborate complication of rules to distinguish somehow between cases of phonetically identical stress, is that C-Sub simply removes X in (239), etc., and is not subject to RAOAC. The remaining element is stressed, but for reasons having nothing to do with C-Sub; cf. (245). If the remaining element happens to be identical with the paired phrase that is its "antecedent," then the sentence is either contradictory (as in (243b) and (245b)), or else must be understood as in the discourses cited. All of this will form part of the rules of interpretation for foci in C-Sub constructions.

Notice now that there is no basis at all for generalizing C-Sub and comparatives, which is just as well in the present framework, for reasons already discussed. But we can go further. Consider the choice of the element X eliminated in C-Sub, as in (239) or more generally, (251):

(251)   ... *than (as)* NP *is* $[[_{QP} X] ...]$

There are several kinds of familiar deletion phenomena. Typical examples are VP-deletion, as in (252); *wh*-deletion, as in (253); and *for*-deletion, as in (254):

(252) *John left early but Bill didn't (leave early)*

(253) a. *the man (who) you met left early*
       b. *John is taller than (what) Bill is*

(254) *John wants (for) to leave*

In such examples as (252), there is typically a variant with the deleted phrase un-stressed. It may well be that this is the only kind of deletion that involves lexical items; namely, deletion "under identity" (cf. p. 81, above) of a phrase that can appear unstressed.[61] Examples (253)–(254) illustrate another major class of dele-tions—perhaps the only other case—namely, deletion of designated terminals, sharply restricted, and often with optional or dialectal variants without deletion.

Let us now return to C-Sub and ask where deletion of X in (251) fits into this pattern. Plainly, it is not a case like (252); there is no variant with an unstressed expression. Nor are there optional or dialectal variants. The deleted element X must simply be absent; period. The rule of C-Sub, as we have seen must refer specifically to X; it does not fall under RAOAC, as in (237). Assuming Bresnan's analysis, X is simply some representative of QP that is obligatorily eliminated.

We do have an element that is obligatorily deleted under some conditions, namely, *wh*-. Suppose, then, that we were to take $X = wh$- or to take *wh*- to be a feature of X. This choice allows us to express the relation between comparatives and C-Sub constructions in terms of presence of *wh*-. Furthermore, the obligatory deletion might fall under a broader generalization or might require no rule at all, given that *wh*- in isolation has no phonetic content. And we can easily formulate RAOAC so that it does not apply to "bare" *wh*- but only to phrases *wh-Y* (*Y* some terminal string) of the form X-bar (with the right number of bars; three in Bresnan's theory). We might, for example, limit RAOAC to cases where *wh*- is a specifier, in the sense of X-bar theory, of some lexical category, as it is in all the cases where RAOAC applies but not in (251), where it does not.[62]

Pursuing this approach, we will have *wh*-movement followed by the familiar *wh*-deletion in C-Sub constructions.[63] It will follow, then, that C-Sub has the proper-ties (49).

Bresnan gives a number of arguments against the assumption that a movement rule such as *wh*-movement applies in C-Sub. There are two basic points. The first is that there are no dialectal variants with *wh*-words in the case of C-Sub; i.e., no examples such as (255) analogous to (256):

(255) *John is more courageous than what Bill is intelligent*

(256) *John is more courageous than what Bill is*

But this argument does not apply to the analysis just suggested. Under this analysis, there is no form such as (255) for the reason that no *wh*-word was moved, but only *wh*-, which cannot be phonetically realized. The second argument is that where there is a lexical string in place of X in (251), extraction of QP is impossible, as illustrated by (238). That is, "certain kinds of left-branch modifiers cannot be moved away from the constituents they modify." Bresnan explains this fact in terms of RAOAC, and we have been relying on her explanation in the case of questions and relatives. But we have already seen that RAOAC does not account for C-Sub; rather, we must reformulate either RAOAC or C-Sub, perhaps along the lines just sketched, so that C-Sub does not fall under RAOAC. Therefore, this class of arguments against a movement rule no longer applies. Whether we have deletion or movement, the left-branch modifier involved in C-Sub is not subject to the general left-branch condition, which Bresnan convincingly explains in terms of RAOAC. In short, it does not matter whether we assume that the designated element X of (251) is deleted in place, or is moved by wh-movement and then deleted by an obligatory rule; in either case, either because it has no phonetic content in principle (and therefore, strictly speaking is not deleted) or as a subcase of the familiar rule illustrated in (253).

We can now see that C-Sub, though an extremely interesting phenomenon, does not seem to be relevant to our current discussion or to the thesis (50). If we decide to rule such "complex" examples as (232c) ungrammatical, then it follows that CNPC, etc., simply do not apply to C-Sub. In accordance with this decision as to the facts, we will formulate C-Sub as a rule deleting X of (251) in place; whatever conditions are established regarding complexity and parallelism will form part of the associated rule of interpretation. The rule is no longer "deletion over a variable"; we therefore do not have to admit this new category of rules into the grammar, and nothing follows concerning the general thesis (50). Or, if we decide, with Bresnan, that (232c), etc., are grammatical, then we will conclude that C-Sub does observe our general conditions subject to some extragrammatical factors that account for the rapid decline in acceptability with complexity and for the focus and parallelism requirements. In accordance with this interpretation of such constructions as (232c), we will stipulate that X of (251) is (or has the feature) wh-; We now have just another bit of evidence corroborating the general thesis (50), though very weak evidence because of the ambiguous status of (232c), etc.

The choice between these two alternatives will have to await a better understanding of the conditions on complexity and parallelism involved in C-Sub constructions. As far as the general thesis (50) is concerned, nothing seems to follow, either way.

If this line of argument is correct, we have then a very welcome outcome. Namely, there seem to be no clear counterexamples to the general thesis (50). The consequences have already been noted several times. We have an explanation for a variety of otherwise unexplained constraints in terms of rather simple conditions on rules, conditions that seem entirely natural as limitations on procedures of mental computation. Furthermore, we can reduce drastically the set of available rules. There will be no asymmetry between rightward- and leftward-movement rules; all are upward-bounded, in Ross's sense. There is no distinction between bounded and unbounded rules. All movement rules are simply subject to subjacency, if they are part of the cycle. There is no clause-mate constraint applicable to certain rules but not others. The only deletion rules are those of the type (252)–(254), and of these, only (252) are non-trivial. Rules of construal and no others are subject to the basic conditions

(4), (5); we thus have a rather natural formulation of an autonomy thesis for formal grammar, as noted earlier. More important still, we have some reason to believe that for the core grammar at least, the expressive power of transformational rules can be vastly reduced so that very few possibilities are available at all. Thus the class of possible grammars is significantly reduced and we have a natural and rather far-reaching explanation for phenomena of the sort under discussion here. Of course, these conclusions will only hold if the problems noted along the way and many others, no doubt, can be overcome.

Reduction of the class of available grammars is the major goal of linguistic theory. To account for the fact that language is acquired as it is, we must find ways to restrict the "space" of potential grammars to be searched by the language learner. Note that reduction of the class of grammars is not in itself an essential goal, nor is restriction of the class of generable languages; it is the class of "available" grammars that is important, We might in principle achieve a very high degree of explanatory adequacy and a far-reaching psychological theory of language growth even with a theory that permitted a grammar for every recursively enumerable language. The reasons are those outlined in Chomsky (1965), chapter 1, section 9. What is important is the cardinality of the class of grammars that are compatible with reasonably limited data and that are sufficiently highly valued. We achieve explanatory adequacy and approach a successful "learning theory" for language to the extent that this class is small, irrespective of the generative capacity of the class of potential grammars. We can try to keep this class "small" by restrictive conditions on the various components of the grammar (e.g., the X-bar theory for the categorial component of the base). The preceding discussion suggests other ways in which the variety of highly valued grammars can be reduced—quite significantly, if the suggestions developed here prove tenable.

Acknowledgments

I am grateful to Leland George, Norbert Hornstein, and Howard Lasnik for helpful comments on an earlier draft of this paper, and to many students whose suggestions and criticisms in the course of lectures and class discussion have been worked into the text.

Notes

1. As noted in Chomsky (1973), the principle of strict cyclicity as there formulated implies that wh-movement is cyclic. Bach and Horn (1976) state that they do not see why this principle implies that wh-movement is successive cyclic. The problem they perceive arises from their conclusion that when I wrote that the principle implies "cyclicity," I really meant "successive cyclicity"; cf. their note 23. But I did mean "cyclicity," and the problem they see does not arise.
2. Kayne suggests a possible deep structure for this case, but it seems rather artificial.

3. Note that there is no way to explain these facts in terms of a "clause-mate" constraint and a rule of raising to object. In the first place, reciprocal interpretation is not subject to a "clause-mate" constraint. cf. (7), (8); in fact, I think there is no credible evidence that any transformational rule or rule of construal is subject to such a constraint, i.e., that there is any reason to permit this option within linguistic theory. Furthermore, in many dialects we have such sentences as "they want very much for each other (themselves) to win," completely ruling out any such analysis. In general, even if there is a rule of raising to object position, which I doubt, it will not apply to *want*-type verbs, for reasons discussed in Bresnan (1970, 1972, 1976c); Lightfoot (1976a). See the latter for a general review of the matter.

4. Cf. note 3. Note that in all dialects, "*they* want very much for *them* to win" requires disjoint reference between the italicized positions. I will assume here that EQUI is correctly analyzed as deletion of "*X*'s self" (*X* a pronoun) in the context *for* − VP, optionally in some dialects, obligatorily in others, yielding the dialectal "they want for to do it" and the standard "they want to do it" with *for*-deletion before −*to*, under conditions that are moderately complex and somewhat variable across dialects. For discussion, cf. Chomsky (1975c), and for an independent argument, cf. Fodor (1975), pp. 141ff.

5. Bach and Horn (1976), in a criticism of Chomsky (1973), argue that "the total effect of the Specified Subject Condition ... (etc.) ... is to block extraction from" noun phrases. This is a rather selective reading. Examples of reciprocal interpretation and disjoint reference, not to speak of many others discussed in Chomsky (1973), have nothing to do with extraction from noun phrases. Thus even if they were correct in their proposals concerning noun phrases, to which I return below, the consequences for the analysis presented in Chomsky (1973) would be slight, it seems to me.
presented in Chomsky (1973) would be slight, it seems to me.

6. The point of these examples is that by reliance on PIC and SSC, which are independently motivated for interpretive rules, we can significantly reduce the expressive power of the theory of transformations, perhaps even to such a level that basic rules can be formulated as in (1). For discussion, cf. Chomsky (1975b,c). Even if this reduction is unattainable, the effect of the conditions discussed is considerable. This is important, since naturally we are concerned to reduce the class of grammars potentially available.

7. These examples are from Kayne (1975), as reanalyzed by Quicoli (forthcoming a,b,c).

8. Such examples as (i) have been suggested as counterexamples:
    (i) *los hombres parece* [*que t estan cansados*]
    But as Quicoli observes, this appears to be a case of topicalization with subsequent deletion of the subject pronoun rather than a case of raising. Under the analysis of topicalization presented below, PIC is irrelevant here. This is another example of the irrelevance of unanalyzed examples to confirmation of conditions on rules.

9. Cf. Kayne (1975), Quicoli (forthcoming b), Pollock (1976). The English examples are cited in Chomsky (1973) from Fauconnier (1971), who gives the French equivalents.

10. One crucial assumption in this analysis is that in English COMP cannot be doubly filled. It follows that no more than one element can be extracted to the matrix sentence from a complement clause. Postal (1976a) argues that this assumption is incorrect, as shown by (i) and (ii):
    (i) *under those conditions, what do you think I should do*
    (ii) *if he comes, what do you think I ought to do*
    He argues that "both of the italicized phrases have been extracted from the complement of *think*." Postal does not formulate the rules that he believes to be operative here, but presumably he is assuming that certain phrases *X* are preposable to sentence initial position in the context (iii):
    (iii) *what you* VP [$_S$ NP V ... *X*]
    Assuming that some such rule is what he has in mind, we see at once that it is incorrect. Cf. (iv), (v):

(iv)   *under those conditions, what did you tell Mary [that I should do t]

(v)   *if he comes, what did you tell Mary [that I should do t]

To be precise, (iv) and (v) are not starred, but rather cannot be interpreted as extraction from the position marked with t, but only as preposing from the matrix clause. Thus the rule that seems to be presupposed by Postal's discussion is wrong. This leaves us with the problem of explaining (i), (ii). Whatever the explanation may be, notice that the phenomena cited have no direct bearing on the conditions on rules that Postal is discussing, for reasons already elaborated several times. Postal's discussion of alleged counterexamples to SSC is a good example of the fallacy that I have noted several times: phenomena do not bear directly on conditions on rules; only rules do. In no case does he propose a rule that violates (or confirms) these or any other conditions. Similar criticisms with regard to Postal (1974a) appear in Lightfoot (1976a); Bresnan (1976c).

As far as (i) and (ii) are concerned, perhaps the explanation is that such phrases as "you think" are subject to a reanalysis as adsentials, so that none of the relevant conditions apply, just as we have "violations" of CNPC under the reanalysis indicated in (vi) and (vii):

(vi)   what did he [make a claim] that John saw (acceptable, for many speakers)

(vii)   what did he [have an opportunity] to do

Such reanalysis is motivated by the familiar analysis of tags; e.g., (viii), (ix):

(viii) I think that John will come, won't he

(ix)   *I told Mary that John will come, won't he

Whether or not this suggestion is correct, I stress again that such examples as (i) and (ii) have no relevance to the question of the adequacy of conditions on rules in themselves, but only indirectly, insofar as they indicate what the rules of grammar might be.

11. Compare *"what did they hear some funny stories about pictures of," blocked because of subjacency. Cf. Chomsky (1973) for discussion of some complications.

12. A more familiar assumption is that relativization in these languages leaves a copy. I am assuming that pronouns are base-generated, and that the power of transformations is so restricted that pronouns (or, for that matter, lexical items in general) cannot be introduced by transformation. For discussion, see Wasow (1972), Lasnik (forthcoming). Perhaps the most convincing argument against a pronominalization transformation, in my opinion, is the one given by Dougherty (1969). He points out that in positions where nouns and non-anaphoric pronouns can freely occur, pronouns that can be understood anaphorically can also be understood nonanaphorically, a fact unexplained under a transformational analysis but immediately explicable on the assumption that pronouns are base-generated (his "anaporn relation"). Thus a transformational analysis is missing an important and obviously nonaccidental generalization. Postal (1972) argues that Dougherty's observation is false, on the basis of examples in which pronouns occur in positions where nouns and nonanaphoric pronouns do not freely occur. Since the proviso italicized above is perfectly explicit in Dougherty's discussion (cf. his note 13) Postal's rejoinder is completely beside the point.

13. It has been noted that English speakers sometimes use a construction with a pronoun where an island constraint would block relativization, as in (23ii); cf. Andrews (1975a) for some discussion. I suppose that this is an ancillary process, not to be incorporated, strictly speaking, within the grammar.

14. On the significance of erasure of trace, as in NP-preposing in (29), cf. Fiengo (1974), Chomsky (1974, 1975b). Note that trace theory introduces no "globality" in any unwanted sense, contrary to what is sometimes assumed. Cf. Chomsky (1975b) for discussion.

15. We may take who, what to be, in effect, wh-person, wh-thing, respectively, Thus who is analogous to "what student." Relations between interrogatives and indefinite pronouns, discussed in Chomksy (1964), Postal (1965), will be expressed, within this framework, as conditions on variables in LF, along the lines of Chomsky (1975c).

16. In Chomsky (1973), section 17, it is suggested that the rule of *wh*-movement might be replaced by an interpretive rule for *wh*-phrases generated in COMP position. The rule of interpretation would then be something like (38). I think that this is entirely possible, but I am not convinced that it is a meaningful alternative to the transformational analysis as a movement rule, for reasons discussed in Chomsky (1975c). The same may be said about the proposal to replace NP-movement rules by interpretive rules. It seems to me that we have three types of rules, each with their separate properties: NP-movement, *wh*-movement, rules of construal (and, of course, others: e.g., extraposition, quantifier-movement or interpretation, FOCUS, predication, etc.). If all are regarded as interpretive rules, we still have the same three collections of properties, which can, in fact, be explained (rather than stipulated) if we take the NP-movement and *wh*-movement rules to be movement transformations meeting the conditions discussed here.

17. Direct application of *wh*-movement to give (41) is blocked by PIC and SSC. Application of *wh*-movement in the embedded clause will give "you told Mary [who she should meet]." Extraction of *who* on the next cycle is blocked by PIC, since the bracketed phrase is a tensed clause, and by SSC, under the present formulation (but not that of Chomksy, 1973), since it contains a specified subject. Cf. notes 37, 38. Bach and Horn (1976) state that in Chomsky (1973) a "special clause" is required "allowing extraction over a specified subject by movement into a COMP node." That is incorrect. Movement to the COMP node in the first cycle does not fall under (11), as explained in Chomsky (1973), because there is no internal cyclic node.

18. Examples (a) and (b) are from Dean (1967). Example (c) is from Erteschik (1973), who gives a detailed discussion of the topic. The oddity of *wh*-movement from certain factives is noted in Kiparsky and Kiparsky (1970).

19. In Chomsky (1973), note 22, I remarked that none of the arguments in the literature appear to apply to the formulation of cyclicity of *wh*-movement proposed. Bach and Horn (1976) dispute this observation, claiming that these arguments do apply. They present one example, which, as they note, is based crucially on the assumption that *wh*-movement is obligatory in the embedded clause. They fail to note, however, that I explicitly assumed the rule to be optional; cf. section 13. Thus the statement to which they object seems to me accurate. They assert that optionality of *wh*-movement undermines arguments for successive-cyclicity, but they present no grounds for this conclusion (they do offer arguments purporting to show that strict cyclicity is untenable, but whatever the merits of these may be, the question is a quite different one). In fact, optionality of *wh*-movement is irrelevant to the arguments for successive cyclicity. My assumption is that all rules of the "core grammar" (excluding what Bach, 1965, calls "housekeeping rules") are optional, the apparent obligatoriness deriving from filters and principles of interpretation, along the lines discussed in Chomsky (1973). Cf. Lasnik and Kupin (forthcoming), Chomsky and Lasnik (forthcoming).

20. Note again that we also must presuppose the "superiority condition" of Chomsky (1973), independently motivated by "I don't remember who saw what," *"I don't remember what who saw."

21. Note that if a language has no transformations, this "escape hatch" is unavailable in principle. Therefore it follows that for such languages, extraction of *wh*-phrases from embedded clauses is impossible. Cf. Hale (1976) for an argument along these lines for Walbiri. Note that the sufficient condition cannot be strengthened to necessary and sufficient.

22. Bach and Horn (1976) suggest a different explanation for CNPC, to which I will return.

23. Bresnan notes that there is no convincing evidence for cross-over in the case of comparative subdeletion, and that some of the cross-over phenomena do not seem to hold for subdeletion. Reanalysis of subdeletion along the lines discussed below has as a consequence that these structures should differ from comparatives in this respect.

24. The analysis that follows is essentially that of Chomsky (1974). It was suggested by material presented in Emonds (1976) based on ideas of Ann Banfield. I am indebted to Ivan Sag for emendations, as noted below.

25. How seriously one should take this last remark I am not sure. There is no particular reason to take the *wh*-phrase of the COMP in relatives to be a quantifier binding the variable, and it may be that a natural semantic interpretation of relatives, along the lines previously discussed, will regard the variable introduced as free whether or not the *wh*-phrase in the COMP is deleted. Cf. discussion following (24) and Vergnaud (1974).

26. E.g., subjects, extraposed clauses, pseudoclefts. Also such structures as *"I'm sad he left" (cf. "I'm glad he left"), *"I muttered he'd better leave," etc.

27. After writing this sentence, I noticed that it illustrates the property of left-dislocation discussed earlier without clear examples, namely, that the proposition need not be "open" but can be about the focused element of the TOPIC in some more vague way.

28. This is ungrammatical, but for independent reasons; namely, free relatives with *who* are excluded in general by a special restriction. Thus "this book is what I want Bill to tell Mary to read" is fine.

29. The last example is from Pinkham and Hankamer (1975). We should have also "pea green is what Tom ordered us to paint our boat"; "pea green, Tom ordered us to paint our boat"; "it was pea green that Tom ordered us to paint our boat." But the last two of these seem to me very questionable. The (d) cases also seem marginal, suggesting that PP might be excluded from subject or TOPIC. I am assuming here that the TOPIC is construed with the embedded clause.

30. With obligatory auxiliary inversion.

31. Pinkham and Hankamer, in their very interesting study of clefts, state that their analysis, which postulates two independent rules that form clefts (one of them structure-building), is intended "as a challenge to any analysis" that is not structure-building. But I think that the data they cite, where judgments are clear, is just as well handled by postulating the underlying structure (85) and no rule of cleft-formation at all, apart from the interpretive rules. Note that this analysis covers two cases, but these do not coincide exactly with their two cases. I am not convinced by some of the crucial data that they offer to demonstrate that the examples divide as they propose, but will not pursue the matter here. They note a parallel between PP-preposing and clefting (p. 438), but it is not exactly the parallel noted here. I am suggesting, in effect, that the parallel is far broader and not limited to extraction from the scope of a negative as they propose.

32. Note that we cannot have *believe* in this position as in (94b). The reason has to do with general properties of infinitives. Nonagentive constructions would be equally odd in "I ordered Bill to believe that Mary left," "John is hard to believe to have left," etc.

33. On the status of embedded finite clauses in these constructions, see below.

34. For discussion of infinitival relatives from a somewhat different point of view, see Emonds (1976).

35. Judgments vary, as is generally the case when *each other* is in subject position: cf. "they wanted each other to win," "they prefer for each other to win," "they would hate it for each other to win," "they would hate it for each other's pictures to be on sale," etc.: see Chomsky (1973) for some discussion. However, there seems no question that (103b) is incomparably more acceptable than (103c). Note that *books* must be plural in (103b), as is generally the case in reciprocal constructions for reasons that remain obscure: cf. "we saw pictures (*a picture) of each other," "we turned the arguments (*the argument) against each other," etc. Cf. Chomsky (1973) for discussion.

36. Similarly, *"who$_2$ did you find a book (which$_1$) for us to give t_1 to t_2," *"[to whom]$_2$ did you find a book (which$_1$) for us to give $t_1 t_2$," *[what book]$_2$ did you find a person (who$_1$ for) to give t_2 to t_1," *[what book]$_2$ did you find a person [to whom]$_1$ (for) to give $t_2 t_1$."

37. The proviso (46) permits escape from COMP in a tensed sentence. If the notion "subject" is so defined that the subject of S is also the subject of $\bar{S}$, then (46) is required to permit escape from COMP in infinitives as well. If the subject of S is not the subject of $\bar{S}$, then nothing will prevent movement from COMP in infinitives. In Chomsky (1973) I made the

latter assumption, in the foregoing discussion, the former, largely for expository reasons. If bridge conditions are limited to finite clauses, as appears to be the case, then "subject of" should be defined only for S, not $\bar{S}$, so that SSC is inapplicable to COMP–COMP movement.

38. The basic observation is due to Ross (1967). He notes that some restriction must be formulated to rule out "this rock is too heavy for us (to try) to claim that we picked up." Cf. also Ross (1973): "Gravel pizza is tough for me to prove that she thought of." Ross stars these examples. Lasnik and Fiengo (1974) note that the restrictions follow from PIC, according to their analysis. In our terms, they follow by withdrawing (46) in these cases. Consider the corresponding infinitivals: "this rock is too heavy for us (to try) to order her to pick up," "Gravel pizza is tough for me to prove her to have thought of." Lasnik and Fiengo block these by SSC. If, in fact, the finite and infinitival embedded clauses give approximately the same degree of "strangeness," then in the present framework we must accept the formulation of "subject of" assumed here rather than in Chomsky (1973) (cf. note 37), and relax the language-specific proviso (46) for all these cases. If the tensed S's are indeed of a different category, then the formulation of Chomsky (1973) must be accepted, and the language-specific proviso (46) relaxed. If there is some independent reason for the "strangeness" in all of these cases, then nothing follows with regard to subject of $\bar{S}$ and nothing need be said about (46). Judgments are sufficiently obscure, to me at least, so that I hesitate to make a definite proposal. Note that all that seems to be involved is a language-specific proviso and the precise formulation of a general principle for a domain of facts that are rather marginal.

39. The following discussion draws heavily on Lasnik and Fiengo (1974), though a somewhat different analysis is proposed.

40. I have been assuming throughout that VP is introduced only under S; thus, that infinitival subjectless complements of *promise-persuade*, etc., are $\bar{S}$, with NP = PRO. Deletion of *for X-self*, as in EQUI, will leave VP under S (cf. note 4). Arguments in support of distinguishing VP infinitival complements in this way appear in Quicoli (forthcoming a,b,c); cf. Chomsky (1975c). There is a similar distinction in Kayne (1975).

41. For discussion of various adjectival constructions, cf. Lees (1960b) and much later work. That the *for*-phrase is within the embedded sentence in both cases of (123c) is argued by Bach and Horn (1976). We will return to this question.

42. These examples suggest that the phenomena that Bresnan discusses under the rubric of the "fixed subject constraint" might preferably be handled by a surface filter (a suggestion that she rejects, but on grounds that can be overcome in terms of trace theory, it seems) rather than as a condition on rule application, since in these cases *wh*-movement takes place after *for*, which then deletes before *to* in standard dialects.

43. A rather similar analysis, but without *wh*-movement, is suggested in Ross (1967), but he later rejected it on gounds that were later shown to be inadequate by Akmajian. Cf. Lasnik and Fiengo (1974) for a review.

44. Cited in Grimshaw (1975) from Berman (1974). Grimshaw attributes the original observation to Huddleston (1971).

45. They do not cite (f), (g), but these are implicit in their analysis. Similarities between *easy-to-please* constructions and others that we have discussed here are noted in the literature. Cf., e.g, Evers (1975).

46. I am indebted to Alan Prince for pointing out this consequence.

47. Postal (1974) aruges to the contrary on the basis of such examples as "John's tendency to talk too much," which he takes to be derived by raising to subject followed by nominalization. But he overlooks the fact that the noun *tendency* must have a different source, as in "John's tendency towards violence," where there can be no raising. In fact, it seems that there is an NP of the form "NP's tendency . . ." wherever there is a structure "NP has a tendency . . .," suggesting either a transformational analysis or a redundancy rule, in

either case, relying on base-generated *tendency*, as implied by the lexicalist hypothesis. For discussion, see Chomsky (1974), Lightfoot (1976a).

48. Perhaps the latter approach will provide a principled explanation for the other major property of *easy*—as distinct from *eager*—constructions, namely, the fact that we have "an easy man to please" but not "an eager man to please." Again, various explanations have been proposed since the basic properties of these constructions were noted (cf. Chomsky, 1962), and the investigation has clearly been a very fruitful one in terms of insights attained along the way, though the original problem remains a challenging one.

49. But see notes 37, 38.

50. Note that the Sentential Subject Constraint of Ross (1967) is a consequence of subjacency whether or not S is cyclic, but the Subject Condition is not.

51. Of course we have "of the students in the class, how many got As" by PP-extraction after *wh*-movement.

52. In their concluding remarks, Bach and Horn note that there are many rules that extract phrases from NP, violating the NP Constraint as they formulated it. They do not consider this a problem for their analysis, apparently because NP is explicitly mentioned in the structural description of these rules. I do not fully understand their point, however, and may have misstated it.

53. Compare "we read stories about each other," "they read stories about them" (cf. Chomsky (1973) for some discussion of the latter as compared with "they read stories about themselves"). Note that SSC is required for NPs quite apart from the reanalysis that Bach and Horn suggest. Cf. note 5.

54. Examples of this sort are difficult to evaluate, since they might arise from passivization of "John — wrote — a book about Nixon" followed by extraposition from subject NP and (perhaps) interchange of PPs. The same is true of *wh*-question; see below. It has sometimes been suggested that (i) is not so deviant as (ii):

    (i)   *of whom was [a picture t] standing on the mantelpiece*
    (ii) *who was [a picture of t] standing on the mantelpiece*

One might attribute this difference, if it is systematic, to extraposition from NP yielding (iii) and then (i):

    (iii) *[a picture t] was standing on the mantelpiece of NP*

To me, (iii) seems to have approximately the status of (i). Alternatively, one might argue that (i) derives by *wh*-movement directly while (ii) is blocked, appealing to the absolute interpretation of the A-over-A condition to make the distinction. If so, then S need not be taken as a cyclic node for subjacency, and (181) will be modified accordingly. Unfortunately, the examples that seem crucial to selecting among these alternatives seem rather marginal.

55. Similar question arise in connection with (209), as noted in Chomsky (1973). See Oehrle (1974) for some relevant discussion.

56. Fauconnier refers to Postal (1974b) for a possible explanation of why quantifier scope should be constrained by islands, but the basic data that Postal assumed seem to be incorrect. Cf. Jackendoff (1975a). That is, the cases he considered seem not to be governed by such conditions as CNPC (as would be expected in the present framework).

57. Cf. Hornstein (1975), note 33, citing observations by G. Horn.

58. Recall that cross-over conditions are in part inapplicable, in part violated by C-Sub, as Bresnan notes. See note 23.

59. Note that the italicized phrases in (243)–(245) must be stressed. However, this is no special property of C-Sub, as we can see from (245).

60. I owe this point to Ivan Sag, who cites the following sentence suggested by Larry Horn:

    (i)   *John drinks more Scotch than Bill does <u>Scotch</u>*

As Horn observes, (i) is quite appropriate in the following discourse:

Speaker A: *John drinks more Scotch than Bill does* Bourbon
Speaker B: *No, you've got it all wrong,* (i)

Boldface type indicates stress throughout these examples.

61. One might consider the possibility that such rules as VP deletion do not belong to sentence grammar at all, but rather to a theory of discourse. Cf. Sag and Hankamer (1976), Sag (forthcoming, 1976), who do not draw this conclusion but provide arguments on which it might be based. If so, then deletions can be narrowly restricted in sentence grammar, perhaps just to deletion of certain grammatical formatives and pronouns. Other deletions, where a variant appears with the deleted string unstressed and the deletion is conditional on discourse factors (hence, in special cases, sentence-internal discourse factors), would then be regarded as on a par with the rules that generate bare NPs, say, as answers to questions. If this proves to be a reasonable course, there will be certain consequences with regard to the effect of deletion rules on generative capacity. Grammars must allow some deletion of designated elements; at least this is true of any grammar that derives "the man I saw" from "the man who I saw," etc. If no constraints are placed on such deletion, then for most classes of grammars it will follow that all recursively enumerable sets can be generated, not a particularly important fact, for reasons discussed in Chomsky (1965) and below. E.g., phrase structure grammars have the weak generative capacity of unrestricted rewriting systems (arbitrary Turing Machines) if one terminal symbol is taken to be "blank." Peters and Ritchie (1973) observe that the same is true of transformational grammars, and state some general properties of grammars with cyclic rules that would suffice to reduce weak generative capacity to recursive sets. Peters (1973) suggests a rather plausible general property of transformational grammars that would suffice for this purpose, namely, his "survivor property." A number of people have observed that there is no algorithm for determining whether an arbitrary transformational grammar has this property, again, neither a surprising nor particularly interesting fact; there is also no algorithm for determining whether an arbitrary rewriting system generates finite sets, but that would not lead us to conclude that a class of "grammars" generating only finite sets cannot be specified. Peters's suggestion poses the problem of finding decidable conditions for grammars that guarantee that the survivor property (or some other sufficient property) is met, if indeed it is true that natural languages are recursive, which is by no means obvious (or, again, particularly important, in itself). Perhaps an approach to deletions of the sort just briefly discussed might provide an answer to this problem, if worked out in detail.

62. As noted by Woisetschläger (1976), Bresnan's RAOAC might be modified so that it applies to all and only "mixed terms" with a designated specifier. Then her analysis would apply at once to such examples as "so tall a man, I have never before seen," *"so tall, I have never before seen a man," where the specifier is *so* rather than *wh-*; etc.

63. Note that *wh*-deletion is vacuous in this case, perhaps, since there may be no terminal string in the first place.

COMMENTS ON THE PAPER BY CHOMSKY

Emmon Bach

Department of Linguistics
University of Massachusetts
Amherst, Massachusetts

Introduction

In a paper published in 1972, Chomsky characterized the state of our field as follows:

> There is an appearance of considerable diversity of points of view—and to some extent, the appearance is correct. However, I think that the dust is beginning to settle, and that it is now possible to identify a number of real, empirically significant theoretical questions that have been raised, if not settled, in this work. I also think much of the apparent controversy is notational and termonological—including many issues that appear to be fundamental and have been the subject of heated, even acrimonious dispute. This is unfortunate, because it sidetracks serious work, and because occasionally certain questions of some interest are embedded, sometimes buried in these terminological debates. (Chomksy, 1972b, 63 ff.)

I think this characterization holds today as well, and I would like to make my remarks in the same spirit. I will first list what I think are uncontroversial general areas of agreement. Then I will look at some specific points of agreement across various current (and not so current) frameworks that emerge from Chomsky's latest paper(s), trying to sort out what are differences of substance and what merely terminological. I have a number of questions about the interpretation of various aspects of Chomsky's current position and some criticisms. Finally, I will try to identify a very broad issue that needs to be worked on in the future.[1]

I am not going to talk much about the parts of Chomsky's paper addressed to the question of comparative deletion since I think they have been adequately treated in the discussion of Bresnan's paper.

1. General Areas of Agreement

Although surely not every linguist would agree about the following assumptions, I think every linguist working within the generative framework would (hence I will not defend them here):

1. The fundamental goal of linguistic work is to delimit as narrowly as possible a class of "rule systems" ("grammars" in the broad sense) that represents the competence of users of natural languages. This assumption characterizes what it is fair to call the Chomskyan paradigm under which most of us have been working for twenty years or so.

II. A grammar is a complex collection of subsystems or "levels" (Chomsky, 1955). The discovery of the structure of these parts and their interrelationship is an empirical matter. We do not know in advance how facts and generalizations are going to fall into line. [2]

III. One part of the task of linguistic theory is to account for the ability of a native speaker to know about an infinite set of pairings of syntactic structures with meanings (in some sense to be defined).

IV. A necessary condition for judging the adequacy of a theory is explicitness, ideally in all subparts of the theory.

V. Given two theories compatible with "known facts" we will a priori choose the more restrictive one (this follows from I).

VI. A necessary condition for choosing between two theories is showing that they are different (not just "notational variants"). This assumption and V presuppose a reasonable degree of explicitness.

VII. Finally, the principal means of finding out about language and languages is to work out reasonably rich fragments of grammars of natural languages.

It seems to me that the present paper contributes a great deal to the task of judging and elaborating what Chomsky calls the extended standard theory[3] against this background of agreement.

Before turning to specifics, I would like to summarize and perhaps clarify the question of the relationship between syntax and semantics so that we will be able to talk about some real issues. I think a good deal of the confusion about these matters has been cleared away in recent work by all sorts of linguists.

There are at least two things that people seem to mean when they talk about "semantics," "rules of interpretation," and the like. On the one hand, they may be talking about the relationships between expression in some language (natural or not) and their interpretation in the logician's or philosopher's sense, This interpretation would fix what are taken to be the truth conditons of sentences, their entailments, and the like. On the other hand, they may be talking about relationships between expression in some object-language (English, surface structures, deep structures) and expressions in some (to-be) interpreted language (Katzian "readings," Montague's intensional logic in PTQ (Montague, 1973)). It is possible to skip this intermediate step (Cooper, 1975) as it is possible to posit further intermediate stages (such as Chomsky's "semantic representation" as distinct from "logical form," 1975c). I will assume here with most linguists and without argument that there is some intermediate language (logical form, "Markerese," deep structure, etc.). Let us call the relation that holds between expressions in the object language and the expressions in the interpreted language the *translation relation*. I think it is profitable to consider various current issues in terms of the way in which they specify the structure of this relationship.

2. Some Specific Agreements

Now let us look at some more specific questions where it seems as if some agreement has been achieved, appearances to the contrary notwithstanding.

2.1 Globality

One of the hotly debated issues of the sometimes more calorific than phosphorescent "interpretive-generative-semantics" battles of recent memory was the question of globality. G. Lakoff and others (1970a, 1971b) claimed that the translation relationship necessarily involved nonlocal constraints (derivational constraints). Despite Chomsky's disclaimer (cf. note 14, cf. also Chomsky 1975b pp. 117 ff.), it seems to me that this claim is recognized as correct and explicitly incorporated into the "revised extended standard theory" (REST). Chomsky (1972b) rightly criticized a theory in which unrestricted use of (undefined) derivational constraints was countenanced (a theory I do not think anyone has ever advocated).

The important question, to my mind, is then not whether a grammar needs global power but rather: how can we restrict the global power of a grammar so as to get a reasonable explanation of the facts?

Let us continue to assume that a derivation involves a sequence of phrase markers $K_1 \ldots K_n$, K_1 a deep structure, K_n a final derived phrase marker. What elements of this derivation are available as input to the translation rules? The standard theory said: there is a distinct set of projection rules $P_1, \ldots P_n$ that apply bottom to top to K_1 to derive a representation that is the projection of the deep structure onto an interpreted language. The inadequacy of this hypothesis soon became apparent, and there were two sorts of modifications in the theory. In one approach K_1 was modified and global conditions were added to ensure the proper matchings of initial phrase markers and K_n's, eventually leading to an identification of K_1 with semantic representations. In the other approach the nature of K_1 was maintained, but other parts of the derivation were made available to the projection rules: end of cycle P-markers, etc. Both extensions thus incorporated global power. The current theory of Chomsky, as I understand it, encodes into the K_i certain information from the entire derivation that was not available in the standard theory (by changing the definition of the elementary transformations (including the reduction operations associated with them) and introduces a new significant level of representation K_i $(1 < i < n)$. I am glad that Chomsky has given up the misleading terminology "surface structure" for this level. Let us call it "intermediate structure." The new theory also incorporates a distinction not available in the standard theory, the distinction between "movement" rules and "deletion" rules. In most formalizations of the standard theory, what was called a movement rule was actually a conjunction of two elementaries: a copying elementary (substitution or adjunction) and a deletion of the source of the copy from its original site. Thus the effect of a deletion was always the same: deletion of the terminal element and automatic reduction of all labeled brackets strictly enclosing the deleted element. In the new theory a "movement" rule is a rule that copies and deletes, but there is no subsequent reduction and the "empty" nodes remain. Since the nodes (or labeled brackets) are indexed the new phrase marker resulting from the rule bears a record of what element has been moved: this is the "trace." As opposed to this type of rule a deletion rule works exactly as before.

Thus the new theory is global in the sense that it can in principle keep track of every position occupied by an element at every stage of the derivation. It provides a notation for the concept of "corresponding node" (G. Lakoff, 1971b).

There is, however, a difference. Deletion and substitution rules can operate to obliterate a trace. It is an open question what difference this makes.[4] I will take up some consequences of this idea for the rules of interpretation later.

As far as I can see this theory of globality is not very restrictive. So the interesting remaining question is still: how can we restrict it?

One way to restrict this power would be to claim that only universal principles, rules, etc., could be global. For example, the specified subject constraint incorporates a certain amount of globality (the indexing of pro-elements and traces is necessary to determine whether the condition is to be invoked, whether as a condition on rules or as a condition on intermediate structures). To the extent that it can be shown to be universal, it will represent a restriction on the expressive power of a grammar.

2.2 Variables

In the middle and late sixties a number of linguists proposed various ways in which quantification and the like could be expressed for natural languages (and many logicians in an informal way had always assumed that the use of variables was a necessary or desirable part of any account of the semantics or syntax of natural language).[5]

Chomsky's most recent papers (cf. also Wasow, 1975) offer a new way to think about this problem. The agreement here is that a necessary task for syntactic-semantic theory is to account for those aspects of the structure–meaning relationship that are related to the interpretation of sentences involving quantifiers and bound elements (variables, pronouns, traces, etc.).

What is important to me about this agreement is that—whatever the details of the proposals for incorporating such matters into linguistic theory—a way is now open for incorporating into the revised theory a rich tradition stretching from Frege to the present. Three specific parts of this tradition are cited in the next sections.

2.3   Open Sentences and the Lambda Calculus

The notion of the open sentence as an essential part of the syntax and semantics of language (formal or natural) is, I believe, due to Frege. I believe linguistics was hampered by a failure to incorporate this insight. Again, I think recent work under a variety of frameworks has recognized the importance of the idea. In Chomsky's present paper the concept comes in the interpretive rules that give parts of logical form as open sentences. It has been used essentially in Montague grammar and various extensions of it (cf. Partee, 1976, for a variety of approaches under this general framework). The lambda calculus has been exploited within transformational-generative theory (in slightly differing ways) by Sag (1976) and Williams (forthcoming).

2.4   Interrogatives as Quantifiers

The idea that question words like *who* and *what* are logically exactly the same as quantifiers is relatively old (Jesperson, 1924, pp. 302-305; Carnap, 1937 [German original, 1934], p. 296; Reichenbach, 1947, p. 340). In more recent work in the transformational framework we find it in Bach (1968); Baker (1970). In the Montague framework, a recent paper devoted to the syntax and semantics of questions by L. Karttunen gives an elegant incorporation of the idea (Karttunen, ms.).

2.5   Quantification in General

Finally, in this general area the current paper of Chomsky (as well as recent work of Edwin Williams) is devoted to an account of the kinds of facts associated with quantifiers first brought to the attention of linguists (in the recent tradition) by (I believe) "generative semanticists" and responded to by workers like Jackendoff.

I am very optimistic about all this work. I will try to outline in a later section what I take to be the major issues concerning the particulars of how to account for all the facts. The common and, I believe, very positive result of all the recent (and not so recent) debates has been an increase in our understanding of what it will take to flesh out a full answer to the question about the nature of the translation relation. We obviously will not be able to answer this until we have fragments worked out (cf. p. 74), but up until recently it seems to me that work has suffered by not paying enough attention to all parts of the system of rules. In a later section I will make a few critical remarks along these lines about Chomsky's current work and also argue that specification of the translation relation is not enough.

3.   Queries and Problems

In this section I will take up a number of questions that arise in my mind about Chomsky's paper (and recent work along the same lines). Some of these questions will, I hope, be answered in the general discussion of the paper. Some are aimed rather at isolating certain problem areas that need to be worked on.

3.1   Rules, Families of Rules, or Subrules?

What does it mean exactly to say that "*wh*-movement" is involved in the generation of sentences with restrictive and nonrestrictive relatives, question words, tough-movement, etc., etc.? Here I am hoping for some clarifying discussion.

I can think of three possible interpretations. One of them is literal: there is a single rule that applies literally and freely to yield all of the derived structures of the types of constructions described in this paper. Whenever a structure is generated to which the rules can apply, it applies (optionally). There are of course vast differences in the details of the particular constructions covered by the rule (as noted by Chomsky himself). For example, all of the following are unacceptable sentences that arise by applying the rule generally (I omit all examples where I have been able to figure out how a particular condition on interpretation discussed by Chomsky would apply):

(1)   *?The people some of whom left were tired.* (restrictive reading)

(2)   *?What did he die during?*

(3)   *?Stories about whom have you heard recently?*

(4)   *?John, that lives in India, is here.*

(5)   *?With whom that is from India did you go to school?* [6]

(6)   *?With whom did you talk that was from India?*

Chomsky writes (p. 86): "There are, of course, some distinctions among these cases. Some of them can be accounted for by considering the contexts in which the *wh*-movement rule applies. E.g., questions but not relatives can have *wh*-movement of adjective phrases, but this distinction will obviously follow from *the rule of relativization* [italics mine] . . . " I cannot make any sense of this statement interpreting it literally, since according to its literal interpretation *wh*-movement *is* the rule of relativization.

Another interpretation is that "*wh*-movement" stands for a family of related rules each applying under varying conditions. But this does not square with the "no-conditions" hypothesis (Perlmutter, 1971) that seems to govern a great deal of recent work.

Finally, it might be that rules like "move *wh*" are actually the smallest (elementary) operations available for constructing "bigger" transformations.

3.2   What Cost Simplification?

A general motivation for much recent work has been the desire to restrict the power of the rule systems available to the learner. Among the restrictions relating to the transformational component have been: the no-conditions hypothesis (Perlmutter, 1971); dropping of various possibilities for Boolean combinations of predicates (Bresnan, 1976a); elimination of so-called "semantic conditions"; the string condition (Chomsky, 1975c); and so on. Chomsky characterizes his work as contributing to the goal of restricting grammars (Assumption I above). About the elimination of "semantic" conditions, I have nothing to say, since I think nothing can be said that does not beg the question of what is semantic and what is syntactic (cf. note 2). But about the other sorts of restrictions I think it is proper to ask about complications of other parts of the grammar. There are two relevant areas: conditions on applicability and rules of interpretation.[7]

The main thrust of Chomsky's present paper (as well as 1975c and 1975a) as opposed to the original Conditions paper (1973) has been to eliminate conditions on applicability in favor of surface filters and rules of interpretation. Quite correctly, Chomsky has stated that there is no a priori reason to think that either of the latter lay more claim to universality than transformational rules. There is, however, a crucial practical difference at the present stage of research. We have a general characterization (in fact quite a few alternatives) of the form of the syntax of a language (narrowly construed) including various notions about the form of the base rules and of transformations. In order to have an explanatory theory in Chomsky's sense this must be supplemented by a general characterization of possible language-particular conditions and rules of interpretation (as well as translation rules and semantic rules). It is pointless to argue about whether or not a simplification in one part is possible or desirable without considering the effects of the simplification on the other parts, and without some notion (or guesses) about what the other parts would look like there is not much hope of coming to any conclusions.

I would like to consider in a little detail just what is going to be necessary in the case that Chomsky appears to favor, where transformations are allowed to apply freely and the weight of culling out unacceptable results is thrown onto the rules of interpretation and "surface" filters.

Consider the rule "move NP." As I understand it, this rule is to be allowed to replace a nonterminal NP structure by some lexically filled NP (the latter carrying along its index). The base freely generates nonterminal NPs and the rule can be used to generate the following well-formed intermediate structures:

(7)   *Dams$_i$ are built t$_i$ by beavers.*

(8)   *Harriet$_i$ seems to John t$_i$ to be very intelligent.*

It will also generate all of the following (again I will try to exclude cases covered by some principle posited by Chomsky):

(9)   *Beavers$_j$ are built dams by t$_j$.*

(10)   *John$_j$ seems to t$_j$ Harriet to be very intelligent.*

(11)   *Sally$_j$ was given a book to t$_j$ by Harriet.*

In fact, take any arbitrary English sentence, move any NP into the position of any other NP, leaving a trace, and there will be a derivation of that intermediate structure from the grammar. Clearly, the adequacy of the system of rules cannot be judged unless we have (in detail) the "surface" filters and rules of interpretation that will sort out the differences between structures (7)–(8) and those like (9)–(11). Suppose it turns out that for every separate rule of a more familiar sort we have to provide a separate filter or rule of interpretation to segregate English from word-salad; then we will have a mere notational variant of the more traditional grammar (with complicated structural conditions, brackets, and the like).

Clearly, the only interesting version of the theory will be one in which filters and rules of interpretation have some measure of generality. A good deal of Chomsky's paper is devoted to arguing that there are such general conditons that apply in a variety of different situations. However, the net effect of an explicit set of rules treating completely a reasonably rich fragment of English will, I suspect, lead to the following question: why should we have any transformations at all? And what conceivable role would deep structure play in such a theory?

Let me try to be a little more explicit. Assume that we have successfully carried out the program of eliminating completely the need for conditions on applicability. The base generates an infinite set of generalized phrase markers including indexed nonterminals, variables (PRO's), and lexically filled structures. The core rules of English apply freely and the rules of interpretation and "surface" filters pick out a reasonable approximation to a set of acceptable English sentences (modulo stuff that we think might be taken care of by translation rules and semantic rules). I claim that the following nontransformational grammar will generate exactly the same set of sentences, assign them the same logical forms and phonetic representation. Allow lexically filled nodes to be freely indexed, generate directly all elements that were introduced by transformations, and eliminate the core transformational rules.

Actually, as far as I can tell, if the program of determining logical form step-by-step from intermediate structures is sucessfully carried out, then there will always be a nontransformational derivation of an intermediate structure directly for every transformational derivation. Structure preservation and free generation of indexed nonterminals ensure that there will always be a directly generated structure of the form:

$$\ldots NP_i \ldots t_i \ldots$$

for every such structure that arises by virtue of a movement rule. Hence, in this model the transformations are completely superfluous.

It seems clear to me that such a system is exactly (to the extent that we can be exact about undefined systems) equivalent to the system envisaged by proponents of "generative semantics." There is a level of representation that provides structures that are input to the rules of translation (or directly to the semantics). It bears a strong resemblance to the predicate calculus (compare McCawley's representations for quantification in McCawley, 1968a). It is called logical form. It is related by certain rules of an unknown sort to another level (shallow structure), which is a level unaffected by certain rules of undefined nature ("scrambling" rules, etc.). It incorporates global power both in the form of certain very general constraints (again of an undefined nature) and in the ability of certain rules (even phonological rules) to have access to various levels of representation at once. (Chomsky, 1972, claimed as much: generative semantics is a less restricted from of EST. Several years ago, I claimed, Bach, 1974, that "generative semantics" and "interpretive semantics" were descriptively equivalent. At the time, there was some doubt in mind as to whether this would turn out to be true if the systems were specified more precisely. Today, I do not have any such doubts.)

I think we can go one step further. An extremely simple context-free base can be set up that will generate all possible structures, something like a universal base to generate $(V*)*$ (by which I mean the set of all possible structures generable over an alphabet of indexed nonterminals and terminals). Following Chomsky's suggestion that the filters and interpretive rules are connected in some way to sentence processing, we can think of a grammar as simply a parser, say an ATN model.

3.3   The Organization of a Grammar

A number of questions remain in my mind about the organization of a grammar. A grammar (sentence grammar) contains all these parts: base rules, lexicon, 'core' transformational rules, other transformational rules, nontransformational syntactic rules, cyclic or postcyclic, "housekeeping" rules. Of these, all but the "scrambling" (and housekeeping?) rules are involved along the thorny path from deep to intermediate structure. Then the rules of intepretation take over, filling in variables, construing, etc. Somewhere along the way a (phonological?) contraction rule operates after some variables have been filled in but before others. (I am assuming that some variable or lambda operator or something has to be introduced to get the logical form of *I wanna go home*; and Edwin Williams (forthcoming) has suggested a derived verb phrase rule to account for the logical form of sentences with VP-deletion). Then come all the other rules of quantifier-raising (the analogue to "lowering" in G. Lakoff et al.), and so on. The chief distinction between the transformations and all other rules is that they are restricted to a simple form of a single "string condition." The other rules appear to do all the things transformations cannot do: change structure without reordering (cf. Chomsky's suggestions for *see a picture of NP*); use labeled bracketings (cf. Rule 38), insert terminal elements over unbounded contexts (ditto); be sensitive to "heaviness," ignore conditions on transformations, etc. They will also have to be able to do things that are not mentioned, for example: find the last occurrence of a trace with a particular index, change all the variables in a structure to avoid variable collision, or examine all the variables used so far and pick a new one.[8]

I am unable to put all this together in my head (let alone imagine how I could *have* it all in my head), and I am not entirely sure it is my fault. I have already mentioned and will take up again the question of how the phonological representation is going to be built up. Another question is where do rules like scrambling come in? And what sort of a rule is the rule of "control" that gets the indices onto PROs?

3.4   The Trace Theory of Movement Rules

The new paper spells out quite explicitly what traces are (with some modifications of earlier ideas). A trace is simply an indexed nonterminal node with no lexical content. I am not altogether clear about how the indexing takes place. In addition to nodes with fixed indices there are trace elements with a (single?) variable index (the old PRO). What work do these trace elements do? As far as I can see there are five things that they do:

A.   An improperly bound trace can block a derivation in which NP-postposing has applies to move a subject NP into the *by*-phrase, but NP-preposing has not replaced the trace in subject position (possibly other similar examples).

B.   They make it possible to recover the initial position of an NP for checking thematic relations, etc., that are determinable only at deep structure.

C.   A trace may act as a specified subject to block certain rules (or interpretations).

D.   They may be turned into variables by rules of interpretation to form part of the input to translation rules dealing with questions, relative clauses, etc.

E.   A trace that has been filled in by a variable (a terminal element of logical form) may block contraction (*wanna-want to*).

The case for (A) rests or falls with the analysis of Passive as an application of two rules (or "move NP" twice). There is an alternative analysis (within EST-oriented syntax) developed by Bresnan (1972) in which the underlying structure of a passive is a sentence with an empty subject and the agent phrase is already in position. In this analysis only one rule applies ("move NP"). I do not know of any compelling evidence one way or the other, but it seems as if it will have to come from the analysis of nominal structures like *the destruction of the city by the enemy* and the extent to which it will be possible (within the $\bar{\text{X}}$-theory) to maintain a parallel analysis of sentential and nominal structures. The Bresnan analysis goes naturally with an analysis of the nominals as having a source in which both the agent and the object are in postnominal position, and no rule at all has applied in the phrase given above. The NP-postposing analysis goes with a source in which the agent is already in determiner position. Taken literally, the trace theory predicts that the phrase above is ungrammatical since it has an improperly bound trace. Fiengo (1974) invokes a rule of trace replacement in which the determiner replaces the trace and in which phrases with no determiner (*destruction of private property is illegal*) are explained as the result of replacing the trace by a null determiner. I find this analysis completely unconvincing and ad hoc and conclude that if trace theory is right, then that analysis is wrong.

The second point (B) has to do with the determination of deep structure relations from intermediate structures. In chapter III of *Reflections*, Chomsky suggests that all semantic interpretation can be done from intermediate structures (via rules of interpretation and translation rules) and in my argument about the dispensability of transformations, I assumed that this is still the favored hypothesis. Jackendoff has pointed out (1975b) that the new conception of the translation relation undermines certain arguments about the derivation of *easy-to-please* constructions. Actually, a much broader consequence can be shown, namely that some alternative analyses available under the older assumptions are indistinguishable, for example, two analyses of Topicalization, one in which teh topic is moved from a position inside a sentence, and another in which it is generated in initial position followed by a sentence containing PRO or else a nonterminal node with the same index as the topic. This may be a good result.

The use of traces to act as specified subjects (C) obviously can be considered evidence only to the extent that the specified subject condition is considered to exist. I do not think it does, but the only convincing argument aginst it will be a better alternative explanation for the facts it is intended to account for, and this is not the proper place to try to present such an alternative even if I had one.[9]

I do not see any problems in principle with the interpretive rules that turn traces into variables (D), but I can see a lot of problems in actually giving the rules. Rule (38) (p. 84) is supposed to give the logical forms as indicated for these samples:

(12)   *Whose book did Mary read?*
         (*for which x, x a person*) (*Mary read x's book*)

(13)   *Who did Mary say that John kissed?*
         (*for which x, x a person*) (*Mary said that John kissed x*)

As far as I can see this rule will also give some undesirable derivations. Thus, example (12) also has a trace in position before *that*, so the rule will give this result:

(14)   (*for which x, x a person*) (*Mary said x that John kissed x*)

And it will also produce, from an example similar to (13)

(15)   (*for which x, x a person*) (*x's book was believed x's book to have been
         x's book likely . . . x's book to have been read x's book*)

Example (14) shows, that without some further elaboration the problem raised by Lightfoot (1976c) still arises. (15) shows that even in those places where we want the *x* to really show up (cf. Lightfoot, 1976c, again), Rule (38) will strew copies of the *wh*-phrase all the way down. What could be done? I am sure it is possible to work out a rule that will get the right results, but it will have to know a lot more than (38) appears to know. Notice that it is Rule (38) that is supposed to account for the contraction facts (E).

It is interesting to notice that a trace theory of movement rules which did not incorporate the hypothesis of successive cyclic *wh*-movement could avoid a lot of these problems. The rule (38) for example would not lead to placing variables and other junk into COMPs where they play no role, either in the phonology or the semantics. Actually, I think that is the wrong way to look at it. It follows from the more familiar unbounded single-movement hypothesis that the only place where traces can play a role is in the original position of the moved element or in some position where it has been moved by a cyclic rule that must yield some successive cyclic derivations (Lightfoot's double moved cases). In other words, the facts follow from one analysis, what follows from the other analysis is the necessity to elaborate more and more machinery to be consistent with the facts. I cannot think of a stronger argument against successive cyclic *wh*-movement.

As a matter of fact, there is a straightforward explanation of the contraction facts that does not make use of traces at all (Bresnan, 1972). In fact, there are two. You can take your pick, depending on whether you want *want* (and similar verbs) to always go with sentential complements or with bare VP-complements as well. Assume that there is a syntactic rule of cliticization that attaches *to* to *want, got*, etc. Assume a non-successive cyclic *wh*-movement rule ordered after this rule which in turn is ordered after EQUI. The rule is cyclic. Then the facts about *wanna–want to* follow if we assume that contraction applies only to cliticized combinations of *V+to*. The other explanation is essentially the same, but assumes that *want* and similar verbs occur with bare VP. (I will take up the question of variables again in a later section.)

3.5   Universal Grammar

So what kind of a picture of the nature of Language, that beast we are all trying to catch, emerges from the latest revised version of the extended standard theory? I mean, you set me out in some odd corner of the world and what am I supposed to expect? The answer that I see is not far off of the answer we all used to quote sniffily from Joos's reader: languages can vary in arbitrary ways. Conditions can vary (COMP-to-COMP). The specified subject constraint may have some claim to universality, but the definition of subject can vary from language to language. The tensed sentence constraint was a nice constraint because you could test it. The propositional island constraint is not so nice because the definition of a propositional island can vary from language to language. There are nontransformational languages and transformational ones. There are regrouping rule languages and, I guess, nonregrouping ones (only they, like English, can have readjustment rules). And apparently (according to Hale, this volume), there are languages that have phrase structure bases (with ordered strings) and other (Shaumjanian) languages that have bases that just generate unordered stuff that you can string out any old way you want.

4.   Internal Problems

In this section I am going to accept the general framework of Chomsky's program and the specific proposals for rules and conditons that he makes, insofar as I am able to understand them and raise some questions about problems that seem to remain.

4.1   The Propositional Island Condition (PIC)

The propositional island constraint (a "parametrized" version of the tensed sentence condition of earlier papers) can be stated thus (5)-(6):

PIC: given a structure

$$\ldots X \ldots [_{\alpha} \ldots Y \ldots] \ldots X \ldots$$

where α is a cyclic node ($\overline{S}$, NP possibly S, $\overline{\overline{S}}$)
no rule may involve X and Y
if α is a propositional island
(for English = finite clause)

I will assume that a finite clause is any clause containing as its main Aux (Aux $_1$): a modal, an auxiliary, or verb marked with Tns (= Past, Pres, Subjunctive [no claims about this last element being made]). Stated negatively, this means any "clause" except those including *to*, Poss-Ing, bare infinitives, Acc-Ing.

On p. 75   this condition is modified to overlook all cases except those in which α is a cyclic node immediately dominating the category of Y (suggested by J. -R. Vergnaud). That is, PIC now applies only to full subjects of tensed sentences.

The notion "involved" is spelled out in detail in the paper. I will not repeat Chomsky's explanation here.

Let us first stick to the restriction on cyclic nodes followed in the first part of the paper, that is, $\overline{S}$ and NP are the only cyclic nodes. The effect of Vergnaud's modification taken together with the specified subject constraint is to restrict application of the condition to the full subject of a tensed sentence. The modification is intended to take care of the problem of (16)–(Chomsky's example (8):

(16)   *The men expected   that   pictures of each other   would be on sale*

In (17) the condition blocks application of the reciprocal rule to *each other* because the cyclic node for the tensed sentence immediately dominates the subject NP.

(17)   *They expected that each other would win.*

In (16) it does not. But now as far as I can see the rule of disjoint reference will also apply freely in structures like (16). Hence, we should not be able to interpret *the men* and *them* as coreferential in sentences like those of (18):

(18)   a.   *The men expected that pictures of them would be on sale.*
        b.   *The men thought that a discussion about them would take place very soon.*

Chomsky's rule falsifies the condition as modified. I suspect that any attempt to state a general condition to cover the construal rules of reciprocal and reflexive interpretation together with the disjoint reference rule will fail for all the reasons that led Jackendoff (1972) to distinguish between optional and obligatory reflexive interpretation and Postal (1974a) and others to distinguish clause-mate cases of reflexive and reciprocal facts from other cases. Chomsky's rules and conditions make a clear prediction: in just those cases where reflexive and reciprocal construal is possible, disjoint reference will be required. This prediction is false.

I suggest that there are probably two rules each at least for reciprocal interpretation and bound anaphora interpretation. The PIC should be left as originally stated (without Vergnaud's revision). The other rules will have to be stated with constants intervening between the antecedent and the anaphor (which will hence not be "adjacent" in Chomksy's sense and will hence not fall under the defnintion of "involvement"). PIC can then be retained in its most general formulation at the cost of some special rules for picture-noun contexts, etc. (cf. Postal, 1974a, pp. 61-76). That changes in the general formulation of PIC are probably not going to work is suggested by these examples:

(19)   *the men expected that discussion about themselves (each other) would take place later.

(20)   I said that as for me/myself, I would prefer to stay in town.

(21)   Bill said that the book was to be written by Justine and him/himself.

(22)   Mary said that Harry would be staying with John and her/?herself.

Alternatively, one could assume that besides the rule for interpreting reflexives and reciprocals that are part of sentence grammar, there are other rules not part of this system at all (cf. Chomsky's remarks on pronouns on pp. 80 - 81). This would appear to work better for reflexives than for reciprocals. Most of the phenomena about reflexives discussed in Ross (1970) as support for his "higher performative" analysis can be turned around in support of a pragmatic account (which would then, like other such phenomena, explain the intrasentence uses of reflexives). Consider for example the *as for* construction.

(23)   As for myself, I like stars better than traces.

(24)   John said that as for himself, he liked squid better than octopus.

Instead of saying that we understand (23) because of its analogy to (24), we can say that we understand (24) because it is *about* a situation like that in which a sentence like (23) can be *used*. (One could use Ross's reasoning to argue that the fact that I am male is a fact of grammar because of the oddity of the sentence: *I am pregnant*.)

This explanation seems credible for a number of the types of sentences cited by Postal (1974a, pp. 61-69):

(25)   This paper was written by Ann and myself.

(26)   Physicists like yourself are a godsend.

But it will not work for picture-nouns or with cases attributed to Lawler by Postal (1974a, p. 66):

(27)   *?A picture of myself is hanging on the wall.*

(28)   *?They are more liberal than myself.*

So it seems that the special rules of construal can be limited to one or two special contexts that will simply have to be built into the rule.

That some instances of reciprocals might be pragmatically controlled is suggested by examples like these:

(29)   *Here's a book to read to each other.* (A handing a book to B and C).

But most of the other kinds of exceptional reciprocals do not seem to be controlled in this way.

I do not know whether the following suggestion is feasible under the constraints that Chomsky wants to impose on construal rules. Suppose we relax the string condition to the extent that the use of parentheses is allowed. Then the special cases (environments) for reflexivization could be collapsed with the general rule:

$$\text{vbl, } NP_i, \text{ vbl, (C), PRO-self, vbl}$$

(in schematic form, where C stands for the picture-noun and symmetric predicate contexts). The rule with the parenthetical stuff expanded would escape the effect of the PIC (and other conditions), but the general case (terms 2 and 4 "adjacent") would not.

The effect of the modified version of PIC (reverting to Chomsky's formulation including the suggestion of Vergnaud) is to restrict application of the condition to the full subject of a tensed clause. (Depending on our analysis of the Auxiliary, it will block rules from relating an Aux with stuff in the higher sentences as well. The only rules I can think of that might do this seem to be ones specifically concerned with Aux elements themselves, hence they would escape application of all conditions, if interpreted as part of the evaluation metric.) Other parts of the clause will be immune to the effect of higher structures by virtue of the specified subject condition unless the rule in question applies to a sentence with a subject under control of the X (of structures like those given in the general scheme above). I will now take up the latter condition.

4.2   The Specified Subject Condition

Crucial contrasts for the specified subject condition (SSC) are examples like these:

(30)   **They** *seem to me* [*t to like* **each other**]
        I* *seem to* **them [*t to like* **each other**]
        what books do **they** *expect* [*to read t to* **each other**]
        what books do* **they *expect* [*t to be read to* **each other**]

For the specified subject condition to be maintined, it is crucial that all instances of movement or deletion out of or into sentences be analyzed as *wh*-movement unless they involve movement of a subject from a nontensed clause. An example of the latter is the application of the rule "move NP" for *seem*-constructions. More familiar analyses of such phenomena as *though*-movement/deletion, *too/enough* deletion, *ready*-deletion, etc., would be blocked by the SSC.

Like PIC, SSC is supposed to apply to all rules of sentence grammar (at least all transformations and construal rules). There is at least one rule mentioned by Chomsky (cf. 1975c) that appears to violate SSC. It is the rule intended to account for wide-scope interpretations of sentences:

(31)   *John is looking for a unicorn.*

The rule must be stated something like this

(32)   (*Wide scope quantification*)

Given a structure $[_\alpha X, [\text{ Quantifier } \overline{N}]_{NP_j} Y]$
$\alpha = S$, etc.

rewrite it as:
Quantifier x_i, x_i a $\overline{N}$ $[X', x_i, Y']$
where x_i is a new variable not in X, Y
and X' and Y' are derived by replacing any traces
marked +anaphoric to j by x_i (or something like that)

(Cf. Williams, forthcoming, and Cooper and Parsons, 1976.)

This rule is not subject to SSC as these examples show:

(33)   *We would like you to answer a few questions about someone*
       (=*there's someone* . . . .)

(34)   *I enjoyed Sally's responses to every question.*

Further, Chomsky's rule (38) (question interpretation) appears to violate SSC (as well as PIC) (perhaps this is to be explained according to the "logic of markedness").[10]

4.3   Subjacency

The subjacency condition is supposed to hold for movement rules only (although I do not quite see how this is going to work if we replace conditions on rules by principles of interpretation). Bresnan (this volume) has given examples purporting to show that the question interpretation rule relating unmoved **wh**-phrases with COMPs is subject to various island conditions, so I will not discuss them. But consider the rule of wide scope quantification just given (32). It seems to obey whatever principles or combination of principles are intended to take care of CNPC. Compare these examples (in each case, the reader is asked to judge whether or not the quantified NP can be given a wide scope interpretation):

(35)   *John thinks that everyone is crazy.*

(36) *John regrets that everyone has a nickel.*

(37) *Sally disputed the claim that everyone had a nickel.*

(38) *Walter knows a man who every woman loves.*

(These, of course, were the kind of phenomena that were supposed to be explained by the quantifier lowering rules of yore.) (35) and (36) exhibit the "bridge" properties discussed by Chomsky. They cannot be explained by a COMP-to-COMP movement analysis (blocked in (37) and (38)) because there is no movement.

4.4 The Analysis of Adjectival Complements

As noted above, Chomsky has to analyze every rule moving or deleting a non-subject as *wh*-movement. Here are some examples of such sentences:

(39) *John is easy to please.*

(40) *This steak is too rare to eat.*

(41) *The meat is ready to take out of the oven.*

If they are the result of *wh*-movement in a structure like this,

$$\text{Adj} \; [_{\overline{S}} \; \text{COMP} \; [_S \quad] \;]$$

then they should exhibit the cluster of properties (49) (Chomsky's numbering) (gaps, apparent violation of PIC and SSC under bridge conditions, observe CNPC, observe *wh*-island constraints). I would like to focus on Chomsky's attempt to explain the relative acceptability of examples like these:

(42) *What piece of music is this instrument easy to play on?*

(43) *What instrument is this piece of music easy (easiest) to play on?*

I find these crashingly different. Chomsky argues that the unexpected acceptability of (43) is to be accounted for by its having a different source, one in which *on what instrument* "is associated with the VP rather than the adjective phrase." He points out that in cases where we must associate the PP with the verb, the result of "second" *wh*-movement should be bad and exhibits these sentences as evidence (=143):

(44) *What table is the book easy to put on?*

(45) *... the table that the book is easy to put on ...*

I frankly do not share his judgments. If we pick more plausible examples, the results appear (if clumsy) fine:

(46) *Which box is this book too big to put into?*

(47) *... the box that this object will be easiest to put into ...*

(48) *Which students is this subject easy to talk about with?*

(49) *... the person that the message is ready to send to ...*

The general pattern seems to be that when we have to associate two items in sequence with two gaps, the pattern (a) is unacceptable, but (b) is relatively good[11]:

$$\text{(a)} \quad A_1 \ldots A_2 \ldots \text{gap}_1 \ldots \text{gap}_2$$
$$\text{(b)} \quad A_1 \ldots A_2 \ldots \text{gap}_2 \ldots \text{gap}_1$$

Notice the differences if we make various rearrangements of (46):

(50)   *Which students is this subject easy to talk with about?*

(51)   *Which subject are these students easy to talk with about?*

(52)   *Which subject is this student easiest to talk about with?*

And potentially ambiguous sentences are rendered unambiguous in such structures:

(53)   *Which patient is that doctor easiest to talk to about?*

(54)   *Who is John ready to talk to about/about to*

Notice that in none of these examples is it possible to imagine that there is a "higher PP" associated with the VP.

I do not know what the explanation is for this pattern of acceptability, probably it is to be explained in terms of processing mechanisms (maybe: if you are storing a phrase looking for its "trace" you cannot start the same subroutine until you have cleared the first one). In any event, I think these facts cast considerable doubt on Chomsky's explanation and hence on this whole analysis of adjectival complements.

4.5   S as a Cyclic Category

Chomsky tentatively suggests that S might be a cyclic category and that much of the evidence in support of G. Horn's NP-constraint (Bach and Horn, 1976; Horn, 1974) can be explained in terms of subjacency. If S is a cyclic category, then any transformational rule that might involve something outside of S with an element properly contained in an NP would be blocked from applying (or the corresponding intrepretive filter would be blocked at intermediate structure).[12]

I want to point out a couple of consequences if S is indeed cyclic. The first is that Bresnan's explanation of contraction facts follows immediately without any use of traces or extrinsic rule ordering. Removal of the *wh*-phrase will necessarily follow any cyclic cliticization rule. Chomsky's version of strict cyclicity will ensure that the cliticization rule will not apply after we have passed the S-cycle.

The other is that Bresnan's ordering hypothesis about stress assignment will give different predictions for sentences like (55):

(55)   *What books has Harriet written?*

Given a structure like this,

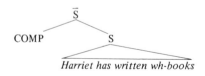

the nuclear stress rule will assign l-stress to *wh-books*, then on the next cycle, the *wh*-phrase will move and main stress will remain on *what books*. If S is not a cyclic node, then main stress will fall on *written*. I think the first result is more nearly correct for "normal" stress, so this seems to support the cyclicity of S.

Finally, I do not understand what Chomsky says about the effect of this hypothesis on the specified subject condition. It seems to me that SSC now predicts that nothing but a subject can be *wh*-fronted.

5. Alternatives

As Chomsky remarks, the only convincing refutation of his hypotheses will be reasonably detailed alternative analyses, and this is obviously not the place to attempt to present any.[13]

However, I would like to mention briefly what seems to me to be a promising and significant alternative to almost all current views of the translation relation.

Practically all linguists within the transformational tradition since the advent of the "standard theory" have shared a particular assumption about the translation relation. This assumption is that there are certain levels of syntactic representation that form the domain of the translation relation, that is to say that the translation rules are structure-dependent. In the standard theory the structures were deep structures, in the framework of generative semantics they were remote structures (or rather the remote structures were intended to be the disambiguated language to which the semantic rules would apply), in the various versions of EST, other levels of representaitons were added: end-of-cycle structures, surface structures. In Chomsky's current position the relevant structures are those of "logical form" (the output of sentence grammar). The generative semanticists tried to build into the remote structure aspects relating to determination of scope, and incorporated quantifier lowering rules and the like into transformations. The REST is doing the converse: instead of lowering rules we have "raising" rules and insertions of variables.

The earliest attempt to incorporate a semantic theory into generative grammar did not make this assumption. Instead it was assumed that some parts of the translation procedure were associated with rules rather than structures (Katz and Fodor, 1964). The alternative that I would like to suggest as worth exploring is one in which the entire translation relationship is conceived of not as a structure-dependent mapping or relation but rather as an association of rules of the translation procedure directly with rules of the syntax. One can conceive of a grammar (again in the broad sense) as a theory in which rules of syntax apply to build up syntactic structures while "simultaneously" rules of translation build up a representation in the interpreted language.[14]

In a system like this it is possible to maintain a sharp separation between syntax and semantics. Syntactic rules have only syntactic representations to work on, the translation rules have only the "logical" representation to work on. (If my interpretation of Chomsky's ideas is correct, his theory permits a kind of "mixed" representation consisting of structures containing partly English morphemes, partly logical elements, quantifiers, and the like.) Moreover, we can place quite severe restrictions on the syntactic and semantic sides of this process: for example, the requirement that the output of a semantic rule associated with a syntactic rule not only be a function of the translations of the input structures but retain those translations intact (up to "alphabetic variance"). This approach fits quite naturally with a pre-*Aspects* picture of syntax (as in Chomsky, 1955), modified along the lines of Fillmore (1963) and with the simple addition of rules of NP-embedding.[15]

The natural way to treat bound anaphora in such a system is by means of syntactic variables (translated into semantic variables). The modifications of Chomsky's latest paper, in fact, suggest a rather nice way to do this. It would involve interpreting an indexed nonterminal as a (syntactic) variable of the appropriate category, translated in the semantics as a corresponding semantic variable. All bound anaphora (in the strict sense required for sentence grammar) would arise by embedding a full noun phrase into the position of the (leftmost) syntactic variable with a particular index in a sentence structure containing one or more variables of the appropriate category. The translation rule corresponding to such an operation (as in Montague) is simply an application of the translation of the NP to the appropriate lambda abstract of the sentence. A syntactic rule would fill in the appropriate pronouns (in the case of noun phrases, an analogous treatment of sentence-embedding to get VPs would not entail this step, what is though of as VP-deletion is simply the result of English not having any pro-VP variables in the syntax, just as Japanese bound anaphora for nominals are not pronounced).[16]

The insight of classical transformational grammar that part of the relevant properties of a sentence were expressed in the way it was derived was expressed in the notion of a T-marker. This same insight is expressed in Montague grammar in the idea of an analysis tree, but it is not necessary to add either a T-marker or an analysis tree to the structural descriptions assigned by a grammar if the buildup of the translation goes hand in hand with syntactic derivation.

It is impossible to evaluate the two approaches at present because we lack detailed sets of rules, including all parts relevant to specifying the translation relation within a transformational framework for a significant fragment of a language. That the details of the semantics (*sensu stricto*) can play a role seems to me beyond question. Montague's uniform treatment of all noun phrases as denoting sets of individual concepts, for example, is crucial for his treatment of intensional verbs like *seek*. Decisions about the semantics of gender in English (Cooper, 1975) will obviously be reflected in the syntax. It is not possible to evaluate Chomsky's treatment of quantification or his use of variables because the details of the translation relation and the interpretation of the ultimate semantic representation are not worked out. Chomsky (1975c) gives an "empirical argument" againt Montague's analysis. But the argument is based on "anaphoric" relations of a sort treated neither by Montague nor himself so we can really draw no conclusions.[17]

6. Conclusion

In closing, I would like to stress again the positive sides of my reactions. I think I understand much better the motivations and the details of Chomsky's current approach as the result of the present paper. Only time will tell whether his program will be successful, but I believe the nature of the issues raised by his work and the directions necessary for a resolution of the issues have been clarified greatly both by his paper and by several others in this volume, as well as by the commentaries and discussions at the conference.

Notes

1. I would like to thank Jane Grimshaw and Edwin Williams for discussing with me many of the questions raised here and Alan Prince and Barbara H. Partee for general discussion as will as for helpful comments on my remarks.
2. Cf. p. 108 (of Chomsky's paper, henceforth cited just by page): "Only if acceptability judgments come marked as 'syntactic', 'semantic', etc., can the objection [i.e., that a certain judgment is a matter of syntax rather than interpretability] be sustained."
3. I find this terminology somewhat objectionable as well as misleading. The current version of EST bears no more resemblance to the Standard Theory than do various versions of "generative semantics" that have been advanced over the years. Furthermore, the term carries with it an unpleasant flavor of orthodoxy. But I will bow to usage.
4. P. Jacobson has pointed out to me that one effect of this system is to ensure that the "cyclic subject" (Postal, 1976) will always leave a trace, unless it is a PRO which may be deleted.
5. Linguists: Bach, 1968; McCawley, 1968a and 1970; Keenan, 1972; Partee, 1972 and 1976b; logicians: Quine, Reichenbach, Carnap *passim*, but see Quine, 1960.
6. Examples (5) and (6) were discovered by Muffy Siegel.
7. As Chomsky notes, it is not very interesting to argue about whether the latter should be called "semantic" or "syntactic." They are clearly not semantic in either of the senses given above. I will try to be consistent in using "rules of interpretation" for Chomsky's rules that determine logical form from "intermediate structure," I will continue to call the rules that get you from there to an interpreted language "translation rules," and I will reserve "semantic rules" for the rules that give the interpretation of this final language, a language that plays the role in the theory that Montague's intensional logic plays in PTQ.
8. The only successful and complete attempt to actually work out rules for the treatment of quantification and bound variable interpretation for a transformational grammar is to be found in Cooper and Parsons (1976), which gives a complete translation of Montague's syntax and semantics for a fragment of English (PTQ) into an interpretive transformational framework of a pre-traces variety.
9. In Bach and Horn (1976) a number of counterexamples to the condition were given (considered, as in Chomsky, 1973, as a condition on applicability). It and other conditions rest heavily on Chomsky's successive cyclic analysis of *wh*-movement, to which I will return.

10. In the discussion at the conference, Chomsky stated that the rule in question was not of the type to be covered by his conditions. In the next section I will show that the rule appears to act like a movement rule with respect to his properties "(49)." In his paper, Chomsky states that only rules can be evidence against conditions (cf. note 13, below). But given the incompleteness of the specification of the whole system, it appears as if no rule can be counterevidential either. Given this "comp(onent)-to-comp escape hatch," it is impossible to refute, hence support, any of his general hypotheses.

11. Cf. Culicover and Wexler, this volume, for a discussion of such examples within the context of the "freezing principle." Kuno and Robinson (1972, fn. 15) credit Arlene Berman with discovery of such examples and the generalization about nested versus crossing patterns. The idea that the unacceptability of the crisscrossed patterns is due to some kind of "push-down store" property of the processing mechanism was suggested to me by Avery Andrews.

12. In note 52, Chomsky expresses some puzzlement about our concluding remarks where we note that rules can be formulated that specifically mention NP-structures that are exempt from the conditions. I am surprised at this puzzlement since we thought we were simply following Chomsky here in his interpretation of such conditions as part of the evaluation metric, cf. his remarks here about the "logic of markedness." I am not going to enter into an extended discussion of the NP-constraint and its ramifications, which obviously involves a lot more than the few remarks devoted to it in Bach and Horn (1976), in particular the analysis of complement sentences. See Horn (1974, 1975, and forthcoming) for a discussion of many of the details. I think Chomsky is probably right about the analysis of structures like *see a picture of NP*, etc. His extraposition ("readjustment") rule might also be involved in a number of other constructions which are problematic both for Horn's principle and a number of other possible explanations, especially NPs with measure phrases: *a bottle of milk*, etc.

13. Nonetheless, one has to make educated guesses about whether a certain program is plausible, has some hope of success, etc. One way to do this is to try to think up problematic cases, counterexamples, and so on. At one point Chomsky dismisses this kind of work with the statement that no phenomena can be crucial evidence against conditions, only systems of rules can be (p.   ). There is a sense in which this is true, of course, but given the fragmentary state of our knowledge about the rules of *any* language, it seems to me counterproductive to dismiss all possible evidence in this way. Moreover, it is sometimes possible to argue that several reasonable alternative sets of rules would violate a condition. A case of this sort against the tensed sentence condition in Amharic was outlined in Bach and Horn (1976). Either of two possible analyses (i.e., rules) for certain structures (as Raising and Nonraising) would constitute counterevidence to TSC (as would any other reasonable alternatives that we were able to think of). To ignore such evidence seems to me to increase the extent to which linguistic theory takes on a completely scholastic character.

14. This is a possible interpretation of systems like those of Montague grammar. Montague himself (and others developing and extending his ideas) have tended to think of the translation rules as being "structure-dependent" where the relevant structures are the analysis trees. Thus Montague in PTQ takes the language of analysis trees as being the disambiguated language to which the translation rules apply.

15. For a preliminary study of the syntax of this model (without semantics and without NP-embedding) see Bach (1976), and for a sketch of a revised version including quantification, see Bach (forthcoming).

16. The mistake made by linguists like Bach (1968), McCawley (1970a), and so on who introduced variables into deep structures was to assume that all full NPs got into sentences by replacement of variables.

17. Barbara Partee has suggested to me that Chomsky's argument may be based on an observation that Montague's fragment in PTQ contains an error of descriptive detail, since his

quantification rules allow binding of pronouns across coordinate structures, cf. Rodman (1976, p. 172–3) for discussion.

VARIABLES IN THE THEORY OF TRANSFORMATIONS
PART I: BOUNDED VERSUS UNBOUNDED TRANSFORMATIONS

Joan Bresnan

Department of Linguistics
Massachusetts Institute of Technology
Cambridge, Massachusetts

1.   The Problem

Although the problem I am concerned with in this study has given rise to a complex theoretical controversy, it can be described in elementary terms.

Natural languages exhibit many syntactic dependencies that hold over unbounded contexts. One such dependency is illustrated in (1):

(1) a. *Should we remove bombs from?*
     b. *Should we remove bombs from **the sacks**?*
     c. ***Which sacks** should we remove bombs from?*

(1a) is ill-formed because the preposition *from* lacks an object, which is present in (1b). (1c) shows that the object can occur displaced from its governing preposition. The dependency is this: the dangling preposition of (1c) can occur if and only if a displaced object also occurs. Compare:

(1) d. *Should we remove bombs?*
     e. **Which sacks should we remove bombs?*

The dependency between the displaced object and the dangling preposition can extend, in principle, over contexts of arbitrary length (unbounded contexts):

(2) a. *Which sacks will they allow us to remove bombs from?*
     b. *Which sacks will they consider allowing us to remove bombs from?*
     c. *Which sacks are they willing to consider allowing us to remove bombs from?*
     d. *Which sacks do they appear to be willing to consider allowing us to remove bombs from?*

It is easy to continue the sequence begun in (2); although the sentences become harder to remember, they are well formed grammatically. In each case, if the dangling preposition is present but its displaced object is absent, the result is an ill-formed sentence:

(3)   *Do they appear to be willing to consider allowing us to remove
        bombs from?

—And vice versa:

(4)   *Which sacks do they appear to be willing to consider allowing us
        to remove bombs?

If the syntactic structures of the sentences in (2) are analyzed, it emerges that the context over which the object can be displaced is not finitely specifiable, in the sense that there is no finite sequence of categories that exhaustively describes all the possible contexts of displacement. See Figure 1.

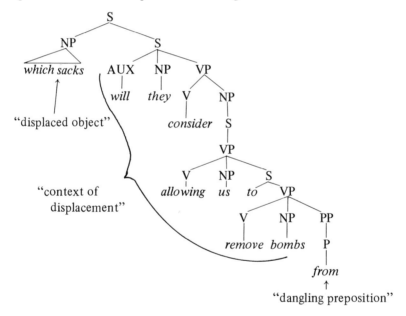

Figure 1: Syntactic Structure for Example (2b)

It is clear from Figure 1 that the context of displacement is a nonconstituent sequence of categories: the sequence of verbs and nouns that intervene between the displaced object and its preposition is not dominated by a single node. Because the VP-embedding shown in Figure 1 is recursive, the nonconstituent sequence lengthens with each layer of embedding, and so the context of displacement is not finitely specifiable. Facts like these can provide one of the most convincing arguments that phrase structure grammars are inadequate for describing the syntactic structure of natural languages.

Transformational grammar has provided basically two means for describing such unbounded syntactic dependencies. One is to permit transformations to have unbounded domains of application by making essential use of syntactic variables. The other is to permit transformations to have unbounded numbers of iterative applications by making use of the transformational cycle. These two analytic options for the example of Figure 1 are illustrated in Figures 2 and 3, respectively.

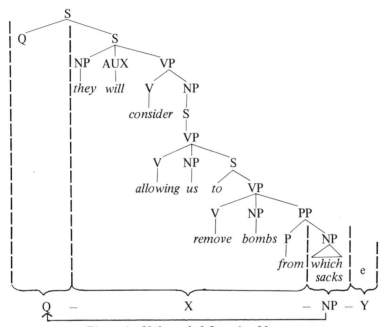

Figure 2: Unbounded Question Movement

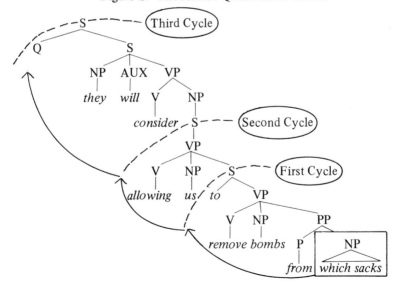

Figure 3: Iterated Question Movement

An unbounded transformational analysis of Question Movement, like that illustrated in Fugure 2, has been adopted by many linguists; see Ross (1967), Postal
(1972), and Bresnan (1976a), for example. An iterative-cyclic analysis has been
advanced recently by Chomksy (1973, 1975), who has proposed that all syntactic
transformations are subject to a bounding condition known as the Subjacency
Condition. This condition limits the domain of application of transformations to
adjacent cyclic nodes, and thus eliminates the type of analysis shown in Figure 2.
Chomsky has also argued that the evidence of Ross (1967) and Postal (1972) can be
explained without unbounded transformation. The problem I would like to consider
is that of finding independent evidence to decide between these two types of analyses.

2.   Significance of the Problem

It is a fundamental assumption of transformational grammar that questions of
linguistic theory are ultimately questions about the nature of the human faculty of
language. But unlike many questions of linguistic theory, the question of whether
there are unbounded transformations has a direct bearing on the construction of
experimentally plausible models of human sentence perception. For example, the
Augmented Transition Network parsing system developed by Woods (1973) has
several facilities for recognizing sentences like (2). In one of them, when the displaced constituent (e.g., *which sacks*) is found in a left-to-right parse, it is held in
temporary memory as the parsing continues until a position is found in the sentence
structure where the constituent would have been accepted if it had not been displaced (e.g., as object of *from*); the displaced constituent is then retrieved and
treated as though it had actually occurred at that position. Woods (1973, p. 110)
notes that the same effects can be achieved alternatively by passing the displaced
constituent up and down from level to level of phrase structure, using a different
set of memory actions. As Woods observes, these two methods of processing questions have a correspondence to alternative linguistic analyses, the first method corresponding to the essential use of variables in unbounded transformations. Since
general parsing systems can be experimentally utilized as psychological models of
sentence perception (see, for example, Wanner and Maratsos, 1974), it is quite
reasonable to ask which parsing operations would more closely approximate the
functioning of the human syntactic processor. This is one way in which the linguistic question of whether there are unbounded transformations could bear on the
characterization of human language processing, or "the nature of the human faculty
of language," as I put it above. There are, of course, many other ways. For example,
a bounding condition on transformations, together with several other constraints
whose empirical justification is currently being explored, has been assumed in a
proof of the 'learnability' of transformational grammars, as discussed in Culicover
and Wexler (1976). (But cf. Baker, 1976, for alternative restrictions that could
yield a different proof of learnability.)

The question of whether there are unbounded transformations is also embedded in theoretical issues within transformational grammar. Chomsky's bounding condition is part of a system of conditions designed to restrict radically the form and functioning of transformations (Chomsky, 1975). Whether the resulting impoverishment of the expressive power of transformations yields a more restrictive overall theory of grammar is questionable, however, because the proposed impoverishment of the transformational component of the grammar must be offset by the enrichment of other components, particularly the surface-structure filtering component; an alternative theory of grammar permitting a somewhat richer class of transformations could drastically limit the class of possible surface-structure filters (Bresnan 1976d). But the bounding condition by itself appears to be a strong constraint on grammars. If it turns out that the bounding condition is empirically unjustified, then to what extent is present transformational theory thereby weakened and made less constrained?

Although a definitive answer cannot be given without comparing total theories, a partial answer is suggested by Friedman (1973) and Woods (1973). Friedman (1973, p. 26) argues that "Peters and Ritchie's proof that every recursively enumerable set is generable by a transformational grammar with minimal base goes through even for grammars without essential variables." In other words, for the model of transformational grammar formalized by Peters and Ritchie (1973) and Friedman et al. (1971), a constant bound on the domain of applicability of transformations does not by itself restrict the weak generative capacity of transformational grammars. (It is assumed that a restriction is desirable, since there is evidence that natural languages are recursive sets; cf. Peters, 1973.) On the other hand, Woods (1973, p. 125) has claimed that "[i]t is relatively easy to place a sufficient restriction on the transition network grammar model to ensure that the class of languages accepted by the restricted model falls completely within the class of recursive languages (for which effective recognition procedures exist), while preserving the power for full and efficient linguistic expression (e.g., the equivalent of the use of 'general variables' in the classical transformational theory)." Because *unrestricted* Augmented Transition Network grammars are equivalent to transformational grammars in weak generative capacity, Woods' claim suggests that a significant restriction in the weak generative capacity of transformational grammars is possible *without* imposing a bounding condition of transformations. So a bounding condition in itself may not be such a strong constraint as it first appears to be. (Ronald Kaplan [personal communication] has also suggested a possible proof of the recursiveness of restricted ATN grammars.)

In any case, if a constraint on transformations is empirically unjustified, leading to losses of generalizations in individual grammars, its theoretical 'restrictiveness' cannot justify it. In general, metagrammatical arguments must not be confused with descriptive grammatical arguments. The argument from restrictiveness (i.e., the argument that theory A is preferable to theory B because theory A is more restrictive, more narrowly characterizing the class of possible languages) is a metagrammatical argument: it presupposes that descriptively preferred grammars meet the proposed universal restrictiveness conditions. To inject an argument from restrict-iveness into a descriptive grammatical argument (e.g., to argue that formulation A of the passive is preferable to formulation B *because* A, not B, is consistent with such and such a 'more restrictive' metagrammatical theory) is to beg the funda-mental empirical question. What must be shown first is that descriptively *preferred* grammars meet the proposed restrictiveness conditions. If they do not meet them, then some other metagrammatical constraints must be sought.

In this study I will give evidence that descriptively preferred grammars of English contain unbounded syntactic transformations, making essential use of variables.

3.   An Unbounded Deletion Rule

There is one immediate consequence of a bounding condition that can be tested directly. A bounding condition on all transformations predicts an asymmetry be-tween transformational movements and deletions. The movement of a constituent over an (in principle) unbounded context can be achieved by iterative bounded movements, but the deletion of a constituent must occur within a bounded context, for unlike a bounded movement transformation, a bounded deletion transformation cannot iteratively reapply to remove the same constituent. As pointed out in Bresnan (1975a), the existence of unbounded deletion transformations applying in compar-ative and relative clause constructions would disconfirm the Subjacency Condition of Chomsky (1973, 1975).

Unbounded deletion transformations have been independently proposed in linguistic analyses of various languages, including Albanian (Morgan, 1972), Basque (deRijk, 1972), Middle English (Grimshaw, 1975), Modern English (Bresnan, 1975a,b, 1976a), Japanese (Kuno, 1973), and Old Icelandic (Maling, 1976). How-ever, it is possible at least in principle that all cases of unbounded deletion are only apparent, in that what appears to be deletion over an unbounded context is analyti-cally decomposed into the iterative movement of some element over an unbounded context followed by obligatory "local" deletion of the moved item. Given this possibility, it is necessary to ask what independent motivation there is for the hypo-thesized movements. In some cases there appears to be not only no independent motivation for such iterative movements, but the movement analysis leads to unnecessary and ad hoc complications in the grammatical description; one such case from Middle English is given by Grimshaw (1975) and also discussed in Bresnan (1976d). In Modern English, too, it can be shown that an iterative-movement anal-ysis of some constructions leads to losses of generalizations and descriptive inade-quacies that do not arise in a theory permitting unbounded deletion rules (Bresnan, 1976d). I will review here briefly some of the evidence for this claim.

There is in English a rule of "Subdeletion" that applies in comparative construc-tions like those shown in (5) and (6):

(5)   *Why were there **more women** on t.v. than there were **men**?*

(6)   *There weren't **as many men** on t.v. as there were **women**.*

I will refer to the boldface phrases in examples like (5) and (6) as the "compared constituents." The one on the left in each pair is the "head" of the comparative (*than* or *as*) clause; the one on the right is affected by the rule of Subdeletion, which deletes an underlying modifier of the compared constituent. Although the missing modifier can be one of several different cateogries, in examples (5) and (6) it is a Quantifier Phrase ('QP') modifier, similar to *x many, x much*.

The existence of such underlying modifiers can be justified in detail; see Bresnan (1973, 1975a,b, 1976a,d). But here I will simply note that the deleted modifiers of examples (5) and (6) can be "detected" in the following way, among others. When *many* or *much* occurs in a partitive phrase, the preposition *of* appears: *many of those men, much of it*. And when the compared constituents are partitives, the *of* appears in both:

(7)   *Why were there **more of those women** on t.v. than there were
        of those men?*

(8)   *There weren't **as many of them** as there were **of us**.*

The rule of Subdeletion removes a subpart *x many* of the compared constituents in the *than* and *as* clauses of (7) and (8), converting *x many of those men* to *of those men*, and *x many of us* to *of us*. Note that Subdeletion in (7) and (8) accounts for the grammaticality of what would otherwise be an ill-formed sequence: compare *there were many of us* and **there were of us*.

Now the compared constituents upon which Subdeletion is defined can be separated by unbounded contexts. This is shown by (9)–(11). The locus of the removed modifier is indicated by a ' __ '.

(9)   a. *Therefore, they can hire more women than they can hire __ men.*
        b. *Therefore, they can hire more women than the Administration
            would allow them to hire __ men.*
        c. *Therefore, they can hire more women than the Administration would
            even consider allowing them to hire __ men.*
        d. *Therefore, they can hire more women than the Administration
            would be willing even to consider allowing them to hire __ men.*
        e. *Therefore, they can hire more women than the Administration
            would appear to be willing even to consider allowing them to
            hire __ men.*
        f. *Therefore, they can hire more women than the Administration
            would ever want to appear to be willing even to consider allowing
            them to hire __ men.*

(10)   a. *You could have twice as many stocks as you now have __ of
            these bonds.*
        b. *You could have twice as many stocks as you want to have __ of
            these bonds.*

    c.   *You could have twice as many stocks as you anticipate wanting to have ___ of these bonds.*

    d.   *Your could have twice as many stocks as you are ever likely to anticipate wanting to have ___ of these bonds.*

    e.   *You could have twice as many stocks as your broker considers you ever to be likely to anticipate wanting to have ___ of these bonds.*

    f.   *You could have twice as many stocks as your broker claims to consider you ever to be likely to anticipate wanting to have ___ of these bonds.*

(11) a.   *We have ordered more warheads built than they have ___ missles.*

    b.   *We have ordered more warheads built than they claim to have ___ missles.*

    c.   *We have ordered more warheads built than we expect them to claim to have ___ missles.*

    d.   *We have ordered more warheads built than they expect us to expect them to claim to have ___ missles.*

    e.   *We have ordered more warheads built than they are reported to expect us to expect them to claim to have ___ missles.*

As with the Question Movement sequences (2), the sequences of sentences in (9)-(11) can be extended to arbitrary lengths.

    Examples (9)-(11) have been chosen to exhibit certain properties. The context between the head of the comparative clauses and the Subdeletion site '___' is a non-constituent sequence of categories. (For brevity, I will call this context "the Subdeletion context.") The Subdeletion contexts in these examples consist solely of infinitival and gerundive construction types that cannot be used "parenthetically." This choice was made to obviate the possible objection that an apparently unbounded Subdeletion context is really just a long parenthetical insertion. And, finally, the Subdeletion context is free of certain obstacles to transformational applications that are known to be "constraints on transformations." (How a range of these constraints can affect Subdeletion is discussed in Bresnan, 1975a.) In particular, the Subdeletion contexts are free of "islands." such as Complex Noun Phrases, in Ross's (1967) terms.

    As Ross (1967) showed (see also Hankamer, 1971; Bresnan 1975a), complex noun phrases—relative clause constructions and nominal complement constructions—prevent the unbounded removal of their parts. The occurrence of such a construction in the Subdeletion context yields an ungrammatical sentence:

(12)   *Therefore, they can hire more women than I met a woman who has ___ boyfriends.*

(13)   *I predict that there will be twice as many of the "minority" applications as I have a report that there are ___ of the "majority" applications.*

The underlying structure for (12) is shown in Figure 4 (with irrelevant details omitted).

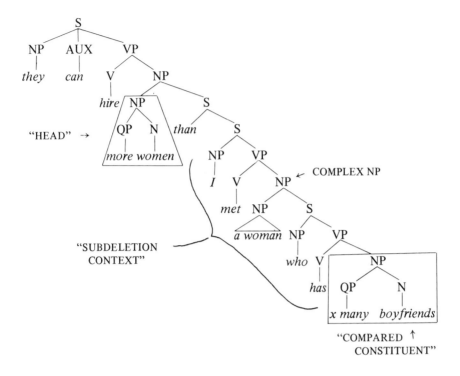

Figure 4: Underlying Structure for Example (12)

Thus, it is the "Complex NP Constraint" that accounts for the contrasts in examples (14)–(17).

(14) a. *Then why have they produced **only half as many job applicants** as they claim to believe that there are ___ jobs?*

 b. ***Then why have they produced **only half as many job applicants** as they believe the claim that there are ___ jobs?*

(15) a. *We have ordered **more warheads** built than we expect them to announce that they have ___ missles.*

 b. ***We have orderd **more warheads** built than we expect the announcement that they have ___ missles.*

(16) a. *You could have **more stocks** than you would ever anticipate wanting to have ___ bonds.*

 b. ***You could have **more stocks** than you anticipate the possibility that you might want ___ bonds.*

(17) a. *He can always avoid this problem by hypothesizing **as many protopropositions** as he needs to assume that there are ___ distinct empty sets of possible worlds.*

b.   *He can always avoid this problem by hypothesizing *as many*
     protopropositions as he needs the assumption that there are
     —— *distinct empty sets of possible worlds.*

The intended meaning of (17a) can be paraphrased: "He can always avoid this problem in the following way. If he needs to assume that there are n distinct empty sets
of possible worlds, then he hypothesizes that there are n protopropositions, whatever n is." And (17b) can be paraphrased: "He can always avoid this problem in the
following way. If he needs the assumption that there are n distinct empty sets of
possible worlds, then he hypothesizes that there are n protopropositions, whatever
n is." I have found that speakers for whom the subject matter of (17a) is complete
gobbledygook can nevertheless construe it perfectly well, judging it much more
acceptable than (17b).

Examples (14)–(17) show that when the underscored compared constituents are
separated by a complex noun phrase, the result is markedly worse than when they
are not. Observe that the a- and the b-examples in each pair of sentences are separated by the same number of "cyclic modes," in Chomsky's (1973) terms. Compare
(18a) and (18b), for example:

(18)   a.   ... [NP *as many job applicants*] [S *as they claim* [S *to believe*
            [S *that there are* [NP —— *jobs*]]]]

       b.   ... [NP *as many job applicants*] [S *as they believe* [NP *the claim*
            [S *that there are* [NP —— *jobs*]]]]

Chomsky (1973) assumes NP to be a cyclic node. Together with his Subjacency
Condition, this enables him to explain the Complex Noun Phrase Constraint as
follows. Apparent unbounded movements are analyzed as iterative bounded movements through complementizer position. As shown in (19), *wh*-movement cannot
apply in the NP-cycle, because NPs lack complementizers (COMPs):

(19)   *Who does Mary believe John saw pictures of?*
       [S_1 COMP$_1$ *Mary believes* [S_2 COMP$_2$ *John saw* [NP*pictures of who*NP]S_2]S_1]

However, on the S_2 cycle in (19), *wh*-movement can move *who* into COMP$_2$, because S_2 and NP are adjacent cyclic nodes. On the S_1 cycle, *who* is moved again
into COMP$_1$. Now compare (20), which contains a complex NP:

(20)   *Who does Mary believe the claim that John saw?*
       [S_1 COMP *Mary believes* [NP*the claim* [S_2 COMP$_2$ *John saw who*S_2]NP]S_1]

On the S_2 cycle in (20), *who* is moved into COMP$_2$. On the next cycle–the NP
cycle–*who* cannot be removed, because NPs lack COMPs. But then on the S_1 cycle,
wh-movement es prevented by the Subjacency Condition from extracting *who* from
S_2. S_1 and S_2 are not adjacent cyclic nodes because the cyclic NP node separates
them. Consequently sentence (20) cannot be derived.[1]

This is an ingenious solution, but it cannot be extended to account for Subdeletion without a significant loss of generalizations. For, as pointed out in Bresnan

(1975a), the measure-phrase modifiers removed by Subdeletion cannot in general be moved from the constituents they modify by known movement rules. Contrast (21) with (22)-(25).

(21)   *She has as many boyfriends as she has ___ books.*

(22)   a. **How many did she send ___ books to you?*
        b. *How many books did she send ___ to you?*

(23)   a. **How many she sent ___ books to you!*
        b. *How many books she sent ___ to you!*

(24)   a. **So many does she have ___ books, that her garage is being converted into a library.*
        b. *So many books does she have ___ , that her garage is being converted into a library.*

(25)   a. **Many though she has ___ books, she wants more.*
        b. *Many books though she has ___ , she wants more.*

Furthermore, there is no *overt* evidence that a constituent is moved in Subdeletion constructions, as was also pointed out in Higgins (1973). For example, the *wh*-movement rule can move phrases superordinate to the *wh*-pronoun, by the so-called "obligatory pied-piping" convention. We see this happening in (26):

(26)   *I asked [Q there was how large a percentage of men] ---→*
            I asked how large a percentage of men there was.

The entire noun phrase including *a percentage of men* is "pied-piped" along with *how large*, into interrogative position. But in (27) we see that the same constituent *cannot* be moved in Subdeletion constructions:

(27)   **There isn't even as large a number of women as ___ a percentage of men there was.*

The "Subdeleted" phrase in (27) is *x large*. If this phrase had undergone movement prior to its deletion, we would expect (27) to be derived by obligatory pied-piping. What we have instead is simply (28):

(28)   *There isn't even as large a number of women as there was ___ a percentage of men.*

In fact, *no* examples like (28) could be derived by *wh*-movement without losing the generalization in English that when a left-branch modifier of a phrase is affected by a movement rule, the entire phrase obligatorily "pied-pipes." The movement analysis can preserve this generalization only at the cost of systematically deriving examples like (29a) *instead* of (29b).

(29)   a. **She has more boyfriends than ___ books she has.*
        b. *She has more boyfriends than she has ___ books.*

In short, Subdeletion cannot be analyzed as a movement rule without a significant loss of generalizations about movement rules. But if so, the applicability of

Subdeletion over unbounded contexts (e.g., (14)–(17)) then disconfirms a bounding condition on transformation.

By contrast, a simple deletion analysis of Subdeletion can preserve these generalizations (Bresnan; 1975b, 1976a,d). The "obligatory pied-piping" mentioned above is an interesting property of a number of movement rules in Englsih, including the preposing rules involved in examples (22)–(25). As observed in Bresnan (1975a), these rules are "cross-categorial": they can affect phrases of several different kinds, such as noun phrases, adjective phrases, and adverb phrases. Although the preposed phrases in the (b) examples of (22)–(25) were all noun phrases, we can just as easily construct examples like "How serenely he sits by the fire smoking his pipe!" or "How tall do you estimate that a ginkgo tree grows?" (with a preposed adverb phrase or adjective phrase). These sets of different kinds of phrases fall into natural classes in the $\bar{\text{X}}$ theory of categories of Chomsky (1970), Bresnan (1973), Selkirk (1976), and others. Further, it has been shown in Bresnan (1975b, 1976a) that if the movement transformations are formulated with natural class predicates in the $\bar{\text{X}}$ notation, the pied-piping effects are a consequence of a general maximality principle governing the application of transformations, the "Relativized A-over-A Principle." Question Movement, for example must move the maximal interrogative phrase that satisfies the natural class predicate in its structural condition. Thus in example (30), *how many* is not the maximal interrogative phrase that satisfied the Question Movement transformation—

(30)   [Q *she sent* [$_{NP}$[$_{QP}$ *how many* $_{QP}$] *books*$_{NP}$] *to you*]

—but *how many books* is, and this accounts for the difference in grammaticality between (22a) and (22b):

(22)   a.   **How many did she send ___ books to you?*
        b.   *How many books did she send ___ to you?*

Now Subdeletion is also a cross-categorial rule, as can be seen from examples like (31)–(33), where it applies to compared constituents that are NPs, APs, or AdvPs.

(31)   *She has* [$_{NP}$*more boyfriends*] *than she has* [$_{NP}$ ___ *books*]

(32)   *She seems* [$_{AP}$ *as happy*] *now as she seemed* [$_{AP}$ ___ *sad*] *before*

(33)   *My sister drives* [$_{AdvP}$ *as carelessly*] *as I drive* [$_{AdvP}$ ___ *carefully*]

Furthermore, Subdeletion can *remove* phrases of these different kinds—an NP in (34), an AP in (35), an AdvP in (36):

(34)   *There isn't as large a number of women as there was ___ of men.*
        [deletion of *x large a number*]

(35)   *There isn't even as large a number of women as there was ___ a percentage of men.* [deletion of *x large*]

(36)   *Your face, I judge, is more nearly oval than it is ___ ogival.*
        [deletion of *x nearly*]

Thus, if Subdeletion *were* a movement rule, as required by the Subjacency Condition, it would necessarily prepose the maximal ("largest") NP, AP, or AdvP that satisfied its structural condition. As a deletion rule, however, Subdeletion can delete a modifier of the compared constituent in place, subject to recoverability. In cases where the entire compared constituent is not recoverable, Subdeletion must delete a proper subpart, the maximal one that satisfies its structural condition.[2] Therefore, given the relativized A-over-A principle and the $\bar{X}$ theory of categories as developed in Bresnan (1975b, 1976a), we can *explain* the contrast in the behavior of these cross-categorial rules (e.g., the contrast between Subdeletion and Question Movement in (21) and (22)) by hypothesizing that the missing subpart of the compared constituent is not moved, but simply deleted.

The preceding argument is quite independent of the issue of whether Subdeletion is a special case of the rule of Comparative Deletion (as suggested in Bresnan 1975a,b; 1976a) or not. There are several unexplained differences between Subdeletion and Comparative deletion. One is that Subdeletion into several tensed clauses "gets worse faster" than Comparative Deletion. (This is noted in Bresnan (1975a, note 10). Another is that Subdeletion into nonextraposed clauses can be nearly incomprehensible:

(37)   *More women than ___ men flunked, passed.*

(38)   *I gave as many women as I had ___ men in my courses, As.*

(This fact was pointed out to me by Jessie Pinkham.)
   On the other hand some cases are acceptable:

(39)   *I can tell you that fewer women than there are ___ fingers on my right hand, passed.*

(40)   *He has as many women as he has ___ horses, in his stable.*

And when the comparative clauses of (37) and (38) are extraposed, the result is fully acceptable: *More women passed than men flunked; I gave as many women As as I had men in my courses.*

   Involving a comparison of "contrasts," Subdeletion constructions have, intuitively, a greater semantic complexity than corresponding Comparative Deletion constructions. It is also clear that strategies for parsing Subdeletion constructions will be harder to devise than for corresponding Comparative Deletion Construction, because the deletion site is not as obviously marked syntactically in cases of Subdeletion. For these reasons I continue to assume that such differences between Subdeletion and Comparative Deletion as those I have just referred to may be attributable to "performance factors." However, it is always possible that a revealing grammatical explanation will be found to require distinct rules of Subdeletion and Comparative Deletion. This would not weaken my argument. See Bresnan (1976d).

4. Summary

As remarked in the first section of Part I, transformational grammar has provided basically two options for describing unbounded syntactic dependencies: one makes essential use of syntactic variables, permitting unbounded domains of transformational application; the other makes essential use of the transformational cycle, permitting iterative transformational applications to the same constituent. A bounding condition on transformations like the Subjacency Condition presupposes the latter analytic option and eliminates the former. But the evidence for an unbounded deletion rule presented in the third section of this Part shows that the "iterative movement" option leads to a significant loss of generalizations in one area of English syntax.

As for the fact that this deletion rule is subject to the same 'island' constraints as movement rules, this shows that it is a mistake to regard such constraints as diagnostics for movements (as argued in Bresnan, 1975a). Instead, the constraints themselves should be revised or replaced by alternatives that apply equally to unbounded movements and unbounded deletions. One such alternative is given in Bresnan (1976d), where it is shown how the Subjacency Condition can be eliminated without losing any of the major theoretical results that have motivated it (assuming these results to be valid generalizations).

My conclusion is that unbounded transformations should remain as a descriptive option in transformational grammar. Whether the "iterative movement" optional should also remain, is an interesting question for further research.[3] Part II of this study will corroborate this conclusion.

PART II: ON CONSTRAINING UNBOUNDED TRANSFORMATIONS

Part I provided evidence of the existence of one unbounded deletion rule in English grammar. Part II provides evidence for a generalization that shows an important class of English transformations to be unbounded, making essential use of variables.

1. A Generalization

It is a frequently observed fact of English that a subject noun phrase cannot be removed from a complement clause marked by the complementizer *that*. This is illustrated by (2a), which is to be understood as deriving from a structure like (1):

(1)   *Jack claimed (that) one of his cats had eaten one of his birds.*

(2)   a.   **Which one of his cats did Jack claim that ___ had eaten one of his birds?*
        b.   *Which one of his cats did John claim ___ had eaten one of his birds?*

('___' indicates any position from which a phrase has been transformationally removed.) (2b) shows that in the absence of *that*, the subject can be successfully removed from the complement. But the removal of NPs other than subjects is not restricted by the presence of a complementizer; for example, with or without a *that*-complementizer, (3) is grammatical.

(3)   *Which one of his birds did Jack claim (that) one of his cats had eaten ___ ?*

Less well known is an observation of Ross's, that a subject NP cannot be removed from a complement clause marked by the complementizer *for* (Ross 1967, 6.3.2). He gives the following examples in illustration:

(4)   *It bothers me for her to wear that old fedora.*

(5)   a.   **The only girl for whom it bothers me ___ to wear that old fedora is Annabelle.*
        b.   **The only girl who it bothers me (for) ___ to wear that old fedora is Annabelle.*

(5a) and (5b) contain relative clauses constructed on the pattern of (4) by relativizing the subject of *to wear*. (5a) shows that the complementizer *for* cannot "pied-pipe" with the relative pronoun. (Contrast the mobility of the preposition *for* in *The only girl for whom I would buy a hat is Annabelle*.) (5b) shows that whether or not *for* remains in complementizer position, the subject NP cannot be extracted from the complement. But observe that the *object* of *to wear* can be relativized:

(6)   *The only hat which it bothers me for her to wear ___ is that old fedora.*

To account for these facts, Ross proposed the following contraint (Ross 1967, example 6, p. 183):

(7)   *Ross's Generalization*

             No element in the environment [*for* ___VP]
             can be chopped.

This means that "chopping" rules like Question Movement, Relativization, and the like, cannot remove the subject of a complement marked by *for*. It is easy to see why the bracketing in Ross's generalization is necessary: without it, (7) would wrongly prohibit the removal of objects of the preposition *for*, which happened to be adjacent to NPs, as in (8) and (9).

(8)   *It will be hardest [PP for the new students] [VP to follow the lectures]*

(9)   a. *For whom will it be hardest ___ to follow the lectures?*
       b. *Who(m) will it be hardest for ___ to follow the lectures?*

For is a preposition in these examples, as in *It will be hardest for the new students.* (Contrast the complementizer *for* in (4): **It bothers me for her.*) Other examples like (9) are (10) and (11).

(10)   *Who(m) would it be good for ___ to take dancing lessons?*

(11)   *For which one of them would it be dangerous ___ to be seen with me?*

The close relation between these two sets of facts involving *that* and *for* has been largely unrecognized. But Ross's generalization (7) can be naturally generalized to account for both sets of facts:

(12)   No element in the environment [COMP___VP]
           can be chopped.

COMP is the category of complementizers. (12) is more general than Ross's statement (7) because (12) extends to the *that*-complementizer as well as the *for*-complementizer. Indeed, if *whether* is also a COMP (see Bresnan, 1974, and the references cited there), then (12) would automatically account for contrasts like the following (from Hudson, 1972):

(13)   *The book that the editor asked whether I'd review ___ for him*
           was very long.

(14)   **The book that the editor asked whether ___ could be reviewed by*
           next month was far too long.

Although, as Chomsky (1964) observed, the removal of any elements from 'wh-complements' is heavily restricted, linguists have given some relatively acceptable examples: in addition to Hudson (1972), see Kuno and Robinson (1972; examples 3-9, 3-10, 3-11), and Bresnan (1976d).

A version of the generalization stated in (12) was formulated in Bresnan (1972) as "The Fixed Subject Constraint":

(15)   No NP can be crossed over an adjacent COMP:

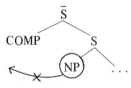

(15) is still more general than (12); it was intended to apply not only to chopping rules, but also to rules like Passive and Subject Raising (see Bresnan, 1972). However, as Ross (1967) pointed out, a constraint on variables would be inapplicable to transformations like Subject Raising, which involves no essential variables. There is interesting evidence that Ross's interpretation of the constraint is correct.

2. A Constraint on Variables

What is a constraint on variables? Given a proper analysis of a structure with respect to a transformation, we can distinguish between 'variable factors' and 'constant factors' of the proper analysis: a variable factor will correspond to a variable in the transformation and a constant factor, to a constant.[4] For example, in Figure 2, the portions of structure described by 'X' and 'Y' are variable factors and the portions described by 'Q' and 'NP' are constant factors. A constraint on variables can be regarded as a condition on variable factors which limits the class of proper analyses.[5]

To formulate (12) more explicitly as a constraint on variables, observe that a chopping transformation that applied in violation of (12) would give rise to a proper analysis of the form shown schematically in (16), where X and Y are variable factors and A is a constant factor.

(16)

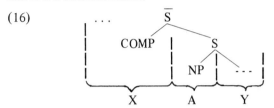

Thus we could restate (12) by saying that in any proper analysis (. . ., X, A, Y, . . .), if A is a constant factor to be chopped, and X and Y are variable factors, then X cannot end in a complementizer. Because rules that delete over a variable are subject to the same kinds of constraints as chopping rules (as argued in Bresnan, 1975a, and 1976d), and because the "chopping" of a phrase involves both copying and deleting it, I will state the constraint as in (17):

(17)   *The Complementizer Constraint on Variables*

For any proper analysis (. . . , X, A, Y, . . .)
such that X and Y are variable factors and A
is a constant factor to be deleted, if
X = --- COMP, then --- must be empty (of terminals).

This means that X can contain a COMP only if it contains nothing else, a condition that permits X to function as an 'end variable' when a transformation applies on $\bar{S}$. For example, imagine that a transformation applies on $\bar{S}$ in (16) and postposes the NP adjacent to COMP; in this case, the variable factor X will contain nothing outside the COMP, and so (17) will not prevent the rule from applying.[6]

Perhaps a more intuitive way of putting this constraint is that factorization must respect clause marking, in the sense that variable factors cannot split off complementizers from the clauses they mark and lump them together with arbitrary material.

Now we are in a position to ask how one can tell whether a generalization like that given is a constraint on variables or some other form of constraint or restriction.

Answering this question will be the object of the remainder of Part II. After presenting positive evidence for formulation (17), I will compare it to alternative accounts.

3. Evidence

The Complementizer Constraint on Variables (17) is not an absolute prohibition
against removing an element adjacent to a complementizer. Rather, it prohibits
removing elements adjacent to a complementizer *if* the complementizer lies (properly) within a variable factor of the proper analysis. Thus an element A could be
removed if, say, the adjacent COMP were not part of a variable factor but were itself
a constant factor, explicitly "mentioned" by the transformation. This hypothetical
possibility could arise if there were a rule that deleted the subjects of designated, or
marked, complement types. An example would be Rosenbaum's (1967) rule of
Equi-NP Deletion:

(18)   X   [$\bar{S}$ for NP   Y]   Z
            1   2 3   4   5 →
            1   2 ϕ 4   5

(For expository convenience, (18) is a modified version of Rosenbaum's (1967)
"Identity Erasure Transformation," which applies to "poss-ing" as well as to *for*-
complements, using a feature analysis of the complementizers.) The Complementizer
Constraint on Variables (17) would not prevent such a rule from applying as in (19):

(19)   *It would bother Annabelle$_i$-[for - her$_i$ - to go]* - e
              X   *for*   NP   Y   Z
              X   *for* ϕ Y   Z

(Subsequent to the deletion of *her$_i$*, *for* deletes.) Note that the complementizer *for*
does not lie in any variable factor in (19); rather, it constitutes a constant factor.
Hence there is no violation of (17).

Although this example shows that the standard transformational treatment of
Equi-NP Deletion is consistent with (17), I prefer a nontransformational treatment
of "equi" cases (Bresnan, 1976b, 1977), but in any case there are more interesting
consequences of (17).

3.1 Relativization

Suppose we accept in its broad outlines the type of analysis of relativization
proposed by Emonds (1976; 142ff), Morgan (1972), and others, wherein the relative
pronoun is either deleted in place or moved to the position of the relative clause
marker, which is *that* in English. This analysis is illustrated in (20).

(20)   a.   *the woman that everybody will vote for* rel
       b.   *the woman that everybody will vote for* ϕ (deletion)
       c.   *the woman who(m) everybody will vote for* ϕ (movement)

Most details of the analysis are unimportant here; thus "rel" is used in (2) as a neutral term for the relativized item, because its specific properties (whether it is a pronoun, a *wh*-pronoun, or a Δ) are irrelevant. We can suppose that if "rel" is deleted rather than moved, the complementizer *that* remains in clause-initial position, itself subject to an optional deletion:

(21)   that $--\rightarrow\phi$ / NP___ NP

The identification of the relative *that* with the complementizer (or conjunctive) *that* in modern English has been adopted by Jespersen (1927), Klima (1964), Emonds (1970, 1976), Bresnan (1970, 1971, 1972, 1974), and others. Among the justifictions for this analysis are that it "accords the same status to all S-intoductory *that*s, explains why prepositions never precede *that* even though they precede other relative pronouns, and limits relative pronouns to being a subset of the WH question words" (Emonds, 1976, p. 142).

The deletion or movement involved in relativization can take place "over a variable":

(22)   a.   *the woman (whom) the committee predicts that everybody will vote for* ___
       b.   *the woman (whom) the committee is likely to predict that everybody will vote for* ___
       c.   *the woman (whom) the committee seems to be likely to predict that everybody will vote for* ___

Therefore, in accordance with this type of analysis, Relativization can be formulated (very approximately) as in (23):

(23)   *Relativization*

NP	[$_{\overline{S}}$ COMP	X	rel	Y]
1	2	3	4	5
1	2	3	ϕ	5	or
1	4	3	ϕ	5

(It is not essential that term 1 in (23) be a full NP; cf. Partee, 1973.) Given such a formulation, the Complementizer Constraint on Variables correctly rules out (24) and allows (25):

(24)   *the woman who the committee predicts that ___ will win the election*

(25)   *the woman who the committee predicts ___ will win the election*

Figure 5 shows that the proper analysis of (24) with respect to (23) violates the Complementizer Constraint on Variables.

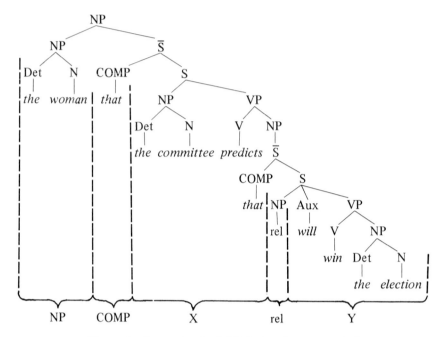

Figure 5: Proper Analysis Violating Constraint (17)

In Figure 5, "rel" is a constant factor to be deleted, but it lies between variable factors X and Y, where X ends in a COMP.

Now it is crucial to observe that the constraint (17) *does* allow removal of a relativized item adjacent to the initial COMP of the relative clause (term 2 in (23)), because the latter does not lie in the variable factor, but is analyzed by a constant in the rule; see Figure 6.

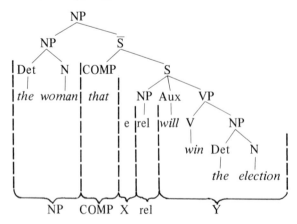

Figure 6: Proper Analysis Not Violating Constraint (17)

Therefore there is no violation entailed in treating the relative-clause marker *that* as a COMP in the well-formed phrase (26):

(26)   *the woman that ___ will win the election*

The motivation for mentioning the COMP in the relativization rule is that the relative pronoun supplants this marker. However, it is natural to question whether in cases of simple deletion the COMP need be mentioned at all. Could a rule of Relativization-by-Deletion not be formulated as in (27)?

(27)   *Relativization-by-Deletion*

NP [$_{\overline{S}}$ X   rel   Y]
1   2   3   4   →
1   2 ϕ 4

The answer is that it could be. Formulation (27) will produce exactly the same pattern of violations and nonviolations with respect to the Complementizer Constraint on Variables as (23). For example, the analysis of (24) would be like that shown in Figure 5, except that the second factor (COMP) and the third factor (X) would not be distinguished. Since the variable factor X would still end in a COMP on the right, a violation would still occur. But now compare Figure 7.

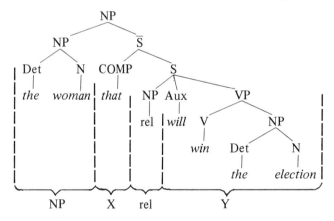

Figure 7: **Proper Analysis Not Violating Constraint (17)**

Here X functions like an 'end variable' (see the comments following (17) above): the X variable factor contains nothing outside of the $\overline{S}$ clause that the COMP is a marker of, so there is no violation of the constraint (17).

Thus we see that there are two ways in which an element can be removed next to an adjacent COMP without violating the constraint (17): either the COMP is a clause-marker mentioned by the transformation in its structural condition and so does not lie in a variable factor at all, or the variable factor does contain the COMP but does not extend beyond the clause the COMP marks. In either case the exceptional COMP has the distinguishing function of marking part of the characteristic domain of the transformation—the relative clause, in the case just considered.

The view that the relative marker *that* is a pronoun is so entrenched (from school grammar, if not theory), that it may be worthwhile to introduce evidence from a different type of relative clause, the *as*-relative, to support this point. Among its many uses, *as* can serve as the marker of relative clauses like those in (28).

(28) a. *Such women as Tom was able to speak to ___ were*
          very unfriendly.
      b. *Such women as there were ___ on the playing field were*
          unfriendly to Tom.
      c. *Such women as ___ were on the playing field were*
          unfriendly to Tom.

It is quite natural to regard *as* here as a nonpronominal, "conjunctive" clause marker—a complementizer, in our terms. Relative pronouns (*who, which*, etc.) do not appear at all in *as*-relatives, so we can assume that simple deletion applies (as in (27), for example). As (28c) already shows, the subject of the *as*-clause itself can be deleted; this does not violate the Complementizer Constraint on Variables for the reasons given above. However, when the deletion applies in a complement clause within the *as*-relative, a violation can be produced:

(29) a. **. . . to give such particulars of Edward as she feared that ___*
          would ruin him forever
      b. *. . . to give such particulars of Edward as she feared ___ would*
          ruin him forever

((29b) is cited by Jespersen (1927: p. 201).) This is in accordance with the Complementizer Constraint on Variables. In connection with the analysis of *as* as a COMP, it is interesting to note that *as* also appears in dialectal examples like (30), which is cited in the *Oxford English Dictionary:*

(30)   *I don't know as you'll like the appearance of our place.*

The Complementizer Constraint on Variables would therefore predict contrasts like the following for dialects with (30):

(31) a. *. . . someone (that) I don't know as I would like to*
          talk to
      b. **. . . someone (that) I don't know as ___ would like to*
          talk to me

To conclude this brief discussion of relativization, I have shown that relativization cannot remove a phrase adjacent to a clause marker except when the clause marker serves to mark the relative clause itself, and this is precisely what is predicted by the analysis of relativization assumed here together with the formulation of the complementizer constraint as a constraint on variables.

3.2 Clefting

The same points can be made with the cleft construction, illustrated in (32).

(32) a. *It's her Alfa that she was driving ___ .*
b. *It's her Alfa that she's likely to have been driving ___ .*
c. *It's her Alfa that the police believe that she is likely to have been driving ___ .*

Relative pronouns may appear in this construction:

(33) *It's her Alfa which she told us ___ was stolen.*

But when a relative pronoun appears, it is positioned initially in the cleft clause, where it supplants the *that*-complementizer. The relative pronoun cannot be stranded in some other COMP position:

(34) **It's her Alfa that she told us which ___ was stolen.*

Now if we assume that, like relativization, clefting makes essential use of variables, moving (or deleting) an element into (or from) a specified position at the extreme of the cleft clause, the Complementizer Constraint on Variables accounts for all contrasts like (35) and (36):

(35) a. *It's her Alfa that she told us ___ was stolen.*
b. **It's her Alfa that she told us that ___ was stolen.*

(36) *It's her Alfa that ___ was stolen.*

The complementizer *that* in (36) marks the cleft clause itself, part of the characteristic domain of the clefting transformation; the second complementizer *that* in (35b) lies in a variable factor with respect to the clefting rule.

Again, the question may arise whether the initial *that* in cleft constructions is truly a COMP and not a relative pronoun. Here we can appeal to a special peculiarity of the English cleft construction: not only NPs but PPs can be "clefted," as in (37).

(37) *It's with Mary that I was sitting.*

And when a PP is clefted, a relative pronoun cannot appear in place of *that*:

(38) a. **It's with Mary who(m) I was sitting (with).*
b. **It's with Mary with whom I was sitting.*

((38a,b) are to be construed as clefts; there is a different, grammatical, but irrelevant construction which can be paraphrased "It (namely, my umbrella) is with Mary, with whom I was sitting.") But if relative pronouns cannot have a cleft PP as antecedent, then *that* in examples like (37) must not be a relative pronoun. It is a complementizer.

Now consider the fact that some PPs can participate in subject–verb inversions, such as (39):

(39) *In these villages can be found the best examples of this cuisine.*

Here the initial PP has inverted with the subject NP, now in postverbal position. We can exploit this fact to derive the following examples:

(40) *It's in these villages that ___ are found the best examples of this cuisine.*

(41) a. *It's in these villages that we all believe ___ can be found the
           best examples of this cuisine.*
      b. **It's in these villages that we all believe that ___ can be found the
           best examples of this cuisine.*

Here we find that the PP can be clefted when it is adjacent to the initial COMP
marking the cleft clause (40), but not when it is adjacent to some other COMP (41b).
This is striking confirmation of the constraint on variables (17).[7]

In Summary, Clefting conforms our previous findings with relativization. The
fact that a phrase adjacent to the *that* complementizer that marks the cleft clause
can "exceptionally" be removed, as in (36) and (40), follows from the Complementizer Constraint on Variables, together with the hypothesis that Clefting makes
essential use of variables.

3.3 Comparative Deletion

Comparative Deletion is another transformation that can be assumed to make
essential use of variables:

(42) a. *Jack cooked more pancakes than we could eat ___ .*
      b. *Jack cooked more pancakes than we believed that we could eat ___ .*
      c. *Jack cooked more pancakes than we'd been led to believe
           that we could eat ___ .*

It also obeys the Complementizer Constraint on Variables:

(43) a. **I solved even more problems than I'd predicted that ___ would
           be solved by all of us.*
      b. *I solved even more problems than I'd predicted ___ would
           be solved by all of us.*

(44) *I solved even more problems than I'd predicted (that) I would
       solve ___ .*

(45) a. **I solved exactly as many problems as I had claimed that ___ could
           be solved by someone with my background.*
      b. *I solved exactly as many problems as I had claimed ___ could
           be solved by someone with my background.*

(46) *I solved exactly as many problems as I had claimed (that) I
       could solve ___ .*

These facts follow, given a formulation of Comparative Deletion like that proposed
in Bresnan (1976a).[8]

3.4 'Across-the-Board' Deletions

Jespersen (1927) argued that *than* and *as* in examples like (42), (43b), (44), 45b),
(46) should be classed as clause marking particles or conjunctions, along with the

relative marker *that* and what we call the complementizer *that*. We can use this analysis to construct a further test of the Complementizer Constraint on Variables. I will assume here for convenience of exposition that *than, as* are members of COMP; but the basic point holds even if they are analyzed as "conjunctive" prepositions: see notes 6, 11.

We begin by noting that on this analysis, the deletion of phrases adjacent to *than* and *as*, as in (47) and (48), is consistent with the Complementizer Constraint on Variables:

(47)   *I solved only as many problems as ___ could be solved without a slide rule.*

(48)   *I saw more people than ___ saw me.*

For if Comparative Deletion is formulated as shown schematically in (49) or (50), then *than* and *as* mark part of the characteristic domain of the transformation—the comparative clause $(\bar{S})$.

$$(49) \quad A \quad [_{\bar{S}} \; COMP \; X \; A \; Y \;], \text{ where } COMP = \left\{ \begin{array}{l} than \\ as \end{array} \right\}$$
$$\qquad\qquad\qquad +F \qquad\qquad\qquad\qquad\qquad +F$$

$$\begin{array}{ccccc} 1 & 2 & 3 & 4 & 5 \quad \rightarrow \\ 1 & 2 & 3 & \phi & 5 \end{array}$$

$$(50) \quad A \quad [_{\bar{S}} \; X \; A \; Y \;]$$
$$\begin{array}{cccc} 1 & 2 & 3 & 4 \quad \rightarrow \\ 1 & 2 & \phi & 4 \end{array}$$

(For a more exact formulation of Comparative Deletion, see Bresnan, 1976a.) Consequently, either *than* and *as* will not lie in a variable factor of a proper analysis with respect to Comparative Deletion (49), or they will be the sole terminal elements in the variable factor (50). In either case, no violation of the Complementizer Constraint on Variables ensues.

Given the analysis of *than* and *as* as members of COMP, we would predict that if another rule could extract something from a comparative clause "over a variable," it would be prohibited from removing an element adjacent to *than* or *as*. Now this prediction is difficult to test, for the following reason. Comparative constructions are like Complex NPs, in that they resist extraction from any position in the clause:

(51)   a.   Q *Freddy is taller than which one of his sisters is* →
       b.   **Which one of his sisters is Freddy taller than ___ is?*[9]

(52)   a.   Q *Freddy is taller than you found which one of his sisters to be* →
       b.   **Which one of his sisters is Freddy taller than you found ___ to be?*

(53)   a.   Q *Freddy is taller than you were believed to be by which one of his sisters* →
       b.   **Which one of his sisters is Freddy taller than you were believed to be by ___ ?*

Question Movement yields ungrammatical results not only where the subject of the *than*-clause is removed, as in (51b), but also where other phrases not adjacent to *than* are removed (52b), (53b).

These facts make it difficult to test our prediction, but not impossible, For, as Ross (1967) observed, there exist what have been called "across-the board" applications of rules like Question Movement or relativization into coordinate clauses, as in (54):

(54)   . . . *a man who Mary called ___ an idiot and June called ___ a cretin*

It is an interesting feature of comparative clauses that they, too, appear to permit such across-the-board applications:

(55)   . . . *a man who Mary called ___ an idiot as often as June*
              called ___ a cretin

In these cases, we *can* extract elements from comparative clauses without creating the ungrammatical effects of violations of "island" constraints.[10]

Now compare (56) with (57):

(56)   . . . *someone that I believe Freddy has visited ___ as many times*
              as my brother has visited ___

              *. . . *someone that I believe ___ has visited Freddy as many times*
              as ___ has visited my brother

In (56), the object of *visit* in both matrix and subordinate clause is deleted, yielding a grammatical examples. In (57), the subject of *visit* in both clauses is deleted, but the second deletion site is adjacent to a clause marker (*as*) which is not distinguished in the relativization rule, and the result is ungrammatical. (Cf. "someone that I believe has visited Freddy as many times as he has visited my brother.") Thus we find that *as* prevents deletion of an adjacent phrase by across-the-board relativization in the same way *that* does:

(58)   a.   . . . *someone that I believe ___ hates me as much as you believe*
              ___ hates you
         b.   *. . . *someone that I believe ___ hates me as much as you believe*
              that ___ hates you

Similar examples can be constructed with *than*.

To sum up this argument, where a clause marker (such as *as* or *than*) marks part of the characteristic domain of a transformation (such as the comparative clause for Comparative Deletion), it permits deletion by that transformation of an adjacent phrase. This is illustrated by (47) and (48). But where the same clause marker lies properly within a variable factor with respect to a transformation, it prohibits the deletion of an adjacent phrase. This is illustrated by (57). The predicted contrast between examples like (47) and (57) thus provides striking confirmation of the Complementizer Constraint on Variables.

3.5 Summary

To conclude this section on evidence, I have now reviewed properties of relativization, clefting, and Comparative Deletion to show that they are subject to the Complementizer Constraint on Variables. By making essential use of variables in these transformations and formulating the constraint as a constraint on variables, we can systematically account for exceptions to the generalization that phrases cannot be removed from clauses by a transformation if they are adjacent to the clause markers. The exceptions are just those complementizers that mark the characteristic domain of the transformation itself and therefore do not lie properly within its variable factors.

The rules that I have discussed are only a small sample of the rules affected by the constraint, but I believe that they sufficiently illustrate the principles involved in my hypothesis. In the next section, I will compare alternative accounts of some of the same phenomena.

4. Alternatives and Counterarguments

4.1 The False-Parsing Hypothesis

Langendoen (1970) makes the following proposal, which I will refer to as the False-Parsing Hypothesis:

> We can account, on similar grounds, for the fact that when the relative pronoun stands for the subject of a subordinate clause inside the relative clause, the subordinating conjunction *that* introducing that subordinate clause must be deleted. Thus the following sentence is grammatical:
> (20) The committee which I understand investigated the accident has not yet made its report public.
> but not:
> (21) *The committee which I understand that investigated the accident has not yet made its report public.
> The subordinating conjunction may, however, be retained in case the relative pronoun stands for some other noun phrase in the subordinate clause. Thus both of the following sentences are grammatical:
> (22) The accident which I understand the committee investigated was the worst in the state's history.
> The ungrammaticality of (21) stems presumably from the fact that the retention of *that* would lead to a false parsing of the sentence, in which *that* is taken to be the subject of the subordinate clause. This means, of course, that (21) fails to provide access to the deep structure underlying both it and sentence (20): the obligatory deletion of the subordinating conjunction may be understood as a means of rendering grammatical certain surface structures which do not provide ready access to their deep structures.

The False-Parsing Hypothesis is clearly limited to *that*, the only one of the sub-ordinating conjunctions which, because it is homophonous with a pronoun (*that*), could give rise to "false parsing" as a subject. *For, whether, as,* and *than* could not be parsed as subjects; hence, the propensity they share with *that* to protect adjacent phrases in their clauses from deletion would have to have a different explanation, on Langendoen's account. The Complementizer Constraint on Variables therfore captures a generalization that the False-Parsing Hypothesis cannot in principle express.

We should also note that the False-Parsing Hypothesis presupposes that relative *that* is a pronoun; even if this explanation holds in relatives, it does not extend to the PP-clefting examples discussed above ((40)-(41)).[11]

4.2   The Missing-Subject Hypothesis

Another type of explanation that has been offered to account for the ungram-maticality of examples like *Who do you think that is coming to town?* is based on the idea that an English clause without its subject is ungrammatical. One version of this Missing-Subject Hypothesis is Perlmutter's (1971, p. 100):

(59)   Any sentence other than an Imperative in which there is
            an S that does not contain a subject in surface structure
            is ungrammatical.

In order to avoid questionable assumptions about pruning (Perlmutter, 1971, Ch. 4, note 16), let us consider instead of (59) the version given in (60):

(60)   *Missing-Subject Hypothesis*

            Every clause beginning with a clause marker must have
            a subject in surface structure.

As a consequence of (60) (and of (59) as well), the *that* in examples like (61) must be analyzed not as a COMP (i.e., a clause marker), but as a relative pronoun:

(61)   . . . *the women that were on the playing field*

Indeed, one of the reasons for which grammarians have distinguished a relative pro-noun *that* from the "conjunctive" *that* has been precisely to uphold the generaliza-tion that every English clause must have a subject.

Jespersen considered false the ganeralization that every English clause has a subject; he argued in effect that the true generalization is that English clauses, whether they are complements, relatives, or comparatives, are syntactically alike. His view of relative *that* is summed up as follows (1927, sec. 8.7$_5$):

We have thus brought together a great many phenomena, which traditional grammar puts into various separate pigeon holes, though they are in reality identical means of connecting a clause with the rest of the sentence, either without any form word or with the empty and therefore in many cases super-fluous particle *that*. We may even say that in *I know you mentioned the man,* and in *I know the man you mentioned* we have clauses with direct contact, and in *I know that you mentioned the man*, and in *I know the man that you mentioned*, we have the same kind of clauses with mediate contact, *that* being used to cement the two closely connected parts of the sentence.

To Jespersen we owe the following counterargument to the view that relative *that* serves as the subject of clauses in cases like (61). Jespersen observes (1927, sec. 9.1), "The conjunction of comparison *as* often serves to introduce clauses which must be termed relative. Many grammarians then call *as* a relative pronoun . . ." He then shows by parallel examples that if *that* and *as* are to be analyzed as relative pronouns, so must *than* and *but* be. The relative use of *but* occurs in such (now nonstandard) examples as *I see none but are shipwrecked*, meaning, approximately, "I see only ones that are shipwrecked." The examples Jespersen gives include the following:

(62)   *such women as knew Tom*
         such women as Tom knew
         such women as Tom dreamt of
         more women than ever came here
         more women than he had seen there
         more women than he dreamt of

Jespersen concludes:

It seems, however, hardly natural to extend the name of pronoun to all these cases. After what was said above (8.7₅) [quoted above—JWB] on *that* it will not surprise my readers if I prefer using the term particle or conjunction in speaking of *as, than*, and *but* in these employments, exactly as in other uses of the same words. This puts all the clauses here mentioned on the same footing and also approximates them to contact clauses [see the above quotation—JWB]. If it is asked what then is the subject of the verb in "such women as *knew* Tom" and "more women than ever *came* here" and "there are no women but *admire* him", the answer must be that there is no subject in these clauses, and that there is the same lack of a subject in "all the women that *admire* him" and in "there's a man below *wants* to speak to you". In the same way there is no object in the other clauses. Nothing is gained in such cases by putting up fictitious subjects and objects [i.e., treating *as, than, but, that* as relative pronoun subjects and objects—JWB] : it is much better to face the simple truth that there are clauses without a subject and others without an object, just as there are sentences without either.

Jespersen's argument, then, is that to preserve the generalization that English clauses must have (surface structure) subjects, one is forced to treat *that, as, than*, and *but* as relative pronouns. One thereby loses the generalization over "relative" and "conjunctive" uses of these particles. For example, if *as* and *than* are the missing subjects in comparative clauses like (63),

(63)   a.   *As many students were flunked **as were passed**.*
       b.   *Fewer students were passed **than were flunked**.*

—then they must certainly have a different function in (64), where subjects are supplied:

(64)   a.   *As many boys were flunked **as girls were passed**.*
       b.   *More boys were flunked **than girls were passed**.*

I think Jespersen's argument alone is a compelling reason for rejecting the Missing-Subject Hypothesis, but there are others. One is the contrast between sentences like (41a) and (41b), in which the subject of *be found* and PP have exchanged positions:

(41)   a.   *It's in these villages that we all believe ____ can be found the
            best examples of this cuisine.*
       b.   **It's in these villages that we all believe that can be found the best
            examples of this cuisine.*

I assume that (41a) is derived from a source something like that in (65):

(65)   *It's △ that we all believe **in these villages** can be found
          the best examples of this cuisine.*

After it has inverted with the subject of *be found*, the PP is clefted. Note that the subject of *be found* is still present in the complement clause in (41b): it is not actually missing, but has merely exchanged places with the PP. But then the ungrammaticality of (41b) must be caused by something other than a missing subject. (I assume that the PP in (65) is not a subject, on the ground that subjects can induce number agreement of the verb: cf. *Near that town were situated two old castles* and *Near these towns is situated an old castle*.) Further reasons for rejecting the Missing-Subject Hypothesis in favor of the Complementizer Constraint on Variables are given in the next section.

4.3   Surface Structure Constraints

Although the previously proposed Missing-Subject constraint on surface structures does not adequately express the generalizations captured by the Complementizer Constraint on Variables, there have been (to my knowledge) two arguments offered in favor of defining the constraint on surface structure. Neither of them establishes this conclusion, however, and there is counterevidence against any surface structure constraint approach, as I will show below.

The first argument, suggested by Chomsky (personal communication), is based on the grammaticality of examples like (66a,b).

(66)   a.   *He's the one that they still want very much to go to Harvard.*
       b.   *You're someone whom we have wanted for a long time to visit us.*

The argument assumes that with *want* (and similar verbs—see Bresnan, 1972), a post-verbal adverb requires the presence of the complementizer *for*, as in (67) and (68):

(67)   a. *They still want very much for him to go to Harvard.*
       b. **They still want very much [him to go to Harvard* s]

(68)   a. *We have wanted for a long time for someone to visit us.*
       b. **We have wanted for a long time [someone to visit us* s]

Now, so the argument goes, given a constraint like the Complementizer Constraint on Variables, which affects transformational applications, the obligatory presence of the complementizer *for* should prevent relativization of the adjacent subject, and therefore (66a,b) should be ungrammatical, like their sources (69a,b):

(69)   a. **He's the one that they still want very much for __ to go to Harvard.*
       b. **You're someone whom we have wanted for a long time for __ to*
           visit us.

But contrary to this prediction (66a,b) are grammatical. On the other hand, if the constraint is defined as a surface structure constraint (like (60), for example), then (66a,b) would have ungrammatical '*for* __ ' sequences, subsequent deletion of *for* before *to* yields structures to which the surface structure constraint can no longer apply.

The flaw in this argument is the implicit and unwarranted assumption that (69a,b) are the only sources for (66a,b). It is assumed that in the derivation of (66a,b) the postverbal adverbs are positioned prior to relativization between the verb and its *for*-complement, as in (67a) and (68a). However, it could be just as well assumed that the adverbs are positioned postcyclically (after relativization), or that they are positioned as in (70a,b):

(70)   a. *?They still want him very much to go to Harvard.*
       b. *?We have wanted someone for a long time to visit us.*

As they stand, these examples are relatively unacceptable. (For discussion of possible explanations, compare Postal, 1974, pp. 134–154, and Bresnan, 1976c.) However, it turns out that removal of a NP from between a verb and its adverbial modifier greatly improves examples like (70a,b), and that this effect holds even in *believe*-complement constructions that give no evidence of an underlying *for* (see Kiparsky and Kiparsky, 1970; Bresnan, 1972):

(71)   *?You believe these things so strongly to be true.*

(72)   *The things which you believe so strongly to be true are not true.*

(71), like (70), is relatively unacceptable, where the adverb modifies the main verb; but (72) is fine. What these facts show is that however the contrasts between (71) and (72), (70) and (66) are ultimately to be accounted for (whether by a surface structure constraint on adverb positions or by late [postcyclic] reorderings of adverbs), there exist possible sources for examples like (66a,b) which entail no violation of the Complementizer Constraint on Variables. Thus this argument for a surface structure constraint is invalid.

Furthermore, the surface structure filtering approach to examples like (66) can be shown to be inadequate. Observe that the claim that (66a,b) derive from (69a,b) requires that a rule deleting *for* before *to* be applicable after relativization. It is the application of this rule—call it "*for*-before-*to* deletion"—that "saves" (66) from the hypothesized surface structure constraint. But then *for*-before-*to* deletion should likewise "save" examples like (73) and (74):

(73)   *This is the dress that it is required for __ to be worn
          on these occasions.
          (Cf. *This is the dress that it is required for us to wear __ on
          these occasions.*)

(74)   *This is one game that it wouldn't matter for __ to be lost.
          (Cf. *This is one game that it wouldn't matter for us to loss __ .*)

But after *for*-before-*to* deletion, the examples are still ungrammatical:

(75)   *This is the dress that it is required to be worn on
          these occasions.

(76)   *This is one game that it wouldn't matter to be lost.

The Complementizer Constraint on Variables can explain these facts, for the only sources for (73) and (74) involve violations of the constraint (17): cf. *It is required this dress to be worn* versus *It is required for this dress to be worn*, and *It wouldn't matter one game to be lost* versus *It wouldn't matter for one game to be lost*. Similarly, the Complementizer Constraint on Variables automatically accounts for the contrast between (75) and (76):

(75)   *It's John that I wouldn't be eager to see me here.

(76)   It's John that I wouldn't be eager to have see me here.

The sources of the cleft clauses in (75) and (76) are similar to (77) and (78) respectively:

(77)   I wouldn't be eager for **John** to see me here.

(78)   I wouldn't be eager to have **John** see me here.

The clefted element *John* is adjacent to the underlying complementizer *for* in (77), but not in (78). Thus the evidence from *for*-complements actually supports the Complementizer Constraint on Variables and disconfirms the surface structure constraint approach. [12]

The second argument for a surface structure constraint is given by Perlmutter (1971, pp. 111–112). Consider (79):

(79)   a. *John is anxious for someone to visit him, but I don't know
              who John is anxious (for) to visit him.
          b. John is anxious for someone to visit him, but I don't know who.

Assuming that (79b) derives from (79a) by means of Sluicing (Ross, 1969), Perlmutter argues, essentially, that if (79a) is ruled out by a constraint on transformations rather than a surface structure constraint, (79b) should also be ungrammatical. However, it is well known that other violations of constraints on transformations appear to be mitigated by the Sluicing transformation—indeed, this was one of

Ross's points, used to justify reanalyzing such constraints as constraints on derivations. Consider (80):

(80)   a. *Press aides revealed that the President would make a surprise
            proposal to disband a certain corporation–**which** corporation
            the President would make a surprise proposal to disband they
            didn't say.
        b. Press aides revealed that the President would make a surprise
            proposal to disband a certain corporation–**which** corporation they
            didn't say.

In (80a) a violation of the complex NP constraint occurs, but it is not reflected in (80b). Thus the argument from Sluicing does not show that the complementizer constraint should be formulated as a constraint on surface structures.[13]

Observe finally that any finite, or "local," surface structure constraint would be incapable in principle of discriminating between examples like (81) and (82):

(81)   This food is still cooked in the same way that ___ is prescribed
        in ancient books.

(82)   *One food that ___ is cooked by the French in the same way that
        ___ is cooked by the Italians is this.
        (Cf. One food that is cooked by the French in the same way that
        it is cooked by the Italians is this.)

(82) is a case of "across-the-board" relativization, as was discussed in section 3.4. When this rule removes the second relative item adjacent to *that*, the result is ungrammatical, as (82) shows; but when the second relative item is not adjacent to the complementizer, the result is grammatical:

(83)   One food that the French cook ___ in the same way that the
        Italians cook ___ is this.

Notice also that removal of the second object depends upon the relativization of the first object:

(84)   *The French cook one food in the same way that the Italians
        cook ___ .
        (Cf. The French cook one food in the same way that the
        Italians cook it.)

The reason that a local surface structure constraint would fail to discriminate between such examples as (81) and (82) is that the same sequences, having the same structures, occur in both examples–*the same way that φ is V-ed;* yet they contrast in grammaticality. As observed in section 3.4, the Complementizer Constraint on Variables can explain such examples, since in (81) *that* marks the characteristic domain of the unbounded rule of relativization, but in (82), the same *that* lies in a variable factor with respect to relativization.

Let me add in conclusion that very little work has been done to make precise exactly what it is that surface structure constraints cannot do. Clearly it would mean nothing to "drastically restrict" the expressive power of transformations while tacitly permitting surface structure constraints to be formulated with labelled brackets, with essential variables, with traces, and with trace binding (in the sense of Chomsky, 1976). In Bresnan (1976d), I have proposed one strong but very natural restriction on surface structure constraints (and transformations as well)— the requirement that they may not refer to traces or trace binding. This would restrict idiosyncratic, language-particular rules from access to "global" information, greatly simplifying the task of the language learner.

In any case, it appears that enriching the surface-structure filtering component with traces and labelled brackets can provide at best only a piecemeal account of the range of evidence explained by the Complementizer Constraint on Variables. [14]

4.4   The Syntactic Nature of the Constraint

Although the Complementizer Constraint clearly affects syntactic movements and deletions of the kinds I have illustrated, it appears to exert no effect on rules for determining quantifier scope and variable-binding. For example, the rule that would give (optional) widest scope to *someone* in the "transparent" reading of (85)—

(85)   *Everyone believes that someone loves Mary.*
           (Ex) (Ay) (y believes that x loves Mary)

—is unaffected by the adjacent COMP *that*. This is in sharp contrast to (86), where a syntactic deletion is involved:

(86)   **There is someone that everyone believes that ___ loves Mary.*
           Cf. *There is someone that everyone believes ___ loves Mary.*)

Similarly, the rule which binds *he* to the quantifier in (87) is indifferent to the adjacent COMP:

(87)   *Everyone thinks that he is right.*
           (Ax) (x thinks that x is right)

Again this contrasts with a deletion (though the element deleted is also bound to a quantifier):

(88)   **someone that everyone thinks that ___ is right*

Further, we can find examples that contrast with respect to the complementizer constraint but have identical logical forms:

(89)   **someone that ___ has visited Mary as many times as ___ has visited June*

           someone that ___ has visited Mary as many times as he has visited June

The logical form for (89) would presumably be identical to that for (90), with *he* bound by *someone*; the contrast between the two cannot therefore be expressed as a condition on logical form itself. Finally, there do exist grammatical nonecho questions like (91):

(91)   a.   *Who recommends that who be fired?*
        b.   *Which man ordered that which woman be fired?*

((91a,b) are counterexamples to Kuno and Robinson, 1972, but I find them perfectly grammatical; cf. Hankamer, 1975.) If these are interpreted along the lines suggested by Chomsky (1973)—e.g., "For which x, for which y, x recommends that y be fired"—then ungrammatical examples like (92) would have the same kind of interpretations—"For which x, you recommend that x be fired"—providing further evidence of the syntactic nature of the constraint.[15]

(92)   *Who do you recommend that ___ be fired?*

Thus the Complementizer Constraint on Variables provides some support for a theoretical distinction between syntactic transformations and interpretive rules.

5. Conclusion

We have now reached by a different route the same conclusion that was arrived at in Part I: that by making essential use of syntactic variables in transformations, we can capture linguistic generalizations that would otherwise be lost.

It should be remarked that the Complementizer Constraint on Variables appears not to be universal: in particular it appears not to hold in languages which have subject pronoun deletion (e.g., Portuguese and Spanish; see Perlmutter, 1971, for some discussion). Although this poses the empirical problem of discovering which properties of given languages determine the presence or absence of the constraint, it does not seem to me to pose a problem in theory. It is known that languages vary in whether they allow prepositions to be "stranded" by transformations under certain conditions (see, e.g. Grimshaw, 1975); and so languages vary in whether they allow clause markers to be stranded by transformations under certain conditions. I see no reason why grammars for these languages might not vary with respect to admissibility conditions on proper analyses. Perhaps the assumption that applicability conditions on transformations could vary among languages or language types will seem more plausible when the problem of incorporating grammars within performance models is considered. In a sentence recognition model in which (unbounded) transformations correspond directly to sentence-processing operations, these operations would be actively used to extract an underlying structure from a surface structure. (See Bresnan, 1976b and 1977, for a discussion of the realization problem for transformational grammars.) General conditions governing the applicability of these operations within a language could well depend upon particular, nonuniversal structural properties of the language.

It is also important to recognize that because the effects of the Complementizer Constraint on Variables vary with the form of the transformation (i.e., with respect to the sequence of variables and constants in its structural condition), the constraint presupposes certain universal formal limitations on transformations. To see this, note that we could "get around" the constraint simply by reformulating all transformations that delete 'A' between variables, as in (93).

(93)   A   X   A   Y
          1   2   3   4   -→
          1   2 ϕ 4

with an extra variable, as in (94),

(94)   A   X   Z   A   Y
          1   2   3   4   5   -→
          1   2   3 ϕ 5

or with an extra constant, as in (95).

(95)   A   X   (COMP)   A   Y
          1   2   3   4   5   -→
          1   2   3 ϕ 5

This is because the proper analyses shown in (96) would be permitted by the constraint:

(96)   a.   A - . . . - COMP - A - . . .
            A - X -   Z   - A - Y

       b.   A - . . . - COMP - A - . . .
            A - X -(COMP)- A - Y

Thus the formulation of the constraint in (17) tacitly presupposes that (94) and (95) are not available transformations, while (93) is.

   Now it is easy to see that without the Complementizer Constraint, (94) and (95) are *descriptively equivalent* to (93): the set of structures immediately derivable by (93) is the same as the set of structures derivable by (94) or by (95). (For every structure s which has a proper analysis $p = (p_1, p_2, p_3, p_4)$ with respect to (93), there is a proper analysis p' of s with respect to (94) or (95) which yields the same derived structure as (93): namely, $p' = (p_1, p_2, e, p_3, p_4)$, where e is the labelled bracketing of length 0. Conversely, for a proper analysis $(p_1, p_2, p_3, p_4, p_5)$ of any s with respect to (94) or (95), there is a proper analysis of s with respect to (93) that yields the same derived structure: $(p_1, p_2 p_3, p_4, p_5)$. For the definitions assumed here, see Bresnan, 1976a.) Thus apart from the effects of the Complementizer Constraint, we would lose no descriptive power by eliminating (94) and (95) from the realm of possible transformations, and retaining (93). One way of restricting the class of possible transformations appropriately would be to take equivalence classes of transformations under a relation of descriptive equivalence and to select from each class one representative transformation (say the shortest), eliminating the others. In defining the relation of descriptive equivalence, only *universal* conditions on transformations would apply. In this way (93)–(95) would belong to the same equivalence class, and (94) and (95) would be eliminated as possible transformations.

The determination of universal formal constraints on transformations is one of the most important and interesting in syntactic theory, but as I hope to have shown in this study, the study of nonuniversal constraints can also shed light on the formal properties of transformations.

Acknowledgments

I would like to thank my fellow participants in the Irvine Conference on Formal Syntax, June, 1976, and especially Noam Chomsky, for very stimulating discussion of the material in this article. I am grateful to the John Simon Guggenheim Memorial Foundation for the Fellowship that made it possible for me to pursue the research of which this study is a part. The illustrative material in part I of this study is drawn from Bresnan (1976d) with permission.

Notes

1. What is produced instead is *Does Mary believe the claim who John saw?*, which is ruled ungrammatical by a surface-structure constraint that requires *claim* to have a *that*-complement.
2. I have given two slightly different formulations of Subdeletion in Bresnan (1975a) and Bresnan (1976a). Both of them are governed by the relativized A-over-A principle, and both of them automatically "collapse" with Comparative Deletion (in which the entire compared constituent is deleted, e.g., *Bill is taller than John is*). However, under the relaivized A-over-A principle as given in Bresnan (1976a), the earlier formulation of Subdeletion also derives, as an option, all examples like *Bill is taller than John is tall*, where the compared constituent contains repeated material. In his contribution to this volume, Chomsky argues that such examples are grammatical, but mistakenly claims that it is a "crucial requirement" of the analysis of Subdeletion in Bresnan (1975a) that such sentences "must be marked ungrammatical, as a violation of [the Relativized A-over-A Principle]." Chomsky's objections to my analysis are therefore inapplicable. The interested reader is referred to Bresnan (1976d) for a full discussion of this issue, as well as a more detailed exposition of properties of Subdeletion that Chomsky's (1976) analysis fails to account for.
3. An interesting alternative to eliminating unbounded transformations would be to eliminate iterative cyclic transformational applications to the same constituent. Although cases like the passive transformation (which applies iteratively to *John* in *John is believed to have been awarded the prize*) seem at first to be obvious counterexamples to such a proposal, a cyclic passive transformation is not necessary to account for these examples, and there is some evidence that a restriction of the transformational cycle will yield a more realistic model of transformational grammar (see Bresnan, 1976b, 1977). It is interesting to note in this connection that within the theory of Bresnan (1976b, 1977), in which deep structures much more closely resemble surface structures, the Passive and Raising rules meet the criteria for *lexical* rules given by Wasow in his contribution to this volume, where he argues

that the Passive must be a transformation. This goes to show that 'criteria' for interpreting phenomena are dependent on theories of the phenomena and cannot be treated as theory-independent diagnostics. I hope to provide a full discussion of this issue in another study.

4. A proper analysis of a structure s with respect to a transformation T is a factorization $(p_1, \ldots, p_n)$ of s which satisfies the structural condition of T and on which the transformational mapping (structural change) of T is defined. (See Peters and Ritchie, 1973.) In terms of the Peters and Ritchie definitions, which do not use variable symbols in structural conditions, we can define a factor p to be a constant factor if there is a basic predicate P in the structural condition of T such that P holds of p_i and to be a variable factor otherwise.

5. —or, conceivably, as one which limits the class of derivations; cf. note 13.

6. As it is formulated in (17), the constraint permits all examples like *Who did she say that tomorrow ___ would regret his words?, an amendment which they say that next year ___ will be law, Which doctor did you tell me that during an operation ___ had had a heart attack?*, in which an adverb intervenes between the deleted phrase and the COMP. If it is considered desirable to rule out these (mildly awkward) examples, (17) could be appropriately modified, for example by having, instead of adjacency of COMP to A, adjacency of COMP to the S which immediately dominates A. Note also that although (17) is formulated in terms of 'COMPs', it could be generalized to include other subordinating conjunctions; cf. note 11.

7. Note that *all* in (41a) can bear heavy stress, suggesting that *we all believe* is not a parenthetical insert. This suggestion is reinforced by the existence of examples like "It's precisely in X's writings that I do *not* believe will be found any evidence for your hypothesis." Negative parentheticals cannot occur in affirmative sentences: *"In X's writings, I do not believe, will be found any evidence for your hypothesis."

8. As formulated, constraint (17) predicts contrasts between Subdeletion examples like (a) *As many men were hired as you had predicted ___ women would be*, and (b) ?*As many men were hired as you had predicted that ___ women would be*, even though (c) *There were as many men as you had predicted that there would be ___ women*, and (d) *There were as many men as you had predicted there would be ___ women* do not contrast. As I have remarked elsewhere (Bresnan, 1975a), I do find a contrast between (a) and (b)—with (b) worse—but it is slight enough that I do not wish to base too much upon it. Let me note, therefore, that the deleted constant factor in cases of Subdeletion is never immediately dominated by the S that the adjacent COMP marks, although it is in the other cases discussed here, so that (17) could be appropriately modified to permit (b), if desired.

9. On the status of examples like *Which one of his sisters is Freddy taller than?, Who wasn't he as tall as?*, see Hankamer (1973), who argues that the structure of these seemingly truncated clauses is not COMP S.

10. It is worth pointing out that Right Node Raising does not provide a plausible source for many examples like (54) and (55). The reason is that Right Node Raising affects only phrases at the right periphery of their clauses. Thus Right Node Raising can derive "I go out with, more often than I stay home with, that kind of friend" from a source like "I go out with *that kind of friend* more often than I stay home with *that kind of friend*." But where *that kind of friend* is not the rightmost phrase in the clauses, the result is ungrammatical: "I meet *that kind of friend* at restaurants for lunch more often that I invite *that kind of friend* to my home for supper" cannot be converted into *"I meet at restaurants for lunch, more often than I invite to my home for supper, that kind of friend." Nevertheless, I find examples like the following perfectly grammatical: "the kind of friend that I meet ___ at restaurants for lunch more often than I invite ___ to my home for supper." This suggests that the latter is not derived by applying Right Node Raising prior to relativization.

11. See Hudson (1972) for other criticisms of Langendoen's proposal. Hudson offers a proposal of his own: "if a clause contains among its immediate constituents both a conjunction

(which must be overt) and a grammatical subject, then they must come in that order, even if the subject has been 'raised' into the structure of the matrix clause." The reliance on reordering biases this proposal toward movements; it would not provide an explanation for the contrasts created by deletion rules, such as Comparative Reduction (on which cf. Vergnaud, 1975 and Hankamer, 1971)–*He ran faster than I'd thought (*that) was possible* –and Comparative Deletion–*He ate more than I had believed (*that) was in the refrigerator.* Nor would this proposal distinguish correctly between the PP-clefting examples (40)– (41). Nevertheless, in its emphasis on "conjunctions," Hudson's proposal is similar in spirit to mine.

One interesting feature of Hudson's analysis is that he extends it to subordinating conjunctions (e.g., *though, if*). Although I argued in Bresnan (1972) that the evidence he gives for this extension is not sufficient, it would be quite possible to generalize (17) further to subordinating conjunctions as well as complementizers: what these have in common is that they are "particles" (members of closed classes) that can be generated as sisters to S. (I presuppose here an analysis of subordinating conjunctions like that given in Emonds, 1976, together with the analysis of complementizers of Bresnan, 1974.) And there is in fact other evidence for such a generalized formulation, as Alex Grosu has pointed out to me. It would explain, for example, contrasts like the following:

(i)   *This is a delicate matter that, quite frankly, I would be surprised if he were to resolve ___ effectively.*

(ii) **This is a delicate matter that, quite frankly, I would be surprised if ___ were to be resolved effectively.*

12. It is important to notice that the Complementizer Constraint on Variables is not disconfirmed by the occurrence in some dialects of constructions like *Who does she long for to visit her?* A number of verbs select the preposition *for*, which, as I have already noted, is not subject to the Complementizer Constraint (see (8)–(11)). *Want*-type verbs, in particular, may, in some dialects, select a complement construction in which the preposition *for* governs the entire complement clause (S). Because this preposition does not form a constituent with the clausal subject, it would not "pied-pipe" under *wh*-movement, but because it is not a complementizer, it would not prevent extraction of the subject. Thus we can attribute this dialectal variation to lexical selectional differences in a natural way.

13. Let me note that it would be possible to regard a constraint on variables as restricting derivations rather than proper analyses. However, I do not view the evidence from Sluicing as compelling, because the types of facts that Ross adduces to show that Sluicing must involve syntactic deletion can also be found in "discourse Sluicing." Compare, for example: **Someone's coming, but I don't know whom.* and A: *Someone's coming.* B: *Whom?* Since pragmatic principles rather different from rules of sentence grammar may be required to account for "discourse Sluicing," and since they might also extend to sentence Sluicing, it could well turn out that (b) is not derived from (a) in either (102) or (103).

14. For example, in the course of discussion at the Irvine Conference on Formal Syntax, Chomsky suggested the following surface structure constraint:

(i)   **[$_{COMP}$ t X] t, where X = *that*, . . . , and t is a trace.

This constraint would account for the contrast between (ii) and (iii)–

(ii) *the man* [$_{COMP}$ *that*] *t was there*

(iii) *the man that I said* [$_{COMP}$ *t that*] *t was there*

–if we assume that *wh*-movement occurs in both these examples, leaving a trace in COMP to the left of *that* in both, and the subsequent *wh*-deletion in relative-clause initial position leaves no trace. However, (i) fails to account for the difference between (82) and (83). For *the same way that* . . . is a "*wh*-island" in Chomsky's (1976) terms:

(iv) *The French cook this in the same way in which the Italians cook that food.*

This means that once *wh*-movement moves *in which* in (iv), no other *wh*-word can move into COMP position. By hypothesis, when *in which* is deleted by *wh*-movement, no trace of it remains. Thus a trace can never be left in the lower COMP of (82), shown in (v):

(v)   *One food that t is cooked by the French in the same way* [$_{COMP}$ *that*] *wh-food is cooked by the Italians is this.*

In this respect, (82) would not differ from (83), shown in (vi):

(vi)   *One food that the French cook t in the same way* [$_{COMP}$ *that*] *the Italians cook wh-food is this.*

Thus, even if we increase the expressive power of surface structure constraints in this undesirable way, we obtain a less general account than the explanation provided by the Complementizer Constraint on Variables.

Obviously, (i) also fails to account for the *for*-deletion examples (75) and (76), since the crucial complementizer has been deleted.

15.   Fiengo and Lasnik (1973) suggest that a rule of Reciprocal Interpretation would be constrained by the complementizer constraint, but examples recorded by Postal (1974: pp. 76–77, n. 24) argue against this: *They arranged for each other to live in comfort, They prayed for each other to prosper.*

COMMENTS ON THE PAPER BY BRESNAN

Barbara Hall Partee

Departments of Linguistics and Philosophy
University of Massachusetts
Amherst, Massachusetts

The main aim of Bresnan's paper is to define the existence of a class of syntactic rules whose existence was not thought until recently to need any defense. Ever since Ross (1967), the class of unbounded movement rules making essential use of variables has been the focus of a great deal of study of constraints on rules, on rule applications, and on derivations, and Bresnan (1975) argues persuasively that there are unbounded deletion rules as well as unbounded movement rules, and that they share the same constraints. The challenge to the existence of unbounded rules came from Chomsky (1973); *wh*-movement when formulated as an unbounded movement rule violates at least two of the constraints there proposed, the Tensed-S Condition and the Specified Subject Condition, but Chomsky argued for a reformulation of the rule as a successive-cyclic movement into COMP, and proposed the Subjacency Condition that rules out unbounded movement (and deletion) rules altogether. Bresnan's present paper, as well as Bresnan (1975), provides arguments in support of the existence of unbounded deletion rules and hence against Chomsky's Subjacency Condition, and since parts of Chomsky's present paper are directed specifically against Bresnan's arguments, I will direct my own comments as much to the relevant parts of Chomsky's paper as to Bresnan's.

My remarks will fall into three sections. The first section contains some general observations that can be made about the semantics of unbounded rules. The second addresses Chomsky's suggested alternative treatments of the rule of Subdeletion and in particular the question of what Subdeletion deletes; the third takes up the problem raised for Bresnan's analysis by sentences like *John is taller than Bill is tall* , discussed by Chomsky. I am raising problems of detail because I do not believe that the nature of the rule of Subdeletion is yet fully understood, particularly those cases that in Bresnan's analysis involve deletion of a constituent larger than X *much* or X *many* but less than the whole compared constituent. I will argue in section 2 that such cases, if admitted, would provide the strongest counterarguments to Chomsky's reanalysis of Subdeletion as *wh*-movement, but in section 3 I suggest that the same cases seem to be counterexamples to the best account I can think of for sentences like *John is taller than Bill is tall* within Bresnan's framework. In

general, I find Bresnan's arguments quite compelling; but further research remains
to be done before the issues will be resolved.

1. Unbounded Rules and Variable Binding

Within a theory in which semantic interpretation is based on syntactic derivation
in such as way that for each syntactic rule there is a unique corresponding semantic
rule, one place to look for constraints is on the form of the interpretation rules that
correspond to syntactic rules of a given form. It is not my place to argue for such a
theory here (see Partee, 1975); I only want to remark that it appears that one general constraint of this sort might be that all and only unbounded syntactic rules are
interpreted semantically by rules that bind variables (either by quantification or by
lambda abstraction.) This holds of relative clause formation (Montague, 1973, and
later extensions by Rodman, 1976, and by Thomason, 1976), *wh*-question formation (Karttunen, 1975), Comparative Deletion and Subdeletion (Davis and Hellan,
1975); it hold equally of unbounded rules that have been formulated within alternative frameworks, such as Quantifier Lowering (Lakoff, 1971b), and the Derived
Verb Phrase Rule (Partee, 1975c); I hypothesize that the constraint holds quite
generally and can be maintained over a considerable range of alternative formulations of syntactic–semantic theory.[1]

If Chomsky (this volume) is able to reformulate successfully all of the traditionally unbounded rules as rules involving *wh*-movement, then it might be possible
to formulate an equivalent constraint relating *wh*-movement and variable-binding,
except that within his framework the semantic interpretation operates on almost-
surface structures rather than in any direct correspondence to syntactic rule applications. It should be noted that among the rules that map the almost-surface
structures onto logical form, there are unbounded rules, e.g., his rule (38) that
interprets a *wh*-phrase as a quantifier and inserts a matching variable in the corresponding trace, which may be arbitrarily far away. Hence a likely candidate for the
corresponding constraint within Chomsky's theory might will be that all and only
the unbounded interpretive rules are variable-binding rules.[2]

As a potentially relevant aside, let me note that there is apparently a theorem,
though I have never seen proof of it, to the effect that the set of closed sentences of
first-order predicate calculus is not context-free, and it is clearly the "unbounded-
ness" of variable-binding that is the only potentially non-context-free aspect of that
language. Variable-binding is obviously a very powerful device, and it would not
surprise me if our competence in coping with it were reflected in a syntactically
powerful device such as unbounded rules as well as in the semantically powerful
devices needed to interpret it. Tying two such powerful devices together by a
universal constraint on the syntax–semantics connection might be a fruitful step
toward limiting the places where such power is to be expected.

2. What Subdeletion Deletes

The first section of Bresnan's paper is devoted to a demonstration that Subdeletion, whether or not it is collapsible with Comparative Deletion, is an unbounded deletion rule and cannot without significant loss of generalization be reformulated as a successive-cyclic movement rule followed by a local deletion rule. Chomsky (this volume) proposes two alternatives to Bresnan's formulation of Subdeletion, the choice between them resting on whether Subdeletion does in fact obey the Complex Noun Phrase constraint as Bresnan (1975) argued (and as she further argues in the present paper.). Both of Chomsky's alternatives result ultimately in the removal just of the special representative of QP which he calls X, which corresponds to Bresnan's "X much" and "X many." If Subdeletion does obey the CNPC, then X is to be identified with or have the feature *wh-*, and is to count as a "bare" *wh-* so that the Relativized A-over-A Condition does not apply to it; then Subdeletion will be treated as another case of *wh-* Movement and will obey all of the associated constraints without violating the relativized A-over-A condition. If Subdeletion does *not* obey the CNPC but is sensitive to some not yet understood conditions regarding complexity and parallelism of structure, then the designated element X is to be freely deleted (locally, in place) and the conditions of complexity and parallelism are to be built into the rules of interpretation. Let me call the first proposal "Bare *wh-*movement" and the second "free X-deletion in place." In the present paper Bresnan gives further evidence that Subdeletion obeys the CNPC, so that the "free X-deletion in place" proposal is not an appropriate alternative, and I will not discuss it further.

The other proposal, bare *wh-*movement, which Chomsky discusses in more detail, seems to me to rest on an unsuitable analysis of the deleted (or moved) element. Bresnan's analysis of comparatives treats the phrases *X much* and *X many* as phrases of the category $\overline{\overline{\text{QP}}}$ (or Q triple-bar); the *X* is the specifier of the QP, as are *as, -er, so, that*, and *too*. Subdeletion always deletes at least *X much* or *X many* (I will return below to the cases where it apparently deletes more besides); it never leaves the *much* or *many* stranded. Now if *wh-* is attached to *X much* or *X many*, the result should be *how much* or *how many*. But Chomsky's bare *wh-*movement analysis depends on the unpronounceability of the bare *wh-*. Both Chomsky and Bresnan refer to the fact that the dialect that allows (1) below does not allow (2).

(1)   *John is more courageous than what Bill is* (=Chomsky's (256))

(2)   *John is more courageous than how Bill is intelligent.* (=Chomsky's (255)).

Bresnan (1975) suggests that such facts argue for the simultaneous existence within a grammar of closely related deletion and movement rules; the dialect in question permits a movement construction in place of Comparative Deletion but no movement construction, only a deletion, for Subdeletion. Chomsky attempts to account for the impossibility of (2) within a movement analysis on the basis of the lack of phonetic realization for a bare *wh-*. But if what must be moved is *wh-X many* or *wh-X much*, what we really should expect to find in this dialect is not (2), but (3) or (4), depending on the formulation of *much*-deletion.

(3)   *John is more courageous than how much Bill is intelligent*

(4)   *John is more courageous than how Bill is intelligent.*

What is a reasonable form for the full adjective phrase, given the similarities of APs and NPs pointed out, for instance, in Ross (1969). The absence of a direct inter-rogative form for adjectives is unexplained, but the existence of interrogative *how much, how many* would certainly seem to argue against the unpronounceability of *wh-X much, many* as the explanation for the absence of any surface form to cor-roborate a movement alternative to Subdeletion.

I would like to know what has been found out about acquisition of comparatives, since I am fairly certain I have heard children use sentences like (5) and (6), which would further confirm the claim that if there were a movement alternative to Sub-deletion, it should show up as (3) or (4), and that the absence of such forms con-firms Bresnan's use of the Relativized A-over-A Condition to rule them out.

(5)   *I want more cookies than how many Sarah got.*

(6)   *I'm bigger now than how big I was last year.*

Whether there is relevant data from acquisition or not, the main point here is that Subdeletion deletes at least *X much* or *X many*, and that adding a *wh-* to them gives *how much* and *how many*, not an unpronounceable abstract form. To suggest that Subdeletion deletes something else, such as a bare *wh-* or *wh-* combined with some different abstract element, would require explaining away both syntactic evidence (such as the partitive remnants like *of the women* from *X many*) and semantic evidence, since Davis and Hellan (1975) provide an elegant semantics that operates on a syntactic structure exactly like Bresnan's in all relevant respects[3] in which Comparative Deletion and Subdeletion are a single rule as in Bresnan (1975).

On Bresnan's view of Subdeletion, an even stronger argument against bare *wh-* movement can be constructed, since Bresnan gives examples in which the deleted material is more than *X much*, while less than the entire compared constituent. In the present paper, there are examples of the deletion of *X (much) large* (35), *X (much) large a number* (34), and *X (much) nearly* (36) (Bresnan omits the *much*, but I assume that is merely abbreviatory); further examples such as *X (much) phony* can be found in Bresnan (1975). If such examples, like (7) below, are indeed instances of Subdeletion, it follows that Subdeletion cannot be reanalyzed as either movement or deletion of just a single designated element; real lexical items are crucially involved.

(7)   *There isn't even as large a number of women as there was ___ a*
             percentage of men. (= Bresnan's (35))

However I do not regard this last kind of evidence as conclusive, because the deletion of these additional lexical items by Subdeletion conflicts with the hypo-thesis that rules of sentence grammar do not delete full lexical items under identity, a hypothesis that Chomsky mentions (cf. note 61 in this volume) and one that I find very attractive and will appeal to in the following section. Bresnan (1975) suggests in a note that it is a separate rule (from Andrews, 1975b), not Subdeletion, that deletes *nuggets* in (8); I do not know whether the same or a similar rule could delete the entire material in the examples cited above, but that possibility needs further discussion.

(8)   *There aren't as many nuggets of gold in that jar as there appear to be ___ of pyrite.*

3.   John is taller than Bill is tall

If Subdeletion deletes only *X much* or *X many*, and Comparative Deletion always deletes the entire compared phrase, then some of Bresnan's arguments in both the present paper and Bresnan (1975) are somewhat weakened; Subdeletion becomes less of a cross-categorial rule, since although it deleted QPs from NPs, APs, and AdvPs, it no longer would *remove* phrases of those kinds, only QPs. And it could not be collapsed so neatly with Comparative Deletion by the use of the Relativized A-over-A Condition in combination with the identity condition.

Chomsky's strongest argument against Bresnan's analysis of Subdeletion, in my opinion, is the fact that the Relativized A-over-A Condition, which is crucial in blocking (9) and (10),

(9)   **How many did John read ___ books?*

(10)   **How (much) is John ___ tall?*

also predicts the ungrammaticality of (11), which is in fact grammatical with emphatic stress.

(11)   *John is taller than Bill is **tall**.* (= Chomsky's (243a)).

A rebuttal to this argument would require showing that the second *tall* in (11), or what underlies it, is not in fact identical to the first *tall*, or what underlies it. I can think of two possible arguments of this sort, although neither one is without problems.

A. *EMPH as a morpheme.* The first possibility is that the head contains just *tall*, while the compared constituent contains *EMPH tall*, with the emphatic morpheme EMPH blocking identity. The reality of EMPH has been widely used to block affix-hopping and trigger DO-support (or block DO-deletion) in sentences like (12).

(12)   *Susan **does** like Tom.*

Similarly, it appears that Chomsky's obligatory rule of non-coreference can be blocked by emphatic stress on either occurrence of *John* in (13), or on *me* in (14).

(13)   *John shot John*

(14)   *I want me to hand him the prize.*

Note that stress on the first *tall* instead of the second, as in (15), similarly makes a sentence like (11) well formed.

(15)   *John is **taller** than Bill is tall.*

  One crucial problem with this proposal is that it cannot account for the well-formedness of (16), with both *tall*s stressed.

(16)   *John is **taller** than Bill is **tall**.*

(Here the preceding discourse should contain something like (17).

(17)   *John is fatter than Bill is heavy.*

If two occurrences of *EMPH tall* counted as identical, as we would suppose they should on this proposal, the second would be deleted and we would get (18), and be unable to generate (16).

(18)   *John is **taller** than Bill is.*

To generate both (18) and (16) while preserving the Relativized A-over-A Constraint, (18) and (16) would have to have distinct sources. And taking all the combinations of *tall* with or without EMPH, there are only four possible source configurations and five distinct grammatical sentences (all mutually nonsynonymous), (11), (15), (16), (18), and the normally unemphatic (19).

(19)   *John is taller than Bill is.*

The problem can be summarized as in (20) below.

(20)   a.   *J is taller than B is*   : ... *er much tall* ... *x much tall*
       b.   *J is taller than B is TALL*   : ... *er much tall* ... *x much EMPH tall*
       c.   *J is TALLER than B is tall* : ... *er much EMPH tall* ... *x much tall*
       d.   *J is TALLER than B is*   ⎫ *?* ... *er much EMPH tall* ... *x much*
       e.   *J is TALLER than B is TALL* ⎭ *EMPH tall*

  Note that (18) would be normal when preceded by (21):

(21)   *John is heavier than Bill is; what is more, _____ .*

The difference between (16) (=20e) and (18) (=20d) is that in (16), the first *tall* and the second *tall* are in contrast with two different adjectives, e.g., *fat* and *heavy*; in (18), both (underlying) occurrences of *tall* are in contrast with the same adjective, e.g., *heavy*. This leads to the second hypothesis.

  B.   *Variables over adjectives.* Just as those who support a transformational analysis of e.g., reflexivization, now generally hold that it applies to variables and not to full lexical phrases, one might argue that Comparative Deletion and Subdeletion also operate on structures with adjective variables rather than full adjectives. Full Comparative Deletion would apply to a structure of the shape (22), Subdeletion to (23) or (24) (the latter a possibility on the assumption that both lexical adjectives and variables can be inserted in the base.)

(22)   *John is -er much* A_1 *than Bill is x much* A_1.

(23)   *John is -er much* A_1 *than Bill is x much* A_2.

(24)   *John is -er much tall than Bill is x much heavy.*

On this account full Comparative Deletion could not apply to (23), but subsequent
"quantifying in" of adjectives might happen to insert the same adjective for both
variables, thus leading to a sentence like (16). The chart (25) below shows a possible
analysis of each of the five sentences of (20), omitting the alternatives with direct
insertion of adjectives; A'_1 and A'_2 refer to variables in preceding discourse.

(25)   a. $(A_1: tall)$ $(\ldots er\ much\ A_1 \ldots x\ much\ A_1)$
        b. $(A_1: tall)$ $(A_2: tall)$ $(\ldots er\ much\ A_1 \ldots x\ much\ A_2)$
              $(A_1 = A'_1 ; A_2 \neq A'_2)$
        c. $(A_1: tall)$ $(A_2: tall)$ $(\ldots er\ much\ A_1 \ldots x\ much\ A_2)$
              $(A_1 \neq A'_1 ; A_2 = A'_2)$
        d. $(A_1: tall)$ $(\ldots er\ much\ A_1 \ldots x\ much\ A_1)$ $(A_1 \neq A'_1)$
        e. $(A_1: tall)$ $(A_2: tall)$ $(\ldots er\ much\ A_1 \ldots x\ much\ A_2)$
              $(A_1 \neq A'_1 ; A_2 \neq A'_2)$

(An interpretive variant of the same proposal could presumably be devised; cf.
Cooper and Parsons, 1976, for analogous translation of Quantifier-Lowering into an
interpretive scheme.)

Independent evidence for positing variables for adjectives can be obtained from
the data discussed in Ross (1969), which includes examples such as (26) and (27),
to which can be added examples with comparatives such as (28).

(26)   *John says that Mary is pretty,* **which** *she is.*

(27)   *John said that Mary is pretty, and she is* **that**.

(28)   *John is still pretty hard to talk to, but he is less* **so** *than he
            used to be.*

This sort of analysis seems somewhat plausible to me, and it would further support
the hypothesis that rules of sentence grammar do not perform deletion under lexical
identity, a hypothesis on which there seems to be welcome convergence from a
number of different theoretical frameworks. But unless there is independent evidence
for a variable corresponding to *nearly* in (29), or to *large a number* in (30), this
analysis raises problems for Bresnan's treatment of Subdeletion as a cross-categorial
rule deleting constituents of various intermediate sizes, although it would preserve
the unity of Subdeletion with Comparative Deletion.

(29)   *Your face, I judge, is more nearly oval than it is ___ ogival.*
            (= Bresnan's (36))

(30)   *There isn't as large a number of women as there was ___of men.*
            (= Bresnan's (34))

4. Conclusion

In general, I find Bresnan's arguments extremely persuasive, and Chomsky's counterarguments less so. But in both of the arguments that I have discussed in some detail, quite a lot turns out to depend on whether Subdeletion can delete a constituent larger than *X much* or *X many* but smaller than the entire compared constituent. In particular, the claims that Subdeletion obeys the RAOAC and is a cross-categorial rule with respect to what it deletes both seem to depend on these intermediate size applications of Subdeletion, and the claim that Subdeletion is an unbounded rule is certainly much stronger if it has both of those properties. Since the best proposal I could think of to answer Chomsky's RAOAC objection, namely the treatment of adjectives as variables, seemed in turn to lead to a new objection to intermediate size Subdeletion, that aspect of the Subdeletion rule stands particularly in need of further study. However, the evidence still seems to favor Subdeletion strongly as a deletion rule over a variable, and not as a movement rule.

In closing, I should note that my comments above were all concerned with the nature of the Subdeletion rule itself, which is the subject of Part I of Bresnan's paper. Part II gives a strong independent argument for the existence of unbounded transformations by showing that the Complementizer Constraint on Variables (a reformulation of the Fixed Subject Constraint of Bresnan, 1972) is an important generalization and that there is no adequate substitute for it in a system that does not include unbounded transformations. Unless an alternative to the Complementizer Constraint on Variables can be found within Chomsky's framework, that constraint provides strong support for the existence of unbounded transformations even if some modification of the particulars of the rule of Subdeletion should prove to be necessary.

Acknowledgments

I wish to thank Emmon Bach for a great deal of profitable and enjoyable discussion of Bresnan's and Chomsky's present papers and for example (14). I am also grateful to Edwin Williams for numerous fruitful discussions that have helped me appreciate the extent to which convergence on particular issues is possible within the quite different frameworks of Montague grammar and the Revised Extended Standard Theory, and to Lars Hellan for lengthy discussions of the semantics of comparatives that he and Charles Davis have worked out.

Notes

1. *Tough-movement* as formulated in Partee (1975) is an unbounded movement rule whose interpretation is the identity mapping (i.e., it preserves meaning) and is hence a counterexample to the hypothesis suggested here. A reformulation that combined the effect of

Tough-movement and the Derived Verb Phrase Rule would not be, nor would a reformulation involving *wh*-movement (cf. Chomsky, this volume) if *wh*-movement were unbounded.

2. Chomsky stated during the discussion period that *all* of the rules of interpretation at that level are unbounded. In that case, of course, no such direct analog of the suggested constraint would be possible.

3. The only point of disagreement is that Davis and Hellan find it preferable to posit the deep structure [*a* [[*how big*] *man*]] where Bresnan posits [[*how big*] [*a man*]] .

ON TRACES AND CONDITIONS ON RULES*

David Lightfoot

Department of Linguistics
McGill University
Montreal, Canada

1.1   In recent studies within the framework of what has come to be known as
the "trace theory of movement rules," one finds the following analyses:

(1)   a. **Xerxes seems to be ill*   (Fiengo 1974, p. 43)
      b. *Jones hit Smith and* Δ *was hit by Brown*   (Fiengo 1974, p. 111)
      c. *John promised Bill* [PRO *to read the book*]   (Chomsky 1975c, p. 26)
      d. [[ϕ]$_{Det}$ [*disrespect of authority by the young*]$_{\bar{N}}$]$_{NP}$
                                                (Fiengo 1974, p. 41)
      e. *the men seem to John* [*t to like each other*]   (Chomsky 1975c, p. 22)
      f. *John wants* [*to read the book*]   (Chomsky 1975c, p. 26)
      g. *we heard about* [*plans* [Δ *to kill Bill*]]   (Chomsky 1973, p. 258)

These analyses hold of various levels of representation. (a,g) are terminal strings of
initial phrase markers: (b,c,d,e, f) are surface structure strings (notice that Chomsky's Δ in (g) is distinct from Fiengo's in (b), and is an "indefinite"). The point is
that we find seven different types of inaudibilia, one of which (f) is also "invisible."
These seven inaudibilia serve different functions and are distinguished for various
reasons. Whatever the merits of the theory, this proliferating inventory is troublesome, particularly when one bears in mind that most proponents of the Extended
Standard Theory would argue against the abstract grammar postulated in the late
sixties by so-called "generative semanticists," on the grounds that they involved a very
loose theory of transformations and therefore imposed a heavy burden on the language learner. If the theory of grammar is loose enough to be compatible with a wide
range of particular grammars, then (assuming that a child is faced with the task of
acquiring a unique grammar for his target language) it follows that the language
learner will consider and reject a large number of grammars. That is, the "learning
process" will involve very many decisions. One approach to account for the speed
of the acquisition process and the limited range of errors made by children, is to
hypothesize that they are endowed with a restrictive theory of grammar and therefore consider only a narrow range of the logically possible grammars. It should be
pointed out that this is by no means a necessary hypothesis. An alternative approach

would posit a loose theory of grammar and a rich evaluation metric that would enable the child to make the relevant choices. I find this an implausible approach and as a matter of historical fact, grammarians arguing for a loose theory of linguistic rules have had very little to say about any evaluation metric. Of course, there are other approaches in the literature. However, I assume here a research program that aims for a highly restrictive theory of possible grammars and postulates only readily learnable systems, i.e., where the learning process would involve only minimal decisions. Hence I am wary of a postulated grammar of English that sets up seven different kinds of phonologically null elements. This introduces a different kind of abstractness and prima facie does not seem to be a readily learnable system. Setting up a new phonologically null element should be regarded as equivalent to extending the power of transformations in some respect, in that it should be something one does only in the face of compelling evidence, something one should be forced into reluctantly.

This paper will address two intimately related questions: (a) Can the null elements *t* and PRO be collapsed? One may think of a trace *t* as something left behind by a moved NP, and PRO as loosely equivalent to the residue of an old style deletion-under-identity. (b) Do the Specified Subject, Tensed S, Subjacency, COMP-to-COMP, and Subject conditions hold as constraints on rule applicability or are they constraints on the well-formedness or interpretability of surface structures? When these conditions were first proposed (Chomsky, 1973), they were viewed as conditions on rule applicability. Thus the Specified Subject Condition (henceforth SSC) blocked *each* Movement from applying to a structure corresponding to (2a) to yield (2b), and blocked RI (a rule specifying disjoint reference for two NPs) from marking (3a) as deviant. Compare (2c) and (3b) where there is no specified subject and the rules are free to apply.

(2)   a.   *the candidates each wanted [Mary to vote for the other]*
        b.   **the candidates wanted [Mary to vote for each other]*
        c.   *the candidates wanted [to vote for each other]*

(3)   a.   *we expected [Mary to wash us]*
        b.   **we expected [to wash us]*

On the other hand, given the trace theory of movement rules, it may be possible to view the SSC etc. as conditions on the interpretability of surface structures. For example, one could distinguish among the sentences of (2) by rejecting *each* Movement and base-generating *each* in its surface structure position. Then one would postulate an interpretive rule that would associate *each* with a plural NP, in this case with *the candidates*. This rule would apply freely to (2a) and (2c) but would be blocked from applying to (2b) by the SSC, leaving *each* uninterpreted, i.e., unassociated with any NP. Movement rules will apply quite freely but the rule interpreting the traces will be sensitive to the SSC. Thus assuming an initial phrase marker along the lines of (4a) and a very general rule of NP Preposing (5) (where lower case indicates an empty node), (4b) or (4c) may be derived. However, the interpretive rule associating *John* with its trace in (4c) will be blocked by the SSC, leaving a trace unassociated with a full NP, hence a deviant structure. (Trace theory specifies that a NP_i, when moved, leaves behind a trace t_i, and that each trace in surface structure must be "properly bound", i.e., preceded and commanded by its NP. For details see Chomsky (1976, Ch. 3), Fiengo (1974).

(4)   a.   *np believe* [*Mary to have seen John*]$_S$
       b.   *Mary was believed* [t_m *to have seen John*]$_S$
       c.   **John was believed* [*Mary to have seen* t_j]$_S$

(5)   np X NP_i $\Rightarrow$ NP_i X t_i

In this way the conditions might distinguish interpretable from uninterpretable surface structures. From these illustrations one can see that in many cases, viewing the conditions as holding of surface structure interpretability appears to be equivalent to the more "traditional" view. If this proves viable, then we can face the possibility of eliminating all cyclic NP-movement rules and of base-generating traces. Under this view traces could be generated in any NP position but would be subject to the same conditions as PRO, namely, that they must be interpretable as coreferential with a full NP which precedes and commands them. In which case, it may be possible to collapse t and PRO. Both would be coindexing functions, "placeholders" for a full NP. This has a certain naturalness and reinforces the analogy between abstract elements and bound anaphora in that the SSC, say, will apply to the pair (NP, t), in the same way as to (NP, *each other*). Hence the two questions posed above are closely related, although logically distinct. Such a view of grammar has many intriguing implications, not the least of which is that as the role of the transformational subcomponent is eroded, so the content of the autonomy thesis is reduced. But it is a plausible and, in many ways, an attractive view of things, made possible by recent work subsuming what were thought to be many different rules under NP Preposing and *wh* Movement (see section 2.3). On the other hand, it might turn out that traces play a crucial role in the syntax, distinct from the role played by PRO.

This paper will examine these two interpretations of the proper role of conditions on rules. In section 2 I shall take one area of grammar and investigate the consequences of viewing the conditions as constraints on rule applicability or on the interpretability of surface structures. In section 3 I shall look at the consequences for the Subjacency Condition of collapsing t and PRO, and in section 4 we shall indulge in some diachrony. The paper will not establish one particular interpretation as clearly preferable, but I shall point to several empirical consequences and, I hope, clarify generally what is at stake in choosing the correct view.

2.1   Consider first the old problem of the contraction of *want to→wanna*, *used to→usta*, *supposed to→sposta*, *have to→hafta*, *ought to→oughta*, *need to→ needa*, *got to→gotta*, *going to→gonna*. The basic observation is that (6a) is ambiguous in that *who* may be interpreted as the subject or object of *succeed*, whereas in (6b) *who* can only be interpreted as the object.

(6)   a.   *who do you want to succeed?*
       b.   *who do you wanna succeed?*

Bresnan (1971a) showed that the facts could be handled neatly by a simple "local" transformation, which I have called *to* Adjunction. The rule adjoins *to* to the preceding verb and then, as a "syntactic dependent," it is liable to phonological reduction. Bresnan argued that the rule must apply as the last of the known cyclic rules.

   to Adjunction

   X   V   *to*   V   Y $\overset{\text{optional}}{\Rightarrow}$ X   [V + *to*]   V   Y

Bresnan's analysis, which she called the Ordering Hypothesis, captures the facts of (6) by postulating two deep structures (7a) and (7b), each of which may surface as (6a). (6b), on the other hand, can be derived only from (7b), i.e., the object interpretation for *who*.

(7)   a. $[_{\bar{S}} + \text{WH} \; [_S \textit{you want} \; [_{\bar{S}} \textit{for} \; [_S \textit{who to succeed}]]]]$
       b. $[_{\bar{S}} + \text{WH} \; [_S \textit{you want} \; [_{\bar{S}} \textit{for} \; [_S \textit{you to succeed who}]]]]$

(6a) is derived from (7a) by applying Complementizer Deletion and then on the final cycle *who* is moved into +WH. Only at this point is the structural description met for *to* Adjunction. It is blocked from applying by the principle of the cycle (Bresnan assumed S and $\bar{S}$ to be cyclic nodes; I shall argue in section 2.3 that S is not cyclic). However, in (7b) on the second S-cycle, after Complementizer Deletion and Equi-NP Deletion, the structural description for *to* Adjunction is met and the rule is free to apply to yield (6b) (with subsequent application of *wh* Movement, Inversion and *do* Support on the final S-cycle). This analysis will also account for the unambiguous object interpretation for *Teddy* and *who* in (8), as compared to the ambiguous interpretations in (9).

(8)   a.   *Teddy, I wanna succeed*
       b.   *Teddy is the man (who) I wanna succeed*
       c.   *the one (who) I wanna succeed is Teddy*

(9)   a.   *Teddy, I want to succeed*
       b.   *Teddy is the man (who) I want to succeed*
       c.   *the one (who) I want to succeed is Teddy*

If we assume, with Bresnan[1], that there is a transformational rule of *to* Adjunction, then clearly trace theory, which I assume to be motivated independently, will be applicable here and the application yields some interesting conclusions.[2] First, it removes the need for a necessary ordering function such that Equi-NP Deletion precedes *to* Adjunction which in turn precedes *wh* Movement, Relativization, Topicalization and Pseudo-cleft (arguably all instances of the same rule; see below). The second relationship follows from the cyclic principle if one assumes (with Bresnan) a base rule $\bar{S} \rightarrow \text{COMP S}$ and that $\bar{S}$ and S are cyclic nodes (where COMP is the final resting place of *wh*-elements and topicalized NPs), but the mechanism for achieving the ordering is irrelevant here, as we shall see. Trace theory requires that NPs moved by *wh* Movement, Relativization, Topicalization and Pseudo-cleft leave behind a trace. Hence (6a), (9a), (9b), and (9c) will each have two possible surface structures. (In this section I shall assume that *wh* elements do not move successive cyclically and therefore that *t* is not also left in the COMP position; we shall return to this in section 2.3)

(6)   a'. *who do you want* [PRO *to succeed t*] (object interpretation)
             who do you want [*t to succeed*]   (subject interpretation)

(9)   a'. *Teddy, I want* [PRO *to succeed t*]
             Teddy, I want [*t to succeed*]

(9)   b'. *Teddy is the man (who) I want* [PRO *to succeed t*]
             Teddy is the man (who) I want [*t to succeed*]

(9)   c'. *the one (who) I want* [PRO *to succeed t*] *is Teddy*
             the one (who) I want [*t to succeed*] *is Teddy*

Recall that Bresnan assumed a rule of Equi, so there would be no PRO in any of the above structures and *to* Adjunction would be unimpeded in the first of each of the above pairs. For the moment we simply assume that the intervening PRO on the object interpretations will not block *to* Adjunction, returning to this question in detail in section 2.2. However in the second of each of the above pairs the intervening trace will block application of Adjunction—a correct result. Not only can the trees not be factorized in such a way as to meet the structural description of *to* Adjunction, but also recall that in the earliest discussion of traces (Chomsky, 1973), they were defined as being specified subjects; they were abstract elements controlled by something other than the elements affected by the rule in question. Hence the SSC will block Adjunction in the second case of each of the above pairs. Notice that *wh* Movement in (6a') will not be blocked by the SSC since it is a rule that moves material into a COMP slot, which is not a possible controller (Chomsky, 1973). However, the important thing to observe is that now the ordering is irrelevant because *to* Adjunction will never be able to apply at any stage of the derivation, being blocked either by the intervening *who, Teddy*, etc., or, if it applies after *wh* Movement, Topicalization etc., by the intervening trace. Hence, given trace theory, all the relevant facts can be handled without recourse to ordering arguments. The same holds of Subject-to-Subject raising cases, where Adjunction will be blocked by either the subject or the trace left behind after the subject has been raised, and no ordering need be invoked: **John is certainna win, *who did John happenna see.*

    Not only *can* the facts be handled without recourse to rule ordering; they *must* be. Assuming $\bar{S} \rightarrow$ COMP S, then *wh* Movement, Relativization, Topicalization and Pseudo-cleft will each apply on the $\bar{S}$-cycle. Therefore *to* Adjunction will be blocked from applying on the internal cycle by the intervening NP, which will still be present. Therefore a crucial test to choose between the ordering and trace theories will be one where no appeal can be made to this extra cycle (still assuming with Bresnan, as noted above, that both S and $\bar{S}$ are cyclic nodes).

The contraction of *use(d) to → usta* works in identical fashion to that of *want to → wanna*, in that it will be blocked just in the event that an NP has been extracted (i.e. moved) from the *used—to* position. Hence contraction is possible in (10), where under either the transformational or interpretive Equi-analysis no extraction is involved, but is not possible in (11), where an NP has been extracted. Similar examples can be constructed with *need: we needa fix this*, but **a wrench we needa fix this*.

(10)   *Tom used _ to meet Harry for lunch*
         Tom used _ to be considered smart
         Tom used _ to seem smart

(11)   [$_{\overline{S}}$ *what* [$_S$ *Tom used _ to take the picture*]] *was a Nikon*
         this is the Nikon [$_{\overline{S}}$ *(which)* [$_S$ *Tom used _ to take the picture*]]
         [$_{\overline{S}}$ *what* [$_S$ *did Tom use _ to take the picture?*]]
         [$_{\overline{S}}$ *the Nikon,* [$_S$ *Tom used _ to take the picture*]]

In (11) Bresnan would argue that the NP is extracted only on the uppermost $\overline{S}$ cycle and is still present on the cycle where *to* Adjunction might apply, hence blocking the rule. However, consider (12a), where contraction is also impossible. Here *a Nikon* is moved out on the same cycle as that on which *to* Adjunction might apply.

(12)   a.   *a Nikon was used _ to take the picture*
         b.   **a Nikon was usta take the picture*
         c.   *Δ used a Nikon to take the picture*
         d.   *a Nikon was used t to take the picture*

If we adopt the trace theory, then either *a Nikon* (c) or a trace (d) will intervene between *used – to*, and the structural description for *to* Adjuction will never be met—a good result, and again no ordering requirements are needed. But if we adopt the ordering hypothesis, we shall need a statement that *to* Adjunction must precede Passive (otherwise Adjunction might apply to (12a)). This would contradict Bresnan's claim that *to* Adjunction applies as the last of the known cyclic rules and would yield an ordering paradox: the required ordering would be Equi - *to* Adjunction - Passive, which conflicts with a solid argument for ordering Passive before *to* Adjunction. We proceed now to that argument.

I shall assume that in infinitive constructions *want* and all verbs of desiring take a *for*-complementizer. This is essentially the proposal of Bresnan (1972).[4] It can be justified by noting that *for* may surface optionally with many desiderative verbs (13), and must surface when lexical material separates the verb from its complement (14), unlike epistemic verbs, which never tolerate *for* (15). Also *for* surfaces in corresponding derived nominals (16), but not in derived nominals corresponding to epistemic verbs (17).

(13)   *I would prefer (for) John to do it*
         I would hate (for) John to do it

(14)   *I want very much for John to come*
         *I want very much John to come
         I would like very much for John to come
         *I would like very much John to come

(15)   *I believe (very much/sincerely) for John to be popular
       *I expected (very much/sincerely) for John to have been elected

(16)   her desire for Mary to come   cf. her desire for fame
       her preference for gin to be available   cf. her preference for gin

(17)   *her belief for John to be popular   cf. *her belief for God
       *her expectation for John to have been elected   cf. *her expectation for
                                                            John

This for-complementizer, so justified, will intervene between want and to and therefore will have to be deleted before to Adjunction can apply to yield wanna. Hence
to Adjunction must be ordered after Complementizer Deletion. But Passive must be
ordered before Complementizer Deletion, in order to block (18). If Passive precedes
Complementizer Deletion, then it will fail to apply in (18), because its structural
description will not be met. Passive requires a NP V NP sequence, and so is blocked
in the structures underlying (18) by the for intervening between the V and the
following NP—a correct result. Compare (19), where there is no for at any stage of
the derivation to block application of Passive.[5]

(18)
$$\text{*John was} \left\{ \begin{array}{l} wanted \\ preferred \\ desired \\ hated \end{array} \right\} to\ do\ it$$

(19)
$$\text{John was} \left\{ \begin{array}{l} believed \\ expected \\ known \end{array} \right\} to\ be\ popular$$

Hence in this paragraph we have demonstrated by an indirect argument (via the
interaction with Complementizer Deletion) that Passive must precede to Adjunction.[6] Hence the ordering paradox.

    This ordering paradox, of course, does not arise in a trace theory account of the
contraction data along the lines of (6a′), (9a′), (9b′) and (9c′). We showed that if
one adopts that account, then no ordering relationship needs to be specified. That
alone is a reasonable argument for using trace theory, assuming trace theory to have
independent motivation, since it yields a simpler grammar. The argument gains
force when it is shown that trace theory provides a way to avoid what would otherwise be an ordering paradox. We have therefore shown that trace theory gives a
superior account of the contraction data. If this analysis as correct, then we have an
argument that there is a crucial distinction between a trace, which marks an "extraction site." and a PRO, which marks a coreferential NP-position where no extraction
has been involved. Traces, but not PROs, block Adjunction. One might take this to
indicate that PROs do not "count" when trees are analyzed to match structural
descriptions of transformational rules. Under this account we do not have to appeal
to the SSC to block Adjunction. It will be blocked by "visible" material intervening
between want and to, either lexical NPs or traces; PROs will be "invisible," perhaps

empty nodes to be filled in by semantic interpretation rules. Thus prima facie, *t* and PRO seem to have different properties. This needs further examination.

2.2   In the light of this analysis, certain consequences follow for the possibility of collapsing *t* and PRO. I shall show in this section that collapsing them requires introducing a new phonologically null element, resulting from the application of a deletion rule. Distinguishing them entails changes in the SSC and in the usual view of a trace and a PRO.

While PROs may not affect the *structural* requirements of transformational rules, it has been argued that they may affect the application of rules in another way, and this should block *to* Adjunction. The SSC specifies that an improperly controlled PRO can block the application of rules.

Specified Subject Condition (Chomsky 1973, p. 254)

No rule can involve X, Y, (X superior to Y) in the structure
... X ... [... Z ... -WYV ...] ...
where Z is the specified subject of WYV.

A "specified subject" is one that is either (a) lexically filled (see Chomsky, 1973, note 39) or (b) one controlled by a category not containing X (p. 262). We shall refer to (a) as the syntactic definition and (b) as semantic since it refers to the property of "control." This constraint predicts that Adjunction will be blocked in, say, (20).

(20)   *what do you want* [PRO *to see t*]

The rule affects *want* (= 'X' of the definition) and *to* (= 'Y'); PRO is controlled not by *want* but by the subject *you*, and therefore is a specified subject. Therefore this analysis is an exception to the SSC, since Adjunction can in fact apply here. This leads me to suggest a revision to the SSC.

The SSC is a constraint on syntactic (and other) rules, which is sensitive to control properties, which in turn are determined in the semantic component. This raises a question about the hypothesis of the autonomy of syntax. It is consistent, of course, with the notion of a "parameterized autonomy thesis" (Chomsky, 1974), whereby there are certain prescribed areas where syntactic and semantic information may be confounded, e.g., the lexicon, conditions on rules. It is also consistent with the notion that conditions on rules may be part of the *theory* of grammar, and not part of specific grammars. Nonetheless, we could construct a plausibility argument for some version of the autonomy thesis, if we could show that syntactic rules are subject only to the syntactic aspect of the SSC and that only semantic rules are sensitive to the notion of control. To do this we would need to show that syntactic rules may be blocked by an intervening lexically specified subject but not by an intervening PRO controlled by something other than 'X' in the definition. It seems to me that this is a plausible position and, if sustained, it would allow *to* Adjunction to take place in (20) and all other structures where only PRO intervenes between the verb and its potential clitic *to*. In fact, under this proposal we may dispense with the symbol PRO, dealing instead with an empty node which may be "filled" by the rules of semantic interpretation. Assuming that empty nodes are "invisible" to the structural descriptions of transformations, then nothing will intervene between *want* and *to*, and *to* Adjunction will not be blocked. Alternatively we might regard PRO as a nonterminal element, as Chomsky (1975, class lectures) treats trace (see section 2.3), or as a feature on an NP (see below).

This position derives its plausibility from the fact that several syntactic rules are not sensitive to the miscontrolled PRO aspect of the definition of a specified subject, and I know of no clear case of a syntactic rule that is. Relevant cases will be syntactic rules which operate across S boundaries and "dip down" into infinitival complements. *To* Adjunction is an example of such a rule and it is blocked only by a trace or intervening lexical matierial and not by an improperly controlled PRO. The same situation obtains for "*tough* Movement," as shown by Chomsky himself.[7] Chomsky (1973) noted the ungrammaticality of (21), where *tough* Movement has taken place over a lexically specified subject, and argued that (22i) and (22ii) have underlying structures of the form of (22a), where *for us* and *for the rich* are part of the matrix sentence and control the lower PRO. The structures of (22a) allow *tough* Movement although the PRO subject is controlled by something other than *it* (which is 'X' in the definition) and therefore counts as a specified subject. Chomsky (p. 263, ff.) suggests various more or less ad hoc ways around this problem, "reaching no firm conclusion."

(21)   (i)   *Latin is a waste of time for us for them to teach us*
        (ii) *the hard work is pleasant for the rich for poor immigrants to do*

(22)   (i)   *Latin is* $\begin{Bmatrix} easy \\ a\ waste\ of\ time \end{Bmatrix}$ *for us to learn*
        (ii) *the hard work is pleasant for the rich to do*

    a. (i)   *it is* $\begin{Bmatrix} easy \\ a\ waste\ of\ time \end{Bmatrix}$ *for us* [PRO *to learn Latin*]
        (ii) *it is pleasant for the rich* [PRO *to do the hard work*]

Thirdly, *wh* Movement is another rule that can affect an element in an infinitival complement, but this obeys neither component of the SSC in sentences and can move elements both over a lexically specified subject (23) and over an improperly controlled PRO (24). However, it is subject to the syntactic version of the SSC in NPs (25); the semantic version will never be applicable since PROs do not occur as the "subject" of NPs (or rather, if they do, they cannot be interpreted by the usual coreference rules, and the uninterpreted PRO (or, under our proposal above, the unfilled node) ensures that the derivation is blocked).

(23)   *who do you want* [*John to visit* __]?

(24)   a. *what is easy for us* [PRO *to learn* __]?
        b. *who did you persuade Bill* [PRO *to see* __]?

(25)   a. *who did you see* [*pictures of* __]?
        b. *who did you see* [*John's pictures of* __]?

Chomsky accounts for this data by moving *wh*-elements into COMP on the innermost cycle and then specifying that COMP acts as an "escape hatch," whereby *wh* may leave its S, if it moves directly to another COMP. In this way *wh* Movement is rendered subject to the SSC and we get an explanation for (25). NPs, of course, have no COMP and therefore no escape hatch; hence, if we assume the Subjacency Condition, extraction of *wh*-elements from within an NP embedded in an NP will be impossible. A possible argument that *wh* Movement is sensitive to an improperly controlled PRO lies in Chomsky's recent explanation for **what sonata is this violin easy to play on* by his generalized *wh* Movement rule (see section 2.3). The structure after the first application of *wh* Movement will be *COMP this violin is easy* [*which for PRO to play what sonata on t*] and *what sonata* now cannot move to the highest COMP, it might be claimed, by virtue of the SSC and the requirement that COMP cannot be double filled. But this is false since, although PRO is not controlled by COMP, i.e., the target of *wh* Movement and therefore 'X' for the purposes of the SSC, COMP is not a possible controller and so PRO will not count as a specified subject. However, such movement would also be blocked by Subjacency on the crucial assumption that either S or AdjP is a cyclic node (for the question of the cyclicity of S, see section 2.3 and Chomsky's paper in this volume), and therefore the SSC is not crucially involved. In the examples cited, PRO is interpreted as indefinite, but it would be controlled in the parallel example **what sonata is this violin easy for you* [*for PRO to play on*] . Notice that the (strict) cyclic principle will block successive cyclic movement of *what sonata* after deletion of *which* on the higher cycle. So we have a solution to the old violin-sonata problem, still maintaining our claim that *wh* Movement is not sensitive to an inappropriately controlled PRO.

In fact, the only syntactic rule which seems to be subject to the semantic aspect of the SSC is *each* Movement and this is by no means a clear case of a syntactic rule.[8] If we claim that *each* is generated in its surface position and is subject to an interpretive rule to determine the NP it binds (the position advocated by Jackendoff, 1972, although not discussed or argued for in detail there), then we lose the earliest motivation for making syntactic rules sensitive to improperly controlled PROs. This seems to me to be a reasonable view, if only because of the high cost of a syntactic *each* Movement rule in terms of special requirements needed for Chomsky's (1973) conditions on rules. Chomsky's contribution to this volume takes the same position.

I know of no syntactic rules which are sensitive to the semantic definition of a specified subject, while three are sensitive to lexically filled subjects, i.e., the syntactic aspect of the definition: *to* Adjunction, *tough* Movement and *wh* Movement. Hence I propose a revision of the SSC: that syntactic rules are sensitive only to the syntactic definition of a specified subject. This (a) solves our problem with *to* contraction in that Adjunction is no longer blocked by the SSC from applying to (20), and our analysis becomes compatible with an interpretive treatment of Equi, (b) yields another plausibility argument for some version of the autonomy thesis, and (c) provides a diagnostic for distinguishing between syntactic and semantic rules. Hence a syntactic rule will be blocked from dipping down into a tenseless structure (S or NP) only if there is lexical material (this includes t, which I take to be a terminal element, but not PRO) in the subject position. Note in particular that *wh* Movement behaves in accordance with this proposal. This takes on importance in the light of recent work by Chomsky, following up suggestions in Chomsky (1975c). He argues that two rules, NP Preposing and *wh* Movement, constitute the core of English syntax and that each has much "broader scope than has hitherto been imagined." "Rules" such as Comparative Deletion (Bresnan, 1973), *tough* Movement, Infinitival Relative Formation, Topicalization, Clefting, are special cases of *wh* Movement. Having so much subsumed under *wh* Movement increases the plausibility of our proposal. Notice that if NP Preposing is given a SD: np V NP, it will never interact with the SSC. This account of the Adjunction data presupposes a crucial destinction between t and PRO; it also refines the SSC and extends the notion of an autonomous syntax.

An alternative approach is to argue for a deletion rule erasing the subject of the complement to *want* etc., so that there will be no PRO intervening between *want* and *to*, and hence no problem. Chomsky (1975c) adopts this approach while maintaining a PRO-analysis for verbs such as *promise, persuade*; he calls this the "EQUI-hypothesis." Thus *I promised Bill to come home, I persuaded Bill to come home* and *I wanted to come home* will have deep structures as in (26).

(26) a. *I promised Bill* [PRO *to come home*]
      b. *I persuaded Bill* [PRO *to come home*]
      c. *I wanted* [*for X-self to come home*]

Chomsky (p. 33) suggests "a general principle that NPs may be realized either as PRO or with lexical material, but not in both ways. We might think of PRO as an optional feature on the category NP; NP can be expanded by rules of the base only when it is [-PRO]." Thus *promise, persuade, try*, etc., will subcategorize a PRO complement subject because one can never have lexical material there: **I promised Bill John to come home. *I tried Bill to come home.* On the other hand, *want* does permit a lexical subject (*I want John to come*) and therefore is ineligible for a PRO-analysis. The same holds for epistemic verbs (*Fred believes John to be popular*), but these verbs may not undergo EQUI (**John believes to be popular / John believes himself to be popular*), whereas EQUI is obligatory for verbs like *want* (for most dialects): *John wants to be popular / *John wants himself to be popular*. The EQUI-hypothesis will handle the contraction data in that after deletion of the designated element *for X-self*, nothing will intervene between *want* and *to*, and *to* Adjunction will be free to apply; also there will be no inappropriately controlled PRO to activate the standard version of the SSC. By Chomsky's general proposal, the other verbs undergoing *to* Adjunction, *have to, be supposed to, use(d) to* (as in (10)), *got to, be going to*, will subcategorize an embedded PRO subject, since no lexical item can occur here: **I have John to go, *Fred is supposed Bill to leave*. One might now propose that these items are followed directly by a VP, not a sentential complement. In that case nothing would intervene at any stage to block Adjunction. Under this view *to* Adjunction will apply if there is no lexical item or abstract element between the V and the infinitive, and so it will not provide any reason to distinguish PRO and t. Therefore this analysis, unlike the one we have just outlined, will be compatible with collapsing PRO and t.

Two independent arguments are adduced for this position. The first concerns clitics in Portuguese and Czech (based on work by Quicoli and Toman, respectively), where a pronominal object of an embedded verb may be cliticized to the matrix verb.

(27)   *o medico nos quer examinar*
         'the doctor us wants [_ to examine t]'

However, such cliticization will be blocked if the embedded subject is lexically specified, a trace, or an inappropriately controlled PRO.

(28)   a.   **Carlos us$_i$ saw [the doctor examine t_i]*
       b.   **the man [who$_i$ Maria us$_j$ saw [t_i examine t_j]] disappeared*
       c.   **the doctor$_j$ us$_i$ promised* [PRO$_j$ to examine t_i]
             *the doctor it$_i$ persuaded us$_j$ [PRO$_j$ to examine t_i]

Cliticization to the matrix verb from the embedded object is possible only with verbs such as *querer* "want." Postulating a deleted subject here will make the appropriate distinctions. If we assume that the grammar of a given language L may be underdetermined by data from L, we may accept an argument of this form, i.e., that given clear evidence from Portuguese, the conclusion may carry over to English on some currently ill-understood general grounds. However, clitics in Old French behave in such as way as to cast strong doubts: here sentences like (27) and (28c) are grammatical. In other words, an inappropriately controlled PRO will not block cliticization, and therefore postulating a deletion rule for *want* etc., will not make the required distinctions. I cite the Old French, the modern equivalents and a gloss.[9]

(29)   a.   *Deus le me doinst venger* (Chanson de Roland)
             Dieu me donne de le venger
             'may God allow me [PRO to avenge him]'
       b.   *qu'i la viegne chacier*
             qu'il y vienne la chasser
             'that he come [PRO to chase her]'

Notice that under Chomsky's general proposal above a PRO-analysis will be required here, as indicated in (29), and EQUI cannot be invoked, because no lexical material can ever occur as the embedded subject: **Deus me donne [Jean partir]*, "God permits me John to leave." This suggests that it can scarcely be argued that the EQUI-hypothesis is motivated for English on universal grounds; it will have to be motivated on internal grounds.

The phenomenon of "clitic climbing" in the Romance (and other) languages has attracted much attention recently. The conditions for clitic climbing vary considerably across languages, but Portuguese as discussed by Quicoli, represents an unusual, perhaps even unique situation. Clitics in Italian seem to have some of the properties of those of Old French; again it appears that they can be promoted over an inappropriately controlled PRO (data from Radford, 1976).

(30)   a.   *lo insegna a fare a Paolo*
            it he-teaches to do to Paolo
            'he teaches Paolo [PRO to do it]'

       b.   *ti vengo a trovare*
            you I-come to find
            'I am coming [PRO to find you]'

There is much more to be said about the Italian data, since it seems possible also to promote certain clitics over a lexically specified subject, although this might be a case of Adverb Preposing since parallel examples do not occur with object clitics.

(31)   *ci ho visto Paolo entrare*
            there I-have seen Paolo enter
            'I have seen [Paolo enter there]'

Modern French does not allow this kind of clitic climbing under any conditions (**je le veux faire*), and Spanish represents yet another situation. Lujan (1976) presupposes a rule which will delete embedded subjects under identity (instead of deleting a designated element, as in Chomsky's version). Then verbs that *must* undergo the rule (*creo, afirmar, admitir, decir*) are distinguished from those that *may* undergo it (*querer, preferir*), and it is claimed that only the latter allow clitic climbing. This is consitent with the EQUI-hypothesis: verbs that in Lujan's terms must undergo his rule, would be subcategorized for an embedded PRO subject in Chomsky's account, unlike verbs like *querer*, which can have a lexical subject and therefore would be analyzed as undergoing EQUI. As with Portuguese, only the EQUI verbs allow clitic climbing.

(32)   a.   *lo quiero hacer bien*, 'I want to do it right'
       b.   *te lo prefiero dar ahora*, 'I prefer to give it to you now'

(33)   a.   *creo hacerlo bien*, 'I think I do it right'
       b.   *afirma habertelo dado*, 'he says that he has given it to you'
       c.   **lo creo hacer bien*
       d.   **te lo afirma haber dado*

Lujan correlates ability to tolerate clitic climbing with the possibility of taking a complement verb in the subjunctive mood. However, Aissen and Perlmutter (1976) look at a wider range of data in Spanish and list some of those verbs that permit clitic climbing (34a) and those that do not (34b). Of the verbs in (34a), only *querer* could be assigned an EQUI-analysis; the rest have an obligatory dummy subject (therefore a PRO). In most cases the PRO will be controlled by the higher subject, but with *ordenar* and *permitir* it will be controlled by the higher object. One valid generalization seems to be that verbs that undergo subject-to-subject raising will not tolerate clitic climbing. Under the assumptions of this paper a trace would be left in the lower subject position, so we can note that a *t*-subject will always block clitic climbing but a PRO usually will not. Of the other verbs which will not allow climbing, the remainder subcategorize a PRO.

(34) a. *soler* 'tend'   b. *parecer* 'seem'
          acabar (de) 'have just'   *deber (de)* 'must (epistemic)'
          querer 'want'   *insistir (en)* 'insist'
          tratar (de) 'try'   *soñar (con)* 'dream of'
          poder 'be able'   *decidirse (a)* 'decide'
          deber 'ought, should'   *evitar* 'avoid'
          empezar (a) 'begin'   *sugerir* 'suggest'
          terminar (de) 'finish'   *pedir* 'ask'
          continuar 'continue'   *decir* 'say'
          seguir 'keep on'   *afirmar* 'affirm'
          dejar (de) 'stop'
          volver (a) 're-, again'
          ordenar 'order'
          permitir 'permit'

A second argument for the EQUI-hypothesis is based on English. Discussing problems in determining the scope of *only*, Fodor (1975) argues against the proposals of McCawley (1970) and for the EQUI-hypothesis on the basis of (35).

(35)   *only Churchill remembers giving the speech about blood, sweat
          and tears*

The descriptive problem is to characterize exactly what Churchill is the only person to remember. Clearly Churchill is not the only person to remember Churchill giving the speech, since millions of others remember the same event. Rather, Churchill is the only one to remember that he himself gave the speech. This seems to be an argument against deleting *Churchill*, but it does not choose between the EQUI-hypothesis above and the PRO-analysis. Since Chomsky allows rules of interpretation to operate on partially determined logical form (LF), the scope of *only* could be prescribed in LF: specifiying that of the people remembering *PRO giving the speech*, Churchill was the only one. In fact, the data seem to be the same with *promise: only Churchill promised to give the speech about blood, sweat and tears.* If one assumes *promise* to be a clear case of a PRO-verb, then the argument for assigning *remember* an EQUI-analysis fails.

Although the independent motivation for the EQUI-hypothesis is weak, we have two functioning accounts for the *to* Adjunction data. Ceteris paribus, the PRO-analysis, if it can be sustained, must be preferable: it permits a more restrictive version of the autonomy thesis (and provides another plausibility argument for it), while the EQUI-hypothesis adds another phonologically null element to the proliferating inventory. The PRO-analysis reflects a somewhat different view of trace theory: that the "residue" of movement rules have some kind of privileged status, as indicated by the contraction data, and in a sense the moved element is always present in its original position, in contrast to the residue of what have been viewed as deletion rules or interpretive rules specifying coreference for phonologically null elements. Chomsky, on the other hand, views a trace and a PRO as essentially the same thing. He regards a trace as a function, a coindexing device: when NP_i moves, it leaves a trace t_i. We may then view PRO as a base-generated $t(x)$, where x is a variable to be filled in by a control rule, and we reduce the proliferation of null elements. The contraction data seems to have crucial consequences in that it is a problem for this view and seems to necessitate the EQUI-hypothesis, thereby adding another type of null element. On the other hand, distinguishing t and PRO entails a change in the SSC (a desirable change, if it can be sustained) and a different view of a PRO, which is regarded as "invisible" to the structural descriptions of transformations and therefore as a nonterminal element. In this way we can give a partial answer to one of the questions posed at the outset. We have shown that the analysis of *to* contraction in section 2.1 has empirical consequences for the question of whether t and PRO can be collapsed. Collapsing t and PRO will require a different and somewhat less desirable treatment of *to* contraction. This question will not be resolved, however, just on the basis of this analysis of a phenomenon involving a small class of English verbs.[10]

2.3   Consider now the logically distinct but intimately related question of the domain of conditions on rules: do they act as constraints on rule applicability or do they hold of well-formedness of surface structures. Again, data involving *to* Adjunction turns out to be crucial. There is a further problem with the analysis adopted in section 2.1. I shall outline three solutions to this problem, showing that two will hold if one views the SSC, etc., as constraining the applicability of rules, while the third will hold under this interpretation only if we make some undesirable moves; this solution is more compatible with viewing the conditions as surface structure constraints.

The analysis adopted in section 2.1 is incompatible as it stands with what Postal (1972a) calls the "successive-cyclic" treatment of *wh* Movement, advocated by Chomsky (1973). One may derive *who do you want to try to visit* either by a single application of *wh* Movement as in (36) or by passing the *wh*-element successively into each COMP node, as in (37).

(36)   COMP *you want* [COMP PRO *to try* [COMP PRO *to visit who*]]

(37)   COMP *you want* [COMP PRO *to try* [COMP PRO *to visit who*]]

Consider, for example, (38a), which derives from (38b).

(38)   a.   *who do you want to beat*
       b.   *who do you want* [PRO *to beat t*]

If one adopts the successive-cyclic hypothesis, then the structure at the end of the first $\bar{S}$ cycle will be:

you want [[*who*]$_{COMP}$ PRO *to beat t*]$_{\bar{S}}$

Who will not be moved out of this position until the final $\bar{S}$-cycle and therefore would serve to block application of *to* Adjunction on the last S-cycle (again assuming S and $\bar{S}$ to be cyclic nodes), the only possible point of application—an incorrect result. Even if application of *to* Adjunction can somehow be delayed until after *who* is moved out of this position, the rule will still be blocked, this time by the intervening trace. On the other hand, if one assumes the single movement hypothesis illustrated in (36), *who* will at no point intervene between *want* and (PRO) *to*, and therefore Adjunction will be free to apply—the correct result. Throughout the analysis of section 2.1 we assumed the single movement hypothesis and that assumption was crucial. Notice that this problem within the successive-cyclic hypothesis arises under both the EQUI-and PRO-analyses discussed in section 2.2.

This corroborates the results of Jenkins (1975). Chomsky (1973) gave an argument that *wh* Movement should be post-cyclic (based on its interaction with *each* Movement) but showed that the force of this argument was avoided under trace theory. Jenkins argues to the same effect and shows that his argument (based on the elimination of the condition (123.c), that anything moved from a COMP must be moved only into another COMP-position) cannot be avoided by appeal to traces. Hence, he argues, the postcyclic treatment of *wh* Movement must be correct, since it gives the correct result in both cases. However, adopting a postcyclic *wh* Movement also entails violations of the Subjacency Condition and the SSC. For example, a single, postcyclic application of *wh* Movement in (39a) will cause the *wh*-element to cross two cyclic nodes; the movement in (39b) contravenes the SSC. But if we make *wh* Movement exceptional to these constraints, we are left with no way to characterize the ungrammaticality of (39c).

(39)   a.   *who do you want* [PRO *to hear* [*stories about t*]$_{NP}$]$_{\bar{S}}$

      b.   *who do you think* [*John saw t*]

      c.   *who do you want [PRO *to hear* [*John's stories about t*]$_{NP}$]

Making *wh* Movement postcyclic and therefore exceptional to Subjacency and the SSC is a high price to pay. Only if the rule is successive cyclic and subject to Subjacency can Chomsky's proposals stand for subsuming so much under it, and successive cyclicity is essential if Ross's Complex NP Constraint, Coordinate Structure Constraint, and *wh* Island Constraints are to be just special cases of Subjacency. To illustrate, consider infinitival relatives such as (40a), which Chomsky proposes to derive by application of *wh* Movement with subsequent deletion of the *wh*-element as in (40b).

(40)   a.   *he is looking for a man to build a pyramid*

      b.   *he is looking for a man* [[*wh*]$_{COMP}$ *t to build a pyramid*]

(41)   a.   **what are you looking for a man to build*

      b.   [ ]$_{COMP}$ *you are looking for* [*a man* [[*wh*$_i$]$_{COMP}$*t$_i$ to build wh$_j$*]$_{\bar{S}}$]$_{NP}$

If *wh* Movement is successive cyclic and subject to Subjacency, (41a) will be blocked: *wh$_j$* cannot move to the highest COMP in (41b) without violating Subjacency. If *wh* Movement is to be postcyclic, it will clearly not be subject to Subjacency or the SSC and therefore the movement of *wh$_j$* will have to be blocked by a not otherwise needed *wh* Island Constraint. Such illustrations can be multiplied by examining the so-called rules of Comparative Deletion, Topicalization, Relativization, Clefting, etc., and showing how the grammar would have to include not only the Subjacency Condition, but also Ross's constraints above, stated separately—an undesirable complication. Some alternatives suggest themselves, although none are wholly satisfactory.[11]

(a)   Under the EQUI-hypothesis let the designated element to be deleted include the *t* in COMP, *[(t) for X-self]*, an effective but surely ad hoc move.

(b)   Postulate that *wh* Movement, unlike NP Preposing as discussed in section 2.1, leaves behind a trace only on the first application of the rule. Again, stated in this form, this is quite ad hoc. However, Chomsky (cf. this volume) has outlined just such a proposal but formulated it in a non-ad hoc fashion. The proposal views a trace as a preterminal element, essentially a coindexing device (as we viewed PRO in section 2.2). A trace left by the first application of *wh* Movement will be spelled out as a variable in LF, but not a trace left in an intermediate (COMP) position. Thus the surface structure (42a) will be mapped into the partial LF (42b), but only the original trace is realized as a variable (Chomsky, 1975c, p. 35).

(42)   a.   *who$_i$ did you tell Bill$_j$* [[t_i]$_{COMP}$ PRO$_j$ *to visit* t_i]
       b.   *for which person x, you told Bill, Bill to visit x*

So in LF the right distinctions are made: a *t* in COMP will not appear as a variable, which is a terminal element. Chomsky proposes that *to* Adjunction and other rules should have access to this distinction: the rule will be blocked by terminal material intervening between *want* and *to*, although some terminal elements may not become such until at least a partial LF has been determined. This raises two major problems: firstly, it weakens the autonomy thesis insofar as a syntactic rule (or perhaps even a phonological rule) will need to "know" what is going on in LF, and secondly it reopens questions about "globality" since *to* Adjunction will have to peek ahead in the derivation to the results of semantic interpretation. We shall return to this point.

(c)   A third and more promising way to make this analysis compatible with a successive-cyclic treatment of *wh* Movement would be to provide no COMP to house the offending trace. One might adopt an analysis along the lines of what Faraci (1974) proposed for various types of purpose clauses, as in (43) and (44) with *wh* Movement applying as indicated.

(43)   [COMP [*I want* [[*for*]$_P$ [PRO *to succeed wh*]$_S$]$_{PP}$]$_S$]$_{\bar{S}}$

(44)   [COMP [*you want* [[*for*]$_P$ [PRO   *to seem* [[*wh*]$_{COMP}$
          PRO *to succeed t*]$_{\bar{S}}$] $_S$]$_{PP}$]$_S$]$_{\bar{S}}$

Faraci (ch. 2) derived *he was hoping to find a good movie* from *he was hoping* [*for* [*to find a good movie*]$_S$]$_{PP}$ on the basis of parallels with *for*-phrases, *he was hoping for a good movie*, and he extended this analysis to other infinitival expressions like *John built a robot to entertain his guests* (cf. *John built a robot for entertainment*). To reinforce this analysis, there is historical evidence that *for* must be a preposition in such constructions and not a COMP. The argument is that if one assumes *for* to be a preposition, one can give a natural account of a cluster of changes taking place simultaneously in late Middle English by showing that they are in fact the surface realizations of a single change in the base component; such an analysis does not seem possible on the assumption that *for* was a COMP, and in that case there would be no way to relate the changes and their simultaneity must be viewed as accidental (for details see Lightfoot, 1976b). There are some difficulties with this analysis; I shall mention three. If all *for*s are prepositions, it is not clear how to derive those in surface subject complement position, *for John to leave would distress me*. Clearly one does not want to permit a base structure $[PP \ VP]_S$, so the PP would have to be moved into subject position by transformation, perhaps by Emonds' (1972b) Subject Replacement or "Intraposition." Secondly, since PPs can normally occur in cleft constructions, something will have to block **it is (for) to see a movie that I want*. Joe Emonds pointed out at the conference that his *for*-phrase Formation rule provides an alternative analysis treating *for* as a transformationally derived preposition and that this may avoid these problems. Thirdly, if the analysis is to be compatible with the Subjacency Condition, S must be treated as a noncyclic node. If S were a cylic node, then the movement in (43) and (44) would violate Subjacency. It is clear that $\bar{\bar{S}}$ and $\bar{S}$ (I assume phrase structure rules $\bar{\bar{S}} \to TOP$ $\bar{S}$, $\bar{S} \to COMP \ S$) must be cyclic, but the evidence is conflicting on the status of S. For example, if S is cyclic, then all COMP-to-COMP movements of *wh* elements will violate Subjacency in its present form.

(45) $[[\ ]_{COMP} \ [\cdots [[wh]_{COMP} \cdots]_{\bar{S}}]_S]_{\bar{S}}$

On the other hand it has been claimed that S needs to be cyclic if **John, I wonder who saw* is to be blocked by Subjacency (assuming Chomsky's reanalysis of topicalized sentences as special cases of *wh* Movement). If only $\bar{S}$ and $\bar{S}$ are cyclic nodes, Subjacency will not block the movement indicated in (46). However, the movement in (46) will also be blocked by the SSC, even by our proposed revision above, whereby a trace but not a PRO will count as a syntactically specified subject. In which case, if such movements will always be blocked by the SSC instead of by Subjacency, we may well be able to claim that S is not cyclic; this seems plausible.

(46) $[[John]_{TOP} [[\ ]_{COMP} \ [I \ wonder \ [[who_i]_{COMP} \ [t_i \ saw \ wh]_S]_{\bar{S}}]_S]_{\bar{S}}]_{\bar{\bar{S}}}$

A serious problem, however, emerges with the sentences of (47).

(47)   a.   **the men want Bill to see each other*
        b.   **the men want Bill to see themselves*
        c.   *the men want Bill to see them*

Only if [*Bill to see . . .*] is dominated by a cyclic node will *each* Interpretation, Reflexive, and R.I. be blocked by the current version of the SSC. There, if one adopts an analysis such as (43) and claims S to be noncyclic, there will be no currently available method of blocking (47a) and (47b), and (47c) will be starred incorrectly by RI. See Chomsky's paper in this volume for further discussion of this question.

We have outlined three solutions to the problem of distinguishing traces in COMP from traces in "subject" position. The first and third solutions essentially avoid the problem of drawing such a distinction in that in each case there is no offending trace in COMP at the time that *to* Adjunction might apply or at surface structure. These two solutions can therefore stand whether the conditions hold on rule applicability or on the interpretability of surface structures. The second solution, however, needs more discussion.

If the SSC is a condition on rule applicability, then under the second solution, globality will be introduced since the SSC will block *to* Adjunction only if there is intervening between *want* and *to* either lexical material or a variable that is to occur later in LF. The structures for the two readings of *who do you want to succeed* will be (48) at the point that *to* Adjunction might apply.

(48)   a.   *who$_i$ you$_j$ want* $[[t_i]_{COMP}$ PRO$_j$ *to succeed* $t_i]$
       b.   *who$_i$ you want* $[[t_i]_{COMP}$ t_i *to succeed*$]$

Under this proposal the traces and the PRO are preterminal elements and therefore "invisible" to the structural description of *to* Adjunction. However, the rule can be blocked from applying to (48b) if it is known that either of the traces will be spelled out as a variable in LF, as in fact will happen with the subject trace: for which person x, you want x to succeed. This globality problem can be avoided by viewing the SSC as a "well-formedness" condition on derivations. At the end of the derivation, it will be clear whether *to* Adjunction has taken place. It will also be known whether a subject of *to succeed* has been spelled out in LF. Let us assume that if a logical variable does occur, the SSC, a well-formedness condition, will be able to detect a violation and will assign *. This treats *to* Adjunction as a kind of interpretive rule but it avoids the globality problem. However, it will fail to handle the contraction data, since LF will not make the right distinctions. If the LF of (48b) is (49b), then presumably the LF of (48a) will be (49a).

(49)   a.   *for which person x, you want* $\left\{ \begin{array}{c} self \\ you \end{array} \right\}$ *to succeed x*

       b.   *for which person x, you want x to succeed*

Notice that this is a claim about LF, which will hold whether one adopts the EQUI-hypothesis or the PRO-analysis (section 2.2). If in LF material intervenes between *want* and *to* for both the subject and object readings, a derivation will be blocked in either case if *to* Adjunction has applied. What is needed is a level of representation where (48b) is characterized as having an embedded subject while (48a) does not. This will not be LF, under the ususal assumptions[12]; it will be surface structure given either my revision of the SSC above or the EQUI-hypothesis. However, the same level of representation must also distinguish a trace in COMP from traces elsewhere, where only the latter can be "visible." LF makes that distinction, but surface structures do not. The problem is that there seems to be no single level of representation that makes both distinctions. We can conclude from this that, under the second solution outlined, if the SSC is to be a condition on rule applicability, globality will be introduced of an undesirable kind; if it is to be a condition on the "interpretability" of surface structures, the right distinctions will not be made.

In section 2 we have demonstrated the attractiveness of a trace-based account of *to* contraction and considered a variety of solutions for two problems that arise within that account. From section 2.2 we may conclude that if a language learner cannot distinguish between two phonologically null elements *t* and PRO, he will be driven to a more complicated analysis of *to* contraction than would be available if such a distinction were made. From section 2.3 we conclude that a language learner endowed with the SSC as a condition on the interpretability of surface structures will be free to select a grammar incorporating "solutions" (a) or (c), but not (b), which is in some ways the most attractive of the three solutions; whereas a language learner endowed with the SSC as a condition on rule applicability will be able to select either (a), (b) or (c), but (b) would entail an undesirable kind of globality. We have entertained only a small set of the possible assumptions, but I hope to have demonstrated that there are empirical issues here: collapsing *t* and PRO and interpreting the SSC as a surface structure condition force us into grammars that give less compelling accounts of the *to* contraction data. This does not mean that the SSC cannot hold of surface structure interpretability. Such a question could not be resolved on the basis of a limited phenomenon. After all, the trace-based account of *to* contraction may not be correct, even though it is superior to Bresnan's Ordering Hypothesis. For example, one might argue, as suggested in section 2.2, that the facts be handled by subcategorization restrictions on complement types, whereby *have, be supposed, use(d)*, etc., must be followed by a VP complement and *want* may be followed by either a VP or a $\bar{S}$. This would avoid the need for either the EQUI-hypothesis or making PRO a nonterminal element (with the concomitant revision of the SSC). There are various problems with such an account but it might be made to work.[13] However the logic of this section has been to take Bresnan's analysis of *to* contraction and to show that appealing to trace theory has desirable consequences for the analysis and illustrates empirical differences in the two views of traces under consideration. Independently of the correctness of Bresnan's analysis, I hope to have clarified what is involved in choosing between these two views of traces.

3.1   Chomsky (1973, p. 247) formulated the Subjacency Condition as a constraint on extraction rules, so one·might expect to motivate a distinction between extraction and other rules on this basis, a distinction that is obliterated if *t* and PRO are to be collapsed and cyclic NP-movement rules abolished. In other words, if the Subjacency Condition is correct there will have to be some way of characterizing the class of rules to which it applies, distinguishing *t* from PRO would permit such a characterization. However, given Chomsky's recent proposals for making NP Preposing and *wh* Movement the core of English syntax, subsuming under these two rules what had been treated as many different rules, it may be possible to modify the Subjacency Condition in a way consistent with collapsing *t* and PRO.

Structures such as (50) and (51) have been taken to indicate that Reflexive, RI, and *each* Movement/Interpretation are not sensitive to Subjacency.

(50)   a. *John wants* [PRO *to try* [PRO *to begin* [PRO *to wash himself*]]]

        b. **I want* [PRO *to try* [PRO *to begin* [PRO *to wash me*]]]

        c. *the men want* [PRO *to try* [PRO *to begin* [PRO*to wash each other*]]]

(51)   a. *John told* [*stories about* [*pictures of himself*]]

        b. **I told* [*stories about* [*pictures of me*]]

        c. *the men told* [*stories about* [*pictures of each other*]]

wh Movement, however, is subject to Subjacency for the reasons given in section 2.3. On the other hand, NP Preposing will never interact crucially with Subjacency if given a SD. np V NP; even if NP Preposing were formulated with a variable between the two NP positions (5), incorrect derivations can always be ruled out without appeal to Subjacency. Consider some examples: *John was expected to appear to win* would normally be derived from an initial phrase marker like (52) by two successive applications of NP Preposing.

(52) np_1 *was expected* [np_2 *to appear* [*John to win*]]

However, if *John* were to move directly to the highest np, violating Subjacency, the empty NP subject of *to appear* would not be filled at any point in the derivation and the derivation would be ruled out by Emonds' theory of empty nodes. If np_2 contained lexical material, the derivation would be ruled out by the SSC, whether that condition holds of rule applicability or interpretability. The one remaining possibility is with np_2 containing PRO. In this case, the resulting surface structure will be (53), which can be interpreted by normal rules with both PRO and *t* associated with *John*; the LF will specify correctly that *John* is the subject of *be expected . . ., to appear . . .* and *to win*.

(53) $John_i$ *was expected* [PRO *to appear* [t_i *to win*]]

(54) $John_i$ *was persuaded Bill* [PRO *to appear* [t_i *to win*]]

If PRO were controlled by something other than *John*, as in the analogous surface structure (54), the derivation would be ruled out by the SSC. Consequently, I cannot imagine any bad application of NP Preposing where one would need to appeal to Subjacency and where independently required mechanisms would not suffice to rule it out. Note further that NP Preposing will never apply to a NP contained within a larger NP, as in (55). Such derivations would be blocked by the A-over-A Condition and therefore have nothing to do with Subjacency.

(55)   a. **John seems to read* [*stories about t*]$_{NP}$

        b. **John was read* [*stories about t*]$_{NP}$

If this is correct, Subjacency would hold only of the generalized *wh* Movement (subsuming the so-called rules of Topicalization, Clefting, Comparative Deletion, etc.). In that case, Subjacency could be collapsed with the COMP-to-COMP condition and made into a condition on the interpretability of an element in COMP such

that it may be coreferential only with an abstract element within its cyclic domain
or with an element in a lower COMP. By "within its cyclic domain" I mean within
the same $\bar{S}$ as the wh-element (wh-elements will occur only in COMP) and separated
from the $\bar{S}$-node by no more than one intervening NP-node. This will suffice to distinguish the sentences of (56).

(56)   a.   *who did you meet t*
        b.   *who did you see [pictures of t]* NP
        c.   **who did you hear [stories about [pictures of t]*NP] NP

If such a view can be sustained, the phenomena handled by the Subjacency Condition will not require the grammar to distinguish *t* from PRO.

4.1   In several papers (Lightfoot, 1974, 1975, 1976b,d, forthcoming), I have
argued that theories of grammar can be made responsible to diachronic change and
that diachronic analyses can provide much insight into ways of restricting further
the activities of the transformational subcomponent. I am particularly interested in
sets of apparently unrelated changes that occur simultaneously, and I assume that
we should prefer a grammar in which the apparently unrelated changes can be
viewed as the consequence of a single change in the abstract system, perhaps the
introduction of a new deep structure category, a new phrase structure rule, a new
transformation, etc. Predictions can be made about possible changes in a given
grammar and these predicitons will be based on the form of the particular grammar,
the general theory of grammar and a few basic statements about the nature of
change. The theory of *grammar* will specify that G_p and G_q are possible grammars
of natural language and a theory of *change* will specify whether G_p and G_q can be
"adjacent" to each other, e.g., whether G_p could hold of the parent's language and
G_q of the child's. It is important to note that the distinction between possible and
impossible changes cannot be based on the formal properties of "rules" relating
G_p and G_q, although most of the current work on language change assumes some
such notion of 'diachronic processes' whose formal properties can be characterized.
I think that this is an entirely fallacious view and a legacy of neogrammarian theories
of change, but the view seems to be almost universally assumed in various forms.
If we concentrate our attention on sets of simultaneous changes and seek grammars
that can relate these changes, we find that grammars within the broad framework of
the Extended Standard Theory provide a good basis for discussing change. However,
the interesting thing from the standpoint of a theory of grammar is that we gain
insight into the "load" that can be borne by the transformational subcomponent. A
radical restructuring will take place when the burden on the transformational subcomponent becomes excessive. To illustrate, consider the history of items like *may,
must, shall, can*, modals in modern English (NE) (Lightfoot, 1974). In Old English
(OE) their syntactic behavior was identical to that of verbs and so there was no
reason to distinguish a deep structure category of modal. However, during the
Middle English (ME) period some changes took place at different times in different

parts of the grammar and the effect of these changes was to distinguish the "pre-modals" from the other verbs. The grammar continued to treat them as verbs, but this necessitated special statements for some rules. These special statements became more numerous until the sixteenth century, when a whole series of changes took place together, all of which follow from saying that *may, must*, etc., were now reanalyzed as a new category distinct from "verb." The evidence for the reanalysis is the simultaneity of the changes. When one looks at several such reanalyses, one sees that the effect is that the transformations are simplified. I have therefore formulated a Transparency Principle which specifies that deep structures must stay fairly close to their corresponding surface structures; transformations cannot carry a great burden. To put it differently, language learners are not capable of construct-ing systems with an elaborate transformational subcomponent, where the deep structures are "far-removed" from their corresponding surface structures. Examin-ing these radical reanalyses can tell us about the load the transformations can bear; the point at which the reanalyses occur will define the upper limits to that load. So data from certain diachronic changes, those involving radical restructuring, provide a window on the language learner's tolerance level for deep structure opacity. Ideally, after examining many such reanalyses, we should be able to quantify this tolerance level in some way. This, in brief, is the view of syntactic change that lies behind my studies of such radical changes. Language learners practice therapy rather than prophylaxis; they perform changes at various points in their grammars without realizing prudently the problems they are creating elsewhere. The point at which therapy becomes necessary tells us about their limits, and the therapy is revealed when one looks at grammars diachronically. One need hardly emphasize the diffi-culties in making claims about the grammar of, say, OE, but it seems to me that if we look at it in this way, there is much to be gained for the theory of grammar. The Transparency Principle will constitute part of the theory of *grammar*, but we shall arrive at it primarily through the study of change.

4.2   With this perspective on the study of syntax diachronically, let us assume for a moment that the grammar of NE has a rule of NP Preposing, as specified in (5). One may ask how this rule was introduced historically. There seems to be no motivation for the rule in the grammars of the earliest stages of English, as we shall see below, so it must have been introduced at some point. It could have been intro-duced in a number of ways: it might have sprung fully armed from the thigh of Zeus, as it were; it might have developed first as a restricted rule, gradually extend-ing its range of application in some principled way; it might have developed first as a non-structure-preserving rule applying only in root Ss and then been assimilated gradually into the grammar, acquiring the more restrictive properties of a standard transformational rule. No doubt there are further possibilities. The second possi-bility outlined would represent a curious development from the point of view of the theory presupposed in this paper, which claims that transformational rules are few in number, maximally simple and general, but subject to severe general constraints on their form and function. In fact, it seems that the first and simplest case holds, that the rule was introduced to the grammar of some stage of English in more or less its present form. Hence the argument for the correctness of NP Preposing is this: saying that there is such a rule and that the rule was introduced at some point yields an explanation for a set of diverse changes occurring simultaneously in the history of English. At this stage of English the grammar changed to yield a new output; positing the introduction of NP Preposing (5) gives an account of the simultaneity of the changes in the output. That is, the properties related by NP Preposing also cluster together in their diachronic development. To fully substantiate this would take more time and more data than I have available, but I hope to present enough material to show the plausibility of the claim.

(a)   The first piece of evidence concerns impersonal verbs later reanalyzed as personals (discussed in detail in Lightfoot, 1976d). *Hine hungreð,* lit. 'to him it hungers', becomes *he hungers; me (dative) thynketh I heare* becomes *I think that I hear; the king liceden peares,* lit. 'to the king were pleasing pears' where *peares* is nominative and *the king* originally a dative, becomes *the king liked pears.* Notice that *like* also undergoes a semantic shift from 'to cause pleasure' to 'to receive pleasure'. For the earliest stage, when English has an underlying SOV order, we may postulate (57) as the relevant initial phrase markers. See Lightfoot (1975) for arguments for generating logical sentential subjects in the rightmost position of the VP for this stage of English. In (57b) a rule of NP Postposing would move *pears* to the right.

(57)   a.

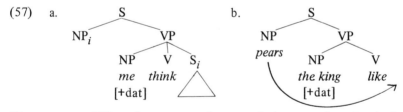

We may posit (58) as the corresponding initial phrase markers for the later stage, after English had adopted underlying SVO order but before the reanalysis and semantic shift had taken place.

(58)   a.

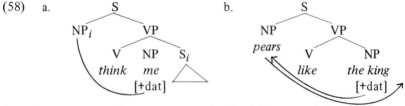

In order to generate the sentences *me thynketh I heare* and *the king liceden peares*, a rule would be needed to move *me* and *the king* into preverbal position, as indicated above. One can see that the derivation of *the king liceden peares* from an underlying sequence *peares liceden the king* (58b) would be opaque to the language learner, and difficult to figure out. However, such a preposing rule was available, and it was NP Preposing. NP Preposing was not involved with these verbs until the SOV→SVO base change had taken effect. At this stage NP Preposing served to move *me* in structures like (58a) and *the king* in (58b). After the reanalysis of these verbs, whereby they become "personal," being derived from structures like (59), NP Preposing was no longer involved. Hence NP Preposing applied in these constructions only during the late ME period.

(59) a.   b.

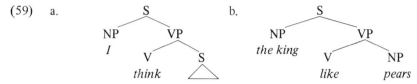

(b)   I turn now to the most difficult case, which is the role of NP Preposing in passive constructions. Under familiar assumptions about the grammar of NE, the rule moves the postverbal NP into the empty subject position. At the earliest stages of English, however. when the base order was SOV, there was no reason to invoke a preposing rule. Keenan (1975) claims that it is a universal principle that the Passive transformation in an OV language is not a movement rule. Also it seems to be a plausible constraint on transformational rules that no rule can be formulated such that it will only change structure without reordering (Lightfoot, 1976a), which would eliminate the possibility of a rule changing (60) into (61). This constraint is implicit in work as early as Chomsky (1965), which restricted transformations to operations of deletion, permutation, substitution, and addition. Even such a loose definition of transformations would not permit a rule to be formulated that would map (60) into (61).[14]

(60)   (61)

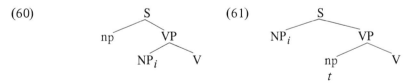

Therefore NP Preposing could be involved in the derivation of passive sentences only after the SOV→SVO base change. Canale (in preparation) dates this change in the late twelfth century. From this point onwards, passive sentences *could* be generated by means of NP Preposing or they could be base-generated. Strong evidence for a movement analysis in NE concerns "idiom chunks," but I have no data on the behavior of idiom chunks in ME with respect to passive sentences. However, clear evidence for movement also comes from corresponding nominals, such as *Rome's destruction*. At all stages of English the "object" of NPs has been generated postnominally, i.e., *destruction of Rome*, even in the SOV period. However, one finds these nouns being preposed only from late ME. The earliest case I know of is *he [deofol] tihte þæra luseiscra manna heortan to Christes slege* 'to the slaying of Christ', Aelfric 1.26, but they start to occur readily only in Chaucer and then

Shakespeare uses them very productively, including with many nouns that no longer tolerate preposing in NE. Jespersen (V 7.5_4) cites several examples: *I burn with thy desire*, (='desire for thee') H6A I 2.108, *least I be suspected of your carriage from the court*, (='of carrying you from the court') Cymb. IV 4.190, *In my despite*, (= 'despite me') Tit. 1.361, *thou didst denie the golds receit*, Err II 2.17, *a great man's memory may outliue his life half a year*, Hml III 2.140. Meanwhile subject NPs had occurred in prenominal possessive form from earliest records, *the Goths' destruction of Rome*. Despite cutting some corners in the discussion, we seem to be justified in claiming that NP Preposing first occurs in the derivation of passive structures in late ME.

(c)   A similar story lies behind causative and "middle" constructions, *ice melts t, the book sells t well*. Under the trace theory of movement rules, these sentences have a (simplified) initial phrase marker as in (62).

(62)   a.   b.

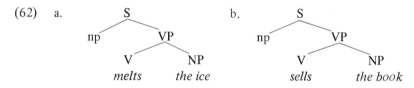

If the subject NPs are lexically filled in the initial phrase marker, a causative and agentive reading will be derived from (a) and (b) respectively: *Fred melts the ice, Fred sells the book*. Again when the underlying structure in the language was SOV, there would have been .no motivation for a movement rule, whether one adopts Keenan's assumptions or the constraint on the form of transformations that no rule may only change structure without reordering elements. Therefore, NP Preposing would not have played a role in the derivation of these constructions until after the late 12th century, i.e., after the base change of SOV to SVO. Sweet labels sentences like *the book sells well, the door doesn't lock*, "passivals." Visser (section 1914) characterizes these as Present-Day English expressions, but they certainly were very productive in ENE and Shakespeare uses the construction with many verbs that will not tolerate it today: *one of our French wither'd peares, it lookes ill, it eates drily*, Alls I 1.176; *thy glasse will shew thee how thy beauties **wear***, Sonn. 77.1 (see Jespersen, III, 16.8, for a long list of such constructions). Therefore NP Preposing became involved with these types sometime between 1200 and Shakespearian English. This is consistent with the general claim that the rule developed in late ME, but I do not have sufficient data to make a more precise claim about the first instance of these constructions after the establishment of the SVO base order. The causative/de-causative relationship (*Fred melts the ice/the ice melts*) also enjoyed its most productive period in the 16th century. Caxton uses as causatives *cease* (*I ceased him* = 'I caused him to cease') *learn, possess* (= 'put in possession'), *succumb* (= 'subject'), *sit* (='set'), *tarry* (= 'delay'), etc. Similarly Shakespeare uses many verbs as causatives where this is no longer possible: *decrease, fall, fear, fly, increase, issue, perish, remember, sup*, etc. In earlier English, of course, the causative/de-causative relation had been indicated by ablaut, which survives in pairs such as *fell-fall, set-sit.* Therefore, as with the "passivals," one can motivate a NP Preposing analysis of decausitives after the establishment of the new SVO base order and after the loss of ablaut as a productive signal for causative verbs. But the analysis would be well motivated by the time of Caxton and Shakespeare. Again I do not have sufficient data on the intervening period to establish the date more precisely.

(d)   Subject-to-subject raising cases like *John seems* [*t to be happy*] have been discussed by Kageyama (1975). Kageyama distinguishes two putative rules: Subject Raising into Object Position and Raising to Subject position (RS). He claims, with Traugott (1972, p. 152), that RS did not exist in OE, but was established in late ME. According to Jespersen (1909-1949 III, Ch. 11) constructions such as *John happened to come, John chanced to come, John was certain to come* all arise for the first time in late ME. *He is sure to come* did occur from earlier times but under the meaning that 'he was sure that he would come', cf. *he was eager to please*, where a deletion analysis would be appropriate but not a preposing rule. Jespersen distinguishes two lines of development for "RS verbs": verbs such as *happen, seem, chance*, were impersonal verbs taking a dative object, as discussed above, unlike *sure, certain, unlikely*, where there was never a dative "experiencer." Therefore it may be the case that the subject-raising constructions with *sure*, etc., developed under the influence of types like *John happened to leave*. The development of *John happened to leave* was part of the demise of the impersonal verbs already discussed. Notice that if *John happened to leave* results from the application of NP Preposing, *John* must be moved not from the dative position but from the subject of the lower clause. Crucial evidence exists in sentences where the dative and embedded subject are not coreferential (63). Here the dative cannot be preposed: **he happened that his life was ended.*

(63)   a.   *þa gelamp **him** þæt his lif wearð geendod*, 'then happened him that his life was ended', OE Blick. Hom X.

       b.   *me þyncheð þæt me fæder nis no whit felle*, 'it seems to me that my father is not . . .', c1205 Layamon 3290.

       c.   *it chaunced **him** that as he passed through Oxfoorde, the schollars picked a quarrell unto his servauntes*, 1568 Grafton: OED.

The properties related by the rule of NP Preposing behave alike from the viewpoint of historical change; they enter the language simultaneously. There is much more to be said before I can make this claim with conviction, but the evidence presented is sufficient to indicate the plausibility of the hypothesis. The historical data discussed here constitutes support for a grammar relating the cluster of properties handled by NP Preposing. However, if NP Preposing did spring fully armed into the grammar of late ME, we should ask why. Can it be viewed as a function of the Transparency Principle? Various possibilities suggest themselves but I find none of them totally satisfactory. The role of NP Preposing with impersonal verbs is an indirect consequence of the earlier SOV→SVO change, and its role in passives, de-causatives and "passivals" is more directly related to the earlier word order change. However, its role in subject-to-subject raising seems to bear no relationship to the order of major constituents. But these are questions which can be postponed.

Let us return now to the two questions posed at the outset. The simultaneity of the changes discussed can be captured by claiming that a rule of NP Preposing was introduced in late ME. Consider now the alternative view of grammar: that there is no distinction between t and PRO, that the conditions hold of rules relating surface structures to logical forms and, in particular, that abstract elements are base-generated, there being no cyclic NP movement rules. Assuming such a theory of grammar, it is difficult to see how the simultaneity of these changes can be interpreted. It is not the case that a new interpretive rule is introduced whereby NP_i ... t_i now becomes an interpretable structure. Such structures were always interpretable, as in (64), and, in any case, the rule associating an abstract element with a full NP is generally supposed to be a special case of what Fiengo (1974) calls an Overrule, as would be involved in (65). In (64) I use t for the abstract symbol collapsing what would be t and PRO in other theories, such as that in section 2.2.

(64)   a.   *John$_i$ wants t$_i$ to leave*
        b.   *John persuaded Bill$_i$ t$_i$ to leave*
        c.   *who$_i$ did you see t$_i$*

(65)   a.   *the candidates voted for each other*
        b.   *the candidates voted for themselves*

In other words, the theory that allows a transformation like NP Preposing permits the distinction needed to capture the changes above; the changes are more easily interpretable within such as framework. It is not clear how such a distinction would be made in a theory that did not distinguish t and PRO or allow cyclic NP-movement rules. Therefore, on the assumption that grammars should be made responsible to diachronic data in the manner indicated in section 4.1, we have shown again that the choice between the alternatives outlined in section 1.1 has empirical consequences: in this case, one supports a superior account of a certain set of changes in the history of English.

Notes

*   This work was partially supported by Canada Council research grant S74-1936. Much of the material in section 2 develops proposals in Lightfoot (1976c), which discusses the same data although it addresses different theoretical questions. Material in section 4.2 is drawn from Lightfoot (1976d). Throughout the paper abstract structures will be given only in simplified form, omitting such details as tense markers, possessives, etc., and containing only information which is crucial to the discussion in hand. I am grateful to Noam Chomsky, Richard Kayne and Jean-Yves Morin for useful discussion.

1. I shall not follow Bresnan strictly nor shall I argue for the very minor differences in formulation of her rule and deep structures.

2. Selkirk (1972, pp. 121–129) also revised Bresnan's treatment of *to* Adjunction by using a notion of "traces." However, her analysis differs from the one adopted here in that the *to* Adjunction data was not used as crucial evidence to support her "traces convention"; the convention was motivated on other grounds and proved applicable to this area and an alternative to Bresnan's description. Furthermore, Selkirk had a notion of "word boundary traces" that she claimed (p. 73) to be quite different from "pronominal traces which are motivated by the syntax" (i.e., traces of the type used here and by Chomsky, Fiengo, and Wasow). The most important differences are that word boundary traces mark "removal sites" (i.e., gaps resulting from the application of *either a deletion or movement rule*), and that they were taken to be "invisible" to all transformations, to be unable to figure in the proper analysis of a string (p. 128). We shall argue below that to handle the *to*-contraction data it is crucial that the grammar distinguish the residue of a movement rule from what may be viewed as the residue of a deletion rule or a semantically interpreted but phonologically null element such as PRO, and that a trace be "visible."

3. Somebody might suggest the following way for Bresnan to avoid the ordering paradox. (ii) and (iii) seem to indicate that the boldfaced portion of (i) is an island, and therefore adjunction of *to* to *used* would be blocked by island constraints.

   (i)   *a Nikon was used to take a picture of the man*

   (ii) *the man who a Nikon was used to take a picture of ___ was tall

   (iii) *Fred, a Nikon was used to take a picture of ___

   Such an analysis assumes the validity of "island constraints," which I dispute. Following Chomsky's reanalysis (1975) of the putative rules of Topicalization, Clefting, *tough* Movement, etc., as special cases of *wh* Movement, then the usual "island" phenomena (e.g., Ross, 1967) can be subsumed under the Subjacency Condition (see Chomsky, this volume, for details; for Subjacency, see Chomsky, 1973, (196)). Application of *to* Adjunction on a structure corresponding to (i) would not be blocked by Subjacency. This analysis is controversial, but attractive from many points of view (see section 2.3 for more discussion).

4. The difference is that Bresnan claims that epistemic verbs take no complementizer, whereas I follow a slight revision made by Chomsky (1974, this volume), and claim that they have an empty complementizer. This is necessary in order to be consistent with the proposal, to be discussed later, that COMP provides an "escape hatch" for *wh*-elements. The empty COMP will be a preterminal element and therefore "invisible" to rules such as Passive (or Adjective Formation, see note 6).

5. See Lightfoot (1976a) for more details of this analysis, which dispenses with the usual Raising rule. Paul Schachter has pointed out two problems for this analysis: the acceptability of *John was desired to do it* in certain dialects (the OED cites some examples) and the fact that *mean* and *intend* are passivisable (*John was meant to do it*) although they take a *for* complementizer (*I meant for John to do it*).

6. This argument assumes (with Bresnan, 1971) that there is a rule of Passive. If instead passive sentences are generated by rules of Agent Postposing and NP Preposing, then we might establish the ordering paradox by arguing that NP Preposing must precede Complementizer Deletion and therefore *to* Adjunction. Chomsky (personal communication) points out that this will follow only if either (a) NP Preposing applies only to immediately postverbal NPs, or (b) Bresnan's Fixed Subject Constraint is correct, i.e., the *for* blocks the preposing rule. (a) is probably wrong if the rule is to be generalized to other construction types such as "*tough* Movement" sentences, and Chomsky argues that also (b) cannot be right. In which case the constraint that in passives the moved NP must originate in postverbal position could be expressed by an Adjective Formation rule, that *-en* can make an adjective out of V + *t*. Thus any effort to 'passivize' after *for* will yield a structure from which no adjective

be formed, *V for t*. If that analysis is correct, then Adjective Formation would have to precede Complementizer Deletion, and NP Preposing, of course, would precede Adjective Formation: the required ordering will be NP Preposing – Adjective Formation – Complementizer Deletion – *to* Adjunction, whereas a non-trace account of (12a) would require *to* Adjunction to precede NP Preposing. Hence there will be an ordering paradox whether one thinks in terms of a Passive rule or a very general rule of NP Preposing. This rule is also involved in the derivation of structures corresponding to passive sentences (*the ice was melted t*), subject raising (*John seems t to be popular*), nominals (*Rome's destruction t*, possibly even *yesterday's lecture t*) and 'middle' constructions (*the book reads t easily*), as discussed in section 4.

7. I ignore here the irrelevant question of whether this is better formulated as a deletion rule, as argued by Lasnik and Fiengo (1974). If one assumes the trace theory of movement rules (as they did not), Jackendoff's (1975) refutation of Lasnik and Fiengo goes through with pleasant consequences, and avoids the need for end-of-cycle semantic interpretation. In any case, more recent work by Chomsky shows that the data handled by a rule of *tough* Movement/Object Deletion can be subsumed under *wh* Movement, as we shall discuss in a moment.

8. If this revision of the SSC is correct it will provide a diagnostic for syntactic and semantic rules. Fiengo and Lasnik (1976) formulate a syntactic rule of Quantifier Floating which seems to be sensitive to what we have called the semantic definition of a specified subject. They do not argue against the possibility of treating this as an interpretive rule and I see no reason not to formulate it in such a way.

9. The Old French data is from Morin (1975), who uses it to make a different claim.

10. There are, after all, alternative analyses; for one example see the end of section 2.3. Chomsky (personal communication) suggests a slight variant on the above, whereby one views *to* Adjunction as a kind of interpretive rule, which would associate *to* with the lower verb. Like all interpretive rules, it will be subject to the usual conditions. We could then argue that it applied (under the EQUI-hypothesis) after the rules associating (NP, *t*) (or, more generally, the rules specifying bound anaphora) but before the rule filling in the "logical subject" where EQUI has applied, assuming these to be distinct interpretive rules. This raises many questions, but it would be consistent with viewing the conditions as holding of the rules relating surface structures to logical form, and not as holding of derivations.

11. Notice that it is not a solution to say that it will take *two* intervening traces to block Adjunction, the first of which would be in COMP. That would suffice to distinguish (48a) and (48b), where only (48a) may undergo Adjunction. However it will not block the rule from applying to (12d).

12. Consider also the sentences of (i)–(iii) and the corresponding (partial) LFs.

(i) *what do you want to melt* (object reading)   (*wanna*)
for what thing$_x$, you want self to melt x

(ii) *who do you want to be arrested by?*   (*wanna*)
for what person$_x$, you want x to arrest self

(iii) *who do you want to be arrested?*   (**wanna*)
for what person$_x$, you want $\left\{ \begin{array}{c} self \\ somebody \end{array} \right\}$ *to arrest x*

The problem in (i) is as in (49), but (iii) has a similar LF and cannot undergo Adjunction. The LF of (ii) would predict incorrectly that Adjunction could not apply because in LF a variable, i.e., a terminal element, intervenes between *want* and *to*. Again wrong predictions are made. However, the correct form of LF is an empirical issue and not a matter for stipulation; the usual assumptions may be wrong. For example, one might claim that LF may contain passive verbs and that the LF of (ii) is: *for what person$_x$, you want self to be arrested by x*. If correct, this reduces the problem to the status of *self* in LF.

13. Presumably PRO would now be a freely occurring item, so there would be a minor problem in eliminating the possibility of an initial phrase marker *John wants for PRO to go*, in addition to *John* [*wants* [*to go*] VP] VP. However, under the subcategorization analysis one could characterize the change in the behavior of French clitics by saying that in Old French *vouloir* subcategorized a VP or S̄ complement, and in Modern French only a S̄ complement. Similarly Portuguese *querer* would subcategorize a VP or S̄ complement. Kayne has pointed out sentences like *there usta be more trees here then*, which suggest that *used to* takes a VP-complement. But neither subcategorization nor my analysis accounts for the distinction between *I've gotta see Joe tomorrow* versus *I got to (*gotta) see Joe yesterday* (the latter sentence pointed out by Kayne).

14. This may not be an accurate interpretation of the *Aspects* theory. It assumes: (a) that transformations refer only to linear analyses and not to higher structure; (b) that a transformation can perform only one of the four operations listed, particularly that no transformation can simultaneously substitute and delete; and (c) that "permutation" means reordering of two non-null elements. I am not sure that it is fair to attribute these three conditions to the "*Aspects* theory."

COMMENTS ON THE PAPER BY LIGHTFOOT

Joseph Emonds

Department of Linguistics
UCLA
Los Angeles, California

1.   One of the central questions David Lightfoot addresses in his paper is whether the "trace" (t) left by an NP-movement rule should be formally distinguished in linguistic theory from an NP that has no surface realization but can be shown to be present in some underlying representation ("null anaphora"). For purposes of this question, "has no surface realization" can be taken to mean "is transformationally deleted" or "is a phonetically null anaphoric expression present in surface structure." This null anaphoric NP will be notated PRO.

Thus, the question is, are t and PRO in the following pairs formally identical?

(1)   a.   *Wilson$_i$ is certain t$_i$ to leave.* (Subject-raising)
        b.   *Wilson$_i$ is eager PRO$_i$ to leave.* (Equi-NP)

(2)   a.   *Which weapons$_i$ would it have been too insightful for them to have bought t$_i$ for such a crime?*
        b.   *Which weapons$_i$ would be too big for them to have bought PRO$_i$ for such a crime?*

In this volume, Chomsky claims that PRO and t can be considered identical, except for how the co-referential index is assigned. The index of t is assigned when the movement rule applies (during the transformational cycle), and the index of PRO is assigned at the end of the cycle (under an interpretive theory of pronominalization) when the rules of anaphora apply. Elaborating on this somewhat, suppose we take the coreferential index as the minimal specification necessary to make both PRO and t dominate a terminal symbol (that is, we let

$$t = \begin{bmatrix} NP \\ PRO \end{bmatrix}$$
$$\mid$$
$$[i]$$

where t is the trace left by the movement of NP$_i$). It then follows that during the part of a given cycle *after* some transformation has given rise to t_i but *before* the end-of-cycle interpretive anaphora rules assign an index to a base-generated PRO, the syntactic rules will automatically distinguish between t and PRO. PRO will be, during this segment of the derivation, "invisible" to the structural descriptions of transformations, since it is not a terminal symbol, but t will be "visible."

Lightfoot's arguments in section 2.1 do not imply that t and PRO need differ beyond the just-described method of assigning the co-referential index (during the cycle versus at the end of the cycle). Even if the various COMP-substitution rules such as question formation are shown to apply before *to* Adjunction, and an interpretive rule of "Equi-NP" is shown to apply after it, the above method of assigning indices will appropriately distinguish between t and PRO.

One of Lightfoot's points, of course, is to establish that traces are in fact involved, and that Bresnan's ordering solution (which involves three ordered rules: Equi-NP deletion, *to* Adjunction, COMP-substitution) is not a possible alternative account of the data. I do not think he succeeds here, which may mean that even the minimal difference between t and PRO implicit in Chomsky's formulation is unnecessary.

To show that traces are involved with *to* Adjunction, Lightfoot argues that the NP-preposing operation that forms passives must precede *to* Adjunction, and that the traces generated by NP-preposing must block *to* Adjunction just as those left by COMP-substitution rules do. This is the point of his examples (12).

One can object here that *used to = usta* is a fixed form, and that Equi-NP deletion is simply not involved. The objection is sustainable because there is no variation with *usta* according to person and tense. By contrast, there is such variation with *want* and *have*, indicating that the contracted forms of the latter are not just fixed lexical entries:

(3)   *Wilson wanna(s) leave.*
            Wilson wansa leave.

            Wilson hafta(s) leave.
            Wilson hassa leave.
            Wilson hadda leave.

The kind of data Lightfoot is looking for here is in principle difficult to isolate, for it would be necessary to find a case where *to* Adjunction cannot apply to the passive participle of the verb across an extraction site induced by NP-preposing, but *can* apply to the finite or infinitive forms of the same verb. He must furthermore show that *to* Adjunction never applies across such an extraction site.

It seems to me, however, that there are examples of *to* Adjunction applying to passive participles. Of course, it must first be determined what constitutes an instance of *to* Adjunction, a matter that is not gone into carefully in Lightfoot's paper. A plausible position is that this process is responsible for, among other things, the loss of the segment t of the morpheme *to* after a stop or a nasal. In (4a), we could say that two phonological t segments block intervocalic voicing, while in (4b) it seems that the $d+t$ combination leads to a phonetic "long" d or perhaps to just a lengthening of the preceding vowel:

(4)   a. *The automatic cameras that they've got to photograph the
            workers are broken.*
            **The automatic cameras that they've gotta photograph the
            workers are broken.*

        b. *The automatic cameras that they need to photograph the
            workers are broken.*
            **The automatic cameras that they needa photograph the workers
            are broken.*

By contrast, in (5a) there is intervocalic voicing of the single *t* resulting from *to*
Adjunction before the unstressed vowel, and in (5b) there is no lengthening of the
vowel *ee* or the consonent *d*:

(5)   a. *These cameras have gotta (= got to) be able to photograph
            my workers.*
        b. *These cameras needa be able to photograph my workers, not
            just my machines.*

Consider now the passive participles that terminate in *en*; certain contrasts can
be described by, for example, saying that *to* Adjunction can apply to (6a), yielding
(6b), but that the rule cannot apply to (6c):

(6)   a. *They were taken to see a better doctor.*
        b. *They were taken 'a see a better doctor.*
        c. *They were shaken to see such a massacre.*
        d. **They were shaken 'a see such a massacre.*

But it suffices to show a single verb which allows *to* Adjunction over the NP-preposing extraction site, as in (6b), in order to disprove the contention that the trace left
by this rule counts as a terminal symbol in strings to which the structural description of *to* Adjunction applies. (Any lack of generality in the applicability of the
rule can be attributed to its admitted idiomatic nature.)

   Thus, it is doubtful that Lightfoot has an argument that NP-Preposing leaves
a "visible" trace; just the opposite seems to be the case. But then, NP-preposing
must precede *to* Adjunction, and the nonapplicability of this rule in Lightfoot's
(11)-(12) must be described by saying that transitive (literal) *use* does not trigger
to Adjunction.

   We are therefore still free to consider the ordering solution of Bresnan, where
the ordering of transformations is, Equi-NP deletion, NP-preposing, *to* Adjunction,
COMP-substitutions.[1]

2.   The weakness of Lightfoot's section 2.1 means that we cannot take his
account of what blocks *to* Adjunction as more than a well-defined alternative hypothesis to Bresnan's ordering hypothesis. Lightfoot claims that certain syntactic
processes such as *to* Adjunction will treat the extraction sites created by movements and deletions differently (analogously to COMP-substitutions and Equi-NP

deletion, respectively), whereas Bresnan's alternative, which is not weakened by the NP-preposing data, is that processes like *to* Adjunction must precede rules whose syntactic domain includes at least the COMP of the clause affected, and tend to follow processes of smaller domain. If in fact my (6b) is an instance of *to* Adjunction, NP-preposing goes counter to Lightfoot's hypothesis and supports Bresnan's.

When we consider further rules, we find that Bresnan's rather than Lightfoot's predictions are confirmed. According to Lightfoot, we might expect that the movement rule of subject-raising would leave a trace that would block *to* Adjunction, whereas Bresnan's analysis would suggest that subject-raising has the same effect as Equi-NP deletion, since the two rules have essentially the same domain. And the latter situation seems to be the case:

(7)   *Wilson is certain 'a take this hard.*
          We just happen 'a like to write on lots of unrelated topics.

Such a similarity between "Equi-NP deletion" infinitives and "subject-raising" infinitives is consistent with taking either PRO = t in some relevant aspect, or with the position that neither is present in the structures to which *to* Adjunction applies.

Not only can we find movement rules whose effects are comparable to Equi-NP deletion, but we can also find deletion rules with effects similar to the COMP-substitution rules. In (8a) the infinitive following *need* is contracted by *to* Adjunction, as in (5b), and in (8b) the material that undergoes COMP-substitution rules (or the trace left by such rules) blocks *to* Adjunction:

(8)   a.   *We needa fix this car.*
       b.   **Three hours we'll needa fix this car.*
             *How many hours did John needa fix his car?
             *The three hours which we needa fix this car can't be found.

Now in (8c) a deletion rule, or in any case a rule whose domain includes at least the COMP of the clause in which *to* Adjunction could apply, gives rise to an extraction site that blocks this latter rule:

(8)   c.   **Take as much time as these cars needa be fixed.*

Similarly in (8d):

(8)   d.   **We've got as many cameras for snapshots as they've gotta
             photograph the workers.*

The examples in (8) do not argue against Lightfoot's hypothesis if one takes comparatives to be formed by a movement rule, as Chomsky does in this volume. However, it is difficult to establish that a movement rule gives rise to the deletion sites in (9):

(9)   a.   *These weapons would be too big for them to have bought
             ___ to be shipped express.*
       b.   *These weapons would be too big for us to want ___ to
             be shipped express.*

And yet such deletion sites, determined by a rule whose domain includes in fact a higher clause, block *to* Adjunction, as Bresnan's ordering hypothesis would predict:

(10)   *These weapons would be too big for us to wanna be shipped express* (≠ 9b).

Since material deleted by the rule operating in (9) blocks *to* Adjunction like COMP-substitution material does, and since material moved by subject-raising does not block *to* Adjunction any more than Equi-NP deleted subjects do, we can only conclude that Bresnan's ordering solution for the rule of *to* Adjunction, based on the principle of the cycle and making no appeal to traces, is superior to one based on a distinction between *t* and PRO.

In particular, Bresnan seems to have isolated successfully the conditioning factor that blocks *to* Adjunction: if the intervening material in V ___ *to* is removed by a rule whose domain includes at least the COMP of the lowest clause containing V, that material is still present when *to* Adjunction applies, and hence blocks the rule. It can be added that any PRO or *t* in this same position is syntactically null with respect to *to* Adjunction.

3.   To my mind, the most interesting section of Lightfoot's paper is section 2.2, which I do not really think is weakened by the possibility that his argumentation in section 2.1 is incorrect. In this section, he suggests that the specified subject condition (SSC) be stated such that only semantic rules of interpretation (having to do with reflexives, reciprocals, disjoint reference of referring expressions in certain domains, etc.) are "blocked" by semantically but not syntactically specified subjects such as PRO. (Since PRO can be taken as a nonterminal, "invisible" syntactic symbol, it is not inaccurate to define it as semantically "specified" only after it comes to dominate a terminal symbol by means of a rule of interpretation.)

I am not going to discuss Lightfoot's argumentation in this section, which on the whole I find convincing. However, there is a logical dependence between the material of his sections 2.1 and 2.2. If Lightfoot is wrong in distinguishing PRO and *t*, but correct in proposing that syntactic transformations do not treat PRO as a terminal symbol, then such rules should not treat *t* as a terminal symbol either. (Thus, *to* Adjunction is not blocked by a trace left by subject-raising, or by PRO, as seen above.)

At the end of this section, Lightfoot does claim that "clitic climbing" in Spanish is not allowed over a trace of a raised subject, even though it is sometimes allowed over a PRO-subject (see his lists 34a–b). However, there are verbs in the "clitic climbing" list that at least in English have been claimed to be subject-raising verbs (*tend, begin, finish, continue*, etc.). Thus, we might find that this putative process in Spanish can take place over a trace as well as over PRO, and this would still be consistent with Lightfoot's proposal that the specified subject constraint is syntactically operative only in phrases whose subject is a terminal element and not PRO *or* trace. [2]

It should be observed that nothing in what is being said here concerning Lightfoot's revision of the SSC is incompatible with keeping PRO and t distinct; I am only saying that it does not seem to me that his suggestion regarding the SSC requires this.

4.   In section 2.3, Lightfoot addresses the problem of ensuring that *to* Adjunction will apply properly in a framework where *wh*-fronting applies in "successive-cyclic" fashion. In accordance with the conclusions of his section 2.1, (11) would have to be derived by the operation of *to* Adjunction across the trace in (12), but the rule should be blocked by the trace in (13).

(11)   *Who do you wanna attack?*

(12)   *Who$_i$ do you want* [$_{COMP}$ t_i] PRO *to attack t_i ?*

(13)   *Who$_i$ do you want* [$_{NP}$ t_i] *to attack?*

But following my conclusions of part I above, a successive-cyclic treatment of *wh*-fronting would mean that lexical material is involved in the COMP-position when *to* Adjunction applies. Therefore, (11) would be dervied from (14):

(14)   *You do want* [$_{COMP}$ *who$_i$*] PRO *to attack t_i ?*

Lightfoot discusses three possible solutions to the problem of deriving (11) from (12), but his solutions (a) and (b) are not compatible with deriving (11) from (14), as seems to me necessary in the successive-cyclic treatment of *wh*-fronting. This is because his (a) and (b) solutions essentially involve eliminating the trace in the complementizer in (12), and this cannot be done without irrecoverably deleting *who* in (14).

Lightfoot's third (c) solution suggests that the infinitival complements under discussion are derived from deep structure Ss, rather than from deep structure $\overline{S}$s.[3] It would then follow that movements out of syntactically (not semantically) subjectless infinitives would be blocked only by Chomsky's subjacency condition on extractions. Since movement out of subjectless infinitival complements is more or less unrestricted, he goes on to propose that S not be considered a cyclic node (hence, it will not contribute to subjacency violations). In this way, (11) would be described directly from (15) rather than from (12) or (14). This is of course assuming that *wh*-fronting is not blocked by "semantically" (as opposed to syntactically) specified subjects.

(15)   *Who$_i$ do you want* PRO *to attack t_i?*

In examining this solution, care needs to be taken in determining exactly what classes of infinitives can profitably be derived from a COMP-less S. Certainly infinitival indirect questions should not be so derived, and quite possibly adverbial infinitives such as those in purpose clauses (which alternate with present subjunctives and full clauses with modals) should not be either. For our present purposes, it is of interest to note that such infinitives do not give rise to *to* Adjunction, nor do they permit other kinds of extractions with any freedom. These considerations actually enhance the proposal, since the replacement of "tensed S" by $\overline{S}$, as in note 3, would predict that clauses with COMP would resist extraction.

Lightfoot points out in his discussion that certain incorrect frontings in infinitives could be avoided as well by appeal to the specified subject condition as by an appeal to subjacency. But he then claims that "the current version of the Specified Subject Condition" will yield the wrong results in his (47a-c) if infinitive clauses with syntactic subjects are not exhaustively dominated by a cyclic node (that is, he is citing evidence against his proposal that only $\overline{S}$ and not S be considered a cyclic node). But I do not see here how cyclic nodes enter into the operation of the SSC at all, if the "current version" is to be taken as what Lightfoot cites at the beginning of section 2.2, since there is no mention of cyclic nodes in the definition of specified subject. Therefore, taking S as cyclic or not cyclic cannot affect the applicability of this condition on transformations in any way.

Thus, from Lightfoot's discussion at least, I do not see any objection to his proposal that S not be considered a cyclic node—as opposed to $\overline{S}$ which would remain cyclic.[4]

For a different view of the importance of S being a cyclic node, consult the paper of Culicover and Wexler in this volume.

5.   Let me turn now to the question Lightfoot poses in section 4: can a theory of grammar without transformations insightfully describe the set of changes in late Middle English that, in a theory with transformations, can be described by saying that the rule of NP-preposing entered the language at a certain moment?

It seems to me, at the level of precision at which this question can be discussed, that the answer is affirmative. Notice that the "NP-preposing" rule or rules are essentially leftward structure-preserving movements of NP into "grammatical relation" positions, whereas the COMP-substitution rules are rules that move constituents into positions that are not potential subcategorized "arguments" to higher predicates.

The fact is, the transformations that move constituents into focus position in cleft and pseudo-cleft constructions (almost certainly there is such a rule for at least cleft constructions) also have in common with COMP-substitution rules that they move elements into positions that are not part of the deep structure–predicate argument configurations. (Focus placement in clefts moves constituents into a position after the verb *be*, which can be considered as semantically empty and probably absent in deep structure; in any case, it would seem to be a grammatical and not a lexical formative.)

Thus, suppose we had a language without "NP-preposing" constructions (subject-raising, transformationally derived "middle" constructions, deep objects as subjects of passives, etc.). In a nontransformational theory with traces and with a PRO to be interpreted in surface structure, we could say that each NP in the enriched surface structures of this language (NP here includes traces and PROs) is subject to the

the following "argument condition":

(16)   Every NP in surface structure is either not an argument to a lexical
        predicate (such would be the case with focused constituents, constitu-
        ents in COMP-position, dislocated constituents, etc.), or it is an argu-
        ment to a predicate which (argument) satisfies the lexical subcategori-
        zation and selectional restrictions imposed by this predicate on argu-
        ents in its structural position.

Semantically, we can add the requirement that the NP-arguments to lexical
predicates (in this language without NP-preposing) are interpretable as standing
in that grammatical relation to the governing predicate indicated by their surface
positions.

Now, suppose such a language were to acquire a set of surface structures such as
those Lightfoot says can be attributed to the introduction of NP-preposing (where
the structural description of NP-preposing is given as, say np–Y–NP, for some set of
contexts Y). We can describe this set of changes as the theory of grammar without
transformations (or the type envisioned by Lightfoot) by saying that for the set of
contexts Y, the NP_i in the surface configurations NP_i –Y–t_i are exempted from the
argument condition (16). In other words, the NP_i may stand structurally in grammatical relations in surface structure in such a way that they are not interpretable
semantically as being in the relation. (For example, the raised surface subject of
seem in Modern English is not interpretable as its semantic subject and does not
satisfy (16).)

This statement of exceptions to the argument condition (16) is the equivalent of
NP-preposing, and it seems to me that it, equally well, in principle, captures the
simultaneous appearance of several syntactic innovations, as Lightfoot desires.
Further, this view is not incompatible with a formal collapse of *t* and PRO; the
antecedents of PRO in, say, "Equi-NP contexts" would not be exceptions to the
argument condition, whereas the antecedents of true "traces" would be exceptions;
beyond this, no formal distinction between *t* and PRO would need to be made.

Acknowledgments

I would like to thank David Lightfoot, Wendy Wilkins, and Richard Oehrle for discussions
of the issues in this paper.

Notes

Notes

1. Suppose one succeeded, by utilizing the various forms of *use* or otherwise, in showing that
    the traces created by NP-preposing blocked some version or part of *to* Adjunction. In such
    a case, an ordering solution of the form: "Equi-NP deletion, *to* Adjunction, NP-preposing,
    COMP-substitutions" still suggests itself, since I do not believe Lightfoot's argument in

section 2.1 against this ordering is valid. He claims that Complementizer Deletion must follow NP-preposing in order to block his examples (18). But these verbs (*want, prefer, desire, hate,* etc.) do not freely passivize anyway, so some independent mechanism may block (18). If so, Complementizer Deletion can precede *both to* Adjunction and the NP-preposing, and is irrelevant to ordering the latter two operations.

Later in the paper, Lightfoot makes the point that the Complementizer *for* may have preposition status, which I agree is the case in surface structure (cf. section V.9 of my *Transformational Approach to Egnlish Syntax*). But the preposition *for* directly following a verb does not generally suffice to block NP-preposing:

(i)   *The guests were prayed for next.*

(ii)   *These things shouldn't even be asked for.*

It is thus ad hoc to appeal to the *for* that intervenes in V_NP in the structures underlying Lightfoot's (13) as the mechanism that blocks NP-preposing.

2. Carlos Piera has provided me with some Spanish examples of "clitic climbing" with verbs that could plausibly be considered subject-raising verbs. He notes that acceptability judgments vary with such examples, but not decidedly more so than with "Equi-NP" verbs. Examples are:

Q.   *When did you begin to feel the pain?*

A.   *Lo empece a notar el ano pasado.*
        'I began to notice it last year.'

A.   *Lo suelo notar por la noche.*
        'I used to feel it at night.'

El mal tiempo lo empezo a molestar.
El mal tiempo lo solia molestar.
'The bad weather began to (used to) bother him.'

3. We could then identify "tensed S" with $\bar{S}$, provided that present subjunctives could be accommodated insightfully.

4. For purposes of discussion, let A^n mean A with n-bars, in the "bar notation" of Chomsky's *Remarks on Nominalizations*.
    One can object to using S^1 ($= \bar{S}$) and S^2 ($= \bar{\bar{S}}$) as the notation for the constituents that contain S if S and S^1 can be generated in a variety of structures other than directly dominated by S^1 and S^2, respectively. For in the framework of the bar notation, A^n is usually generated only directly under A^{n+1}, with the sole exception of A^{maximum}
    Thus, if S is generated in places where S does not dominate it directly, as suggested by Lightfoot and others, then S is not an appropriate notation. Similarly, if VP is always generated as a daughter to S, we could take that as an indication that if VP = V^n, then S = V^{n+1}. Finally, S^2 is not appropriate for a nonrecursive initial symbol (of the type proposed in Banfield, 1972), for the same reason.
    The objection might be overcome if a principled way were found to relate the distribution of these various constituents to the properties of the heads of phrases that can govern them as complements, such as that explored in Ronat (1973).

CONSTRAINTS ON PHRASE STRUCTURE RULES

Ray Jackendoff

Department of English
Brandeis University
Waltham, Massachusetts

In the search for constraints on the theory of grammar, there has been much concern over the years with the problem of constraining transformations, since their power is so clearly excessive. But little attention has been paid to how the phrase structure component is to be constrained. This paper will address itself to that problem.[1]

We will be asking the following sorts of questions: what counts as a possible phrase structure rule of a natural language? What is the relation between phrase structure and grammatical relations? How does the theory express the traditional grammatical distinction between heads and modifiers?

Chomsky's important paper "Remarks on Nominalization" (1970) sketches a theory of phrase structure called the X-bar ($\overline{X}$) Convention, which deals with many of these questions, and which will be the basis of the present discussion. In attempting to flesh out Chomsky's proposal, I will separate it into a number of parts, some of which will be supported, others not. Essentially, I will retain what I take to be the conceptual core of Chomsky's theory, but will modify most of the details.

The theory presented here is what I take to be quite a conservative version of the $\overline{X}$-Convention: the formally simplest and most restrictive statement of the theory that appears adequate for the description of English. In adopting this approach and thus requiring reformulation of many well-accepted analyses that weaken the theory, I an consciously adhering to the research strategy prescribed by Chomsky in the Preface to *Syntactic Structures*:

> Precisely constructed models for linguistic structure can play an important role, both negative and positive, in the process of discovery itself. By pushing a precise but inadequate formulation to an unacceptable conclusion, we can often expose the exact source of this inadequacy and, consequently, gain a deeper understanding of the linguistic data. More positively, a formalized theory may automatically provide solutions for many problems other than those for which it was explicitly designed.

After reformulating the $\overline{X}$ Convention, I will outline how it deals with a few of the more familiar parts of English phrase structure. I will then present some

249

examples for which even the improved notation for phrase structure rules appears
to be inadequate.

1.   Reformulation of the $\overline{\text{X}}$-Convention

The $\overline{\text{X}}$-Convention can be taken as a theory of syntactic categories in universal
grammar, making three principal claims. First, universal grammar includes a set of
syntactic distinctive features which define the possible lexical categories of human
languages. A particular language chooses its repertoire of lexical categories from
among those provided by universal grammar, just as it chooses a phonological repertoire from the possibilities provided by universal grammar. Presumably the choice
must be made in a constrained way—one would hardly expect a language with adverbs but no nouns. But this too is parallel to phonological theory, where one does
not expect a language with the sound $\ddot{u}$ but without a.

The second claim of the $\overline{\text{X}}$-Convention is that each lexical category X defines a
set of syntactic categories $X', X'', \ldots, X^p$, the *supercategories* of X, related by
phrase structure rules of the form (1).[2]

(1) $X^n \rightarrow \ldots X^{n-1} \ldots$

(1) is a phrase structure rule schema provided by universal grammar. It results in
phrase structure configurations of the form (2).

(2)
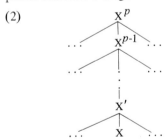

The *head* of a phrase of category X^n can be defined in two different ways, either
as the X^{n-1} that it dominates or as the lexical category X at the bottom of the
entire configuration. We make use of both senses here, making it clear when necessary which sense is meant. Both reflect traditional usages of the term. Refinements
of (1) in section 3 will guarantee that the head is unique, that is, each X^n will dominate one and only one X^{n-1}. Section 7 will take up a number of exceptions to this
generalization.

The third claim of the $\overline{\text{X}}$-Convention is that rules of grammar are stated in terms
of syntactic feature complexes and the prime notation. To be more precise, each
term of any rule of grammar must be either a specified lexical or grammatical
formative or of the form

$$\begin{bmatrix} \alpha F_1 \\ \beta F_2 \\ \vdots \end{bmatrix}^i$$

This third claim gives substance to the other two claims, since it is by attempting to write rules of grammar in these terms that we test hypotheses about the feature system and the hierarchical organization of categories.

To flesh out these claims, we must answer at least these four questions: What are the syntactic distinctive features? Is there a maximum value for i in (1), and is it the same for each category? Are there any constraints on what may appear in place of the ellipses in (1)? Does (1) provide the only phrase structure rules of the language, or are there other types? The rest of this paper is devoted to formulating one possible set of answers to these questions and to defending them on the basis of the grammar of English.

2.   The Syntactic Distinctive Features

The choice among competing systems of distinctive features should be made on the basis of how easy it is to state actual rules of the language in terms of the proposed systems. One presumes that rules are more likely to generalize to "natural classes," those that take fewer features to pick out. This criterion is essentially the same as in used in justifying phonological feature systems, and should therefore be altogether familiar.

In "Remarks on Nominalization" Chomsky analyzes the major lexical categories N, A, and V into the features $\pm N$ and $\pm V$ in the following way:

(3)

	+N	-N
+V	A	V
-V	N	

A fourth major lexical category is preposition; presumably Chomsky's system would analyze it as $[-N, -V]$, completing the matrix in (3).

In distributing two distinctive features over four major categories, there are actually only two systems possible other than (3):

(4)   a.

N	V
A	P

b.

N	V
P	A

The choice between the three must be made on the basis of what categories go together in the rules of English (and other languages, of course). Anticipating the generalizations that appear in Jackendoff (forthcoming), we will adopt (4a) as our feature system. It emerges that there are many rules that generalize across supercategories of N and V, and this is not expected in a feature system like (3). Similarly, there are many rules that generalize across supercategories of N and A, and many to

V and P, and this is not expected in (4b). Probably the only rule that makes (3) and (4b) look more natural than (4a) is the formation of cleft sentences, in which the clefted item can be only an NP or a PP. Since the combination of N and P is so rare, and the combination of V and A at least equally rare, we will feel justified in provisionally accepting (4a) as the major division of lexical categories.

Feature system (4a) has the interesting property of corresponding to two significant divisions in the phrase structure rules of English. Though these divisions may strictly speaking not obtain in other languages, we will for convenience name the features after the corresponding properties of English phrase structure. The first division is between those categories that have a subject, N and V, and those for which no subject relation exists, A and P. We will accordingly call the feature ±*subj*, and designate N and V as +*subj* and A and P as –*subj*.

One might question the claim that adjectives do not have a subject, since it is often assumed that *John* in *John is tall* is the subject of *tall*. This assumption is incorrect. Although *tall* imposes a selectional restriction on the NP in *NP is tall*, the NP bears the grammatical relation "subject-of" to the verb *be*, not to the adjective. This becomes clearer if other verbs are substituted for *be*, e.g., *John became tall, John made it tall*, etc. An NP bearing the "subject-of" relation to an adjective would have to be contained in the AP, as the subject of a noun is contained in the NP. Since there is no AP **John('s) fearful* corresponding to the NP *John's fear*, for example, we conclude that adjectives do not have grammatical subjects.[3]

To emphasize the heuristic, nontheoretical significance of the names for the features, it is worth pointing out that in French, for example, nouns cannot take NP subjects (other than possessive pronouns, which may be articles). Nevertheless, we assume that French nouns and English nouns have the same syntactic features, and that it is only the way these features appear in the grammar that differs from one language to another.

The second division in the phrase structure of English is between those categories whose complements may include a surface NP direct object after the head, i.e., V and P, and those categories whose complement cannot contain surface NP, i.e., N and A. The feature will be named ±*obj*; V and P are +*obj* and N and A are –*obj*. Again, the use of the term "direct object" is strictly syntactic: since there is no NP **his consideration the offer* and no NP **afraid Bill*, but only *his consideration **of** the offer* and *afraid of Bill*, these categories are not considered to have syntactic direct objects.

Next consider the "minor" lexical categories of English. Adjectives and adverbs clearly should be related, and we will designate them both as [–subj, –obj]. Since their major difference with respect to associated phrase structure is in the ability to take a complement (adjectives may, and adverbs nearly always may not), we will invent a feature to distinguish them and call it ±*comp*: adjectives are +*comp* and adverbs are –*comp*.

We will also use the feature *comp* to describe other minor lexical categories in the language. The clearest case is the category Particle: particles such as *up, on*, and *away* are morphologically identical to prepositions but permit no complements. To express this relationship, we designate both particles and prepositions as [-subj, +obj] ; prepositions are +*comp* and particles are -*comp*.

The difference between modal verbs and ordinary verbs must be stated somewhere in the grammar, and ±*comp* is a good place to localize it, calling verbs [+subj, +obj, +comp] , and modals [+subj, +obj, -comp] . This analysis makes them separate categories, yet their close feature relationship makes plausible the historical creation of the category of modals in English (cf. Lightfoot, 1974): a particular class of verbs underwent change in one syntactic feature, moving into a category available in universal grammar but previously unrealized in English. We will deal with the English auxiliary in a little more detail in section 5.

Finally, there is a clear candidate for a -*comp* category associated with nouns: the rather heterogeneous system of articles, quantifiers, and numerals. These can be further divided into two classes, which we may call Articles (Art) and Quantifiers (Q). Although the actual division will not be determined here, we introduce the relevant feature for completeness: articles are [+subj, -obj, -comp, +det] ; quantifiers are [+subj, -obj, -comp, -det] ;

We may use the feature *det* also to pick out a special class of adverbs, the "degree words" *so, too, as*, etc. We may call this category "Degree" (Deg) and designate it by the features [-subj, -obj, -comp, +det] , ordinary adverbs will be [-det] ; This choice is again made for reasons that will not be elaborated here.

There is no place in this system for coordinating conjunctions and complementizers. However, they do not participate in the grammar in the same way as the other categories, in that they do not strictly subcategorize complements and specifiers, so their exclusion is motivated. Section 7 will suggest places for them in the general theory. Subordinating conjunctions, on the other hand, can be described as prepositions with sentential complements, so they do participate in the feature system.

The feature system thus looks like this:

(5)

	Subj	Obj	Comp	Det
V	+	+	+	
M	+	+	-	
P	-	+	+	
Prt	-	+	-	
N	+	-	+	
Art	+	-	-	+
Q	+	-	-	-
A	-	-	+	
Deg	-	-	-	+
Adv	-	-	-	-

3.   The Phrase Structure Rule Schema

As stated in section 1, the second claim of the $\overline{\text{X}}$-Convention is this: every lexical category X must be dominated in phrase structure by a hierarchy of categories X', X'', . . . , X^p; furthermore, the set of syntactic categories in a language is completely determined by the lexical categories plus the hierarchical categories projected from them. In formal terms, the claim is that all possible phrase structure rules are of the form

(1) $X^n \to \ldots X^{n-1} \ldots$

We will weaken this claim slightly in section 7. But aside from minor exceptions, we will claim that (1) represents the canonical form for all phrase structure rules.

Notice what sorts of rules (1) excludes. One kind of phrase structure rule that has been widely accepted in the literature is so-called Chomsky-adjunction,[4] which appears in a popular source for relative clauses (6a), one account of the verb-particle construction (6b), one theory of manner adverbs (6c), and many other places.

(6)   a.   NP→ NP – S
         b.   V → V – Prt
         c.   VP→VP – Adv

Since these rules generate a category on the right-hand side that also appears on the left-hand side, they are impossible within schema (1).

In Vergnaud's (1974) account of relative clauses, there is a phrase structure rule of the following form:

(7) $N'' \to \pm\text{def} - N''' - S$

Such a rule is impossible within schema (1), since (1) requires a rule expanding N'' to contain an N' somewhere on its right-hand side.

Berman (1974, p. 109) proposes a number of structures for comparative constructions that illustrate violations of (1) and that seem in general counterintuitive. There is nothing in the standard theory of phrase structure to rule them out, though:

(8)   (= Berman's (127))

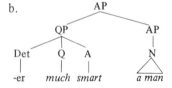

c.

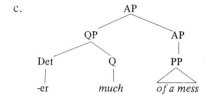

In (8a), AP dominates QP, but immediately dominates no category A^i. In (8b), in addition to the Chomsky-adjunction, the lower AP dominates N rather than an A^i; in (8c), the lower AP dominates only PP and no A^i.

Thus (1) is a relatively restrictive theory of phrase structure rules, ruling out many counterintuitive structures as well as a number that have been taken rather seriously in the literature. In particular, the Chomsky-adjoined source of relative clauses (6a) enjoys a wide following. Jackendoff (forthcoming) shows that (1) permits well-motivated descriptions for a wide variety of these constructions.

Schema (1) leaves open two issues: first, what is the maximum value of n and does it differ from category to category? Second, what is permitted on the right-hand side besides X^{n-1}, filling in the ellipses in (1)?

Various answers to the first question appear in the literature. In Chomsky's original formulation, n equals 2 for nouns and 3 for verbs (assuming the verb is the head of the sentence). Vergnaud (1974) and Siegel (1974) have n equal to 4, at least for nouns; Dougherty (1968) has n equal to 3 for nouns and 6 for verbs; Jackendoff (1969, 1974a) has n equal to 2 for all categories. The best theory, of course, provides just enough structure to make the relevant structural differences and no more. It now appears to me that n must equal 3 for verbs and nouns. For reasons of structural parallelism with the syntax of NPs, n must equal 3 for several other categories as well; thus, at the expense of some otherwise superfluous structure, the most uniform hypothesis is that n equals 3 for all categories. We will call an X''' a *major syntactic category*.

This hypothesis makes possible an answer to the second question above, which has not (to my knowledge) been addressed seriously. We will claim that every category to the left or right of X^{n-1} in (1) is either a major syntactic category or a specified grammatical formative, such as *have, tense,* or *number,* and probably that it is optional. Thus the canonical form (1) for phrase structure rules can be refined to (9).

(9) $X^n \rightarrow (C_1) \ldots (C_j) - X^{n-1} - (C_{j+1}) \ldots (C_k)$,
        where $1 \le n \le 3$, and for all C_i, either $C_i = Y'''$
        for some lexical category Y, or C_i is a specified
        grammatical formative.

We will refer to rule schema (9) as the Uniform Three-Level Hypothesis.

(9) rules out many further phrase structure combinations, for example the situation in (8a,b) in which QP dominates two lexical categories, Q and A. More generally, (9) guarantees that no two categories can have the same expansion: no situation

such as (10a,b) can arise, in which two different categories dominate precisely the same constituents.

(10)   a.    b.

We combine the feature notation of section 2 with the prime notation to arrive at distinctive feature analyses of all syntactic categories. For example, NP (now N $'''$) is designated as [+subj, -obj, +comp]$'''$; a rule applying either to P$'$ or V$'$ will mention the feature complex [-obj, +comp]$'$. The combination of the two notations makes the desired claim about possible cross-category syntactic generalizations: generalizations must be across categories of the same level, so it is impossible, for example, to pick out both N$''$ and Q$'$ with a single term of a structural description. This hypothesis can be crucial, in the absence of other evidence, in deciding which of a number of possible structures to assign to a construction, in that parallelisms with the structures associated with other lexical categories constrain the choices in interesting ways.

Before going on, let us clarify our terminology. We will continue to use the traditional terms S, NP, AP, AdvP, PP, and QP informally for the major syntactic categories associated with V, N, A, Adv, P, and Q respectively; the Three-Level Hypothesis claims that these traditional symbols for the major categories are equivalent to what rule schema (9) defines as V$'''$, N$'''$, A$'''$, Adv$'''$, P$'''$, and Q$'''$.

Chomsky uses the term *specifier* to refer to the material in a phrase to the left of the head. According to the tree structures in "Remarks," Chomsky considers *specifier* to represent a syntactic category, but *complement* is simply an abbreviatory term for some concatenation of ordinary syntactic categories. However, there is to my knowledge no evidence that either complements *or* specifiers function as constituents—they do not move or delete as units, and unlike normal constituents, no part can be designated as a head. Consequently, I will use the terms *specifier* and *complement* for expository convenience only, with no theoretical significance implied. In (9), the concatenation $(C_1) \ldots (C_j)$ will be referred to as an X^n *specifier*, and $(C_{j+1}) \ldots (C_k)$ as an X^n *complement*.

This terminology is suitable for discussion of English, though not perhaps for other languages, since it calls the direct object in an SOV language part of a specifier, not of a complement. In fact, we will see even in English that there are a few cases where a particular grammatical relation is defined as part of an X^i specifier for some categories and part of an X^i complement for others. It must be understood, therefore, that the distinction between specifier and complement is to be regarded here as only a convenience.

4.   The Generalized Subject Relation

One of the desiderata under the lexicalist hypothesis is that there be appropriate generalizations of the projection rules, so that selectional restrictions can be generalized over sentences and derived nominals. The grammatical relation "subject-of (an S)" is defined by Chomsky (1965, p. 71) as [NP, S], that is, in a string exhaustively dominated by S; the subject is a substring exhaustively dominated by NP; and that occurrence of NP is directly dominated by the S. We would like to define the relation "subject of an NP" for derived nominals in such a way that it generalizes with the relation "subject of an S," so that the projection rule for subjects need not be stated twice.

Compare the sentence *John has proved the theorem* with the derived nominal *John's proofs of the theorem*. We would like to say that *John* is subject in both cases. First, observe that the possessive affix *'s* occurs with all NPs in initial position in nominals, including not only those NPs that function as subjects but those that function as possessors and those that arrive in initial position by a transformation (e.g., *the city's destruction by the enemy*). This suggests that a relatively late oblig-atory transformation attaches the affix to whatever NP occupies initial position.[5]

Next, suppose we take the view of specifiers proposed in the last section: there is no category specifier; rather "specifier" is simply an abbreviation for a concatenation of nodes. Then we need not subordinate the NP subject to [Spec, N'] as Chomsky does:

(11)

```
                    NP
              _____/_____
      [Spec, N']            N'
         |             ____/\____
         NP         proofs of the theorem
         |
        John
```

We may instead attach it directly as a daughter of the higher NP.

Third, Chomsky claims that the phrase structure rule for S is (12),

(12) $S \rightarrow N'' - V''$

which makes it impossible to attach subjects in parallel positions in S and NP. Under the reasonable assumption that the head of S is the verb, the subject of S is at the V''' level and that of NP is at the N'' level. To create parallelism we must modify one or the other of the structures so that *John* is attached the same number of nodes up from the head. By dropping a node in the S we get a parallelism of the form (13); by adding an extra node in the NP we get the pair (14).

(13)   a.

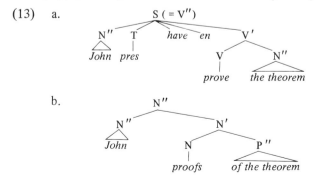

    b.

(14)   a.

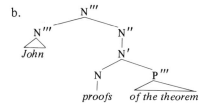

    b.

(13) is the two-level hypothesis of Jackendoff (1974a); (14) is the three-level hypothesis proposed in section 3. In either pair, *John* is in precisely parallel positions in NP and S; we can therefore define the generalized grammatical relation "subject-of" as [N″, [+subj]″] in (13) or as [N‴ , [+subj]‴] in (14). The choice of (14) over (13) receives considerable support in Jackendoff (forthcoming), and we will mention a number of the most important considerations here.

Here are some arguments which favor the uniform-level theories (13) or (14) over Chomsky's mixed-level theory. The arguments all show that where rules generalize across categories, it is invariably Ss, not NPs, that behave like NPs, APs, and PPs. First, observe that the rule of Topicalization preposes the major syntactic categories NP, AP, and PP:

(15)   a.   *My brother (,) everyone expects Bill to like.*
        b.   *Taller than Marvin (,) no one ever expected you to be.*
              (in "Yiddish" English)
        c.   *Into the bucket (,) we asked you to put the bananas.*

Topicalization also applied to sentences, not to VPs:

(16)   a.   *That you were coming (,) no one ever expected Bill to find out.*
        b.   **Coming tomorrow (,) no one ever expected Bill to find out
               that you were.*

If the rule of Topicalization is to generalize across categories, the appropriate generalization thus is to sentence, arguing that it is of the same level as the other major syntactic categories.

The pronoun *it* can have as its antecedent an NP, an AP, or an S:

(17)   a.   *A car drove up and I looked at it.*
        b.   *She is heavy, but she doesn't look it.*
        c.   *Bill came, but I didn't know it.*

The anaphoric expression for VP is *do so* or *do it*, which does not generalize directly with any other category. Hence the generalization calls for S rather than VP being similar to NP and AP.

Similarly, NPs, APs, PPs, and Ss serve as antecedents of appositives.

(18) a. *Charlie talked to Wendy, who was carrying the groceries.*
b. *Karl is famous, which you'll never be.*
c. *The tree was in the clock tower, which was certainly an odd place for it to be.*
d. *Harold left abruptly, which surprised no one.*

If the rule which determines antecedents of appositives is to be stated in the simplest fashion, it should generalize over all four categories. In the $\overline{X}$ convention this is possible only if all are of the same level.

Certain predicates permit a PP to replace the subject *it*.

(19) a. *It's a long way to Tipperary* ⇒
To Tipperary is a long way
b. *It's not too long from Groundhog Day to Purim* ⇒
From Groundhog Day to Purim is not too long.

This PP movement appears to generalize with the movement of S into subject, called Subject Replacement or Intraposition.[6]

(20) a. *It's no wonder that Harry's so brilliant.* ⇒
That Harry's so brilliant is no wonder.
b. *It's a marvel that they ever get along* ⇒
That they ever get along is a marvel.

Again there is no generalization of this sort between PP and VP. Thus the phrase structure rule schema demands that PP and S be of the same level if this generalization is to be captured.

PP and S generalize again in a rule that extraposes certain PPs from within the subject and also extraposes relative clauses.[7]

(21) a. *A review of that book appeared yesterday* ⇒
A review appeared yesterday of that book.
b. *A man who was from Philadelphia came in* ⇒
A man came in who was from Philadelphia.

The rule of Gapping applies in conjoined Ss and NPs, with precisely parallel conditions (see Jackendoff, 1971, for details).

(22) a. *Max plays saxophone and Medusa (,) sarrussophone.*
b. *Max's recording of Klemperer and Medusa's of Bernstein*

There is no corresponding generalization with VP. Again, the way in which the rule generalizes argues that S, not VP, should be of the same level as NP.

Thus there are numerous reasons to consider S rather than VP as structurally parallel to the other major syntactic categories, arguing for the uniform-level theory. One difference between Ss and NPs is that subjects are obligatory in Ss but not in

NPs. The former case is an apparent counterexample to the claim of section 3 that only heads are obligatory constituents. However, let us examine the constraints on S subjects a little more closely. It is generally considered to be the case that those sentences lacking surface subjects, namely *to*-infinitives, do so because the underlying subject has been deleted or is the phonologically null form PRO. However, at least two recent articles, Lasnik and Fiengo (1974) and Brame (1975), have argued that certain constructions contain surface infinitives with no deep subject. Their claim is that these infinitives are VP complements in deep structure, not Ss. Such a solution violates the phrase structure rule schema (9), since it involves generating a V″ to the right of a head. But an alternative is to generate them as subjectless Ss, i.e., as Ss that do not even contain a PRO in subject position. This alternative is equally consistent with Lasnik and Fiengo's and Brame's arguments. Then the phrase structure rules could generate an optional subject in S, its obligatoriness under most conditions being due to conditions extrinsic to the phrase structure rules. Whether such conditions can be independently motivated must be left for future research; but it provides a way of generating so-called VP-complements within in the present framework. Should this solution not prove viable, we can, of course, always accept a weakening of the optionality condition to allow obligatory subjects.

One problem that remains in justifying the uniform-level hypothesis is the treatment of the complementizer. The question is where the complementizer is attached to the sentence. All the movement rules cited above move the sentence with complementizer, and no rule ever leaves the complementizer behind. Thus the simplest hypothesis is that the complementizer is a left sister of the subject, attached to V″ in (13a), or to V‴ in (14a). Unfortunately this hypothesis appears to run afoul of the analysis of Gapping, for Gapping applies only if the complementizer is absent from the second clause:

(23) a. *It is hard to believe that Jack hates swimming and (*that) Fred fishing.*
      b. *For Jack to hate swimming and (*for) Fred fishing would be a tremendous surprise.*

One explanation of this is that the difference in structures is (24a) versus (24b).

(24) a.

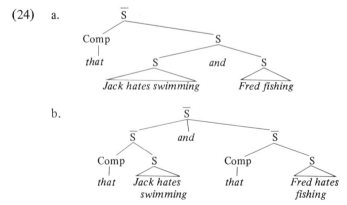

      b.

If Gapping were defined over S conjunction but not over $\overline{S}$ conjunction, the difference would be immediately accounted for.

Other evidence is provided by Bresnan (1974), who shows that Right Node Raising applies only to single constituents, but that it can apply to sentences with or without their complementizers:

(25) a. *Mike wouldn't tell us, but Randy readily volunteered,*
          that Jenny was drinking again.
      b. *I've been wondering whether, but wouldn't positively*
          want to state that, your theory is correct.

Again this argues that the complementizer is a sister of the entire S, not of the subject.

This raises a difficulty for the generality of movement rules under the $\overline{X}$-Convention: since $\overline{S}$ is one level higher than NP, i.e., apparently V^4, it cannot be moved by the same rule that moves an N''', P''', or an A'''. There are two possible ways to deal with this problem. One would be to claim that $\overline{S}$ is indeed V^4 (assuming a three-level S and NP), but that the A-over-A convention actually generalizes over category levels: the structural description of a rule would be met by the highest-level constituent of the category mentioned by the rule. For instance, by mentioning V in a rule, the structural description would be met by V^4; by mentioning N, the structural description would be met by N'''. In order to pick out the lexical category *verb*, a rule would have to mention specifically V^0. This is not an unattractive way out, although some care would be necessary in checking its feasibility. It has the interesting property of vitiating all the above arguments for parallelism based on movement rules, since a rule mentioning, say, +*subj* will apply to either N''' or V^4. [8]

A less drastic solution is to claim that both S and $\overline{S}$ are instances of V''':

(26)

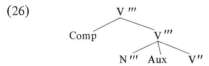

Under this proposal, the A-over-A convention would guarantee that any movement rule would move $\overline{S}$ rather than S, while preserving the generalization with the movement of other X'''. Such a structure represents a weakening of the theory of phrase structure, since it contains the forbidden configuration of a category dominating itself. Section 7 will show, however, that this exception can be accommodated within a highly constrained class of rules generated by a second phrase structure rule schema of considerable interest.

Which of these two solutions to the complementizer turns out to be correct, however, does not seem to be of major importance to the main hypothesis. For simplicity, we will assume the second solution, in which the complementizer is Chomsky-adjoined to S. This problem disposed of, there appears to be no evidence barring the uniform-level hypothesis, and, under certain assumptions, there is considerable evidence for it.

5.   The Auxiliary

The problem of this section is where the various parts of the auxiliary are attached and whether they provide evidence for the general structure of the S. The
position adopted here is a modification of the analysis in Jackendoff (1972, section
3.8), based in part on 1966 lectures by Klima and on Emonds (1970); other revi-
sions have been proposed by Akmajian and Wasow (1975). In turn, these are all
variants of the original analysis of Chomsky (1957).

The verb and its complements apparently form a constituent that does not
include the modal, since there is a rule (pointed out by Ross 1967) that fronts a
VP after modals under certain conditions:

(27)   *They said she may attempt to leave, and attempt to*
          leave she will.

The rule of VP-deletion provides evidence that the verb and its complements form
a constituent that does not include the aspectual verbs *have* and *be*, since a VP may
delete leaving aspect intact.

(28)   a.   *We asked them to stay, and they would have, if it hadn't*
              been for your idiocy.
        b.   *Michael said he had been practicing, but I don't really believe*
              he had been.

Jackendoff (1972) gives evidence that the first auxiliary is a daughter of S, but
that subsequent auxiliaries are not daughters of S. The evidence is that sentence
adverbs such as *frankly, probably*, and *evidently* occur in all possible positions as
daughter of S—initial, final with comma intonation, and before the auxiliary. They
also occur after the first auxiliary, but not after subsequent ones.

(29)   a.
$$\text{George will} \begin{Bmatrix} frankly \\ probably \\ evidently \end{Bmatrix} \begin{Bmatrix} have\ amused \\ be\ amusing \end{Bmatrix} \text{the children by the time}\\ \text{we get there}$$

        b.
$$\text{George will} \begin{Bmatrix} have \\ be \end{Bmatrix} \begin{Bmatrix} frankly \\ probably \\ evidently \end{Bmatrix} \begin{Bmatrix} amused \\ amusing \end{Bmatrix} \begin{matrix} them\ when\ we \\ get\ there \end{matrix}$$

A simple way to account for this difference is to claim that the second auxiliary
forms a constituent with the verb and its complements; then an adverb following
the second auxiliary cannot be a daughter of S, but an adverb preceding the second
auxiliary can be.

These three arguments for constituency lead to a three-level theory of the S:

(30)

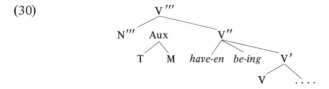

One of the problems in Chomsky's original analysis of the English auxiliary is the recurrence of the configuration

$$\left\{ \begin{array}{c} \text{M} \\ \textit{have} \\ \textit{be} \end{array} \right\}$$

in transformational rules as the first verbal element, including all uses of *be* and the aspectual use (and in some dialects the possessional use) of *have*. The solution of Klima, Emonds (1970), and Jackendoff (1972) is an obligatory transformation *Have-Be* Raising which moves the appropriate uses of *have* and *be* to a position under Aux, just in case there is no modal present. After this transformation, any transformation can refer to the first auxiliary by mentioning the node Aux in its structural description, and the need for the repetitive braces is eliminated.

McCawley (1975) objects to the rule of *Have-Be* Raising on the grounds that it is entirely arbitrary to treat *have* and *be* as unlike other verbs in undergoing this rule; and that if modals are a category separate from verbs, there is no reason for modals, *have* and *be* to behave alike. The theory of categories of sections 2 and 3, however, makes possible a refinement of the analysis that meets McCawley's objections in a rather interesting way.

Recall that the syntactic distinctive features of Modal are [+subj, +obj, −comp], contrasting with verbs only in the last feature. Now suppose that the lexical entries for the appropriate uses of *have* and *be* are assigned the syntactic features [+subj, +obj], being unmarked for *comp*. Then, by the usual conventions for applying rules, any rule which applies to the feature complex for modals, [+subj, +obj, −comp] will also apply to *have* and *be* but to no other verbs. In other words, [+subj, +obj] corresponds to Chomsky's (1957) category v; [+subj, +obj, +comp] to V; [+subj, +obj, −comp] to

$$\left\{ \begin{array}{c} \text{M} \\ \textit{have} \\ \textit{be} \end{array} \right\}$$

The exceptionality of *have* and *be* and their falling together with modals is expressed naturally in terms of such a lexical feature analysis; and the description of the auxiliary thus looks considerably less arbitrary than before.[9]

For a further refinement, observe that the phrase structure rule schema claims that Modal is the progenitor of a series of larger categories M', M'', ... The category Aux, which so far has not played any role in the $\overline{\text{X}}$ convention, can therefore be analyzed as M^i, for some i. If we adopt a uniform three-level hypothesis of phrase structure rules, i.e., rule schema (9), the phrase structure rule for S may contain no category besides V'' of level other than three; hence Aux must be analyzed as M'''. Although there is no empirical evidence that so many levels are necessary, the superfluous structure is harmless and makes a more highly constrained theory possible; furthermore, the extra rules are part of universal grammar, so add no cost to particular grammars. We will arbitrarily attach Tense as a daughter of M''' rather than at any of the lower levels, yielding the following phrase structure rules:[10]

(31)   a. $V''' \rightarrow N''' - M''' - V''$
       b. $M''' \rightarrow T - M''$
       c. $M'' \rightarrow M'$
       d. $M' \rightarrow M$

$$
\begin{array}{c}
V''' \\
N''' \quad M''' \quad V'' \\
T \quad M'' \\
M' \\
M
\end{array}
$$

Now since the phrase structure rule schema also predicts that a head is obligatory in M''', the only way a modal can be omitted from a tensed sentence is to generate the empty node Δ under M. Thus both *Have–Be* Raising and *Do*-Support can be stated in such a way as to fill this empty node with a category nondistinct from M, making one further peculiarity of the English auxiliary somewhat less peculiar. [11]

One further minor point: the phrase structure rule schema (9) claims that all complements and specifiers are optional, at least from the point of view of phrase structure rules. This is certainly true of M''' in rule (31a), since in infinitive clauses there is no evidence that there has ever been a tense or modal present. We can thus feel justified in regarding the obligatoriness of Aux in main clauses as a semantic condition, or at least as a condition extrinsic to the phrase structure rules proper.

It is a little more difficult to justify making Tense optional in (31b), since the accepted syntactic treatment has always required it. Its obligatory presence seems in any event to be a minor exception to the overall generalization that only heads are obligatory in phrase structure expansions.

6.   The Three Levels of Complements

The three-level hypothesis predicts that complements to a phrase can be attached in three possible places—to X', X'', or X'''. Since any constituent following the head of a phrase could in principle be attached in any of the three complement positions, we must be concerned with how the theory picks out the correct position for a complement phrase.

Complements can in fact be divided up on essentially semantic grounds, corroborated in part by syntactic evidence. There are three distinct ways in which a complement may be integrated into a semantic interpretation: as a functional argument, as a restrictive modifier, and as a nonrestrictive modifier. We will attempt to identify these respectively with X'-, X''-, and X'''-complements.

Those lexical items that strictly subcategorize phrases in their environment can be thought of as semantic functions that take as their arguments the interpretations of the strictly subcategorized phrases. For example, the verb *give* strictly subcategorizes a subject, an object, and an indirect object, and can be thought of as a semantic function $f(x, y, z)$ that maps ordered triples of terms into propositions. Such an approach is developed in Katz (1966, 1972) and Jackendoff (1972, 1976), among other places, and has been used implicitly in almost every approach to semantic interpretation in generative grammar. Similarly, the noun *part of* strictly subcategorizes an NP, and can be treated semantically as a function $g(x)$ that maps terms into terms; the adjective *proud (of)* maps terms into properties (or predicates, or whatever kind of object the intension of adjectives is); the preposition *to* maps terms into (intensions that select) directions. Aside from subjects, functional arguments in English come immediately after the head, typically preceding all other modifiers, and many grammarians have had the intuition that they are the most "tightly bound" to the head of all the complements. This intuition can be expressed by assigning all and only the strictly subcategorized phrases other than subjects to the X'-complement in deep structure.

In many cases a phrase can be identified as structly subcategorized by the fact that it cannot be omitted from the sentence without incurring ungrammaticality. For example, the PP in *Joe put the book on the table* must be strictly subcategorized, since **Joe put the book* is ungrammatical. However, this is only a sufficient condition for strict subcategorization, not a necessary condition, since many words optionally subcategorize phrases. For example, *tell* occurs in contexts *John told Bill a lie* and *John told Bill*, but *a lie* appears to operate semantically as a functional argument in the former sentence and hence must be strictly subcategorized. Similarly, when adjectives and nouns strictly subcategorize, their arguments are usually optional.

A second criterion for X'-complements in Ss and NPs is provided by certain anaphoric processes. The phrase *do so* appears to be a pro-V', and may be followed only by material outside the V'-complement (usually part of the V''-complement.) [12] Consider (32).

(32)   a.   *Joe bought a book on Tuesday, but Sim did so on Friday.*
        b.   **Joe put a book on the table, but Sim did so on the chair.*

The ability of *on Tuesday* to follow *did so* indicates that it is a V'' or V''' complement in this sentence; the inability of *on the chair* to follow *do so* indicates that it must be inside of V' in the antecedent sentence.

A parallel anaphoric process in NPs is the use of the pro-N' *one*. Lakoff (1970a) observes that there is a contrast in the applicability of *one* that depends on the nature of the complement.

(33)   a.   *Jack met the king from England, and I met the one from France.*
        b.   **Jack met the king of England, and I met the one of France.*

Notice that the PPs *of England* and *from England* play different semantic roles, since there may be a king of England from France. *Of England* appears to be a functional argument, since it specifies part of the function of the king; *from England*, on the other hand, specifies a somewhat inessential part of kingliness. Notice further that the two PPs may appear together only in one of the two possible orders: we cannot get **the king from France of England*. These facts can be described simultaneously if we suppose that *of England* is an N'-complement and *from England* is an N''-complement. An N''-complement would automatically follow an

N'-complement, the different positions would correspond to different semantic roles.

Based on this reasoning, the proper formulation of the difference between (33a,b) appears to be this: the pronoun *one* cannot be followed by the phrase *of NP* within the N'-complement. It can however be followed by other N'-complements, as will be seen shortly.[13] Thus the inability of a particular *of NP*-phrase to follow the pronoun *one* is a sufficient test for its being an N'-complement.

This test requires some care. At first glance it would appear that *of water* must be an N''-complement in (34), since it follows *one*.

(34)   *Bill has two quarts of wine and one of water.*

However, we notice that *one* can be pluralized in (33a) but not in (34).

(35)   a.   *I met the ones from France.*
        b.   **The quarts of wine and the ones of water were left behind.*

The difference is explicated if we realize that there are two morphemes *one* that can function anaphorically in an NP: a numeral (a kind of Q, alternating with *two, three*, etc.) and a pronoun. Only the latter, which takes the place of the head of the NP, can be pluralized to *ones*. (35b) shows that the *one* in (34) is the numeral one_Q, and that in fact the pro-N' one_N cannot be followed by the complement *of water* here. We conclude therefore that *of water* is indeed an N'-complement in (34), and so, by parallelism, is *of wine*.

There are certain cases that appear to be ambiguous between N'- and N''-complements without appreciable difference in meaning. For example, because of the parallel between the direct object in (36a) and the PP in (36b), one would want to claim that the PP is an N'-complement.

(36)   a.   *Bill pictured Fred*
        b.   *Bill's picture of Fred*

Yet *the pictures of Fred and the ones of Harry* is also acceptable, arguing that *of Fred* must be an N'' complement, similar to *the pictures which are of Fred*. The simplest solution is to accept both sources for such a case.

Another test to distinguish N'- from N''-complements is based on a distinction noticed by Lakoff (1970b):

(37)   a.   *Fathers of few children have any fun.*
        b.   **Fathers with few children have any fun.*

Notice that *of few children* is, by our previous criterion, an N'-complement, since **ones of few children* is ungrammatical. But *with few children* can be paraphrased by the relative clause *who have few children*, suggesting that it is an N''-complement. This conjecture correctly predicts that only one order will be possible with both complements, i.e., *fathers of few sons with many daughters* but not **fathers with many daughters of few sons*. To describe the difference in grammaticality between (37a,b), then, one is led to the hypothesis that a quantifier may extend its scope out of an NP dominating it if it is in the N'-complement but not if it is in the

N"-complement. Thus *any* could be in the scope of *few* in (37a) but not in (37b); since *any* must be within the scope of negation, (37b) is unacceptable. I can offer no reason why this distinction should be so, but it is confirmed by considering the possibility of *wh*-questions and relatives: according to the previous criterion, only N'-complements can be *wh*-ed.

(38)   a.   *Fathers of which children had fun?*
            I met some children the fathers of whom like them.

       b.   **Fathers with which children had fun?*
            *I met some children the fathers with whom like them.

Another pair with this contrast is (39).

(39)   a.   *Arguments with few people yield any satisfaction.*
            Arguments with which people satisfy you?
            He is a person arguments with whom are fruitless.

       b. *?*Arguments with few premises yield any satisfaction.*
           ?*Arguments with which premises satisfy you?
           ?*This is a premise arguments with which are useless.

(39b) is all right if it is read "arguments *against* which premises," parallel to "arguments with which people," but impossible if read "arguments *employing* which premises." It is plausible to assume that a person or premise against which an argument is directly is strictly subcategorized, i.e., an N'-complement, but that the instrument of argument, the premise employed, is an N"-complement like other instrument phrases. This is supported by the grammaticality of *arguments with Bill with few premises* and the ungrammaticality of **arguments with few premises with Bill*. Thus this distinction between complement types supports the proposed interaction between level of complement and quantifier or *wh*-scope, and inability of quantifiers or *wh* to extend scope outside the NP seems to be a sufficient condition for N"- rather than N'-complements.

Since there has been little study of a possible distinction between different kinds of NP-complements, I am not familiar with enough strong cases to verify completely the validity of the two tests described above, nor to explain why these particular distinctions should obtain. However, the proposed distinction between N'- and N"-complements does seem to be fairly well borne out by the few examples examined here.[14]

The distinction between X"-complements and X'''-complements is somewhat more straightforward. In sentences, the V"-complements are the expressions of manner, means, accompaniment, instrument, purpose, and other so-called VP-adverbials. Semantically, they map predicates into predicates of the same number of arguments, and they contribute to the main assertion of the sentence. As such, they can be focused, clefted, and affected by sentence negation:

(40)   a.   *John hit the nail **softly**.*
            It was with a hammer that John hit the nail.
            *We didn't buy this for **your** benefit.*

Because they add extra truth conditions to the assertion of the sentence, restricting the extension of the sentence, V″-complements can be called *restrictive modifiers*.

V‴-complements, by contrast, add no conditions to the assertion of the sentence, but rather add some sort of auxiliary assertion (one of whose arguments is usually the main assertion). They include sentence adverbials of all sorts, sentential appositives, parentheticals (e.g., *John is a fink, I think*), and various other subordinate clauses. When they occur at the end of a sentence, they are set off by comma intonation. Since they are not part of the main assertion of the sentence, they cannot be focused, clefted, or affected by sentence negation:

(41)   a.   *John hit the nail, **of course**.

     b.   *It was $\begin{cases} probably \\ in\ my\ opinion \end{cases}$ that John hit the nail.

     c.   *John didn't hit the nail, **I think**.
        (cf. *John didn't hit the nail, I don't think.*)

The geometry of the sentence predicts that V‴-complements must follow V″-complements, and this prediction is obviously borne out (except for some stylistic inversions).

(42)   *John hit the nail softly, of course.*
      ?*John hit the nail, of course, softly.

      ?John ran away quickly, probably.
      *John ran away, probably, quickly.

      John hit the nail with a hammer, which surprised no one.
      *John hit the nail, which surprised no one, with a hammer.

      John hit the nail with a hammer, I think.
      ?John hit the nail, I think, with a hammer.[15]

Similar contrasts can be found in NPs. The paradigm example is the difference between restrictive and nonrestrictive (appositive) relative clauses; the former follow previous modifiers without a break, may contain foci, and may be affected by sentence negation; the latter are separated by comma intonation, may not contain foci, and may not be affected by sentence negation.

(43)   a.   *I didn't see the man who brought the **strawberries**.*
     b.   **I didn't see the man, who brought the **strawberries**.*

I would like to claim therefore that restrictive relative clauses are deep structure N″-complements and that appositives are deep structure N‴-complements.[16]

However, other constructions besides relative clauses can appear in N″- and N‴-complements. For example, the PPs in *the king from England, the weather at 6:00, the man with a big nose*, etc., are not in the N′-complement, follow the head without a break, and can be focused and affected by sentence negation.

(44)   *We didn't mention* $\begin{cases} the\ king\ from\ \textbf{England} \\ the\ weather\ at\ \textbf{6:00} \\ the\ man\ with\ a\ big\ \textbf{nose} \end{cases}$

They are thus candidates for N''-complements. Descriptive adjectives, despite their prenominal position, have similar semantic properties to these PPs, arguing that they are attached to N''. This of course makes them parallel in structure and function to preverbal VP-adverbs, which are in V'', consistent with the predictions of the $\overline{\text{X}}$-Convention.

By contrast, there are certain nonsentential appositives that can be characterized as N'''-complements:

(45) a. *I will sell you these bagpipes, the finest in all Poland,*
          for only 4000 zloty.
      b. *Perhaps you have heard of my brother, known the world*
          over as a notorious womanizer.
      c. *She presented Picasso, then in his blue period, with a blueberry pie.*

One might want to argue that all these are reduced nonrestrictive relative clauses, and this is certainly conceivable. In any event, they have the characteristic comma intonation and inability to be affected by sentence negation that we identify with an X'''-complement.

Again, the N'''-complements must follow the N''-complements, as predicted by the geometry of the NP:

(46)   *the man that brought the strawberries, who was dangerous*
          *the man, who was dangerous, that brought the strawberries

          these bagpipes from Poland, the finest known
          *these bagpipes, the finest known, from Poland

          the man with a big nose, then in his blue period
          *the man, then in his blue period, with a big nose
          (only ok as two appositives)

We see therefore that there are three distinct kinds of complements in both sentences and NPs, corresponding to the three levels predicted by the phrase structure rule schema. Furthermore, the parallels in structure and function across the two categories S and NP are clear and confirm the view of grammatical parallelism we have advocated here.

In the remaining major categories, AP and PP, the complements are less productive, but the three types are distinguishable. Both adjectives and prepositions strictly subcategorize arguments, as was pointed out above. Most of the modifiers at the A''- and P''-level are part of the degree system, preceding the head; they are treated in some detail in Jackendoff (forthcoming). At the A'''- and P'''-level, there are appositive clauses again, as usual marked by comma intonation.

(47) a. *Martha is proud of her height, which you'll never be.*
      b. *We went from Aspen to Denver, which seems like a long*
          way, in less than four weeks.

As usual, the order of the appositive and the strictly subcategorized arguments cannot be reversed:

(48)   a.   *proud, which you'll never be, of her height
        b.   *from, which seems like a long way, Aspen to Denver
              *from Aspen to, which seems like a long way, Denver

Thus the facts of APs and PPs are consistent with the three-level hypothesis, although they do not push it to its limits as do Ss and NPs.

7.   Two Other Phrase Structure Rule Schemata

One obvious exception to the theory of phrase structure presented so far is coordination. It is generally agreed that the node dominating conjoined Ss is an S, that the node dominating conjoined NPs is an NP, and so forth.

(49)   a.   b.

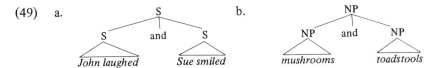

This violates even the hierarchic arrangement of categories predicted by (1), the primitive version of the phrase structure rule schema. Furthermore, no constituent of a coordinate construction can be identified as its head. Clearly a separate phrase structure rule schema is necessary. (50) is one possible form.

(50) $X^i \rightarrow X^i - (\text{conj} - X^i)^*$

This permits coordination of any syntactic category. Whether it can be refined to a more restrictive form is left for future research.

A different sort of exception to the phrase structure rule schema emerges from considering the structure of gerundive nominals such as Noam's inventing a new theory. Chomsky shows that gerundives, unlike derived nominals, are closely related to sentences, having the same possibilities for modification as sentences and having interpretations with direct and productive relationships to the corresponding sentences. Emonds (1970) shows, furthermore, that (unlike that and for-to complements) they have precisely the distribution of NPs. Hence a first approximation to the structure might be (51).

(51)

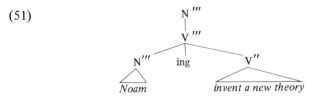

Schachter (1976) and Horn (1976) independently suggest an alternative structure, in our terms best represented as (52).

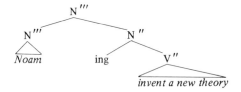

(52) has at least two advantages over (51). First, it enables the rule inserting *'s*
(POSS) on the subject of an N''' to be generalized to the subject of gerunds without further ado. Second, it makes possible a certain limited class of gerunds such as
(53) (quoted from Schachter).

(52) a. *There is no enjoying this world without thee.*
      b. *This telling tales out of school has got to stop.*

The replacement of the subject by a normal NP determiner is inexplicable in structure (51), but is an expected possibility in (52).

The differences between gerundive and derived nominals observed by Chomsky
can still be explained in terms of (52), since they all depend on the difference
between the internal structure of V'' and N'', which difference is still present under
the theory (52). Since the Lexicalist Hypothesis generalizes the subject relation
to NP, *Noam* can still be interpreted as the subject of the verb *invent*, at worst by
ignoring the feature +*obj* at some point in the derivation. Hence (52) appears to be
a viable alternative theory of gerundive nominals, with a certain amount of evidence
in its favor.

Observe, however, that neither (51) nor (52) conforms to the phrase structure
rule schema, since the main N''' has no noun head. Hence it is necessary in either
case to treat gerundives as an exception to the schema, by adding phrase structure
rule (54a) to generate (51) or (54b) to generate (52).

(54) a. N''' → V'''
      b. N'' → ing - V''

Either of these rules provides a way to use a verb phrase as a noun phrase, i.e.,
not as a verb phrase with respect to the upper context. The literature contains at
least two other recent proposals for which such "deverbalizing rules" are an appropriate formulation.

There are a few -*ing* complements which, unlike most gerundives, alternate with
PPs rather than NPs:

(55) a. *John kept Bill* $\left\{ \begin{array}{l} running \\ at\ a\ run \end{array} \right\}$

      b. *Bill remained* $\left\{ \begin{array}{l} working \\ at\ work \end{array} \right\}$

      c. *Moe went on* $\left\{ \begin{array}{l} working \\ with\ his\ work \end{array} \right\}$

There is no possibility of a subject in these -*ing* complements; further, like the
corresponding PPs and unlike most gerunds, they do not cleft: **it was running that*

John kept Bill. The subcategorization of the verbs in (55) would be simplified if in fact these complements were not NPs but PPs. Jackendoff (1976) shows that they behave semantically as expressions of Location, so PP constituency is not semantically implausible.

There are two possible structures, given in (56) along with the necessary additions to the phrase structure rules.

(56) a.

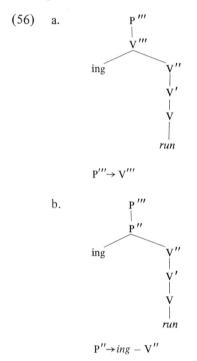

$$P''' \to V'''$$

b.

$$P'' \to ing - V''$$

These correspond to the possibilities in NP, (54a) and (54b) respectively. Of the two, (56b) makes automatic the absence of a subject, a tense, and a modal within the complement in (55), since a PP does not allow a subject.[17] However, since it is not clear that these gaps are syntactic rather than semantic in nature, this does not really decide between the analyses at this stage. For the present, however, we will adopt the *b*-analysis.

Emonds (1970) suggests that the progressive *be* belongs to the class of verbs that take this sort of *-ing* complement. The main attraction of Chomsky's (1957) analysis of the progressive auxiliary was that it explained the inability of progressive to be followed by modals, *have* or another progressive. But Emonds shows that this need not be a particular syntactic idiosyncrasy of the progressive but may rather be part of a more general set of semantic restrictions. He points out that, like *be*, the verbs of (55) cannot be followed by perfective or progressive aspect:

(57) a. *John kept Bill* $\left\{ \begin{array}{l} \textit{having run} \\ \textit{being running} \end{array} \right\}$

b. *John remained $\left\{ \begin{array}{l} \textit{having worked} \\ \textit{being working} \end{array} \right\}$

c. *Moe went on $\left\{ \begin{array}{l} \textit{having sung} \\ \textit{being singing} \end{array} \right\}$

Notice also that *be* takes a semantically parallel PP: compare *John is working* to *John is at work*. Hence, however these restrictions are accounted for (presumably semantically), they can be generalized to progressive *be* with no difficulty if the progressive *John is singing* is assigned the structure (in present terms) (58).

(58)

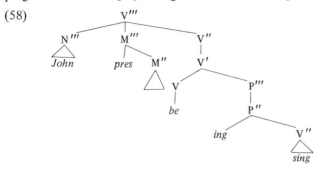

As further support for this analysis, Jackendoff (1976) shows that the verb *be* fills a gap in the semantic paradigm given by the verbs in (55), and that the interpretation of the progressive given by assigning it to this gap is not implausible, at least for some of its uses. Hence we have some reason to consider progressive *be* a main verb taking a PP complement, and we can eliminate it from the phrase structure rule for V″.

Finally, Fiengo (1974) revives a proposal from the inner depths of Chomsky (1955), in which the passive verb phrase is an AP. The passive auxiliary is present in deep structure, and the necessity of preposing the direct object is guaranteed by semantic constraints (which, however, Fiengo does not spell out in much detail). The deep structure of a passive is (59a) or (59b); its surface structure is (59c), in the present framework.

(59) a.

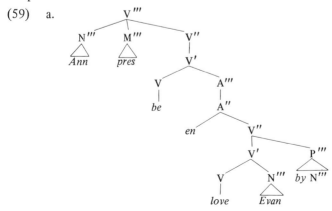

b.

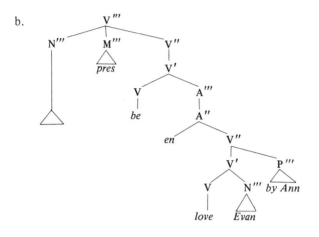

c.

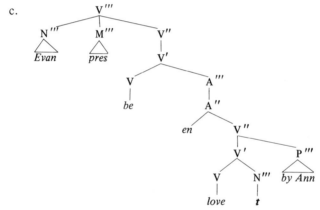

The *t* in direct object position in (59c) is the "trace" left behind by movement rules in Fiengo's theory, a pronoun anaphorically bound to the NP originally occupying that position. We need not go into Fiengo's motivation for this theory, as it goes far beyond the scope of the present study. However, we observe that the analysis requires a deverbalizing phrase structure rule, here represented as (60), in that there an AP without an adjectival head.

(60)   A″ → en – V″

One piece of evidence for identifying the passive verb phrase as AP is that passive verb phrases occur, with the correct meaning, after certain verbs other than *be*, for example (61).

(61)   a.   *Fred got arrested by the cops.*
        b.   *Mary got Kathy arrested by the cops.*
        c.   *George had Jerry studied by a team of shrinks.*

Since these environments also permit APs (*Fred got sick, Mary got Kathy sick, George had Jerry angrier than a swarm of bees*), an A‴ -structure like that in (59) would make the generation of these otherwise troublesome examples rather simple. Such a theory would, of course, have to develop a semantic explanation of why passive VPs do not occur in all adjectival environments, a problem I must leave for future research.

With the relatively scanty evidence at hand, it is difficult to form any well-motivated hypothesis about possible constraints on "category-switching" phrase structure rules such as the deverbalizing rules (54), (56), and (60). A fairly restrictive conjecture might be the following rule schema:

(62) $X^i \rightarrow$ af $- Y^i$

That is, a category-switching rule must replace one category with another of the same level, and there may be no complements or specifiers other than an affix or other morphological marker indicating the change of category.

As Emonds has pointed out (personal communication), schema (62) provides a solution to the problem pointed out in section 4 concerning what category dominates the complementizer. In order to state generalizations about movement rules, it was necessary to say that the complementizer is attached to the sentence as in (63a). But this presupposes the phrase structure rule (63b), which is not an instance of rule schema (9), since the head is not V'' but V'''.

(63)   a. V'''
                 /   \
            Comp V'''

        b. $V''' \rightarrow$ Comp $- V'''$

(63b) is, however, an instance of rule schema (62), where X happens to be identical to Y, and the complementizer is a particular kind of affix.[18] Thus the choice of (62) as the formulation of category-switching rules receives independent motivation.

The limiting case of (62), of course, is when $i = 0$, in which case it defines a class of word-formation rules such as nominalizations. One can imagine, for example, a construction becoming more "nounlike" and less "sentencelike" as i becomes less in progressing from a structure like (64a) through (64b,c) to (64d).

(64)   a.

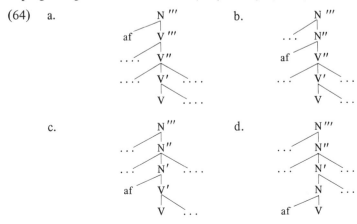

(64a) or (64b) is the English gerundive nominal; (64d) the derived nominal.[19] Whether all these structures exist in English, or whether further phrase structure rule schemata are necessary, must be a matter for future research.

8.   A Problem with the Evaluation Measure

If the parallelism of grammatical relations from one category to another is a linguistically significant generalization, the evaluation measure for the theory of grammar ought to be constructed in such a way as to favor grammars with such parallelisms over those lacking them. The usual way to construct an evaluation measure is to develop notational conventions such that the more general case takes fewer symbols to state. This is the purpose of the use of parentheses, braces, and distinctive feature notation to collapse rules.

However, a detailed investigation of the phrase structure of English uncovers quite a number of cases in which the ordinary abbreviatory conventions are to no avail. One case involves the rule for expanding X'. There is a strong generalization about order in the English X': when there is an NP in the X'-complement, it precedes all other X'-complements. PPs invariably follow NPs and precede $\overline{S}$s, which in turn always come last in the complement. But expressing this generalization in the grammar is difficult.

Suppose, for example, that we try to collapse just the V'- and P'-rules so that the appropriate parts of the complement coincide; The rules are worked out in full detail in Jackendoff (forthcoming), but the relevant parts are these:

(65)   a. $V' \rightarrow V - (N''') - (P''') - (\overline{S})$

   b. $P' \rightarrow P - \left\{ \begin{array}{l} (N''') - (P''') \\ (\overline{S}) \end{array} \right\}$

The elements of the V'-complement are self-explanatory (though it is interesting and so far unexplained that they can occur only two at a time, not all at once). The upper expansion of P' includes such things as *across the road from Bill's house, to Bill in New York*, and *from one end to the other*; this structure is motivated in Jackendoff (1973). The lower expansion includes *since you came, after the ball is over*, etc. I know of no examples which include NP-$\overline{S}$ or PP-$\overline{S}$ complements, and the brace in (65b) is the usual notation used to express this fact.

However, the only likely abbreviation of (65a,b) is the rule (66).

(66) $\begin{bmatrix} X \\ \langle +\text{subj} \rangle_1 \\ \langle -\text{subj} \rangle_2 \\ +\text{obj} \\ +\text{comp} \end{bmatrix}' \rightarrow X - \left\{ \begin{array}{l} (N'') - (P''') \\ \langle \overline{S} \rangle_2 \end{array} \right\} - \langle (\overline{S}) \rangle_1$

Capturing the generalization about the relative order of N''' and P''' misses the generalization about the presence of $\overline{S}$ in the complement. In (66), the two occurrences of $\bar{S}$ have nothing to do with each other, and either could be changed to something else without affecting the complexity of (66). This is clearly an incorrect result. The only way to improve on this is with a complex Boolean condition such as in (67), simulating the effect of the braces in (65b) within the constraint of a linear string.

(67)
$$\begin{bmatrix} X \\ +obj \\ +comp \end{bmatrix}' \rightarrow X - (N''')_1 - (P''')_2 - (\bar{S})_3$$

Condition: If $X = P$, not (3 and (1 or 2))

Apparently, then, the rules for all X' can be collapsed, while preserving the generalizations about order, only by means of a rule essentially like the rule for V', but supplemented by numerous negative Boolean conditions. It is hard to judge how good such a solution is. The introduction of more or less arbitrary Boolean conditions increases the power of a phrase structure grammar considerably, and one would have to ask very seriously how they can be constrained. Furthermore, it is not clear how one would define an evaluation measure over such a set of conditions, so as to know exactly what is a generalization and what is not. Nonetheless, the numerous partial generalizations of English seem to require some such rather complex solution. I can offer no interesting suggestions for alternatives to Boolean conditions. A serious study of the phrase structure rules of a number of other languages would no doubt elucidate what problems must be solved by an explanatory theory of cross-category phrase structure rules.

A more striking case concerns word order in X''. Consider phrases like *two parts steel, three quarters alcohol, five percent goo*, which contain the measure phrases *two parts, three quarters*, and *five percent*. Since *part* and *quarter* are nouns, one would suspect that these measure phrases are NPs somewhere in the specifier of the larger NP. Since they precede adjectives (e.g., *two thirds cold water*), which are in N'', they cannot be in the N'-specifier; since they do not receive the possessive affix, it would be advantageous to distinguish them structurally from NPs in the N'''-specifier, which are invariably possessive. This suggests that the measure phrase is attached to N''; thus it is further evidence that the NP must contain three levels.

Similarly, certain quantifiers can be argued to be X''-specifiers, namely those that can be preceded by an article: *many, few, several, little*, and the numerals. Since they cannot co-occur with measure phrases, we may use feature notation to collapse the phrase structure rules introducing the two categories:

(68)
$$N'' \rightarrow \left(\begin{bmatrix} +subj \\ -obj \\ -det \end{bmatrix}''' \right) - \ldots N' \ldots$$

In fact, it turns out that all [+comp] categories except verbs permit either a measure phrase or a quantifier phrase to precede the head:

(69) a.   *two parts steel*   (NP–N)
           little steel   (QP–N)
      b.   *two miles long*   (NP–A)
           little interested   (QP–A)
      c.   *two miles down the road*   (NP–P)
           far down the road   (QP–P)

By parallelism of grammatical relations, we are led to assign all of these cases to the X″-specifier.

In the verb phrase there is also an alternation of a measure phrase and a quantifier phrase in V″, but this time it is to the right of the head:

(70) a.   *He jumped into the air two times*   (V′–NP)
      b.   *He talked about sex too much*   (V′–QP)

To make matters worse, the measure phrase and (under certain conditions) the QP can follow the head in PP:

(71) a.   *down the road two miles*   (P′–NP)
      b.   *down the road quite far*   (P′–QP)

There is thus a generalization that $[\text{+subj, -obj, -det}]'''$ can be generated as a daughter of X″. But traditional phrase structure rules cannot express this generalization at all, because of the difference in word order. In this case even Boolean conditions do not provide much help. The best one could do is something like (72) (relying on semantic conditions to prohibit both at once in PP).

$$(72) \qquad X'' \rightarrow \ldots \left(\begin{bmatrix} \text{+subj} \\ \text{-obj} \\ \text{-det} \end{bmatrix}''' \right)_1 - \ldots - X' - \ldots - \left(\begin{bmatrix} \text{+subj} \\ \text{-obj} \\ \text{-det} \end{bmatrix}''' \right)_2 \ldots$$

Conditions: If X = V, not 1
                If X = [–obj], not 2

But this does not capture the generalization that the same expression appears on both sides of X′; the grammar would be no more complex (in terms of number of symbols) if the subscripted terms in (72) were of entirely different categories but used the same number of features. One might suggest instead that all these modifiers are generated before the head, and a transformation permutes them obligatorily around a V′ and optionally around a P′. Such a rule, however, would be non-structure-preserving, and besides would be supported by no independent syntactic evidence, at least in the case of V′.

Though this is the only such case I know of in English, there is reason to believe that it is not such a rare situation. It would arise most drastically in a language with a verb-final V′ but a noun-initial N′; German, if it is SOV, as has been rather persuasively argued by many people, is such a language. Languages in which adjectives follow nouns but adverbs precede adjectives would be another such case; so would SOV languages with prepositions rather than postpositions. Such languages are cited by Greenberg (1963).

Greenberg points out, however, that such languages are relatively rare; his "universals" say that the opposite correlations occur with "overwhelmingly greater than chance frequency." This suggests that the evaluation measure for phrase structure rules counts parallelisms of word order across X^n as generalizations, as we have come to expect here. But it appears also that parallel grammatical relations with differing orders across X^n also count as generalizations, though not as strongly; present notations have no way at all to express this. Again, detailed study of the phrase structure of languages other than English is necessary, in order to establish exactly what generalizations there are and how the formalism for phrase structure rules should be constrained so as to explain why these and no other generalizations appear.

9.   Closing Remarks

The $\overline{\text{X}}$-Convention as formulated in section 1 makes three claims: the class of possible lexical categories is determined by a set of distinctive features; the class of syntactic categories is determined by elaborating the lexical categories in terms of the prime notation; rules of grammar are to be stated in terms of these features and primes. We have argued here that this theory can be strengthened into the Uniform Three-Level Hypothesis: for every lexical category X, there are syntactic categories X', X'', and X''' , and no more, and the major phrase structure rules elaborating these categories are of the form given by rule schema (9):

(9) $X^n \rightarrow (C_1) \ldots (C_j) - X^{n-1} - (C_{j+1}) \ldots (C_k),$
             where $1 \leqslant n \leqslant 3$, and for all C_i, either
             $C_i = Y'''$ for some lexical category Y,
             or C_i is a specified grammatical formative.

Three arguments have appeared that bear on the need for three levels. First, the constituent structure of the auxiliary requires a level for aspectual verbs between the S-level and the V'-level (section 5). Second, complements can be divided into three semantic types whose ordering suggests the geometry of a three-level NP and S (section 6). Third, the position of measure phrases in NP specifiers requires a level intermediate between NP and N' (section 8).

Rule schema (9) provides the bulk of the phrase structure rules of the language, but there are at least two other schemata that generate possible configurations ruled out by (9): the schemata for coordination (50) and for "category-switching" rules (62).

(50) $X^i \rightarrow X^i - (\text{conj} - X^i)^*$

(62) $X^i \rightarrow \text{af} - Y^i$

These provide places in universal grammar for the parts of speech that do not play a rule in the $\overline{\text{X}}$-Convention, namely coordinating conjunctions, which appear in (50), and complementizers, which appear as one type of affix in (62). (62), with $i = 0$, also provides the prototype for a large class of word-formation rules.

I will conclude by mentioning a number of questions this theory leaves in my mind. The first group concerns the feature system. It is clear that a theory of markedness for syntactic categories is necessary, which will predict the relative probability of the parts of speech across languages: nouns and verbs are presumably universal, adjectives and prepositions less common, adverbs rarer, modals rarer still. Also, one of the drawbacks of the present feature system is that it incorrectly predicts that generalizations across *-comp* categories should be as common as those across *+comp* categories. Is this a question of markedness? Or are there substantive universals outside the feature system (such as the presence of Tense in sentences and deictic elements in NPs) that simply override possible generalizations?

A second group of questions concerns the adequacy of the constraint on the form of C_i in schema (9). Is it necessary to weaken the claim that all C_i are optional, and if so, how? Is the restriction to X ′′′ viable?[20] If not, what is a properly restrictive way of weakening it?

A third group of questions concerns the interpretations associated with various levels of specifiers and complements. To what extent are they universal? In English, as we have seen, complements are fairly consistent and well differentiated; but specifiers are less so, since (for instance) the quantifiers *few* and *every* seem to appear at the N′′ - and N′′′ -levels, respectively, despite their similar interpretations. Are the scope constraints illustrated in section 6 fundamentally syntactic or semantic in nature? Note that the answers to these two questions are related, since if interpretations of particular levels are not universal, the scope restrictions will correlate with varied level if they are syntactic and with varied interpretation if they are semantic.[21]

Finally, this theory suggests a somewhat novel approach to the complementizer. Most current work, for example Chomsky's and Bresnan's papers in this volume, assumes that there is a category $\bar{S}$ distinct from S that expands to *comp* - S. As has been shown here, the simplest version of the present theory is forced to claim that there is no difference in category status between $\bar{S}$ and S; rather the rule introducing the complementizer is V ′′′ → *comp* - V ′′′ , a special case of schema (62). This has immediate bearing on the issue of cyclicity of $\bar{S}$ and S addressed in Chomsky's paper.

But there are further interesting consequences. All examples of "category-switching" rules above the word level that have come to my attention involve deverbal constructions, i.e., the right-hand side of the rule is V^i, for some i. If this is generally the case, (62) can be further constrained. But this constraint predicts in turn that the only categories that can dominate themselves (in non-conjoined constructions) are V^i. Hence the phrase structure schema explains why only sentences have complementizers, and therefore, if *wh*-fronting is movement to Comp, why *wh*-fronting takes place only in sentences. Up to now this fact has been accounted for with the ad hoc rule expanding S; it now appears more principled.

To close, I will observe that many of these consequences and conjectures arise from the fact that I have attempted to formalize a maximally constrained version of the theory, as advocated in the opening citation from *Syntactic Structures*. I take it as a measure of my success that so much falls out from such relatively simple assumptions. If nothing else, the theory should provide a useful normative proposal against which to measure particular phrase structure analyses, an analytic tool that up to now has been unavailable.

Notes

1. The material in this paper is for the most part excerpted from my forthcoming monograph $\bar{X}$ *Syntax: A study of Phrase Structure*, where many specific points made here are elaborated in greater detail. Among those I would like to thank for valuable criticism and comment, Adrian Akmajian, Noam Chomsky, Peter Culicover, Joe Emonds, Lisa Selkirk, and Henk van Riemsdijk spring immediately to mind. My thanks to them and to many others I have not singled out.
2. For typographical convenience, I adopt Selkirk's "prime notation" $(X', X'', \text{etc.})$ instead of Chomsky's "bar notation" $\bar{X}, \bar{\bar{X}}$, etc.). No theoretical or ideological point is intended.
3. For a discussion of how the selectional restriction is imposed without a grammatical relation, see Jackendoff (1974b), especially section 5.
4. This term has nothing to do with Noam Chomsky, and he regrets its existence (personal communication). However, since it seems to be firmly established in common linguistic usage, I will retain it, sparingly, with apologies.
5. In section 7 the structure of gerundive nominals will be developed in such a way that they too receive their *'s* by this transformation.
6. I assume here the analysis of Emonds (1970), not that of Emonds (1976).
7. Or, if there is not an extraposition transformation, the generalization is in the projection rule. See Akmajian (1975) for evidence that this rule applies also in NP, a further generalization of NP and S.
8. Joe Emonds has pointed out (personal communication) that this solution is in some sense a return to one attractive aspect of Harrisian transformations: one would state, say, an NP movement rule as "move N"; all the modifiers would be moved along automatically. This emphasizes the centrality of the notion "head" to syntax in a highly suggestive fashion.
9. Wendy Wilkins has pointed out (personal communication) that this analysis brings to mind the arguments in SPE (pp. 382–385) that show a possible illegitimacy in the use of partially specified phonological feature matrices. However, examination of those arguments reveals that they depend on the fact that phonological rules may alter distinctive features. Since, under the assumptions of the lexicalist hypothesis, syntactic category features are never changed by transformations, the use of partially specified syntactic features is not susceptible to Chomsky and Halle's criticisms.
10. During the conference, Akmajian objected to this approach to the auxiliary on the grounds that it is a distortion of the actual facts of English and that there are auxiliary constituents in other languages that show no evidence of a modal. The approach taken here, however, is forced on me by the highly restrictive phrase structure rule schema (9). The citation from Chomsky in the introduction to this paper is relevant here: either this analysis will prove that the theory must be weakened in a highly specific way, or else it will provide a new analysis of what is otherwise an unprincipled exception to the general theory.

Akmajian further suggested that if the Modal is excepted from the phrase structure rule schema, perhaps all the other minor categories should be too. But since at least adverbs, quantifiers, and degree words have a rich specifier system governed by the $\bar{\text{X}}$-Convention (see Jackendoff, forthcoming, as well as Bresnan, 1973, and Selkirk's paper in this volume), I find this proposal questionable.

11. If there are no auxiliaries, and Affix Hopping attaches Tense to the main verb, presumably the entire M''' is deleted; but the empty node M is never filled in the course of the derivation, violating Emonds' (1970, 1976) condition on empty nodes. If the condition on empty nodes is modified to prohibit them *in surface structure* unless they have been filled at some point in the derivation, all is well again. Whether such a modification is desirable on independent grounds is unknown to me.

12. This distinction in the use of *do so* was first observed by Lakoff and Ross (1966). I assume that the interpretation of *do so* will be carried out by focus-dependent anaphoric processes such as Akmajian (1973) describes.

13. I am grateful for Noam Chomsky for pointing out this latter distinction to me. See note 14.

14. Notice, by the way, that (39) provides evidence that the *ones* test is valid only for *of-NP* complements, not for other PPs in N', since both of the following examples are acceptable.

    i.   *Arguments with Bill are less fruitful than ones with Harry.*
        (N'-complement)

    ii. *Arguments with many premises are less impressive than ones with few premises.*
        (N''-complement)

15. The insertion of parentheticals in V'' may be what Banfield (1973) calls a "stylistic transformation," one of a class of rules with somewhat different properties from ordinary transformations.

16. The bulk of Chapter 7 of Jackendoff (forthcoming) is devoted to defending this assertion against a number of other popular analyses. In particular, it is argued that the interpretation of so-called "stacked" relative clauses (e.g., *the man you saw who was from Philadelphia*) is not to be accounted for by syntactic stacking, but by the system that interprets focus and presupposition. As preliminary evidence, observe that the order of "stacking" in the example above changes if *saw* is stressed instead of *Philadelphia*, and recall that the sytem of focus and presupposition is based heavily on just such stress distinctions.

17. The subject would be interpreted by whatever principle assigns a subject to the nouns in (55a,b)—possibly the Complex Predicate Rule of Jackendoff (1974b).

18. Schachter (1976) also suggests that at least some infinitives are instances of deverbalized constructions, in which case the complementizer *to* is the relevant morphological marker.

19. Similarly, if N is replaced by A throughout (64), the transformational passive is (64b) and the lexical passive (discussed by Wasow in this volume) is (64d). The possibility of accounting for the historical connection between the constructions is quite evident: the addition of verbal rather than adjectival modifiers to a lexical passive would force a reanalysis of the structure to a more "sentencelike" configuration.

20. Selkirk's paper in this volume proposes the structure (i) for *many of the men*. Jackendoff (forthcoming, Chapter 5) defends instead the structure (ii), which obeys the constraint on C_i.

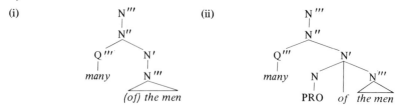

Akmajian's paper in this volume proposes two underlying structures which violate the C_i constraint:

(iii)   NP   (iv)   VP

I believe that (iii) can be replaced with (v) without losing the virtues of Akmajian's solution. This is argued in Jackendoff (forthcoming, Chapter 9).

(v)

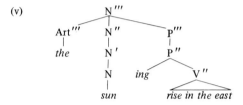

However, no attractive alternative solution to the "bare-infinitive" complement in (iv) immediately presents itself to me, and this may be a genuine exception to (9). See also note 10.

21. The scope restrictions also have a bearing on Chomsky's account of extraction in his paper in this volume. It was not pointed out in section 6 that complement level corresponds not only to possibility of scope extension but also to extractability of *wh*:

   (i)   *Who did you meet a brother of?*   (N'-complement)

   (ii)   **What did you meet a man with?*   (answer: *a scar*)   (N''-complement)

Is it a coincidence that scope and extraction are restricted in the same way? In Chomsky's theory it would appear to be, since the violation in **the man with what did you meet?*, a scope violation, must be accounted for by Chomsky's rule (38), which assigns logical form to traces; yet the violation in (ii) appears to be an extraction constraint of some sort. Since other environments, e.g., the interior of complex NPs, are also islands for both extraction and extension of scope outward, one would hope for a more general account.

SOME REMARKS ON NOUN PHRASE STRUCTURE

Elisabeth Selkirk

Department of Linguistics
University of Massachusetts
Amherst, Massachusetts

Perhaps the single most important contribution to the development of linguistic theory in this century has been the demonstration of the inadequacy of phrase structure grammars as a model of linguistic structure. This demonstration, made first by Chomsky in *Syntactic Structures*, and subsequently reiterated by Chomsky, Postal, Lees and others[1] in a number of classic papers, laid the ground for the emergence of a new theory of linguistic structure. According to this new theory, the grammar of a language includes not only a set of phrase structure rules (PS-rules) but, in addition, a set of transformational rules, rules that perform operations on the phrase markers generated by the PS-rules. This theory, the theory of transformational grammar, has come to dominate linguistic work in the United States and elsewhere in the last twenty years.

Transformational rules so captured the interest and the imagination of workers in the field that the greater part of the syntactic investigation carried out in this recent period has focused on the transformational component of a grammar. Attention has primarily been directed toward the discovery of transformations, the study of their formal properties, and the conditions on their application. Constituent structure per se took the back seat.

This is not to say that advances were not made in our understanding of the constituent structure of natural languages. There have been advances in this area, but those aspects of sentence structure that are now best understood are precisely those that have been relevant to the operation of some transformation or other. We may know, for example, that some PP is dominated by NP, if a transformation moves that PP along with the rest of the NP. Or we may discover from the operation of a transformation like VP-deletion whether or not some complement is dominated by VP, or some higher node. For quite a period of time, however, the internal structure of a category like NP went unstudied, for the simple reason that so few of the better known transformations were relevant to it. Questions of phrase structure were addressed insofar as they bore on the study of transformations.

Chomsky's *Aspects of the Theory of Syntax* (1965) was exceptional in its concern with the role of PS rules in a generative grammar. Indeed, the view soon emerged, under the name of generative semantics, that there was *no* role for PS-rules in a generative grammar. The debate centered on the existence of an underlying level of syntactic structure where significant generalizations about the canonical syntactic form of a language could be captured, by means of PS-rules. The proponents of generative semantics denied the existence of such a level, and claimed instead that all languages have a same underlying structure, one identical to logical form. In doing so they entrusted to the transformations of particular languages the central task of generating the language-specific peculiarities of syntactic form revealed in their surface structure; I mention this debate not to add anything of substance to it, but only to point out the extremes to which some linguists have gone in their zeal to give transformations the leading role in a grammar.

In recent years, many linguists have come to a renewed understanding of the primordial role of PS-rules in a grammar. The base-schema hypothesis, an innovative theory of phrase structure put forth in Chomsky (1970) has provided the impetus for new and original research on the phrase structure of English, in particular, and on the notion "possible phrase structure rule." [2] This line of research has led to a re-evaluation of many earlier transformational analyses, and one has increasingly seen the role of transformations diminished in the derivation of a sentence. It has been shown, for instance, that nominalizations must be generated as such in the deep structure (Chomsky, 1970), that quantifiers, among them comparative elements, should be generated in deep structure in the prenominal position that they occupy in surface structure (Stockwell et al., 1973, Jackendoff, 1968, forthcoming, Selkirk, 1970, Bresnan, 1973), and that prenominal adjectives must be generated in prenominal position in deep structure (Bresnan, 1973). This trend we see unfolding is one of the reaffirmation of the integrity of linguistic form, as expressed in phrase structure rules.

The present paper falls within this trend, and its primary goal is to make a contribution to our understanding of certain aspects of noun phrase structure in English. The investigation of noun phrase structure—the determination of the constituents that compose the noun phrase—is not without its difficulties, for few transformations, those invaluable tools of constituent structure analysis, ever apply within this domain. The investigator of the noun phrase thus has very few of these tools, and so must search for other sorts of arguments in articulating his or her hypothesis about noun phrase structure. One of the morals of the story to be told here is that syntactic arguments *can* be found for and against competing hypotheses concerning the hierarchical relations within this phrase category. In this light, an examination will be undertaken of noun phrases of the types *many women, many of the women, a bunch of flowers, a bunch of the flowers*. It is also hoped that the analysis to be offered will permit certain points to be made about the theoretical issues providing the focus of this conference—the thesis of the autonomy of syntax.

The autonomy thesis receives support from any demonstration that there is not a one-one mapping between syntactic form and semantic interpretation. These demonstrations can be made quite readily, if one assumes that the grammar includes a level of deep structure, with a fully articulated theory of phrase structure such as has been developed in recent research. Two examples stemming from some of this research might help demonstrate this point:

(i) *Mary is a more outrageous dancer than Andrea is.*

(ii) *The presentation of the Palestinian delegation made a big impression.*

In both cases, it is claimed, the boldfaced noun phrases are syntactically unambiguous, with surface structures that are furthermore almost identical to the deep structures. Yet the semantic component must assign two rather different interpretations to these collocations of constituents. In the first case, the adjective phrase *more outrageous* may be describing Mary's qualities as a dancer; here the adjective combines with the noun to make a derived property of sorts. But *more outrageous* may also be being predicated of Mary, in general, independent of her dancing. This distinction in prenominal adjective function has long been recognized, and it has been thought that prenominal adjectives in surface structure may have two different deep structure sources—one prenominal, the other in a relative clause of the form NP *be* AP (cf. Siegel, 1976, for example). However, Bresnan's (1973) demonstration that a NP with a prenominal "compared" adjective in surface structure must also have that shape in deep structure rules out this latter explanation for the source of the ambiguity in (i). One must conclude that two different semantic operations must be performed on that single adjective phrase/noun configuration.

In the second example above, the complex noun phrase in boldface may be given two interpretations depending on what grammatical relations are assigned to *the Palestinian delegation*. The delegation may be either the object of *presentation*, i.e., the Palestinians may be being presented, or the delegation may be the subject of *presentation*, i.e., doing a presentation. It seems clear by now that nominalizations like that in (ii) are not derived from a sentence, but rather are generated in the deep structure. And it seems desirable to argue that both the object and the subject instances of *the Palestinian delegation* are generated in their postnominal position in deep structure. As a consequence, it is up to the semantic component to provide a representation of the two different functions of the delegation.

The subject function must also be assigned to noun phrases appearing in two other structural configurations within the NP, as illustrated in (iii) and (iv).

(iii) *The Palestinian delegation's presentation . . .*

(iv) *The presentation by the Palestinian delegation . . .*

The possessive NP in English may play the role of a subject; the NP contained within a *by*-phrase must play that role. It is quite likely that there is no common deep structure source for *the Palestinian delegation* in (iii) and (iv) and the one with the subject interpretation in (ii).[3] If this is indeed true, then the autonomy thesis receives support once more. A one-one mapping between syntactic form and semantic interpretation is impossible, this time because one type of semantic function must be assigned to a NP appearing in a number of distinct syntactic configurations.

The noun phrase constructions investigated in this paper do bear on the issue of the autonomy of syntax. It is shown that expressions like *many women* have a structure distinct from that of *many of the women*, and that *a pound of potatoes* has a structure different from *a pound of the potatoes*. Yet it is not entirely clear that the semantic properties of the members of these pairs are all that different. The point is that whatever these similarities in semantic representation are, they will have to be obtained through the operation of the semantic rules to two distinct sytnactic configurations.

1. The QP within NP

English noun phrases may be divided into two types according to the syntactic characteristics of the quantifier and determiner elements specifying the head noun. The first type, that will be called the simple noun phrase, is exemplified by *some people, each woman, an objection*. Here the determiner precedes the head noun directly, or is separated from it only by an adjective phrase, as in *some rich people*. These simple noun phrases are generally thought of as having roughly the underlying structure in (1).

(1) $_{NP}$[*some* $_{Det}$ $_{\bar{N}}$[*people* $_N$]$_{\bar{N}}$]$_{NP}$

(Until we have accumulated further information regarding the internal structure of the NP, we will refrain from making precise what other nodes, if any, dominate Det and/or $\bar{N}$ under NP.) The second type of noun phrase is called the partitive noun phrase. Typical examples of partitives are the following: *many of these people, each of the women, some of her objections, three of the chapters*. Common to most every analysis of the partitive noun phrase is the claim that it contains a noun phrase within a noun phrase, i.e., that it has at least the structure of (2).

(2) $_{NP}$[*some* $_{Det}$ (*of*)$_{NP}$[*her* $_{Det}$ $_{\bar{N}}$[*objections* $_N$]$_{\bar{N}}$]$_{NP}$]$_{NP}$

(Again, we leave any further specification of the internal structure of these phrase types until later.) The simple noun phrase and the partitive noun phrase are thus significantly different in underlying (and surface) structure.

The question I would like to pose is this: how do noun phrases like *many objections, three chapters, the two objections* fit into this scheme? Do they have the deep structure of (3) or of (4)?[4]

(3) $_{NP}$[*many* $_{QP}$ $_{\bar{N}}$[*objections* $_N$]$_{\bar{N}}$]$_{NP}$

(4) $_{NP}$[*many* $_{QP}$ (*of*) $_{NP}$[[△]$_{Det}$ $_{\bar{N}}$[*objections* $_N$]$_{\bar{N}}$]$_{NP}$]$_{NP}$

The answer is that noun phrases like *many objections* are simple noun phrases like (3); and in this section arguments will be adduced that demonstrate that they cannot be derived from structures like (4). The hypothesis according to which (4) or something like it underlies *many objections* or *two dogs* will be dubbed the Hidden Partitives Hypothesis, or HPH. It has had a number of advocates (Jackendoff, 1968, Selkirk, 1970, Bresnan, 1973).

The hypothesis that will be defended here may be dubbed the Simple Noun Phrase Hypothesis, or SH. The feature of this hypothesis most important for our immediate concerns is the generation of the quantifier phrase containing *much, many, little, few*, and the numerals as sister to $\bar{\text{N}}$ within the NP. In contrast to the SH, the HPH asserts that there is no source for QP as sister to $\bar{\text{N}}$ within NP, rather that any noun phrase containing one of these QP will have to have the structure of a partitive. With the HPH, identical deep structure configurations will be assigned to *many objections* and *many of the objections*. Compare (4), the HPH-source for *many objections* to (5), the deep structure for *many of the objections*.

(5) $_{\text{NP}}$ [*many* $_{\text{QP}}$ (*of*) $_{\text{NP}}$ [*the* $_{\text{Det}}$ $_{\bar{\text{N}}}$ [*objections* $_{\text{N}}$] $_{\bar{\text{N}}}$] $_{\text{NP}}$] $_{\text{NP}}$

The first set of arguments that can be made against the HPH and in favor of the SH-analysis of *many objections* involves impermissible combinations of Quantifier plus Noun. These ungrammatical noun phrases can be ruled out in a quite general and natural fashion by the SH, but require the HPH to invoke ad hoc constraints to eliminate them. Compare first the sentences of (6a) and (6b).

(6)   a.   *She doesn't believe **much of that story**.*
            *We listened to **as little of his speech** as possible.*
            *How **much of the frescoes** did the flood damage?*
            *I read **some of the book**.*

       b.   **She doesn't believe **much story**.*
            We listened to **as little speech as possible.*
            How **much frescoes did the flood damage?*
            I read **some book.*   (as [–count])

The partitives of the (a) sentences allow a mass, i.e., non-count, quantifier phrase to co-occur with a lower noun phrase containing a singular count noun. But the (b) sentences show that mass quantifiers (or determiners) may not directly precede such count nouns. These facts are easily explained within the SH-theory, which assigns different deep structures to the (a) and (b) types. Within the SH-theory we will impose the condition that in a simple noun phrase like those of (1) or (3), all specifier elements (quantifiers, determiners) are required to agree with the head noun in their specificiation of the syntactic feature [count] . In fact, as will become clear, the specifier elements and the head noun of a simple noun phrase must agree for *all* syntactic features—count, number gender, case. Thus agreement for syntactic features is an entirely general condition on the well-formedness of simple noun phrases, and is undoubtedly a syntactic universal, hence not part of the grammar of of English per se. In partitives, like those in (a), this condition on agreement is inapplicable. No agreement between the higher quantifier and the lower noun phrase is required, and mass and count elements can therefore co-occur.

Within the HPH, the agreement condition for simple noun phrases will also be required. But this condition would do no work in ruling out the (b) sentences, which are not simple noun phrases for the HPH, but partitives. So, in addition, the HPH requires a constraint ruling out mass–count combinations in some partitives, but not in others. Those where the additional constraint must apply are those where the determiner is null, i.e., those in (b); the constraint would apply nowhere else.

The next set of troublesome facts centers on the difficulties the HPH encounters when it derives Quantifier–Noun combinations where the quantifier is the numeral *one*. The noun phrase *one book* is to be derived from *one (of)* [Δ] $_{Det}$ *books*, with a change in number of the head noun from plural to singular, according to Jackendoff (1968). But the results produced are ungrammatical when the lower noun is conjoined, as in (7), is a collective noun, as in (8), or is modified by a semantically plural adjective, as in (9). Compare the (a) and (b) sentences of the sets below.

(7)   a.   { *One* / *Many* } *of her brothers and sisters was/were arrested for disturbing the peace.*

            { *One* / *Several* } *of the workers and artisans in Via del Corno was/were in the party.*

            { *One* / *Few* } *of the men and women there was/were a fascist(s).*

       b.   { **One* mother(s) and sister(s) / Many brothers and sisters* } *was/were arrested . . .*

            { **One* worker(s) and artisan(s) / Several workers and artisans* } *in Via del Corno was/were . . .*

            { **One* men (man) and women (woman) / Few men and women* } *there was/were . . .*

(8)   a.   { *Many of the cattle / One of the people / Several of the womenfolk* } *was/were dying of thirst.*

       b.   *Many/*one* { *cattle / people / womenfolk* } *was/were dying of thirst.*

(9)   a.   *After* { *two / one* } *of her successive failures on the New York stage, Mary did a short stint in a suburban night club.*

            { *Two / One* } *of the consecutive blasts of the whistle was/were enough to wake her from a deep sleep.*

b. $After$ $\begin{Bmatrix} two \\ *one \end{Bmatrix}$ *successive failure(s) on the New York stage, Mary did a short stint in a suburban night club.*

$\begin{Bmatrix} Two \\ *One \end{Bmatrix}$ *consecutive blasts of the whistle was/were enough to wake her from a deep sleep.*

In all cases, the partitives of (a) are grammatical, whether the quantifier is *one, two, many*, or whatever. But the (b) noun phrases, while allowing plural quantifiers, are ungrammatical with *one*. The head nouns are inherently plural—for a variety of reasons—and therefore cannot undergo the number change that the HPH requires. So the HPH must add some mechanism to the grammar to exclude them. No such additional mechanism is required by the SH, however. With the SH it is simply the agreement condition on simple noun phrases that rules out the (b) sentences.[5]

To summarize, in the sentence sets (6-9) the examples of (b) show ungrammatical combinations of mass quantifier with count noun and singular quantifier with plural noun (or $\bar{N}$). The ungrammatical noun phrases of (6) though (9) can be ruled out by the SH merely by imposing what is undoubtedly a universal condition on simple noun phrases—that the specifier elements and head noun agree for all grammatically relevant syntactic features such as count, plural, gender, case, etc. Such a condition must be available to the HPH as well, for its own simple noun phrases where the specifier is Det. But, the HPH must appeal to an additional mechanism in order to rule out as ungrammatical the (b) sentences, which are generated as partitives, not simple noun phrases. Such a mechanism would have to exclude mismatches in the syntactic features [count] and [plural] between the higher quantifier and lower head noun just in case the lower Det is null, that is, just in case, at surface structure, that partitive would end up looking like a simple noun phrase. Only the SH provides a unified explanation for the ungrammaticality of the (b) sentences. Based on this evidence alone, then, it is to be preferred to the HPH. Further investigation will show additional drawbacks with the HPH while revealing the SH to be eminently capable of accounting for all the data.[6]

Recall that the HPH must allow for the conversion of (10) into (11).

(10)   *one (of)* $_{Det}[\Delta]$ $[\,^{N}_{+plur}]$

(11)   *one* $[\,^{N}_{-plur}\,]$

Notice now that the HPH has problems when relative clauses are taken into consideration. As has been pointed out in the literature (Dean, 1967, Jackendoff, 1968, Selkirk, 1970, Stockwell et al., 1973), in partitive noun phrases relative clauses may "modify" both the lower and upper noun phrases. The sentences in (12) where the number agreement in the restrictive relative clauses is not the same, should suffice to demonstrate this point.

(12)   *(That) one$_i$ of the politicians$_j$ that were$_j$ arrested together last week who is $_i$ willing to talk thinks he's going to save his skin.*

Each of those liberal candidates who were in favor of ecology who was known to have a compost heap was elected.

What would happen if the lower noun *politicians* or *candidates* had an indefinite determiner? According to the HPH, the *of* would fail to appear, producing the sentences of (13), which are ungrammatical.

(13)   *(That) one **politician that were arrested together last week**
         who is willing to talk thinks he's going to save his skin.

         *Each liberal candidate who were in favor of ecology who was
         known to have a compost heap was elected.

Similar problematic noun phrases are listed in (14).

(14)   *One leftist worker that were murdered one by one by the generals
         *One teacher who got to know each other last summer

The sentences (15) and (16) are not generated at all by the SH-grammar, for since *one politician* is an underlying singular simple noun phrase, it will never be associated with a relative clause with plural number agreement.

Notice furthermore that the HPH would generate the ungrammatical

(15)   *Two people that had left the meeting in a threesome

deriving it from the partitive source in (16)

(16) $_{NP}$[*two (of)* $_{NP}$[*people* $_S$ [*that had left in a threesome*] $_S$] $_{NP}$] $_{NP}$

Because both sentences of (17) below are grammatical, it appears the HPH would require some ad hoc surface filtering out of (15).

(17)   The people that had left the meeting in a threesome were
         rounded up by the DINA.

         Three people that had left the meeting in a threesome were
         rounded up by the DINA.

A final argument attesting to a structural difference between *many objections* and *many of the objections* is provided by the behavior of the transformation of extraposition from NP in its application to these different phrase types. In (18) and (19) we see examples of partitive noun phrases and what we have been claiming to be simple noun phrases.

(18)   How many of the answers to this classical mechanical
         problem have been found?

         Two of those reviews of Helen's first symphony have been reprinted.

(19)   How many answers to this classical mechanical problem have
         been found?

         Two reviews of Helen's first symphony have been reprinted.

In all of these noun phrases, the head noun has a PP-complement. The partitive noun phrases of (18) do not allow extraposition of that PP:

(20) ?*How many of the answers have been found to this classical
      mechanical problem?

  ?*Two of those reviews have been reprinted of Helen's first
      symphony.

But the simple noun phrases of (19) do allow extraposition of PP:

(21) How many answers have been found to this classical
      mechanical problem?

  Two reviews have been reprinted of Helen's first symphony.

In this way, the noun phrases of (19) are just like the simple noun phrases of (22),
which also permit extraposition, as shown in (23).

(22) $\begin{Bmatrix} Answers \\ The\ answers \end{Bmatrix}$ to this classical mechanical problem have been found.

  $\begin{Bmatrix} Reviews \\ Those\ reviews \end{Bmatrix}$ of Helen's first symphony have been reprinted.

  $\begin{Bmatrix} Answers \\ The\ answers \end{Bmatrix}$ have been found to this classical mechanical problem.

  $\begin{Bmatrix} Reviews \\ Those\ reviews \end{Bmatrix}$ have been reprinted of Helen's first symphony.

The explanation for this difference in extraposability of the PP is to be found in the
difference in the internal structure of the noun phrases of (18) and (19). In particular, it lies in the difference in the depth of embedding of the PP-complement
within the noun phrases of the two types. As has been pointed out by Ross (1967)
and Akmajian (1975), extraposition from noun phrase is upward-bounded. Akmajian
formulates the constraint on movement in the following way:

(24) No element may be extraposed more than one cycle up
      from the cycle containing it. (p. 119)

where the cyclic domain is S or NP. Accordingly, given a structure like that of (25),

(25)

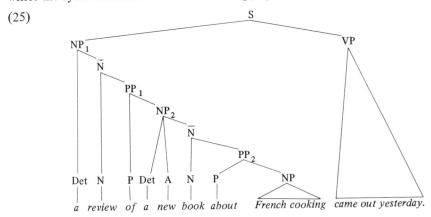

Akmajian points out that only PP_1 and not PP_2, may be extraposed to the end of the main clause:

(26)   a.   *A review came out yesterday of a new book about French cooking.*
       b.   **A review of a new book came out yesterday about French cooking.*

To extrapose PP   is to move it "more than one cycle up," and this creates ungrammaticality.

Notice now that in a partitive phrase, a PP-complement to the head N will always be "two cycles down":

(27) $_{NP_1}$[*how many of* $_{NP_2}$[*the*$_{\overline{N}}$[*answers*$_{PP}$[*to this . . . problem*]$_{PP}$]$_{\overline{N}}$]$_{NP}$]$_{NP}$

Thus, according to the Ross/Akmajian boundedness principle, a PP should never be able to be extraposed out of a partitive noun phrase. With this explanation for the lack of extraposability of the partitive noun phrases, one is obliged to accord the noun phrases of (19), which allow extraposition, a structure where that PP will not be "two cycles down." This structure is the structure of the simple noun phrase:

(28) $_{NP_1}$ [*how many*$_{\overline{N}}$[*answers* $_{PP}$[*to this . . . problem*]$_{PP}$]$_{\overline{N}}$]$_{NP_1}$

It seems that the Simple Noun Phrase Hypothesis does indeed account for all the syntactic characteristics of the *many objections* type of noun phrase.

What is it, then, that recommends the HPH to our attention? There is one argument that at first glance may seem to rule in its favor (cf. Jackendoff, 1968). The HPH will not allow for the generation, as a surface structure, of the ungrammatical partitive (29).

(29)   **many of objections*

for the structure that would underlie (29) as a surface structure is instead realized by the noun phrase (30).

(30)   *many objections*

The HPH seemingly requires no constraint on partitives in order to rule out (29). (29) is simply not generable in an HPH-grammar, which (on the version we are assuming here) would never insert *of* into a partitive that has a lower null Det. The SH-grammar, on the other hand, will require some kind of deep or surface constraint to rule out (29), which will be generated along with all the other partitives.

It must be realized, however, that any grammar of English will require certain constraints to be imposed on partitive constructions, for it is simply not the case that just any Det may be present in the lower noun phrase. Witness the ungrammaticality of the noun phrases of (31).

(31)   **three of some men*
            *many of all women
            *several of no books
            *two of too many acquaintances
            (versus *two of her many acquaintances*)

The HPH-grammar will require some constraint to rule these out, just as the SH-grammar will. Though the precise character of this partitive recursion constraint is not yet known, it may be safely assumed that, along with ruling out the noun phrases of (31), it could also rule out that of (29), which has an indefinite Det in the lower noun phrase.[7] It is this single constraint that the SH-grammar will contain. Since the HPH-grammar also requires this constraint, its superiority over the SH has not been demonstrated.

A further look at possible partitive constructions reveals that the HPH would be inconsistent in the use it made of any partitive recursion constraint(s). The HPH must derive a noun phrase like *many objections* from the underlying partitive (32)

(32) $_{NP}$ [*many (of)* $_{PP}$ [Δ_{Det} *objections*] $_{PP}$] $_{NP}$

and must therefore avoid invoking any partitive recursion constraint here, where the lower Det is null. But in other cases some constraint must indeed be invoked by the HPH to rule as ungrammatical partitive constructions with a null lower Det. Contrast the noun phrases in (33) to those in (34).

(33)   i.   *several (of) twenty of his roses that were sick*
        ii.   *nine (of) many of the lathe operators who were from Sicily*
        iii.   *three (of) nine planets of the solar system*
        iv.   *not much (of) little of Jane's wine that remained*
        v.   *few (of) many question*
        vi.   *any (of) many answers*

(34)   i.   several of those twenty of his roses that were sick
        ii.   nine of the many of the lathe operators who were from Sicily
        iii.   three of the nine planets of the solar system
        iv.   not much of the little of Jane's wine that remained
        v.   few of her many questions
        vi.   any of their many answers

The noun phrases of (33) are ungrammatical, with or without the parenthesized *or*, because *twenty, many, nine* etc., are preceded by a null Det. Deep structures will be generated for the noun phrases in (33), but they have no grammatical surface realization. The HPH must therefore appeal to a partitive recursion constraint to rule these out, and then somehow prevent that constraint from applying to rule out (32).

The SH provides a unified approach to the definition of a possible partitive construction, i.e., a unified definition of the possibilities for recursion in partitives, and is hence to be preferred over the HPH.

In concluding this section, I would like to remind the reader that the strongest arguments that have been adduced for choosing a simple noun phrase analysis for *many objections* and the like have been syntactic in character. To review, the arguments were that the SH provides an explanation for (i) the agreement in syntactic features between the Q and the head N, (ii) the number marking on verbs and relevant adverbials within relative clauses associated with these NPs, and (iii) the extraposibility of PP-complements to the head. The last argument in this section, namely that the SH will allow for the most general statement of a partitive recursion constraint, may be thought of as a "semantic argument," in that it is based on the application of the simplicity criterion to two solutions that will ultimately be expressed in semantic terms.

Before proceeding to the next section, it must be pointed out that all that has been established here is that the QP of *how many answers* and *two reviews* is sister to the N̄ within NP, and not sister to an NP. In other words, we have shown that QP and N̄ are dominated by a common node. Whether or not that node is itself NP, as in (35), or yet another nominal node mediating between NP and N̄, as in (36), has yet to be decided.

(35)   NP   (36)   NP

            QP   N̄   N̄̄

                                                        QP   N̄

This question forms the subject matter of the following section.

2.   Determiners and the Possessive in NP

Where do the NP-determiners (e.g., *the, that, those, a, any, some, no, each, every,* etc.) and the possessive NP "hang" within the NP? A number of possibilities present themselves; two promising candidates are depicted below:

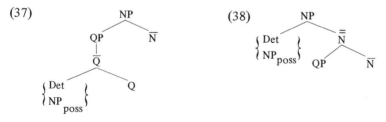

(37)   NP   (38)   NP

            QP   N̄   { Det }   N̄̄

            | { NP_poss }   QP   N̄

            Q

    { Det }   Q

    { NP_poss }

According to the first, which I have advocated in earlier, unpublished work,[8] QP and N̄ compose the NP, the Det and Poss being generated within the Det-position in the QP. According to the second, which has been proposed by Jackendoff (forthcoming) and K. Ross (1976), the QP and N form a constituent unto themselves, this constituent being sister to Det or Poss under NP. The principle drawback of (37) is that it provides only one source for Det in the NP-specifier (inside the QP). The principle drawback of (38) is that the only Det generable in QP would be the degree determiners *so, too, as,* etc. In what follows, it will emerge that there should be two sources for NP determiners—one inside the QP, and one outside the QP. This means that neither (37) nor (38) provides an adequate representation of the NP specifier.

Instead, the correct analysis is in some sense an amalgamation of these two. (As for the Poss, the discussion below indicates that it should have its source outside the QP.)

The "compromise" solution could be represented as in (39a). It should be kept in mind, however, that the extra level $\overline{\overline{N}}$ which contains just QP and $\overline{N}$ remains controversial, and that arguments must be provided that permit one to choose it instead of (39b), which lacks a level of $\overline{\overline{N}}$.

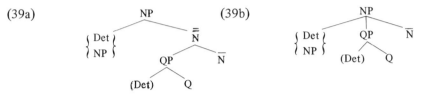

Such arguments are available.

In developing support for either version of (39), we review the reasons for generating noun phrase determiners in QP. In what follows we assume the correctness of the analysis according to which the degree particles *as, so, too, -er, that,* etc., are generated within the QP as sister to the quantifiers *much, many, little,* and *few* (Selkirk, 1970, Bresnan, 1973). The category dominating them will be called $\overline{Q}$, where $\overline{Q} \rightarrow (\text{Det}_{deg})$ Q. In addition, following Bresnan's (1973) analysis, the left-branching recursion of QP will be assumed to be generated by the rule $QP \rightarrow \left\{ \begin{matrix} QP \\ NP \end{matrix} \right\} \overline{Q}$. The question is whether degree particles and the noun phrase determiner have the same phrase structure source.[9]

One sort of argument of favor of a QP source for NP is based on the fact that the degree particles and noun phrase determiners seem to belong to the same sort of syntactic category, and that they appear to have much the same distribution. Note first that the complement clauses associated with these words (relative clauses, comparative clauses, *that*-clauses with *so*, and *for/to*-clauses with *too*) share a number of important syntactic and semantic properties that distinguish them as a group from other sorts of complement clauses (cf. Selkirk, 1970, Bowers, 1970). Now, it is within the specifier category QP, whether in AP or in NP, that the determiners of degree find their source.

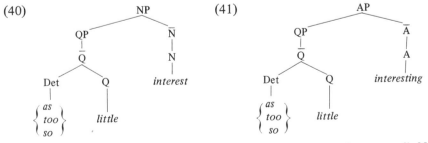

And it seems entirely plausible to generate the NP determiners here as well. Note that some noun phrase determiners actually must be said to crop up in the QP.

Consider first the *the* that appears with superlatives like those in (42):

(42)   *Mary spoke the most convincingly.*
               She ran the fastest.
               We thought this was the most interesting.

What is this *the*? It does not find its source in the noun phrase, for there is none here in the relevant positions. The most reasonable assumption is that *the* is a (surface) Det of the QP of AP. One might propose that this occupies the position in the tree that in deep structure was occupied by the superlative Det *-est*, and that this *-est*, which we take to be [+Definite], is postposed and encliticized to the Q. In so doing, it leaves behind an empty [+Definite] determiner node; it is into this position that *the* is inserted. This analysis is represented schematically below.

(43) $_{AP}[\ _{QP}[\ _{Det}[\ \text{-est}\ ]\ _Q[\ much\ ]_Q\ ]_{QP}\ _A[\ \cdots\ ]_A\ ]_{AP}$ ==>
         +def

     $_{AP}[\ _{QP}[\ _{Det}[\ \phi\ ]\ _Q[\ _Q[\ much\ ]_Q\text{est}\ ]_Q\ ]_{QP}\ _A[\ \cdots\ ]_A\ ]_{AP}$ ==>
           +def

     $_{AP}[\ _{QP}[\ _{Det}[\ the\ ]_Q\ [\ much\text{-est}\ ]_Q\ ]_{QP}\ _A[\ \cdots\ ]_A\ ]_{AP}$
          +def   ⇓
                          most

Now if this analysis is correct for *the most convincingly*, it could quite likely be correct for *the most conviction*, or *the most money*, which would have the surface structure of (44).

(44) $_{NP}[\ _{QP}[\ _{Det}[\ the\ ]\ _Q[\ most\ ]_Q\ ]_{QP}\ _{\bar N}[\ _N[\ conviction]_N\ ]_N\ ]_{NP}$

One might reasonably ask why, if *the* is generated in QP in superlatives, it should not be generated there all the time? [10]

Yet another sort of noun phrase determiner—the demonstrative—makes an appearance in the QP specifying AP.

(45)   a.   *Was it really **that much** more interesting?*
        b.   *The board's **this long.***
        c.   *The food isn't **that awful.***

Here, the demonstratives are determiners of Q, as in (46), and function in part as degree particles.

(46)

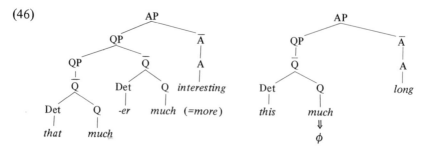

In addition to specifying degree, these demonstratives are still demonstratives, i.e., referential, and in cases like (45b) clearly deictic.

The demonstrative degree determiners are to be found in the QP of NP as well, generated in the same place as *as, so, too*, etc.

(47)   *There were* $\left\{ \begin{array}{l} \textit{these} \\ \textit{that} \end{array} \right\}$ **many fewer people** *at the meeting this time.*

          Is there really **that little** *to do?*

          I don't want **that much heat***.*

The appearance of these demonstratives in QP lends more credence to the idea of having NP–Det elements generated there.

It seems that those NP–Det that can be reasonably said to be generated within the QP are given a "degree" interpretation, akin to that involved with the determiners *so, as*, etc. Let us suppose that whenever any NP–Det is generated in QP it has a degree interpretation, and that when it is generated outside of QP it does not have this sort of interpretation. A dual source like that allowed by (39) could thus provide an appealing explanation for the puzzling ambiguities displayed by the bold-faced determiners in the following sentences.

(18)   **Those** *many friends of J. Mensch were there at the meeting.*

(19)   *I was amazed at* $\left\{ \begin{array}{l} \textit{the} \\ \textit{the few} \end{array} \right\}$ *people who showed up.*

(30)   **Some** *people were observed entering through the back door.*

In each case, the determiner may or may not be given a "degree" interpretation. *Those many friends* may mean "those numerous friends" or "that many friends." In the latter case, the determiner is functioning as a degree particle, modifying *many*. And in (49), while one reading may be roughly paraphrased as "I was amazed at something about those (few) people who showed up," the other is something like "I was amazed at how $\left\{ \begin{array}{l} \text{many} \\ \text{few} \end{array} \right\}$ people showed up.[12]" The *the* itself seems to have a degree modifier function in the latter case. Finally, as is well known, one of the interpretations of *some* in (50) is a quantity-like interpretation. It is this interpretation that will be associated with the QP-source.[13, 14]

The dual-Det hypothesis has one glaring deficiency: it allows for the generation of the ungrammatical sequences *NP$_{\text{poss}}$ Det and *Det–Det, e.g.,

(51)   **those how many heroes of bygone days*

          **his as few virtues*

          **the so little interest*

          **the too many kids*

The grammar containing the phrase structure rules generating (39) will have to include a constraint that rules these sequences out. I will not attempt to formulate this constraint here, but only wish to mention that by including a provision in the grammar for excluding *Det–Det sequences, we might at the same time rule out infelicitous sequences produced when a NP-determiner and the Det that may be generated in the QP of a prenominal AP co-occur in the same noun phrase, e.g., *the as ingenious arguments, *her so much more appealing traits, *any too strenuous efforts. So there may be independent motivation for this constraint.

Turning now to the question of the source of NP$_{poss}$, recall that either analysis of (39) gives it a source under NP, not within QP. The NP$_{poss}$ functions in no way like a degree modifier, and so it seems semantically inappropriate to give it a source in QP. (The analysis of (37) required such a source, cf. (52).)

(52)

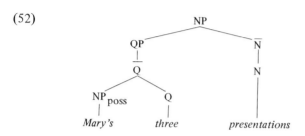

Note that given this analysis, it is an NP embedded way down in the QP that must be given the interpretation of "subject of NP" in an example like (52). This result seems counterintuitive, for there is no resemblance between the configuration upon which the subject relation is defined here within NP and that on which it is defined in S.

In principle, this lack of parallelism between subject in NP and subject in S is not problematic. We have already mentioned that the subject relation must be defined on the post-head N noun phrase the Palestinian delegation in the noun phrase the presentation of the Palestinian delegation. And there is no comparable post-V parallel in the S to the of-phrase in NP. Evidently, the grammar must include a semantic projection rule specific to NP which interprets such of-phrases as subjects.

The question to be asked is whether still another NP-specific rule for subject is required in order to give the proper interpretation of Mary in Mary's three presentations. Just such an additional rule is necessary, if Mary is generated within the QP. If, however, either alternative phrase structure analysis of (39) is adopted, then a semantic rule can be defined that ranges over both NP and S, interpreting as subject that NP immediately dominated by NP or S.

A choice still remains to be made between (39a) and (39b). The grammaticality of a NP such as (53) would seem to indicate that (39a) provides the correct analysis.

(53)   Mary's three sisters and two brothers

The phrase structure hypothesis of (39a) would allow (53) to be analyzed as an NP containing a conjunction of N̿, each one composed of a numeral and a head noun, as in (54).

(54)

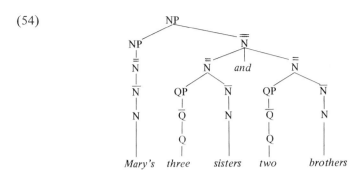

(the conjunction analysis imposed by (39b) would involve a coordination of NPs and, presumably, a deletion or interpretation of an identical Poss in the second conjunct.)

Now notice that if the category S is indeed merely the verbal category $\overline{\overline{V}}$, as has been argued by Williams (1971), Jackendoff (1973, forthcoming) and others, and if NP is a "three-level" category, as in (39a), then the subject relation in noun phrase and sentence is defined on syntactic structures that are parallel:

(55)

$$\overline{\overline{N}} \; (=NP) \qquad\qquad \overline{\overline{V}} \; (=S)$$

If the analyses of (55) are correct, they permit one to entertain a rather strong hypothesis about the possible phrase structure configurations of a language such as that proposed by Jackendoff (forthcoming):

(56)   If parallel grammatical relations exist in two different categories, the categories must be syntactically parallel. pp. 3–18

He calls this the Uniform Level Hypothesis. The formulation of this hypothesis could be elaborated somewhat, so as to allow for rather specific predictions about the structure of the parallel categories. (One could also give the hypothesis a some-what more perspicuous name, e.g., the Syntactic Parallellism Hypothesis.) It might read as follows:

(57)   If parallel grammatical relations obtain in two different categories, and the constituents over which these relations are defined have the same, i.e., parallel, syntactic distribution within those cate-gories, then the categories must be syntactically parallel, that is, the relevant constituents must enjoy the same, i.e., parallel, hierarchical relations within the categories.

This hypothesis lies at the heart of the base schema hypothesis of Chomsky (1970), and has been implicit in most of the work carried out in this framework. We have every interest in adopting it in something like the form above, for it makes extremely strong predictions about the syntax of related categories. It is to be expected that the investigator will, on occasion, encounter situations where no syntactic evidence is available to permit a choice to be made between two (or more) competing phrase structure hypotheses. In such cases the theory, i.e., the Syntactic Parallelism Hypothesis, could provide the answer. Before this hypothesis can play such as decisive role, however, support for it from a wide variety of languages must accumulate.

3.   Measure Phrases

In this last section, the syntax of partitives and partitive-like constructions will be examined. First I would like to argue that measure phrases like those in (58) are simple noun phrases, not partitives,

(58)   *a number of objections*
            three pounds of stew meat
            a bushel of apples
            loads of time

and that they have the underlying structure of (59), parallel to that of *many people*, in (60).[15]

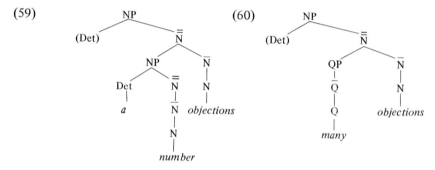

(A transformation will have to insert *of* in the context NP___ N̄. The Det under the highest NP will have to be either optionally developed, or null and "indefinite," were this permitted by the constraint on Det in sequence.) The noun phrases of (58) will be called pseudopartitives. It will be shown that much is to be gained by not considering the subsequent *(of) objections* to be a NP composed of null indefinite Det plus N.[16] The claim is therefore that the noun phrases of (58) do not have a structure identical to those of (61), which are partitives.

(61)   *a number of her objections*
            three pounds of that stew meat
            a bushel of the apples
            loads of them

Second, a brief review will be made of the evidence, drawn in large part from Akmajian and Lehrer (1975) and K. Ross (1976), that phrases like *a bunch of flowers* and *a bunch of the flowers* are syntactically ambiguous. These phrases are semantically ambiguous: on one interpretation *a bunch* is a "measure phrase," indicating the amount of flowers; on the other *bunch* functions as a head noun and is further characterized or qualified by the phrase *(of) the flowers*. Were the syntax of these phrase types always the same (as some have thought[17]), then we would have yet another example of the lack of a one–one mapping between syntactic form and semantic interpretation. These phrase types can be shown to have two different syntactic analyses, however, one in which *bunch* is a head N under $\bar{\text{N}}$ with a complement *of*-phrase, and the other where *bunch* is a measure noun, generated either in a partitive or pseudopartitive construction. As a consequence they do not provide additional evidence for the autonomy thesis.

Let us turn now to our first question about the distinction between partitives and pseudopartitives. Notice first that by considering *five pounds of apples, a bunch of flowers* and the like, to be simple noun phrases we are able to obtain a completely general statement of the partitive recursion constraint, valid for both measure phrase and quantifier phrase partitives. Recall that the base rules advocated here will generate the following array of noun phrases with quantifiers.

(62)   **Partitive**

   a.
   $$\text{many of} \left\{ \begin{array}{l} \text{the} \\ \text{those} \\ \text{her} \end{array} \right\} \text{apples}$$

   b.   *many of $\left\{ \begin{array}{l} \text{some} \\ \text{all} \\ \text{no} \\ \Delta\text{-indef} \end{array} \right\}$ apples

   Simple

   c.   *many apples*

The noun phrases of (b) containing the lower determiners *some, all, no,* Δ (=indef), and so on, must be ruled out by a partitive recursion constraint. The very same constraint can apply in measure phrase partitives if *five pounds of apples* is considered to be a simple noun phrase.

(63)   **Partitive**

   a.
   $$\text{five pounds of} \left\{ \begin{array}{l} \text{the} \\ \text{those} \\ \text{her} \end{array} \right\} \text{apples}$$

   b.   *five pounds of $\left\{ \begin{array}{l} \text{some} \\ \text{all} \\ \text{no} \\ \Delta\text{-indef} \end{array} \right\}$ apples

   Simple

   c.   *five pounds apples* > *five pounds of apples*

This constraint could be given the initial rough formulation of (64). (In its present state it is merely a descriptive statement.)

(64)   Rule out as ungrammatical any partitive construction containing
             some, all, no, Δ (= indef), and so on, in the lower noun phrase.

However, it would require some modification if *five pounds of apples* were really a partitive with a null indefinite Det on *apples*; it would have to allow the null indefinite determiner in measure phrase partitives but not in quantifier phrase partitives. I contend that there is no such asymmetry between the two partitive types and would now like to adduce certain types of syntactic evidence showing that *five pounds of apples* is a simple NP.

The first bit of evidence is provided by the transformation of Extraposition from NP, which treats partitives and "pseudopartitives" differently. Extraposition may postpose the *of NP* sequence of partitives, but cannot postpose the *of $\overline{N}$* sequence of the pseudopartitives.[18] The following examples illustrate this difference.

(65)
   a.   *A lot of* $\left\{ {the \atop \phi} \right\}$ *leftover turkey has been eaten.*

   b.   *A lot had been eaten of* $\left\{ {the \atop *\phi} \right\}$ *leftover turkey.*

   a.   *Only a handful of* $\left\{ {those \atop \phi} \right\}$ *questions concerning electromagnetism were asked.*

   b.   *Only a handful were asked of* $\left\{ {those \atop *\phi} \right\}$ *questions concerning electromagnetism.*

   a.   *How many pounds of* $\left\{ {those \atop \phi} \right\}$ *apples did you buy?*

   b.   *How many pounds did you buy of* $\left\{ {those \atop *\phi} \right\}$ *apples?*

   a.   *They devoured seven boxes of* $\left\{ {your \atop \phi} \right\}$ *delicious fudge last night.*

   b.   *They devoured seven boxes last night of* $\left\{ {your \atop *\phi} \right\}$ *delicious fudge.*

   a.   *He gave a rather large number of* $\left\{ {his \atop \phi} \right\}$ *books by famous authors to Mary.*

   b.   *He gave a rather large number to Mary of* $\left\{ {his \atop *\phi} \right\}$ *books by famous authors.*

If both types of noun phrase are given the structure of partitives then the transformation, which displaces a Prep–NP sequence, should be applicable to both. Note that it is not possible to maintain that extraposition does not move noun phrases whose determiners are indefinite, for sentences like (66), where extraposition has applied to a non-partitive, non-measure phrase construction, are common.

(66)   *Atlantic Richfield was originally scheduled to start **delivery** this month **of coal from its Thunder Basin Mine south of town.***

The failure of extraposition to apply to a sequence like *of leftover turkey* must be viewed simply as a consequence of the fact that such sequences do not meet the structural description of the rule. Extraposition displaces a *noun phrase*, i.e., NP, which is preceded by a preposition. It will not apply to *of leftover turkey*, for according to our hypothesis this string has the structure *of*-N̄.

Yet another set of facts connected with extraposiiton provides further support for the pseudopartitive analysis. In the (1975) article mentioned above, Akmajian observed that examples such as the (b) sentences of (67) and (68) may be problematical for Ross's upward-boundedness constraint, as long as it is assumed that in those noun phrases the noun *number* is a head noun with a prepositional complement, as in (69).

(67)   a.   *A number of pictures of John were taken yesterday.*
         b.   *A number of pictures were taken yesterday of John.*

(68)   a.   *A number of stories about Watergate soon appeared.*
         b.   *A number of stories soon appeared about Watergate.*

(69)

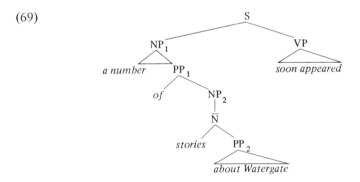

In these cases the PP$_2$ does extrapose, and given a structure like (69), it is moving more than one cycle up. Akmajian leaves the problem unresolved, suggesting that (69) may be the incorrect structure for "quantifier-like elements (such as *a number of*)." There is a solution available to this problem, one that allows the generalization in (24) to be maintained. It amounts to giving the noun phrases of (67) and (68) the deep structure I have suggested, that of (70). (Akmajian and Lehrer, 1975, also arrived at this solution.)

(70)

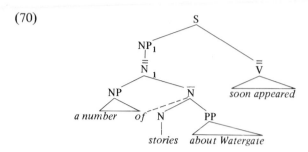

Given this structure, where only NP is a cyclic node, the extraposition of PP does not involve moving it more than one cycle up. The PP is contained within the cyclic domain NP_1, and it is moved up into the S. Thus, the behavior of the sentences (67) and (68) does not represent counterevidence to the generalization about boundedness if one adopts the analysis proposed here.

What is significant in this connection is that what are being claimed here to be real partitives in measure phrases like *a number of*, and so on, do *not* allow extraposition. The sentences of (ii) below show a difference in behavior between what I am calling pseudopartitives in (a), and the real partitives in (b). (The examples of (i) are designed to show that in a non-pseudopartitive noun phrase, extraposition is possible in both cases.)

(71) a. (i)   *Answers have been rediscovered to this classical mechanical problem.*
      (ii) *The answers have been rediscovered to this classical mechanical problem.*

    b. (i)   *A variety of answers have been rediscovered to this classical mechanical problem.*
      (ii) *?*A variety of the answers have been rediscovered to this classical mechanical problem.*

(72) a. (i)   *Objections soon emerged against these kinds of tactics.*
      (ii) *The (traditional) objections soon emerged against these kinds of tactics.*

    b. (i)   *A bunch of objections soon emerged against these kinds of tactics.*
      (ii) *?*A bunch of the (traditional) objections soon emerged against these kinds of tactics.*

(73) a. (i)   *Commentaries have appeared on Anne's latest book.*
      (ii) *The commentaries have appeared on Anne's latest book.*

    b. (i)   *A number of commentaries have appeared on Anne's latest book.*
      (ii) *?*A number of the commentaries have appeared on Anne's latest book.*

(74) a. (i)   *Reviews were published today of Helen's first symphony.*
      (ii) *The reviews were published today of Helen's first symphony.*

    b. (i)   *A lot of reviews were published today of Helen's first symphony.*
      (ii) *?*A lot of the reviews were published today of Helen's first symphony.*

We know that partitives have a structure something like that in (75), with an NP inside an NP. (We will be more specific later.)

(75)

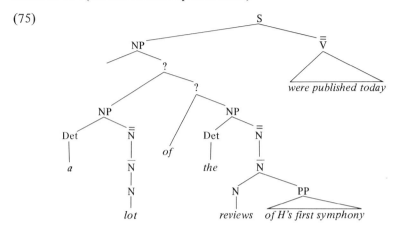

Because of the embedded structure of the partitive, the PP would have to be extraposed more than one cycle up on its way to the end of the sentence. This is not permitted, following (24), and the sentence becomes ungrammatical. So it is that the assignment of the different structures (70) and (75) to the (i) and (ii) sentences allows for a straightforward explanation of the differences in extraposability of the Prep–NP sequences contained within them.[19]

Let us turn now to another sort of argument that noun phrases like *a whole lot of famous paintings* and *dozens of daffodils* are not partitives. The evidence is provided by the interpretation of nonrestrictive relative clauses in association with such noun phrases. Observe first that relative clauses of the sentences (76) and (77) are ambiguous.

(76)   *In the Uffizi they saw a whole lot of the famous paintings, several of which were by Sienese artists.*

(77)   *She bought him dozens of those daffodils, only two of which were faded.*

In (76) the several paintings by Sienese artists were either among the paintings they saw, or simply among the famous paintings in the museum and not necessarily seen by them. In (77), the two faded daffodils could either have been among the ones she bought, or among the group designated by *those daffodils*, and not necessarily chosen by her. Observe next that the lack of a determiner after *of* is correlated with a reduction in the number of relative clause interpretations available.

(78)   *In the Uffizi, they saw a whole lot of famous paintings, several of which were by Sienese artists.*

(79)   *She bought him dozens of daffodils, only two of which were faded.*

Each relative clause has only one interpretation. The paintings by Sienese artists were among the "whole lot" seen by them, and two of the purchased daffodils were faded. The sentences of (76) and (77) are ambiguous because the relative clause may be associated with either of two NPs—the entire partitive noun phrase, *dozens of those daffodils*, or the lower one, *those daffodils*. In (78) and (79) there is no lower NP. The relative clause cannot associate with *of daffodils*, only with the full noun phrase, *dozens of daffodils*.[20]

A final argument in favor of the contention that the category $\overline{\overline{N}}$ may be rewritten as [NP $\overline{N}$] is based on the observation that in certain circumstances the *of* may in fact be absent from "pseudopartitives" while it is never allowed to be absent from real partitives. We take this to mean that the rule inserting *of* in partitives knows no exception, while the rule inserting *of* in the context NP-$\overline{N}$ may be subject to exception. There are lexical exceptions to this latter *of* insertion rule. The measure phrase *a dozen*, when in a pseudopartitive, requires the absence of *of*. Contrast (80) and (81).

(80)   *She bought him a dozen (*of) daffodils.*

(81)   *She bought him a dozen* $\left\{ \begin{matrix} of \\ *\phi \end{matrix} \right\}$ *those daffodils*

The measure phrase *a couple* optionally permits *of* to be absent.

(82)   *Can I borrow a couple (of) sheets of paper?*

Aside from these lexicalized exceptions, one also encounters locations like the following, expecially in recipes.

(83)   *A pound cake is one pound butter, one pound sugar, one*
          pound eggs and one pound flour.

These too have the air of fixed expressions, so it is perhaps most important that the *of* may disappear in constructions like those below, which are indisputably derived from nonidiomatic noun phrases.

(84)   *I met a larger number of high school students than*

          I did $\left\{ \begin{matrix} college\ students. \\ ?of\ college\ students. \end{matrix} \right\}$

          They sold as many pounds of apples as they did $\left\{ \begin{matrix} pears.^{21} \\ of\ pears. \end{matrix} \right\}$
          A word has the same number of tone specifications that
          it has $\left\{ \begin{matrix} syllables.^{22} \\ ?of\ syllables. \end{matrix} \right\}$

Note that the absence of *of* is not allowed in the real partitives.

(85)   *I met a larger number of the high school students than*

          I did $\left\{ \begin{matrix} *the\ college\ students. \\ of\ the\ college\ students. \end{matrix} \right\}$

          They sold as many pounds of those apples as they did $\left\{ \begin{matrix} *those\ pears. \\ of\ those\ pears. \end{matrix} \right\}$

According to my analysis, there is an identifiable structural configuration, [NP N̄], where the *of* may sometimes be absent. On the other hand, in the structures associated with partitives, the *of* must always be present.

In sum, a variety of syntactic arguments lead one to the conclusion that *five pounds of apples* is structurally distinct from *five pounds of the apples*. The second is a partitive, so the first must not be. The evidence suggests that the first is a simple noun phrase with the measure noun phrase NP sister to the constituent N̄.

Let us turn now to a comparison of pseudopartitives and the noun complement construction. Many of the points to be reviewed have been made by other linguists in their work on the noun phrase, e.g., Jackendoff (1968), Stockwell et al. (1973), Akmajian (1975), Akmajian and Lehrer (1975), and K. Ross (1976), and I hope I will be pardoned if I do not mention the exact source at every juncture of the observation to be made.

As was pointed out above, noun phrases whose *of*-phrase is a complement to the head noun do not have the same behavior with respect to the transformation of extraposition from NP as do noun phrases containing pseudopartitives. To review, compare the pairs (86) and (87).

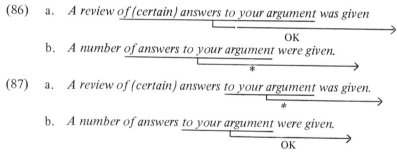

(86) a. *A review of (certain) answers to your argument was given*

          OK

      b. *A number of answers to your argument were given.*

          *

(87) a. *A review of (certain) answers to your argument was given.*

          *

      b. *A number of answers to your argument were given.*

          OK

This difference is explained by assigning a different syntactic structure to the noun phrase of the (a) and (b) sentences. In the (a) sentences, *review* is the head noun, generated under N̄, with an *of*-NP complement. In the (b) sentences, *answers* is the head noun, while *number* is a measure noun generated in an NP sister to the N̄ containing the head.

In general, the other tests permitting one to distinguish between pseudopartitives and noun complement constructions involve processes that crucially refer to the head noun of a noun phrase. So, for example, the number agreement of a verb is (usually) determined by the head N of the subject NP. Notice in the sentences in (86) and (87) that the sentences with *review* as a head N have the auxiliary *was* while those with the head N *answers* have *were*.

Some nouns may function either as a head noun or a measure noun. In a sentence such as (88), it is in the number agreement on the verb that one finds a clue to the structure of the noun phrase.

(88)
   An assortment of responses to those questions of yours $\begin{Bmatrix} were \\ was \end{Bmatrix}$ *considered.*

Notice that number agreement correlates in a rather nice way with the possibilities for extraposition with the two noun phrases underlying (88). In (89), *responses* is the head and thus the extraposition of its complement is permitted; *were* agrees with *responses*.

(89)   *An assortment of responses* $\left\{\begin{array}{c} was \\ were \end{array}\right\}$ *considered to those questions of yours.*

In (90), *assortment* is the head, takes *was*, and allows its complement to be extraposed.

(90)   *An assortment* $\left\{\begin{array}{c} was \\ *were \end{array}\right\}$ *considered of responses to those questions of yours.*

Other phenomena that make crucial reference to the head of a noun phrase are pronominalization and selectional restrictions. First compare the sentences (91) and (92).

(91)   *That group of crazies really got **itself** in hot water, didn't **it**?*

(92)   *That group of crazies really got **themselves** in hot water, didn't **they**?*

(91) and (92) do not mean the same thing. In (91), *group* is the head N, requiring the reflexive *itself* and the tag pronoun *it*, and may be taken to mean something like "organization." In (92), *crazies* is the head N, requiring the reflexive *themselves* and the tag pronoun *they; group* in this sentence is a measure noun, having a meaning more like "bunch" or "lot."

Finally, compare the sentences (93) and (94).

(93)   *A cup of sugar was strewn on the floor.*

(94)   *A cup of sugar smashed on the floor.*

In the first sentence only the quantity of sugar, equivalent to a cupful, was on the floor (but not necessarily the cup itself); *sugar* is the head noun. In the second, *cup* is the head noun, has itself fallen, and broken into pieces. Notice that a noun phrase cannot allow both interpretations at once. The sentence (95) demonstrates that the noun of an NP determining the selectional restrictions in a matrix sentence must also determine them in a relative clause.

(95)   *The cup of sugar that this recipe requires* $\left\{\begin{array}{l} \text{*crashed to the floor.} \\ \text{was strewn on the floor.} \end{array}\right\}$

Whichever noun is interpreted as the head is fixed for any sentence.

Taken together, then, the transformation of extraposition and the head-sensitive phenomena of number agreement, pronominalization, and selectional restrictions provide evidence that an NP like *a bunch of flowers* may be ambiguous between the pseudopartitive and the noun complement construction. It remains now to show that the real partitives are syntactically distinct from the noun complement construction. The operation of the extraposition transformation does not give evidence for a syntactic distinction. But the facts available from number agreement, pronominalization, and selectional restrictions indicate that in a partitive the "measure noun" cannot be considered to be the head of the noun phrase, and so I believe we are forced to posit a syntactic distinction between partitives and the noun complement construction.

With respect to extraposition from NP, both these types behave similarly:

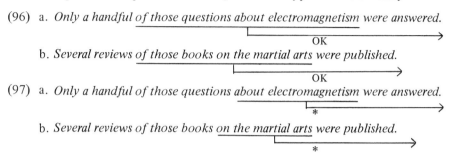

(96) a. *Only a handful of those questions about electromagnetism were answered.*

OK

    b. *Several reviews of those books on the martial arts were published.*

OK

(97) a. *Only a handful of those questions about electromagnetism were answered.*

*

    b. *Several reviews of those books on the martial arts were published.*

*

It is not necessary to attribute this similarity to an identity of structure between these two phrase types, however; it would simply result from the fact that both contain an NP embedded within an NP.

The other tests may be taken to show that noun phrases of the type Det–N *of* Det–N are syntactically ambiguous:

(98) **Number Agreement**

    A bunch of those flowers $\left\{ \begin{array}{c} was \\ were \end{array} \right\}$ *thrown out on the back lawn.*

(99) **Pronominalization**

    A bunch of those flowers could be put in the vase, couldn't $\left\{ \begin{array}{c} they \\ it \end{array} \right\}$ *?*

(100) **Selectional Restrictions**

    She $\left\{ \begin{array}{c} broke \\ drank \end{array} \right\}$ *a bottle of that good wine.*

From this we conclude that the measure noun of the partitive construction, be it *handful, bottle,* or *bunch* is not to be considered the head N of NP, and thus that partitives are syntactically distinct from the noun complement construction. (I am assuming that "head N of NP" is a *syntactic* notion, defined perhaps as that first N dominated by $\overline{\text{N}}$ dominated by $\overline{\overline{\text{N}}}$ dominated by NP. (This definition will be modified below.) As a consequence of this assumption, NPs having different heads must have different syntactic structure.)

Our last task is to offer some hypothesis about the structure of partitives. We know that the partitive construction (i) contains an NP within an NP, (ii) is recursive, and (iii) is right-branching. Furthermore, it has been shown that partitives like *three of the women* or *some of the women* cannot derive from a source like **three* *women of the women* or *some women of the women* (cf. Selkirk, 1975). We would like to suggest that the structure in (100), which resembles a structure proposed by K. Ross (1976), best represents the properties described.

(101)

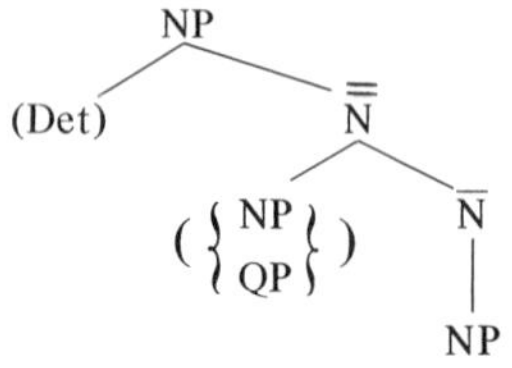

$$
\begin{array}{c}
\text{NP} \\
\diagup\quad\diagdown \\
(\text{Det}) \qquad \overline{\overline{\text{N}}} \\
\diagup\quad\diagdown \\
(\{^{\text{NP}}_{\text{QP}}\}) \qquad \overline{\text{N}} \\
| \\
\text{NP}
\end{array}
$$

The phrase structure rules we have developed so far for noun phrase are gathered together in (102).

(102) $\text{NP} \rightarrow (\{^{\text{Det}}_{\text{NP}_{\text{poss}}}\}) \, \overline{\overline{\text{N}}}$

$\overline{\overline{\text{N}}} \rightarrow (\{^{\text{NP}}_{\text{QP}}\}) \quad \overline{\text{N}}$

$\overline{\text{N}} \rightarrow \text{N} \, \{^{\text{PP}}_{\text{S}}\}$

To allow for the generation of partitives, we have only to add the rule (103).

(103) $\overline{\text{N}} \rightarrow \text{NP}$

To sum up, *a bunch of the flowers*, which may be either a partitive or a noun complement construction, will be assigned one of the two following structures:

(104)   *Partitive*   (105)   *Noun Complement*

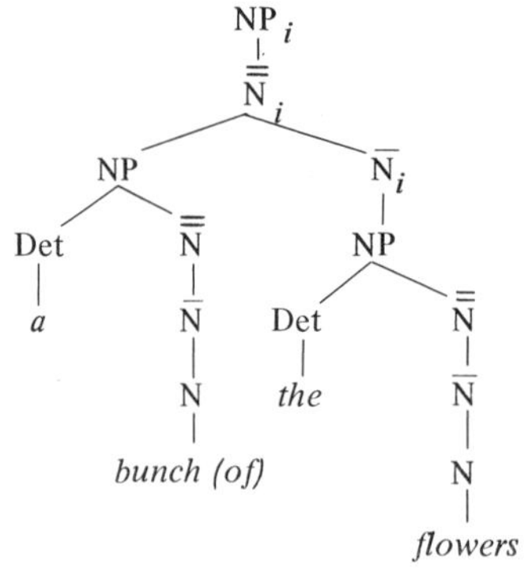

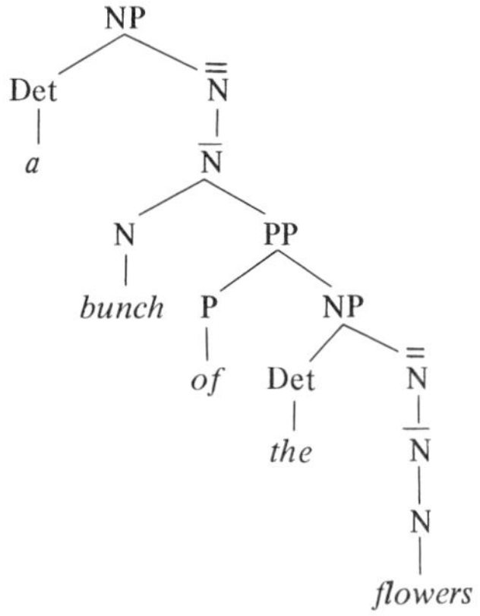

(Note that given the rules (102) and (103) "head N" will have to be defined in the following way (roughly): the *head noun* N of NP$_i$ is that N that is dominated by $\overline{\text{N}}_i$ and $\overline{\overline{\text{N}}}_i$, both dominated by NP$_i$, and that is not dominated by any category PP, VP or AP which is dominated by NP$_i$. A look at (104) will satisfy the reader that this definition allows *flowers* to be picked out as the head N of NP in (104). *A bunch of flowers* on the other hand, has the syntax of either a pseudopartive of a noun complement construction:

(106) *Pseudopartitive*   (107)   *Noun Complement*

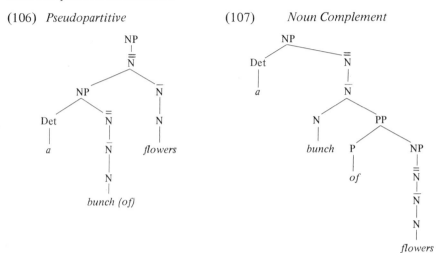

I would like to conclude by remarking that the demonstration that there are three distinct syntactic structures associated with partitives, pseudopartitives, and noun complements is of some relevance to the issue of the relation between syntactic form and semantic interpretation. It seems quite likely that we will find that NPs in English with a structure like that of partitives will always be interpreted as partitives, or that NPs in English with the structure of pseudopartitives will always be interpreted as pseudopartitives. In other words, with these phrase types the semantic interpretation may be fixed; here there may be a one–one mapping between form and meaning. It certainly is not the case that head nouns and the complements under $\overline{\text{N}}$ that follow them are always given the same sort of semantic interpretation, however. A whole variety of grammatical relations may obtain, and so a one–one mapping between form and meaning is not possible at this level. It would be nice to know whether it is an accident of English that partitives and pseudopartitive constructions each have a single type of interpretation, or whether this limitation follows from deeper principles concerning the types of interpretation that can be assigned by the semantics at the various levels (X, $\overline{\overline{\text{X}}}$, XP) inside the major phrase category. Hopefully, continued research on the constituent structure of natural languages will provide an answer to this question.

Acknowledgments

I would like to thank Joan Bresnan, Ray Jackendoff, Dick Oehrle, Jean-Roger Vergnaud, and Edwin Williams for discussions and commentaries that contributed to the development of this paper. All deficiencies are, of course, my own.

Much of the research for this paper was carried out during the tenure of a NATO Postdoctoral Fellowship in Science, in Paris, January 1973–January 1974. I am grateful to the Laboratoire d'Automatique Documentaire et Linguistique, and in particular to Maurice Gross, for providing me with research facilities during this time.

I would also like to extend my deepest thanks to Sally Hollens and Terry Sachs, who were responsible for typing and reproducing an earlier version of this paper.

Notes

1. Chomsky (1964, for example), Postal (1964a, 1964b), Lees (1957).
2. Bowers (1970, 1968), Selkirk (1970, 1972, 1974, forthcoming), Williams (1975), Bresnan (1973, 1975, 1976), Jackendoff (1974, forthcoming), Vergnaud (1973), Stockwell, Schachter and Partee (1973), Ronat (1973), Halitsky (1975), Hornstein (1975), Milner (1975), and Emonds (1976), among others.
3. Given an analysis of the Passive like that of Bresnan (1972), the agent originates and stays in the *by*-phrase that is generated in postverbal position in deep structure. Carried over to the noun phrase this analysis would have the *by*-phrase generated with the agent in postnominal position. The "subject" in Poss-position in NP would be generated in that position in deep structure, and would not be postposed, according to this analysis.
4. In asserting that there is a syntactic category Quantifier Phrase, I am drawing on Bresnan (1973). This fundamental insight of Bresnan's, that there exists a QP distinct from NP and AP, has been of immense importance in my work on the structure of Noun Phrase and Adjective Phrase.

    It should be pointed out that the analysis of Noun Phrase, Adjective Phrase, and Quantifier Phrase being proposed here differs in certain ways from that of Bresnan (1973). The reasons for these differences will become clear below. I would like to emphasize, however, that the research reported on in this paper owes a very great deal to Bresnan's work, and continues much in the same vein.

5. Notice also that the boldfaced noun phrase of (i) is problematical for the HPH.

    (i)   *She didn't do one single thing.*

    The alleged source for this, according to Jackendoff (1968) is (ii),

    (ii)   *She didn't do one of ϕ_{Det} single things.*

    where the lower noun phrase in the partitive is plural, yet containing the adjective *single*. In general, though, *single* is prohibited from appearing with plural nouns, cf. (iii)

    (iii) *two of the single things*
           single things

    So it is puzzling that lexical insertion of *single* into an underlying structure like (ii) should even be permitted.

    For the SH, the derivation of (i) presents no such puzzles. The noun phrase *one single thing* is simple generated as such, as a simple noun phrase, with the requirement that *single* have a singular head noun being met.

6. The proponent of the HPH might conceivably argue that the conditions for agreement among quantifiers, determiners, and head nouns should be stated at surface structure, after the transformation that determines the presence (or absence) of the *of* operates. The claim might be that the Q N combinations derived from underlying partitives are made to agree because of their juxtaposition in surface structure. Such a claim would be based on the assumption that agreement would be determined only by the linear arrangement of the elements in surface structure, not by their hierarchical relations, for, according to the HPH, the Q N sequence is still a partitive of the form $_{NP}[_{QP}[Q]_{QP} _{NP}[N]_{NP}]_{NP}$ in

surface structure, not a simple noun phrase. This account is unsatisfactory, for it seems highly unlikely that the mere absence of the *of* should cause agreement to be defined over a syntactic configuration totally different from the Simple NP where agreement usually obtains.

7. It does seem to be possible for the lower noun phrase of a partitive to contain a null determiner, as (i) shows.

(i)   *I heard too much of one speech and not enough of the other.*

This possibility is only available when that noun phrase is interpreted as [+specific].

8. Cf. Selkirk (1975) and talks delivered at University College London and Cambridge University in December 1973. Cf. also Bresnan (1976).

9. This is Bresnan's (1973) posititon, which I think is correct. For a dissenting view, see Jackendoff (forthcoming), whose proposal is more in the spirit of Selkirk (1970) and Bowers (1970) in that it involves a rule AP → Det A, where Det is not introduced under QP. Unfortunately space does not permit me either to pursue the discussion of this dispute or resolve it.

10. The *the* generated in the QP of AP in superlatives is undoubtedly deleted when the AP is generated within the NP, as in *the three most interesting reports*. According to the *Det in QP* hypothesis, such a noun phrase would have the underlying structure of (i), which is transformed into (ii).

(i)

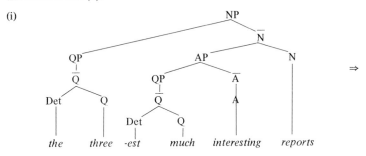

(ii)

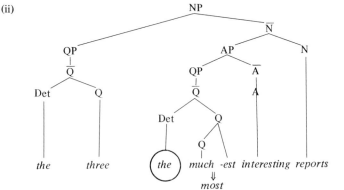

The circled *the* in (ii) is deleted.

Notice also that, according to this analysis, the noun phrases of (iii) would derive from those in (iv), by *the*-deletion in the QP of AP.

(iii) $\left\{\begin{array}{l} Jane's \\ the \end{array}\right\}$ *most interesting contribution*

(iv) $\left\{\begin{array}{l} Jane's \\ the \end{array}\right\}$ AP[QP[*the most*] QP*interesting*] AP *contribution*

11. Many speakers allow only the singular *that* to be used as a degree determiner: *that many people*. For others, myself included, the forms *these, those*, and *this* may also be used, deictically, in pointing out the quantity being discussed. I can put out four fingers of my right hand and declare "There were only these many people there!"

12. See Carlson (1975) for an extremely interesting account of "amount relatives" such as *We were surprised at the water that there was in the streets*.

13. In Selkirk (1975), I proposed that the "quantitative" *some* be generated as a Det in a QP whose head Q was underlying *much* or *many*. This *much* or *many*, whose interpretation would be similar to the *much/many* of *how much/many*, was argued to be deleted after *some, any* and *no*.

    Cf. Carlson (1975), where it is argued that an abstract quantifier is generated (and deleted) after *the* and other determiners in amount relatives.

14. Consider the following sentence, in which *those* has two possible sources: *Did only those few black people get to go?* Pronounced with more prominence than *few* (not contrastively), *those* is interpreted as the degree determiner. When *those* and *few* have comparable prominence, *those* is interpreted as a normal demonstrative, i.e., as an NP–Det. We can expect that such facts will help provide arguments for syntactic analyses like those being discussed here, when the intonation of English noun phrases is better understood.

15. In his work on the specifier system of the noun phrase in Fench, Milner (1975) gives an analysis similar to this pseudopartitive analysis to measure phrases in constructions like:

    Trois kilos de pommes   'three pounds of potatoes'
    une grande quantite de vin blanc   'a large quantity of white wine'
    un nombre incroyable de spectateurs   'an incredible number of spectators'

In this analysis, too, the measure phrase is generated as sister to the $\overline{\text{N}}$, and the particle *de* is inserted by transformation.

16. This latter view is commonplace (cf. Jackendoff, 1968, Selkirk, 1970, Stockwell et al., 1973, Bresnan, 1973).

17. This for example is the position adopted by Jackendoff (1968).

18. This observation has been made independently by Akmajian and Lehrer.

19. A possible counterexample to this extraposition analysis was brought to my attention by Dick Oehrle: *How much of a proof actually exists of this theorem.* Assuming that *How much of a proof of this theorem* is a partitive construction, exptaposition should not be allowed to move *of this theorem* up and out of the NP. I might point out that another, similar sort of counterexample is provided by sentences such as: *A hell of a report came out on the secret activities of the CIA.* In both cases we have a noun phrase that, semantically speaking, is not like a partitive, and it is perhaps not unreasonable to imagine assigning them a syntactic structure distinct from real partitives. Time will tell. (For some discussion of the *how much of a . . .* construction, cf. Bresnan, 1973.)

20. Jackendoff (forthcoming) and K. Ross (1976) assign to nonrestrictive relatives a source immediately under the NP node, e.g.,

It follows from this analysis that a simple NP can have only one nonrestrictive relative, while a partitive, which is an NP containing yet another NP, could have more than one.

21. The sentence below is actually ambiguous:

    They sold as many pounds of apples as they did pears.

It may mean that the number of pounds of apples sold was equivalent to the number of pounds of pears sold, or simple to the number of (individual) pears sold. Only the first interpretation is of relevance here.

22. This example is due to Mary Clark, its unwitting utterer.

COMMENTS ON THE PAPER BY SELKIRK

Richard T. Oehrle

Department of Linguistics
Stanford University
Stanford, California

1.   As the structural configurations of various syntactic constituents provide the requisite level of generality at which to state conditions on syntactic well-formedness, the question of what internal structure to assign to English noun phrases is an important one. Selkirk demonstrates effectively in her paper that the choice of one structure over another for certain classes of NPs has interesting consequences with respect to an optimal account of such grammatical phenomena as mass/count/concord, subject-verb agreement, various issues concerning selectional restrictions, and the proper applicability of the rule known as Extraposition from NP. In the three main sections of her paper, Selkirk puts forth several hypotheses which involve distinctions between various structural configurations. Although by and large I agree with her on where such distinctions are to be drawn, there are a number of cases in which I think the distinctions at issue should be expressed in a fashion somewhat different from that she suggests. In the discussion to follow, while I shall touch briefly on her basic points, I wish to demonstrate a conflict between two of her implicit assumptions and to offer some speculations on how this conflict might be satisfactorily resolved.

1.1   Selkirk's first point is that in such phrases as *how many answers* and *two reviews*, the QP (i.e., *how many* in the first case, *two* in the second) is sister to N^1 and not sister to an NP. [1] In other words, they have the structure illustrated in (1):

(1) $_{NP}$ [$_{QP}$[*how many*] $_{QP}$ $_{N^1}$ [*answers*] $_{N^1}$] $_{NP}$

Her arguments concerning the mass/count distinction and various problems concerning number agreement provide sufficient evidence to favor this conclusion over the alternative "Hidden Partitive Hypothesis" found in Jackendoff (1968) and elsewhere.

1.2   In the second section of the paper, Selkirk discusses two ways of generating the possessive NP determiner and various other elements of the NP specifier system.

On one account, these elements are to be generated in the left branch of the QP generated under N^2. On another account, there is a higher node N^3, which dominates the source of these specifier elements as well as N^2. These two alternatives are illustrated below in (2) and (3).

(2)   (3)

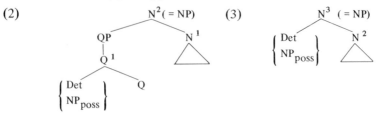

Although Selkirk presents two arguments based on distributional evidence which seem to favor (2) over (3), she ultimately opts for (3), partly on the basis of the Syntactic Parallelism Hypothesis due to Jackendoff. Insofar as we assume that for any given well-formed syntactic constituent (under a given interpretation) there is a unique structure, Selkirk is certainly correct in urging that we endeavor to develop general principles that will settle questions of constituent structure in cases where the correct choice is underdetermined. This assumption is open to question on a variety of grounds, however. For example, diachronic changes in the syntactic structure assigned to certain sentences suggest that the structure assigned is not always uniquely determined. Hence either we may find cases in which more than one structure is compatible with whatever general principles we adopt, or we must allow the possibility of indeterminacy in some cases.[2] In the case at hand, however, there is evidence to settle the relevant aspect of the constituent structure independently of the Syntactic Parallelism Hypothesis.

Selkirk notes in her first section that "the specifier elements and the head noun of a simple noun phrase must agree for *all* syntactic features—count, number, gender, case." If this is true, then it is difficult to see how the hypothesis embodied in (2) could account for the distinction between phrases like *a bare 50 people* and **a people*. On the other hand, structure (3) allows us to express the required distinction just as long as we allow the agreement rule to express compatibility between the heads of phrases and the determiners of that head—not between determiners of one phrase and heads of another. In other words, in *a bare 50 people*, the word *a* is a determiner element in a QP headed by *50*, whereas in **a people, a* acts as the determiner of a phrase whose head is incompatible with it. The same phenomenon can be seen, I believe, in the distinction between *these many people* and *that many people*. Contrary to what Selkirk suggests, I find these phrases unambiguous and nonequivalent.

If this argument is correct—and it has roughly the same form as some of the arguments in Selkirk's first section—there is good reason to choose (3) over (2) as the source of the class of specifier elements Selkirk is concerned with. That this decision is in conformity with the Syntactic Parallelism Hypothesis provides some independent evidence in its favor, of course—a more interesting result than one that merely employs it as a methodological principle.[3]

1.3   In the final section of the paper, Selkirk shows that such phrases as *a bunch of flowers* and *a bunch of the flowers* can be analyzed in two ways: in one structure *bunch* is the head of the phrase as a whole, and *(the) flowers* is its complement; in the other structure, *a bunch* is analyzed as a measure phrase and is generated in exactly those positions in which we find quantifier phrases in such expressions as *some flowers* and *some of the flowers*. Selkirk presents a variety of arguments in favor of this analysis, yet certain difficulties arise with respect to the structures Selkirk chooses to express the distinctions at issue. The conflict in assumptions discussed in the next section will clarify in part exactly what these difficulties are.

2.0   Throughout her paper, Selkirk draws on conclusions inferred from the behavior of the rule of Extraposition from NP (hereafter 'E-NP'), a rule discussed recently by Akmajian (1975). The fact that this rule, like other rightward movement rules, is upward-bounded, makes it an obvious choice for analyzing the complexity of constituents from which material can be extracted: a natural way of accounting for the failure of the rule to apply in certain cases is to assume that the upward-bounded property prevents the rule's application, i.e., that the phrase to be extracted is too deeply embedded.

There is a difficulty in this sort of reasoning, since from a purely syntactic point of view, there are a variety of constraints on the applicability of E-NP. Among these we note: 1) the shape of the determiner of the matrix NP; 2) the relation between the matrix N and its complement; and 3) the predicate of the S into which the extracted PP is to be extraposed. These three properties are illustrated in the following examples.

(3)   a.   *A review of Claudia's book was sent to me.*
       b.   *A review was sent to me of Claudia's book.*
       c.   *?*The review was sent to me of Claudia's book.*

(4)   a.   *A proof of this theorem would be easy to develop.*
       b.   *A taste for figs would be easy to develop.*
       c.   *A proof would be easy to develop of this theorem.*
       d.   **A taste would be easy to develop for figs.*

(5)   a.   *No proof of this theorem will ever be found.*
       b.   *No proof of this theorem will ever be sound.*
       c.   *No proof will ever be found of this theorem.*
       d.   **No proof will ever be sound of this theorem.*

The nature of these constraints—their substantive character and the difficulty of stating them as syntactic conditions on E-NP—suggests that we attempt to subsume at least some of them under a single semantic condition. It is an interesting and instructive exercise to try to formulate such a condition, an exercise I shall forego for the present since the exact statement of the constraints on E-NP is irrelevant to the argument that follows.

What is clear, however, is that while a certain phrasal constituent structure provides a necessary condition for the applicability of E-NP, it does not constitute a sufficient condition: the inapplicability of E-NP in a given case may be due to other factors than the depth of embedding of the target subconstituent. Hence from E-NP's failure to apply acceptably in a given case, we cannot jump to conclusions about the constituent structure of the phrase from which extraction was to take place.

Of particular interest for our purposes here is the interaction of the upwrad-bounded character of E-NP with one other critical assumption, embodied in the following passage from Selkirk's paper:

(6)   Common to most every analysis of the partitive noun phrase is the claim that it contains a noun phrase within a noun phrase, i.e., that it has at least the structure of (2).

(2) $_{NP}[$ *some* $_{Det}$ *(of)* $_{NP}[$ *her* $_{Det}$ $_{\bar{N}}[$ *objections* $_N]_{\bar{N}}]_{NP}]_{NP}$

It would seem, then, that the presence of the determiner following *of* is taken as an indication of the presence of an embedded NP. If the rule E-NP is in fact upward-bounded, however, this assumption cannot be correct.

Consider first noun phrases containing a quantifier phrase which have a 'predicative' interpretation, such as *(not) much of an argument, quite a fool, a hell of a drummer*. In certain cases, at least, such phrases admit the application of E-NP, as the following examples show:

(7)   a.   *How much of a proof of this theorem actually exists?*
        b.   *How much of a proof actually exists of this theorem?*

(8)   a.   *One hell of a review of Mary's book has just appeared.*
        b.   *One hell of a review has just appeared of Mary's book.*

In line with (4), we might expect that the analyses in (9) would be unobjectionable:

(9)   a. $_{NP}[$ *(how much of)* $_{NP}[$ *a proof of this theorem*$]_{NP}]_{NP}$

        b. $_{NP}[$ *(one hell of)* $_{NP}[$ *a review of Mary's book* $]_{NP}]_{NP}$

Yet on the assumption that E-NP is upward-bounded, such a structure is untenable, since E-NP may clearly apply in spite of the infraction that its application would incur in moving the subconstituent *of this theorem* out of more than one cyclic domain.

This problem is not limited to cases in which the noun phrase as a whole has a 'predicative' interpretation." Thus, in the following pairs of sentences, there seems to be little difference in acceptability between the case in which the subject NP contains a quantifier and the case in which it doesn't, although on Selkirk's assumptions, there should be a sharp distinction since in the former case the application of E-NP should violate the upward-boundedness condition.

(10)   a.   *Have all of the commentaries appeared already on Mary's work?*
        b.   *The commentaries have finally appeared on Mary's work.*

(11)   a.   *None of the reviews have appeared yet of this important work.*
       b.   *The reviews are finally beginning to come out of Mary's new book.*

Again, given the well-formedness of these examples, we cannot maintain both that
E-NP is upward-bounded and that the expressions *all of the commentaries on
Mary's work* and *none of the reviews of this important work* both constitute cyclic
domains as a whole and properly contain cyclic domains in which the expressions
on Mary's work and *of this important work* (respectively) are embedded.

   In short, the assumption embodied in the passage quoted in (6) conflicts with
the assumption that E-NP is upward-bounded.

2.1   There are several ways to attack this dilemma. One is to maintain the sort of
structure given in (6) and deny the upward-bounded character of E-NP. Of the ways
I can think of, however, this is by far the least attractive: it denies us a reasonable
account of the inapplicability of E-NP to a class of structures for which there is
otherwise no obvious treatment, while at the same time segregating E-NP from the
class of other rightward movement rules, all of which have the upward-bounded
property.

   The basic problem is to present an analysis of the expressions in question which is
consistent, then, with the assumption that the expression moved by E-NP is contained within only one cyclic domain. There are many conceivable ways of doing
this: I shall concentrate here, however, on two broad approaches to the problem.

2.1.1   One possibility is to leave the form of the constituent structure given in (9)
relatively untouched and merely change the category symbol around *a proof of
this theorem* in such a way that it does not constitute a cyclic domain. In particular,
if N^k represents the cyclic domain NP and N^0 is the lexical category noun, we
need available some intermediate level of structure lying between N^0 and N^k,
call it N^j, where $0 < j < k$. Since by hypothesis, N^j is not a cyclic domain, our reanalysis poses no barrier to the application of E-NP. In short, what this solution
attempts is to exploit the inherent power of the bar notation, a theory of categorial
substructure which allows us to draw distinctions that are impossible in a theory that
distinguishes only between the lexical node N $(=N^0)$ and the phrasal node NP $(=N^k)$.

   As noted, the crucial aspect of this first proposal is that it allows constituents of
the form *Det . . . N . . .* to be generated in ways which do not involve considering
the full expression a cyclic domain: they are not immediately dominated by N^k.
This is a somewhat radical departure from current practice, but not one that lacks
historical precedent. In fact, the proposal is analogous to the question of whether
it is possible to generate the node VP $(=V^2)$ elsewhere than immediately under S
$(=V^3)$. Whether the difficulties and prospects involved in the two cases are precisely
the same is unlikely, however: a more thorough study of this question than I am
able to provide here would have to investigate in some detail the precise role of the
categorial hierarchy in subcategorization, to cite just one obvious problem.

   Whatever the empirical status of this proposal may turn out to be, however, it does have points of interest. For instance, we can apply it in an interesting way to certain problems that arise with respect to Chomsky's subjacency condition (cf. Chomsky, 1973, this volume). As Chomsky notes, *wh*-movement, constrained by the subjacency condition, is unable to extract material from within cyclic domains to COMP position. Hence in order to account for the (grammatical) sentences in (12) below, Chomsky proposes that a lexically governed restructuring rule applies to the complements of certain noun phrases (in certain contexts), thus placing the NP to which *wh* is attached within the domain of *wh*-movement as constrained by the subjacency condition. (The symbol *t* identifies the position from which the constituent moved by *wh*-movement is extracted.)

(12)   *Who did you see a picture of t?*
         What were you watching movies about t?
         Which sets did Zermelo deny the existence of t?

An alternative to Chomsky's proposal is to regard such phrases as *a picture of t, movies about t, the existence of t* (at least in the contexts in which they appear in (12)) as not constituting cyclic nodes (i.e., N^k) but rather as instances of N^j. Note that if possessive determiners and demonstratives are generated only along a left branch stemming from N^k, then one consequence of this proposal is that extraction is automatically excluded from nominal expressions specified by these elements.

More generally, however, the proposal sketched here is worth exploring independently of this particular application merely because it attempts to apply the resources of the bar notation to certain long-standing syntactic problems.

2.1.2   A second way out of the conflict described in section 2.0 also denies that the subexpression *a proof of this theorem* is a full noun phrase—in fact, this way out is consistent with a variety of assumptions concerning the (derived) constituent structure of the full expression *how much of a proof of this theorem*; For example, we might suppose that the structure underlying this expression is roughly that of (13):

(13) $_{NP}[\,^a\text{Det}\,_{QP}[\,$ *how much* $\,]_{QP}\,_N\,[$ *proof of this theorem* $]_N\,]_{NP}$

On this account, the QP *how much* shifts to the left of the article, with a concomitant insertion of *of* between Q and Det. A more interesting theory of the structure of this expression involves construing *how much of a* as a kind of complex determiner, reminiscent of the treatment found in Chomsky (1970). Hence the constituent structure would be grossly as in (14).

(14)   [[*how much of a*] [*proof of this theorem*]]

Although the first way out sketched above suggests a possible solution to the problem of extraction from (apparent) noun phrases, the second way out suggests a syntactic account of a rather different set of problems: namely, the rather special behavior of singular count nouns in a variety of "comparative" structures. Consider the following paradigms:

(15)   *How much of a doctor is he exactly?*
         How much (of) water is that? [amount interpretation only]
         *How much (of) doctors are they?

(16)   *How good a doctor is she?*
         *How pure water is that?
         *How good doctors are they?

(17)   *Angelica is quite a doctor.*
         *That stuff in your sink is quite water.
         *Angelica and Mathilde are quite doctors.

The point of these examples is that they illustrate some of the ways in which the degree/kind interpretation of QP is intimately associated with the article *a*. It is by no means inconceivable, of course, that we could find some sort of semantic account of this. Yet the problems in doing so are almost self-evident. For example, it seems perfectly possible to construe plurals "predicatively" (whatever this may mean exactly) in such sentences as

(18)   *Mary and Max are lawyers.*

On the other hand, suppose that the degree interpretation is available only when the QP forms a syntactic constituent with the article, along the lines suggested above. In this case, we need not concern ourselves with such problems, and at the same time we find, happily enough, that there is no bar to the operation of E-NP.

2.2   Reviewing the discussion in this section briefly, we have seen that the assumption embodied in (6)—namely, that the presence of an article indicates the presence of an NP whose left bracket is immediately to the left of the article—leads to certain difficulties if we accept the upward-bounded character of E-NP. I have tried to suggest several possible reanalyses, which seem to warrant further investigation.

3.   Returning now to the difficulties alluded to in section 1.3 and their relation to the problem discussed in section 2, let us examine how the grammar Selkirk proposes generates partitive constructions. We have at our disposal the following set of phrase structure rules:

(19) $(N^3=) \quad NP \rightarrow (\left\{ \begin{array}{c} Det \\ NP_{poss} \end{array} \right\}) \; N^2$

(20) $N^2 \rightarrow (\left\{ \begin{array}{c} NP \\ QP \end{array} \right\}) \; N^1$

(21) $N^1 \rightarrow NP$

The major source of difficulty here is rule (21), since it is by this rule that the troublesome aspects of the phrases discussed in section 2 are introduced. For example, the phrase *none of the reviews of Mary's book* is assigned the structure:

(22)   NP [QP[*none*] QP *(of)* N¹ [NP [*the reviews of Mary's book*] NP] N¹]NP

A further indication of the infelicity of this way of generating partitive constructions is the fact that it allows of ambiguities in analysis. Consider such a phrase as
a couple of jars of mustard, on the interpretation on which both *a couple* and *jars*
are construed as measure phrases. (That this is possible is shown by the existence of
such sentences as *A couple of jars of mustard would spice up your sandwich consid-*
erably, at least if the selectional relation between *mustard* and *spice up* is a reliable
indication of which noun is the head of the phrase as a whole.) In accordance with
the rules Selkirk suggests, this phrase can be assigned the following two structures
(on this interpretation):

(22)   (23)

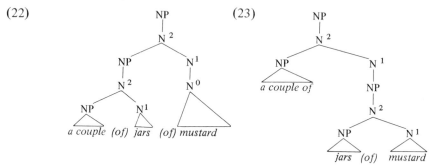

It is difficult to see any noticeable empirical consequence of this distinction in
structure, and the existence of such dual structures has the unfortunate theoretical
consequence of forcing a complication of Selkirk's definition of head, since according to her definition, the head of the highest NP in (23) is not uniquely identifiable.

Thus, phrase structure rule (21) seems to have little to recommend it. As for
possible reanalyses of the structure of partitive constructions, I suspect that the
choice among competing solutions will depend in part on a deeper understanding of
the problem of recursion in partitive constructions.

In regard to expressions like *none of the reviews*, if we introduce the quantifier
by means of a rule such as (24),

(24)   NP → QP   NP

then we only complicate matters as far as the upward-bounded property of E-NP is
concerned. An alternative is to accomplish the recursion through the left branch of
QP itself. Thus, instead of generating structures like (25), we will have structures
like (26).

(25)

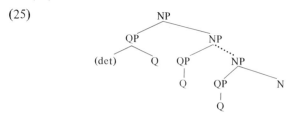

(26)

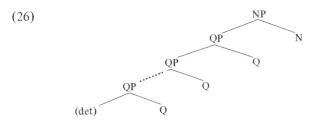

One interesting aspect of (26) is that it has closer affinities than (25) to Bresnan's (1973) proposals concerning the expansion of QP in comparative structures.

The interesting question, however, is how to state the recursion restriction in an exact way. If (25) is correct, we might expect that the recursion restriction would be expressed through dependencies between each QP and its sister NP as a whole. On the other hand, if (26) is a better model, then we might expect the dependencies to involve each Q and the QP to its left. I believe that this is the more promising approach, but the problem deserves a more complete treatment than is possible here.

4.   In the preceding discussion, I have tried to explore one way in which Selkirk's analysis is open to improvement. My remarks have been somewhat speculative. Yet this is not altogether inappropriate, since Selkirk's work suggests several other lines of potentially fruitful research: it provides not only a foundation for future research, but a model of careful and detailed investigation as well.

Notes

1. Like Selkirk, I shall employ a somewhat mixed notation. I use superscript numerals, rather than the typographically inconvenient bars, to represent various levels of categorial structure. Since it is not altogether clear, however, what numeral to assign to the maximal major phrasal categories, I employ the symbol 'NP' as well.
2. The utility of Jackendoff's principle is, of course, also dependent on such factors as how broadly we construe the notion "grammatical relation."
3. Actually, if our argument is correct, we have only provided evidence that the class of determiners involved is not generated inside the QP generated under N^2.

TRANSFORMATIONS AND THE LEXICON

Thomas Wasow

Departments of Linguistics and Philosophy
Stanford University
Stanford, California

1. Introduction

A favorite weapon among critics of the Extended Standard Theory (EST) has been Occam's razor. McCawley (1973) and Postal (1972), among others, have argued that Generative Semantics is to be preferred over EST because it makes use of a more limited inventory of rule types. Chomsky's (1972b) rebuttal to this sort of argument is, I think, fundamentally a sound one.

> If enrichment of theoretical apparatus and elaboration of conceptual structure will restrict the set of possible grammars and the class of sets of derivations generated by admissible grammars, then it will be a step forward . . . . Although one wants the 'simplest' linguistic theory [footnote omitted], in some sense that cannot be specified in a useful way, elaborations and complications of linguistic theory are all to the good insofar as they narrow the choice of grammars and the range of admissible languages (i.e., sets of derivations). (pp. 68-9)

While Chomsky's point is correct in principle, it does not suffice as a defense of current practice by advocates of EST. The fact is that EST allows grammars to include at least four supposedly distinct syntactic and/or semantic rule types: phrase structure rules, transformations, rules of semantic interpretation, and lexical redundancy rules. In order to justify this multiplicity of rule types, it is necessary to distinguish empirically the functions of different types of rules. In other words, if all of these rule types are to be admitted and considered distinct, then constraints must be placed on the form and functions of each type of rule, and these constraints must be shown to have correct empirical consequences. Otherwise, by Occam's razor, some of the rule types should be conflated.

There seems to be no real problem of justifying phrase structure rules as an independent category. It is universally agreed that sentences should be represented at some level by means of labeled bracketings or trees. This being the case, some mechanism is needed for generating these structures, and no other rule type in EST can do this. Hence, the problem is to distinguish among transformations, interpretive rules, and lexical redundancy rules. I will not consider here the question of what distinguishes interpretive rules. My purpose in this paper is to propose a set of criteria for distinguishing between transformations and lexical redundancy rules and to show that these criteria lead to surprising and correct predictions.

2.   Lexical Rules versus Transformations

2.1   Why They Might Be Confused

It is obvious that transformations fulfill one function that cannot be assumed by lexical redundancy rules. Transformations may deform base-generated structures, but items related by lexical redundancy rules must be inserted into structures generated by the phrase structure rules. Hence a transformation that might be reformulated as a lexical redundancy rule would have to produce outputs isomorphic to base structures.

It has long been recognized (see, e.g., Chomsky, 1955, p. 444, 1957, p. 73) that many of the standard examples of transformations are in fact of this type, which I (following Emonds) will call "structure-preserving." The primary motivation for structure-preserving transformations has been to account for regularities in co-occurrence restrictions. More specifically, when there are two syntactic constructions with the following three properties, then their relationship can be formulated as a structure-preserving transformation: (i) they both can be generated by the rules of the base; (ii) the morphological forms that appear in one construction are predictable from those that appear in the other; and (iii) the co-occurrence restrictions in one construction are predictable from those in the other. Recently, several linguists have pointed out that it is, in general, also possible to relate constructions satisfying (i)–(iii) by means of lexical redundancy rules. This is accomplished by isolating a key word in each construction (generally a verb) and expressing the regularities between the constructions in terms of the lexical entry for that word, especially the contextual features in the entry for that word. Freidin (1974, 1975) and Bresnan (1976) have suggested that all structure-preserving transformations can be reformulated as lexical redundancy rules. They further suggest that doing so is desirable for a number of reasons, among them that it provides an explanation for the fact that these rules preserve structure. Without dealing directly with either Freidin's or Bresnan's arguments for this position, I will argue below for a less radical departure from the usual version of EST. Before doing so, however, I would like to illustrate how the same relationship may be expressed either transformationally or lexically within EST. I will do this by sketching very briefly the analyses of causatives presented by Fiengo (1974) and Jackendoff (1976).

Fiengo (1974) proposes that the relationship between the transitive and intransitive forms of such verbs as *break, change, drop, end, grow, melt, move*, etc., can be captured transformationally by means of a rule of NP preposing that moves the object into the position of a dummy subject (represented by an asterisk). Thus, (2) would be derived from (1).

(1)   *broke the glass   ⇒

(2)   the glass broke.

This seems like a simple and elegant way of expressing the fact that the subject of the intransitive form corresponds semantically to (and hence obeys the same selectional restrictions as) the object of the transitive form. It is not subject to the objections which have been raised (see, e.g., Fodor, 1970) against the "predicate-raising" analysis of the same phenomenon (see McCawley, 1968).

Jackendoff (1975, p. 659) suggests instead that this relationship should be handled in the lexicon, and proposes (3) as the necessary lexical redundancy rule.

(3)
$$\begin{bmatrix} +V \\ +[NP_1 \text{ ---- }] \\ NP_1 W \end{bmatrix} \longleftrightarrow \begin{bmatrix} +V \\ +[NP_2 \text{ ---- } NP_1] \\ NP_2 \text{CAUSE} (NP_1, W) \end{bmatrix}$$

The indexing of the NPs expresses the fundamental fact that the subject of the intransitive form corresponds to the object of the transitive form.

Both of these analyses are formulable within EST, and they express essentially the same facts. It is clear that the theory would be more restrictive (and hence better) if it offered a principled means of choosing between these analyses. This becomes all the more desirable in view of the fact that many other alternations can also be analyzed either transformationally or lexically within EST. In the next section, I will present a set of criteria for distinguishing these rule types.

2.2   Distinguishing Criteria

The criteria I wish to propose are based on my assumptions regarding what the functions of the different components of EST should be. In other words, they are meant to express what seem to be "natural" properties of transformations or lexical redundancy rules. Hence, I will try to provide for each proposed criterion some reasons why I believe it to be a priori plausible.

My first criterion is the one given above, namely that transformations but not lexical redundancy rules can result in structures not generable by means of the rules of the base. My justification for this criterion has also been given.

My second criterion is that lexical redundancy rules but not transformations may be used to relate items from different grammatical categories. The justification for this is largely historical: the lexicalist hypothesis was first propsed in order to account for the relationship between derived nominals and their associated verbs or adjectives, and it has generally been assumed by lexicalists (see Jackendoff, 1972, p. 13) that transformations may not change the label on an existing node. Nor do any of the standard transformtions discussed in the literature involve label-changing (see, e.g., the rules given by Akmajian and Heny, 1975). In keeping with this, the standard formalizations of transformations (e.g., Peters and Ritchie, 1973, pp. 57-62) do not allow rules to alter the label on a node. In contrast, lexical redundancy rules may readily relate items of different grammatical categories.

A third difference between the two rule types is that lexical rules must be more "local" than transformations. Whereas transformations are mappings between entire phrase markers, lexical redundancy rules are mappings only between lexical items. Hence, lexical rules ought not to be able to refer to aspects of the environments in which the lexical items appear, other than those aspects that must for independent reasons be included in the lexical entries anyway. Only those properties of an element's deep structure environment that condition its appearance ought to be available for the formulation of lexical rules it undergoes.

In trying to make fully precise this property of "localness" that should characterize lexical rules, one rather strong hypothesis to put forward is that the only elements of a verb's[1] environment that may enter into the statement of lexical redundancy rules are the NPs bearing deep structure grammatical relations to it (viz., its subject, direct object, and indirect object). In an intuititve sense that is hard to pin down, these NPs are the elements of a verb's environment most closely associated with it. There can be little doubt that they must enter into the statement of contextual features; indeed, informal statements of both selectional restrictions and strict subcategorization are typically formulated in terms of these relations (see, e.g., Chomsky, 1965, p. 155). Thus, I claim that a natural way of stating the "localness" property of lexical rules is to insist that they be "relational" in this sense. I assume that transformations, in contrast, are defined in the usual way, in terms of structural relations of phrase markers.[2]

A fourth difference between lexical and transformtional rules is that the latter but not the former may be fed by transformations. This follows automatically from the organization of grammars within EST, which requires that lexical rules relate items in the lexicon, while transformations must operate on phrase markers into which lexical items have been inserted. Hence, if transformation T feeds rule A, then A cannot be a lexical rule; and if rule B feeds lexical rule L, then B cannot be a transformation.

A final criterion is that transformations are more productive than lexical rules. This follows from the conception of the lexicon as the receptacle of idiosyncratic information about the elements of the vocabulary of a language. It was largely the idiosyncracy of English nominalizations that orginally motivated the lexicalist hypothesis, so it is natural that lexical rules should be conceived of as freely allowing unsystematic exceptions. Jackendoff's (1976) proposals for formulating lexical rules are designed to accommodate this feature. I would like to claim that transformations, in contrast, are exceptionless, in the sense that apparent singularities are in fact systematic and predictable. Admittedly, this is a claim to which there are numerous prima facie counterexamples, so the burden of proof lies heavily with me (see Lakoff, 1970, Kayne, 1969, Bresnan, 1972, 1976b, and Baker, in preparation, for some interesting discussion of exceptions to transformation; see also section 4.5 below). Should this strong (and, on the face of it, wrong) position prove untenable, I still want to maintain that lexical rules are generally far less productive than transformations.[3] That is, I assume that if a tree satisfying the structural conditions of a transformation is prohibited from undergoing the structural change, then some explanation is called for, but a lexical item that does not undergo a lexical rule whose conditions it satisfied is perfectly normal. Transformations are crucial to the generation of all and only the sentences of the language (and hence have infinite domains); in contrast, lexical rules express subregularities within a finite lexicon (though they may at times be used in forming new words—cf. Aronoff, 1974). Hence, I assume (following Jackendoff, 1975c) that lexical rules are part of the evaluation metric and will typically have unsystematic exceptions. In what follows, the existence of numerous idiosyncratic exceptions to a relationship will be taken as evidence for handling it in the lexicon.

The following table summarizes the criteria I have proposed for distinguishing between lexical rules and transformations.

	Lexical Rules	Transformations
Criterion 1	do not affect structure	need not be structure preserving
Criterion 2	may relate items of different grammatical categories	do not change node labels
Criterion 3	"local"; involve only NPs bearing grammatical relations to items in question	need not be "local"; formulated in terms of structural properties of phrase markers
Criterion 4	apply before any transformations	may be fed by transformations
Criterion 5	have idiosyncratic exceptions	have few or no true exceptions

3.   Two Applications of the Criteria

In the remainder of this paper, I will apply these criteria to three constructions in English, showing that they lead to some surprising and correct predictions.

3.1   Causatives

Consider first the question of causatives, mentioned above. The first two criteria are clearly irrelevant, since Fiengo's proposed transformation does not alter node labels and is structure-preserving. Criterion 3 is relevant, however. If the causative rule is lexical, then it should only turn direct objects into subjects. Even when another NP occupies the normal direct object position (namely, immediately after the verb), it could not become the subject of the intransitive. Fiengo's transformational derivation of causatives would lead one to expect that any immediately postverbal NP, whether a direct object or not, should be preposable.

One sort of case in which the immediately postverbal NP is not a direct object involves the accusative plus infinitive construction with verbs like *believe, consider, find*, etc. The arguments for calling the postverbal NP the complement subject rather than the direct object are well known (see Akmajian and Heny, 1975, Chapter 9) for a summary and references). I will refer to this construction as the "accusative subject" construction.[4] The only verb allowing this construction I have been able to find that also exhibits the transitive–intransitive (causative) alternation is *show*.

(5)   a.   *John showed hostility*
       b.   *Hostility showed.*
       c.   *John showed hostility to be a result of cold weather.*

According to Fiengo's analysis of causitives, (5b) is transformationally derived from (6).

(6)   *showed hostility.*

Nothing in Fiengo's analysis could prevent a completely parallel derivation of (7b) from (7a).

(7)   a.   *showed hostility to be a result of cold weather.*
       b.   *Hostility showed to be a result of cold weather.*

If the causative rule is lexical, however, Criterion 3 would prevent the subject of the intransitive form from being related to the complement subject of the transitive form.

A second type of case in which the immediately postverbal NP is not the direct object is the double object construction, in which the indirect object precedes the direct object. *Drop* is a verb that both exhibits the causative alternation and appears in the double object construction.

(8)   a.   *They dropped the rope 100 feet.*
       b.   *The rope dropped 100 feet.*
       c.   *They dropped John the rope.*

According to Fiengo's analysis, (8b) would be derived from (9).

(9)   *dropped the rope 100 feet.*

In a completely parallel fashion (10b) could be derived from (10a).

(10)   a.   *dropped John the rope.*
       b.   *John dropped the rope.*

Although (10b) is a grammatical sentence of English, it is doubtful whether anyone would want to derive it from (10a), since *John* in (10b) is the agent, not the goal of *drop*. Assuming that any analysis of causatives must capture the correspondence between the intransitive subject and the transitive object, the derivation of (10b) from (10a) must be excluded, for no such correspondence holds. A lexical causative rule conforming to Criterion 3 would, of course, exclude such a derivation of

(10b), since *John* is the indirect object, not the direct object, in examples like (8c).

(7b) and (10b) could also be taken as evidence bearing on Criterion 4, if one believes in the existence of transformations of Raising (to object position) and Dative Movement. If (7b) and (10b) are so construed, then, according to Criterion 4, they still support the lexical analysis of causatives, for they show that neither Raising nor Dative may feed the causative rule. It is interesting to note, by the way, that Newmeyer (1974) argues that even the Predicate Raising analysis of causatives requires that no transformations feed the causative rule.

Criterion 5 also supports the lexical analysis of causatives, for they exhibit a good deal of lexical idiosyncracy, as evidenced by the following:

(11)
  a. *John* $\begin{Bmatrix} dropped \\ lowered \end{Bmatrix}$ *the rope.*

  b. *The rope* $\begin{Bmatrix} dropped. \\ *lowered. \end{Bmatrix}$

(12)
  a. *John* $\begin{Bmatrix} shattered \\ demolished \end{Bmatrix}$ *the light bulb.*

  b. *The light bulb* $\begin{Bmatrix} shattered. \\ *demolished. \end{Bmatrix}$

(13)
  a. *John* $\begin{Bmatrix} darkened \\ tinted \end{Bmatrix}$ *his hair.*

  b. *His hair* $\begin{Bmatrix} darkened. \\ *tinted. \end{Bmatrix}$

(14)
  a. *We* $\begin{Bmatrix} moved \\ transported \end{Bmatrix}$ *the boxes.*

  b. *The boxes* $\begin{Bmatrix} moved. \\ *transported. \end{Bmatrix}$

In short, the criteria I propose for distinguishing lexical rules from transformations unequivocally favor a lexical analysis of the causative alternation over Fiengo's transformational derivation.

3.2 *-able* Adjectives

A large number of English verbs have corresponding adjectival forms ending in *-able*. Since the rule relating the verbs to the adjectives relates items in different grammatical categories, Criterion 2 forces me to analyze it as a lexical rule. Before exploring the consequences of doing so, I will comment briefly on the suggestion of G. Lakoff (1970c, p. 32) that the *-able* rule should be a transformation operating on the output of the Passive transformation. This is necessary because, if the rule were in fact fed by a transformation, then, by Criterion 4, it would have to be a transformation itself. This would show my criteria to be mutually incompatible.

Lakoff's discussion is so brief that I can repeat it here in full (omitting only some of the examples):

> The rule which forms *readable* from *able to be read* is also a minor rule. (Call it ABLE-SUB.) Thus we get:
>
> (5-5) a. *His handwriting can be read* ⇒ *His handwriting is readable.*
>   b. *He can be depended on* ⇒ *He is dependable.*
>   ⋮
>   ⋮
>
> Most verbs, however, cannot undergo this rule. Thus we do not get:
>
> (5-6) a. *John can be killed* ⇏ **John is killable.*
>   b. *John can be shot* ⇏ **John is shootable.*

"Minor rules" in Lakoff's terminology are "rules . . . that apply only to exceptions and not to ordinary lexical items" (Lakoff, 1970c, p. 30). Notice that this property of the *-able* rule would lead me (by Criterion 5) to assign it to the lexicon quite independently of the fact that it changes category membership.

Inexplicit though the quoted remarks are, they do make certain predictions. Clearest among these is that verbs that do not passivize should not have corresponding *-able* adjectives. This appears to be a correct prediction: verbs like *resemble, cost,* and *last* have no *-able* forms.

(15) a. *Bill resembles John.*
        b. **John is resembled by Bill.*
        c. **John is resembleable.*

(16) a. *This car costs too much.*
        b. **Too much is cost by this car.*
        c. **Too much is costable.*

(17) a. *The party lasted all night.*
        b. **All night was lasted by the party.*
        c. **All night is lastable.*

There are, however, other verbs whose passives sound significantly worse than the coresponding *-able* adjectives:

(18) a. ??*Your unfortunate remarks can be regretted.*
        b. *Your unfortunate remarks are regrettable.*

(19) a.??*This car can be afforded.*
        b. *This car is affordable.*

(20) a. ?*The condition of the library can be deplored.*
        b. *The condition of the library is deplorable.*

(21) a. ?*Triscuits can be munched.*
        b. *Triscuits are munchable.*

While it is hard to draw firm conclusions from such marginal data, they do serve to weaken the argument for ABLE-SUB based on (15)–(17).

Another prediction which follows from Lakoff's proposal is that any contexts in which V*able* adjectives may appear should allow either *able to be Ven* or *can be Ven* to appear. This prediction is not borne out.

(22)   *This book promises to* $\left\{\begin{array}{l} \textit{be readable.} \\ \textit{*be able to be read.} \\ \textit{*can be read.} \end{array}\right\}$

(23)   *I was expecting the evening to* $\left\{\begin{array}{l} \textit{be tolerable.} \\ \textit{*be able to be tolerated.} \\ \textit{*can be tolerated.} \end{array}\right\}$

(24)   *The bottles began* $\left\{\begin{array}{l} \textit{being returnable} \\ \textit{??being able to be returned} \\ \textit{*canning be returned} \end{array}\right\}$ *last year.*

(25)   *The ordeal seemed* $\left\{\begin{array}{l} \textit{endurable} \\ \textit{??able to be endured} \\ \textit{*can be endured} \end{array}\right\}$ *until now.*

No doubt, a sufficiently abstract version of Lakoff's analysis could accommodate facts like (22)–(25), but it is clear that they are a problem for the proposal as stated.

A more serious difficulty for Lakoff's analysis is the existence of verbs whose -*able* adjectives may not be substituted for *can be Ven* in all environments which allow the latter.

(26)   a.   *This book can be read.*
        b.   *This book is readable.*
        c.   *Johnny can be read this book.*
        d.   **Johnny is readable this book.*

(27)   a.   *Such behavior cannot be allowed.*
        b.   *Such behavior is not allowable.*
        c.   *Such behavior cannot be allowed him.*
        d.   **Such behavior is not allowable him.*

(28)   a.   *Shirley can be elected.*
        b.   *Shirley is electable.*
        c.   *Shirley can be elected President.*
        d.   **Shirley is electable President.*

(29)   a.   *John's conjecture can be proved.*
        b.   *John's conjecture is provable.*
        c.   *John's conjecture can be proved to be wrong.*
        d.   **John's conjecture is provable to be wrong.*

(30)   a.   *John's arguments can be believed.*
        b.   *John's arguments are believable.*
        c.   *John's arguments can be believed to be plagiarized.*
        d.   **John's arguments are believable to be plagiarized.*

(31)   a.   *This seven notrump contract can be made.*
        b.   *This seven notrump contract is makeable.*
        c.   *This seven notrump contract can be made too much of.*
        d.   **This seven notrump contract is makeable too much of.*

Lakoff could not mark these verbs as exceptions to ABLE-SUB without incorrectly excluding the (b) examples. Therfore, given the well-formed (c) examples, his analysis incorrectly predicts that the (d) examples should be grammatical. There appears to be no way to rule out the (d) examples under Lakoff's analysis. Hence, the analysis is rendered extremely suspect, and my claim that transformations may not feed category-changing rules is saved from this apparent counterexample.

If -able adjectives are derived from the corresponding verbs by means of a lexical rule (as Criterion 2 says they must be), then the other criteria make certain predictions about them. Criterion 1 predicts that -able adjectives should be able to appear only in normal adjective positions; Criterion 3 predicts that the subject of an -able adjective must correspond to the underlying direct object of the associated verb, and not to any other NP that might occupy the same position; Criterion 4 says that no transformation may feed the -able rule; and Criterion 5 allows for idiosyncratic exceptions to the -able rule; All of these predictions are borne out by the facts.

Consider first the prediction of Criterion 1. There are at least three different constructions in which adjectives appear: following a copula, prenominally in NPs, and as the complements to a small class of verbs like *act, become, look, seem*, and *sound*. They never appear in sequences of *be*-adjective-NP.[5] This accounts for the ungrammaticality of the (d) examples of (26)-(28)[6] and (31). (29d) and (30d) are ungrammatical because their subjects do not correspond to the underlying direct objects of the associated verbs. In both cases the subject corresponds to the underlying subject of the verb's complement, so they are excluded by Criterion 3. (26d) and (27d) would also be ruled out by Criterion 3, since their subjects correspond to underlying indirect objects of the associated verbs. If the purported transformations of Dative Movement or Raising (into object position) exist, then examples (26d), (27d), (29d), and (30d) are relevant to Criterion 4. Otherwise, it is sufficient to note that there are no counterexamples to Criterion 4, i.e., no transformations may feed the -able rule. Finally, the same facts that led Lakoff to call his ABLE-SUB transformation a "minor rule" show that the -able rule has idiosyncratic exceptions, as Criterion 5 predicts that it might. Thus, the data in (26)-(31), which presented serious problems for Lakoff's analysis of -able adjectives, are predicted by my criteria 1-5.

The facts in (18)-(25), awhich also created difficulties for Lakoff's analysis, present no special problem to a lexical analysis, since it predicts no particular correlation between the environments allowing passives and those allowing -able adjectives. The fact that -able adjectives may often be paraphrased by *can be Ven* constructions is due to two facts: first, that the semantic content of the suffix -able is close to that of one meaning of *can*, and second, that the lexical rule relating verbs to the corresponding -able adjectives identifies the subject of the latter with the direct object of the former, just as the Passive usually turns a direct object into a subject. However, these facts do not constitute sufficient justification for applying Passive to modal constructions in the derivation of -able adjectives, as the earlier discussion showed.

3.3 A Digression Regarding Criterion 3

So far, I have not made really crucial use of Criterion 3, for every prediction I derived from it would also follow from Criterion 4, under the assumption that Dative Movement and Raising (to object) are transformations. Although I find the arguments aginst Dative Movement convincing (see Oehrle, 1975, and Baker, in preparation), it would be nice to have a perfectly clear insance requiring Criterion 3. This is especially true because it is perhaps the least intuitive of the criteria, and because there is currently a good deal of discussion regarding the proper role of grammatical relations in linguistic theory (see Postal, 1976, and Fiengo and Lasnik, 1976).

It is natural, therefore, to ask whether any verbs in English may be immediately followed by a single NP that is not the direct object. A plausible candidate would be *tell*, in constructions like (32b), since the object here clearly corresponds to the indirect object in double object constructions like (32a).

(32) a. *I told John the story.*
      b. *I told John.*

If this is correct (and, further, if we assume that (32b) does not involve deletion of a direct object), then the contrast in (33) supports Criterion 3.

(33) a. *That story isn't tellable.*
      b. **John isn't tellable.*

Unfortunately, however, applying the same sort of reasoning to *teach* yields an apparent counterexample to Criterion 3.

(34) a. *John teaches handicapped children manual skills.*
      b. *John teaches handicapped children.*
      c. *Manual skills are teachable.*
      d. *Handicapped children are teachable.*

In order to maintain Criterion 3, I must insist that though *handicapped children* is an indirect object in (34a), it is a direct object in (34b). Counterintuitive though this may at first appear, I think there is some support for it. For one thing, there is a subtle difference between the two examples in the relationship between *teach* and *handicapped children*: (34a) entails that the children learn some of the skills, but (34b) carries no comparable entailment of success. Significantly, no such difference exists between the sentences of (32). In addition, if (34b) is nominalized, then *handicapped children* is preceded by the preposition *of*, which is the normal marker of direct objects in nominals, but the only nominal corresponding to (34a) marks *handicapped children* with *to*, which is usally a marker of indirect objects.

(35) a. *John's teaching* $\left\{ \begin{array}{c} of \\ ??to \end{array} \right\}$ *handicapped children is admirable.*

      b. *John's teaching of manual skills* $\left\{ \begin{array}{c} *of \\ to \end{array} \right\}$ *handicapped children*
      is admirable.

In contrast, (32b) has no nominalized form at all.

(36)   a.   *My telling of the story to John took three hours.*

b.   **My telling* $\left\{ \begin{array}{c} of \\ to \end{array} \right\}$ *John took three hours.*

I conclude, tentatively, that *handicapped children* in (34b) is the direct object, and that (34c) is therefore no counterexample to Criterion 3.

Returning now to the question of whether there are any English verbs that take only an indirect object, I would like to suggest two further candidates, namely, *help* and *thank*. These are, of course, natural choices, since the corresponding verbs in many other Indo-European languages take dative objects; this is particularly clear in German, where the relevant verbs are cogantes (*helfen* and *danken*). A shred of evidence that the objects of these verbs are indeed indirect objects is provided by the choice of prepositions in nominals.

(37)   *Our* $\left\{ \begin{array}{c} help \\ thanks \end{array} \right\} \left\{ \begin{array}{c} ?to \\ *of \end{array} \right\}$ *the hostess went unacknowledged.*

If it is true that the objects of *help* and *thank* are indirect objects, Criterion 3 predicts that there should be no adjectives **helpable* or **thankable*, and indeed there are none. More consequences will emerge in the next section.

4.   Passives

4.1   Two Types of Passives

Before applying my criteria to passives, I woud like to show that English must have two sources for passives. I will do this by showing that some passive participles are adjectives while others are verbs.

It is by no means a novel observation that passive participles exhibit both adjectival and verbal behavior. Indeed, my dictionary defines a participle as "an adjective form derived from verbs . . ." Among generativists, the adjectival behavior of passives has been observed by Chomsky (1955, 1957), Aronoff (1972), Freidin (1975), and Bresnan (1976), among others. I will repeat the relevant observations here anyway, for they are crucial to my theoretical arguments below.

The most obvious piece of evidence suggesting that passive participles are adjectives is that they may appear in prenominal adjective position.

(38) $\left\{ \begin{array}{c} A \\ The \end{array} \right\} \left\{ \begin{array}{c} broken \\ filled \\ painted \\ cherished \end{array} \right\}$ *box sat on the table.*

Of course, this construction is widely thought to be transformationally derived from a relative clause in which the Passive transformation has applied. However, such an analysis is motivated primarily by the assumption that all passive partciples are transformationally derived from active verbs; if prenominal passive participles are analyzed as lexical adjectives, then little (if any) motivation remains for the relative clause reduction analysis.

Another typically adjectival position in which passive participles may appear is as the complement to certain verbs, including *act, become, look, remain, seem*, and *sound*.

(39)

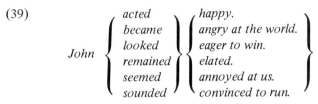

This construction has also been analyzed as a reduced transform of a more complex structure. The necessary transformation, referred to as *To be* Deletion, has never to my knowledge actually been formulated, presumably because it would be so highly idiosyncratic. It is therefore difficult to assess the merits of such an analysis with any certainty. The problems involved in determining when it would apply obligatorily (e.g., to complements of *seem*), and when it may not apply (e.g., to complements of *tend* or to most complements containing progressives) are enormous (see Borkin, 1973, Baker, in preparation, and Hubbard and van den Heuvel, 1974, for some discussion of these questions). These problems do not arise in an analysis that assumes that these verbs are strictly subcategorized to take AP-complements, and that some passive participles are lexical adjectives.

A stronger argument for calling some passive participles adjectives is given by Siegel (1970), who attributes it to Edwin Williams. Siegel notes that there is a substantial class of verbs to which *un-* may be prefixed only when they are in the passive.

(40) a. *Our products are untouched by human hands.*
      b. *The island was uninhabited by humans.*
      c. *All his claims have been unsupported by data.*
      d. *Her whereabouts may be unknown.*
      e. *?He was being unconcerned.*
      f. *Their potential would have been untapped.*

(41) a. **Human hands untouch our products.*
      b. **Humans uninhabited the island.*
      c. **Data have unsupported all his claims.*
      d. **They may unknow her whereabouts.*
      e. **It was unconcerning him.*
      f. **Someone would have untapped their potenital.*

The prefixing of *un-* to these verbs depends crucially on the voice. This is shown most clearly by the (b), (c), and (f) examples, in which the superficial forms of the items to which *un-* is prefixed are the same in (40) as in (41), yet they differ with respect to grammaticality.

Aside from the kind of examples illustrated in (40), there are two large classes of lexical items that may take the prefix un-. One is a class of verbs, including *buckle, do, fold, leash, lock, seat*, and *tie*, which take un- in all tenses, aspects, and voices.

(42)   a.   *John unlocks the door every morning.*
       b.   *Mary undid the knot.*
       c.   *Senator Green has unseated ex-Senator White.*
       d.   *That decision could unleash powerful forces.*
       e.   *John is unbuckling his belt.*
       f.   *The flag was unfolded by the committee.*

The other class is a class of adjectives, including the following:

(43)   *breakable, eventful, happy, lucky, palatable*, etc.

It would obviously be desirable to assimilate the class illustrated in (40) to one of the other two classes. If one says that the passive participles to which un- can be prefixed are in fact adjectives, then examples like (40) can be assimilated to examples like (43). Further, the apparently strange restriction that the prefix is only attached to passives ceases to seem strange.

Another adjectival characteristic exhibited by passive participles involves the behavior of degree modifiers. McCawley (1970c, footnote 3) notes that verbs and adjectives differ with respect to the form of degree modifiers.

(44)

a.   *John very *(much)* $\left\{ \begin{array}{l} \textit{respects} \\ \textit{frightens} \\ \textit{appreciates} \\ \textit{resents} \end{array} \right\}$ *your family.*

b.   *John is very (*much)* $\left\{ \begin{array}{l} \textit{fond of} \\ \textit{grateful to} \\ \textit{angry with} \end{array} \right\}$ *your family.*

(An asterisk outside of parentheses is used here to indicate that the sentence is ungrammatical unless the parenthesized material is included.) Passive participles may behave like either adjectives or verbs.

(45)

Your family was very (much) $\left\{ \begin{array}{l} \textit{respected.} \\ \textit{frightened.} \\ \textit{appreciated.} \\ \textit{resented.} \end{array} \right\}$

The crucial point for present purposes is that *much* may be absent in (45). This would follow from any analysis which could account for (44b), if these passive participles can be analyzed as adjectives.[8]

These observations suffice, I think, to show that some passive participles are adjectives.[9] There are equally compelling reasons for believing that some passive participles are not adjectives, to which I now turn.

As Freidin (1975, p. 401) observes (numbering changed):

The most serious drawback to analysing [all] passive predicates as adjectives involves double-object verbs such as *give*. For these verbs, passives may be followed by NP, e.g.,

(46)   *The turtle was given an ear of corn.*

If *given* is an adjective here, then the phrase structure rule that expands AP must allow for an optional NP complement. The rule would have to look something like

(47)   AP → A (NP) (PP)

This analysis is extremely dubious. There is no other construction in English that requires rule (47).[10] I will show below that phrases like *given an ear of corn* do not in general behave like APs, as Freidin's analysis suggests that they should.

Another problem with this analysis of passives of double object constructions is that it makes it extremely difficult to specify the subcategorization features on "adjectives" like *given*. Consider the following facts.

(48)   a.   *The United Fund was given *($10).*
        b.   *$10 was given (to the United Fund).*

In order to account for this with the standard machinery of selection and strict subcategorization, it would be necessary to make the obligatoriness of the presence of an NP-complement to *given* dependent on the selectional features of its subject. If, instead, these examples are derived transformationally, (48) follows from (49), which can be captured quite straightforwardly with the standard machinery.

(49)   a.   *Someone gave the United Fund *($10).*
        b.   *Someone gave $10 (to the United Fund).*

Passive participles followed by predicative expressions like those in (50) also provide an argument against analyzing all passive participles as adjectives, for those predicative expressions may not appear directly after adjectives.

(50)   a.   *John is considered a fool.*
        b.   *Mary was elected President.*

(51)   a.   **John is obvious a fool.*
        b.   **Mary was happy President.*

Whether or not *a fool* and *President* in (50) are NPs (cf. note 6), the advocate of an adjectival analysis for all passives would have to explain why these expressions can appear after passive participles, but not after ordinary adjectives. Of course, such expressions may appear after verbs (with or without direct objects intervening), so if *considered* and *elected* are verbs, (50) is no problem (irrespective of whether Passive is a transformation).

These two constructions suffice to establish that some passive participles are not adjectives. More evidence for this conclusion will be given in section 4.3 below, where it will be shown that many passives exhibit none of the syntactic behavior characteristic of adjectives.

4.2   Classifying the Two Passive Rules

I assume without argument that an adequate grammar of English must be able to relate all passive constructions to some corresponding active construction. Since some passive participles are adjectives and others are not, there must be at least two rules in English relating transitive verbs in the active voice to passive constructions. Knowing of no reason to think that there are more than two passive rules, I will assume that there are exactly two. I will now consider to which rule type each of them belongs.

The rule deriving adjectival passives must be a lexical redundancy rule, according to my criteria. This is quite evident, since Criterion 2 prevents transformations from changing grammatical categories.

My criteria require that the rule for nonadjectival passives be transformational. This follows most clearly from Criterion 3. Though the derived subject of passive constructions usually corresponds to the underlying direct object of the active, in examples like (46), the subject of the passive corresponds to the underlying indirect object of the active. This suggests that the passive rule operating in (46) is not formulated in terms of grammatical relations. The following facts support the conclusion that a nonrelational passive rule exists.

(52)   a.   *There is believed to be a monster in Loch Ness.*
        b.   *Advantage has been taken of John by unscrupulous operators.*
        c.   *John was* $\left\{ \begin{array}{l} helped \\ thanked \end{array} \right\}$ *by Bill.*

In (52a) the derived subject is *there*, which cannot be an underlying object of *believe*, since it may only be inserted into subject position.[11] In (52b) the derived subject is a chunk of an idiom, which bears no grammatical relation in the active.[12] In (52c), if my claims in section 3.3 are correct, the derived subject corresponds to the indirect object of the active. Assuming that there are only two rules for deriving passives, Criterion 3 entails that one of them must be a transformation.

4.3   Some Correct Predictions

My criteria lead me to classify certain passives as lexically derived and others as transformationally derived. Certain empirical predictions follow from this classification. The purpose of this section is to show that these predictions are borne out by the facts.

The criteria I used in making this classification were numbers 2 and 3: passives were called lexical when they displayed behavior that was demonstrably adjectival, and passives were called transformational when their derived subjects were not their underlying direct objects. It follows that passives whose derived subjects are not their underlying direct objects should be unable to exhibit adjectival behavior. This is the clearest prediction of my analysis. Criterion 4 predicts that there may be cases in which a transformation feeds the Passive transformation, but that no transformation may feed the lexical passive rule. It also predicts that lexical but not transformational passives may undergo lexical rules (e.g., category-changing rules). Finally, Criterion 5 suggests that lexical passives may exhibit idosyncracies not found in transformational passives.

I have cited the following kinds of passives as requiring a transformational derivation: passives of double object constructions, passives of the "accusative subject" construction, passives of idiom chunks, passives of *help* and *thank*, and passives followed by predicative expressions like *a fool* or *President*. (All but possibly the last of these are cases of non-direct objects becoming the subject). I have used the following four diagnostics for adjectives as evidence for lexical derivation of passives: prenominal position, appearance as complements to verbs like *act, look,* and *seem*, prefixing of *un-*, and degree modification by *very* (without *much*). My analysis predicts that passives in the first list should never be able to appear in the environments of the second list. In principle, then, there should be twenty kinds of test cases for this claim; in fact the number is smaller. This is because only the participle itself (plus adverbial modifiers) may appear prenominally, while most of the tests for transformationally derived passives involve other aspects of the context. For example, the "accusative subject" construction could be excluded from appearing prenominally quite independently of my criteria, because no participle or adjective may appear prenominally with a complement. Thus, whatever excludes (53b and c) will also rule out (53a), quite apart from my predictions.

(53) a. *The (widely) believed to be a communist man turned out
           to be an FBI agent.
      b. *The (recently) persuaded to turn state's evidence man got
           off on probation.
      c. *The eager to win woman lost.

This eliminates four possible tests. In addition, some of the others can be ruled out on other grounds. Nevertheless, quite a few specific predictions can be tested.

Consider first the passives of the double object constructions. As predicted, they cannot occur as complements to verbs taking AP-Complements.

(54) *John $\left\{ \begin{array}{l} looks \\ acts \\ seems \end{array} \right\}$ $\left\{ \begin{array}{l} given\ first\ prize\ every\ time\ we\ have\ a\ contest. \\ told\ the\ bad\ news. \end{array} \right\}$

There is no apparent independent reason for ruling (54) out, as the grammaticality of the very similar examples in (55) shows.

(55) John seems to $\left\{ \begin{array}{l} be\ given\ first\ prize\ every\ time\ we\ have\ a\ contest. \\ have\ been\ told\ the\ bad\ news. \end{array} \right\}$

Incidentally, the contrast between (54) and (55) is another difficulty facing advocates of *To Be* Deletion.

There are a few verbs that can appear in both double object constructions and in *un*-passives. As my analysis predicts, these verbs may not appear in both constructions at once.

(56)   a.   *John told* $\begin{Bmatrix} Bill\ (the\ story). \\ the\ story. \end{Bmatrix}$
        b.   *Bill was told (the story).*
        c.   *The story was told (to Bill).*
        d.   **Bill was untold (the story).*
        e.   *The story was untold (?to Bill).*

(57)   a.   *Mary sent Sue the letter.*
        b.   *Sue was sent the letter.*
        c.   *The letter was sent (to Sue).*
        d.   **Sue was unsent the letter.*
        e.   *The letter was unsent (?to Sue).*

Incidentally, the ungrammaticality of (56d), even without the parenthesized material is predicted by my contention (section 3.3) that *tell* may take an indirect object without a direct object. My claim that *many talented musicians* in examples like (58a) is a direct object predicts that (58b) should be as good as (58c), and I think it is;

(58)   a.   *John teaches many talented musicians.*
        b.   *?Many talented musicians are untaught.*
        c.   *?The love of music is untaught.*

No passives of double object verbs sound fully acceptable to me with degree modifiers, though some sound no worse than rather awkward. Without *much*, however, they are totally unacceptable, as predicted.

(59)   a.   *?John was very *(much) taught the value of a dollar.*
        b.   *?John was very *(much) sold a bill of goods.*

The behavior of double object verbs, then, is just about what my criteria predict it should be. I know of no other existing analysis that makes these predictions.

The behavior of passives of the "accusative subject" construction fits the predictions at least as well. They may not occur as complements to verbs like *act* or *seem*.

(60)   a.   *There* $\begin{Bmatrix} is \\ *seems \end{Bmatrix}$ *believed to be corruption in high places.*

        b.   *Mary* $\begin{Bmatrix} is \\ *appears \end{Bmatrix}$ *thought to be a genius.*

        c.   *John* $\begin{Bmatrix} is \\ *sounds \end{Bmatrix}$ *considered to be a scoundrel.*

        d.   *Nixon* $\begin{Bmatrix} was \\ *acted \end{Bmatrix}$ *found to be not guilty.*

Again, these facts would be surprising to advocates of *To Be* Deletion:

(61)   a.   *Mary appears to be thought to be a genius.*
        b.   *John seems to be considered to be a scroundel.*

I have found only one verb (namely *know*) that may appear in both the "accusative subject" construction and in *un*-passives. As predicted, the *un*- form may not appear in the "accusative subject" environment.

(62) a. *John is unknown.*
      b. *John is known to be a communist.*
      c. **John is unknown to be a communist.*

Few verbs taking the "accusative subject" construction permit degree modifiers, but none is acceptable without *much*.

(63) a. *We were very *(much) expected to be model citizens.*
      b. *The war was very *(much) believed to be wrong.*

Some speakers may find these examples less than fully acceptable, but the contrast between the forms with *much* and those without it is undeniable. My analysis predicts the ungrammaticality of the forms without *much*. The "accusative subject" construction behaves exactly as my criteria predict.

Passives of idiom chunks provide much less clear evidence. Although all the forms my criteria rule out are indeed impossible, there are several related forms not so excluded which are far from fully acceptable.

The clearest test with the idioms is the one involving verbs with AP-complements.

(64) a. *Advantage* $\left\{ \begin{array}{l} \textit{is} \\ \textit{*sounds} \end{array} \right\}$ *easily taken of John.*

      b. *An example* $\left\{ \begin{array}{l} \textit{was} \\ \textit{*seemed} \end{array} \right\}$ *(unfairly) made of John.*

In contrast, the examples of (65) are far better.

(65) a. *John sounds easily taken advantage of.*
      b. *John seemed unfairly made an example of.*
      c. *An example seems to have been made of John.*

If *take advantage of* and *make an example of* are lexical verbs (presumably with internal structure, e.g., $[_V [_V take] [_{NP} [_N advantage]] [_P of]]$ —see Bresnan (1972, p. 147)), then the contrast between (64) and (65) follows from Criterion 3, for *John* is the direct object of these verbs, whereas *advantage* or *an example* is part of the verb itself.

No passives of these idioms may be prefixed with *un*-.

(66) a. **A great deal was unmade of the dinner.*
      b. **The dinner was unmade a great deal of.*
      c. **Advantage was untaken of the offer.*
      d. **The offer was untaken advantage of.*

This can be attributed, at least in part, to the marginal character of *un*-passives of the verbs within the idioms, viz., *take* and *make*.

(67) a. *?Dinner was unmade.*
      b. *?The offer was untaken.*

These facts do not provide confirmation for my criteria, but neither do they provide counterevidence.

The evidence from degree modifiers is only slightly less equivocal. The forms my criteria rule out are indeed ungrammatical, but other forms sound only a bit better.

(68)   a. *??Advantage was very *(much) taken of us.*
       b. *??An example was very *(much) made of John's blunder.*
       c. *??We were very *(much) taken advantage of.*
       d. *??John's blunder was very *(much) made an example of.*

The evidence based on passives of idiom chunks is, in general, not very conclusive. Although all the forms my criteria rule out are indeed ungrammatical, there is reason to believe that many of these would also be excluded by independently necessary factors. Passives of *help* and *thank* bear out the predictions of my criteria more clearly.

The may not appear prenominally.

(69)   *??A *(recently)* { *helped* / *thanked* } *person is usually in a good mood.*

They may not be complements to verbs like *act* or *seem*.

(70)   *John always* { *acted* / *seems* } { *helped* / *thanked* } *by his friends.*

This last example contrasts with (71), providing further problems for the *To Be* Deletion analysis.

(71)   *John always seems to be* { *helped* / *thanked* } *by his friends.*

Neither *unhelped* nor *unthanked* is an English word, as predicted.[13]

Finally, as expected, *much* is required in degree modifiers of passives of *help* or *thank* (though the examples with *thank* are admittedly marginal, even with *much*).

(72)   a. *I was very *(much) helped by your comments.*
       b. *?John was very *(much) thanked for his generosity.*

Passive participles followed by predicative expressions like *President* or *a fool* also behave as predicted. They may not appear as complements to verbs requiring AP-complements.

(73)   a. *Teddy already acts elected President.*
       b. *??John seems considered a fool.*

These examples contrast with those in (74), providing yet another challenge to the defender of *To Be* Deletion.

(74)   a. *Teddy already acts elected.*
       b. *John seems to be considered a fool.*

The verb *elect* may appear in *un*-passives, but not when it is followed by a predicative expression.

(75)   a.   *The present administration is unelected.*
        b.   **Jerry is unelected President.*

Degree modifiers provide a less clear test, since they sound less than perfect with these verbs, even when *much* is present.

(76)   a.   *?John is very *(much) considered a fool.*
        b.   *?John was very *(much) acclaimed a hero.*

Once again, however, the forms ruled out by my criteria are indeed ill-formed.
The table given in (77) summarizes the results of the last few pages.

(77)

	prenominal	after V [_ AP]	un- passives	degree modifiers w/o *much*
double objects	NA	+	+	?
"accusative subjects"	NA	+	+	+
idiom chunks	NA	+	NA	?
help and *thank*	+	+	+	+
predicative expressions	NA	+	+	?

"+" designates a case in which the prediction is clearly borne out; "NA" designates a case in which independent factors suffice to account for the ungrammaticality of the relevant examples, so that no meaningful test is possible; "?" designates a case in which it is unclear whether such independent factors exist. The important point is that there are no counterexamples to the predictions. Further, over half of the test cases provide clear confirmation of the predictions. This constitutes extremely strong empirical support for my criteria.

My criteria make some further predictions about passives. Criterion 4, for example, entails that no transformation may feed the lexical passive rule and that the passive transformation may not feed any lexical rules. Anyone who believes in the existence of transformations of Raising (to object position) or Dative Movement could use all of the arguments given above involving what I have been calling the "accusative subject" and "double object" constructions to show that these rules cannot feed the lexical passive rule. In any event, I know of no well-established transformation that can feed the lexical passive rule.

The failure of transformational passives to undergo the rule prefixing *un-* can be taken as support for the prediction of Criterion 4.[14] I have not been able to discover any other clear cases of lexical rules fed by the lexical passive rule. Criterion 4 predicts that all such rules should apply only to lexically derived passives, not to transformationally derived passives. One possible family of candidates consists of nominalization rules; it is tempting to argue that passive nominals like those in (78) result from nominalizing lexically derived passives.

(78) a. *John's rejection (by Harvard)*
      b. *The city's destruction (by the enemy)*
      c. *Mary's dismissal (by the school board)*
      d. *Our acquittal (by the jury)*
      e. *His enlightenment (by the guru)*

However, as Chomsky (1970) points out, such examples could also be derived by applying the Passive transformation to lexically derived nominals. Such an analysis is supported by the existence of examples like *Aristotle's portrait (by Rembrandt)*, in which the nominal is not deverbal. On the other hand, it does seem to be the case that those passive participles that must be transformationally derived never have nominal counterparts.

(79) a. **John's gift (of) $10 by Mary*
      b. **John's belief to be a genius*
      c. **Advantage's taking of John*
      d. **My* $\left\{\begin{matrix} help \\ thanks \end{matrix}\right\}$ *by Mary.*
      e. **Jerry's election (of) President*

The assumption that passive nominals must be derived entirely within the lexicon would predict the ungrammaticality of the forms in (79). Hence, (79) might be taken as support for Criterion 4. Whether such a position is tenable is not at present clear to me (see Jackendoff, 1971, and Akmajian, 1975, for evidence showing that some transformations must apply to nominals as well as sentences).

Criterion 5 predicts that transformational passives should be completely regular, whereas lexical passives might exhibit idiosyncracies. As noted above, the existence of transitive verbs that do not passivize at all (e.g., *resemble*) may ultimately prove Criterion 5 to be too optimistic. Nevertheless, I believe that it can be maintained that transformations are far less idiosyncratic than lexical rules. In the case of passives, this manifests itself in two ways: first, lexical passives may require adverbial modifiers, and second, lexical passives may use prepositions other than *by* to mark the NP corresponding to the subject of the associated active.

A number of English verbs appear quite freely in passive constructions, but may appear in environments diagnostic of lexical passives only if accompanied by an adverb.

(80) a. *An example was constructed by the teacher.*
      b. *These specimens were found by students.*
      c. *Two errors were noticed by every reviewer.*
      d. *This book was read by the entire class.*
      e. *The chicken was killed by the butcher.*

(81) a. *A ??(carefully) constructed example illustrated the point.*
      b. *These specimens look *(recently) found.*
      c. *Two *(widely) noticed errors have been corrected.*

    d. *This *(rarely) read book is a gem.*
    e. *The chicken smells *(freshly) killed.*

There are a number of puzzling aspects to this phenomenon (e.g., that the other adjectival environments I have cited do not exhibit it clearly), and I do not pretend to understand it fully. I merely wish to note here that a lexical derivation of the participles involved makes it possible to mention an obligatory adverb in the strict subcategorization features. The fact that transformationally derived passives do not have similar restrictions is what Criterion 5 leads one to expect. Incidentally, there is also a small number of verbs whose passive participles cannot behave like adjectives, even in the presence of adverbial modifiers.

(82)   a. *Three wishes were granted to the young man.*
    b.*??The (recently) granted wishes all came true.*

Such cases come as no surprise.

The other idiosyncracy of lexical passives is more interesting. A number of passive participles may utilize prepositions other than *by* in marking the NP corresponding to the subject of the active. Examples include *annoyed at, bored with, contained in, disappointed with, elated at, frightened at, horrified at, interested in, known to, overjoyed at, pissed off at, relieved at, surprised at, tired of*, and *upset with*. Quite generally, an alternative with *by* is also possible. Since the choice of these other prepositions does not seem to be very systematic, Criterion 5 leads to the prediction that they should not be able to appear in environments requiring a transformational analysis. Further, one might expect that environments allowing only lexical passives would sound better with the other prepositions than with *by*. (Notice that this latter expectation may sometimes fail, since there is nothing to prohibit a lexically derived passive from taking *by* as its associated preposition, or as one of several alternatives).

With one exception, verbs whose passives take prepositions other than *by* do not appear in environments diagnostic of transformationally derived passives. The one exception is *know*, which may appear in the "accusative subject" construction. As predicted, *known* may not take *to* in the passive of the "accusative subject" construction.

(83)   a. *John is known* $\left\{ \begin{array}{l} to \\ by \end{array} \right\}$ *everyone.*

    b. *John is known to be a CIA agent.*

    c. *John is known* $\left\{ \begin{array}{l} ??to \\ by \end{array} \right\}$ *everyone to be a CIA agent.*

The expectation that passive participles taking prepositions other than *by* will sound better in adjectival environments than the same participles with *by* appears to be borne out, in general, though the judgments are rather delicate.

(84)

a. *He acted* $\left\{\begin{array}{l} \textit{annoyed at} \\ \textit{bored with} \\ \textit{interested in} \\ \textit{tired of} \end{array}\right\}$ *the news.*

b. *He acted* $\left\{\begin{array}{l} \textit{?annoyed} \\ \textit{?bored} \\ \textit{??interested} \\ \textit{*tired} \end{array}\right\}$ *by the news.*

c. *He has become known* $\left\{\begin{array}{l} \textit{to} \\ \textit{*by} \end{array}\right\}$ *everyone.*

(85)

a. *I was surprised* $\left\{\begin{array}{l} \textit{at} \\ \textit{??by} \end{array}\right\}$ *your remarks*

b. *This was unknown* $\left\{\begin{array}{l} \textit{to} \\ \textit{*by} \end{array}\right\}$ *the ancients.*

(86)

a. *I am very* $\left\{\begin{array}{l} \textit{annoyed at} \\ \textit{bored with} \\ \textit{interested in} \\ \textit{tired of} \end{array}\right\}$ *these developments.*

b. *I am very* $\left\{\begin{array}{l} \textit{?annoyed} \\ \textit{??bored} \\ \textit{??interested} \\ \textit{*tired} \end{array}\right\}$ *by these developments.*[15]

Thus, the idiosyncratic behavior of passive participles seems to be largely restricted to those I have proposed to derive lexically. This is just what Criterion 5 predicts.

4.4   Semantic Evidence

The claim that there are two kinds of passives gains a good deal of credibility when one investigates the interpretation of passives. Consider (87).

(87)   *The door was closed.*

(87) is ambiguous; its two interpretations can be roughly paraphrased as (88a) and (88b).

(88)   a.   *The door was not open.*
        b.   *Someone or something closed the door.*

The analysis of the previous section provided two different sources for (87); it is natural to conjecture that each interpretation is associated with one of the derivations.[16] This gains support from the fact that adjectival (hence lexical) environments strongly favor the interpretation paraphrased by (88a).

(89)   a.   *The closed door blocked the way.*
        b.   *The door remained unclosed.*

    c.   *The door looks closed.*
    d. *?The door was very closed.*

Though not all cases are as clear as this one, these semantic considerations do lend support to the postulation of a dual source for passives, which my criteria required.

4.5   Two Possible Objections

    Since I have claimed that only underlying direct objects may become the subjects of lexical passives, one might expect that no adjectival passive could have prepositional adjuncts. However, this is clearly not the case.

(90)   a.   *John is the most talked about player in the game.*
          b.   *The bed looks slept in.*
          c.   *Just ten years ago this would have been unheard of.*
          d.   *Their living room is very lived in.*

These examples might be taken as counterevidence to Criterion 3, since they appear to involve turning the object of the preposition into the subject by means of a lexical rule.[17]
    In order to accommodate such examples, I must claim that *talk about, sleep in, hear of, live in*, etc. are transitive verbs, each with its own lexical entry, and each taking a direct object. While this requires quite a large lexicon, it seems rather plausible to me on independent grounds, for these verb–preposition combinations typically have meanings not fully predictable from the meanings of their parts. For example, when one sleeps in a bed, one is actually on top of it, not in it; correspondingly, one can make an adjectival passive out of *sleep in*, but not *sleep on*.

(91)   a.   *John slept* $\left\{ \begin{array}{c} in \\ on \end{array} \right\}$ *that bed.*

          b.   *That bed looks slept* $\left\{ \begin{array}{c} in. \\ ??on. \end{array} \right\}$

Similarly, while (92a) may mean either that the room in question serves as our residence or that we make heavy use of it, (92b) has only the latter interpretation.

(92)   a.   *We live in this room.*
          b.   *This room is very lived in.*

In both cases, the idiomatic interpretation is the one associated with the lexical passive, just as one would expect if idiomatic interpretations require separate lexical entries. *Hear of* is less clearly noncompositional, but its idiosyncratic character is evident from the fact that *hear* is the only verb of sensation that may take *of* to indicate indirect evidence. Thus, if someone shows me a picture of John kissing Mary, I may not describe this with (93) (analogous to *I heard of John('s) kissing Mary*

(93)   **I saw of John('s) kissing Mary.*

Somehow the lexicon must record this distinction; if it does so by listing *hear of* as a verb, then the existence of (90c) becomes unproblematic. Though I cannot at present provide arguments for the idiosyncratic character of all verb–preposition pairs that allow lexical passives (e.g., *pay for*), the analysis sketched here strikes me as a plausible answer to the problem raised by examples like (90).

Another possible objection to the theory sketched here is based on the existence of exceptions to passivization. My Criterion 5, in conjunction with my claim that there is a structurally defined Passive transformation, leads to the conclusion that any verb immediately followed by an NP should be passivizable. As I noted above, this conclusion is false. For example, verbs expressing symmetric predicates (e.g., *resemble* and one sense of *equal*) do not allow passives; nor do "measure" constructions like *last all night* or *weigh ten tons*. Hence, one might argue that Criterion 5 is incompatible with my analysis of passives.

I noted earlier that Criterion 5 might be too strong as stated, but I am not yet prepared to accept that conclusion solely on the basis of exceptions to passivization. Not all ungrammatical passives need to be accounted for in terms of the formulation of the Passive transformation. General constraints or rules of semantic interpretation may interact with the transformation so as to account for the apparent exceptions. While I cannot, at present, provide a full account of exceptions to Passive in this way, I would argue that the rather systematic character of these exceptions provides cause for optimism. Unlike the quite idiosyncratic exceptions to the lexical passive, the *-able* rule, the *un-* rule, or such dubious transformations as Dative Movement or *To Be* Deletion, the constructions that take no passives fall into a small number of relatively well-defined classes. It seems reasonable to me to hope that each of these classes can be accounted for in some non-ad hoc way.

To illustrate, I will consider one particularly interesting class of exceptions to Passive that is discussed by Bresnan (1976b). Bresnan cites (94)–(97), noting that the contrast between (96) and (97) has never been satisfactorily explained by proponents of the Passive transformation.

(94) a. *His friends regard him as pompous.*
      b. *Aunt Mary made the boys good little housekeepers.*
      c. *Her friends had failed her in some unclear way.*
      d. *The vision struck him blind.*
      e. *Frank persuaded Mary to leave.*

(95) a. *He strikes his friends as pompous.*
      b. *The boys made Aunt Mary good little housekeepers.*
      c. *Max failed her as a husband.*
      d. *The vision struck him as a beautiful revelation.*
      e. *Mary promised Frank to leave.*

(96) a. *He is regarded by his friends as pompous.*
      b. *The boys were made good little housekeepers by Aunt Mary.*
      c. *She has been failed by her friends in some unclear way.*

      d. *He was struck blind by the vision.*
      e. *Mary was persuaded to leave by Frank.*

(97)   a. **His friends are struck by him as pompous.*
      b. **Aunt Mary was made good little housekeepers by the boys.*
      c. *??She was failed by Max as a husband.*
      d. **He was struck by the vision as a beautiful revelation.*
      e. *??Frank was promised to leave by Mary.*

The examples in (97) are instances of the following generalization, which Bresnan attributes to Visser (1973):

(98)   A passive transform is only possible when the complement relates to the immediately preceding (pro)noun.

In other words, passive senetences are ungrammatical when they contain a complement that is subject-oriented. Assuming this generalization to be correct, I wish now to consider how it can be captured in the theory proposed here, i.e., in a theory including a Passive transformation satisfying Criterion 5.

The contrast between (96) and (97) can be accounted for with the following two assumptions: first, that the semantic component must relate subject-oriented complements to the deep structure subject, and second, that passive sentences have no deep structure subjects. If passives contain no deep structure subjects for subject-oriented complements to be related to, then they cannot be interpreted, and will be marked anomalous. I know of no independent arguments for the first assumption, but neither do I know of any reasons for not accepting it.

The second assumption calls for a bit more comment, for it is widely taken for granted that the object of *by* in passivized sentences is the deep structure subject. However, a survey of the arguments that have been offered for having a Passive transformation (see, e.g., Akmajian and Heny, 1975, for such a survey) reveals that the only argument for having a subject-postposing component to the rule is that the object of the passive *by* obeys the same selectional restrictions as the subject of the corresponding active sentence. As I (and others before me) have noted elsewhere (Wasow, forthcoming) this sort of argument does not suffice to establish the existence of a transformtional operation, at least within EST. Other arguments for Passive, such as those based on strict subcategorization or the prior application of other transformations justify only the object-preposing portion of the rule. This being the case, I see no obstacle in the way of assuming that passive *by*-phrases are present in deep structure, and the Passive consists only of object-preposing. Interestingly, very similar proposals have been made by several other investigators (Bresnan, 1972, pp. 139–143, Keenan, 1975, and Langacker and Munro, 1975), though for rather different reasons.

If the analysis sketched here is correct, then examples like (97) are not counterexamples to Criterion 5. Under this analysis, the Passive transformation applies quite freely, generating forms like (97), but the rules of semantic interpretation will not be able to assign a reading to such examples. I am hopeful that other exceptions to Passive can also be accounted for without requiring abandonment of Criterion 5.

5. Conclusions and Residual Questions

Sections 3 and 4 have shown that the criteria proposed in section 2.2 for distinguishing lexical rules from transformations not only select one type of analysis over
the other in some controversial cases, but make a substantial number of correct and
otherwise unanticipated predictions as well. This lends strong support to the postulation of both rule types by proponents of EST, and it provides a reason for stopp-
ing short of the position taken by Freidin (1974) and Bresnan (1976b), that all
structure-preserving transformations should be reanalyzed as lexical redundancy
rules. I hope that further research on other constructions and other languages will
provide additional support for the proposed criteria.

Before closing, I would like to address myself very briefly to some obvious
questions that have been left unanswered.

First and foremost is the question of how to specify which NPs bear which
grammatical relations. One possible partial solution to this problem is provided by
Chomsky's (1965) definitions of "subject" and "direct object." Whether these
definitions are satisfactory is a question I cannot attempt to answer here (but notice
that the discussion in section 3.3 implicitly rejects Chomsky's definition of "direct
object"). In any event, it is by no means obvious how one would go about defining
"indirect object" along the same lines. If Chomsky's definitions are rejected, an
alternative is needed. I have none to offer, at present. However, I take it as generally
accepted that these relations must play a role in an adequate linguistic theory (see
Osherson and Wasow, 1976), so the problem of characterizing them is not mine
alone. In the worst case, of course, each lexical entry for a verb could indicate what
grammatical relations the nearby NPs bear. In conjunction with relational lexical
rules, plus universal constraints that refer to grammatical relations, such lexical
markings would be making empirical claims.

A second important question concerns lexical rules not involving verbs. My
Criterion 3 requires that NPs mentioned by lexical rules bear grammatical relations
to the items undergoing the rules. This requires either that all lexical rules involve
verbs, or that grammatical relations be defined for items of other categories. The
former alternative is probably untenable (since, e.g., there are de-adjectival nouns),
and the latter alternative further complicates the already difficult problem of defining grammatical relations. A third possibility might be to find some other way of
characterizing the "localness" property of lexical rules. Notice, however, that some
"localness" criterion is necessary. Even if one accepts the controversial transformations of Dative Movement and Raising (to object position), the other criteria will
not serve to account for the nonexistence of -able adjectives or lexical passives of
idiom chunks and help and thank. Hence, Criterion 3 or some other "localness"
condition is needed. Dick Oehrle (personal communication) has suggested that
lexical rules might best be stated in terms of thematic relations (see Jackendoff,
1972, 1975c), rather than grammatical relations. Since existing characterizations of
thematic relations are even less precise than those of grammatical relations, I will

not attempt to evaluate this suggestion. I leave the matter open, noting only that the question of how to characterize "localness" needs to be considered in greater depth.

A related problem is that of formalizing lexical rules. Jackendoff (1975c) proposes a formalism, but it does not, of course, incorporate the "localness" property of Criterion 3. Borrowing from Postal and Perlmutter the notation 'I', 'II', and 'III' for "subject," "direct object," and "indirect object," respectively, one might formalize the lexical rules discussed in this paper as follows:

(99)   a. $\Lambda_{VV}(I) = II$

       b. $-able_{V_A} (II) = I$

       c. $-en_{V_A} (II) = I$

How this formalism is to be interpreted can most easily be illustrated with an example: (99b) says that members of some class of verbs can be turned into adjectives by suffixing *-able*, and that the direct object of the verb corresponds semantically (and hence selectionally) to the subject of the adjective. "Λ" stands for the null string. Notice that (99a) could also be formulated as $\Lambda_{VV}(II) = I$; I know of no basis for choosing between these formulations. An adequate theory of lexical redundancy rules will undoubtedly require a more elaborate formalism[18], but the one I propose here suffices to capture the facts discussed in this paper. I reiterate the need to study a broader range of constructions within the framework proposed here.

Another point I would like to touch upon is the relationship between the ideas put forward here and the theory of "relational grammar" currently being developed by Postal, Perlmutter, Johnson, and others. It is clear that they have much in common: both ascribe a much greater importance to notions like "subject" and "object" than the standard theory did; both reformulate in relational terms many rules that had earlier been formulated in structural terms; and both claim that all relational rules precede all structural rules.[19] There are, however, important differences between the two proposals. This is clearest when one considers the passive: relational grammar does not permit a structural passive rule in addition to the relational one. Hence, it encounters much the same problem as Freidin (1975), in that it cannot make the distinctions necessary to account for the facts discussed in section 4.3 above.

Finally, I want to raise the question of why there should be two passive rules in English, whose effects are so often identical, but which cannot be collapsed. This sort of duplication of effort would seem to be most undesirable. Nevertheless, it is demanded by the facts. An obvious hypothesis is that English once had only lexical passives (Elizebeth Traugott, personal communication, has suggested to me that this was the case), and that it is currently in transition, drifting towards a state in which it will have only transformational passives. Thus, the current duplication of effort may be merely a stage in the simplification of the grammar of English produced by the regularization of the active–passive relation. This is a hypothesis that deserves careful investigation. If it proves tenable, it would be interesting to see whether there are other similar cases in syntax (for a somewhat analogous case in phonology, see Robinson, 1976).

I hope this paper will serve as a stimulus to further research on all of these questions.

Acknowledgments

Valuable feedback on the ideas in this paper and on an earlier version was provided by a number of people, including Adrian Akmajian, Joan Bresnan, Joe Emonds, Jim Gee, Dick Oehrle, and Sue Steele. Of course, they are not to be blamed for any of its shortcomings. Some of the research that went into the paper was supported by a Summer Stipend from the National Endowment for the Humanities.

Notes

1. In the present work I deal only with lexical rules involving verbs, leaving open how to generalize this claim to other lexical rules—see section 5.
2. I thus reject the claim of Postal, Perlmutter, Johnson, and others, that many transformations should be formulated in terms of grammatical relations—see section 5.
3. See Aronoff (1974) for a discussion of some problems encountered in trying to characterize the notion of productivity precisely.
4. This terminology is meant to reflect my neutrality on the controversial issue of whether the complement subject gets raised into object position in this construction. See Postal (1974), Lightfoot (1976a) and references cited there for discussion of this question.
5. Freidin (1975) argues that this sequence does exist, but his argument for this is defective. See note 10 below.
6. Hankamer (1971) argues that expressions like *President* in constructions like *elect Shirley President* are not NPs. Even if he is right about this, there is no reason to believe that these expressions can be generated immediately following an adjective, so the ungrammaticality of (28d) still follows from Criterion 1.
7. I do actually know of one fairly persuasive argument for the existence of *To Be* Deletion. If is based on examples like (i).

   (i)   *There seems little reason to expect an improvement.*

   Since *seem* does not ordinarily allow *There* Insertion (*Optimistic people seem to expect an improvement* → **There seem optimistic people to expect an improvement*), it is hard to come up with a source for (i) without *To Be* Deletion.
8. The fact that *much* is excluded in (44b) but not in (45) follows, under my analysis, from the fact that the examples in (45) have two derivations: one in which the participles are lexical adjectives (in which case *much* is excluded), and one in which a passive transformation operates (in which case the verb remains a verb, and *much* is hence obligatory). Note also that the examples in (45) all lack *by*-phrases; this will be discussed below in connection with Criterion 5.

9. Some other constructions that might be taken as diagnostic for adjectives have been pointed
    out to me. Adrian Akmajian (personal communication) mentions "*Though* Movement"
    (Ross, 1967) and the context *portray NP as* __, illustrated in (i) and (ii).

    (i)   *Handsome though John is, Mary finds him repulsive.*

    (ii)   *The newspaper portrayed Jerry as honest but dumb.*

    I have not used these tests, however, since I can get progressives in the same contexts.

    (iii)   *Living in the country though he was, he kept up with the news.*

    (iv)   *The newspaper portrayed Jerry as having taken bribes.*

    (A very limited range of *-ing* forms—which I take to be adjectives—are possible in the other
    contexts I have designated as adjectival, but these contexts seem to accept progressives
    more freely). It may be that there are speakers for whom these environments do serve as a
    test for distinguishing adjectives from verbs; such speakers could use these environments to
    test the predictions my criteria make regarding passives.

        Joe Emonds (personal communication) has pointed out to me that certain verbs may
    appear in the environment __ NP AP, and he suggests that this construction may provide
    another diagnositc for adjectives. I have not used this test because some such verbs will not
    take passive participles as their AP-complements, while others take too wide a range of
    complements (i.e., not just AP).

    (v)   *John makes everyone* $\begin{Bmatrix} mad \\ *annoyed. \end{Bmatrix}$

    (vi)   *Tom painted the fence* $\begin{Bmatrix} white. \\ *whitewashed. \end{Bmatrix}$

    (vii)   *I saw John* $\begin{Bmatrix} alive. \\ beaten\ by\ the\ police. \\ run(ning)\ away. \\ being\ beaten. \end{Bmatrix}$

    I believe that this construction might, in fact, provide a further test for my criteria, but
    this would require a more thorough study of the construction than I am prepared to
    undertake at present. See Gee (1975) and Akmajian's paper in this volume.

10. Freidin gives (i) as examples of other APs that have an NP following the head, but he
    offers no arguments for calling the predicates NPs.

    (i)   a.   *This is too difficult a problem to give a beginner.*
          b.   *Harold is so obnoxious a person that not even his analyst can
                stand listening to him.*

    In fact, there are good reasons for thinking that these phrases are NPs, not APs. For
    example, the same expressions may appear as subjects, direct objects, and objects of
    prepositions.

    (ii)   *I don't believe that* $\begin{Bmatrix} so\ obnoxious\ a\ person \\ too\ difficult\ a\ problem \end{Bmatrix}$ *derserves much of my time.*

    (iii) $\begin{Bmatrix} I\ have\ never\ encountered \\ You\ shouldn't\ waste\ your\ students'\ time\ on \end{Bmatrix}$ $\begin{Bmatrix} so\ obnoxious\ a\ person \\ too\ difficult\ a\ problem \end{Bmatrix}$

             $\begin{Bmatrix} that\ not\ even\ his\ analyst\ can\ stand\ listening\ to\ him. \\ to\ give\ John. \end{Bmatrix}$

    Notice that none of these positions allows APs.

    (iv)   **I don't believe that* $\begin{Bmatrix} obnoxious \\ difficult \end{Bmatrix}$ *deserves much of my time.*

(v) * { *I have never encountered* / *You shouldn't waste your students' time on* } { *so obnoxious that not even* / *too difficult to give* }

       { *even his analyst can stand talking to him.* / *John.* }

In contrast, the postcopular position in (i) admits both APs and NPs, so it is not diagnostic of the constituent structure. Even more problematical for Freidin's analysis are sentences like (vi).

(vi) *John was given too difficult a problem to give a beginner.*

Under Freidin's analysis, this would require yet another unmotivated phrase structure rule something like (vii).

(vii)   AP → A (AP) . . . .

The only thing I know of that lends any plausibility to (vii) is the existence of examples like (viii) and (ix).

(viii)   *John is happy poor.*

(ix)   *He was lonely single.*

Examples like these do not, however, justify (vii), since they are far worse if the second adjective is replaced by a full AP.

(x)   *??John is happy too poor to pay his bills.*

More plausible condidates for examples of (47) were brought up by Paul Schachter at the Irvine conference:

(xi)   *Juliet was born a Capulet.*

(xii)   *I'm missing the ace of spades.*

(xiii)   *I'm short ten dollars.*

I think it can be plausibly argued that (xi) and (xii) are instances of verbs with defective paradigms, rather than adjectives. (xiii) is more difficult, but several possible analyses suggest themselves, e.g., deletion of *of.* In any event, a single lexical item (or even two or three) appearing in a given environment seems like very weak justification for adding a phrase structure rule to the grammar.

11. Freidin (1975) suggests that examples like (52a) are compatible with a purely lexical analysis of passives if participles like *believed* are treated as adjectives allowing Raising (to subject position). This proposal suffers from three defects. First, it fails to capture the fact that all verbs that take the "accusative subject" construction allow passives with *there*; that is, it would have to say that it just so happens that the adjectives corresponding to the "accusative subject" verbs always take Raising (to subject). Second, it fails to predict that the restrictions on the verbs that may appear in the complement of the "accusative subject" construction apply by and large to the passives of this construction as well.

(i)   *We believe John to* { *be lazy.* / *??avoid work.* }

(ii)   *John is believed to* { *be lazy.* / *??avoid work.* }

cf. (iii)   *John is likely to* { *be lazy.* / *avoid work.* }

Third (and worst of all), it incorrectly predicts that phrases like *believed to be lazy* should behave syntactically like APs (see section 4.3).

12. I assume that any reasonable definition of "direct object" would make *John* the direct object of *Unscrupulous men took advantage of John.*

13. In the discussion, Paul Schachter disagreed with this claim, pointing out that both words appear in the *OED*, with ample historical citations. This undermines the already weak case for treating objects of *help* and *thank* as indirect objects. On the other hand, I think it may be the case that there are historical and dialectical variations on this issue, in which case my claims about *help* and *thank* may hold only for some dialects.

14. I assume that the *un-* rule is lexical. One piece of evidence for this is that it feeds category changing rules, e.g., the rule turning adjectives into adverbs by suffixing *-ly* (If forms like *unhappily* and *unhappiness* resulted from prefixing *un-* to *happily* and *happiness*, then the *un-* rule could not be restricted to adjectives). Another is that the *un-* rule is quite idiosyncratic; compare *unable* versus **uncapable, unattractive* versus **unbeautiful, unbeaten* versus **unvictorious, unconditional* versus **uncontingent, unhappy* versus **unecstatic, uninteresting* versus **unboring, unjust* versus **unright, unspoken* versus **untalked,* etc.

15. An interesting fact about the participles under discussion (pointed out by G. Lakoff (1970c)) is that many of them have grammatical nominals only in their passive forms.

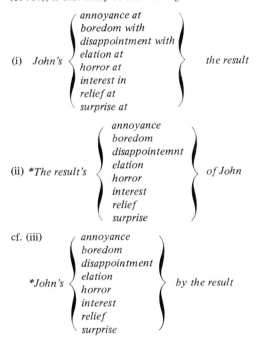

(i)   John's { annoyance at / boredom with / disappointment with / elation at / horror at / interest in / relief at / surprise at }   the result

(ii) *The result's { annoyance / boredom / disappointemnt / elation / horror / interest / relief / surprise }   of John

cf. (iii)   *John's { annoyance / boredom / disappointment / elation / horror / interest / relief / surprise }   by the result

A plausible analysis of these facts would be that the nominalization rules involved take the participial forms as input. The contrast between (ii) and (iii) would then provide more evidence for Criterion 4.

16. I remain neutral here on the question of whether the relevant interpretation should take place at deep structure, surface structure, or somewhere else. Since the two derivations are distinct at every level (because of the difference in the category membership of *closed*), any possibility can be accommodated.

17. Siegel (1970) makes a related objection to deriving *un*-passives lexically.

18. Adrian Akmajian (personal communication) has pointed out to me that a number of other lexical rules seem to apply only to transitive verbs, though some do not involve any change in grammatical relations. For example, *pre-* may not be prefixed to intransitive verbs: e.g.,

*predie, *pre-elapse, *prevanish, prefreeze (transitive only), precook (transitive only). This could be accommodated in my formalism as follows: pre-$_{VV}$(II) = II.

19. These points of similarity are not coincidental, for many of the ideas put forward here began to take shape while I was attending Postal and Perlmutter's course on relational grammar at the 1974 Summer Linguistics Institute. David Perlmutter (personal communication) has informed me that the version of relational grammar I was exposed to at that time has since been superseded. I have no idea whether my position in this paper bears any resemblance to current versions of relational grammar.

COMMENTS ON THE PAPER BY WASOW

Stephen R. Anderson

Department of Linguistics
UCLA
Los Angeles, California

Wasow's extremely stimulating paper is concerned with an issue of central importance to syntactic theory: the character of the distinction between redundancy rules operating over the lexicon and transformational processes involved in the derivations of individual sentences. Much recent research in the theory of grammar has tended toward the conclusion that many of the relationships between sentence types that were once considered appropriate for transformational treatment should instead be described in terms of distinct but related lexical items, inserted into distinct but related underlying structures. A question then arises as to the potential scope of such descriptions: is it in fact possible to do away with all (or at least a major class of) traditionally posited transformations? And if not, what formal characteristics differentiate those systematic relations that should be described transformationally from those that should be described lexically?

Wasow starts from the basic conception of a lexical rule, and elucidates the formal properties we would expect such rules to display. He then goes on to consider particular cases, and to show that the distinction between transformations and lexical rules is substantive and significant. In the case treated in most detail, he shows that the traditional rule of Passive is in fact two quite distinct systematic relations: one transformational, and the other lexical, each with its own well-defined set of properties. The distinction between transformations and lexical rules made within the Extended Standard Theory is thus seen to be a valid and important one.

In these remarks, I would like to discuss briefly the properties of lexical rules that Wasow deals with, and then to comment on one issue he raises: the question of the nature of the structural relations in terms of which lexical rules are to be formulated. Wasow concludes that such rules should be allowed to operate on grammatical relations ("Subject," "Direct Object," etc.), while transformations on the other hand are insensitive to these. I will suggest, on the contrary, that lexical rules are more appropriately formulated in terms of "Thematic Relations," of the sort developed by Gruber (1965) and further by Jackendoff (1972, 1976). I will further suggest that when the central term of this system of relations, the "Theme" itself, is taken into account, some problems that might arise in Wasow's framework are naturally taken care of and interesting descriptive insights can be obtained.

In considering the formal properties of rules that relate lexical items within the lexicon, it is clearly necessary to start from a consideration of what a lexical item is, in most conceptions of generative grammar. Most discussions (e.g., Chomsky, 1965; Jackendoff, 1975) assume that an entry in the lexicon of a language consists of an association of the idiosyncratic properties of the item: its phonological form, the syntactic frame in which it may occur, and its semantic representation. In principle, some of this information may not be explicitly present in the entry for a given item, but rather computable in terms of systematic references to other items in the lexicon (e.g., the semantic representation of a nominalization will be at least partly computable from the semantics of the associated verb); but all is at least potentially present. In addition, some aspect of the lexical entry must allow for the systematic operation of projection rules that perform argument substitutions: thus, the association between elements in the syntactic environment and the role played by their readings in the reading of the element under consideration must be provided for. Lexical entries may (or may not) also contain information about idiosyncratic properties such as exceptional behavior with respect to particular rules of grammar, but this problem will not concern us here.

Since the phonological form, the syntactic frame into which the item may be inserted, and the semantic representation are the essential components of a lexical entry, it is clear that the natural form of a lexical redundancy rule could only be a statement of relations among these things, establishing correlations among these terms across distinct items in the lexicon. From this, certain formal defining characteristics of lexical rules can be seen to fall out.

It is obvious, for example, that the relations between lexical items described by a lexical redundancy rule must meet Wasow's first criterion by being "structure-preserving," at least within the context of the Extended Standard Theory. This is because in this theory (as opposed, for example, to that of McCawley, 1968, where this conclusion would not hold) lexical items are all inserted in base structures. A relation between such items could thus not involve as one term a structure that could not be generated by the base rules without violating this fundamental defining criterion for the elements of the lexicon.

A corollary of this observation is Wasow's fourth condition: that all lexical relations have to be ordered "before" all transformations. In the absence of evidence for McCawley's proposal that lexical insertion takes place at many different stages of a derivation, we presume that the claim of the Standard Theory is correct, and lexical items are inserted into base structures. But since base structures form the input to the transformational rules of the grammar, it is clear that no transformation could apply "before" a lexical rule. Again, the condition is not a special fact about lexical redundancy rules, but rather a consequence of the overall organization of grammars within the (Extended) Standard Theory.

Wasow's third criterion, called "localness," is more specifically related to the organization of the lexicon. The syntactic material that can be relevant to defining the frame in which an item can be inserted (its "subcategorization" features) is generally taken, following Chomsky (1965), to be limited to other constituents of the same clause. Since such subcategorization features are part of the lexical entry for a given item, it follows that lexical rules might refer to them: indeed, this is the only element of a lexical item that allows such rules access to syntactic (as opposed to phonological or semantic) structures. But in that case the limitation on the scope of subcategorization features entails that the syntactic reference of lexical redundancy rules must be similarly limited: in other words, such lexical rules cannot possibly involve reference to elements outside of the immediate clause in which the item is inserted. Thus, non-clause-bounded processes such as wh-movement or topicalization could not possibly be restated as lexical redundancies, since such a rule would have to violate the condition that it could only refer to the (clause-bounded) information present in the lexical entries related.

In addition to the limitations imposed by clause-boundedness, there are presumably other limitations on subcategorization features that extend a fortiori to lexical relations: thus, there are apparently some limitations on what material in a clause can be relevant to the insertion of lexical items. Certain sorts of adverbial material, in particular, do not seem to be tied to the possibilities of occurrence of particular lexical items, but are related rather to more general conditions of well-formedness on semantic representations. If there are no subcategorization features referring to such material, it would follow that lexical relations cannot involve it either, and hence processes of adverb movement or positioning are probably not generally describably as lexical redundancies. More generally, if any particular item does not require subcategorizational specification of a given constituent type, a lexical redundancy rule involving that item could not involve that constituent either.

We neglect for the moment the other aspect of Wasow's localness criterion: the proposal that lexical relations refer specifically to grammagical relations. While it is probably the case that subcategorization restrictions refer to such notions as "Subject," "Direct Object," etc., and thus that lexical rules *could* have access to them as well, it is not obvious that these are the *only* relations to which such rules could refer, and we will in fact suggest otherwise below.

Wasow's other criterion for distinguishing the two types of rules is that lexical rules, but not transformations, can relate items belonging to distinct lexical categories. It is immediately clear that lexical rules can do this, since category membership is part of the syntactic information that characterizes a lexical entry. The claim that transformations cannot change such category membership is one that most (Standard Theory) grammarians have accepted, and that leads to the posited difference between lexical and transformational rules. Note, however, that the acceptance of this restriction on the power of transformations does not entail the further claim that the category label associated with a *phrasal* node may not be changed as the result of a transformation; see Anderson (1967) for an early formulation of the structure-preserving hypothesis in which such phrasal category shifts are an automatic consequence of certain structural changes.

In any event, we can see that the criteria Wasow proposes for distinguishing rules of the two types are entirely natural and well-motivated ones within the general conception of grammar developed as the Extended Standard Theory. Most of them, in fact, would appear to be essential to the very notion of a relation between lexical items in the context of such a theory. The question that naturally arises then is, what else goes with this set of properties? That is, how large a subset of the class of bounded, structure-preserving relations between sentence types ought to be formulated as lexical, rather than transformational rules? It is in giving an answer to this question that we give independent substance to the notion of lexical redundancy rules.

There is an obvious advantage to making the subclass of lexical redundancy rules as large as possible, Wherever a transformation can be equally well reformulated as a lexical relation, the number of steps between underlying and surface structure is reduced, along with the degree of abstractness of the former. The approximation of underlying to (independently observable) surface structures thus follows from Occam's razor, again assuming that lexical and transformational formulations are descriptively equivalent. It is understandable, therefore, that the trend in grammatical theory since lexical redundancy rules were first proposed has clearly been in the direction of replacing transformational relationships with lexical ones.

An initial step toward defining a class of nontransformational relations of this type is provided by Wasow's criterion 2, just discussed. From the limitation on the ability of transformations to alter category membership, it follows that any bounded structure-preserving rule that relates items from distinct lexical categories must be a lexical redundancy rule. This already substantially narrows the class of possible transformations. We might further observe that, given the logic of the situation, there is no way to describe a rule that relates items of distinct lexical categories that is not bounded and structure-preserving, since such a rule could only be lexical. Thus again the theory of lexical redundancy rules allows us to exclude a class of (conceivable) rules of grammar.

Another recent proposal, that of Bresnan (1976), would allow us to extend further the class of rules that are to be treated as lexical. Bresnan suggests that any rule to which individual items may be idiosyncratically exceptional should be treated as a lexical, rather than transformational relationship. It is not immediately obvious that this must be the case, though it is clearly an attractive proposal. Where the government of particular relations is idiosyncratic, it must clearly be provided for in lexical items; and it would be pleasant if we could dispense with it elsewhere. Indeed, ever since the notion of rule government was first extensively discussed (by Lakoff, 1965), linguists have been trying to relegate it to some more or less unobtrusive corner. A case in point is the history of analyses of the dative relation in English, a rule with obvious lexical idosyncracies. The extensive discussion of this rule by Green (1973) is largely devoted to reducing the idiosyncracy from arbitrary lexical classes to semantically defined ones; the equally extended treatment by Oehrle (1975) tends to the conclusion that the relationship is purely lexical, and not a transformational one. The general project of reducing all lexically governed rules to lexical redundancies is one for which Wasow expresses hope and enthusiasm, but to which he is not committed. If possible, however, this would clearly extend the class of nontransformational relationships in a natural and interesting way.

Now of course, we would know that such a project was incorrect in the general case if we could show a rule with lexical exceptions that could not be formulated as a lexical redundancy by virtue of its violating some of the basic conditions discussed above. If there is a rule of subject-to-subject raising, for example, involved in the derivation of sentences such as (1),

(1)   a. *It seems to be raining.*
        b. *This bed appears to be believed to have been slept in*
            by Noam Chomsky.
        c. *The cat looks like it's got his tongue.*

then this rule could not be formulated as a lexical relation insofar as it relates structural positions not in the same clause. Since this rule gives every appearance of having lexical exceptions, it is a prima facie counterexample to such a proposal, at least in its strongest and most interesting form, until an adequate clause-bounded formulation of these facts can be provided.

Nonetheless, it is clearly incumbent on any syntactician who admits the possibility of lexical redundancy rules to justify in detail the positing of *any* bounded, structure-preserving transformation, in the face of the apparent virtues of making all such rules lexical. As soon as lexical rules are admitted to the grammar at all, then, the burden of proof shifts to the analysis in which a transformational account of such a process is suggested.

Wasow assumes that there is one overriding difference between lexical and transformational rules that motivates the existence of the latter: at least in the framework of most of those attending this conference, and in the Extended Standard Thoery in general, transformational rules are insensitive to grammatical relations, and apply simply to the terms of a proper analysis of the string representing a sentence. Lexical rules, on the other hand, are stated in terms of relations between elements such as subcategorization features, which refer to grammatical relations rather than to the terms of a proper analysis, and hence lexical rules ought to be sensitive to grammatical relations. As a consequence, we can assume we have to deal with a transformation, rather than with a lexical rule, whenever the process in question, relating structures X and Y, has the property that the elements filling a given unitary position in Y are related to ("come from") a whole host of distinct positions in X (in terms of grammatical relations, at least). Thus, a transformational rule of Passive is motivated by the existence of systematic structural relations between "actives" and "passives," where the subjects of the passives correspond to direct objects, indirect objects, idiom chunks, NPs from other clauses (e.g., the subject of an accusative+infinitive construction), etc.: here there is no unitary definition in terms of grammatical relations of the class of NPs that can be passivized, though there is (arguably) such a definition in terms of the proper analysis of a terminal string. At least in the case of bounded, structure-preserving rules, this is the basic motivation given for positing a class of transformations.

Now of course it would be of great interest to identify a class of structurally significant relations with the property that all and only lexical redundancy rules (to the exclusion of transformations) can make reference to them. We should note, however, that if the class in question is to be that of traditional grammatical relations, the case is a weak one. While a number of writers have recently emphasized the independence of transformations from grammatical relations (as opposed, for instance, to the claims of those working within the framework of Relational Grammar), this independence is more apparent than real. As Chomsky has noted in his contribution to this conference (Chomsky, 1976) one of the major conditions on rules necessary in this framework is the Specified Subject Condition; but as reformulated in that paper, the primary thrust of that condition is to allow rules to distinguish between subjects and nonsubjects. Thus, while the relation "Subject" may not appear in the structural descriptions of individual transformational rules, it does appear in the theory of transformations, and in such a way as to make rules apply differentially to subjects and nonsubjects. Thus, if one examines simply the overt character of grammatical relationships (rather than their formulation within a theory), one may well find some that are apparently sensitive at least to the notion of subject, and that are furthermore formulated as transformations in the Extended Standard Theory (inevitably, apparently, since not all such processes are bounded or structure-preserving). The criterion of sensitivity to grammatical relations (at least to "Subject") is therefore not a sufficient condition for the assignment of a rule to the category of lexical redundancy rules.

The question I would like to address here is the other side of this coin: is it in fact appropriate for lexical relations to be formulated in general in terms of grammatical relations such as "Subject," "Direct Object," etc., and more particularly, only in terms of these? I would like to suggest that if we recognize the role of Thematic Relations in lexical structures, we arrive at a narrower and more interesting conception of the lexical redundancy rules, and that some of the problems arising in Wasow's paper receive a satisfying account. In addition, some more general problems in the theory of grammar can also be accounted for in the same framework.

Let us first recall that Thematic relations (similar in many ways to Fillmore's case relations) were posited by Gruber (1965) as the basic structural relations at a "Pre-lexical" semantic level of representation. Jackendoff (1972) subsequently showed that a number of problems in syntax and semantics could be dealt with neatly by paying attention to the thematic relation a given NP bears within its clause. In subsequent work, Jackendoff (1976) has shown that several of the basic thematic relations can be satisfactorily formulated in terms of fairly orthodox semantic representation: thus, the relation *Agent* can be defined as the element filling the first argument position of a predicate CAUSE (x,e) (and/or a predicate LET(x,e)); *Source and Goal* as the second and third arguments (respectively) of a predicate GO(x,y,z), etc. Such elements of semantic structure are not, of course, to be redefined ad hoc for each individual lexical entry, but rather represent recurrent components found in the semantic representations of large numbers of items, as shown in some detail by Jackendoff.

It is interesting to note, however, that one of Gruber's relations is conspicuously absent from Jackendoff's (1976) discussion: the relation *Theme* itself. The *Theme* of a clause, as identified by Gruber (1965) and Jackendoff (1972) is a central participant in the proposition the clause expresses: with a motion verb, it is the entity that moves (perhaps in some abstract sense); with a verb specifying location it is the entity whose location is thus defined; with many transitive verbs it is the "patient," or entity that undergoes the action described; etc. We could thus specify the Theme as the element filling the first argument position of $GO(x,y,z)$, $STAY(x,y)$, or $BE(x,y)$, etc. In a sense, the *Theme* is the "logical topic" of the clause: the element that the clause is about, in a purely logical sense divorced from any particular use of the clause in discourse. This sort of logical topicality must thus be kept rigorously distinct from discourse topicality: thus, while a sentence such as "John took his books back to the library" could be used in discourse to make a statement about *John* ("Where did he go?"), the *books* ("What happened to the ones that were on this desk?"), the *library* ("Why are all of its shelves full suddenly?"), or even some entity not mentioned at all explicitly ("Why is John's desk so clean?"), it is still a statement about the *books*, in a logical sense, whose motion or location are described independently of such discourse factors. Various extensions of Jackendoff's framework suggest themselves as ways to capture this notion of "logical topic," but for our purposes it is sufficient to indicate simply its existence. We will assume, that is, that part of the process of semantic interpretation involves identifying the *Theme* of the clause.

We can note immediately that there are some rather general correlations between grammatical and thematic relations in English. Thus, the *Agent* of a (nonpassive) sentence is generally the Subject NP, regardless of transitivity of the verb or the presence of other oblique NP in the clause. Of course, not all Subjects are Agents, but the vast majority of verbs whose semantic representation contains $CAUSE(x,e)$ or $LET(x,e)$ will fill the x-position from the syntactic Subject if the verb is nonpassive. This association between grammatical and thematic relations, then, ought not to be stated in each lexical entry, but ought rather to be stated once and for all as a general rule: part of the semantic component of a grammar of English, or (conceivably) part of a semantic metatheory.

Just as the *Agent* relation bears a consistent association with syntactic position, so also does the *Theme* relation: the Theme is quite generally to be found in Subject position if the verb is intransitive, and in Direct Object position if the verb is transitive. In some cases, a few of which will be noted below, the Theme of an individual verb may be associated with syntactic structure in some other way, but it is clearly a general rule that Themes are to be found in the position of intransitive Subject or of transitive Direct Object. This rule too, then, ought to appear somewhere in the grammar (or in linguistic theory) rather than ad hoc for each lexical entry of which it is true: it is only for exceptional items that the grammatical–thematic relational correspondence should have to be listed explicitly.

Again, various possibilities are apparent for formalizing rules of the sort just noted, which associate thematic and grammatical relations; but we see no advantage to be gained at the present state of our knowledge by taking a stand on this issue. For our purposes, it is sufficient to note that such relations are in fact overwhelmingly regular, and hence that grammatical theory must provide for what we will refer to as the Agent-Rule and the Theme-Rule (as well, perhaps, as others of the same sort). The question of formalization is particularly muddled by the observation that in fact practically all known languages make virtually the same associations as English. Thus, the fact that the Theme is to be found in the position of intransitive Subject or of transitive Direct Object is not simply an idiosyncracy of English, but is rather true of virtually all languages. For a tiny fraction of the world's languages, however (e.g., Dyribal: cf. Dixon, 1972, and Anderson, 1976), it may be that the *Theme* is associated with the Subject for *all* verbs, while the *Agent* is associated with the intransitive Subject or with the structural analog of the transitive Direct Object. These considerations make the role of universal factors in the formulation of grammatical–thematic associations unclear, but do not at all undermine the proposal that semantic interpretation in English makes use of the Theme-Rule and the Agent-Rule.

A consequence of the existence of the Theme-Rule is a reduction in the work that must be performed by some lexical redundancy rules. Consider the large number of transitive/intransitive pairs of the familar type *break/break*, for which a syntactic causative analysis is considered and (rightly, to my mind) rejected by Wasow in his paper. He proposes instead, following Jackendoff, that such pairs ought to be related in the lexicon by means of a redundancy rule, given (approximately) as (2):

$$(2) \quad \begin{bmatrix} +V \\ +[NP_1 \underline{\quad}] \\ BREAK\,(NP_1) \end{bmatrix} \leftrightarrow \begin{bmatrix} +V \\ +[NP_2 \underline{\quad} NP_1] \\ CAUSE\,(NP_2,\,(BREAK\,(NP_1))) \end{bmatrix}$$

Now we can note that, among the information provided by this rule, it explicitly establishes the fact that the NP in Direct Object position in a clause with *break* $_{trans}$ corresponds semantically to the NP in Subject position in a clause with *break* $_{intrans}$. In light of the Theme-Rule, however, we can see that this association is exactly the natural one; and that it need not be stated as part of the lexical relation at all. In fact, neither verb need contain any explicit association of particular NP in its syntactic environment with particular positions in the semantic representation, for these will follow directly from the Theme-Rule and the Agent-Rule. Assume that the argument of the semantic function BREAK(x) is not directly identified with any syntactic position, but rather is simply identifiable as a Patient, from considerations entirely internal to its semantic structure. As noted above, Patients usually correspond to Themes; and we know that the Theme-Rule will associate intransitive Subjects with Themes. Thus, the semantic structure of the function BREAK(x) is sufficient to establish the connection $BREAK(x) = BREAK(NP_1)$ in the intransitive case, and this connection need not be entered in the lexical entry itself. Similarly, in the transitive case, the Agent-Rule will establish the connection $CAUSE(x,e) = CAUSE(NP_2,e)$, where we retain (though no longer with justification) the notation

NP_2 for the transitive Subject. The Theme-Rule will also establish the connection $BREAK(x) = BREAK(NP_1)$, since NP_1 is the Direct Object and hence the Theme. Thus, the representation $CAUSE(x,(BREAK(y)))$ will be directly interpreted as $CAUSE(NP_2,(BREAK(NP_1)))$ without the necessity of making this association explicit in the lexical entry itself. The relation (2) can thus be simplified to that in (3):

(3)
$$
\begin{bmatrix} +V \\ +[NP\_\_\_] \\ BREAK(x) \end{bmatrix} \leftrightarrow \begin{bmatrix} +V \\ +[NP\_\_\_NP] \\ CAUSE(y,(BREAK(x))) \end{bmatrix}
$$

The syntactic relations between sentences involving such intransitive/transitive pairs will follow automatically from the Theme-Rule and the Agent-Rule.

The Theme-Rule (and the Agent-Rule) will thus make it possible to make a number of significant simplifications in individual lexical items and in lexical rules, simplifications that are not merely formal but that reflect general facts about (the) language. It seems clear, furthermore, that the operation of this rule underlies a number of other systematic processes in language. Recall that the Theme-Rule associates the relation of Theme precisely with a *Direct* Object. This suggests that if a NP occupying Direct Object position were to be shifted into some other structural position (such as an oblique relation or prepositional phrase), it should cease to be Theme. In fact, there are a large number of pairs of just this sort in English: instances in which a given NP representing the Patient of a verb can appear either as the Direct Object of that verb or in an oblique relation to it:

(4)   a.   i.   *The farmer plowed the field.*
            ii.   *The farmer was plowing in the field.*

       b.   i.   *John painted my picture this morning.*
            ii.   *John painted on my picture this morning.*

       c.   i.   *A vandal smeared the paint on my house.*
            ii.   *A vandal smeared my house with the paint.*

These cases have been discussed in more detail in a previous paper (Anderson, (1971); in summary, there is a difference in interpretation between the members of such pairs as to whether the patient is interpreted as completely or "holistically" affected by or involved in the action. Thus, in the (i) sentences in (4), the field was completely plowed, the picture finished, and the paint used up (though the house may not have been covered); while in the (ii) sentences, the field may or may not have been finished, the picture may still be only half done, and there may well be some paint left (though the house was completely covered or ruined). The same sort of contrast can be seen in the famous pair (5):

(5)   a.   *Bees swarmed in the garden.*
       b.   *The garden swarmed with bees.*

Here, the implication that the garden was completely full of bees is only present in (5b), where *garden* occupies (intransitive) Subject position.

We can suggest, it seems, that the difference in interpretation in pairs such as those we have been discussing is related to the possibility of applying the Theme-Rule to a given NP. That is, the relevant interpretive property seems to correlate with the NPs occupying intransitive Subject or transitive Direct Object position, exactly those to which the Theme-Rule would apply. The existence of such an independent property, furthermore, suggests that *Theme* is not simply to be identified with "Patient," since a NP can be Patient without being Theme (as in (4bii), for example), though this is clearly the unusual case. This might well suggest the existence of a semantic function THEME(x,e) distinct from those discussed by Jackendoff (1976), though this conclusion may not be warranted in the absence of more precise characterization of the semantic consequences of Themehood. In any event, it is the Theme-Rule we have been discussing that is responsible for the semantic differences in the pairs above, depending on whether it can or cannot assign a given NP to the role of Theme based on its structural position in the clause.

It is worth noting, incidentally, that the sort of relation just exemplified is by no means unique to English. Languages as diverse as Avar, Finnish, Maori, and Walbiri demonstrate essentially the same phenomenon in more or less sytematic fashion: when a Patient NP appears in the normal Direct Object position, it is interpreted as the Theme and thus (potentially) holistically; where the same NP can also appear in an oblique position, the Patient is no longer so interpreted. The semantic effects of such changes are well correlated with the interpretation proposed here: when the object is "demoted" in such a way, the logical structure of the clause changes so that it is no longer "about" the Patient, but rather "about" the NP in Subject position. This follows, of course, from the fact that when the verb's Direct Object becomes oblique, the verb ceases to be structurally transitive; and hence the Theme-Rule comes to assign Themehood to the Subject instead. For further discussion and exemplification of this relationship, in which the same Theme-Rule applicable in English plays a central role, cf. Anderson (forthcoming).

Let us now proceed to consider the facts discussed by Wasow in connection with his argument that English has two sources of "passives": a transformational rule and a lexical relation. When we consider the latter, we can see immediately that part of the work Wasow's lexical passive rule must perform is a natural consequence of the operation of the Theme-Rule. In particular, the fact that the Subject of such a lexical passive corresponds semantically to the Direct Object of the related transitive verb follows from the structure in which adjectives appear. Let us characterize the required lexical rule as follows:

$$(6) \quad \begin{bmatrix} /x/ \\ +V \\ +[NP \underline{\quad} NP] \\ w \end{bmatrix} \longleftrightarrow \begin{bmatrix} /x/, \text{[+Past Participle]} \\ +Adj \\ +[NP \; be \; \underline{\quad}(by \; NP)] \\ w \end{bmatrix}$$

In this expression, w represents the semantic characterization of the verb (which is common to verb and adjective), and the feature [+Past Participle] determines the operation of the morphological rules creating the appropriate phonological form by suffixing, Ablaut, etc.

Now observe that the syntactic frame in which the adjective appears has a Subject, but no Direct Object. The Theme-Rule would thus assign the NP in Subject position to the role of Theme; and in the absence of any overt rule to the contrary, the Theme would then be associated with the Patient, first argument of $GO(x,y,z)$, $STAY(x,y)$, or $BE(x,y)$, etc. On the other hand, in the case of the associated transitive, a Direct Object is present; this would thus be associated with the relation Theme, and hence with Patient, first argument of GO, STAY, BE, etc. The result is that the Direct Object of the transitive verb will be assigned the same semantic role(s) as the Subject of the associated (intransitive) adjective through the independent operation of the Theme-Rule, and thus the structural change associated with Passive need not be indicated explicitly.

Furthermore, other differences between lexical and transformational passive rules follow from the same observation. Of central importance is the fact that the subject of the adjectival form is assigned the status of Theme. From this it follows that the Subject of the lexical passive can never be the NP corresponding to the Indirect Object, to a chunk of an idiom, or to a constituent of another clause (such as the subject of an accusative+infinitive construction), since these NPs are not Themes of the relelvant clause: Indirect Objects are rather *Goals* (usually); idiom chunks have no thematic status, and NPs from a lower clause bear no thematic relation in a higher one. The fact that lexical passives are restricted in this way thus follows from the role of the Theme-Rule in their interpretation, without any reference to other properties of lexical rules. As Wasow's discussion of lexical passives demonstrates beyond doubt, these predictions are abundantly validated.

A generalization that arises from several of the preceding observations is the following: when an otherwise transitive verb appears in an intransitive structure, the Theme-Rule predicts that the most natural reading for such a structure to have is a "passive" one, where the Subject NP of the intransitive structure corresponds to the Direct Object NP in the transitive one. The situation may of course be more complex than this: in the "demoted-object" constructions considered before, the Theme-Rule operates as usual to assign Themehood to the (structurally intransitive) Subject, although other semantic properties of the Patient relation are associated with the oblique object phrase. Nonetheless, the most natural reading for an intransitive derived lexcially from a transitive verb is the "passive" one.

We can use this observation to account for another fact cited by Wasow in his discussion. He notes the existence of a number of verbs whose participles are associated with an oblique phrase marked with some preposition other than the usual passive *by*: *annoyed at, bored with, horrified at, disappointed with, interested in*, and a number of others. Following Lakoff, he then observes that these verbs have only "passive" nominalizations: thus, *John's annoyance at the result*, but not **the result's annoyance of John*. Wasow proposes to account for this fact by a lexical rule that derived these nominalizations not directly from the verbal root, but rather from the participle (which, being an intransitive adjective as we have seen above, would have "passive" sense). There are two problems with this analysis, however. First, it fails to account for the fact that it is just this class of verbs, those with oblique phrases involving idiosyncratic, lexically determined prepositions (rather than the general *by*) that undergo this derivation. That is, what differentiates verbs like *annoy* from verbs like *persuade*, where both active and passive senses are possible (cf. *John's perusasion by Mary* and *Mary's persuasion of John*)? This difference would not appear to follow if all nominalizations are derived from participles, since participles of both types of verb are passive: *persuaded* just as much so as *annoyed*.

The second defect in the analysis that derives *annoyance*, etc., from *annoyed*, etc., is a rather obvious one: the formation of past participles involves morphological changes in the verb (the addition of a suffix, typically *-ed*, and/or Ablaut). The morphology of the participle is never, however, reflected in the shape of the nominalization, even when the nominalization clearly involves no morphological changes beyond the addition of a suffix: thus, *disappointment* and not **disappointedment*. The lexical rule for nominalizations, then, would have to first undo the morphological changes effected in the derivation of the participle, and then perform its own morphological change. This convoluted procedure suggests that there is not, in fact, any advantage to be obtained by deriving the nominalization from the participle rather than directly from the root.

We can, however, make the facts concerning this class of verbs follow from the apparatus sketched above. First we note that these verbs have to contain, in their lexical entries, information concerning idiosyncratic preposition selection. Let us simply assume, then, that this information must also be carried over to the corresponding nominalizations. The syntactic subcategorization frame for a verb such as *annoy*, then, when it occurs in nominalized form, will be something like +[NP ___ *at*+NP]. The interpretation of such a structure will now proceed along the expected lines for intransitive clauses (and their nominalized analogs), and the first NP will be interpreted as an intransitive subject. This entails its assignment as Theme by the Theme-Rule; and further, its association with the semantic properties assigned to the Theme/Object of the basic transitive construction *the result annoyed John*. The oblique NP, object of the preposition *at*, will then be assigned to the role of *Source*. Notice that the requirement of listing the preposition in the subcategorization frame entails the conclusion that such nominalization always appear in structurally intransitive construction, and hence always have "passive" sense.

In the case of a verb like *persuade*, however, there is no lexically selected preposition; both the *by* of *John was persuaded by Mary/John's persuasion by Mary* and the *of* of *Mary's persuasion of John* are the normal ones inserted by the syntax in passives and nominalizations, respectively. Hence, the subcategorization frame for the nominalization of *persuade* can be simply +[NP ___ NP]. Such a structure will be interpreted as "active" if nothing else applies (*Mary's persuasion of John*) and as "passive" just in case (the NP-analog of) Passive applies. Of course, some verbs may appear in both the idiosyncratic and the neutral construction: thus, *John's disappointment of his audience, the audience's disappointment by John* reflect the fact that *disappoint* can appear in [NP___NP], while *John's disappointment at the audience's response* reflects its appearance in [NP___ *at*+NP]; We have a natural account, however, of the fact that the restriction of a nominalization to the "passive" sense should be associated with the class of verbs involving a lexically selected preposition. Furthermore, since we can now derive the nominalizations directly from the verbs, rather than from the participles, the morphological shape of the nominalizations is no longer an embarrassment. Central to this derivation, however, is the fact that structurally intransitive constructions such as [NP ___at+NP] most naturally have "passive" sense, which in turn depends on the operation of the Theme-Rule.

Another construction to which the notion of Theme appears relevant is brought up by Wasow as a possible objection to his analysis. He discusses the well-known cases of sentences such as *The bed looks slept in*, in which it appears that Passive has applied not to a Direct Object, but rather to the object of a preposition. He notes that these passives can appear in environments that must be, on his analysis, diagnostic for lexical as opposed to transformational passives; this is clearly inconsistent with the observation that the Subject of a lexical passive must correspond to the Direct Object of the associated transitive verb. He suggests that the way to reconcile these facts with his account is to claim that *sleep in*, etc., are in fact transitive verbs, and thus that their object is not an oblique one but rather a normal Direct Object.

The suggestion that *sleep in*, etc., can be treated as lexical items (distinct from the simple verb *sleep* followed by a locative expression) receives some support from the observation that there is a subtle difference of sense associated with the passive structure. A sentence such as *This bed has been slept in (by George Washington)*, for example, does not simply report an act of sleeping, together with the location of that act; rather, it reports something that has happened to the bed, which has led to its present state. In fact, such passives of apparent objects of prepositions are by no means generally possible, but rather can only occur where the sort of interpretation just hinted at is possible: where the object in question has been affected by the action or has acquired some characteristic as a result of it, and where furthermore the sentence is logically "about" that effect or characteristic. Thus, **Cleveland seemed run amok in by John* is not acceptable, since John's action is unlikely to have had significant consequences for the basic identity and characteristics of Cleveland; while *The room seemed lived in* is possible, since the basic state of a room is definitely affected by its being inhabited.

It should be clear by now that the semantic difference we are concerned with is related to the notion of Theme. The relevant passives, that is, are possible just in case it is possible to assign the role of Theme to the apparent object of a preposition in the clause. This would be exactly what we would expect if, in fact, in these constructions the NP we are concerned with is Direct Object (and not object of a preposition), given the Theme-Rule. The semantics of the constructions, then, is entirely consistent with the claim that *sleep in*, etc., is treated as a transitive verb.

It is not hard to see how the lexical items we posit here (*sleep in*, etc.) can be justified. The crucial fact about English that allows them is the existence of a verb+ particle construction for (clearly lexical) transitive verbs of the type *John threw up his lunch*, *The CIA brought off a coup*, etc. As a result of this construction, the sequence Verb+Prep+NP in derived structure is ambiguous between the interpretation [intransitive verb + prepositional phrase] and the interpretation [[transitive verb–particle] + Direct Object]. We might suggest, therefore, that English has a local transformation (in the sense of Emonds, 1976) that readjusts the structure [V [$_{PP}$ Prep NP]] to [[$_V$V + Prep] NP]. The function of this rule can be acacounted for if we assume, following a suggestion attributed by Chomsky (1976) to J. Goldsmith, that thematic relations are interpreted in derived structure rather than in underlying structure. The proposed adjustment has the effect of making the erstwhile locative NP into a Direct Object, and hence qualifies it for assignment to the role of Theme by the Theme-Rule, as we have seen above is necessary. In order to account for the lexical passives of verbs like *sleep in*, then, we need only assume that the lexicon contains a corresponding redundancy rule, performing the same function as the local transformation just suggested:

(7)
$$
\begin{bmatrix} /x/ \\ +V \\ +[NP \_ (Prep+NP)] \\ w \end{bmatrix}
\longleftrightarrow
\begin{bmatrix} /x/+Prep \\ +V \\ +[NP\_NP] \\ w' \end{bmatrix}
$$

This rule allows for a relation between intransitive verbs that can take a PP-complement and corresponding transitive verb+particle combinations. The resulting lexical units (of the type *sleep in*) can then serve further as the input to the lexical rule of Passive, yielding the sentence type *The bed looks slept in* as required.

The notion of Theme turns out to be relevant to another question addressed by Wasow, that of exceptions to the Passive rule. He notes first that there are a number of verbs that cannot undergo Passive: e.g., *resemble, equal, last, weigh (ten tons,* as opposed to *weigh the meat*). We can see immediately that these verbs have something in common: their apparent Direct Object (the NP which immediately follows the verb) does not meet the semantic conditions of a Theme. Thus, in *John resembles his father*, or *the square root of nine equals three, his father* and *three* are not patients, objects in transition, objects whose location is specified, etc.: they are characteristics rather or qualities or abstract locations or identities assigned to their Subjects. The reading of *John resembles his father* thus includes a function like BE(JOHN, HIS FATHER); and the theme of the clause is thus *John*. Similar observations appear to apply to the other systematic exceptions to the rule of Passive, suggesting the generalization that verbs with nonthematic objects cannot undergo this rule.

Of course, this conclusion would follow in any event from the Theme-Rule if it were only the lexical passives that we were concerned with; but it appears that the transformational Passive rule must be prevented from applying to them as well. This latter fact, however, could be accounted for if we assumed that the lexical Passive rule was in fact responsible for deriving a "passive participle" form, and not simply an adjective as we have assumed thus far. We could then say that the transformational rule of Passive, in addition to performing whatever permutations of NP and changes in the auxiliary were required, also marked the verb as a "passive participle."

For the verbs that fail to undergo Passive, however, no such passive participle form could be derived by the lexical rules, and thus the sentence would block at the level of surface structure. This solution would be similar to that which has occasionally been proposed to account for e.g., the nonappearance of modals in infinitive and gerund constructions by saying that these verbs are defective in not having any non-finite forms. This suggestion for blocking the formation of transformational Passives for verbs whose lexical Passive would be ill-formed (because their objects are non-thematic) seems promising, but must be regarded as tentative in the extreme until more is known about the interaction between morphology and syntactic structure.

Another class of exceptions to Passive, however, appears to have a straightforward solution in terms of the notion of Theme. This is the class of sentences involving a transitive verb and a following complement of some type, discussed by Bresnan (1976), and by Wasow. A number of examples of this type can be adduced, which fall into one or the other of the following two paradigms:

(8)   a.   i.   *Aunt Mary made the boys good little housekeepers.*
              ii.   *The boys were made good little housekeepers by Aunt Mary.*

       b.   i.   *The boys made Aunt Mary good little housekeepers.*
              ii.   **Aunt Mary was made good little housekeepers by the boys.*

Bresnan suggests that these examples illustrate a generalization made by Visser (1973): "A passive transform is only possible when the complement relates to the immediately preceding (pro)noun." Such a generalization may indeed be observationally adequate, but seems (to my mind at least) somewhat unsatisfying as an explanation. A more promising account might be constructed along the following lines: we might say that a rule of semantic interpretation attributes the complements in these sentences to the Theme of the clause (that is, the rule assigns as Subject of such a complement the Theme from the clause). In sentences of type (8ai), this is the Direct Object NP; when (8ai) is passivized, it becomes intransitive, and thus the (derived) Subject becomes the Theme. Since this NP corresponds to the object of the nonpassive clause, however, the complement is correctly assigned in (8aii) as well as in (8ai).

In sentences of the type (8bi), however, the Direct Object is not Theme: *Aunt Mary* in this case does not undergo action or motion, nor is her identity described. She is rather more of an oblique relation: in this sentence it is *the boys* that is Theme, since the sentence basically asserts a quality assignable to them. Sentence (8bii) is now impossible. This can be attributed to the fact that the Direct Object in (8bi), the presumed source, in nonthematic; and we have observed above that such verbs generally do not passivize. Furthermore, in the derived structure (8bii), the intransitive subject *Aunt Mary* is the only NP eligible for assignment as Theme by the Theme rule; but if *Aunt Mary* is taken to be theme, the complement cannot be correctly associated with the appropriate NP. Thus, even if the proposal that verbs with nonthematic Direct Objects do not undergo Passive turns out to be an oversimplification, (8bii) would still be ruled out by the fact that it would not be

possible to interpret the complement correctly here by associating it with the
Theme of the clause.

We note here a possible objection that could be made to our analysis of the facts
of (8) and related constructions. Consider the contrast between (9a) and (9b):

(9)   a.   *John asked Bill to leave.*
        b.   *John asked Bill to be allowed to leave.*

Here we have apparently the same main clause structure, but a difference in the
interpretation of the complements: in (9a), the complement subject is interpreted
as *Bill*, but in (9b), as *John*. Such a contrast would appear to make it impossible to
associate complements uniquely with the Theme, for, whichever NP we treat as
theme, one of the sentences in (9) will be interpreted incorrectly.

It is not hard to see that this argument is fallaciaous and that the facts of (9) do
not impugn the generalization that complements are associated with Themes. (9a)
and (9b) clearly have very different thematic structures: in (9a), what is being
described is an act of ordering, close to the sense of *John ordered Bill to leave*. In
such a case, *Bill* is plausibly regarded as the "undergoer" or the Patient of the act.
He is thus the Theme of the clause, just as in a sentence like *John expelled Bill*.
The complement *to leave* is thus correctly associated with *Bill*. In (9b), on the other
hand, Bill does not undergo anything; rather he is the Goal of a request: the request
that (Theme) be allowed to leave. In this sentence, then, Bill is an Indirect, rather
than a Direct Object; and hence nonthematic. The remaining NP in the clause, the
Subject, thus is the only candidate for Theme, and the complement is associated
with this. Observe further that the passive of (9b), *Bill was asked by John to be
allowed to leave*, if at all well formed, has the interpretation in which Bill is the one
to be allowed to leave, as predicted by our account. Contrasts such as **What John
asked Bill was to leave* versus *What John asked Bill was to be allowed to leave*
further support the difference in thematic structure posited between (9a) and (9b),
and we conclude that the facts of (9) do not invalidate the account of sentences
involving complements given above.

We should note here that this account hinges on our saying that the Theme-Rule
applies to the structure which results from Passive in cases analogous to (8aii, 8bii).
If correct, therefore, this would lend further support to the proposal noted above
that thematic relations are assigned at the level of derived structure rather than in
underlying structure.

A number of other possible cases of the application of the Theme-Rule in English can also be noted. We cite here only one: it has somethimes been claimed that
English contains some rules organized along "ergative" lines, in that they apply to
Direct Objects or to intransitive Subjects, but not to transitive Subjects. For example, in noun compounds, we find the type *bird-call* and the type *lion-hunt* (by
riflemen), but not the type **lion-hunt* (of gazelles). We might suggest, then that
there is a rule of ergative-type that forms such compounds (for further discussion of
such rules, cf. Anderson, forthcoming). When we look at such instances, however,
we can see that they are apparently all semiproductive processes at best, and clearly

candidates for assignment to the status of lexical rather than transformational processes (in the framework developed by Wasow). Insofar as this is the case, it is possible to claim that such processes are not "ergative" in any syntactically relevant sense: rather than applying to Direct Object and intransitive Subject as grammatical relations, they apply interpretively to Themes. When we thus sharpen the definition of "transformation" or "syntactic rule" that might be relevant to the question of whether languages contain ergative rules, it becomes plausible to claim that such cases as may appear to be of this type are not syntactic at all, but rather rules of interpretation that depend upon the relation Theme.

Our conclusion, then, is that the system of thematic relations has a significant role to play in the description of lexical structure, and that the relation Theme itself is of particular importance. Once this relation is recognized, and the existence of the Theme-Rule in English (and other languages) acknowledged, a great deal of the material that might be assigned to individual lexical entries can be seen to follow from general principles. Furthermore, it is no longer necessary to claim that transformations cannot be sensitive to grammatical relations (which is, as observed above, contrary to the spirit of the Specified Subject Condition); or that lexical relations must be. Lexical rules may well be sensitive to grammatical relations; indeed, the fact that the subcategorization information present in lexical items may refer to a substantially larger number of these than just the Subject/non-Subject distinction suggests that that should be the case. Lexical relations may also depend on thematic structure, however, and perhaps the most general cases of what we call lexical redundancy rules depend on thematic, rather than grammatical realtions. The distinctions posited by Wasow between syntactic and transformationa rules are an invaluable clarification of the overall structure of a grammar, and make much clearer the domains of fact that may be relevant to the resolution of fundamental questions in syntax.

THREE CASES OF OVERGENERATION*

Kenneth Hale
LaVerne Masayesva Jeanne
Paul Platero

Department of Linguistics
Massachusetts Institute of Technology
Cambridge, Massachusetts

1. Introduction

It is possible to imagine two diametrically opposed positions concerning the fundamental nature of language. We will characterize these positions in rather extreme terms, though we would not wish to claim that any linguist necessarily adheres totally to either extreme. Our characterizations are to be understood as convenient abstractions that are, to some extent at least, consistent with observable extremes in actual linguistic work.

1.1 The Autonomous Systems View [1]

According to this view, language consists of a number of distinct systems, each possessing inherent principles of organization that are essentially independent of factors relating to any other linguistic system or to extralinguistic considerations. The systems alluded to here inlcude, for example, the categorial rules of the base, the lexicon, the transformational component, the system of rules that assign obligatory coreference, or construal, and other systems. To say that the systems are independent, or autonomous, is to say, for one thing, that the rules belonging to each system apply without constraint—with the exception, of course, of those constraints and conditions that are general for grammatical rules of all kinds and whose identification is one of the important tasks of linguistic science (e.g., general constraints of the sort identified in Chomsky, 1964, 1973, and in Ross, 1967). What the Autonomous Systems thesis specifically rules out, we would suggest, is the local, rule-particular, constraint of the type often seen appended to transformational rules (compare the No-Condition Principle of Perlmutter, 1971, p. 128), or the sort of constraint represented by the environmental specification in a context-sensitive phrase structure rule. The relatively early abandonment by generative grammarians of context-sensitive phrase structure rules can, we believe, be seen as belonging intellectually, though not historiographically, to the tradition that most clearly approximates the Autonomous Systems position. And the thesis of the autonomy of syntax, which informs much of the work of Noam Chomsky and his students, is certainly within this tradition.

1.2   The Dependent Systems View

According to a conceivable opposite extreme, a language consists of a single unified system—or else a set of tightly integrated systems—whose inherent principles of organization are often intimately related to factors belonging to conceptually distinct realms, including extralinguistic factors. Under this conception of language, it is very much to be expected that a **transformational** rule might, for example, be **lexically** governed—i.e., restricted in its application to particular lexical items (e.g., Lakoff, 1970c)—or be subject to one or another of a variety of semantic, pragmatic, or even cultural constraints (e.g., Lakoff, 1971a), or that the internal structure of a phrasal category, say NP, might be dependent upon the grammatical relation it bears to the verb, or upon some semantic factor such as, for example, its use in a generic, as opposed to a specific, sense; and so forth.

1.3   Overgeneration

As preliminary illustration of the distinction between the Autonomous Systems view and the Dependent Systems view, we wish to offer what our imagination tells us would be the treatment of a certain Navajo fact under the two conceptions of language.[2]

Navajo possesses a rule whose effect is roughly that of the passive in English. The rule relates sentences of the form represented in (1) below to corresponding "inverted" sentences of the form represented in (2):

(1)   *Ashkii at'ééd yizts'ǫs.*
         (boy girl yi-kissed)
         'The boy kissed the girl.'

(2)   *At'ééd ashkii bizts'ǫs.*
         (girl boy bi-kissed)
         'The girl was kissed by the boy.'

In addition to inverting the linear order of the subject and object noun phrases, the rule also involves a change in the object marking prefix in the verb work—/yi-/ is replaced by /bi-/, as can be seen in the example. The rule is further exemplified by (3)-(4) below:

(3)   *Łį́į' dzaanééz yiztał.*
         'The horse kicked the mule.'

(4)   *Dzaanééz łį́į́' biztał.*
        'The mule was kicked by the horse.'

Thus, the effect of the rule is to convert a sentence of the form:

        S(ubject) O(bject) *yi*-V(erb)

into a new sentence of the form:

        O(bject) S(ubject) *bi*-V(erb).

We are evidently justified in relating the two forms, since they are cognitively synonymous and, moreover, exhibit the same selectional relationships between their verbs and noun phrases. Let us assume, for the sake of this discussion, that we are correct in relating the two by means of a transformational rule that inverts the subject and object noun phrases—there is, in fact, evidence to support this conclusion, though it will not be detailed here—and let us refer to the rule as Subject-Object Inversion, or SOI.

The interesting fact about this process in Navajo is that while cognitively synonymous pairs

        S   O   *yi*-V
        O   S   *bi*-V

exist to describe many events appropriately described by transitive sentences in Navajo, there are many cases in which only one or the other, but not both, of the two forms can be used. Thus, for example, the circumstance in which a boy kicks a stone can be described in Navajo with a sentence of the form S O *yi*-V, but not with a sentence of the form O S *bi*-V:

(5)   *Ashkii tsé yiztał.*
        'The boy kicked the stone.'

(6)   **Tsé ashkii biztał.*
        'The stone was kicked by the boy.'

On the other hand, the circumstance in which a bee stings a boy may be described in Navajo with a sentence of the form O S *bi*-V, but not with a sentence of the form S O *yi*-V.

(7)   **Tsís'ná ashkii yishish.*
        'The bee stung the boy.'

(8)   *Ashkii tsís'ná bishish.*
        'The boy was stung by the bee.'

The principle is roughly this. Nominal concepts are ranked in Navajo with reasoning beings (humans) at the top of the hierarchy, and unreasoning entities (inanimates and abstract concepts) at the bottom. For sentences in which the subject and object are unequal in rank, the acceptable surface form is that in which the higher ranking NP precedes the lower ranking one.

How would this phenomenon be handled under the two conceptions of language contrasted above? Let us first imagine how it would he handled in the Dependent

Systems view, since this is the way we originally conceived of the problem when it first came to our attention. In this conception, the rule of SOI is subject to the following conditions of application:

(a)   Optional if the subject and object are equal in rank;

(b)   Obligatory if the object outranks the subject;

(c)   Inapplicable if the subject outranks the object.

The Autonomous Systems treatment of this Navajo process, we would propose, is roughly as follows. Assuming that SOI is in fact a bonafide transformational rule in Navajo, it applies **without constraint**. Thus, from the perspective of the transformational system of Navajo syntax, **all** of the sentences (1)-(8) are equally, and perfectly, well formed. This is not to say, of course, that they are all of the same status from a global perspective; far from it. The deviance of sentences (6)-(7), however, does not pertain to the realm of syntax. Rather, it has to do with the **meaning** of the inverted form of the sentences in Navajo. Witherspoon (forthcoming) has argued, persuasively we feel, that the inverted form is used when a being denoted by the object noun phrase, either on purpose or inadvertently, **relinquishes control** of the situation described by the sentence. Thus, the Navajo version of (2) is very poorly represented by the English passive—a more apt rendition would be something like 'The girl let the boy kiss her.' Witherspoon maintains, correctly, we feel, that the ill-formedness of (6) has nothing to do with syntax but rather with the impossibility, from the Navajo point of view, of a stone relinquishing control—a stone does not reason, so it cannot be in control of the situation to begin with. The inappropriateness of (6) can be appreciated, Witherspoon points out, when the sentence is translated 'The stone let the boy kick it.' Correspondingly, the inverted form (8) is required because, in order for a boy (human, and therefore reasoning) to be stung by a bee, he must relinquish his inherently greater control.

Whether Witherspoon is right or wrong about the Navajo semantics involved here is beside the point, actually. Whatever the facts, his assertion that it is not a matter of syntax, or even of grammar, would be represented in the Autonomous Systems view by permitting the syntactic rule of SOI to operate entirely without constraint.

The present paper proceeds from a view of language which, it seems to us, is most consistent with the Autonomous Systems thesis. In the ensuing discussion, we present three cases—one each in Papago, Hopi, and Navajo—in which rules of grammar, if allowed to apply without constraint—that is to say, in conformity with the Autonomous Systems thesis—produce sentences that are in one sense or another unacceptable. For each case, we will propose that the principle which accounts for the unacceptability properly belongs to a system which is entirely separate from that to which the rule itself belongs.

2. Papago Extraposition [3]

Each of the cyclic phrasal categories of Papago—i.e., sentence ($\bar{\bar{\bar{V}}}$), noun phrase ($\bar{\bar{\bar{N}}}$), and postpositional phrase ($\bar{\bar{\bar{P}}}$)—is expanded by means of phrase structure rules conforming to the following schemata:

(9) *Base Rules:*

  a. $\bar{\bar{\bar{A}}} \rightarrow \text{Spec } \bar{\bar{A}}$
  b. $\bar{\bar{A}} \rightarrow (\bar{\bar{\bar{B}}}) * \bar{A}$
  c. $\bar{A} \rightarrow (M) \ A.$

These rules are to be understood as comprising the X-bar theory of Papago phrase structure—the symbols A, B, C, . . . , are used in place of X for expository reasons. The rules embody the claim that Papago is basically nucleus-final. That is to say, the sentence is basically verb-final, the noun phrase is basically noun-final, and the postpositional phrase is basically just that, i.e., postpositional rather than prepositional. The initial expansion of each category introduces the appropriate specifier— "auxilliary" for the sentence, determiner for the noun phrase and spatial determiner (cp. English *"there* in the house") for the postpositional phrase. The second expansion introduces the complement(s)—e.g., arguments of the verb (subject, object, etc.) for the sentence, possessor expression (optional) for the noun phrase, and the object of the postposition for the postpositional phrase. The final expansion introduces the head (V, N, P) and an optional pre-head modifier (M, omitted from ensuing examples, since it plays no role in the discussion).

The tree diagram offered in (10) illustrates the underlying structure-type produced by the proposed Papago base rules.

(10) *Base Structure:*

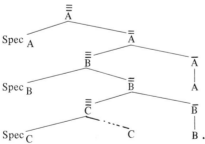

However, this nucleus-final arrangement is not the only one observed in Papago surface structures. Among the actual surface structures underlain by (10) are those included in (11) below.

(11) *Well-formed Surface Structures:*

  a. Spec_A (Spec_B) (Spec_C) C B A
  b. Spec_A A Spec_B (Spec_C) C B
  c. Spec_A A Spec_B B Spec_C C

The first of these is the nucleus-final arrangement produced by the rules of the base. The parenthesis around Spec_B and Spec_C are included to reflect the fact that the generalized N–category specifier /g/ (/heg/ in some Pima dialects and under certain conditions in Papago) is deleted when immediately preceded by a N- or P-category specifier belonging to an immediately superordinate phrase—the rule that effects this deletion may be formulated roughly as follows:

(12)   *g-Deletion:*

$$\overline{X} - \text{Spec}_{N,P} \quad - g - X$$
$$1 \qquad 2 \qquad\quad 3 \quad 4$$
$$1 \qquad 2 \qquad\quad 0 \quad 4$$

Clearly, this rule applies only to nucleus-final structures, since only those structures provide the necessary conditions. In other words, *g*-Deletion must apply after any process that effects non-nucleus-final structures.

The second arrangement in (11) above can be assumed to be produced by extraposing the $\overline{\overline{B}}$-phrase—on the $\overline{\overline{A}}$-cycle. Since $\overline{\overline{B}}$ itself contains a three-bar structure, $\overline{\overline{C}}$, the conditions for *g*-Deletion are met within the extraposed phrase—hence the parentheses around Spec_C.

Finally, the arrangement observed in (11c) above may be assumed to be produced by first extraposing $\overline{\overline{C}}$ on the $\overline{\overline{B}}$-cycle, and then extraposing $\overline{\overline{B}}$ on the $\overline{\overline{A}}$-cycle. This "maximal" application of the putative extraposition process results in the circumstance that no specifier appears in a position from which it would be deleted by (12)—hence, all of the original specifiers are present in the surface structure (11c).

We now formulate the proposed extraposition rule involved in the derivation of (11b–c). We assume that it is cyclic, that it is optional, and that it applies at the first opportunity—i.e., at the two-bar level of structure—to move a three-bar structure into postnuclear position.

(13)   *Three-bar Extraposition:*

$$X - \overline{\overline{A}} - X$$
$$1 \quad 2 \quad 3$$
$$1 \quad 0 \quad 3 \quad 2$$

This rule applies in identical fashion to all phrasal categories of Papago. Thus, given a sentence ($\overline{\overline{V}}$) of the form:

(14) $\overline{\overline{V}}\,[no\ \overline{\overline{N}}\,[g\ \overline{\overline{N}}[g\ h\acute{u}si]\overline{\overline{N}}\ k\acute{\imath}\acute{\imath}]\overline{\overline{N}}\ g\acute{e}\,'ej]\overline{\overline{V}}$

          'Is Joe's house large?'

the following well-formed surface structures are observed (with *g*-Deletion applied where necessary):

(15)   i.   *no g húsi kĭ gé'ej.*
       ii.   *no gé'ej g húsi kĭ.*
       iii. *no gé'ej g kĭij g húsi.*

(The suffix /-j/ appearing on /kii/ in (15iii) is a third person singular agreement marker that regularly appears on the head N when a possessor NP is moved to its right. We leave unformulated the mechanism that accounts for this, since it is not relevant here, insofar as we are aware.)

Similarly, given a noun phrase ($\overline{\overline{\text{N}}}$) of the form:

(16) $\ldots \overline{\overline{\text{N}}}[g\ \overline{\overline{\text{N}}}[g\ \overline{\overline{\text{N}}}[g\ \text{húsi}]\overline{\overline{\text{N}}}\ \text{'óog}\ ]\overline{\overline{\text{N}}}\ \text{kíi}]\overline{\overline{\text{N}}}$

'Joe's father's house'

the following well-formed surface structures are observed (again, with g-Deletion applied where necessary):

(17)   i.   ... g húsi 'óog kíi
       ii. ... g kíij g húsi 'óog
       iii. ... g kíij g 'óogaj g húsi.

And finally, given a postpositional phrase ($\overline{\overline{\text{P}}}$) of the form

(18) $\overline{\overline{\text{P}}}[\ \text{'am}\ \overline{\overline{\text{N}}}[g\ \overline{\overline{\text{N}}}[g\ \text{húsi}]\overline{\overline{\text{N}}}\ \text{kíi}]\overline{\overline{\text{N}}}\ \text{wúi}\ ]\overline{\overline{\text{P}}}$

'to Joe's house'

the following well-formed surface structures are observed (with g-Deletion, as usual):

(19)   i.   ... 'am húsi kii wúi
       ii. ... 'am wúi g húsi kíi
       iii. ... 'am wúi g kíij g húsi.

We have assumed that Three-Bar Extraposition applies in cyclic fashion to produce (11c) and the corresponding actual Papago surface structures—that is, we have assumed that it applies first on the innermost cycle in producing those forms. If we are correct in this assumption, then, since the rule is optional and may therefore be skipped on any higher cycle, there is a further surface form the rule will produce—i.e., that resulting from the application of the rule **only** on the inner cycle. The resulting surface structure in this case, however, is ill formed.

(20)   *An Ill-formed Surface Structure*

$*\text{Spec}_A\ (\text{Spec}_B)\ \text{B}\ \text{Spec}_C\ \text{C}\ \text{A}$
*no g kíij g húsi gé'ej   (from (14))
*... g 'óogaj g húsi kíi   (from (16))
*... 'am kíij g húsi wúi   (from (18)).

There is another consequence of our assumption also. If the rule is indeed cyclic, then there is no way in which a constraint can be placed upon the rule itself in order to avoid the ill-formed surface structure in (20)—apart, that is, from appending a condition to the rule to the effect that it applies obligatorily if the factor $\overline{\overline{\text{A}}}$ is of the form $\overline{\overline{\text{A}}}[\text{Spec}_A\ \text{A}\ \overline{\overline{\text{B}}}]\overline{\overline{\text{A}}}$, which amounts to saying that the rule is obligatory if the category affected by it has itself undergone the rule. Such a condition would be entirely counter to the spirit of the Autonomous Systems view of language. It is, moreover, an extremely unusual and potentially overpowerful sort of condition; in fact, it is the very sort whose riddance inclines us toward the Autonomous Systems position. The reader may well wonder at this point why extraposition is not simply postcyclic, thereby precluding (20). The answer to this question will become evident later.

We would like to propose that the surface structure (20) is, from the point of view of the Papago system of rules to which extraposition belongs, perfectly well formed and that its unacceptability from a more global perspective is to be explained in terms of another system entirely—namely, the system that assigns intonation to linguistic forms in Papago.

In preparation for the description of the mechanisms that assign intonation contours in Papago, it is convenient first to discuss the assignment of stress.

With marginal exceptions, the assignment of primary stress in Papago words is entirely regular—the first vowel of the stem receives primary stress. Thus:

/'ó'odham/	'person'
/gátwid/	'to shoot (imperfective)'
/ṣópolk/	'short'

Prefixes and suffixes do not receive primary stress:

/ha-jéweḏ-ga/	(their-land-alienable) 'their land'

The independent pronouns and the demonstrative determiners receive primary stress on the first vowel, e.g.:

/'áacim/	'we'
/hégam/	'those'

And certain particles also receive primary stress on the first vowel, e.g. :

/hémho (a)/	'necessarily'

But a large number of particles are unstressed:

/o/	'future'
/cem/	'unachieved intention, past'
/wuḏ/	'equational'

The elements commonly referred to by the term "auxiliary" are also unstressed:

/'añ/	'imperfective first person singular'
/no/	'imperfective third person singular interrogative'
/nap/	'imperfective second person singular interrogative'

and so forth. Certain unstressed short, as opposed to extrashort, vowels have associated with them a readily perceptible tertiary stress (also predictable), but this plays no role in the intonational phenomena with which we are concerned here. We will refer to all vowels not assigned primary stress as "unstressed" in the context of this discussion. The role of primary stress in the phonology of Papago—particularly in relation to vowel reduction—is described briefly in Hale (1965).

Certain Papago lexical items receive two primary stresses, the first somewhat subordinated to the second. These items include compounds—both partially fossilized ones like /hóasá'a/ (basket + s + earthen bottle) 'plate', and thoroughly perspicuous ones like /páal-wákon/ (priest-wash) 'to baptize (imperfective)', /síil-mó'ŏ/ (saddle-head) 'saddle horn', and /cúkuḍ-ṣóṣa/ (owl-snot) 'date (i.e., the fruit)'—in which each member receives a primary stress on its first vowel. In addition, there are loans from Spanish—like /pápalóodi/ (<*papalote*) 'windmill, kite', and /'ískóobli/ (< *es-coblo*) 'chisel'—that receive primary stress both on the first vowel, in accordance with the Papago rule, and on a vowel later in the word (to wit, the vowel that bore the primary stress on the form as it was spoken in the source language). It should also be pointed out that the process of compounding, as well as other productive processes, give rise to lexical items with more than two stresses—in fact, there is no theoretical upper limit:

/cúkuḍ-ṣóṣa-kóstal/   ((owl-snot)-bag) 'bag for dates'
/tóki-béhĕdam-máagĭna/   ((cotton-picker)-machine) 'mechanical cotton picker'
/tóki-béhĕdam-máagĭna-mélcuddam/   ((cotton-picker)-machine)-driver)
                                          'operator of a mechanical cotton picker'

Impressionistically, at least, the final stress is more prominent than those preceding it, although the details of stress subordination in Papago have not been worked out. For the purposes of this discussion, it is sufficient merely to speak of "stressed" vowels (those to which the diacritic is assigned in the above examples) as opposed to "unstressed" vowels (those not supplied with the acute accent diacritic).

The assignment of intonation contours is, for the most part, entirely mechanical. Considering first the intonation of stress-bearing lexical items spoken in isolation, the facts are extremely straightforward. In words with a single stressed vowel, the pitch on that vowel is relatively high (H), while the pitch on unstressed vowels is relatively low (L). (We will assume that extrashort vowels and the epenthetic schwa-vowel, when voiced, are assigned a pitch value, like other vowels.) Thus:

/'ó'odham/   (HLL)
/gát[ə]wid/   (HLL)
/ṣópolk/   (HL)
/ha-jéwed[ə]-ga/ (LHLLL)
/'áacim/   (HLL)
/hégam/   (HL)
/hémo (a)/   (HL (L))

Following Goldsmith (1976) and Haraguchi (1975), we will assume that there exists a basic pitch pattern, independent of particular segmental sequences, and that this pattern is mapped in a straightforward fashion onto a segmental string by asso-ciating Hs and Ls with the syllabic segments. For Papago, we will assume that the basic pitch pattern is HL and that the domain to which it is assigned is any string that intervenes between, but does not itself contain, # -boundaries—where the symbol # is used here to designate, not word boundary (as is traditional for this symbol), but rather the class of boundaries that includes those defining the left and right margins of a sentence, or of a word or phrase spoken in isolation.

The procedure that associates the basic HL pitch pattern to segmental sequences may be expressed in the following rule:

(21)   *Intonation Assignment*
         Given the basic pitch pattern HL, associate the H with
         the rightmost stressed vowel.

We then assume there to exist a convention whereby H is also associated with each syllabic segment preceding the rightmost stressed vowel, if there are any, i.e., the H is, so to speak, "spread" to the left, and L is associated with each syllabic segment that follows the rightmost stressed vowel, assuming any do, i.e., L is "spread" to the right. Accordingly, the intonation associated with the word /pápalóodi/ 'windmill, kite', spoken in isolation, say, is assigned in the following manner. First, H is associated with the segment /ó/:

$$\begin{array}{c} \text{H} \\ | \end{array}$$
pápalóodi

Then, the H is further associated with each syllabic to the left of the pivotal position defined by (21), and L is associated with each vowel to the right:

HL
pápalóodi

This gives an intonation which we might symbolize HHHLL, that is to say, high from the beginning of the word up to and including the rightmost stressed vowel, falling to low on the subsequent vowels. Precisely the same intonation assignment procedure operates in the case of compound lexical items, regardless of their internal complexity. Thus, for example,

tóki-béhĕdam-máagĭna

which exhibits the intonation HHHHHHLLL.

If the rightmost stressed vowel is also the last syllabic (capable of bearing a perceptible pitch—voiceless vowels and the voiceless epenthetic schwa-vowel may, perhaps, not be capable of that), as in a word like /mą́d/ 'offspring of female', the H is associated with the stressed vowel, as usual, but the L is also associated with it. This produces a falling intonation (which we might symbolize HL), albeit one sometimes difficult to perceive:

mą́d

We have one final adjustment to make in order to complete the picture for intonation assignment within the domain # . . . # . If the leftmost stressed vowel in the domain is not also the leftmost syllabic, then any H that precedes it as a result of the leftward spreading described above must be lowered (whether to L or to M[id] we cannot tell, precisely, but we will assume the former). This adjustment is accomplished by the following rule:

(22)   *Lowering*
             H → L/ __ XVQ #

This produces the LHL pattern associated, for example, with prefix-initial words spoken in isolation:

The examples offered to this point illustrate cases in which the domain of intonation assignment corresponds to lexical items spoken in isolation. In such a case, the pattern (L)HL is assigned to the item as a whole, regardless of its length or internal complexity. Precisely the same is true of larger constructions (with certain exceptions, one of which will be detailed below).[5] That is to say, the pattern (L)HL is assigned to entire constructions, not to the individual words, or even phrases, of which they are composed. Thus, for example, while the noun /húsi/ 'Joe', spoken in isolation (and therefore constituting the entire domain of intonation assignment), would receive the intonation HL, it does not receive this intonation when it appears as the possessor in the possessor–possessed construction /húsi 'óog/ 'Joe's father'. Considered in isolation (as will be the case for all construction types in the immediately ensuing discussion), the larger possessive construction would, as a whole, be assigned an intonation in accordance with rule (21) and the associated conventions.

/húsi 'óog/ (HHHL)

(The absence of the N-category specifier here is due to another *g*-Deletion process that removes an utterance-initial /g/.) And, if this were itself the possessor phrase in a larger possessive construction, e.g., /húsi 'óog kñ/ 'Joe's father's house', it would not be assigned its own intonation; rather, the larger construction, as a whole, would constitute the domain of intonation assignment.

/húsi 'óog kíi/ (HHHHHL)

And if this construction, in turn, appeared within a postpositional phrase, e.g., /'am húsi 'óog kíi wúi/ 'to Joe's father's house', the intonation would, again, be assigned to the more inclusive construction.

/'am húsi 'óog kíi wúi/ (LHHHHHHHL)

Finally, if this postpositional phrase appeared as a preverbal complement within a sentence, e.g., /namt 'am húsi 'óog kíi wúi o híhi/ 'Are you (pl.) going to go to Joe's father's house?', its own intonation would yield to that of the sentence as a whole.

/namt 'am húsi 'óog kíi wúi o híhi/ (LLHHHHHHHHHHL).

In general, therefore, the basic intonation pattern of Papago is assigned to constructions. In any given case, the construction may consist of a single word—as is necessarily the case when a word is spoken in isolation—or it may consist of an entire
sentence.

Our discussion so far implies that all Papago constructions bounded by pauses
are intoned with an uninterrupted (L)HL pitch profile. This is not the case, however. While the basic pitch pattern is always assigned to Papago constructions, true
enough, it is not always the case that it is assigned "umbrella fashion" to the most
inclusive phrase. That is to say, there are circumstances under which the basic pattern is observed to repeat itself within a construction. One such circumstance, we
would like to suggest, is intimately related to the central issue of this discussion—
namely, the principle that accounts for the ill-formedness of the surface structures
characterized in (20) above.

The reader will have noticed, no doubt, that all of the examples so far used to
illustrate the assignment of intonation in Papago share the property that they are
nucleus-final. More to the point, none of them has, at any level of structure, undergone the rule of Three-Bar Extraposition, which would move a constituent into
pastnuclear position.

Let us now consider the intonation assigned to structures that have undergone
the extraposition rule. First, observe the intonations assigned to (15b-c):

(15) b. *no gé'ej[ə] g húsi kíi.*   (LHLL HHHL)
      c. *no gé'ej[ə] g kíij[ə] g húsi.* (LHLL HLL HL)

The intonation assigned to (17b-c) and to (19b-c) exhibit the same sort of pattern:

(17) b. *. . . g kíij[ə] g húsi 'oog*   (. . . HLL HHHL)
      c. *. . . g kíij[ə] g 'oogaj[ə] g húsi* (. . . HLL HLLL HL)
(19) b. *. . . 'am[ə] wúi g húsi kíi*   (. . . LLHL HHHL)
      c. *. . . 'am[ə] wúi g kíij[ə] g húsi* (. . . LLHL HLL HL).

In each case it can be seen clearly that the constituent moved by extraposition
comprises its own domain for the purposes of intonation assignment. Or, to put this
another way, when extraposition moves a three-bar structure to the left of a nuclear
element, the latter defines the right-hand margin of an intonational domain. We
might express this in terms of a rule which states simply that the double cross
boundary symbol # is inserted after any nuclear element which appears **medially**
within an endocentric phrase of which it is the nucleus:

(23)   *Partitioning by Extraposition*
          $\bar{\bar{A}}[\ldots A \ \# \ X]\bar{\bar{A}}$, X is non null

This rule (convention, or whatever) has the effect of inserting a # -boundary into
any two-bar structure in which extraposition has applied, thereby accounting for
the intonational facts—specifically, the repeated (L)HL pattern—observed in the (b-
(b-c) sentences of (15), (17), and (19).

We have now set the scene for the presentation of our proposal concerning the
ill-formed surface structures represented in (20). In those cases, (23) will have the

effect of inserting a # -boundary into the innermost two-bar structure, thereby effecting the partitioning observed in (24) below:

(24)   *no [g kíij # g húsi] gé'ej   (from (14))
        *... g ['óogaj # g húsi] kíi   (from (16))
        *... 'am [kíij # g húsi] wúi   (from (18)).

Notice that there is a property, related to the partitioning by #, which distinguishes these ill-formed surface structures from the well-formed ones. Specifically, the ill-formed structures have the property that a partitioned phrase precedes the nucleus of an immediately superordinate phrase. This is not the case in any of the well-formed surface structures. We would like to suggest that it is precisely this property that accounts for the ill-formedness of the structures (20). We propose, in short, that there is a surface structure constraint that identifies as ill formed any surface structure in which a partitioned phrase precedes the nucleus of a larger phrase of which it is an immediate constituent. The constraint might be expressed as follows:

(25)   *A Surface Structure Constraint*

$$*_{\overline{\overline{A}}} [\text{Spec}_A \; _{\overline{\overline{B}}} [\dots \; \# \; \dots]_{\overline{\overline{B}}} \; A]_{\overline{\overline{A}}}$$

Thus, we claim that the surface structures of (20) are ill formed not by virtue of the application of Three-Bar Extraposition on an internal cycle, but rather by virtue of the relationship between phrase structure and the position of the # -boundary. It is almost certainly true that this is related to intonation, whose domain of assignment is defined by # -boundaries. Observe that in well-formed surface structures it is necessarily the case that the first (i.e., leftmost) nuclear element that has a falling intonation (i.e., H to L transition) associated with it is also the nucleus of the entire structure; that is to say, it is the nucleus of the maximally superordinate structure. This, as the reader may easily verify, is simply an automatic consequence of the way in which the well-formed surface structures arise, given the mechanisms and principles we are assuming. However, if the rules of intonation assignment applied to the structures that exhibit the illicit partitioning of (24), the first nucleus with falling intonation would **not** be the nucleus of the maximally superordinate structure. It does not seem unreasonalbe to suggest that this fact, i.e., this failure of correspondence between "main nucleus" and "first intonationally marked nucleus," is the essential source of the ill-formedness of the surface structures represented by (20) (equivalently, (24)) and, therefore, the primary motivation for the surface structure constraint (25).

Be this as it may, in order to support our contention that a surface structure constraint is the proper way to account for the ill-formedness of (20), (24), we must demonstrate that Three-Bar Extraposition in fact applies in cyclic fashion. This follows, since we must allow the rule to apply on an internal cycle in order to produce the ill-formed surface structures in the first place. If the rule were not cyclic—if it were, say, postcyclic—then presumably we could arrange matters in such a way as to prevent the generation of (20), (24), and the like.

To put this another way, in order to show that the surface structure constraint expressed in (25) is necessary, we must show that a structure of the type represented in (20), (24) is itself a necessary intermediate form in some derivation. To show that such a structure is, in fact, a necessary intermediate form, we must briefly describe another extraposition rule—actually a subvariety of the extraposition already studied and expressed in (13). This variant extracts a two-bar structure, rather than a three-bar structure. Accordingly, we will give it the name Two-Bar Extraposition. It may be expressed as follows:

(26)   *Two-Bar Extraposition*[6]

$$X - \bar{\bar{A}} - X$$

1	2	3	
1	0	3	2

Rule (26)   operates in all essential respects just like (13), except of course it leaves a specifier behind in the original prenuclear position. For example, from a structure of the form,

(27) $\bar{\bar{V}}$ [*nap* $\bar{\bar{N}}$ [*hég(ai) 'ó'odham*]$\bar{\bar{N}}$ *s-máac*]$\bar{\bar{V}}$

            'Do you (sg.) know that man?'

it produces the surface structure

(28)   *nap hég s-máac 'o'odham.*[7]

And from a structure of the form

(29) $\bar{\bar{V}}$ [*no* $\bar{\bar{P}}$ ['*am* $\bar{\bar{N}}$ [*g míisa*]$\bar{\bar{N}}$ *wéco*]$\bar{\bar{P}}$ *wó'o*]$\bar{\bar{V}}$

            'Is it lying under the table?'

it produces the following:

(30)   *no 'am wó'ŏ míisa wéco.*

An important fact to notice about surface structure (30) is this. The specifier /g/, associated with the object of the postposition, is **missing** in the structure produced by Two-Bar Extraposition. This fact is an automatic consequence of the way in which the rule must apply—assuming that it is in fact a subvariety of Three-Bar Extraposition and, therefore, according to our claim, cyclic, and assuming that *g*-Deletion is also cyclic. To see this, consider the structure of (20), the source of (30), in a tree diagram:

(31)

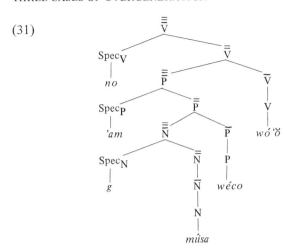

The derivation of (30) involves extraposition of the two-bar structure $\bar{\bar{P}}$. But, notice, this cannot take place until we have reached the $\bar{\bar{V}}$-cycle. At that cycle, we have already passed the $\bar{\bar{P}}$-cycle at which the condition for g-Deletion is met. We account naturally for the deletion of /g/ by assuming that it applied at the first opportunity —that is to say, at the $\bar{\bar{P}}$-cycle and, therefore, **prior** to the extraposition of $\bar{\bar{P}}$ that must be delayed until the $\bar{\bar{V}}$-cycle is reached.

Suppose, however, that we apply Three-Bar Extraposition on the $\bar{\bar{P}}$-cycle, and then Two-Bar Extraposition on the $\bar{\bar{V}}$-cycle. This is a theoretically possible derivation, given our assumptions. Consider, however, the intermediate structure produced by extraposition on the $\bar{\bar{P}}$-cycle:

(32) $\bar{\bar{V}}[no \; \bar{\bar{\bar{P}}}[\text{'}am \; wéco \; \bar{\bar{N}}[g \; múisa] \; \bar{\bar{\bar{N}}}]_{P} \; wó\text{'}ŏ]\bar{\bar{V}}$

This is precisely the ill-formed structure with which we are concerned. Since the #-boundary will be inserted following the postposition /wéco/, which is the nuclear element in the postpositional phrase, the surface structure constraint (25) will come into play to identify (32) as ill formed. And it is indeed the case that (32) is ill formed.

But, if the extraposition processes are cyclic, as we have claimed, then (32) is a possible intermediate form. Our claim makes a rather clear prediction. If we can produce a well-formed surface structure by applying Three-Bar Extraposition on the $\bar{\bar{P}}$-cycle and then Two-Bar Extraposition on the $\bar{\bar{V}}$-cycle, then we would expect the specifier /g/, belonging to the object of the postposition, to remain overt in the derived structure. This follows, since the application of Three-Bar Extraposition on the $\bar{\bar{P}}$-cycle will have the effect of protecting the /g/ from deletion—by moving it away from the superordinate P-category specifier /'am/. [8]

Our proposed derivation does in fact produce a well-formed surface structure, to wit:

(33) $\bar{\bar{V}}[no \; \bar{\bar{P}}[\text{'}am]\bar{\bar{\bar{P}}} \; wó\text{'}ŏ \; \bar{\bar{P}}[wéco \; \bar{\bar{N}}[g \; múisa]\bar{\bar{\bar{N}}} \;]\bar{\bar{P}}]\bar{\bar{V}}$

And, as we predict, the N-category specifier /g/ is not deleted.

We conclude, therefore, that (32) (and by analogy (20), (24)) represents a necessary intermediate form in the derivation of well-formed surface structures in Papago. It follows, then, that no constraint can be imposed directly on Three-Bar Extraposition, to prevent the generation of the ill-formed surface structures with which we have been concerned in this discussion. Instead, the surface structure constraint (25), itself perhaps explicable in terms of perceptual considerations, is required to account for the observed overgeneration.

3.   Hopi Relative Clauses [9]

There is an apparent constraint on the use of the Hopi complex noun phrase structure that functions as the relative clause. The structure can be used freely in constructing sentences of the type that correspond to the English sentences of (34):

(34)   a.   *The man who wrote the book addressed us.*
       b.   *I introduced the man who wrote the book.*
       c.   *I introduced the man whom you brought with you.*
       d.   *I introduced the man with whom I work.*

It cannot, however, without recourse to periphrasis, be used to construct sentences corresponding to the English sentences of (35):

(35)   a.   *The man whom you brought with you will address us.*
       b.   *The man with whom I work will address us.*

The point is essentially this. When the complex noun phrase, as a whole, functions as the subject of the main clause, the relative noun phrase (i.e., that noun phrase in the subordinate clause that is coreferential with the complex noun phrase) must likewise function as the subject within its own clause. No such constraint is observed when the complex noun phrase is a nonsubject within the main clause. Thus, it would appear that Hopi exhibits a curious limitation on the accessibility of noun phrases to relativization (cf. Keenan and Comrie, 1972); when the complex noun phrase is itself a subject, relativization is limited to subjects, otherwise not. This is a rather curious picture, and it is not at all like NP accessibility limitations observed in other languages of the world, since it is tied to the grammatical relation the complex NP bears to the main verb, rather than solely to that which the relative NP bears to the verb of the subordinate clause.

In any event, the particular instance of overgeneration in the Hopi case with which we are concerned is that in which a relative NP is a nonsubject while the complex NP containing it is a subject.

By way of introduction to the problem, we must first present a preliminary theory of Hopi base structures, since it is, we feel, the base which is responsible for the overgeneration of interest here. We will use the bar notation, though we do not wish to imply by our facile use of the latter that the theory of the Hopi base has been adequately worked out or that it is understood in other than superficial terms. Our preliminary theory of Hopi base structures contains the rules embodied in (36) below:

(36)   *Base Rules*

    a. $\overline{\overline{\overline{A}}} \rightarrow (\overline{\overline{\overline{N}}})\ \overline{\overline{A}}$

    b. $\overline{\overline{A}} \rightarrow (\overline{\overline{B}})\ \overline{A}$

    c. $\overline{A} \rightarrow (\overline{C}) * A$

As in Papago, so in Hopi, phrasal categories are nucleus-final. Otherwise, however, the Hopi base is rather different from that of Papago. The initial expansion does not introduce a specifier, as it did in Papago, rather, it introduces an optional noun phrase in "pleonastic" structures, similar to those produced by left-dislocation in English—e.g., 'That man, I can't stand him'—but Hopi generalizes this to give pleonastic structures corresponding to 'that man, his horse', and 'that man, with him'. The core of phrasal categories in Hopi is the two-bar level of structure. These are developed initially by the second expansion, which introduces the subject in a sentence (i.e., in a $\overline{\overline{V}}$-structure), the determiner, or alternatively the possessor expression, in a noun phrase (i.e., in a $\overline{\overline{N}}$-structure), and the object in a postpositional phrase (i.e., in a P-structure). The third and final expansion, which develops the one-bar structure, introduces the nuclear element (V, N, P) and, in the case of $\overline{V}$, the nonsubject dependents of the verb (object and postpositional complements). We assume that the N- and P-categories also have preposed dependents: a preposed modifier, certainly, in the case of N, though we have not studied the internal structures of $\overline{N}$ and $\overline{P}$ in any detail as yet.

Examples of structures developed by the rules of (36) are presented below:

(37)   a. *Pleonastic*   *Plain*

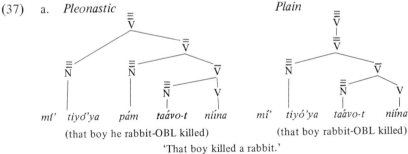

(that boy he rabbit-OBL killed)   (that boy rabbit-OBL killed)

'That boy killed a rabbit.'

    b. *Pleonastic*   *Plain*

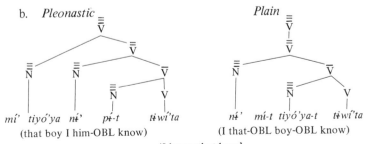

(that boy I him-OBL know)   (I that-OBL boy-OBL know)

'I know that boy.'

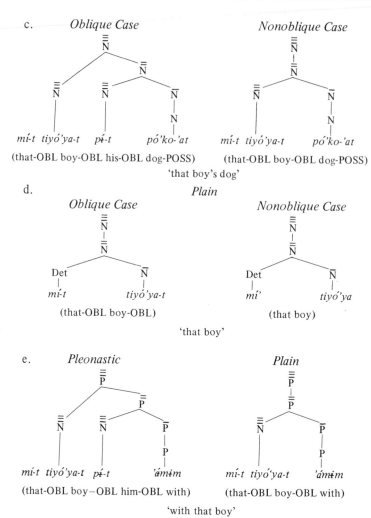

c. *Oblique Case* / *Nonoblique Case*

(that-OBL boy-OBL his-OBL dog-POSS)   (that-OBL boy-OBL dog-POSS)

'that boy's dog'

d. *Plain*

Oblique Case / *Nonoblique Case*

(that-OBL boy-OBL)   (that boy)

'that boy'

e. *Pleonastic* / *Plain*

(that-OBL boy—OBL him-OBL with)   (that-OBL boy-OBL with)

'with that boy'

A pleonastic structure is well formed only if, somewhere within the two-bar or one-bar structure following the "dislocated" noun phrase, there appears a pronoun that can be construed as coreferential with the latter. The reader will have noticed that Hopi noun phrases are, under certain conditions, marked for a generalized oblique case. We will use a feature notation to represent this fact, and we will devise a set of rules to account for case marking. The oblique case will be designated by means of the feature [+obj], and the unmarked, or nonoblique case will be designated [−obl]. The following elementary case marking rule will account for the assignment of [obl] to noun phrases:

(38) $\overline{\overline{N}} \rightarrow \left\{ \begin{array}{l} [-obl] / \_\_\_ \overline{\overline{V}} \\ [+obl] \end{array} \right\}$

That is to say, a noun phrase is assigned the unmarked case of it immediately precedes $\overset{=}{V}$ or $\overset{-}{V}$; otherwise, it will be assigned to oblique case. This will account for the association of oblique case marking (the overt manifestation of which is here glossed OBL) in the structures of (37) above.

In addition to the case assignment rule itself, we must recognize a rule of Case Concord, which ensures that the immediate constituents of a [+obl] noun phrase are also assigned the feature [+obl]. The details of Case Concord, when worked out, will, among other things, ensure that a determiner and the head noun of a [+obl] noun phrase are each supplied with the oblique ending. For the present, however, we will simply assume that a rule of Case Concord exists, without attempting, at this stage of our understanding, to give it explicit formulation.

The overt manifestations of the oblique case category are not particularly straightforward. Limiting ourselves to the singular,[10] and to noun phrases of the type so far considered (i.e., other than those involving relative clauses), the endings are two: /-t/ and /-y/. The latter appears on the head noun in a [+obl] possessive construction, as in sentences like the following:

(39) a. *nɨ' mɨ́-t tiyó'ya-t pó'ko-y-at tɨwa.*
          (I that-OBL boy-OBL dog-OBL-POSS saw)
          'I saw that boy's dog.'

      b. *mɨ' tiyó'ya 'i-vôko-y tɨwa.*
          (that boy my-dog-OBL saw)
          'That boy saw my dog.'

Otherwise, for noun phrases not involving relative clauses, the ending /-t/ is used (as is amply exemplified in (37)).

The same two alternants of the singular oblique ending are used on the head noun in a relative clause, but their selection is rather more complex. Before discussing this, however, we must present our theory of the base structures of Hopi relative clauses. We assume that the relative clause is produced by means of the following rule:

(40) $\overset{\overset{=}{=}}{N} \rightarrow \overset{=}{V}\ \overset{-}{N}$

That is to say, we permit rule (40) to be one of the possible forms of (39b). Accordingly, a relative clause has the following structure:

(41)

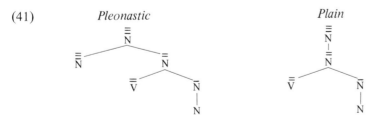

Actually, this structure is used in Hopi not only for the relative clause, but also for the factive nominal complement (i.e., not only for sentences corresponding to 'I know the boy who killed the rabbit', but also for sentences corresponding to 'I know that the boy killed the rabbit'). Notice further that there exist both pleonastic and plain varieties. The pleonastic variety must, of course, conform to the general condition on well-formedness; in this case, the V-structure must contain a pronoun, or else a NP-gap, which can be construed as coreferential with the left-dislocated noun phrase. It happens that the pleonastic variety is much preferred in the relative clause case, and the plain variety is preferred in the factive case. We do not understand fully the conditions under which the plain variety of the relative clause can be used, but there are in fact circumstances in which either variety is well-formed: for example:

(42)   a.   *Pleonastic*

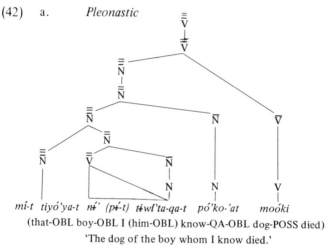

mí-t tiyó'ya-t nɨ' (pɨ-t) tɨwɨ́'ta-qa-t pó'ko-'at moóki
(that-OBL boy-OBL I (him-OBL) know-QA-OBL dog-POSS died)
'The dog of the boy whom I know died.'

       b.   *Plain*

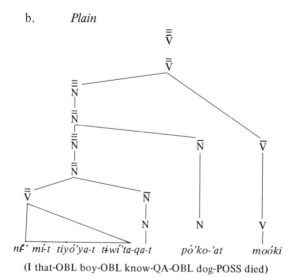

nɨ' mí-t tiyó'ya-t tɨwí'ta-qa-t   pó'ko-'at   moóki
(I that-OBL boy-OBL know-QA-OBL dog-POSS died)

In both of these cases, the complex noun phrase appears in a possessive construction, the most favorable to the use of the plain form of the relative clause.

The following structures illustrate the pleonastic and plain forms of the factive complex noun phrase; in this case, the latter is preferred over the former:

(43) a.   *Pleonastic*

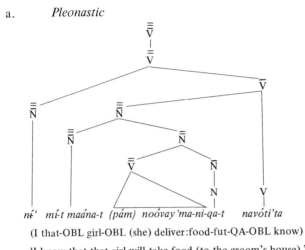

ní' mí-t maána-t (pám) noóvay'ma-ni-qa-t   navóti'ta

(I that-OBL girl-OBL (she) deliver:food-fut-QA-OBL know)

'I know that that girl will take food (to the groom's house).'

  b.   *Plain*

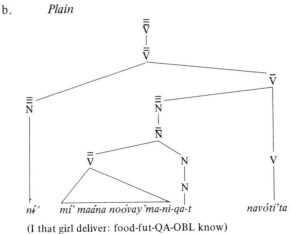

ní'   mí' maána noóvay'ma-ni-qa-t   navóti'ta

(I that girl deliver: food-fut-QA-OBL know)

In (43a), incidentally, we observe that Case Concord has correctly applied to assign the [+obl] case marking to the left-dislocated noun phrase /mí-t maána-t/ in the pleonastic factive complement, itself [+obl] by virtue of its appearance in the environment___ V. By contrast, the very same noun phrase in (43b), i.e., /mí' maána/, is [-obj], because it is in subject position (that is to say, it is in the environment __ V̄) within its clause.

A property that these complex noun phrases have in common, and that must be discussed in some detail, is the peculiarity of the nuclear element, or head noun. Notice that the head noun is uniformly the element /-qa/, a defective noun with no special semantic content.[11] In surface structure, it is unlike any other noun in that it is phonologically bound to the verb word of the subordinate clause. Its only nounlike qualities are the fact that it inflects for case and number and the fact that it appears in precisely the position the X-bar theory predicts for the nuclear element of endocentric phrasal categories in Hopi.

A very special property of the /-qa/ element is the case marking it exhibits. The fact is, Case Concord will not account for the peculiarities of qa-case marking. Rather, case marking in this instance is intimately interwoven with the phenomenon of obviation that prevails in Hopi complex sentences of all kinds.[12] That is to say, to fully determine the appropriate case marking of the defective head noun /-qa/, it is not sufficient merely to know the grammatical relation which the complex noun phrase bears to the main verb; one must also know: (1) the grammatical relation the relative noun phrase bears to the subordinate verb; and (2) whether the main and subordinate clauses share subjects, i.e., whether the subjects of the main and subordinate clauses are coreferential. The principles of qa-case assignment can be expressed roughly as follows (limiting ourselves to the singular):

(44)   *qa-Case Assignment*

    a.   [-obl] (/-qa/): shared subjects, and relative
        NP is subject in its own clause;

    b.   "proximate" [+obl] (/-qa-y/): shared subjects, and
        relative NP is nonsubject in its own clause;

    c.   "obviative" [+obl] (/-qa-t/): otherwise.

The following three sentences illustrate the three cases subsumed under (44a–c):

(45)   a.   *mɨ' tiyó'ya (pám) 'acáta-qa pákmɨmɨya.*
          (that boy (he) lied-QA cry)
          'The boy who lied is crying.'

      b.   *nɨ' taávo-t (nɨ') (pɨ-t) niína-qa-y sískʷa.*
          (I rabbit-OBL (I) (it-OBL) killed-proxOBL skinned)
          'I skinned the rabbit that I killed.'

      c.   *nɨ mɨ-t tiyó'ya-t (pám) 'acáta-qa-t hoóna.*
          (I that-OBL boy-OBL (he) lied-QA-obvOBL sent:home)
          'I sent home the boy that lied.'

We have now set the scene for a discussion of the case of overgeneration that concerns us. Let us consider the offending structure in abstract terms, to begin with. Such a structure would be the following, in which the circled noun phrase is the relative noun phrase:

(46)

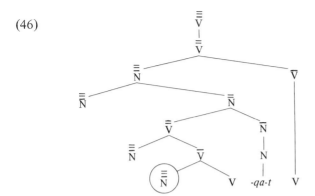

The Hopi fact is this: the structure (46) cannot be used, directly, to render the Hopi equivalent of an English sentence like, say, 'The boy whom I saw has gone home'. Why is this? Notice that the complex noun phrase itself is well formed; it appears in object position in the following sentence:

(47)   'itá-na mí-t tiyó'ya-t nɨ́'(pɨ́-t) tɨ́wa:-qa-t hoóna.
         (our-father that-OBL boy-OBL I (him-OBL) saw-QA-obvOBL sent:home)
         'My (lit., our) father sent home the boy whom I saw.'

But the same complex noun phrase may not appear in subject position, cf. (46).

One might, conceivably, attempt to place a constraint on the base rules of Hopi so as to preclude the development of a complex noun phrase of this offending type in subject position. It is not at all clear how such a constraint could be formulated. But even if it were possible, such a move would be entirely at variance with the Autonomous Systems thesis, which forbids the use of context-sensitive phrase structure rules, or of global conditions linked to specific phrase structure rules. It happens, however, that such a constraint cannot be placed on the development of Hopi relative clauses anyway, for the imagined constraint would identify as ill-formed certain structures that are perfectly grammatical.

Consider the following variant of (47), which we assume is produced by extraposing the relative clause to a position following the main verb:

(48)   'itá-na mí-t tiyó'ya-t hoóna, nɨ́: (pɨ́t) tɨ́wa:-qa-t.
         (our-father that-OBL boy-OBL sent:home, I (him-OBL)
         saw-QA-obvOBL)

Let us assume that we are correct in our guess that (48) is produced by an extraposition rule of roughly the following form:

(49)   Extraposition[13]
         X$\overset{\overline{\overline{}}}{\text{N}}$ – $\overline{\overline{\text{V}}}$-QA – X
         1   2   3
         1   0   3   2

Now consider the following fact. While (50), directly underlain by a structure of the form stipulated in (46), is ill-formed–

(50)   *mi' tiyó'ya ni' (pi-t) ti'wa:-qa-t pay níma.
          (that boy I (him-OBL) saw-QA-obvOBL already went:home)
          'The boy whom I saw has gone home.'

—the corresponding extraposed variant is well-formed:

(51)   mi' tiyó'ya pay níma, ni' (pi-t) ti'wa:-qa-i-t.

If we are correct in assuming that (51) is derived by means of the extraposition
rule, the only conceivable source for the sentence is (50). Therefore, the ill-formed
surface structure (50) must, from the point of view of the base rules of Hopi, be
perfectly well formed.

    We are left, of course, with the problem of explaining the surface ill-formedness
of sentence (50). We would like to suggest that the answer is to be found in a
consideration of the case marking exhibited by the relative clause in (50), and in its
extraposed counterpart (51). Notice that the /-qa/ element is marked with the obviative oblique ending /-t/—this is exactly as it should be, since the sentence as a whole
—cf. (46), its structure in skeletal form—conforms to case (c) of the qa-Case Assignment principles. In the case of sentence (50), this results in the circumstance that a
complex noun phrase **in subject position** terminates in an oblique ending. This is in
defiance of the prevailing surface fact of Hopi that noun phrases in subject position
are unmarked for case. It is conceivable (and we suggest that this is indeed the
answer) that the ill-formedness of (50) is due to the fact that it violates this otherwise general principle of surface structure case marking.[14]

    In any event, it seems quite clear to us that no special constraint need, or in fact
can, be placed upon the rules of the base which are responsible for the development
of structures functioning as relative clauses in Hopi.

4.   Noun Phrase Gaps in Navajo.[15]

    In Navajo surface structures, relative clauses are either of the "headed" type,
with the head following the subordinate clause, as in (52a) below, or else they are
of the "headless" type, as in (52b):

(52)   a.   *Deezhtlizh-ęę ashkii yicha.*
              (stumbled-REL boy cry)

        b.   *Ashkii deezhtlizh-ęę yicha.*
              (boy stumbled-REL cry)
              'The boy who stumbled is crying.'

That the complex noun phrase in sentences like (52b) is headless, and not merely
left-headed as the English analogue would suggest, is shown by sentences of the
type represented by (53)—

(53)   *Ashkii łééchąą'í bi-shxash-ęę nahał'in.*
        (boy dog bi-bit-REL bark)
        'The dog that the boy was bitten by is barking.'

—in which /ɫééchąą'í/ 'dog' is clearly within the subordinate clause, being flanked by material belonging thereto. It is further shown by the ambiguity observed in sentences like (54a–b):

(54) a. *Ashkii at'ééd yi-zts'ǫs-ę́ę́ yáɫti'.*
          (boy girl yi-kissed-REL speak)
          'The boy who kissed the girl is speaking.'
          'The girl whom the boy kissed is speaking.'

      b. *At'ééd ashkii bi-zts'ǫs-ę́ę́ yáɫti'.*
          (girl boy bi-kissed-REL speak)
          'The girl who was kissed by the boy is speaking.'
          'The boy by whom the girl was kissed is speaking.'

The ambiguity here is due to the fact that, since the noun phrase that is understood as coreferential with the complex noun phrase as a whole is within the subordinate clause, rather than in head position, it is not possible to tell, from the surface structure itself, which of the two noun phrases in the transitive subordinate clause is to be construed as the subject of the main verb. For many speakers of Navajo, to be sure, there is a clear preference for construing the **first** subordinate noun phrase with the main verb, but for most, if not all speakers, the other interpretation is also clearly available. This sort of ambiguity is, of course, lacking in the case of corresponding sentences using the headed relative clause—though this alternative, exemplified by (55a–b) below, is greatly disfavored in actual Navajo usage:

(55) a. *At'ééd yi-zts'ǫs-ę́ę́ ashkii yáɫti'.*
          (girl yi-kissed-REL boy speak)
          'The boy who kissed the girl is speaking.'

      b. *Ashkii bi-zts'ǫs-ę́ę́ at'ééd yáɫti'.*
          (boy bi-kissed-REL girl speak)
          'The girl who was kissed by the boy is speaking.'

We are not sure how the headed relative clause is developed in Navajo—whether by deletion of a noun phrase from the subordinate clause, by permitting the base rules to introduce a null proform in the subordinate clause, or by raising a subordinate noun phrase rightward into head position.[16] In any case, an NP-gap is present in the subordinate clause; that is to say, a noun phrase is missing from the subordinate clause. Also, under any of the alternative conceptions of the headed relative clause, we are faced with a minor problem—namely, that of explaining why sentences of the type represented by (55a–b) are not ambiguous. The single possible interpretation of each of the sentences of (55) indicates clearly that the **first** noun phrase in the subordinate clause is the one that is missing—i.e., the NP-gap is initial. In principle, surely, the NP-gap could be in second position—the fact is, however, the gap-second interpretations are simply absent for (55a–b).

An identical observation can be made in the case of the mechanism that accounts for NP-gaps in sentences like the following:

(56)   *Ashkii yah'íīyá áádóó at'ééd yi-zts'ǫs.*
        (boy entered and:then girl yi-kissed)
        'The boy came in and then he kissed the girl.'

This sentence consists of an intransitive (first) clause conjoined to a transitive (second) clause. Again, there is an NP-gap in a transitive clause. And the sole interpretation associated with the compound sentence indicates that the gap is initial in the transitive clause, the theoretically possible gap-second interpretation being entirely absent.

It would appear, therfore, that a constraint must be placed upon the mechanisms that produce NP-gaps in transitive sentences. One might propose, for example, that an NP-gap must be initial within a transitive sentence. Such a constraint would also account for the interpretations of sentences involving adverbial clauses, as in:

(57)   a.   *Ashkii yah'íīyáa-go at'ééd yi-zts'ǫs.*
             (boy entered-SUBORD girl yi-kissed)
             'When the boy came in, he kissed the girl.'

        b.   *Ashkii yah'íīyáa-go at'ééd bi-zts'ǫs.*
             (boy entered-SUBORD girl bi-kissed)
             'When the boy came in, he was kissed by the girl.'

        c.   *At'ééd yi-zts'ǫs-go ashkii dahdiiyá.*
             (girl yi-kissed-SUBORD boy left)
             'When he kissed the girl, the boy left.'

        d.   *At'ééd bi-zts'ǫs-go ashkii dahdiiyá.*
             (girl bi-kissed-SUBORD boy left)
             'When he was kissed by the girl, the boy left.'

A constraint disallowing gap-second transitive clauses would account for the observations we have made so far, but it would not also account for the interpretations of sentences of the type represented by (58) below:

(58)   *Ashkii at'ééd yi-zts'ǫs-ę́ę̌ hastiin yi-yiłtsą́.*
        (boy girl yi-kissed-REL man yi-saw)
        'The boy who kissed the girl saw the man.'
        'The girl whom the boy kissed saw the man.'

This sentence is ambiguous in two ways, which is understandable given the fact that the subject of the main verb is a complex noun phrase consisting of a headless relative clause. The problem is this: why is the sentence not ambiguous in three ways, permitting a reading in which the object of the main verb consists of the otherwise perfectly well-formed relative clause /at'ééd yi-zts'ǫs-ę́ę̌ hastiin/ 'the man who kissed the girl'? It would appear that we must extend our constraint on the occurrence of NP-gaps to disallow also an initial gap if it appears in a transitive relative clause that is itself in second position within the matrix. This cannot be, however, since (59) below is perfectly well formed, and surely its complex noun phrase object exhibits a clause-initial NP-gap:

(59) *Ashkii at'ééd yi-yiɬtsá(n)-ę́ę yi-zts'ǫs.*
      (boy GAP girl yi-saw-REL yi-kissed)
      'The boy kissed the girl whom he saw.'

These observations by no means spell the doom of a constraint on the appearance of NP-gaps in Navajo. In fact, a rather simple constraint can be placed on NP-gaps that will account for all of the observations made thus far—namely, (60) below, in which the symbol 0 represents an NP-gap, and in which the structural description is to be understood as applicable in the order given and in the mirror image order:

(60)   *Constraint on NP Gaps*

         No structure is permitted that can be factored as follows:
         $$X - NP - Y - 0 - Z$$
         if (1) 0 is construed as coreferential with NP, and (2) a variable immediately preceding 0 ranges over a string terminating in a noun.

This will not only account for the interpretations of complex sentences of the type we have been considering, but it will also account for the fact that simple sentences like (61a–b) are unambiguous with respect to coreference between a full noun phrase and an NP-gap:

(61) a. *Ashkii bizhé'é yi-yiɬtsą́.*
          (boy his-father yi-saw)
          'The boy saw his father.'

      b. *Ashkii bi-zhé'é b-iɬtsą́.*
          (boy his-father bi-saw)
          'The boy was seen by his father.'

The crucial point here is that the constraint embodied in (60) will ensure that (61a) cannot receive an interpretation in which the NP-gap immediately precedes the verb ('The boy$_i$'s father saw him$_i$'), structurally parallel to:

(61) c. *Ashkii bi-zhe'é at'ééd yi-yiɬtsą́;*
          (boy his-father girl saw)
          'The boy's father saw the girl.'

The nonambiguity of (61b) is, of course, explained by the general constraint on proforms—i.e., that they may not both precede and command their full NP-anaphors, which rules out a reading in which the NP-gap is sentence initial (*'He$_i$ was seen by the boy$_i$'s father'), as well as by the constraint (60), which rules out an interpretation in which the NP-gap immediately precedes the verb ('The boy$_i$'s father was seen by him$_i$'), structurally parallel to:

(61) d. *Ashkii be-zhé'é at'ééd b-iɬtsą́;*
          (boy his-rather girl bi-saw)
          'The boy's father was seen by the girl'

A simple modification of (60), permitting the use of clause (2) without clause (1), would also account for the fact that transitive fragments, with or without a postposed "afterthought" noun phrase, are unambiguous, at least with respect to the position of the NP-gap:

(62)   a.   *At'ééd yi-zts'ǫs.*
              (girl yi-kissed)
        b.   'He/she kissed the girl.'

              At'ééd yi-zts'ǫs, ashkii.
              (girl yi-kissed, boy)
              'He kissed the girl, i.e., the boy.'

        c.   *Ashkii bi-zts'ǫs.*
              (boy bi-kissed)
              'He/she was kissed by the boy.'

        d.   *Ashkii bi-zts'ǫs, at'ééd.*
              (boy bi-kissed, girl)
              'She was kissed by the boy, i.e., the girl.'

These sentences do not admit of an interpretation according to which the NP-gap is other than in absolute initial position.

We do not know whether the proposed constraint could be formulated as a condition on particular rules which are responsible for creating NP-gaps—more to the point, we are not at all certain, as yet, how NP-gaps are in fact to be produced, whether by movement rules, deletion rules, both, or by rules introducing null pro-forms in the base. But this is not a serious hindrance to the fundamental idea of a constraint like (60). We could, for example, think of it as a constraint on surface strucutres in which a NP-gap is understood as coreferential with a full noun phrase— sentences that violate the stricture on the variable preceding the gap would, by the constraint, be identified as ill-formed. Alternatively, we might recast the constraint as a limitation on the interpretation of NP-gaps: "No NP-gap may be construed as coreferential with NP' if it is preceded by a string terminating in a noun that is not the head of NP'." This would simply leave uninterpreted (rather than strictly speaking, ill-formed) certain sentences produced by the syntax.

Either way, the constraint works quite well. However, we would like to suggest that this is entirely the wrong way to look at the matter. First of all, if it is conceived as a constraint on rules of Navajo syntax or semantics, it is clearly out of keeping with the Autonomous Systems thesis. As a constraint on surface structures, in roughly the form given in (60), it is not clearly inconsistent with the autonomous position, but, we submit, it is still misguided, since it is formulated in terms of an NP-gap in construal with a full noun phrase. Surely the problem is not in the **construal** of NP-gaps, but rather it is related in some way to the problem of **locating** them. This must be so, since the entire problem can be understood in terms of interpretive principles that must surely exist independently of the question of relating NP-gaps to flll noun phrases.

Consider Navajo sentences of the sort introduced in the beginning section of this essay. Surely there must exist principles of interpretation that permit Navajo speakers to determine the grammatical relations the noun phrases bear to the verb in structures which exhibit the surface profiles:

$$\text{NP} \quad \text{NP} \quad yi\text{-V}$$

and

$$\text{NP} \quad \text{NP} \quad bi\text{-V}$$

in which the noun phrases are third person. The principles might be worded roughly as follows:

(63)   *The Interpretation of Grammatical Relations*

NP is:
a.   object/___ *yi*-v
     subject/___ *bi*-V
b.   subject/___ NP *yi*-V
     object/___ NP *bi*V.

If we assume that these principles apply alike to surface profiles in simple and complex sentences, we can begin to see that the problem, as we have been thinking of it heretofore, simply vanishes.

We can locate an NP-gap in the following way: if part (b) of (63) cannot apply, there is an NP-gap in the environment:

$$\underline{\quad\quad} \quad \text{NP} \quad \left\{ \begin{array}{c} bi\text{-} \\ yi\text{-} \end{array} \right\} \quad \text{V}$$

Let us imagine now that, once we have located the gap in this way, we replace it with some symbol, say "NP" (i.e., noun phrase in quotes) and then apply (63b) to determine the grammatical relation "NP" bears to the verb. We can then proceed to what remains of the so-called construal problem, which, presumably is now nothing more than the well-known process of associating an NP-proform with a possible full NP-anaphor—in the Navajo case, general principles of coreference will determine with which overt noun phrase, if any, the proform "NP" can (or must, as the particular case requires) be understood as coreferential; this is a separate issue, and is not directly germane to the questions with which we are concerned here.

Let us see how this works in actual practice. Consider, for example, sentence (56). The relevant substring is /at'ééd yi-zts'ǫs/. Notice that, since no noun phrase immediately precedes this string, (63b) will fail to apply. We therefore know that there is an NP-gap preceding the noun phrase /at'ééd/. Our gap-substitution procedure will insert "NP" into that position, permitting (63b) now to apply and to determine the grammatical relation which the missing noun phrase bears to the verb—subject, in this instance. Quite general principles of coreference will allow "NP" to be associated anaphorically with the noun phrase /ashkii/ in the first conjunct clause, giving the reading corresponding to the English of (56). They will also, as it happens, permit a distinct reading according to which "NP" refers outside the sentence. The reading that is **not** allowed is that in which an NP-gap is located between /at'ééd/ and the verb /yi-zts'ǫs/. But notice that this is not, in our revised conception of the problem, a matter of construal; rather, it is related to the operation of (63), which simply rules out the possibility of a parsing of (56) that locates the gap in object position. A question remains, therefore. What **is** the status of the theoretically possible structure in which an NP-gap is in fact located between /at'ééd/ and /yi-zts'ǫs/? Is the sentence in fact structurally ambiguous in this way, or should this alternative structure be ruled out in some way?

This is a crucial juncture in our discussion.

We feel that the only position we can possibly take that is consistent with the Autonomous Systems thesis is that (56) *is* structurally ambiguous. It is simply the case, we wish to claim, that the force of (63) is so compelling in cases of this sort that it renders inaccessible an interpretation corresponding to the structure in which the gap follows, rather than precedes, the overt noun phrase.[17]

Before concluding, let us observe the operation of (63) in a situation of a different sort, one in which both clauses of (63) are immediately applicable. Consider, in this connection, sentence (58). The relevant substring here is /ashkii at'ééd yi-zts'ǫs/. Notice that both clauses of (63) will apply in this instance, and therefore, crucially, will fail to locate an NP-gap. This explains why the sentence admits only readings according to which the boy kissed the girl. Yet we know that a theoretically possible syntactic structure associated with the terminal string (58) is one in which an NP-gap occurs between /ashkii/ and /at'ééd/—thereby admitting a reading according to which the man (/hastiin/) kissed the girl. This follows from the well-formedness of the complex noun phrase /at'ééd yi-zts'ǫs-ęę hastiin/. In line with our announced position on this matter, we would contend that sentence (58) is in fact structurally ambiguous and that it is the force of (63) that limits the range of interpretations to those reflected in the English translations we have provided.

We have not sought here to develop the full complement of surface structure interpretation (or parsing) principles whose existance we feel it is surely reasonable to imagine. Nor have we fully explored the capabilities of (63). We would, however, maintain that the Navajo phenomena with which we have been concerned in this discussion are best understood in these terms and not in terms of constraints on rules of syntax or semantics.

5.   Conclusion[18]

Our conclusion will have relatively little to do (directly, that is) with the three cases of overgeneration we have used to illustrate the tactical approach to linguistic problems that we feel is consistent with the Autonomous Systems view of language: briefly, the tactic of scepticism toward local, or global but rule-linked, conditions on the application of specific rules of formal grammar. We would like here to make certain remarks of primarily methodological character concerning the tasks of a linguist—particularly one who is interested in language typology—in the context of a conception of language as an autonomous system of Autonomous Systems. And our concrete examples will be drawn from a language that is "worlds apart" from those used in the foregoing sections—namely, Walbiri, of Central Australia.

We find the typological work of C. F. Voegelin to be of considerable interest in that it poses rather clearly the questions that must be addressed by a linguist working within the Autonomous Systems framework. Voegelin's typology is **subsystem** typology, a tradition that he himself traces back to the work of Trubetzkoy (Voegelin, 1955). This is contrasted with the **whole language** typology of the 19th century, continued in the 20th by Sapir. The distinction between whole language and subsystem typology quite clearly depends upon the recognition of a degree of autonomy for linguistic (sub)systems in the latter tradition. By contrast, the former tradition "was set up under the assumption that some morphosyntactic features of a given language will serve as an index or indication of the type of that language as a whole. Such typology attemts to measure the whole language—by implying a correlation between parts of the language treated in the typology and parts not treated" (Voegelin, Ramanujan, and Voegelin, 1960, p. 198). Voegelin does not deny that there are, or may be, correlations between parts of a language: "We move cautiously from one part of a language typologized to another part. If the typology of one part implicates that of another part, that would be important—but discoverable only after preliminary typologizing of more than one subsystem across languages" (Voegelin, Ramanujan, and Voegelin, 1960, p. 199). Clearly, this entire enterprise rests upon the assumption of a degree of autonomy among the parts, or systems, within a language.

If this is correct, and we think it is, then there is a clear challenge present for the linguist in the study of language universals. In the Autonomous Systems tradition, the issue of comparability of systems across languages is critical, as is the problem of identifying the systemic "primes" in language. We will not attempt to address these issues here—since that is the whole science of language typology on the Autonomous Systems view—but we would like to explore very briefly one of the themes which Voegelin has identified as important in the tradition of subsystem typology, i.e., the question of the implicational relations among the systems of language. He offers, among others, the following task for typological work: "To discover laws of implication (functional relations) among subsystems. The question of what constitutes equivalence beweeen languages, aside from cognates . . . , can be considered under implication." (Voegelin, 1955, p. 360).

Let us imagine that we are able somehow to answer the question of cross-language equivalence for particular subsystems and that we can, therefore, proceed directly to the task of discovering laws of implication. Let us then consider the following (partially, but not entirely hypothetical) typological difference in the base structure systems of languages:

Type I Base Structure

The categorial rules of the base are of the form

$$X^n \rightarrow \ldots \widehat{\ } A \widehat{\ } X^{n-1}$$

or

$$X^n \rightarrow X^{n-1} \widehat{\ } A \widehat{\ } \ldots .$$

That is, the rules that develop phrasal categories define (1) a labelled constituent (or bracketing) structure, and (2) a concatenation (or linear ordering) of constituents. This is presumably the type which English, Papago, and Hopi, for example, represent. By contrast, languages of the second type conform to the following scheme:

(65)   *Type II Base Structure*

The categorial rules of the base are of the form

$$X^n \rightarrow \ldots, A, X^{n-1} .$$

In this type, the rules that develop phrasal categories define a labelled constituent structure, but they do not specify a concatenation of constituents. Instead, the observed surface word order for any actual sentence is specified by an entirely distinct system, a schema that assigns linear precedence relations among the words of a sentence, subject to general constraints (such as the constraint that a word from one tensed clause may not be ordered among the constituents of another clause, and so on). A candidate for this type is Walbiri. It is typical of Type II languages, like the "scrambling" Walbiri, that they exhibit highly variable surface word order. We would claim, however, that this is not necessarily so. We would claim, rather, that there could be Type II languages with relatively rigid surface word order and, conversely, Type I languages—e.g., Papago—with relatively variable surface word order.

What implications does this base structure typology have for other linguistic systems? It will, for one thing, necessarily be the case that while a Type I language may or may not have a transformational component, a Type II language will definitely **not** have a transformational component. This follows from the definition of the notion "grammatical transformation"—as a structure-dependent operation on concatenated constituents.

What are the empirical reflections of this, say in a language like Walbiri, which is a putative candidate for membership in Type II? Consider the following. While it is a fact about content questions in Walbiri that the question word appears in initial position, typically, it is very unlikely that it arrives in that position through the action of a movement transformation. Since word order is variable in Walbiri, the initial position of question words can be effected by merely choosing **that** word order for content questions. If this is so, then we can perhaps understand why Walbiri is able to form question-word-initial interrogative sentences corresponding to the English "Where did John tell Bill to go?"—i.e., with the question word extracted from an infinitival clause—but not question-word-initial interrogative sentences corresponding to "Where did John say (that) Bill went?"—i.e., with the question word extracted from a tensed clause. This follows from the Tensed Sentence Condition (Chomsky, 1973)–or a version thereof–which, in this instance, would prevent the word ordering schema from positioning any constituent belonging to a tensed clause out of that clause and into the matrix.

There are other ways of conceiving of these Walbiri facts, but the proposal we have just made seems to us to be the most plausible, all things considered. Now, there may be languages of Type I that are essentially like Walbiri, by virtue of their lacking a transformational component. However, we would maintain that if, on some grounds or other (and there are additional grounds in the Walbiri case, we believe), a given language is determined to belong to Type II, then it will necessarily be like Walbiri with respect to the process of content question formation, i.e., it will fail to form questions by extraction from a tensed clause. (For a somewhat similar observation, but from a different theoretical perspective, dealing with better-known languages, see the extremely interesting paper by Bechhofer, 1975.)

If this is correct, then what we have here is an instance of **necessary implication** in association with a typological characteristic, following (1) from the nature of the base in the typologically distinct languages and (2) from the notion "transformational rule," strictly defined. It is reasonable to enquire whether, in the Autonomous Systems conception of language, all intersystemic implications will be necessary implications–that is to say, does it follow from the Autonomous Systems view that this will be the case? Are there implications of another sort–implications that might be termed **relative**? We do not know the answer to this question, but we would like, nevertheless, to speculate that there are, in fact, relative implications and that their existence is in no way inconsistent with the Autonomous Systems thesis. Let us consider Walbiri again–as a possible exemplar of Type II.

In Walbiri, as in most languages of which we have any direct knowledge, the grammatical relations *subject* and *object* play a vital role in the rules of grammar. However, it seems quite clear to us that the definition of these notions, with respect to the rules that make use of them, cannot be the same as in a language with a Type I base structure. Thus, while in a Type I language, the subject, for example, might correspond to "the first noun phrase in the sentence," or "the last noun phrase in the sentence," or some such thing, in a Type II language such positional definitions of grammatical relations are impossible, by the very nature of the Type II base structure. In Walbiri (according to the null hypothesis, at any rate), the notion subject can adequately, and we think quite correctly, be identified in terms of the case system. The subject is the ergative noun phrase, if there is one, otherwise the absolutive. The object is defined in analogous fashion as the dative, if there is one, the absolutive otherwise. These disjunctive definitions function correctly in most, if not all, areas of Walbiri grammar in which the grammatical relations subject and object play a crucial role. Nevertheless, there is commonality between the Walbiri grammatical relations and those of other languages, which is not at all captured in the scheme we have just outlined here, i.e., in which the subject, say, is defined in terms of the linear order in one language, but in terms of the case system in another. This is cause for concern, since the scheme fails to reflect certain universal, or

near-universal, observations about grammatical relations, such as the observation
that in most languages the semantic agent is the subject (in the basic form of a
sentence), while the patient is typically the direct object; and the observation that,
in languages with an ergative-absolutive type of case system, the semantic agent in
a transitive sentence is typically (perhaps always) in the ergative case; and so on.

Our feeling is that the universals in this case belong properly to the category of
relative implications within the typology that grows out of the Autonomous
Systems view of language. That is to say, these universals are not to be represented
directly in the grammars of specific languages. Rather, we would suggest, they are
to be represented by means of a system analogous to the "marking" or "linking"
conventions of phonology (cf. Chomsky and Halle, 1968, Chapter 9) which specify
the degree of markedness—the naturalness—of particular phonological processes,
morpheme structures, and phonological segments. In relation to case systems, for
example, such linking or marking conventions would specify the extent to which
the use of a particular case, or the case array associated with a particular verb, is
marked or natural within the context of a general theory of naturalness for case
categories vis à vis functional, or thematic, structure. And with respect to
grammatical relations, analogous conventions would define the extent to which
such notions as subject and object, defined for a particular base structure, are
marked or natural within the context of a general theory of naturalness for the
association of grammatical with logical and thematic relations.

To give somewhat more substnace to this suggestion, let us imagine a proposal
along the following lines. The notions *subject* and *object* (not in quotes) properly
belong to the system of representation that defines the logical form of sentences—
assuming that logical form specifies a subject–predicate partitioning for sentences.
We might, for example, represent the logical form of a transitive sentence like
"Japangardi speared the kangaroo," using the λ-notation of Church (1941, and
very successfully developed for a wide variety of long-standing problems in English
grammar by Sag, 1976), as follows:

(66)   *Japangardi, λx(the kangaroo, λy(x speared y))*

Correspondingly, the logical form of an intransitive sentence like "the kangaroo ran
away" might be represented as follows:

(67)   *the kangaroo, λx(x ran away)*

The notion *subject* corresponds to the term directly preceding the maximal λ-pred-
icate, i.e., *Japangardi* in (66), *the kangaroo* in (67). The notion *object*, in a transitive sentence, corresponds to the term directly preceding the minimal, or innermost,
λ-predicate, i.e., *the kangaroo* in (66).

Now let us see how the notions "*subject*" and "*object*" (in quotes) are defined
for Walbiri—e.g., for sentences whose logical form corresponds to (66–67):

(66′)   *Japangardi-rli wawirri pantu-rnu.*
          (Japangardi-ERG kangaroo spear-PAST)

(67′)   *Wawirri parnka-ja-rra.*
             kangaroo run-PAST-away)

We have devised a feature system to represent the case categories of Walbiri, a minimal departure from the surface case marking occasioned by a certain degree of syncretism in case morphology. The features we have chosen are [subj] and [obj]. Ergative case is represented [+subj, -obj] (for mnemonic purposes, read this roughly as "capable of being the subject, but not the object"); the absolutive case is represented [+subj, +obj] (read "capable of being the subject or the object, depending upon the transitivity of the verb"); and the dative case is represented [+obj, -subj] (read, "capable of being the object, but not the subject"). These are the "pure grammatical" cases; all other cases, i.e., the "thematic cases" (e.g., locative, allative, elative, etc) are represented [-subj, -obj]. Using this feature system, we can define the Walbiri notions *"subject"* and *"object"* by means of the following disjunctions:

(68)   *"subject"*: [+subj (-obj)]
                  "object":   [+obj (-subj)]

In accordance with the use of parenthesis to express disjunction (as in phonology), these will correctly select the ergative, if there is one, otherwise the absolutive, for *"subject,"* and they will select the dative, if there is one, otherwise the absolutive, for *"object."* In the normal case, Walbiri *"subject"* and *"object"* will correspond exactly to logical *subject* and *object*. This is not a logical necessity, however. In fact, Walbiri weather sentences, like (69a-b) may be exceptional in this regard:

(69)   a.   *Ngapa ka wanti-mi.*
              (rain PRES fall-NONPAST)
              'It is raining.'

        b.   *Payi ka wangka-mi.*
              (wind PRES speak-NONPAST)
              'It is windy, the wind is blowing.'

While these sentences have *"subjects"* (/ngapa/ 'water, rain', and /payi/ 'air, wind'), it is not at all clear that these are to be identified with the *subject* in the corresponding logical form of weather sentences.

Now let us imagine the sorts of things the naturalness conventions might say in this connection. The lexical representation of each Walbiri verb, we assume, will have associated with it a strict subcategorization stipulating the case categories of its pure grammatical dependents. In addition, the lexical representation will stipulate the thematic relations the dependents bear to the verb. The unmarked, or natural situation for a transitive verb, we suggest, would be that in which, say, the ergative dependent is the agent, the absolutive is the patient, and so on. Given this, we might go on to suggest that grammatical and logical relations are associated with thematic relations in ways that can be characterized as marked or unmarked as well. Thus, for example, the grammatical relation *"subject"* (and the logical relation *subject*) in a transitive sentence will, in the unmarked or natural case, correspond to the thematic relation *agent*—in the basic form of sentences, that is. Walbiri conforms to this expectation, by and large, as do most languages with which we are acquainted. Again, however, this is not a logical necessity. It is at least logically possible for a particular verb, a class of verbs, or even an entire language, to depart from this norm to some extent. A strong case has been made by Dixon, for example, that the Dyirbal language of North Queensland exhibits a basic form of transitive sentences in which the *"subject"* (corresponding to logical *subject*, as expected) is identified not with the *agent*, but with the *patient* (Dixon, 1972). We suggest that the naturalness conventions, once they are fully elaborated, would identify this as a highly marked system, perhaps accounting for the relative rarity of the Dyirbal type among the languages of the world.

Notes

* This work was supported in part by the National Institute of Mental Health Grant No. MH-13390-08.

    The division of labor in preparing this paper has been as follows. Hale is responsible for the prose of the paper as a whole and for sections 1, 2, and 5. Section 3 is a condensation and slight recasting of parts of LaVerne Masayesva Jeanne, "A Reconsideration of the Relative Clause in Hopi" (1975). Section 4 is based on work by Paul Platero (1974), Hale and Platero (1974), and subsequent investigations by Hale and Platero.

1. These introductory sections are taken, with only slight revision, from Hale (1976).

2. For further information concerning this aspect of Navajo grammar, see Hale (1973) and Creamer (1974).

3. This section comprises a thorough revision of a paper by Hale entitled "Papago Intonation and Word Order," prepared originally for inclusion in the volume of *IJAL* dedicated to Stanley Newman. Unfortunately, the paper was not finished in time to appear in that volume. Hale would like now to dedicate this section to Stanley Newman in gratitude for benefits derived from Newman's teaching and general scholarship, both in the context of a study of his published works and in the context of his excellent courses while Hale was his student in 1956–57.

    Hale owes his current understanding of the cyclic nature of the Papago extraposition rule described here almost entirely to discussions with other linguists—especially Lisa Selkirk, Ivan Sag, and Erich Woisetschlaeger. These people are not responsible for Hale's mistakes, however.

    The orthography used in this section is essentially that of Alvarez and Hale, 1969, with the exception that long vowels are written double rather than with a colon.

4. For a discussion of the auxiliary in Papago, see footnote 3 of Hale, 1969, the grammar section of Saxton and Saxton, 1969, or the relevant sections of Steele, 1975.

5. A second class of exceptions is treated briefly in Hale (1975), namely, the phrase-internal fall in pitch from a stressed specifier Spec_A in the context $/ \underline{\quad} \bar{\bar{A}}$. It is omitted from the present discussion, since it does not bear directly on the case of overgeneration with which we are concerned.

6. It is possible to collapse Three-Bar and Two-Bar Extraposition into a single rule schema, as follows, assuming that the structural description below is a legitimate one, and assuming further that the parentheses designate an option merely, rather than a disjunctive ordering relation between the two rules:

$$X - (Spec) \bar{\bar{A}} - X$$
$$\begin{array}{ccc} 1 & 2 & 3 \\ 1 & 0 & 3 \quad 2 \end{array}$$

Ivan Sag has pointed out to us that the intent of this formulation may constitute a violation of his Immediate Domination Principle (Sag, 1976) and Bresnan's Relativized A-over-A Principle (Bresnan, 1976).

7. The stressed singular specifiers have short and long forms—/hégai, hég/ 'that' /hída, ʼíd/ 'this'. The short forms are used in preverbal position when $\bar{\bar{N}}$ is missing from the $\bar{\bar{N}}$ to which the specifier belongs. The phonologically weaker and semantically empty N-category specifier /g/ appears in its augmented form /heg/ when $\bar{\bar{N}}$ is extracted from it.

8. It is remotely possible that there exists a noncyclic analysis that would lead to the same expectations. This would entail, we would imagine, a strict separation of the two extraposition processes and the establishment of an extrinsic ordering relation between them. We have sought in vain for such an analysis that would account for the range of facts successfully handled by the cyclic theory. Another possibility that should not be entirely overlooked is that suggestion by the Saxtons that Papago is basically nucleus-initial (Saxton and Saxton, 1969) and that the movement rules discussed here operate leftward, rather than rightward as we suggest. We have not fully investigated this possibility in our work on Papago, though cases of rightward extraposition that violate subjacency—e.g., /ʼan ʼóoḍ ʼán g káwyu/ (Spec$_P$ (Spec$_N$) N P Spec$_N$ N) 'on the horse's back' (lit., 'there its back on the horse'), presumably produced by successive cyclic extraposition (cf. the nucleus-final variant /ʼan káwyu ʼóo ʼán/—seem to us to be more tractable within the nucleus-final theory than within the nucleus-initial theory.

   Joel Rotenberg is currently working out an alternative analysis of Papago that would account for the total range of possible surface word orders *without* generating the ill-formed (20) at all; his analysis assumes the nucleus-final base but uses a leftward, rather than a rightward, movement rule. Hale is also exploring the possibility that Papago has a Type II base structure (see section 5 of the text) and that the ill-formed (20) is precluded by conditions on word order, rather than on the appearance of #-junctures in surface structures.

9. The Hopi orthography used in this section is one consistent with the findings in Jeanne (1974). We have indicated stress, though this is for the most part redundant. The sequence /VV/ is perceived as a level tone, and the sequence /V̂ʼ/ is perceived as a falling tone, at least in the Third Mesa dialect to which these data belong.

10 The oblique case ending is universally /-y/ in the plural.

11. Our original conception of the /-qa/ element was that it was a complementizer and that the head of a relative clause appeared, if at all, to the left of the subordinate clause. However, evidence from factive complements indicates rather clearly that the noun phrase appearing to the left of a *qa*-terminated sentence cannot be the true head (Jeanne, 1975). Moreover, left-headed relative clauses would fail: (1) to reflect the parallelism between relative clauses and other structures in the use of pleonastic forms; and (2) to conform to the otherwise universally nucleus-final base structure of Hopi. It is possible, however, that we are wrong in our reanalysis; for an interesting discussion of Hopi /-qa/ from a different point of view, see Voegelin and Voegelin (1975).

12. Discussions of obviation in Hopi are to be found in Voegelin and Voegelin (1975) and (though not under that name) in Whorf (1946). The extension of the Algonquianist terms "obviative" and "proximate" to Uto-Aztecan is due to Grimes, under the influence of

Hockett (Grimes, 1964, p. 64). The Voegelins were first in recognizing clearly the fact that obviation is involved in the case marking of the /-qa/ element (Voegelin and Voegelin, 1975).

13. Work in progress by Jeanne indicates cl⁻ rly that extraposition is a bonafide process in Hopi. Her evidence comes from a study of anaphora and from a study of the phonology of the so-called pausal forms (cf., Whorf, 1946, p. 165).

14. Kiparsky (personal communication) has suggested that surface structure constraints of the type alluded to here might be explicable in terms of opacity (Kiparsky, 1973, pp. 57–86). In the Hopi situation, the case marking of the head noun /-qa/, in the ill-formed surface structures, renders opaque the rule that assigns the case category [–obl] to noun phrases appearing in the environment /__ V, i.e., in subject position. This is an extremely interesting idea that, if pursued, might lead to a theory that successfully delimits the class of possible surface structure conditions on well-formedness.

15. The orthography used in this section, and in the introduction, is that which is now traditional in the Navajo community. It is described, among other places, in Young and Morgan (1943). Our usage here adopts certain modifications introduced recently, e.g., the deletion of word-initial glottal stop and omission of the bar from /ł/ in the transcription of aspirated and glottalized, laterally released stops.

16. Processes described by Ellen Kaufman in her important work on questions in Navajo (Kaufman, 1974) involve, virtually without question, **movement** of an element from within a subordinate clause rightward into roughly head position. Hale and Platero (1974) attempted to extend Kaufman's analysis to relative clauses. Other processes that create NP-gaps in Navajo—e.g., that corresponding to pronominalization—quite clearly do not involve movement. It is worth mentioning, perhaps, that our overall case in this section is somewhat strengthened if it can be shown that more than one process is involved in creating NP-gaps.

17. The effects of (63), perhaps expectedly, can be overridden by selectional and NP-hierarchy considerations, for some speakers, at least. Thus, the sentence

(i)   *Hastiin yi-ztał-ę́ę łééchąą'í nahał'in.*
(man GAP yi-kicked-REL dog bark)
'The dog that the man kicked is barking.'

has NP-gap in a "forbidden" position. Nonetheless, for some speakers, the sentence is interpretable in accordance with the reading which locates the NP-gap between /hastiin/ and /yi-ztał/. At work here, among other things, is the fact that the NP-gap associated with /łééchąą'í/ 'dog' could not be located in absolute initial position, since that would violate the principle that the form S O yi-V is not used where the object outranks the subject. Thus, sentence (i) is able to receive the given interpretation (for some people) for the same reason that the following sentence is questionable:

(ii) *?*Łééchąą'í hastiin yi-ztał.*
(dog man yi-kicked)
'The dog kicked the man.'

The reading is, of course, aided by the greater likelihood of a man kicking a dog over that of a dog kicking a man.

This observation also strengthens our contention that constraints on NP-gaps cannot be constraints on rules of grammar.

18. Material appearing in this section constitutes a revision and extension of a discussion appearing in Hale, 1976.

COMMENTS ON THE PAPER BY HALE, ET AL.

Susan Steele

Committee on Linguistics
University of Arizona
Tucson, Arizona

1.   With minor and relatively unimportant exceptions,[1] my questions and comments about the paper by Hale, Masayesva-Jeanne, and Platero have to do with the assumptions that underlie it. In the spirit of the conference at which it was presented. this paper is informed by the thesis of autonomous syntax, that is, as stated by Hale et al., ". . . language consists of a number of distinct systems, each possessing inherent principles of organization that are essentially independent of factors relating to any other linguistic system or to extralinguistic considerations" (p. 379). Besides my doubts about this thesis, this position has had a questionable effect on methodology, less in this paper, to be sure, than in many others written within the same framework. My questions about the methodology and my doubts about the thesis are taken up in sections 2 and 3 respectively. In the last section of these comments, I want to address the typology suggested in the conclusion of this paper.

2.   There is an inherent tension in linguistics between allowing the data to inform hypotheses about the form of the grammar and allowing hypotheses about the form of the grammar to inform the data. The problem most basically is whether it is possible to begin with a set of carefully selected examples and build from that to a theory or whether it is even possible to tell what the data might be without a theory. It is probably impossible to do either consistently, but we should be careful not to let one dominate excessively. Insofar as the assumptions that accompany the autonomy thesis produce arguments or require analyses that are otherwise unsupported. I have objections.

   In the discussion of the data for each of the three languages considered in Hale et al.'s paper, certain analyses or interpretations of analyses are rejected, at least in part because they violate the autonomy thesis. For Papago, " . . .appending a condition to the rule [13] to the effect that it applies obligatorily if the factor $\bar{\bar{A}}$ is of the form $\overline{\overline{A}}[\text{Spec}_A \ \overline{\overline{B}}]\overline{\overline{A}}$ ... amounts to saying that the rule is obligatory if the category affected by it has itself undergone the rule. Such a condition would be entirely counter to the spirit of the Autonomous Systems view of language" (p. 385). For Hopi, "But even if it were possible [i.e., to place a constraint on the base rules to preclude a certain type of complex noun phrase in subject position], such a move would be entirely at variance with the Autonomous Systems thesis" (401). And for Navajo, ". . . we would like to suggest that . . . [the Navajo constraint on NP-gaps (60)] is entirely the wrong way to look at the matter. First of all, if it is conceived as a constraint on rules of Navajo syntax or semantics, it is clearly out of keeping with the Autonomous Systems thesis" (p. 406). Other arguments are adduced in each case against the particular analysis in question, but I find arguments of this sort totally unconvincing ways of ruling out an analysis.

There is another consequence of assuming a theory and arguing from it to an analysis: assumptions about the base form that may be theoretically elegant need not have independent support. Specific to this paper, the bar notation and the assumptions about parallelism it depends on make for some less than satisfactory results in the analysis of Papago. Hale et al. call the AUX a specifier on the verb and generate it clause initially.[2] By so doing, they maintain an elegant parallelism with the relationship between determiners on noun phrases and spatial determiners on postpositional phrases.[3] However, each of the assumptions as regards the AUX is open to question. First, there are no arguments here for why the AUX is a specifier on the verb rather than a specifier on the sentence; in fact, it is a function of the elegance of the parallelism. But the AUX contains elements (aspectual clitics and clitic subject pronouns) that pertain, at least semantically, to the sentence—that is, they are in some sense sentential in scope—and could easily be argued to be a specifier on the sentence. Second, whether the AUX should be a specifier at all is still an open question. The answer may depend ultimately on what is meant by *specifier*, but is is not obvious that it is a specifier in the way that, say, a determiner on a noun phrase is. Finally, it is not at all clear that the AUX should be generated clause-initially. The AUX in Papago does occur initially, but only under specific conditions. (The example sentences in this paper are chosen to illustrate a clause initial AUX and thus meet those conditions.) Rather, the AUX in Papago is essentially a sentential second position element.

(1)   *wákial ?at g wísilo cépos*
        (cowboy AUX article calf brand:perfective)
        'The cowboy branded the calf.' (Hale, 1975, p. 17)

Second position must be defined at a late point in the derivation of the sentence, since the positioning of the AUX must follow all reordering processes that affect the consitutents of the sentence. In (2) below the subject and object noun phrases of (1) have changed positions.

(2)   *wísilo ?at g wákial cépos*
        (calf AUX article cowboy brand:perfective)
        'The cowboy branded the calf.'

In light of the strong trend in linguistics at the moment toward generating more and more transparent deep structures, we need to take a close look at the position of the AUX and the problem of where it is generated.[4] It is not enough to assume a parallelism with specifiers on other phrase types.

3. Insofar as the autonomy thesis turns out to be right, these two objections to methodology will be unimportant. In this section, then, I want to air my doubts about the autonomy thesis. The most important concern the feasibility of actually separating the subsystems of language, but putting those doubts aside for the moment, let me consider one problem that the thesis has to face, even if it turns out to be right.

Hale et al. argue that transformations apply without exceptions; the cases of overgeneration are to be ruled out by some independent linguistic principle. Let me make clear at the outset that my sympathies lie with this approach. The problem, of course, is to rule out the cases of overgeneration in some revealing, and independently motivated, fashion. Here, autonomous syntax runs into the problem that faces anyone who steps outside the formalism for an explanation; which assumptions are valid is not at all intuitively obvious. For a specific example, consider the Hopi case in this paper. The problem in Hopi is to rule out sentences which correspond to the English:

(3)   *The man whom you brought with you will address us.*

"When the complex noun phrase, as a whole, functions as the subject of the main clause, the relative noun phrase (i.e., that noun phrase in the subordinate clause that is coreferential with the complex noun phrase) must likewise function as the subject within its own clause" (p. 394). Hale et al. claim such sentences are ruled out because they violate an otherwise general principle of surface case marking—that noun phrases in subject position are unmarked for case. This argument depends indirectly on the assumption that it is necessary that subject and object be distinguished (either by case marking or by adposition), an assumption not peculiar to this particular paper. Hypotheses about syntactic change have been based on a similar assumption. (See, e.g., Vennemann, 1974.) But I am not convinced that the assumption is justified. There are languages with no overt distinction on the nouns to indicate which is subject and which is object, yet word order is relatively free.[5] Papago is one such language; Classical Aztec, another. And neither language is particularly unusual in this respect. Now it may be the case that context will distinguish between subject and object in such languages; it may also be the case that the assumption that subject and object must be uniformly distinguished is valid as it applies to Hopi. The point is simply that we cannot assume that the distinction between subject and object is necessary, or that it will be expressed in some obvious way.

Let me return to the major issue of the autonomy thesis—the assumption that the systems of language are distinct. It cannot be denied that there is an interface between certain of the subsystems of languages; it is difficult for me to assess the effect of evidence in this regard on the autonomy thesis, but, at the very least, it raises serious questions which will have to be answered. I will briefly consider two examples of the interface, the first of which involves a connection between syntax and semantics; the second, a connection between syntax and phonology.

Akmajian's paper in this volume considers a semantic class of English verbs, the complements of which have syntactic properties peculiar to them. Specifically, the complements of perception verbs are untensed and yet do not have the usual indications of subordination. It is enough that the syntax of English perception verbs is peculiar, but the problem for the autonomous syntax position is clearer when we notice that in other, totally unrelated, languages the same semantic class of verbs has complements with similar properties. In Luiseño, for example, subordinate clauses are never tensed; the verb of the subordinate clause has affixed to it one of a set of suffixes that indicate its time relative to the main clause.

(4)   *noo ngeengi pitoowali teetila - wunut*
         I left still talk-Subordinator:Same:Time
         'I left when I was still talking.'

Some such suffixes require that the subjects of the two clauses be the same, as e.g., *wunut* in (4). Those that do not, require that the subordinate verb have a possessive pronoun prefixed to it.

(5)   *noo poy čakwax wam po-huluqa-qala*
         I him caught already his-fall-Subordinator:Same:Time
         'I caught him as he was falling.'

The subordinating suffixes that require that the subjects of the two clauses be the same consist of an old nominalizer and in some forms, an equivalent to English *be*. Not only do the verbs in the complements of perception verbs have suffixed to them a form that occurs just in the complements of perception verbs—*qal*:[6]

(6)   *čaam tiiwyax hunwuti huluqa-qal*
         we saw bear:object fall-QAL
         'We saw the bear fall.'

but *qal* includes no old nominalizer nor is there a possessive prefix on the verb to which it is suffixed. That is, if subordination in Luiseño is some form of nominalization, indicated either by a nominalizing suffix or by a possessive prefix, the complements of perception verbs are not nominalized. Even if subordination in Luiseño is not to be viewed as nominalization, the complements of perception verbs are aberrant.

The second example of a potential problem for the autonomous syntax position is cliticization. Generally, in languages, a small set of elements either can reduce and attach to some word in the sentence or are obligatorily unstressed and attached. The set includes pronouns, prepositions and postpositions, conjunctions, and indications of tense, aspect, and modality. (7) is an example of the optionally clitic pronouns of English, (8), of the obligatorily clitic pronouns of Luiseño. (9) is an example of the optionally clitic aspectual elements of English; (10), of the obligatorily clitic tense/aspectual elements of Luiseño.

(7)   *I hit'em*

(8)   *noo=n mariyi ?ariq*
         I=Clitic:Subject:Pronoun Mary:object am:kicking
         'I am kicking Mary.'

(9)   *I'd've hit John (if I had a chance).*

(10)   *noo=nu=po mariyi ?arin*
         I=clitic:pronoun=Tense/Aspectual:Clitic Mary:object will:kick
         'I will kick Mary.'

Cliticization of the elements of this set is probably indicative of their grammatical as opposed to lexical category status, assuming that the two concepts can be defined in some precise way. The phonological reduction, be it optional or obligatory, is thus a function of certain syntactic properties.

Chomsky (personal communication) has suggested that the first problem, the perception verb problem, is simply one of the considerations that led him to parameterize the autonomy thesis. I take parameterization of the thesis to be a weakening of it. I do not know whether the second problem, the cliticization problem, would involve further weakening, but I do not see how it is avoidable. The point here is not to recast the autonomy thesis in light of such considerations; it is to raise questions about the entire theoretical construct. And since the framework for Hale et al.'s paper is the autonomy thesis, the question of its ultimate validity must be raised.

4.   In the conclusion, Hale et al. address questions of typology and language universals. As they see it, there are two major issues for the study of language universals: "the issue of comparability of systems across languages" and "the problem of identifying the systemic 'primes' in language" (p. 409). They choose not to address this issue directly; they address it rather indirectly through a subissue: how, and if, the various systems of language are implicationally related. My remarks will consider this subissue of implicational relationships, but I will confront the issue of language typology directly as well.

As Hale et al. see it, a characteristic of one system can have as its consequence either necessary or relative implications for the characteristics of another. That this is true is fairly well established in other typological work; it is the example Hale *et al.* use to illustrate their claim that is problematic. They claim that a language may be one of two types, the types being distinguished (1) by whether the base rules specify a concatenation of constituents and (2) by the presence or absence of transformations. One type orders constituents in the base and has transformations; the second does not order constituents in the base and has, as a result, no transformations. This typology has necessary implications, it is argued, for the sort of reorderings of constituents that will be allowed. Walbiri, as a language of the second type, will not question out of tensed clauses. However, Hale et al. explicitly exclude the possibility that an implication of the typology will be that languages of the first type necessarily have rigid word order and languages of the second necessarily will not. Whether this last is not, in fact, a necessary implication of the typology is at least an open question. More important is the question of whether any substantive distinction can be made between languages on the basis of the types of reorderings allowed; that is, the implication that is supposed to follow from the typology may not be valid. Finally, there is the question of whether the typology can be maintained in the first place.

Three languages are given as examples of Type I; one language, as an example of Type II. The Type II language (Walbiri) has free word order; of the three languages classified as Type I, the only one with relative freedom of word order, Papago, is not decisively of this type. In an earlier paper, Hale suggests that what is handled in this paper by a rule of extraposition is a function of extralinguistic considerations which determine word order.[7] That is, it is not clear that the distinction is not between languages with grammaticalized word order, languages like English and Hopi, and languages without, languages like Walbiri and, probably, Papago.

It is certainly true that different reorderings of constituents are possible across languages; the second problem raised in regard to the typology questions not this fact but rather the conclusions drawn thereby. Clearly, certain reorderings of the constituents of clauses are favored cross-linguistically and others are disfavored, although they are still found sporadically. For example, in a cross-linguistic examination of word order variation among nominal subject, nominal object, and verb in main clauses, I found that the vast majority of reorderings are subject to the following:

A.   A variation on the basic word order which places the verb either initial or final to the clause is to be avoided, if the verb was neither initial nor final in the basic order.

That is, a language with a basic SOV word order may allow SVO word order and a language with a basic VSO word order may allow SVO word order, but a verb initial order for the first and a verb final word order for the second is not common. However, some languages have stronger restrictions on word order variation, where something like the following holds:

B.   A variation on the basic word order in which the verb occurs other than in its position in the basic word order is to be avoided.

and still others allow more variation, subject to the following:

C.   A variation on the basic word order in which the object precedes and the subject follows the verb is to be avoided.

A relatively small number of languages have word order variations beyond those allowed under (A), (B), and (C). I fully expect that other general patterns can be established for other clause- and phrase-types. The problems foreseen for the implication claimed in this paper are two. First, the reordering possibilities distinguish languages scalarly rather than bipolarly. Second, the reorderings favored seem a result not of any typological considerations but rather of certain sentential properties.

Finally, there are questions about the typology itself. The questions raised above in regard to the implications create some problems for the typology; if the implications that are supposed to follow from the typology are not obviously substantiated, the orginal distinction that led to those expectations is suspect. More important, though, is the fact that the typology assumes both ordered bases and transformations. Saunders has raised substantial questions about the existence of an ordered base. The existence of transformations is at best a hypothesis; the role and number of transformations has reduced considerably in current theoretical work. The point is that to accept Hale et al's typology, we have to be willing to accept the construct upon which the distinction between the language types is made. And the existence of those theoretical constructs is open to question.

These implicational relationships are, as already stated, a subissue. Let us turn then to the larger issue of language universals. I noted above that Hale et al. claim that there are two major issues from the study of language universals: the issue of language comparability and the issue of systemic primes. Although these are tacit issues in much of the current work on language universals, they are not issues exclusive to autonomous syntax. Anyone who works on language universals has to come to terms with how to compare systems and with how to define the systemic primes. A difference does exist, however, between most of this work (even that within the framework of autonomous syntax) and the paper under discussion. Hale et al, raise an at least implicit question about the possibility of comparing languages and establishing systemic primes; other work is based on the a priori assumption that both are indeed possible. A major thesis of this paper is that languages differ in nontrivial ways. For example, although both the Hopi and the Papago analyses assume and depend on the X-bar notation, the core of Hopi syntax is supposed to be the double-bar level of structure and the core of Papago syntax is supposed to be the triple-bar level of structure. The necessary and relative implications discussed in the concluding section are meant to argue for substantial differences among languages. At the very least, in the view of the authors of this paper, if languages are comparable, the comparisons are much less obvious than other work on language universals suggests. It may follow from this that the systemic primes of one langauge are not those of another. I do not object to either possibility in the abstract; raising the issue can have the healthy effect of making us look more closely at what we consider comparable constructions cross-linguistically. My own investigations and the investigations of others into language universals does not support such pessimism, however. To take a concrete example, AUX, defined roughly as it is in *Syntactic Structures*, appears to be a universal category. In Luiseño, modality, tense/aspect, and agreement—notions parallel to those analyzed as part of the English AUX—occur in a surface syntactic unit.

(11)   *nanatmalum xu m po henge?malumi ?ari*
            girls MODAL=AGREEMENT=TENSE/ASPECT boys kick
            'Girls should kick boys.'

Admittedly, what comprises the AUX will differ in certain respects from language to language, e.g. in some languages the AUX is more verblike than in others and the "verbiness" of the elements of the AUX corresponds to the semantic notions expressed. But, the existence of such (largely) predictable differences does not detract from the necessity of recognizing a unit AUX in a particular language. I choose the AUX to underscore my lack of pessimism because it is an abstract construct, yet the evidence for its universal category status is drawn from the surface. Support for my optimism is available from other quarters as well. (See e.g., Langacker and Munro's, 1975, analysis of passives.)

5.   My objections to this paper have, as promised, focused on the assumptions that underlie it. I have spent no time praising the paper; it is unnecessary. Small details of analysis aside, the paper is a beautiful piece of work—within its paradigm.

Notes

1. Primary among these minor questions and comments are my questions about the assignment of pitch in Papago. I am not particularly happy with assuming that the basic intonation contour is HL and that the first high pitch is reduced to low if the syllable to which it is assigned is not also stressed. The reduction of pitch under this assumption always occurs on a specifier or (in the case of a word) on a prefix. Under the assumptions of this paper, this is a mechanical result of the pitch reduction rule. Even assuming that reduction is the best way to handle this fact, the type of elements it applies to should be noted somewhere in the grammar. Better still would be a pitch contour that never assigns high pitch to these elements in the first place. Two ways to do just that are immediately obvious. Either assume a (L)HL pitch contour—something that Hale did in an earlier paper. (See Hale, 1975.) Or assume a HL pitch contour, but remove specifiers (and prefixes) from the pitch contour altogether.
2. Hale et al. state that what they refer to as the AUX is "commonly" called the AUX. On the contrary, there is very little agreement on what constitutes an AUX; many linguists assume implicitly that an AUX contains auxiliary verbs. Their assumption is incorrect and the authors of this paper are right, but the arguments in support of that claim are not relevant to this particular paper.
3. Although I admit to difficulties with viewing a preposition or postposition as the head of a prepositional or postpositional phrase, Hale has argued (personal communication) that in Papago, at least, this claim is justified.
4. This point is particularly interesting, since the analysis of the AUX in *Syntactic Structures* is at the very root of transformational grammar. Apparently questions that plagued the field then are still with us.

5. Such languages often have clitic pronouns that either attach to the verb or occur in sentential second position. However, with third person singular nouns, the presence of such clitic pronouns will do little to disambiguate which of the nouns is subject and which is object.
6. -qal can precede other subordinators in regular subordinate clauses, but alone it never occurs in anything but the complements of perception verbs.
7. At the conference at which this paper was presented, Hale argued on other grounds for Papago to be a Type II language.

THE COMPLEMENT STRUCTURE OF PERCEPTION VERBS IN AN AUTONOMOUS SYNTAX FRAMEWORK

Adrian Akmajian

Committee on Linguistics
University of Arizona
Tucson, Arizona

1. Introduction

The purpose of this paper is to present a detailed example of syntactic analysis carried out within the framework of autonomous syntax, in the general sense of Chomsky (1975a). In particular, we will be concerned with the complement structure of perception verbs such as *see* and *hear* (and a number of others[1]), as indicated in boldface in the examples below:

(1) a. *We saw **the moon rising over the mountain***
     b. *We heard **the bells ringing at sunset***

We will present a syntactic analysis of phrases such as *the moon rising over the mountain* in (1a), in which the phrase does not have a sentential source (as might be expected), but rather in which the NP *the moon* functions as the *head* of a single constituent NP, with *rising over the mountain* as its VP-complement. The best analysis, we argue, is based on purely formal, syntactic criteria, i.e., arguments from syntactic constituent structure tests and arguments from overall simplicity of the statement of transformational rules, and we make no appeal to semantic information in determining the underlying structure of perception verb complements (henceforth PVCs).

In arguing for this particular analysis of PVCs, we find that the well known heuristic strategy for syntactic analysis first proposed by Katz and Postal (1964, p. 157) either consistently leads to the wrong results or is simply irrelevant to syntactic analysis:

> Given a sentence for which a syntactic derivation is needed; look for simple paraphrases of the sentence which are not paraphrases by virtue of synonymous expressions; on finding them, construct grammatical rules that relate the original sentence and its paraphrases in such a way that each of these sentences has the same sequence of underlying P-markers. Of course, having constructed such rules, it is still necessary to find *independent syntactic justification* for them.

This heuristic strategy—and indeed the broader Katz–Postal hypothesis—has led to the view that the primary explanatory function of underlying syntactic structure is to provide a coherent basis for deriving a representation of the meaning of a sentence. This is carried further in the framework of generative semantics, where the underlying structure of a sentence is itself postulated as the representation of its meanings, and not merely an intermediate level of structure ("deep structure") from which that representation may be derived.

In contrast, within the autonomous syntax framework, there is a rather different heuristic principle for syntactic investigation: namely, that the formally motivated syntactic rules (both PS- and T-rules) of the grammar will demand that certain syntactic structures (both deep and intermediate) be postulated if the simplest possible statement of those rules is to be maintained. A syntactically well-motivated deep structure is not intended to be a "representation of meaning." Nevertheless, deep and surface syntactic structure, once independently established within a grammar, must mesh in a natural fashion with a plausible semantic description of the sentences in question. Independently motivated syntactic descriptions that mesh in a straightforward fashion with plausible semantic descriptions will be more highly valued than those that do not. The purpose of this paper is to show, by specific example, what it means for a syntactic analysis to be "independently motivated" (i.e., independent of primitive concepts of semantics).

Two observations should be made here. First, the two heuristic strategies outlined above are by no means diametrically opposed, since the Katz–Postal strategy itself demands independent syntactic justification. Second, one cannot "prove" or "disprove" a heuristic strategy: one can only hope to show that analyses suggested by one strategy are descriptively more adequate than those suggested by another strategy. In spite of these qualifying factors, it will nonetheless be convenient for expository purposes to bear in mind the tension between the different emphases of the two strategies. In the next section, section 2, we will discuss in detail the formal criteria that lead us to the specific analysis of PVCs we ultimately posit. In section 3, we will consider alternative, more "semantically based" analyses, and show how these are inadequate. (We will address oursleves more specifically to the Katz–Postal heuristic strategy in that section.) Finally, in section 4, we will discuss how the proposed syntactic analysis might mesh with certain semantic observations regarding PVCs, and in general, how the analysis illustrates the tenets of the so-called autonomy thesis.

2. The Complement Structure of Perception Verbs

Before turning to the relevant evidence for the structure of PVCs, it would be useful, at the very outset, to rule out two constructions as possible sources for PVCs, namely relative clauses and gerunds. That PVCs cannot derive from restrictive relative clauses is shown by the fact that proper names and unique NPs can occur within PVCs, but these may not be heads of relative clauses:

(2)   a.   *We saw John playing the piano*
      b.   *We saw the wind blowing through the trees*

(3)   a.   **We saw John who was playing the piano*
      b.   **We saw the wind which was blowing through the trees*

Furthermore, examples such as the following show that PVCs cannot derive from appositive relative clause structures:

(4)   a.   *We didn't hear anyone playing the piano*
      b.   **We didn't hear anyone, who was playing the piano*

Finally, as noted quite some time ago by Chomsky (1964), there are sentences that are in fact structurally ambiguous between a relative clause and a PVC structure:

(5)   *We saw the boy eating the ice cream cone*

The structure of (5) is ambiguous between the kinds of structures illustrated in the following examples:

(6)   a.   *We saw the boy who was eating the ice cream cone* (REL)
      b.   *We saw the boy eat the ice cream cone* (PVC)

Since (5) is in fact simultaneously ambiguous between a PVC-structure and a relative clause structure, we cannot derive one structure from the other. The facts of (2)–(6) thus militate against a relative clause source for PVCs.

With regard to a gerundive source for PVCs, it was noted by Fillmore (1963) that PVCs differ from gerunds in not allowing the characteristic possessive marking of the subject of the gerund, or allowing auxiliary *have*:

(7)   a.   *I can't hear John playing the piano*
      b.   **I can't hear John's playing the piano*
      c.   **I couldn't hear John's having played the piano*
      d.   cf.: *I regret John's having played the piano* (true gerund)

The lack of possessive marking in PVCs is especially clear when personal pronouns are used:

(8)   a.   *I regret my saying such foolish things* (true gerund)
      b.   **I heard my saying such foolish things*
      c.   cf.: *I hear myself saying such foolish things*

The possessive pronoun *my*, which characteristically shows up in gerunds, is impossible in the PVC-construction, which instead manifests a characteristic reflexive (i.e., *myself*) form. Thus, it has been recognized for some time that PVCs do not derive either from relative clause sources or gerundive sources. The question now arises as to what exactly the source for PVCs should be, and we now turn to evidence bearing on this question.

One set of well-known syntactic tests establishes that PVCs such as those in (1), are single syntactic constituents:[2]

(9)   a.   *What we saw was **the moon rising over the mountain*** (Pseudo-Cleft)
       b.   *We saw what we had all hoped to see: **the moon rising over
             the mountain*** (Equative "Colon" Construction)
       c.   *You can **see**, but you certainly can't **hear**, **the moon rising
             over the mountain***   (Right Node Raising[3])

The postcopular and "postcolon" positions in pseudo-cleft sentences and equative
sentences are usually assumed to contain only single constituents (cf. (9a) and (9b));
and the rule of Right Node Raising operates only on single syntactic units (9c).
Further, another set of diagnostic tests establishes PVCs not only as single constituents, but also as single NP-constituents:

(10)   a.   *It was **the moon rising over the mountain** that we saw*
             (Cleft Sentence)
       b.   ***The moon rising over the mountain** was a breathtaking sight
             to see ___.* (Object Deletion[4])
       c.   ***The moon rising over the mountain** has been witnessed by many
             a lover here on Lover's Lane* (Passive)

It is generally held that only NP-constituents can be inserted into "clefted" position, as in (10a)[5]; only NPs can be deleted by the rule of Object Deletion, as in
(10b) (where, furthermore, the phrase *the moon rising over the mountain* occurs as
the underlying subject of the main clause, another indiciation of its NP-status);
and finally, only NPs can be fronted into derived subject position by the Passive
rule, as in (10c). Consistent with the fact that PVCs behave transformationally as
NPs is the fact that they also occur in deep structure NP-positions (as partially
shown by (10c)):

(11)   a.   ***The moon rising over the mountain** is a beautiful sight*
       b.   *The sight of **the moon rising over the mountain** was breathtaking*

The boldfaced phrase in (11a) is a deep structure subject, and that in (11b) is a
deep structure complement to the head noun *sight*.

   The initial evidence, then, suggests that sentence (1a) has the following gross
(deep) structure:

(12)

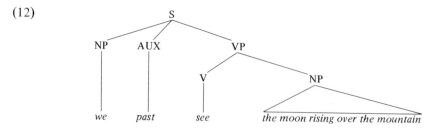

If the PVC, as a whole, is an NP, the question immediately arises as to what the
internal structure of that NP is. The following would be a rather natural first guess,
given many of the assumptions of current work in syntax:

(13)

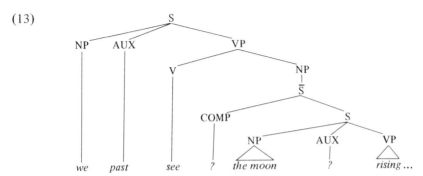

The NP-over-S structure is certainly consistent with the syntactic constituent structure tests given in (9)-(11). Moreover, for many linguists this structural analysis would be confirmed by the fact that the PVC in the sentence *We saw the moon rising over the mountain* is semantically parallel to the sentence *The moon is rising over the mountain*, in that in both, for example, the NP *moon* is interpreted as the subject of the verb *rising*. The definition of *subject of* given in Chomsky (1965, pp. 68-74) stipulates that a subject NP is one directly dominated by S (and only S) in deep structure, i.e., is the NP in the configuration $_S$[NP-AUX-VP]$_S$. By this definition, deep (or "logical") subject status is correctly assigned to the NP *the moon* in structure (13). Hence, this analysis makes the fundamental claim that PVCs are *sentential* in origin.

As plausible as this may seem initially, there are four basic facts about PVCs that are inconsistent with the idea that sentences such as (1a) are structured as in (13). First of all, as noted a good number of years ago by Fillmore (1963), the auxiliary *have* never occurs in PVCs:

(14)   *I heard Mary having played my song*

Indeed, a more general claim can be made: no deep structure auxiliary verb (that is, auxiliary generated by the PS rule *AUX → Tense (Modal) (have en) (be ing)*) may occur in PVCs.[6] This fact is anomalous and totally unexplained if PVCs derive from a sentential source of the sort shown in (13).

A similar and related fact is that PVCs never contain any overt complementizer (i.e. never occur with *that, for-to*, or *poss-ing*[7]). While the verb of the PVC occurs with the affix *-ing*, it is clear that this does not derive from the gerundive complementizer *poss-ing* (cf. sentence (14)). Hence, on a sentential source for PVCs one assumes either that the underlying complementizer generated as part of the embedded sentence is *always* deleted, or that a special "φ"-complementizer exists for PVCs. Neither alternative seems particularly motivated. More importantly, the entire question of complementizer choice seems irrelevant, given the total lack of complementizers in PVCs, and hence our theory should, ideally, avoid the entire issue automatically.

The second troublesome area, and a much more serious one, for the sentential analysis of PVCs, has to do with the nature of Number Agreement when PVCs are in subject position. We have already noted the fact that Passive may front PVCs:

(15)   a.   *The astronomers at Kitt Peak have often* $\left\{\begin{array}{l} observed \\ photographed \end{array}\right\}$
          the moon and Venus rising in conjunction

       b.   ***The moon and Venus rising in conjunction*** *have (*has) often*
            been $\left\{\begin{array}{l} observed \\ photographed \end{array}\right\}$ *by the astronomers at Kitt Peak*

Note that in (15b) the PVC in derived subject position triggers Number Agreement
in the main clause. The very same phenomenon is seen when PVCs function as
underlying subjects:

(16)   a.   ***The moons of Jupiter rotating in their orbits*** *are (*is)*
                beautiful to watch ___ .
       b.   ***The moons of Jupiter rotating in their orbits*** *are (*is) a*
                breathtaking sight.

It is clear that verb agreement in the matrix sentence is triggered by the supposed
"embedded subject" NP of the PVC. But the trouble is precisely that true *embedded*
subjects never trigger Number Agreement in the matrix sentence:

(17)   *That **the moons of Jupiter** rotate in their orbits wasn't (*weren't)*
                obvious.

On the hypothesis that PVCs are structured as in (13), a sentence such as (15b)
would have the following rough structure at the time Number Agreement applies:

(18)

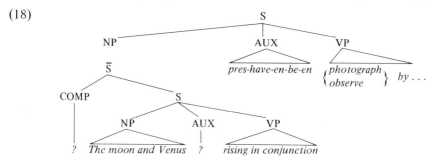

In this structure the NP *the moon and Venus* functions as an embedded subject
(parallel with the NP *the moons of Jupiter* in (17)), and hence (18) predicts that
Number Agreement in the matrix sentence should not be triggered by that NP. The
prediction is false, as shown by the examples in (15) and (16).[8]

    The same Number Agreement phenomena show up in pseudo-cleft sentences as
well:

(19)   a.   *What we saw were (*was) the moons of Jupiter rotating in*
                their orbits

Once again, this phenomenon is not observed with true embedded sentences:

(19)   b.   *What wasn't obvious was (*were) that the moons of Jupiter*
                rotate in their orbits

This then, is formal evidence suggesting a basic structural dissimilarity betwen PVCs and true embedded sentences: the initial NP of the PVC behaves as though it is a constituent of the *main* clause, and not of an embedded clause.

So far, then, the evidence from Number Agreement suggests that in sentence (15b) the NP *the moon and Venus* is not am embedded subject, but rather the *head* of the larger NP of which it is a part (given that only heads of NPs trigger Number Agreement). The minimal hypothesis dictated by these facts is that PVCs are structured not as in (13), but rather as in the following:

(20)

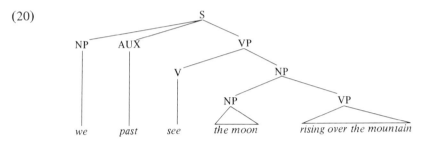

This structure entails a PS-rule of the form $NP \rightarrow NP\ VP$, where the NP on the right of the arrow is the head of the larger NP. If (20) is correct, then example (15b) is structured as in (21):

(21)

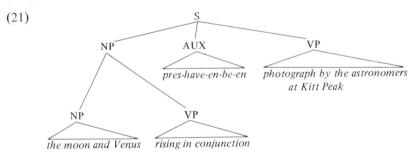

Structure (21) is the result of the application of the Passive rule, and the subject of the matrix sentence contains a plural head noun (*the moon and Venus*). Hence Number Agreement will apply in the main clause as expected.

The agreement phenomenon is not the only one which reveals the *head*-like nature of the "subject" of the PVC. Equally revealing is the fact that the VP that follows the head NP within the PVC can be extraposed to the end of the main clause:

(22) a. *The moon **rising over the mountain** looks spectacular*
      b. *The moon looks spectacular **rising over the mountain***

(23) a. *The bells **ringing at sunset** make a soothing sound*
      b. *The bells make a soothing sound **ringing at sunset***

Exposition of this sort is characteristic of *complements* to heads of noun phrases:

(24) a. *A review **of a new book about China** will appear soon*
      b. *A review will appear soon **of a new book about China***

(25) a. *A man **who we all knew** walked in*
      b. *A man walked in **who we all knew***

(26) a. *New evidence **that NPs are cyclic** was presented*
      b. *New evidence was presented **that NPs are cyclic***

These examples illustrate the extraposability of PP-complements, relative clauses, and *that*-complements, which are all adjuncts to *heads* of noun phrases.[9] The bold-faced VPs in examples (22)–(23) behave identically. On the other hand, VPs contained within true embedded sentences may never extrapose in that fashion:

(27) a. *For the moon **to rise over the mountain** wouldn't be surprising*
      b. **For the moon wouldn't be surprising **to rise over the mountain***

These facts illustrate another important distinction between PVCs and true embedded sentences.

The fourth kind of evidence that suggests a structural dissimilarity between PVCs and true embedded sentences has to do with the contrast in anaphoric relations illustrated by (28) and (29):

(28) a. *That **John** is fairly stupid is a fact that **he** can't bear to live with*
      b. *That **he** is fairly stupid is a fact that **John** can't bear to live with*

(29) a. ***John** playing the piano is a sight as funny as the sight of **him**
          dancing on the tables*
      b. ****Him** playing the piano is a sight as funny as the sight of **John**
          dancing on the tables*

In spite of the fact that *he* precedes *John* in (28b), an anaphoric relation between them is still possible, since *he* does not command *John*: it is contained within a preceding subordinate clause. On the other hand, if we accept the head-complement analysis proposed in this paper for PVCs, then *him* in (29b) is not contained within a subordinate clause, but is a syntactic constituent of the main clause itself. Hence, it both precedes and commands the following NP *John*, and anaphora between the two is blocked.

Evidence from Reflexivization also suggests that the head of a PVC is a member of the main clause in examples such as:

(30) a. *I saw myself (*me) trembling all over (in the mirror)*
      b. *John saw himself trembling all over (in the mirror)*
          John saw **him trembling all over (in the mirror)*

On the assumption that the reflexive form and its antecedent must be "clause-mates"—however that notion is to be expressed in syntactic theory—then the facts of (30) suggest, again, the head-complement analysis of PVCs.[10]

To sum up so far, then, we have adduced four pieces of evidence to argue for the head-compement analysis of PVCs given in (20) and (21):

(A)   The lack of such sentential markers as complementizers and auxil-
        iaries in PVCs. Our analysis has this as an automatic result, since
        NPs, unlike Ss, lack both kinds of constituent.

(B)   Facts from Number Agreement. We expect that Number Agreement
        in the matrix can be triggered by an NP within the PVC, since the
        relevant NP is the *head noun*, not an embedded subject.

(C)   Extraposition of the VP-constituent in PVCs. This fact is inconsist-
        ent with a sentential analysis of PVCs, and suggests strongly that the
        extraposable VP is in fact a complement to the head NP.

(D)   Evidence from anaphora, of the sort given in (29). The head-
        complement structure of PVCs entails that the command relations
        defined from a PVC will differ from those defined from an em-
        bedded sentence.

We take this as fairly conclusive evidence against a sentential structure for PVCs. Of
course, one might propose the following alternative: that PVCs, in deep structure,
derive from a sentential source; but that the sentential structure is later transformed
into a syntactically appropriate one (i.e., of the sort proposed here). We will consider such alternatives in section 3.

    Let us now briefly consider examples alluded to in note 6, in which the Passive
transformation has operated within the PVC:

(31)   *We saw the rebels being executed by the army*

One might argue that the presence of the so-called "passive auxiliary" *be-en* in (31)
is inconsistent with the fact that our analysis provides no node AUX under which
to attach the passive auxiliary. How, then, are sentences such as (31) generated?

    First of all, we will assume that an active–passive pair such as that given in (32)
derives from an underlying structure such as (33):

(32)   a.   *The army executed the rebels*
        b.   *The rebels were executed by the army*

(33)

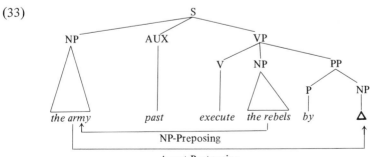

Agent Postposing

Following Chomsky (1970, 1973) and Emonds (1970), we assume that the passive
sentence is generated by the application of Agent Postposing and NP-Preposing.

When NP-Preposing applies, *be-en* is transformationally inserted. It is argued in
Akmajian and Wasow (1975), on completely independent grounds, that *be-en* is
inserted within the VP, and not under AUX. Hence, the passive structure that
results from these various operations is as follows:

(34)

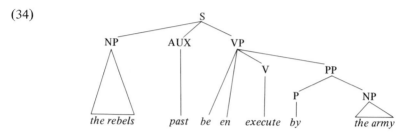

(See Akmajian and Wasow, 1975, for a detailed justification of this attachment of
be-en.)

This analysis of the passive can be extended to perception verb complements if
we assume underlying representations such as the following:[11]

(35)

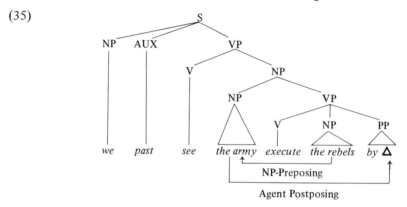

Notice that if the PS-rules generate VPs of the sort shown in (33), then such rules
will automatically generate the same VPs even when they are internal to PVCs, as
in (35). We need only assume that the crucial factorization for the operations
involved in the passive is *NP-X-V(Y)-NP-by-Δ*. That is, as long as the operations
subsumed under the "passive transformation"–i.e., Agent Postposing and NP-
preposing–do not crucially refer to AUX, or some other constituent exclusive to
sentences, then these operations will generalize to PVCs, as shown, and NPs in
general (Cf. Chomsky (1967, 1973) and Emonds (1970) for discussion of this issue).

Having discussed cases of passive PVCs, it is now relevant to consider examples
such as the following:

(36)   *We saw the rebels executed by the army*

It is tempting to postulate a rule deleting *be* (or more precisely, *being*), so that such
examples derive from fuller passive examples:

(37)   a.   *We saw the rebels **being** executed by the army*
               ↓
       b.   *We saw the rebels ∅ executed by the army*

If the putative rule, call it BE-Deletion for reference, were to generalize to cases of main verb *be* as well as passive *be*, then PVCs such as those in the following examples could be derived:

(38)   a.   *We saw Gerald Ford in a general's uniform*
       b.   cf. *Gerald Ford **was** in a general's uniform*

(39)   a.   *I've never seen John so sick*
       b.   cf. *John **was** so sick*

The (a) examples show that PVCs can contain prepositional phrases and adjective phrases following the initial NP of the complement. The (b) examples show that just these constituents are complements to the verb *be*. We might, then, assume the existence of underlying structures such as the following:

(40)   a.

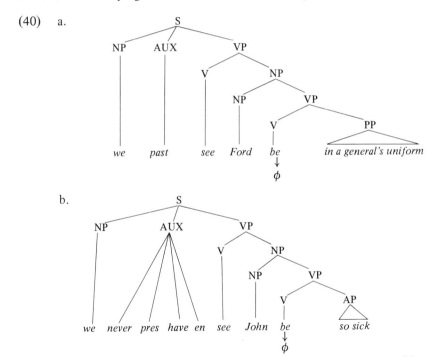

There is in fact nothing to prevent the generation of such structures, and by postulation of a rule of BE-Deletion we could account for the presence of various complements to the copula in PVCs.[12] In any event, we will return now to a discussion of PVCs with *-ing* verb forms.

We noted above, in connection with examples (22)–(26), that Extraposition from PVCs was possible. Consider now the possibility of Extraposition applying ("vacuously") in examples such as the following:

(41) a.

EXTRAPOSITION

b.

The effect of Extraposition in this example is to break up the single constituent *the moon rising over the mountain*. Although we noted earlier that PVCs are single syntactic constituents according to standard constituent structure tests, it turns out that these same tests can also be used to show that PVCs behave as though they were made up of two independent constituents. That is, what we have termed the head of the PVC can be shown to act independently of its following VP:

(42) a. *What we saw rising over the mountain was **the moon*** (Pseudo-Cleft)
      b. *It was **the moon** that we saw rising over the mountain* (Cleft)
      c. ***The moon** was seen rising over the mountain* (Passive)

In these cases, the NP *the moon* has been "clefted" independently of its VP (42a,b), and the Passive rule has fronted it independently of its VP (42c). The following shows that this NP can be deleted independently:

(43)   ***The moon** is beautiful to watch ___ rising over the mountain*
          (Object Deletion)

Unbounded movement rules can also treat this constituent as an independent element:

(44) a. *What did you see ___ rising over the mountain?* (*Wh*-Fronting)
      b. *The moon, I'd love to see ___ rising over the mountain*
          (Topicalization)

Finally, interjections of various sorts may be interpolated between the NP and its following VP:

(45)   *Observe the moon, my dear, rising over the mountain*

What would appear to be something of a syntactic paradox—i.e., that constituent structure tests show PVCs to be both single constituents and at the same time, separate, independent constituents—will follow automatically from our analysis as long as we assume that Extraposition has the effect shown in (41a,b).

So far we have considered only PVCs containing verbs with the suffix *-ing*. However, we should also note the existence of PVCs in which the verb form is the bare infinitive (i.e., tenseless) form:

(46)   a.   *We saw the moon **rise** over the mountain*
        b.   *We heard the bells **ring** at sunset*

It is interesting to note that PVCs with simple tenseless verb forms consistently test out as *nonconstituents*:

(47)   a.   **What we saw was Raquel Welch take a bath*
        b.   **It was Raquel Welch take a bath that we saw*
        c. **?We could **hear**, but we couldn't **see**, Raquel Welch take a bath*
        d.   **Raquel Welch take a bath is a breathtaking sight to see____ .*
        e.   **Raquel Welch take a bath has been witnessed by many a moviegoer*

The reader can see that adding *-ing* to the verb *take* in any of these examples will restore grammaticality. Thus, while PVCs with the *-ing* affix can either be single NP-constituents or sequences of *NP-VP*, those PVCs with plain infinitive verb forms are never constituents, but only (independent) sequences of *NP-VP*, as illustrated in (47). To account for this, we will propose that PVCs with simple tenseless verb forms originate in deep structures such as the following:[13]

(48)

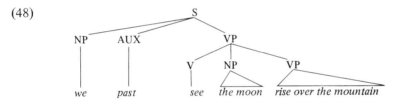

This will mean that perception verbs such as *see* and *hear* have the following subcategorization frames:

(49)   a.   [—— NP]
        b.   [—— NP VP]

Frame (49a) is that in which the PVC is a single constituent, whereas (49b) is that in which the PVC is two independent constituents.[14]

A nice result of this view is that we can account rather naturally for the presence of—or absence of—the suffix *-ing* in PVCs. That is, following Emonds (1970), we will assume that any VP immediately dominated by NP (or N̄) in deep structure automatically has *-ing* attached to it. (This is presumably also the source for *-ing* in the gerund, as in *John's driving the car*.) In contrast, a VP-complement such as that in (48) is not dominated by NP, nor is it adjacent to AUX; hence the verb form remains entirely unmodified (i.e., in its simple infinitive form). The verb morphology, then, provides confirming evidence for the view that PVCs fall into two general types, illustrated in (49).

Arguments of a formal nature i.e., arguments from syntactic constituent structure tests and from verb morphology, have led us to posit for the "infinitive" PVC a deep structure distinct from that of the "gerund" PVC. We can now ask whether there are any semantic differences between the two types of PVC as well. One semantic difference is that "infinitive" PVCs must refer to perceivable events or actions, but cannot refer to states, while "gerundive" PVCs can refer to all three:

(50)   a. $We\ saw\ John \begin{Bmatrix} looking \\ *look \end{Bmatrix} pretty\ sick$

       b. $I\ saw \begin{Bmatrix} John \\ *the\ lamp \end{Bmatrix} stand\ on\ the\ table$

A similar distinction holds between *get* and *be* passives in "infinitive" PVCs:

(51) $We\ watched\ the\ rebels \begin{Bmatrix} get \\ *be \end{Bmatrix} executed\ by\ the\ army$

As Lasnik and Fiengo (1974) point out (p. 553), the VP-complements of verbs such as *force* and *try* also exclude "stative" predicates and *be*-passives, and this seems to be a property of all "basic" (i.e., not de-sentential) VP-complements. If so, the facts in (50)–(51) will be a consequence of VP-complement structures such as that in (48), and hence, the independently determined syntactic structure for "infinitive" PVCs will predict an important semantic property of the construction.

Other semantic differences between "gerundive" and "infinitive" PVCs have been noted as well. For example, Emonds (1972b) notes that in certain specific contexts (i.e., depending on the complement verbs involved) there is a distinction between incompleted and completed action:

(52)   a.   *We watched the prisoners dying* (incompleted)
       b.   *We watched the prisoners die* (completed)

This distinction also holds for certain nonperception verbs as well:

(53)   a.   *We had them marching into the mess hall* (incompleted)
       b.   *We had them march into the mess hall* (completed)

(54)   a.   *We kept them marching into the mess hall* (incompleted)
       b.   *We made them march into the mess hall* (completed)

It appears, then, that the semantic distinction between incompleted and completed action is not restricted to perception verb contexts, but seems rather to be a function of a more general structural distinction between "gerundive" and "infinitive" verb phrase complements. Hence, we can say that at best, our syntactic analysis of PVCs predicts the semantic distinctions we have noted; at worst, our syntactic analysis seems at least consistent with the semantic distinctions that must be drawn. The important point is that the syntactic analysis has in no way been *determined* by semantic facts, and at the same time it appears that semantic facts do not disconfirm the syntactic analysis.

Notice now that while some perception verbs take either subcategorization frame (49a) or (49b), others will allow only (49a):

(55)   a.   Verbs that take both [____ NP] and [____ NP VP]:

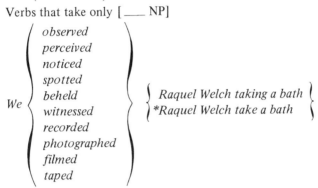

$$We \begin{Bmatrix} saw \\ heard \\ watched \\ listened\ to \end{Bmatrix} \begin{Bmatrix} Raquel\ Welch\ taking\ a\ bath \\ Raquel\ Welch\ take\ a\ bath \end{Bmatrix}$$

       b.   Verbs that take only [____ NP]

$$We \begin{Bmatrix} observed \\ perceived \\ noticed \\ spotted \\ beheld \\ witnessed \\ recorded \\ photographed \\ filmed \\ taped \end{Bmatrix} \begin{Bmatrix} Raquel\ Welch\ taking\ a\ bath \\ *Raquel\ Welch\ take\ a\ bath \end{Bmatrix}$$

Hence, the two subcategorization frames in (49) not only serve to provide two different structures for "infinitive" and "gerundive" PVCs, but they also serve to define verb classes.

It is important to note that PVCs, as we have been calling them, can also occur with predicates that are not, strictly speaking, predicates of "direct perception." For example, PVCs can occur as object complements with predicates such as the following:

(56)   a.

$$We \begin{Bmatrix} caught \\ found \\ discovered \\ came\ upon \\ filmed \\ painted \\ photographed \\ taped \\ recorded \\ imitated \\ portrayed \\ studied \end{Bmatrix} Raquel\ Welch\ taking\ a\ bath$$

PVCs can also occur as subject complements with predicates such as the following:

(57)   a.   *The NY Philharmonic playing the Internationale*
$$\begin{Bmatrix} is\ an\ impossible\ dream\ ^{15} \\ is\ a\ thrilling\ idea \\ was\ an\ experience\ we\ would\ not\ soon\ forget \end{Bmatrix}$$

It is pretty clear, then, that the complement structures we have proposed for the class of "true" perception verbs actually occur with a larger class of predicates, including predicates that are not predicates of direct perception. To the extent that this is true, our proposed structures are needed in English grammar independently of the grammar of perception predicates.

However, we must also note that there are numerous nonperception predicates which cannot co-occur with PVCs. Note the following contrasts:

(58) a. We $\begin{Bmatrix} came\ upon \\ *greeted \end{Bmatrix}$ Raquel Welch taking a bath

b. The NY Philharmonic playing the Internationale
$\begin{Bmatrix} is\ an\ impossible\ dream \\ *was\ seated\ on\ the\ stage \end{Bmatrix}$

Such facts indicate that subcategorization of these predicates must be sensitive to the *internal structure* of complements.   That is, a simple subcategorization frame such as (49a), namely [___ NP], cannot distinguish between the predicates listed above in (58). Rather, we must assume that (49a) and (49b) are restated as follows:

(59) a. [___$_{NP}$ [NP VP] $_{NP}$]
      b. [___ NP VP]

With the subcategorization features restated as in (59) we can now distinguish lexically the different verb classes which co-occur with PVCs, from those that do not (e.g., the predicate *come upon* would have the subcategorization feature [___$_{NP}$ [NP VP] $_{NP}$], while *greet* would not).

3. Some Alternatives

We have so far argued that sentences such as *We saw the moon rising over the mountain* and *we saw the moon rise over the mountain* derive from the following (syntactic) deep structures:

(60) a.

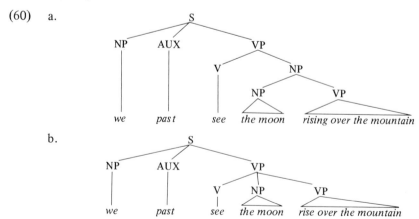

b.

Keep in mind that structures such as (60a) will be optionally transformed by Extra-position into structures such as (60b), hence "gerundive" PVCs are structurally ambiguous (though not so at the deep structure level). In the absence of evidence to the contrary, it would be conceivable, of course, that these structures represent a level of representation that is post-deep structure, i.e., that they are both derived transformationally. However, the simplest hypothesis, given the evidence so far, is that these structures are in fact deep structures, since, as far as one can tell, there are no compelling syntactic reasons to suppose that the underlying structures are any more abstract or complex.

3.1   It might be useful to illustrate what we mean by considering some possible alternative analyses for PVCs. For example, many linguists, citing the parallels in *semantic interpretation* between PVCs and sentences—e.g., in *The moon is rising* and *I saw the moon rising*, the NP *moon* is the subject of the verb *rise*—would insist that PVCs derive from a sentential source. Otherwise, the argument runs, how could such parallels in interpretation be captured? We will address this question more directly below. But here, once again, we must note that a sentential source for PVCs is syntactically quite unmotivated. To make quite sure this point is clear, suppose, once again, that one wished to maintain a sentential source for PVCs. The structural ambiguity of "gerundive" PVCs would not result from Extra-position, but rather from the application of an optional "raising" transformation, having roughly the following effect:

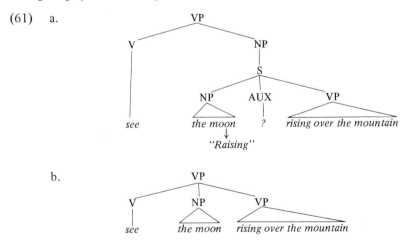

(61)   a.

b.

Ignoring problems with auxiliary elements and complementizers, we could say that if the raising rule optionally did not operate, the PVC would act as a single constit-uent; however, if the rule were to operate, then the PVC would behave as a sequence of independent constituents. This explanation might work for PVCs in object position, but any of the examples of PVCs in subject position (derived or underly-ing) will show the incorrectness of the raising hypothesis.

To see why, let us first note that PVCs in subject position are *always* single constituents, according to the standard tests. For example, corresponding to sentence (62a), we have the other sentences of (62):

(62)   a.   *The moon rising over the mountain is a beautiful sight*

      b.   *It's **the moon rising over the mountain** that's a beautiful sight*

      c.   *What's a beautiful sight is **the moon rising over the mountain***

By using clefting (as above), along with other tests, we can establish that subject PVCs are single constituents. The same tests also show that subject PVCs *cannot* be nonconstituents:

(63)   a.   **It's the moon* that rising over the mountain is a beautiful sight*

      b.   **What rising over the mountain is a beautiful sight is **the moon***

      c.   **What rising over the mountain is a beautiful sight?*

These examples show that the NP *the moon* in a subject PVC cannot be clefted or *Wh*-fronted independently of its following VP.

If PVCs in subject position are always single constituents, then such complements cannot undergo the effects of a raising rule of the sort alluded to above. Hence, subject PVCs would always remain as intact sentential subjects on the raising analysis. But precisely this has been disconfirmed by evidence we have presented above, indicating that PVCs have a head-complement structure, and not a sentential structure. For this reason the raising hypothesis cannot be correct.

3.2   Despite the defects of a sentential source for PVCs, one might be tempted to pursue this line of analysis for other reasons. That is, following Fillmore (1963) and Emonds (1970), one might argue that PVCs with -*ing* derive from underlying structures that contain the progressive, roughly on the following model:

(64)   a.   *We saw [the moon -be-rising over the mountain]*
                     ↓

      b.   *We saw [the moon rising over the mountain]*

The so-called "telescoped progressive"analysis might be correct; however, it might also be irrelevant to the question of whether PVCs derive from sentential sources. For Emonds (1970) has argued that progressive *be* is generated within the main VP-constituent of a clause, not within the AUX constituent. Hence, before the telescoped progressive analysis could be adduced in favor of a sentential source for PVCs, it would have to be shown that progressive *be* is generated only within AUX in *S*-constituents.

However, just such an argument is made in Akmajian and Wasow (1975) (i.e., that progressive *be* is generated within AUX and not VP), and for this reason we must consider the implication of the "telescoped pregressive" analysis of PVCs. I think there is some evidence that this analysis is not correct, but before considering that let us note that one reason that Fillmore cites for this general kind of analysis is that the ungrammaticality of (14) (repeated here as (65a)) will follow from the ungrammaticality of the corresponding progressive sentence, (65b):

(65) a. *I heard Mary having played my song
      b. *Mary is having played my song

Recall, however, that our syntactic analysis of PVCs automatically excludes auxiliary elements, and thus (65a) is always blocked anyway.

The basic syntactic prediction of the telescoped progressive analysis is this: that verbs that do occur in the progressive should be able to occur in PVCs, and verbs that may not occur in the progressive may not occur within PVCs. The first part of the prediction is incorrect, as it stands:

(66) a. My foot is $\left\{ \begin{matrix} bleeding \\ hurting \end{matrix} \right\}$ badly

      b. The doctor watched my foot $\left\{ \begin{matrix} bleeding \\ *hurting \end{matrix} \right\}$ badly

(67) a. They're $\left\{ \begin{matrix} looking \\ feeling \end{matrix} \right\}$ pretty sick

      b. We saw them $\left\{ \begin{matrix} looking \\ *feeling \end{matrix} \right\}$ pretty sick

(68) a. The subject is $\left\{ \begin{matrix} listening\ to \\ hearing \end{matrix} \right\}$ some noises

      b. We watched the subject $\left\{ \begin{matrix} listening\ to \\ *hearing \end{matrix} \right\}$ some noises

In (66)–(68) we see cases of verbs that do occur in the progressive (in simple sentences) and yet that may not occur in PVCs (cf. (66b)–(68b)).

However, this is not a counterexample to the telescoped progressive analysis. These examples simply illustrate the fact that *any* syntactic analysis of PVCs— telescoped progressive or not—will be subject to an independent *semantic* constraint to the effect that only verbs denoting perceivable phenomena can be properly interpreted in PVCs. The verbs in the PVCs in the starred examples of (66)–(68) do not denote perceivable states, but rather denote internal "private" states that are not physically perceivable in any *direct* way by external persons. If this is indeed the basis for the ill-formedness of the starred examples above, then surely we are dealing with a semantic restriction and not a syntactic one, i.e., we are framing our proposed explanation of ill-formedness in terms of the nature of perception, and not in terms of the grammar of perception verbs in the English language. Since the putative semantic explanation in this case seems to cut across the syntactic analyses we are discussing, it will not help in choosing between syntactic analyses. Hence, among the syntacticically well-formed PVC-structures generated by any plausible syntactic grammar of PVCs will be found certain PVC constructions that receive either an anomalous interpretation, or no interpretation at all.

Turning now to the second prediction of the telescoped progressive analysis (i.e., that verbs that cannot occur in the progressive may not occur in PVCs), it turns out that this prediction, too, is incorrect, and this is in fact a counterexample to the proposal. To see how, consider the verbs *picture* and *see*, as used in examples such as the following:

(69)   a.
        I just can't picture John $\left\{ \begin{array}{l} \textit{owning a mansion} \\ \textit{knowing the answer} \\ \textit{weighing 300 lbs.} \end{array} \right\}$
       b.   *I just can't see myself needing any more drugs*

In these examples, of a sort first noted in Rosenbaum (1967), *picture* and *see* have
a sense akin to the verb *to imagine*. Examples such as the following show that their
complements have a PVC-structure:

(70)   a.   *What I just can't picture is **John weighing 300 lbs***
       b.   ***John weighing 300 lbs** is pretty hard to picture*
       c.   *I just can't picture **myself** owning a mansion*
       d.   ***John** is pretty hard to picture **weighing 300 lbs***

Examples (70a,b) show that the complement of *picture* is a single NP-constituent;
(70c) shows that the complement cannot be a gerund (i.e., poss-ing) clause, given
the following contrasts with that example:

(71)   a.   **I just can't picture my owning a mansion*
       b.   cf. *I regret my owning a mansion* (true gerund)
       c.   cf. **I regret myself owning a mansion*

The complement of *picture* in (71a) cannot take the plain genitive *my*, as a true
gerund does (cf. (71b)). On the other hand, a true gerund such as (71b), does not
allow the reflexive *myself* (cf. (71c)), whereas the PVC does (cf. (70c)). Finally,
extraposition of the complement in (70d) reveals a diagnostic property of PVCs,
not shared by gerunds.

   Granting that the verb complements in the examples of (69) are true PVCs, note
now that the verbs within them do not occur in the progressive:

(72)   a.   **John is owning a mansion*
       b.   **John is knowing the answer*
       c.   **John is weighing 300 lbs*
       d.   **I am needing more drugs*

Hence, the telescoped progressive analysis would incorrectly exclude the examples
of (69) as ungrammatical, given that the examples of (72) are ungrammatical. Our
analysis, however, predicts that the examples of (69) are grammatical, since it does
not entail that the complement verbs co-occur with the progressive verb *be*. Other
examples on a par with (69) can also be constructed:

(73) $\left\{ \begin{array}{l} \textit{John owning a mansion} \\ \textit{John knowing the answer} \\ \textit{John weighing 300 lbs.} \end{array} \right\}$ *is an impossible dream*

Again, granting that the subject complements here are PVCs (cf. example (57)), the
telescoped progressive analysis would incorrectly exclude the sentences of (73),
whereas the PVC-analysis presented here would not. To sum up, we take the
examples of (69)–(73) as evidence against the telescoped progressive analysis, and

until further evidence can be adduced, we find no syntactic reason to suppose that PVCs contain progressive *be* in underlying structure.

If what we have said so far is correct, then the result meshes nicely with the syntactic analysis of the auxiliary system presented in Akmajian and Wasow (1975). That paper argues that while auxiliary *have* and progressive *be* are generated under the AUX node in deep structure, the main verb *be* and the passive auxiliary verb *be* are dominated by the main VP-node. It is precisely the latter two—i.e., main verb *be* and passive *be*—that occur overtly in PVCs, whereas auxiliary *have* and progressive *be* never occur overtly in PVCs. This is just what would be predicted on the hypothesis advanced in Akmajian and Wasow (1975), since PVCs contain VPs but not AUX.

3.3   Turning now to other alternative analyses of PVC-constructions, one might well be led to consider the Katz–Postal "paraphrase strategy" more explicitly, for so far we have only discussed the possibility of a sentential source for PVCs (and additionally, a possible progressive source) without making explicit reference to semantic paraphrases. Given that the Katz–Postal strategy has become so widely accepted, it would indeed by interesting to pursue a paraphrase analysis of PVCs.

Note that in our analysis of PVCs so far we have not considered semantic evidence as a determining factor of the analysis. However, keep in mind that we are now going to explore a research strategy that explicitly demands semantic information as part of the heuristic procedure. Hence, in this section, we not only can, but we must, consider semantic evidence for given analyses of PVCs, since that is what the strategy—to be rejected later on—calls for.

An obvious candidate for a paraphrastic source for sentences with PVCs involves sentences which contain *while*-clauses, as in the following:[17]

(74)   a.   *We saw the moon while it was rising over the mountain*
                         ↓
        b.   *We saw the moon rising over the mountain*

(75)   a.   *The moon (,) while it is rising over the mountain (,) is a*
                 beautiful sight
                                      ↓
        b.   *The moon rising over the mountain is a beautiful sight*

The details of this putative transformational process are obscure and probably complex. Regardless of such details, the analysis fails for a number of reasons.

In the first place, the *while*-clause analysis gives no source for sentences such as those in (76):

(76)   a.   *The moons of Jupiter rotating in their orbits have been a*
                 wondrous sight for many centuries

        b.
              The moons of Jupiter (,) while they $\left\{ \begin{array}{l} *are \\ *were \\ *have\ been \end{array} \right\}$ *rotating in*
              their orbits (,) have been a wondrous sight for many centuries

Secondly, numerous sentences with *while*-clauses that are semantically well-formed have no well-formed PVC-counterparts:

(77) a. *We watched John while he was hearing noises*
      b. **We watched John hearing noises*

(78) a. *They were looking at me while I was feeling that pain in my foot*
      b. **They were looking at me feeling that pain in my foot*

Thirdly, as Mike Harnish has pointed out to me (personal communication), there are numerous examples wherein sentences with *while*-clauses and sentences with superficially similar PVCs have quite distinct meanings. Consider, for example, the following:

(79) a. *We saw John while he was dying of cancer*
      b. *We saw John dying of cancer*

Sentence (79b) is true only if we perceived both John and his dying at the time referred to in the sentence. On the other hand, sentence (79a) could be true even if we had no idea of John's malady at the time we saw him. The following contrast illustrates these interpretations quite nicely:[18]

(80) a. *We saw John while he was dying of cancer, but we had no idea*
          that he was dying of cancer (at that time)
      b. **We saw John dying of cancer, but we had no idea that he was*
          dying of cancer (at that time)

Hence, the material contained within the *while*-clause ("he was dying of cancer") need not form any part of the perception referred to in the main clause ("we saw John"). On the other hand, in the PVC-construction, the entire PVC ("John dying of cancer") must be understood as part of the direct perception of the subject (more on this aspect of interpretation below).[19] In any event, what intially seemed like a fairly plausible semantic paraphrase for PVC sentences has turned out to be semantically quite inappropriate.

The *while*-clause analysis for PVC-constructions also runs into syntactic problems, in that PVCs can be single constituents (and in subject position, they are only single constituents), whereas an NP followed by a modifying *while*-clause is a sequence of two constituents. This can be shown by the usual syntactic constituent tests:

(81) a. **It was the moon, while it was rising over the mountain, that we saw*
      b.*?*You can see, but you can't hear, the moon, while it is rising*
          over the mountain[20]

3.4   Continuing in our search for paraphrastic sources for PVCs, we might assume that PVCs derive from nominalizations with abstract head nouns of perceptions, such as *sight, sound*, etc.:[21]

(82)   a.   *We saw **the sight of** the moon rising over the mountain*

                             ↓

      b.   *We saw the moon rising over the mountain*

The transformational machinery involved in this analysis would again be complex. But the machinery is quite necessary, in that a structural source with the properties of (82a) would be syntactically inappropriate, i.e., it could not account for the Number Agreement or Extraposition facts we have previously discussed:

(83)   a.   *The sight of the moons of Jupiter rotating in their orbits*
              is (*are) a beautiful sight (cf. (16))

      b.   *What we saw **was** (*were) the sight of the moons of Jupiter*
              rotating in their orbits (cf. (19))

(84)   a.   *The sight of the moon rising over the mountain is spectacular*
      b.   **The sight of the moon is spectacular rising over the mountain*
          (cf. (22)–(23))

In other words, the abstract nominal structure does not allow Number Agreement or Extraposition, both of which, as we have seen, are triggered by true PVCs. Hence, on this hypothesis, the noun that is the head in underlying structure (*sight*) must be deleted, and the noun embedded in underlying structure (*the moon*) must be transformed into the new head of the NP, with the remainder of the nominal becoming its complement, i.e., the structure underlying (82a) must be converted into a structure like our (60a).

More seriously, the actual nature of the head of the abstract nominal source is quite unclear. For example, consider the implication of the following sentence:

(85)   *You can **see**, but you can't **hear**, the moon rising over the mountain*

This sentence, involving Right Node Raising, cannot derive from either of the following sources:

(86)   a.   **You can see **the sight of the moon rising over the mountain**, but you*
              *can't hear **the sight of the moon rising over the mountain***

      b.   *You can see **the sight of the moon rising over the mountain**, but you*
              *can't hear **the sound of the moon rising over the mountain***

The rule of Right Node Raising requires identical constituents in both clauses as part of its input. In (86a) the nominal objects of *see* and *hear* are identical, but in the case of *hear* the nominal object is semantically inappropriate. In (86b), where the object of *hear* is appropriate, the nominals in the two clauses are no longer identical. Hence, one of two conclusions follow: (a) that the superstructure of the nominal underlying the PVC is deleted and reorganized prior to the rule of Right Node Raising, or (b) the head of the abstract nominal is not literally *sight, sound*, or any other existing lexical item, but is some general proform for perception nouns that never appears on the surface of the language.[22] Whichever conclusion is correct, the important point to notice is that underlying structures such as (82a) are *syntactically* unmotivated, in that the specific underlying structure, proposed for essentially semantic reasons, must be destroyed and reorganized at some early stage in order to provide for a syntactically correct input to rules such as Number Agreement, Extraposition, and Right Node Raising.

Notice further that there are nonperception verbs which also co-occur with PVCs, as we have seen. The abstract nominal analysis would exclude all such cases, since the nonperception verbs never occur with perception nominals:

(87) a.

We
$\left\{\begin{array}{l}\textit{discovered}\\\textit{found}\\\textit{filmed}\\\textit{painted}\\\textit{photographed}\end{array}\right\}$
the moon rising over the mountain

b.

*We
$\left\{\begin{array}{l}\textit{discovered}\\\textit{found}\\\textit{filmed}\\\textit{painted}\\\textit{photographed}\end{array}\right\}$
the sight of the moon rising over the mountain

The verbs in (87a) may occur with PVCs, but never co-occur with abstract perception nominals, as shown in (87b) and in simple sentences such as the following:

(88)

*We
$\left\{\begin{array}{l}\textit{discovered}\\\textit{found}\\\textit{filmed}\\\textit{painted}\\\textit{photographed}\end{array}\right\}$
the sight

Perhaps a more serious flaw in the abstract nominal analysis of PVCs is that it entails that a simple sentence such as (89a) would have to derive from a source such as (89b):

(89) a. *We saw the moon*
      b. *We saw the sight of the moon*

Hence, every simple perception sentence (i.e., a sentence in which the perception verb has a simple NP-object) would derive from the abstract nominal source, and in every case the abstract head noun would have to be transformationally deleted. (Notice that if one wanted to avoid this consequence by arguing that simple sentences, such as (89a), were not in fact analyzed along the lines of the abstract nominal deep structure, then there would be no justification for analyzing the more complex cases along these lines.) This analysis not only imposes unnecessary complexity on our analysis of simple sentences such as (89a), but there are also cases in which the analysis leads to semantic anomaly:

(90) a. *My host showed me his pornographic magazines*
      b.*#*My host showed me the sight of his pornographic magazines*

In my judgment, (90b) is semantically anomalous or simply meaningless. In all, I can find little justification—either syntactic or semantic—for the abstract nominal analysis.

3.5   To recapitulate the theme of this section, we have posited structures such as (60a) and (60b) as the underlying forms for sentences with PVCs, essentially on the grounds that such structures represent the minimal hypothesis (i.e., the one involving the least amount of grammatical machinery) consistent with the syntactic facts of the situation. A number of initially plausible alternatives (some of which are designed to capture more "semantic" facts) have been shown to be more complex and empirically invalid, a result which further confirms the analysis arrived at here.

It is very tempting at this point to argue that we have invalidated the Katz–Postal research strategy given at the beginning of this paper. Indeed, the "paraphrase strategy" has apparently led to consistently wrong results in our effort to discover the deep structure for PVCs: no "semantically based" analysis of PVCs that I am aware of is empirically adequate on wider investigation. However, there is a sense in which we have not demonstrated any negative consequence of adopting the K–P strategy, since we have shown that the initially plausible "paraphrases" for PVC-constructions have not turned out to be paraphrases at all—and thus we have not really followed the K–P strategy. But this is perhaps an interesting point: namely, that we have not been able to find any adequate paraphrase for the PVC-construction that might begin to serve as an underlying form for the construction. The evidence we have examined suggests the possibility that there are no *true* paraphrases at all for the PVC-constructions we have been studying. Hence, it might be the case that the Katz–Postal heuristic strategy is simply incoherent, since it is based on a dubious and possibly nonexistent concept ("paraphrase").

4.   The Analysis of PVCs in an Autonomous Syntax Framework

We have argued for our analysis of PVCs on purely syntactic grounds (i.e., from facts manifested by constituent structure tests, and rules such as Number Agreement and Extraposition; hence, from simplicity of the overall system of syntactic rules), and we have made no explicit attempt to link the syntactic analysis of PVCs with a semantic or logical analysis of them. However, it would be a mistake to conclude from this that the semantic analysis of PVCs is totally irrelevant to the syntactic analysis. Although no semantic concepts have entered into the determination of the structure of PVCs on our analysis, it would be rather surprising to claim that the formal analysis had no relation whatever to the semantic analyis of PVCs. Along more general lines, Chomsky (1957, p. 102) has noted:

(91)   The fact that correspondences between formal and semantic features exist, however, cannot be ignored. These correspondences should be studied in some more general theory of language that will include a theory of linguistic form and a theory of the use of language as subparts . . . . Having determined the syntactic structure of the language, we can study the way in which this syntactic structure is put to use in the actual functioning of the language . . . . We can judge formal

theories in terms of their ability to explain and clarify a variety of facts about the way in which sentences are used and understood. In other words, we should like the syntactic framework of the language that is isolated and exhibited by the grammar to be able to support semantic description, and we shall naturally rate more highly a theory of formal structure that leads to grammars that meet this requirement more fully."

And again (1975, 94):

(92)   To show this strong (autonomy) thesis to be false, it will not suffice, then, to show that there are systematic relations between semantic and syntactic notions. This assumption is not and has never been in question; on the contrary, it was formulated explicitly in conjunction with the thesis of absolute autonomy (of syntax). It would be surprising indeed to find important formal elements that are devoid of semantic import . . . . Rather, the crucial question is whether these systematic relations involving the full range of semantic concepts enter into the *determination* (and perhaps the function) of the categories and rules of formal grammar, or whether they simply *set conditions on the construction of a theory of linguistic form*. [italics mine, AA]

The syntactic analysis we have proposed for PVCs does relate in fact in interesting ways to an informal semantic description of these complements, and we will discuss aspects of this relationship here. However, it should be noted at the outset that we will consider only a fragment of the semantic analysis of perception verbs, which is a formidable topic, both in linguistic and philosophical semantics (see Gee (1975) for a detailed survey and discussion of important ideas in the semantics of perception verbs). Further, this paper makes no contribution to the problem of arriving at a "semantic representation" of sentences with perception verbs. The very concept of semantic representation is itself a controversial issue, and at the present time in linguistics there is no firmly established semantic theory or theory of semantic representation.[23] It is fairly clear that syntactic structure will play a role in the overall determination of the meaning and use of sentences; but it is far from clear exactly how this will be done, and exactly what a "semantic representation" might look like.

We will limit ourselves to a discussion of two topics relevant to the semantic interpretation of PVCs: (a) the distinction between "direct" and "indirect" perception, and (b) the notion "subject of" as it applies to PVCs. Beginning with (a), let us first of all note the contrast, often cited, between sentences such as the following:

(93)   a.   *I saw the moon*
       b.   *I saw that the moon was rising*

When *see* (or a similar perception verb) occurs with a simple direct object, as in (93a), the interpretation is one of "direct perception," i.e., (93a) is true only if I directly perceived (i.e., actually saw) the moon. On the other hand, when *see* occurs with a sentential complement, as in (93b), the interpretation is that of "indirect perception"; i.e., (93b) can be true even if I never saw the moon itself, but only inferred its presence by means of indirect evidence. Indeed, a similar contrast between direct and indirect perception is manifested in certain other perception verbs as well:

(94)   a.   *I could hear John*
        b.   *I could hear that John was singing*

(95)   a.   *I could feel John*
        b.   *I could feel that John was near me*

In (94b) it is not necessary that I heard John directly (for example, it might be the case that every time John sings in the apartment below me, the windows in my own apartment rattle); and in (95b) it is not necessary that I felt John (directly).

Incidentally, the interpretation of indirect perception is not dependent upon the perception verb occurring with a tensed clause. Infinitival complements (presumably de-sentential) will also lead to this sort of interpretation:[24]

(96)   a.   *We saw him to be a complete charlatan*
        b.   *He was seen to be a complete charlatan*

(97)   *I felt him to be a rather timid individual*

The constructions in (96) and (97) are quite reminiscent of the accusative-infinitive (i.e., "raising") construction, and are probably derived in an analogous manner.

Given what we have said so far, it appears that the following two types of structure are necessary:

(98)   a.   *Direct Perception*

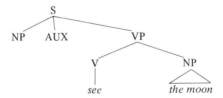

        b.   *Indirect Perception*

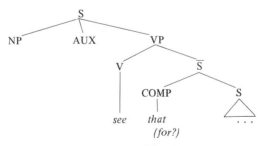

The relevant generalization, then, is this: (a) when perception verbs occur with a simple NP-direct object in deep structure, the interpretation is one of direct perception; (b) when perception verbs occur with sentential complements in deep structure, the interpretation is one of indirect perception.

If these generalizations are valid, then the prediction embodied in our proposed structure for PVCs is that such complements should have the direct perception interpretation:

(99)   a.   *"Gerund" PVC:*

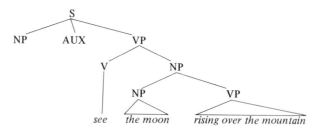

b.   *"Infinitive" PVC:*

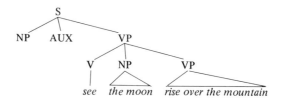

On our analysis of PVCs, the NP occupying the position of *the moon* in (99a–b) is not an embedded subject, but is rather a direct object of the main verb *see*, i.e., is a constituent of the *main clause*, not a separate embedded clause. Hence, the prediction is that perception verbs with PVC-structures should be parallel with the simple direct object structures in having a direct perception interpretation—a prediction that is correct. Further, we predict that PVC-structures should not have the interpretation that sentential complements do—again correct.

Earlier in this paper we argued against a sentential source for PVCs on syntactic grounds. Now we can bring in a new argument against a sentential source for PVCs. Consider again the following putative deep structure for the sentence *we saw the moon rising over the mountain*:

(100)

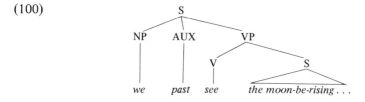

Aside from the fact that this sort of structure is syntactically incorrect, it also fails to mesh in any reasonable way with the semantic description of PVCs, i.e., it makes the wrong semantic predictions. If our generalizations about direct and indirect perception are correct, then structure (100) should receive the interpretation of indirect perception, given that the perception verb has a sentential complement. This is clearly false. Perhaps even more seriously, structure (100) would appear to receive an incoherent or anomalous semantic interpretation due to the fact that the object of *see* in this case is semantically an abstract, nonreferential proposition (i.e., the proposition *The moon is rising over the mountain*). I take it as obvious that when we see the moon rising we surely see the moon (as it rises), we do not see the abstract proposition that the moon is rising.

The analysis we have proposed for PVCs on syntactic grounds has turned out to make correct semantic predictions; and the analysis of PVCs that at first seems so plausible, i.e., a sentential source, turns out to be wrong not only on syntactic grounds, but for semantic reasons as well. Yet, there are parallels between the interpretation of PVCs and related full sentences, as with the following pair:

(101) a. ***The moon is rising over the mountain***
            *We saw **the moon rising over the mountain***

In both the full sentence and in the PVC the understood grammatical relations are identical (i.e., *moon* is the subject of *rising*). Since we have ruled out the possibility that PVCs derive from underlying sentential clauses, we cannot appeal to the definition of "subject of" given in *Aspects*. On our analysis, the NP *the moon* is not the leftmost deep structure NP in an S. How, then, can we properly identify this NP as being the subject of the VP that follows it?

I propose that for given lexical entries of verbs that take complex complements, there exist lexical redundancy rules that specify networks of grammatical relations for the verbs. For example, the lexical redundancy rule that is relevant here would be as follows:

$$(102) \qquad [NP^1\_\_ \ NP^2 \ VP^1] \rightarrow [NP^1 \qquad NP^2 \qquad {}_{VP^1}[V \ X]_{VP^1} \ ]$$

$$\underset{\text{SUB \ OBJ}}{\underbrace{\qquad}} \quad \underset{\text{SUB}}{\underbrace{\qquad}}$$

This rule is to be interpreted as follows: for all verbs with the subcategorization feature $[NP^1\_\_ \ NP^2 \ VP^1]$ [25], interpret NP^1 as the subject of the verb that fills the __ slot, interpret NP^2 as the object of the verb that fills the __ slot, and also interpret NP^2 as the subject of the main verb of the following VP^1. Thus, given a certain syntactic subcategorization feature, the redundancy rule establishes a network of grammatical relations that is to be associated with that particular feature.[26] The redundancy rule given in (102) will not only be relevant to verbs of the perception class and others we have cited in the nonperception class that take PVCs, but will also generalize to the verb class(es) including *force, persuade, help, make, let,* and so on, as in *We let him eat the cake*.

We are essentially proposing, then, that the definition of grammatical relations given in *Aspects* should be replaced by a system in which networks of grammatical relations are lexically specified for given classes of verbs. It will probably be the case that NP^1 and NP^2 in any subcategorization feature will always be interpreted as subject and object, respectively, of the verb that fills the __ slot. Hence, this information probably does not need to be listed in (102), but will be derived by an even more general redundancy rule. Notice that since subcategorization features refer to deep structure constituent positions, "logical" grammatical relations will essentially still be defined on deep structures. Further, since the information available to the determination of grammatical relations is limited entirely to subcategorization features, it will be the case that the NPs that a verb is strictly subcategorized for are those NPs that bear a basic grammatical relation to it, and vice versa. In this system it will be impossible to define grammatical relations in any wider way, e.g., it will be impossible to define a grammatical relation for the NP *5 o'clock* in *I saw John at 5 o'clock*, since the temporal phrase is not part of the subcategorization feature of *see*. Although our proposal for the determination of grammatical relations must be subjected to a good deal of testing (especially cross-linguistically), we have at least been able to specify a procedure for defining grammatical relations as precise as that given in *Aspects*.[27]

Given that there is a means of specifying the subject status of the relevant NP within the PVC, a number of facts will fall into place. First of all, there are verbs, such as the weather verbs, that take idiosyncratic subjects:

(103)   *It rained yesterday*

(104)   *I saw it raining yesterday*

This kind of phenomenon might once have been assumed to argue for a sentential source for PVCs, as follows: since weather verbs require *it* in subject position, then *it* must be a subject in the deep structure of (104), therefore the PVC must have a sentential source, since only sentences have subjects. But we have shown that the last step in unwarranted. Since we can identify *it* in (104) as a deep subject, we can still maintain the restriction that weather verbs require *it* as subject, even though the PVC is not sentential in nature.

Secondly, there is an interesting aspect of the semantic interpretation of PVCs that has been pointed out by Gee (1975, p. 306 ff.), illustrated by examples such as the following:

(105)   *I felt John hitting me with a rock*

According to his interpretation of this sentence, I didn't necessarily feel John, but rather I felt *John hitting*. In other words, Gee points out that it is a general property of PVCs that in some sense it is what is denoted by the entire PVC *as a whole* that we interpret as being perceived. Thus, in a sentence such as,

(106)   *I could smell the toaster burning the toast*

we do not necessarily smell just the toaster, but in some sense we smell whatever is denoted by the entire expression *the toaster burning the toast* (as a single semantic unit). Notice that these examples in no way affect our previous discussion of direct versus indirect perception. In both (105) and (106) the interpretation is definitely one of direct perception, as we would predict. However, Gee's observations show that in determining *what* is directly perceived, we cannot simply say that it is the direct object of the perception verb. Rather, it is what is denoted by the direct object in combination with its associated VP as a semantic unit.

What leads to this sort of interpretation? Why should PVCs be "semantic units" in this sense? The answer seems to be that the subject relation that holds between the NP of the PVC and its following VP causes the PVC to be interpreted as a "unit" in the sense described. If this is the case, we now have more of a basis for explaining the semantic differences between examples such as the following, examined earlier:

(107)   a.   *We saw John while he was dying of cancer*
        b.   *We saw John dying of cancer*

Recall that the content of the *while*-clause need not be part of the perception involved in (107a); however, in (107b), the sentence is true only if we perceived what is denoted by the entire expression *John dying of cancer*. This correlates with the generalization stated at the beginning of this paragraph: in (107b) *John* is assigned by rule (102) as the direct object of *see* and as the subject of *die*; hence, the interpretation of a "semantic unit" *John dying* . . . . On the other hand, in (107a), *John* is the direct object of *see* but is not the subject of *die*, in that it is not even a constituent of the clause containing *die*, and bears no grammatical relations whatever to the *while*-clause or its constituents. Of course, since we interpret *John* and *he* as anaphorically related, and since *he* is the subject of *die*, then, by inference, *John* is semantically associated with *die*. But the relation is clearly an extended, indirect one, and no direct grammatical relation can be said to hold between *John* and *die*. The difference in interpretation of the cases given in (107) seems to correlate nicely with the assignment of grammatical relations in the two cases.

An adequate treatment of the semantics of perception verbs is beyond the scope of this work, but we have at least been able to show, albeit informally, how two important aspects of the interpretation of PVCs, (i.e., the contrast between direct and indirect perception, and the assignment of subject status to the relevant NP within the PVC) relate to the syntactic structure we have proposed. Our aim has been to at least suggest informally how the syntactic analysis might "link up" with a semantic description of PVCs.

In conclusion, I hope to have shown that the required underlying structure of PVCs is one in which the PVC has a head-complement analysis, and not a sentential analysis; that the correct underlying structure is determined by purely syntactic, formal evidence, and that semantic facts do not play a crucial role in arriving at this structure; and finally, that the independently motivated syntactic structure seems to provide an adequate basis for certain important aspects of the semantic description of PVCs. In light of the widely (and uncritically) accepted doctrine that grammars are "semantically based," the analysis of even one construction within an autonomous syntax framework is an important step in establishing the autonomy thesis.

Acknowledgments

I am grateful to Peter Culicover, Jim Gee, Susan Steele, Tom Wasow, Frank Heny, Ray Jackendoff, Joe Emonds, Adrienne Lehrer, Mike Harnish, James McCawley, and Dwight Bolinger for invaluable comments on earlier versions of this work. Only the author is responsible for errors, however. The research contained in this paper was supported in part by Fellowship F-74-106 from the National Endowment for the Humanities. Part of the research contained here was presented in a paper to the winter meeting of the Linguistic Society of America, San Franciso, December 1975.

Notes

1. Other verbs of relevance here include *watch, notice, look at, spot, listen to, witness, behold, perceive, record, photograph, film, tape, study, imitate, portray, catch, discover,* and *find.* Barring idiosyncracies of subcategorization of individual lexical items, any of these predicates could be substituted for *see* or *hear* in the examples of this paper.

2. The syntactic constituent tests we refer to in this paper have been discussed at length in a wide range of papers in the transformational literature, and we will assume familiarity with these tests here. Recent textbooks that discuss constituent structure tests include Bach (1974); and Akmajian and Heny (1975).

3. For discussion of the rule of Right Node Raising, and its use as a constituent structure test, see Postal (1974a) and Bresnan (1974).

4. For a detailed discussion of this rule see Lasnik and Fiengo (1974). Incidentally, the use of Object Deletion as a constituent structure test is just as valid if the rule turns out to be a movement rule (akin to "Tough Movement").

5. More accurately, both PPs and NPs may occur in clefted position, but in (10a) it is obviously an NP that has been clefted. See Emonds (1970), (1972b).

6. Despite this fact, in Fillmore (1963) PVCs are analyzed as deriving from underlying sentential sources that contain the progressive auxiliary, an analysis later elaborated by Emonds (1970). We will discuss the defects of the "telescoped progressive" analysis in section 3. An apparent problem for our analysis can be found in sentences in which the Passive transformation has applied *within* the PVC, as in *We saw the rebels being executed by the army.* If, as we shall claim, there is no auxiliary structure within PVCs, how, then, can the passive auxiliary *be* appear in sentences such as the one just cited? We will address this issue below.

7. Sentences such as *I suddenly saw that I had been wrong about her,* contain perception verbs with the complementizer *that.* However, as discussed in sections 3 and 4, this usage of perception verbs is that of cognition or indirect perception, not direct perception (with which we are concerned here).

8. Some informants have indicated to me that number agreement in examples such as (15) and (16) can optionally be singular as well, and hence such speakers accept both plural and singular verb forms in the relevant cases. The important point is that such speakers still *allow* plural number agreement, and hence the argument here is not affected.

9. A discussion of the restrictions on extraposition of such complements can be found in Akmajian (1975).

10. The "clause-mate" idea is specifically rejected in the framework of Chomsky (1973). Nevertheless, taken in conjunction with facts such as (29b), the reflexive facts of (30) are supportive of the view I am arguing for.

11. To be more specific, we assume that the affix *-ing* is inserted into any VP directly dominated by NP or $\bar{\text{N}}$. Hence, the complement structure of (35) is more accurately shown below, with an indication of how the Passive operates:

    (i)

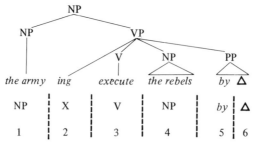

(ii)

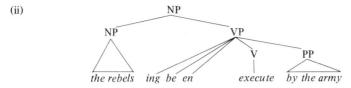

The rule of Affix Hopping on (ii) produces the correct results.

12. I am grateful to James McCawley for brining the BE-Deletion possibility to my attention. This possibility is also discussed by Gee (1975), who takes up in detail the problems connected with BE-Deletion.

13. This same structure for "infinitive" PVCs is also proposed by Gee (1975, Chapter 6).

14. In spite of the fact that "infinitive" PVCs are structured as in (48), i.e., as a sequence of independent constituents NP–VP, the object NP may not be fronted by the Passive transformation:

    (i) a.   *They saw John read the book*
        b.   **John was seen read the book*

15. I am grateful to Joe Emonds for bringing this example to my attention, and for valuable discussion on ideas connected with subcategorization of PVCs.

16. This is argued for independently by Bresnan (1972).

17. I have chosen examples with "full" adverbial clauses, i.e., clauses that contain subjects, rather than examples with subjectless clauses, given that for our purposes subjectless adverbials have the wrong interpretation, as seen in examples such as the following:

    (i)   *I saw the moon while rising over the mountain*

If (i) is possible at all, it can only have the interpretation wherein I, and not the moon, rise over the mountain.

18. These examples are due to Make Harnish.

19. This contrast is brought out in an interesting way in examples such as *I felt my hand hurting* versus *I felt my hand while it was hurting.*

20. The arguments given in this section will also carry over to other adverbial sources for PVCs, such as the following possibility:

    (i) a.   *I saw John in the process of crawling over the wall*
              ↓
        b.   *I saw John*   ϕ   *crawling over the wall*

The source given in (1a) not only runs into the kinds of problems we have mentioned with respect to the *while*-source, but also the following sort of problem:

    (ii) a.   *I saw the lamp standing on the table*
        b.   **I saw the lamp in the process of standing on the table*

21. An analysis similar to this is suggested in Newmeyer (1969).

22. The same sort of argument can be made with examples involving conjunction, as in:

I neither saw, nor heard, $\left\{ \begin{array}{l} \textit{*the sight of} \\ \textit{*the sound of} \end{array} \right\}$ *the dog barking*

23. Although a unified level of "semantic representation" has been tacitly assumed in the majority of linguistic research in recent years, the psychological reality of such a notion has recently been questioned by Fodor, Fodor, and Garrett (1975).

24. Such cases of direct versus indirect perception are discussed at length by Bolinger (1974), who uses the terms "concept" versus "percept."

25. This also includes the subcategorization feature $[NP^1 \underline{\quad\quad} _{NP}[NP^2 \ VP^1]_{NP}]$.

We assume the following convention: if the redundancy rule mentions a subcategorization feature without internal bracketing, then any feature with a matching linear order of constituents will be relevant to the rule, including features with internal bracketing. But, if a redundancy rule should mention a feature with internal bracketing, we assume that the rule would not generalize to cases without that bracketing.

26. Following Jackendoff (1972) we also assume that a network of so-called "thematic relations" is lexically associated with the network of assigned grammatical relations.

27. Keep in mind that the grammatical relations assigned by (102) are "deep" or "logical" grammatical relations. Syntactically, the NP *the moon* in *I saw the moon rising* is a syntactic direct object (of *see*), and not a syntactic subject. Rule (102) assigns it "logical subject" status, not syntactic subject status.

COMMENTS ON THE PAPER BY AKMAJIAN

James Paul Gee

Department of Linguistics
Stanford University
Stanford, California

1.   Akmajian starts out by telling us what PVCs (perception verb complements) are not.[1] Among the things he mentions that they are not are the following:

(1)   Restrictive Relative Clauses
(2)   Appositive Relative Clauses
(3)   Gerunds
(4)   (Reduced) *While/When* Clauses
(5)   Underlying Nominalizations

Akmajian gives syntactic evidence that PVCs are not any of the above five structures.[2] Another piece of syntactic evidence can be added against (4). One cannot make a question out of *while-* or *when*-clauses, nor out of structures that appear to be reduced version of these:

(6)   *What did the policeman shoot John $\left\{ \begin{array}{c} while \\ when \end{array} \right\}$ he was crossing?*

(7)   *What did the policeman shoot John crossing?*

(8)   *What was John shot crossing?*

but you can make a question out of the VPs of PVCs:

(9)   *What did the policeman see John crossing?*

(10)   *What did the policeman see John cross?*

(11)   *What was John seen crossing?*

Akmajian argues that PVCs of the form "the moon rising over the mountain" are (1) single constituents (on evidence from Pseudo-Clefts, Equative "Colon" Constructions, and Right Node Raising) and (2) single NP-constituents (on evidence from Clefts, Object Deletion, Passive, and the fact that they occur in deep structure NP-positions).

He goes on to argue that they have the structure in (12), not that in (13), on the basis of (1) lack of auxiliary verbs; (2) lack of overt complementizers; (3) number agreement facts, and (4) extraposition of the VP from the head of the larger NP:

(12)

(13)   NP
                                                            |
                                                            S

Akmajian acknowledges that while GPVCs like "the moon rising over the mountain" do behave like constituents, they also do *not* behave like constituents. To resolve this paradox, Akmajian appeals to extraposition, applied vacuously, to go from a structure like that in (14) to one like that in (15):

(14)   ⇒   (15)

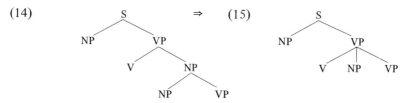

The same tests that show GPVCs are constituents show that they also are not, e.g.:

(16)   a.   *It was the moon rising over the mountain that we saw.*

       b.   *It was the moon that we saw rising over the mountain.*

Other tests, besides Clefting, are Pseudo-Cleft, Passive, Object Deletion, *Wh*-Fronting, Topicalization, and Interjections. These same tests show that IPVCs are *always not* constituents (they always have structures like that in (15) above), as does their failure to occur in deep subject positions:[3]

(17)   a.   **It was the moon rise over the mountain that we saw.*
       b.   *It was the moon that we saw rise over the mountain.*

(18)   **The moon rise over the mountain is a beautiful sight (to see___).*

2.   I will not question for now the status of Akmajian's constituent structure tests (summarized above). Rather, I will show that if we assume that Akmajian is correct about the structures of GPVCs (NP-over-NP VP) and IPVCs (see below), still problems arise.

Akmajian's argument from Number Agreement for (12) over (13) as a source for GPVCs (prior to extraposition) raises some interesting issues, especially in conjunction with the claim that GPVCs undergo extraposition. The evidence is not unequivocal here. Akmajian argues that GPVCs are NPs with heads rather than Ss because they take plural verb agreement when their heads are plural. He acknowledges that some speakers get either singular or plural agreement in these cases. But I believe there are some sentences that most or all speakers would accept wtih singular agreement:

(19)   *The girls getting along together so well after all these years*
         is (?are) a sight to warm the heart.

(20)   *Little children starving in our streets at night is (are) a*
         sight we shouldn't tolerate.

(21)   *Our students beating up an old professor in the courtyard*
         like that is (are) quite a bad sight.

Akmajian's analysis does not account for the possibility of singular agreement. When they take plural agreement they act like NPs, when they take singular agreement they act like Ss. Furthermore, I am not sure that the two do not differ in meaning. Notice though that if GPVCs are Ss when they take singular agreement, then Akmajian's arguments for NP as against S from lack of complementizers and auxiliaries are vitiated.

When the head of the GPVC is a plural pronoun, singular agreement is much better for me than plural agreement:

(22)   *Them trying to play Brahms together* $\left\{ \begin{matrix} *are \\ is \end{matrix} \right\}$ *quite a sight.*

(23)   *Us trying to make up and be friends* $\left\{ \begin{matrix} *were \\ was \end{matrix} \right\}$ *quite a sight.*

(24)   *The two of them trying to play Brahms together* $\left\{ \begin{matrix} were \\ was \end{matrix} \right\}$ *quite a sight.*

Notice that these GPVCs allow Extraposition, but then only take plural agreement:

(25)   *They* $\left\{ \begin{matrix} were \\ *was \end{matrix} \right\}$ *quite a sight trying to play Brahms together.*

Akmajian's argument for an NP as against an S-structure from extraposition is, then, quite crucial. It is one of his strongest arguments. The extraposition process he refers to is an interesting one, while there are problems with it, it appears that there is some sort of extraposition going on here. One problem is that extraposed and unextraposed versions mean different things, which is not in general the case with extraposition:

(26)   *Three of the girls playing in peace and harmony together*
         would be quite a sight.

(27)   *Three of the girls would be quite a sight playing in peace*
         and harmony together.

One argument for extraposition here though is this: quantifiers can float off the head of GPVCs. They can then end up after the VP. Extraposition would account for how they get to this position:

(28) a. *All of the children playing together in peace and harmony*
          are (is) quite a sight.
      b. *The children all playing together in peace and harmony are (is)*
          quite a sight.
      c. *The children are quite a sight all playing together in peace*
          and harmony.

Gerunds with empty subjects have the property of allowing the subject to stay if a quantifier is attached:

(29) a. *The boys left the pary thinking about Mary.*
      b. *The boys left the party all thinking about Mary.*
      c. *The boys left the party, all of them thinking about Mary.*

But (28c) is not, it would seem, equivalent to (30) below:

(30)   *??The children are quite a sight all of them playing together*
              in peace and harmony.

So it seems (28c) must arise through extraposition.

An interesting possibility arises here of tying Akmajian's theory to Emonds' (1976) Structure-Preserving Hypothesis. Akmajian argues that IPVCs have the following deep structure:

(31)

```
                    S
                  /   \
               NP      VP
                      / | \
                     V  NP VP
                     |
                    see
```

Notice that this could render Akmajian's extraposition process structure-preserving:

(32)

```
                    S
                  /   \
               NP      VP
                      / | \
                     V  NP  VP
                     |  / \   △
                    see NP  VP ↑
                           |___|
```

A problem of sorts arises with Right Dislocation. When we Right-Dislocate an NP, the pronoun left behind agrees in gender with the dislocated NP. A dislocated S, on the other hand, leaves behind the unmarked pronoun "it":

(33) a. *The girl who I love has left me.*
      b. $\begin{Bmatrix} *It \\ She \end{Bmatrix}$ *has left me, the girl that I love.*

(34) a. *It was regrettable, John's having said that.*
      b. *It was surprising, for John to have done such a thing in public.*
      c. *It proves that John is guilty, that he lied (that is).*

When GPVCs are Right Dislocated they leave behind an unmarked pronoun, not a gender-agreeing pronoun:[4]

(35)   a.   *A little boy getting his first haircut is quite a sight.*
       b.   *Mary trying to play the tuba is quite a sight.*
       c. $\left\{ \begin{array}{c} *He \\ It \end{array} \right\}$ *is quite a sight, a little boy getting his first haircut.*
       d. $\left\{ \begin{array}{c} *She \\ It \end{array} \right\}$ *is quite a sight, Mary trying to play the tuba.*

Case marking brings out another interesting problem. Consider the facts below:[5]

(36)   a. $\left\{ \begin{array}{c} Him \\ *He \end{array} \right\}$ *trying to play Brahms would be quite a sight.*
       b. $\left\{ \begin{array}{c} *Him \\ He \end{array} \right\}$ *would be quite a sight trying to play Brahms.*

Actually, Akmajian could give an account of this in terms of Klima's and Emonds' principle that a pronoun is nominative if it is immediately dominated by S. This principle would even give some support to Akmajian's NP-over-NP VP structure, since if the GPVC was an embedded S we might expect a nominative pronoun in (36a). Unfortunately, when appositive relatives undergo extraposition they do not act like (36):

(37)   a. $\left\{ \begin{array}{c} *Him \\ He \end{array} \right\}$ *who steals my purse steals trash.*
       b. $\left\{ \begin{array}{c} *Him \\ He \end{array} \right\}$ *steals trash who steals my purse.*

Presumably, the same principle should apply here as in (36), if appositives are NPs (probably NP-over-NP S versus relative clauses that are NP-over-Det N S).[6]

There is some evidence that GPVCs are not always constituents at deep structure. GPVCs occur with *catch, find, discover,* and *come upon*. In these cases, by Akmajian's tests, they are *never* constituents:

(38)   a.   *We caught John stealing the car.*
       b.   **What we caught was John stealing the car.*
       c.   **It was John stealing the car that we caught.*
       d.   **John stealing the car was caught by the police.*
       e.   **John stealing the car would be hard to catch.*
       f.   **John stealing the car was a find.*
       g.   **We tried to catch, but couldn't catch, John stealing the car.*

Note:

(39)   a.   *What we caught was John.*
       b.   *It was John that we caught.*
       c.   *John was caught by the police.*
       d.   *John would be hard to catch.*
       e.   *John was a find.*
       f.   *We tried to catch, but couldn't catch, the thief who made off with the diamonds.*

(40) a. *John was who we caught stealing the car.*
      b. *It was John that we caught stealing the car.*
      c. *John was caught stealing the car by the police.*
      d. *John would be hard to catch stealing a car.*

(38)–(40) would indicate, then, that we have to derive some GPVCs as non-constituents in object position at deep structure. Since this is so we can get rid of Akmajian's appeal to vacuous extraposition for GPVCs in object position of perception verbs. We can either dually subcategorize perception verbs for both $_{NP}$[NP VP]$_{NP}$ and NP VP (or NP S ?) complements, or always generate the latter in complement position after the verb (depending on the status of constituency tests and the passives of perception verbs when they have GPVC-complements, note ?*"John stealing the car was seen by all the neighbors"):

(41)

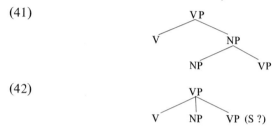

(42)

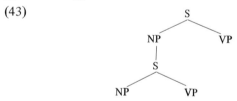

Given the evidence in (6)–(11), (42) is probably NP VP, not NP S.

Finally, the Number Agreement and Right Dislocation facts either must be handled semantically, or we must assume some GPVC-complements in subject (and perhaps other) position(s) to have a structure like (43) below, as well as $_{NP}$[NP VP]$_{NP}$ in other cases:

(43)

In fact structures like (43) may be related to gerunds with no Poss-marker on the subject, e.g.,:[7]

(44) a. *With even John saying (having said) such things, we*
             may be in trouble.
      b. **With even John's saying (having said) such things, we*
             may be in trouble.

3.   It is time now to look more closely at IPVCs. Akmajian claims IPVCs are always not constituents. And indeed they are invariably bad in subject position, but at best this would indicate that they are not NPs. Interestingly enough, in Brazilian

Portuguese IPVCs do act like constituents. For example, both GPVCs and IPVCs passivize with "see." When they passivize, GPVCs have verb agreement with the head of the GPVC and IPVCs take unmarked agreement, i.e., like an S:

(45)   *Maria roubando o carro foi vista (??visto) por todos os vizinhos.*

(46)   *Maria roubar o carro foi visto (*vista) por todos os vizinhos.*

One of the problems with Akmajian's account of IPVCs is that there are several other possibilities concerning their structure that he does not consider. In addition to the nonconstituent structure he offers, other possibilities are (1) they are bare Ss (or object-raising verbs or $\bar{S}$ with a zero complementizer—i.e., like the structure Chomsky, 1973, assigns to infinitival complements to verbs like *believe*) and (2) they are like Equi-verbs.[8] Both of these latter alternatives have the problem of accounting for the absence of "to." But Emonds (1976) argues that they have had "to" deleted, since it shows up systematically when you passivize the subject:

(47)   a.   *We saw John leave early.*
         b.   *John was seen to leave early.*
         c.   **John was seen leave early.*

(48)   a.   *We made John leave early.*
         b.   *John was made to leave early.*
         c.   **John was made leave early.*

"To" does show up in some active sentences:

(49)   a.   *We all saw John to be suicidal on that occasion.*
         b.   **We all saw John (be) suicidal on that occasion.*

One could also appeal to the close correspondence between "to" and non-"to" versions with "help":

(50)   a.   *I help my plants grow by using Ortho.*
         b.   *I help my plants to grow by using Ortho.*

However, it is not completely clear that NI-constructions are related to "to"-constructions. There are several ways in which NI-constructions do not act at all like Equi-verbs for instance:

(51)   a. $\left\{ \begin{array}{l} Make \\ Let \end{array} \right\}$ *it rain.* ("weather *it*")
         b.   **Force it to rain.*

(52)   a. $\left\{ \begin{array}{l} ?Make \\ Let \end{array} \right\}$ *there be peace on earth.*
         b.   **Force there to be peace on earth.*

(53)   a. $\left\{ \begin{array}{l} Make \\ Let \end{array} \right\}$ *it be known that John is a fool.*
         b.   **Force it to be known that John is a fool.*

Also:

(54)   a.   *We saw it rain.*
       b.   *I've never seen there be so many complaints from students before.*
       c.   *I would like to see it (be) proven that John was there that night.*

But NI-verbs are also not like object-raising verbs (like *believe*) in some regards:

(55)   a. $\left\{ \begin{array}{l} Make \\ Let \end{array} \right\}$ *John examine Mary.*
       b. $\left\{ \begin{array}{l} Make \\ Let \end{array} \right\}$ *Mary be examined by John.*

(56)   a.   *We believe John to have examined Mary.*
       b.   *We believe Mary to have been examined by John.*

(55a,b) mean different things, (56a,b) do not.

Another interesting fact is that NI-verbs take deletion or anaphora patterns that are separately, but not together, characteristic of Equi- and Raising-verbs:

(57)   a.   *I saw you try to hit that little girl and Mary saw you too.*
       b.   *I tried to persuade John to make a last attempt and Mary tried to persuade him too.*
       c.   **I believe Mary to have lied and John believes her too.*

(58)   a.   *I saw John hit the little girl and Mary saw it too.*
       b.   **I tried to persuade John to make a last attempt and Mary tried to persuade it too.*
       c.   *I believe Mary to have lied and John believes it too.*

Incidentally, the "it" in (58) appears to be an S-anaphor in (58c), but cannot be one in (58a) on Akmajian's account. Indeed, in (58a) it is, on his account, an anaphor for nonconstituents.

It is interesting to note that only NI-taking verbs that have to do with perception allow "it" anaphora, e.g., *have, make, help, let, discover, find*, and so forth, do not.

(59)   **I would have let Mary smoke cigars, but her mother wouldn't let it.*

But note:

(60)   *I would have let Mary smoke cigars, but her mother wouldn't allow it.*

"Allow" is not an NI-verb but the "it" in (60) appears to refer back to the content of the NI-complement of *let*.

An argument against a bare S-analysis (or zero complementizer S̄-analysis) is that NI-complements will not take sentential adverbs (while raising verbs will for instance):

(61)   a.   *I* $\left\{ \begin{array}{l} knew \\ saw \end{array} \right\}$ **that** *John certainly (clearly, without doubt) had murdered the woman.*
       b.   *I believe John certainly (clearly, without doubt) to have murdered the woman.*
       c.   **I saw John certainly (clearly, without doubt) murder the woman.*

Also:

(62) a. $I \begin{Bmatrix} know \\ see \end{Bmatrix}$ *that it is true that John murdered the woman.*

     b. *I believe it to be true that Mary has murdered her husband.*

     c. **I saw it be true that Mary had murdered her husband.*

However, this may be something we want to handle in the semantics.

Prepositions often have a very verbal meaning with NI-verbs, which is not at all characteristic of the verbs taking S-complements:

(63) a. *Let John (*be)* $\begin{Bmatrix} in \\ out \end{Bmatrix}$

     b. *I believe John *(to be) out.*

(64) a. *I saw John off in the distance.*
       I saw John inside the box.

     b. *I believe John *(to be) off in the distance.*
        I believe John *(to be) inside the box.

Notice also:

(65)   *I forced John inside the box = I forced John to go inside the box.*

(66)   *I saw John inside the box ≠ I saw John go inside the box.*

(67)   *We saw John friendly for once.*

(68) a. *We believed John *(to have been) friendly for once.*
     b. *We forced John *(to be) friendly for once.*

Another fact that may tend to confirm Akmajain's analysis of GPVCs as constituents and IPVCs as nonconstituents, as well as the difference between PVCs and complements to raising verbs comes from Right Dislocation:

(69) a. *I saw it–John cheating on his test.*

     b. **I saw it–John cheat on his test.*

     c. *I believe it–the square root of 2 to be 4 (that is).*

Notice also Right Node Raising:

(70) a. *You can see, but you can't hear, someone doing pantomime.*
     b.*??You can see, but you can't hear, someone do pantomime.*
     c. *You can believe, but you can't prove, Ford to be the best President.*

It is too bad that the evidence from Right Node Raising is so marginal. Right Node Raising is one process that clearly will effect bare Ss:

(71)   *I didn't say that, but merely asked whether,* **John had lied**.

Thus is (70b) was dramatically bad we would have some strong evidence that IPVCs were not base Ss (nor zero complementizer S̄s). But interestingly enough, Right Node Raising of IPVCs is not all that bad, not clearly worse, to me at any rate, than Right Node Raising of complements to *believe* (70c).

A final point can be raised here about the relationship of PVCs and infinitives. One of the most obvious things we sould like to account for is why PVCs do not have a "to." Now one explanation for this fact would be to say that "to" signals

subordination or embedding. PVCs do not have a "to" because they are not subordinated or embedded Ss. This, of course, will not be true if we assign the same
structure to infinitival complements to *believe, prove, think*, etc., and to NI-
complements of perception verbs (or assign them bare Ss). Emonds, for instance,
wants to delete "to" from NI-constructions like "made John leave" (see Emonds,
1976). Akmajian's structure for IPVCs would account automatically for the absence
of "to" vis-à-vis embedded nonfinite clauses, if "to" is the mark of these. But there
is one problem. Lasnik and Fiengo (1974) propose that verbs of the *force* class do
not take an object and embedded S-complement, on which Equi applies, but rather
take an object and a VP-complement. This is the same structure Akmajian assigns to
IPVCs. Yet, of course, a "to" shows up on the VPs of *force*-type verbs. If Emonds
or Lasnik and Fiengo are right, then we would have to look to the semantics or the
logic for the reason of the nonappearance of "to." But the logic, with its limited
operator/predicate-argument structures is not, in my opinion, liable to offer much
help here for a perspicuous distinction of these three cases (*see, believe, force*). But
this is a fairly long story, and I cannot go into in here (see Gee, 1975). I will just
mention that one logical possibility is that perception verbs involve quantification
over predicates (or events), while *believe* and *force* do not. Of course, some may
feel that the problem of "to" is a completely trivial one, merely a matter of a minor
governed syntactic deletion rule. This will, however, not explain why perception
verbs are so commonly among the class of marked infinitive taking verbs in other
languages besides English.

4.   Akmajian accounts for passives in the complements of perception verbs by
generalizing the passive rule to NPs as well as Ss:

(72)   *We saw the rebels being executed by the army.*

He then speculates that we can account for (73) below by getting it from (74) by
deleting *being*:

(73)   *We saw the rebels executed by the army.*

(74)   *We saw the rebels being executed by the army.*

However, this is wrong. (73) and (74) differ in meaning just as (75) and (76) below
do, the *-ing* signalling incompleted action:

(75)   *We saw the army execute the rebels.*
(76)   *We saw the army executing the rebels.*

(73) clearly comes from (75) not (74). This is clear when we notice that the passive
be can show up in many such cases:

(77) a. *Have you ever seen anyone be cross-examined by*
            Melvin Belli before?
      b. *Have you ever seen anyone cross-examined by Melvin Belli?*
      c. *I've seen lots of cars (be) towed away by the police before*
            for no reason at all.

So it seems clear that (73) is derived from (75) via passive and *be*-deletion (not
being-deletion). The patterns of *be*-deleting with perception verbs are quite interesting, but this is not the place to discuss them. I will note the following facts as a
sample:

(78) a. *I've never seen John (*be) drunk, before tonight.*
      b. *I've never seen John ?*(be) obnoxious, before tonight.*
      c. *I've never seen John (be) so* $\left\{ \begin{array}{l} drunk \\ obnoxious \end{array} \right\}$ *, before tonight.*

Now the problem arises that if IPVCs are not constituents, as Akmajian argues, it
is not enough to generalize passive to NPs. It must be allowed to apply to nonconstituents in order to get (73) from (75). Of course, the passive rule Akmajian gives
(i.e., NP-X(Y)-NP-by-Δ) will apply to nonconstituents if we do not constrain such
rules to have to apply to constituents. In (75) an NP immediately follows a V. This,
of course, fits in perfectly with a constraint that Chomsky has for some time put on
transformational rules, i.e., (in loose terms) that they do not know or care what
nodes dominate the nodes in their structural description (that is, there are no
brackets in the SDs of transformational rules). Thus, even if two elements were not
constituents they could undergo a rule like passive just so long as no generalized
constraint on transformations (such as the A/A principle) was broken. Of course,
we could want to make it a requirement that the domain of a transformation was
always defined on a syntactic constituent (S or NP for example, or on cyclic nodes).
    Now transformations apply quite freely to NI-complements (besides passive):

(79) a. *I've never seen John be so easy to please before* (Tough Movement).
      b. *I've never seen it be so easy to please John before.*

(80) a. *The Dean won't let there be any party this year* (There-Insertion).
      b. *I've never seen there be so many complaints from students*
            before (There-Insertion).

(81)   *I've never seen John appear (seem) to be so out of it*
            before (Raising).

(82)   *I saw John want to be President so bad that he could*
            taste it (Equi).

(83) a. *I saw it gradually get clearer and clearer that John was*
            guilty (Extraposition).
      b. *??I saw that John was guilty gradually get clearer and clearer*
            (breaks center-embedded S-constraint).

(84)   a.   *I heard the little boys all begging for ice-cream* (Q-Float).
       b.   *I heard all the little boys begging for ice-cream.*

So either transformations can apply to a domain made up of nonconstituents, or Akmajian is wrong about the structure of IPVCs.

5.   Akmajian realizes, given that IPVCs are not constituents, that the relations of *subject* and *object* have to be defined in the lexicon. We cannot say that a subject is [NP, S] or [NP, $\bar{\bar{X}}$] or any such thing, since in "John saw me steal the car," "me" is the subject of "steal the car," but is not dominated by S or NP.

   Now the NP in the position of "me" in the above sentence does act like a subject vis-à-vis basically syntactic phenomena. For example, this NP obeys the Specified Subject Constraint:

(85)   "each"
       a.   *We saw Mary kiss each other.*
       b.   *We each saw Mary kiss the other(s).*
       c.   *We helped carry each other's groceries.*
       d.   *We each helped carry the other's groceries*
       e.   *We helped Mary carry each other's groceries.*
       f.   *We each helped Mary carry the other's groceries.*

(86)   "Unlike Person Constraint"
       a.   *I saw me.*
       b.   *I saw Mary kiss me (in the mirror).*
       c.   *I saw Mary kiss myself.*
       d.   *I helped get myself (*me) through school by . . .*
       e.   *I helped my parents get me (*myself) through . . .*

Furthermore, as has already been pointed out, IPVCs and GPVCs take elements that are deep subjects:

(87)   a.   *We saw it snow in Columbia.*
       b.   *We heard it raining outside.*
       c.   *We heard all hell break loose.*
       d.   *Then we saw the shit hit the fan.*

(87c,d) contain idioms that can occur only in subject position.

   What does all this indicate then? One thing it indicates is that more evidence must be given against a structure like (88) for IPVCs (it is possible that the $\bar{S}$ in (88) should be an S, but see note 3):

(88)

```
                    S
                 /     \
              NP        VP
                      /    \
                     V      S̄
                          /    \
                       Comp     S
                        |
                        φ
```

This structure would account for the applicability of transformations to IPVCs, as well as the applicability of the Specified Subject Condition, without any modification. The semantics would have to rule out the occurrence of *have* as an auxiliary (for a way in which the semantics could do this, see Gee, 1975), and things like "John saw Bill be stealing the car" would have to be ruled out some way (see Gee, 1975, for a way to do this). Further, we would have to account for the constituent structure tests that Akmajian appeals to (see note 3 for a suggestion of N. Chomsky's here).

6.   The semantics of perception verbs is of a good deal of interest, but we cannot go into this area in any depth whatsoever here. Akmajian does touch on this area towards the end of his paper.

Akmajian gives a semantic argument against a sentential source for PVCs. He claims that there is a generalization to the effect that when perception verbs occur with a simple NP-direct object in deep structure (direct object construction), the interpretation is one of direct perception, on the other hand, when perception verbs occur with sentential complements in deep structure ("We saw that John had been there," "We saw him to be a complete charlatan"), the interpretation is one of indirect perception (for a more detailed discussion of the sense in which the *that*-construction is "indirect" see Gee, 1975). On syntactic grounds, Akmajian has argued that PVCs are not embedded Ss. Thus he predicts, correctly, that they have a direct perception interpretation like the direct object construction and not an indirect perception interpretation like the *that* and raising constructions. An embedded S analysis of PVCs would make the wrong prediction.

Now I believe, and have argued elsewhere at some length (see Gee, 1975), that NI-constructions with perception verbs belong conceptually and logically with the direct object construction and not the *perceiving that*-construction.

However, the contrast between direct perception (NP) and indirect perception (S) here is too simple. *See* can take both headless relatives and indirect questions (note the ambiguity in "I see who John sees"). Consider the following indirect question, presumably an S-complement, uttered after I have gone into a room with a group of men around a table:

(89)   *Now, I see who Smith is.*

This sentence has two readings. It can mean that I already know which one is Smith and I have recognized some relevant descriptive information about Smith (Now I see who he is—he's the guy running for Congress from my district). It can also mean that I already know some relevant descriptive information about Smith and I have seen which one of the men around the table is Smith (now I see who he is—he's that guy over there). On this reading it means "Now I see which one is Smith." The question "Who is Smith?" has the same "ambiguity." These are both different cases of perceptual recognition. But I really do not know if they both, or if one but not the other, or if neither count as "direct perception." If the latter reading is direct perception, then, of course, so is the indirect question sentence "Now I see which one is Smith." Of course, these constructions sometimes do have "indirect perception" readings, as in "Now I see what the problem is (you're talking about)" or "Now I see what to do." Note also, "Can you see who's at that table over there?", which is another hard case to classify. Thus, Akmajian's semantic generalization is not clearly correct until we have a less vague characterization of it than the notions "direct" and "indirect" give us. I rather think different complement types have different meanings (*that*, *for-to*, indirect question, etc., what Bloomfield would have called constructional meanings). In this regard, see Bresnan (1972) and Gee (1975).

Another interesting fact here is this: with NI-constructions one need not perceive the NP-object, one need only perceive the VP. Take a case where John is behind an opaque screen where we can not see him, but we all know he is there. He can, with magnets, move small geometrical objects on the front side of the screen from the back. In this case I can say, it seems to me, when John moves some objects:

(90)   *Now, I can see John moving the little figures.*

(91)   *I just saw John move one of the little figures.*

I do not see John at all. Notice that the NP is inside the scope of "see" still, as is necessitated by the use of the first person subject. Now in a reverse situation, where John is standing in front of the screen, obscuring the figures, with his back to us, and capable of moving the objects without our seeing them or him move at all, I cannot say, when he moves one (even if I somehow know he is moving one, say by being told by someone else that he is doing it) either (90) or (91). All I could say would be "I saw John when he was moving the figures." In NI-constructions I need not see the VP as described (as I will show below), but I must see the action the VP refers to. Note also:

(92)   *I felt Mary hit me with a stone* (Mary could be out of sight,
                 I clearly do not feel her).

The salient point here is this. It is the VP of NI-constructions that is like the NP of direct object constructions with perception verbs.

There is an interesting semantic phenomenon that shows a way in which PVCs do not act like (tensed or untensed) embedded Ss though. As is now well known, intentional verbs can create scope ambiguities (actually of various sorts—see Gee, 1976a,b). The scope ambiguity I am here concerned with is the case where the descriptive content of a phrase ("the sense" in one sense) can (but may not) be outside the scope of the intentional verbs, the phrase in this case belonging to someone other than the subject of the intentional verb (usually it belongs to the speaker). Within the intentional verb, the phrase in this case serves mainly to pick out something that the subject of the intentional verb knows under another descriptive content.

While it is well known that we can get such intentional ambiguities with NPs syntactically inside intentional verbs:

(93) a. *John believes **your brother** stole his car, though he doesn't*
          *know it was **your brother**.*

it appears that when a VP is dominated by S it cannot enter into these sorts of ambiguities, always being inside the scope of the intentional verb:

(93) b. *#John believes your brother **stole** his car, though he doesn't*
          *know it was **stealing** (or: he was **stealing** it).*

This is true also of nonfinite complements:

(94) a. *John believes Mary to dislike **your brother**, though he doesn't*
          *know Sam is **your brother**.*
      b. *#John believes Mary **to dislike** your brother, though be doesn't*
          *know it is **disliking** (or: he is **disliking** someone).*

It is also well known now that perceptual verbs set up such intentional contexts (see Anscombe, 1965):

(95) a. *John (actually) saw **your brother** steal the car, though he didn't*
          *know Sam was **your brother**.*

But notice that the VPs in NI-constructions can also be transparent with respect to the higher intentional verb (of perception):

(95) b. *John (actually) saw your brother **steal** that car, though he*
          *didn't know he was **stealing** it (or: it was **stealing**).*

This seems to have to do with the fact that the VP is dominated by S or not, not with the higher verb itself:

(96) a. *John saw that **your brother** was stealing the car, though he*
          *didn't realize it was **your brother**.*
      b. *#John saw that your brother was **stealing** the car, though he didn't*
          *realize he was **stealing** it (or: it was **stealing**).*

Note also:

(97)   *Bill saw John steal a red car, but he didn't see that it*
            was (a)   a RED car
            *   (b)   a red CAR*
            *   (c)   a RED CAR*

Note also that it is not the presence of "to" in nonfinite complements that makes the VP opaque:

(98) a. *John* $\begin{Bmatrix} demanded \\ asked \end{Bmatrix}$ *that **your brother** steal the car, but he*
          *didn't, or course, know it was **your brother**.*
      b. *#John* $\begin{Bmatrix} demanded \\ asked \end{Bmatrix}$ *that your brother **steal** the car, but he didn't*
          *realize that it was that he **steal** the car that he was asking for.*

Another way in which NI-constructions behave differently than structures with embedded Ss can be seen from how inferences can or cannot be saved in the two cases. Consider Wittgenstein's duck-rabbit (see Wittgenstein, 1958):

(99)   The Duck-Rabbit:

The following inferences are not necessarily valid without the additional premise added at step 3, but with that premise they are, in the general case, valid (see Hintikka, 1969):[9]

(100)   a.   *a knows that the duck is F*
              a believes that the duck is F
              a believes the duck to be F
              a sees the duck to be F
              a sees that the duck is F
              (a knows d—in one sense)

        b. $(d = r)$

        c.   *a knows that* $(d = r)$
              a believes that $(d = r)$
              a sees that $(d = r)$

        d.   ⇒   *a knows that the rabbit is F*
                    a believes that the rabbit is F
                    a believes the rabbit to be F
                    a sees the rabbit to be F
                    a sees that the rabbit is F
                    (a knows r—in one sense)

In other words, a premise of *knowing* (*seeing, believing*) *that* will secure the inference (cf. (3)). But this is not the case with NI or direct object constructions with perception verbs. After experimenting for some time with forms like the duck-rabbit, we can come to see, in looking at the figure (and, of course, seeing either the duck or the rabbit), *that* the duck = the rabbit. But:

(101)   a.   *At* t_4 (after some experience with the figure)
                    a sees d (*wink*)
        b. $(d = r)$
        c.   *At* t_4 *a sees that* $(d = r)$
        d.   ⇏   *At* t_4 *a sees r* (*wink*)

Some concrete examples:

(102) a. *I believe (saw) that the duck winked.*
           I believe the duck to have winked.

       b. $(d = r)$

       c. *I believe (see) that* $(d = r)$

       d. ⇒   *I believe (saw) that the rabbit winked*
               I believe the rabbit to have winked

(103) a. *I saw the duck wink at* t_4
       b. $(d = r)$
       c. *At* t_4 *I (can) see that the duck = the rabbit*
       d. ↛   *I saw the rabbit wink at* t_4

There is a sense in which the inference in (103) goes through, i.e., if we take (103d) in the extensional sense (where "the rabbit" is outside the scope of "see"), but the important point is that there is a sense in which the inference is invalid and there is no sense of (102d) in which the inference in (102) fails (in one sense of "see," at t_4 I saw either the winking of the rabbit or the winking of the duck, but I cannot have seen both).[10]

This is one way (among others) we can show direct object and NI-construction with perception verbs are not reducible to sentential constructions like those in (100a) (contrary to Hintikka's propositional thesis, see Gee, 1975, for discussion and references).

Semantically, I believe NI-constructions have a particularly close relationship between the VP in the complement and the higher perception verb (an almost "direct object"-like relationship. In the way in which "John felt Mary" means that what John felt was Mary, "John felt Mary hit him" means that what John felt was the hitting of Mary on him. If IPVCs have complementizerless or bare Ss or have zero complementizer S̄s, then there may be something of a lack of correspondence between syntax and semantics here, while if they have an NP VP structure (both IPVCs and GPVCs in complement object position), there will be a somewhat better correspondence, I would think.

7.   Finally, let me take up Akmajian's remarks on the autonomy thesis and try to tie together some of the above remarks.

What we have seen is that PVCs behave in a somewhat dichotomous manner. In some ways they behave like Ss and in other ways not (the difference between them is this: GPVCs behave in various respects like Ss [NP over S], NPs [not dominating S], and nonconstituents; IPVCs like S's and nonconstituents).

If IPVCs (and possibly GPVCs in object position) are not constituents, we need to account for the ways in which they act like Ss ("it" anaphora, Right Dislocation, Singular Verb Agreement, some transformations applying to them as they do to Ss and NPs, the Specified Subject Condition, Deep Subjects, Case Marking, and so forth). One hypothesis here would be this: certain phenomena in the grammar are defined upon domains (whether NP, S, or nonconstituents) that have subject–predicate (–object) relations defined for them. Since NI-complements have grammatical relations defined for them, they will behave in certain respects like Ss, the classic domain of grammatical relations. Certain other grammatical phenomena may be defined merely for phrasal categories irrespective of grammatical relations. On the other hand, if IPVCs are Ss, these Ss will not act very much like *propositions* in the semantics (not like *that*-clauses with *know* or infinitives with *believe*). Either way there is interesting ground here for the study of the autonomy thesis. The first solution above seems to have a closer "fit" between the semantics and the syntax, the latter a less close "fit." But the issue of "fit" is not in itself all that relevant to the autonomy thesis, as no one has ever denied that the semantics will in various ways "fit" the syntax. In any case, I think when a decent semantics of perception verbs is at hand, it will be shown that the semantics does not in this case completely (though it well may partially) determine the syntactic structure of PVCs. Their semantics may turn out to be (roughly) something like this, I believe:

(104) a. I can see the wood burning (note that the wood need not be visible, i.e., it may be hidden).

   b. I know on the basis of certain "protoknowledge" (which may be previous perceptual evidence, in the limiting case it may be perceiving the entity in the present case) that a certain entity is involved in a certain act X and I perceive X.

A full discussion of this proposal here would carry us way too far afield.[11] At any rate, it is not at all clear that the semantics given in (104b) renders NI-constructions a completely perspicuous syntactic structure to express this semantics. My guess is that the semantics determines to some extent the NI-form (the absence of "have," the lack of "to," the lack of propositional adverbs, etc.), but that the syntactic structure of the language also plays a prominent independent part in rendering the form as it is. Of course, we could go around saying things like (104b) (or, for another example, the explication offered by Russell's theory of definite descriptions). It seems to me that the autonomy thesis says in part that we will not.

Notes

1. At the conference I did not present the full text of may comments. Some small sections were deleted throughout and all of section 7. I have made no substantive changes in the text, save to relegate parts of it to the notes, delete a section on extraposition, and add some notes to make reference to some of the points made in discussion at the conference.

   Throughout the paper I use "NI-verbs" for "naked infinitive verbs" (a not altogether happy term I picked up from Jespersen). This term is meant to cover all verbs that take what Akmajian calls IPVCs (e.g., *see, hear, feel, help, let, make, have*, and a very few others). The structure that Akmajian proposes for IPVCs has also been independently proposed by Gee (1975) and Milsark (1974).

I wish to thank Richard Oehrle for discussing some of the things in this paper with me, and Mariza Pimenta Bueno for the examples from Brazilian Portuguese.

2. A possible (more abstract) source that Akmajian does not consider is that PVCs are the result of clause union ("verb raising") from an intermediate source like that below:

(i)   *I saw steal(ing) the car (of) John

It is an interesting fact that in English as in some other languages, there are among the nonperception verbs that take NI-complements (usually a small set like *make, have, let,* and *help*), some that do typically exhibit structures like (i) in some languages. For example, Brazilian Portuguese has the following sorts of sentences:

(ii)   *Eu fiz sair o gato.*

(iii)   *Eu deixei ser levado o piano.*

(iv)   *Eu o farei ler a todos.*

It appears though in Brazilian Portuguese that (v) and (vi) below are both bad, though (vi) is better than (v):

(v)   **Eu vi roubando o carro (a) Joaõ.*

(vi)   *Eu vi roubar o carro (a) Joaõ.*

I do not know of any languages that do exhibit structures like (v) and (vi) for perception verbs.

Another possibility for GPVCs is to get "I saw John stealing the car" from "I saw John PREP (at ?) stealing the car."

3. N. Chomsky questioned the status of Akmajian's constituent structure tests in discussion at the conference. He claimed that complementizerless sentences cannot occur in focus position. For example, when *for* is deleted from a *for/to*-complement, the complement cannot occur in a Pseudo-Cleft:

(i)   *What we wanted was for John to tell the truth for a change.*

(ii)   *?*What we wanted was John to tell the truth for a change.*

(iii)   *We wanted (*for) John to tell the truth for a change.*

Thus, it might be suggested that IPVCs are simply bare Ss and as such could not occur in Clefts, Pseudo-Clefts, and so forth (nor, of course, in subject position). However, a problem arises if we assign perception verbs bare S-complements. We can question out of these complements. If they were bare Ss, they would have no Comp-node and so we could not do question movement here Comp-to-Comp as Chomsky wants. Thus, it would seem that a question like that below would break the Specified Subject Condition and Subjacency (with S̄ and S cyclic) if it had a bare S-complement:

(iv)   *What did you see John steal ___?*

Now we might think of assigning IPVCs an S̄- (rather than S-) complement, but with a null complementizer. This is the structure Chomsky (1973) assigns to complements to "raising verbs" like *believe*. In general, complements to *believe* are not very good in focus position, though better than IPVCs I believe:

(v)   *??What we believed was Ford to be a poor President.*

(vi)   *??What physicists believe today is the orbit of the moon to be a parabola.*

(vii)   *??What I believe is four to be the square root of two.*

(viii) cf. *?*What we saw was John steal the car.*

Now it may be correct to say that sentential complements with no overt complementizer cannot appear in focus position. Note also:

(ix)   *What I know is that John lied.*

(x)   *?*What I know is John lied.*

(xi)   *I know (that) John lied.*

If this is true, it would mean that Pseudo-Clefts, Clefts, and so forth, are not tests for the constituency or lack of it of IPVCs, as either way they would not occur there.

Some of the remarks in my paper bear on the question of assigning an $\bar{S}$-complement to IPVCs. One of the things such an analysis would have to account for is the differences below, where I assume the "to" versions do have $\bar{S}$-complements, like that assigned to infinitival complements to *believe*:

(xii) a.   *We saw John to be an obnoxious person.*
      b.   **We saw John (be) an obnoxious person.*

(xiii)a.   *We all saw John to be suicidal on that occasion.*
      b.   **We all saw John be suicidal on that occasion.*

(xiv)a.   *We saw John steal the car.*
      b.   **We saw John to steal the car.*

(xv) a.   *We saw John being polite for a change.*
      b.   **We saw John to be being polite for a change.*

(xvi)a.   *We've never seen John be so happy before.*
      b.   **We've never seen John to be so happy before.*

However, these facts are not really explained in any account as of yet, and are clearly, I believe, connected, at least in part, with the semantics.

4. N. Chomsky brought to my attention that sentences with definites (though not proper names) are better than (35b,c) with gender-agreeing pronouns. However, sentences like:

(i)   *He is quite a sight, that little boy getting a haircut.*

may have simply a reduced relative clause structure in "that little boy getting a haircut."

5. R. Oehrle brought to my attention the case marking facts here.

6. J. Emonds mentioned a way out of the facts in (36) and (37) for his case marking proposal. Emonds' point involves the fact that the head NP in GPVCs is subcategorizationally involved with the VP in the GPVC, while the head of the appositive is not so related to the VP in the relative clause, but to the main VP of the sentence. This is probably correct.

7. There is an additional point here about GPVCs we can bring up. Akmajian claims that the *-ing* of GPVCs does not represent the progressive, and he cites sentences like "I can't see myself needing anymore drugs," and so forth, as evidence for this conclusion. However, I am not convinced that the *-ing* in GPVCs is not the progressive *-ing*. Note that with *let, make*, and *have* we can get "stage direction" sentences with a *be* in them:

(i)   *Let's let Othello be thinking of his next move at this point in the play.*

(ii)   *We'll have Joan be thinking of her long lost love at the opening of Act II here.*

(These facts were brought to my attention by R. Oehrle.) Furthermore, we can note the following facts:

(iii)   *John jumped once (one time).*

(iv)   **John was jumping once (one time).*

(v)   *I saw John jump once.*

(vi)   **I saw John jumping once.*

(vii)   *John's jumping (having jumped) once was sufficient to convince us that he was uncoordinated.*

If the *-ing* here is a progressive and Akmajian is right about the structure of GPVCs, it has, of course, consequences for our analysis of the auxiliary in English (e.g., we would have to modify the account in Akmajian and Wasow, 1975). A structure like that below might be plausible (we would have to rule out *have* on semantic grounds in PVCs—see Gee, 1975, for an analysis of the auxiliary along the lines of (viii)):

(viii)

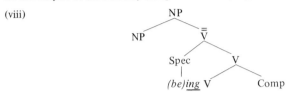

8. Fiengo (1974) orginally proposed that perception verbs with IPVCs were Equi-verbs.
9. For the inferences in (100) to be valid, we must restrict what can replace F. If F is, for example, "is cute" then the inferences are not necessarily valid. Predicates that are (related to) perceptual characteristics will not let the inference go through. This is related to the fact that the inference in (101) is invalid. In turn both these facts are related to the fact that the "objects of perception" are different from the "objects of propositional attitudes." Far from vitiating the point I want to make with the duck-rabbit, *this* is the point.
10. I said above that with a first person subject, the NP inside the intentional verb would have to be inside the scope of the intentional verb. With perception verbs we can get an interesting split in transparent–opaque phenomena (that was not relevant to the previous example). If someone tells me the blur I saw was a rabbit, I can say "I actually saw the rabbit it turns out." Here "the rabbit" is opaque in the sense that it is *my* description (the subject of the intentional verb) bur extensional in the sense that it is not the description that describes what I saw *as* I saw it.
11. The notion of "protoknowledge" in perceptual judgments is developed in Dretske (1969) and modified somewhat in Gee (1975).

REFERENCES

Aissen, J. & D. Perlmutter (1976), "Clause reduction in Spanish," paper read at the Romance linguistics Conference, Universite de Montreal.

Akmajian, A. (1973), "The role of focus in the interpretation of anaphoric expressions," in Anderson and Kiparsky (1973).

Akmajian, A. (1975), "More evidence for the NP cycle," *Linguistic Inquiry* 6, 115-129.

Akmajian, A. & F. Heny (1975), *Introduction to the Principles of Transformational Syntax*, MIT Press, Cambridge, Mass.

Akmajian, A. & A. Lehrer (1975), "NP-like quantifiers and the problem of determining the head of an NP," paper presented at the LSA, December, 1975.

Akmajian, A. & T. Wasow (1975), "The constituent structure of VP and AUX and the position of the verb *be*," *Linguistic Analysis* 1, 205-246.

Alvarez, A. & K. Hale (1969), "Towards a manual of Papago grammar: some phonological terms," *IJAL* 36, 83-97.

Anderson, S. R. (1967), "Concerning the notion 'base Component of a transformational Grammar'," to appear in J. McCawley (ed.), *Syntax & Semantics* VII: *Notes from the Linguistic Underground*, Academic Press, New York.

Anderson, S. R. (1971) "On the role of deep structure in Semantic interpretation," *Foundations of Language* 6, 387-396.

Anderson, S. R. (1976), "On the notion of Subject in Ergative Languages," in C. Li, ed., *Subject & Topic*, Academic Press, New York.

Anderson, S. R. (forthcoming), *Ergativity and Linguistic Structure.*

Anderson, S. & P. Kiparsky, eds. (1973), *Festschrift for Morris Halle*, Holt, Rinehart and Winston, New York.

Andrews, A. (1975), *Studies in the Syntax of Relative and Comparative Clauses*, unpublished doctoral dissertation, MIT.

Andrews, A. (1975), "One(s) deletion in the comparative clause," in *Proceedings of the Fifth Meeting of the Northeastern Linguistics Society*, Harvard University, Cambridge, Mass.

Anscombe, G. E. M. (1965), "The intentionality of sensation," in R. J. Butler, ed., *Analytical Philosophy*, second series, Blackwell, Oxford.

Aronoff, M. (1972), "Studies in analogical pseudo-syntax I," unpublished ditto.

Aronoff, M. (1976), *Word Formation in Generative Grammar*, Linguistic Inquiry Monograph No. 1, MIT Press, Cambridge, Mass.

Bach, E. (1965), "On some recurrent types of transformations," in C. W. Kreidler, ed., *Sixteenth Annual Round Table Meeting on Linguistics and Language Studies*, Georgetown University Monograph Series on Language and Linguistics 18.

Bach, E. (1968), "Nouns and noun phrases," in Bach and Harms (1968).

Bach, E. (1971), "Questions," *Linguistic Inquiry* 2, 153-166.

Bach, E. (1974), *Syntactic Theory*, Holt, Rinehart and Winston, New York.

Bach, E. & R. T. Harms, eds., (1968), *Universals in Linguistic Theory*, Holt, Rinehart and Winston, New York.

Bach, E. (forthcoming), " 'The position of embedding transformations in a grammar' revisited," in a volume of papers from the International Summer School of Computational Linguistics (Pisa), ed. by A. Zampolli.

Bach, E. (forthcoming), "An extension of classical transformational grammar."

Bach, E. & G. G. Horn (forthcoming), "Remarks on 'Conditions on transformations'," *Linguistic Inquiry* 7, 265–299.

Baker, C. L. (1970), "Notes on the description of English questions: the role of an abstract question morpheme," *Foundations of Language* 6, 197–219.

Baker, C. (1976), "Comments on Culicover and Wexler's paper" in this volume.

Baker, C. L. (forthcoming), *Introduction to Generative-Transformational Syntax*, Prentice-Hall, Englewood Cliffs, N.J.

Banfield, A. (1973), "Narrative style and the grammar of direct and indirect speech," *Foundations of Language* 10, 1–39.

Beckhofer, R. (1975), "WHO said WHAT to WHOM?? . . . in Turkish," in S. Kuno, ed., *Harvard Studies in Syntax and Semantics* I, Cambridge, Mass.

Bell, S. (1976), *Subjects in Cebuano in Two Frameworks*, unpublished doctoral dissertation, MIT.

Berman, A. (1974), *Adjectives and Adjective Complement Constructions in English*, doctoral dissertation, Harvard University Formal Linguistics Report NSF–29, Susumu Kuno, principal investigator, Harvard University, Department of Linguistics.

Bolinger, D. (1971), *The Phrasal Verb in English*, Harvard University Press, Cambridge, Mass.

Bolinger, D. L. (1974), "Concept and percept: two infinitive constructuions and their vicissitudes," in *World Papers in Phonetics: Festschrift for Dr. Onishi's KIJU*, Phonetic Society of Japan, Tokyo.

Borkin, A. (1973), "To be and not to be," *Proceedings of the North Regional Meeting of the Chicago Linguistics Society*, University of Chicago.

Bowers, J. (1968), "Some adjectival nominalizations in English," unpublished ditto, MIT.

Bowers, J. (1970), "Adjectives and adverbs in English," unpublished ditto, Indiana University Linguistics Club, Bloomington, Ind.

Brame, M. (1975), "On the abstractness of syntactic structure: the VP controversy," *Linguistic Analysis* 1, 191–203.

Bresnan, J. (1970), "On complementizers: toward a sytactic theory of complement types," *Foundations of Language* 6, 297–321.

Bresnan, J. (1971), "On 'A non-source for comparatives'," *Linguistic Inquiry* 2

Bresnan, J. (1971a), "Contraction and the transformational cycle in English," unpublished mimeo, MIT.

Bresnan, J. (1971b), "On sentence stress and syntactic transformations," *Language* 47, 257–281.

Bresnan, J. (1972), *Theory of Complementation in English Syntax*, unpublished doctoral dissertation, MIT.

Bresnan, J. (1973), "Syntax of the comparative clause construction in English," *Linguistic Inquiry* 4, 275–343.

Bresnan, J. (1974), "On the position of certain clause-particles in phrase structure," *Linguistic Inquiry* 5, 614–619.

Bresnan, J. (1975a), "Comparative deletion and constraints on transformations," *Linguistic Analysis* 1, 25–74.

Bresnan, J. (1975b), "Transformations and categories in syntax," in R. Butts and J. Hintikka, eds., *Proceedings of the Fifth International Congress of Logic, Methodology, and Philosophy of Science*, University of Western Ontario, London, Ontario (forthcoming).

Bresnan, J. (1976a), "On the form and functioning of transformations," *Linguistic Inquiry* 7, 3–40.

Bresnan, J. (1976b), "Toward a realistic model of transformational grammar," paper presented at the MIT-AT&T Convocation of Communications, March 1976 at MIT.

Bresnan, J. (1976c), "Nonarguments for raising," *Linguistic Inquiry* 7.

Bresnan, J. (1976d), "Evidence for a theory of unbounded transformations," *Linguistic Analysis* 4, 353–394.

Bresnan, J. (1977), "A realistic transformational Grammar," in M. Halle, J. Bresnan, and G. Miller, eds., *Linguistic Theory and Psychological Reality*, in press, MIT Press, Cambridge, Mass.

Canale, M. (forthcoming), *Word Order Change: Base Re-analysis in Generative Grammar*, McGill University, Montreal.

Carlson, G. (1976), "Amount relatives," unpublished ditto, University of Massachusetts, Amherst.

Cattell, R. (1976), "Constraints on movement rules," *Language* **52**, 18–50.

Chomsky, N. (1955), *The Logical Structure of Linguistic Theory*, Plenum Press, N. Y.

Chomsky, N. (1957), *Syntactic Structures*, Mouton, The Hague.

Chomsky, N. (1961), "On the notion 'rule of grammar'," *Proceedings of Symposia in Applied Mathematics* **12**, *Structure of Language and its Mathematical Aspects*. Reprinted in Fodor and Katz (1964).

Chomsky, N. (1962), "Explanatory models in linguistics," in Nagel, Suppes, and Tarski, eds., *Logic, Methodology and Philosophy of Science, Proceedings of the 1960 International Congress*. Stanford University Press.

Chomsky, N. (1964), *Current Issues in Linguistic Theory*, Mouton, The Hague.

Chomsky, N. (1965), *Aspects of the Theory of Syntax*, MIT Press, Cambridge, Mass.

Chomsky, N. (1970), "Remarks on nominalization," in Jacobs and Rosenbaum (1970).

Chomsky, N. (1971), *Problems of Knowledge and Freedom*, Pantheon Books, New York.

Chomsky, N. (1972a), *Language and Mind*, Harcourt Brace Jovanovich, New York.

Chomsky, N. (1972b), "Some empirical issues in the theory of transformational grammar," in Peters (1972).

Chomsky, N. (1972c), *Studies on Semantics in Generative Grammar*, Mouton, The Hague.

Chomsky, N. (1973), "Conditions on transformations," in Anderson & Kiparsky (1973).

Chomsky, N. (1974), "The Amherst lectures," (Lectures given at the 1974 Linguistic Institute, University of Massachusetts, Amherst, June 1974.) Université de Paris VII, Département de Recherches Linguistiques.

Chomsky, N. (1975a), "Questions of form and interpretation," *Linguistic Analysis* **1**, 75–109.

Chomsky, N. (1975b), *Reflections on Language*, Pantheon, New York.

Chomsky, N. (1975c), "Conditions on rules of grammar," to appear in R. Cole, ed., *Current Issues in Linguistic Theory*, Indiana University Press.

Chomsky, N. (1976), "On *wh*-movement," in this volume.

Chomsky, N. & M. Halle (1968), *The Sound Pattern of English*, Harper and Row, New York.

Chomsky, N. and H. Lasnik (forthcoming), "Filters and Control," *Linguistic Inquiry*.

Chomsky, N. & G. Miller (1958), "Finite state languages," in Luce, Bush & Galanter, eds., *Readings in Mathematical Psychology*, John Wiley and Sons, 1964.

Church, A. (1941), *The Calculi of Lambda Conversion*, Princeton University Press, Princeton, New Jersey.

Cooper, R. (1975), *Montague's Semantic Theory and Transformational Syntax*, unpublished doctoral dissertation, University of Massachusetts, Amherst.

Creamer, M. H. (1974), "Ranking in Navajo nouns," *Diné Bizaad Nániłįįh/Navajo Language Review* **1**, 29–38.

Culicover, P. W. (1976), "A constraint on coreference," *Foundations of Language* **12**, 53–62.

Culicover, P. W. (forthcoming), "Comparative movement."

Culicover, P. W. & K. Wexler (1973a), "An application of the freezing principle to the dative in English," *Social Sciences Working Paper* **39**, University of California, Irvine.

Culicover, P. W. & K. Wexler (1973b), "Three further applications of the freezing principle in English," *Social Sciences Working Paper* **48**, University of California, Irvine.

Culicover, P. & K. Wexler (1976), "Some syntactic implications of a theory of language learnability," in this volume.

Davidson, D. & G. Harman, eds., (1972), *Semantics of Natural Languages*, Reidel, Dordrecht, Holland.

Davis, C. & L. Hellan (1975), "The syntax and semantics of comparative constructions," unpublished paper, Notre Dame University.

Dean, J. (1967), "Noun phrase complementation in English and German," unpublished mimeo, MIT.

deRijk, R. (1972), *Studies in Basque Syntax: Relative Clauses*, unpublished doctoral dissertation, MIT.

Dixon, R. M. W. (1972), *The Dyirbal Language of North Queensland*, Cambridge University Press, Cambridge.

Dougherty, R. C. (1968), *A Transformational Grammar of Coordinate Conjoined Structures*, unpublished doctoral dissertation, MIT.

Dougherty, R. C. (1969), "An interpretive theory of pronominal reference," *Foundations of Language* 5, 488-519.

Dougherty, R. C. (1974), "The syntax and semantics of *each other* constructions," *Foundations of Language* 12.

Dretsky, F. (1969), *Seeing and Knowing*, University of Chicago Press, Chicago, Illinois.

Emonds, J. E. (1970), *Root and Structure Preserving Transformations*, unpublished ditto, Indiana University Linguistics Club, Bloomington, Indiana.

Emonds, J. E. (1972a), "Evidence that indirect object movement is a structure-preserving rule," *Foundations of Language* 8, 546-561.

Emonds, J. E. (1972b), "A reformulation of certain syntactic transformations," in Peters (1972).

Emonds, J. E. (1974), "Parenthetical clauses," in C. Rohrer & M. Ruwet, eds., *Actes du Colloque Franco-Allemand de Grammaire Transformationelle*, Max Niemeyer Verlag, Tübingen.

Emonds, J. E. (1976), *A Transformational Approach to English Syntax: Root, Structure-preserving, and Local Transformations*, Academic Press, New York.

Erteschik, N. (1973), *On the Nature of Island Constraints*, unpublished doctoral dissertation, MIT.

Evers, A. (1975), *The Transformational Cycle in Dutch and German*, Utrecht, Holland.

Faraci, R. (1974), *Aspects of the Grammar of Infinitives and For-Phrases*, unpublished doctoral dissertation, MIT.

Fauconnier, G. (1971), *Theoretical Implications of Some Global Phenomena in Syntax*, unpublished doctoral dissertation, University of California, San Diego.

Fauconnier, G. (1975), "Pragmatic scales and logical structure," *Linguistic Inquiry* 6, 353-376.

Fiengo, R. (1974), *Semantic Conditions on Surface Structure*, unpublished doctoral dissertation, MIT.

Fiengo, R. & H. Lasnik (1973), "Logical structure of reciprocal sentences," *Foundations of Language* 9, 447-468.

Fiengo, R. & H. Lasnik (1976), "Some issues in the theory of transformations," *Linguistic Inquiry* 7, 82-191.

Fillmore, C. J. (1963), "The position of embedding transformation in a grammar," *Word* 19, 208-231.

Fillmore, C. J. (1965), *Indirect Object Construction in English and the Ordering of Transformations* (Monographs in Linguistic Analysis 1), Mouton, The Hague.

Fodor, J. A. (1970), "Three reasons for not deriving 'kill' from 'cause to die'," *Linguistic Inquiry* 1, 429-438.

Fodor, J. A. (1975), *The Language of Thought*, Crowell, New York.

Fodor, J. D., J. A. Fodor, & M. F. Garrett (1975), "The psychological unreality of semantic representations," *Linguistic Inquiry* 6, 515-531.

Fodor. J. D., & J. J. Katz (1964), *The Structure of Language: Readings in Philosophy of Language*, Prentice-Hall, Englewood Cliffs, N. J.

Freidin, R. (1974), "Transformations and interpretive semantics," in R. Shuy & N. Bailey, eds., *Towards Tomorrow's Linguistics*, Georgetown University Press, Washington, D.C.

Freidin, R. (1975), "The analysis of passives," *Language* 51, 384-405.

Friedman, J. (1973), "Essential variables in mathematical and computational models of transformational grammar," in R. Rustin, ed., *Natural Language Processing*, Prentice-Hall, Englewood Cliffs, N.J.

Friedman, J. et al. (1971), *A Computer Model of Transformational Grammar*, American Elsevier, New York.

Gee, J. (1975), *Perception, Intentionality and Naked Infinitives: A Study in Linguistics and Philosophy*, unpublished doctoral dissertation, Stanford University.

Gee, J. P. (1976a), "The de dicto/de re and transparent/opaque distinctions," Stanford University.

Gee, J. P. (1976b), "De dicto readings, generics and concrete logic," unpublished paper, Stanford University.

Gold, E. M. (1967), "Language identification in the limit," *Information and Control* **10**, 447–474.

Goldsmith, J. (1976), *Autosegmental Phonology*, unpublished doctoral dissertation, MIT.

Green, G. (1973), *Semantics and Syntactic Regularity*, Indiana University Press, Bloomington.

Greenberg, J. (1963), "Some universals of grammar with particular reference to the order of meaningful elements," in J. Greenberg, ed., *Universals of Language*, MIT Press, Cambridge, Mass.

Grimes, J. (1967), *Huichol Syntax*, Mouton, The Hague.

Grimshaw, J. (1975), "Adjectival complements in noun phrases," unpublished mimeo, University of Massachusetts, Amherst.

Grimshaw, J. (1975) "Relativization by deletion in Chaucerian Middle English," in *Proceedings of the Fifth Annual Meeting of the Northeast Linguistic Society*, Harvard University, 1974.

Grosu, A. (1975), "The position of fronted WH phrases," *Linguistic Inquiry* **6**, 588–598.

Gruber, J. (1965), *Studies in Lexical Relations*, unpublished doctoral dissertation, MIT, available from Indiana University Linguistics Club.

Hale, K. (1969), "Papago čim," *IJAL* **35**, 203–212.

Hale, K. (1973), "A note on subject–object inversion in Navajo," in Kachru et al., eds., *Issues in Linguistics: Papers in Honor of Henry and Rene Kahane*, University of Illinois Press.

Hale, K. (1975), "Information and word order in Papago," unpublished paper, MIT.

Hale, K. (1976), "Linguistic autonomy and the linguistics of Carl Voegelin," *Anthropological Linguistics*, forthcoming.

Hale, K. & P. Platero (1974), "Aspects of Navajo anaphora: relativization and pronominalization," *Diné Bizaad Nániłįįh/Navajo Language Review* **1**, 9–29.

Halitzky, D. (1975), "Left branch S's and NP's in English; a Bar Notation analysis," *Linguistic Analysis* **1**, 279–296.

Hamburger, H. & K. Wexler (1973), "Identifiability of a class of transformational grammars," in Hintikka, Moravcsik, and Suppes (1973).

Hamburger, H. & K. Wexler (1975), "A mathematical theory of learning transformational grammar," *Journal of Mathematical Psychology* **12**, 137–177.

Hankamer, J. (1971), *Constraints on Deletion in Syntax*, unpublished doctoral dissertation, Yale University.

Hankamer, J. (1973), "Why there are two than's in English" in *Papers from the Ninth Regional Meeting of the Chicago Linguistics Society*, University of Chicago.

Hankamer, J. (1975), "On Wh-indexing," in *Proceedings of the Fifth Annual Meeting of the Northeastern Linguistic Society*, Harvard University, Cambridge, Mass.

Haraguchi, S. (1975), *The Tone Pattern of Japanese*, unpublished doctoral dissertation, MIT.

Helke, M. (1971), *The Grammar of English Reflexives*, unpublished doctoral dissertation, MIT.

Higgins, F. (1973), "On J. Emonds's analysis of extraposition," in J. Kimball, ed., *Syntax and Semantics* **II**, Seminar Press, New York.

Hintikka, J. (1969), *Models for Modalities*, D. Reidel, Dodrecht, Holland.

Hintikka, J., J. M. E. Moravcsik, & P. Suppes, eds. (1973), *Approaches to Natural Language*, D. Reidel, Dodrecht, Holland.

Horn, G. M. (1974), *The Noun Phrase Constraint*, unpublished doctoral dissertation, University of Massachusetts, Amherst.

Horn, G. M. (1976), "On the nonsentential nature of the poss-ing construction," *Linguistic Analysis* **1**, 333–388.

Horn, G. M. (forthcoming), "The nonapplicability of certain transformations into noun phrases."

Hornstein, N. (1975), "S and the $\overline{X}$ convention," *Recherches Linguistiques à Montréal/Montreal Working Papers in Linguistics* 4

Hubbard, P. & R. van den Heuvel (1974), "Deletion of to be deletion," unpublished paper, Stanford University.

Huddleston, R. (1971), "A problem in relative clause reduction," *Linguistic Inquiry* 2, 115–116.

Hudson, R. (1972), "Why it is that that that that follows the subject is impossible," *Linguistic Inquiry* 3, 116–118.

Jackendoff, R. S. (1968), "Quantifiers in English," *Foundations of Language* 4, 422–442.

Jackendoff, R. S. (1969), "Speculations on presentences and determiners," Indiana University Linguistics Club, Bloomington, Ind.

Jackendoff, R. S. (1971), "Gapping and related rules," *Linguistic Inquiry* 2, 21–35.

Jackendoff, R. S. (1972), *Semantic Interpretation in Generative Grammar*, MIT Press, Cambridge, Mass.

Jackendoff, R. S. (1973), "The base rules for prepositional phrases," in Anderson & Kiparsky (1973).

Jackendoff, R. S. (1974a), "Introduction to the $\overline{X}$ convention," unpublished ditto, Indiana University Linguistics Club, Bloomington, Ind.

Jackendoff, R. S. (1974b), "A deep structure projection rule," *Linguistic Inquiry* 5, 481–506.

Jackendoff, R. S. (1975a), "On belief-contexts," *Linguistic Inquiry* 6.

Jackendoff, R. S. (1975b), "*Tough* and the trace theory of movement rules," *Linguistic Inquiry* 6, 437–446.

Jackendoff, R. S. (1975c), "Morphological and semantic regularities in the lexicon," *Language* 51, 639–671.

Jackendoff, R. S. (1976), "Toward an explanatory semantic representation," *Linguistic Inquiry* 7, 89–150.

Jackendoff, R. S. (forthcoming), *X Syntax: A Study of Phrase Structure*, Linguistic Inquiry Monograph No. 2.

Jackendoff, R. S. & P. W. Culicover (1971), "A reconsideration of dative movement," *Foundations of Language* 7, 397–412.

Jacobs, R. & P. Rosenbaum (1970), *Readings in English Transformational Grammar*, Blaisdell, Waltham, Mass.

Jeanne, L. M. (1974), "Reduplication and tone in Hopi Nouns," unpublished paper, MIT.

Jeanne, L. M. (1975), "A reconsideration of the relative clause in Hopi," unpublished paper, MIT.

Jenkins, L. (1975), "The COMP condition." in G. Drachman, ed., *Akten der I. Satzburger Frühlingstagung für Linguistik*, Narr. Tübingen.

Jespersen, O. (1909–49), *A Modern English Grammar on Historical Principles*, Vols. 1–7, Allen and Unwin, London.

Jespersen, O. (1965), *The Philosophy of Grammar*, W. W. Norton, New York.

Kageyama, T. (1975), "Relational grammar and the history of Subject Raising," *Glossa* 9, 165–181.

Karttunen, L. (1975), "Syntax and semantics of question," unpublished paper, University of Texas, Austin, Texas.

Katz, J. J. (1966), *The Philosophy of Language*, Harper and Row, New York.

Katz, J. J. (1972), *Semantic Theory*, Harper and Row, New York.

Katz, J. J. & J. A. Fodor (1964), "The structure of a semantic theory," in Fodor and Katz (1964).

Katz, J. J. & P. Postal (1964), *An Intergrated Theory of Linguistic Descriptions*, MIT Press, Cambridge, Mass.

Kayne, R. (1969), "On the inappropriateness of rule features," *Quarterly Progress Report, RLE* 95, MIT.

Kayne, R. (1975) *French Syntax: The Transformational Cycle*, MIT Press, Cambridge, Mass.

Keenan, E. (1972), "On semantically based grammar," *Linguistic Inquiry* 3, 413–461.

Keenan, E. (1975), "Some universals of passive in relational grammar," *Papers from the Eleventh Regional Meeting of the Chicago Linguistics Society,* University of Chicago.

Keenan, E. & B. Comrie (1972), "NP accessibility and universal grammar," *Linguistic Inquiry* 8, 63–100.

Kim, W. C. (1976), *The Theory of Anaphora in Korean Syntax*, unpublished doctoral dissertation, MIT.

Kiparsky, P. (1973), "Phonological representations," in O. Fujimura, ed., *Three Dimensions of Linguistic Theory*, TEC Company, Tokyo.

Kiparsky, P. & C. Kiparsky (1970), "Fact," in M. Bierwisch and K. Heidolph, eds., *Progress in Linguistics*, Mouton, The Hague.

Klima, E. (1964), "Relatedness between grammatical systems," reprinted in Reibel & Schane (1969).

Kuno, S. (1973), *The Structure of the Japanese Language*, MIT Press, Cambridge, Mass.

Kuno, S. (1973), "Constraints on internal clauses and sentential subjects," *Linguistic Inquiry* 4, 363–386.

Kuno, S. & J. Robinson (1972), "Multiple WH questions," *Linguistic Inquiry* 3, 463–488.

Kuroda, S.-Y (1969), "English relativization and certain related problems," in Reibel & Schane (1969).

Lakoff, G. (1970a), "Global rules," *Language*, **46**, 627–639.

Lakoff, G. (1970b), "Repartee," *Foundations of Language*, 6, 389–422.

Lakoff, G. (1970c), *Irregularity in Syntax*, Holt, Rinehart and Winston, New York.

Lakoff, G. (1971a), "Presupposition and relative well-formedness," in Steinberg & Jakobovits (1971).

Lakoff, G. (1971b), "On generative semantics," in Steinberg & Jakobovits (1971).

Lakoff, G. (1974), Interview in H. Parret (1974) *Discussing Language*, Mouton, The Hague.

Lakoff, G. & J. R. Ross (1966), "A criterion for verb phrase constituency," in A. Oettinger, ed., *Mathematical Linguistic and Automatic Translation*, Report NSF-17, Harvard Computation Laboratory.

Langacker, R. and P. Munro (1975), "Passives and their meaning," *Language* **51**. 789–830.

Langerdoen, D. (1970), "The accessibility of deep structures," in Jacobs & Rosenbaum (1970).

Lasnik, H. (forthcoming), "Remarks on coreference," *Linguisitc Analysis* 2. 1–22.

Lasnik, H. & J. Kupin (forthcoming), "A restrictive theory of transformational grammar."

Lasnik, H. & R. Fiengo (1974),"Complement object deletion," *Linguistic Inquiry* 5, 535–571.

Lees, R. B. (1957), "Review of Syntactic Structures," *Language* 33, 375–407.

Lees, R. B. (1960a), *The Grammar of English Nominalizations*, Mouton, The Hague.

Lees, R. B. (1960b), "A multiply ambiguous adjectival construction in English," *Language* **36**, 207–221.

Lightfoot, D. W. (1974), "The diachronic analysis of English modals," in J. Anderson & C. Jones, eds., *Historical Linguistics I: Proceedings of the First International Conference on Historical Linguistics*, North Holland, Amsterdam.

Lightfoot, D. W. (1975), "Diachronic syntax: extraposition and deep structure reanalyses," *Proceedings of the Fifth Meeting of the Northeastern Linguisitc Society*, Harvard University, Cambridge. Mass.

Lightfoot, D. W. (1976a), "The theoretical importance of subject raising," *Foundations of Language*, **14**.

Lightfoot, D. W. (1976b), "The base component as a locus of syntactic change," in W. Christie, ed., *Proceedings of the Second International Conference on Historical Linguistics*, North Holland, Amsterdam.

Lightfoot, D. W. (1976c), "Trace theory and twice moved NP's." *Linguistic Inquiry* 7, 559–582.

Lightfoot, D. W. (1976d), "Syntactic change and the autonomy thesis," in C. Li, ed., *Mechanisms of Syntactic Change*, University of Texas Press, Austin.

Lightfoot, D. W. (forthcoming), *Diachronic Syntax and Generative Grammar*.

Lujan, M. (1976), "Proclisis and mood in Spanish," Paper read at the Romance Linguistics Conference, Université de Montréal.

Maling, J. (1976), "Old Icelandic relative clauses," unpublished paper, Brandeis University.

McCawley, J. D. (1968a), "The role of semantics in a grammar," in Bach and Harms (1968).

McCawley, J. (1968b), "Lexical insertion in a transformational grammar without deep structure," in *Papers from the Fourth Regional Meeting of the Chicago Linguistics Society*, University of Chicago.

McCawley, J. (1970a), "Where do noun phrases come from," in Jacobs & Rosenbaum (1970).

McCawley, J. (1970b), "Syntactic and logical arguments for semantic studies," in O. Fujimura, ed., *Three Dimensions of Linguistic Theory*, TEC Company, Tokyo.

McCawley, J. (1970c), Introduction to Lakoff (1970c).

McCawley, J. (1973), "The annotated respective," in J. McCawley, *Grammar and Meaning*, Taishukan Publishing Co., Tokyo.

McCawley, J. (1975), "The category status of English modals," *Foundations of Language* **12**, 597-601.

Milner, J.-C. (1975), *Quelques Opérations de Détermination en Français: Syntaxe et Interprétation*, These de doctorat d'état, Paris.

Milsark, G. L. (1974), *Existential Sentences in English*, unpublished doctoral dissertation, MIT.

Montague, R. (1973), "The proper treatment of quantification in ordinary English," in Hintikka, Moravcsik, & Suppes (1973).

Morgan, J. (1972), "Some aspects of relative clauses in English and Albanian," in *Chicago Which Hunt, Papers from the Relative Clause Festival, April 13, 1972*, available from The Chicago Linguistic Society, Foster 19, 1130 East 59th Street, Chicago, Illinois 60637.

Morin, J.-Y. (1975), "Old French clitics and the Extended Standard Theory," in *Papers from the Eleventh Regional Meeting of the Chicago Linguistic Society*, University of Chicago.

Newmeyer, F. (1969), "English aspectual verbs," *Studies in Linguistics and Language Learning*, **VI**, University of Washington, Seattle, Washington.

Newmeyer, F. (1974), "The precyclic nature of predicate raising," presented at the USC Causative Festival, May, 1974.

Oehrle, R. (1974), "Some remarks on the painting of Rembrandt," in *Papers from the Tenth Regional Meeting of the Chicago Linguistic Society*, University of Chicago.

Oehrle, R. (1975), *The Grammatical Status of the English Dative Alternation*, unpublished doctoral dissertation, MIT.

Osherson, D. & T. Wasow (1976), "Task-specificity and species-specificity in the study of language: a methodological note," *Cognition* **4**.

Partee, B. (1972), "Opacity, coreference, and pronouns," in Davidson & Harman (1972).

Partee, B. (1973), "Some transformational extensions of Montague Grammar," *Journal of Philosophical Logic* **2**; reprinted in B. Partee, ed., *Montague Grammar*, Academic Press, New York.

Partee, B. (1975a), "Comments on Chomsky's address," in R. Austerlitz, ed., *The Scope of American Linguistics*, Peter de Ridder Press, Lisse.

Partee, B. (1975b), "Deletion and variable binding," in E. Keenan, ed., *Formal Semantics of Natural Language*, Cambridge University Press, Cambridge.

Partee, B. (1975c), "Montague Grammar and transformational grammar," *Linguistic Inquiry* **6**, 203-300.

Partee, B., ed., (1976), *Montague Grammar*, Academic Press, New York.

Perlmutter, D. (1971), *Deep and Surface Structure Constraints in Syntax*, Holt, Rinehart and Winston, New York.

Peters, S. (1972), *Goals of Linguistic Theory*, Prentice-Hall, Englewood Cliffs, N. J.

Peters, S. (1973), "On restricting deletion transformations," in M. Gross, M. Halle, & M.-P. Schutzenberger, eds., *The Formal Analysis of Natural Language*, Mouton, The Hague.

Peters, S. & R. Ritchie (1973), "On the generative power of tranformational grammars," *Information Sciences* **6**.

Pinkham, J. & J. Hankamer (1975), "Deep and shallow clefts," in *Papers from the Eleventh Regional Meeting of the Chicago Linguistics Society*, University of Chicago.

Platero, P. (1974), "The Navajo relative clause," *IJAL* **40**, 202–246.

Pollock, J.-Y. (1976), "Théorie des traces et syntaxe du francais: quelques problemes," unpublished mimeo, Vincennes.

Postal, P. (1964a), *Constituent Structure*, Indiana University Research Center Publications in Anthropology, Folklore, and Linguistics **30**.

Postal, P. (1964b), "Limitations of phrase structure grammars," in Fodor & Katz, (1964).

Postal, P. (1965), "Developments in the theory of transformational grammar," mimeo, MIT. Translated as "Novy vyvoj teorie transformacni grammatiky," *Slovo a Slovesnost*, Ceskoslovenska Academie fed, **26** (1965).

Postal, P. (1971), *Cross-Over Phenomena*, Holt, Rinehart and Winston, New York.

Postal, P. (1972a), "On some rules that are not successive cyclic," *Linguistic Inquiry* **3**, 211–222.

Postal, P. (1972b), "Some further limitations of interpretive theories of anaphora, *Linguistic Inquiry* **3**, 349–372.

Postal, P. (1972c), "The best theory," in Peters (1972).

Postal, P. (1974a), *On Raising*, MIT Press, Cambridge, Mass.

Postal, P. (1974b), "On certain ambiguities," *Linguistic Inquiry* **5**, 367–424.

Postal, P. (1976), "Avoiding reference to subject," *Linguistic Inquiry* **7**, 151–181.

Quicoli, A. C. (forthcoming a), "Conditions on clitic movement," *Linguistic Analysis* **2**, 199–224.

Quicoli, A. C. (forthcoming b), "Conditions on quantifier movement in French," *Linguistic Inquiry* **7**, 583–608.

Quicoli, A. C. (forthcoming c), "Clitic movement in French causatives."

Quine, W. V. O. (1966), "Variables explained away," in W. V. O. Quine, *Selected Logic Papers*, Random House, New York.

Radford, A. (1976), "Constraints on clitic promotion in Italian," Paper read at the Fourth Romance Linguistics Seminar, Cambridge.

Reichenbach, H. (1947), *Elements of Symbolic Logic*, Macmillan, New York.

Reinhart, T. (1974), "Syntax and coreference," in *Proceedings of the Fifth Annual Meeting of the Northeastern Linguistic Society*, Harvard University, Cambridge, Mass.

Robinson, O. (1976), "A 'scattered' rule in Swiss German," *Language* **52**, 148–162.

Rodman, R. (1976), "Scope phenomena, 'Movement transformations and transformational grammar'," in Partee (1976).

Ronat, M. (1973), "Une contrainte sur l'effacement du nom," in *Recherches Linguisticques*, **III**, Université de Paris VIII, Vincennes.

Rosenbaum, P. (1967), *The Grammar of English Predicate Complement Constructions*, MIT Press, Cambridge, Mass.

Ross, J. R. (1967), *Constraints on Variables in Syntax*, unpublished doctoral dissertation, MIT.

Ross, J. (1969a), "Guess who?," in *Papers from the Sixth Regional Meeting of the Chicago Linguistic Society*, University of Chicago.

Ross, J. R. (1969b), "Adjectives as noun phrases," in Reibel & Schane (1969).

Ross, J. R. (1969c), "A proposed rule of tree-pruning," in Reibel & Schane (1969).

Ross, J. R, (1970), "On declarative sentences," in Jacobs & Rosenbaum (1970).

Ross, J. R. (1970), "Primacy," unpublished mimeo, MIT.

Ross, J. R. (1973), "Nouniness," in O. Fujimura, ed., *Three Dimensions of Linguistic Theory*, TEC Company, Tokyo.

Ross, K. (1976), "Quantifiers and the structure of the noun prhase in English," unpublished paper, University of Massachusetts, Amherst.

Sag, I. (1976), *Deletion and Logical Form*, unpublished doctoral dissertation, MIT.

Sag, I. (forthcoming), "A logical theory of verb phrase deletion," in *Papers from the Twelfth Regional Meeting of the Chicago Linguistics Society*, University of Chicago.

Sag, I. & J. Hankamer (1976), "Deep and surface anaphora," *Linguistic Inquiry* **7**, 391–428.

Sanders, G. (ms), "Invariant ordering," Indiana University.

Saxton, D. & L. Saxton (1969), *Dictionary, Papago and Pima to English, English to Papago and Pima*, University of Arizona Press, Tucson.

Schachter, P. (1976), "A nontransformational account of gerundive nominals in English," *Linguistic Inquiry* 7, 205–241.

Selkirk, E. (1970), "On the determiner system of noun phrase and adjective phrase," unpublished paper, MIT.

Selkirk, E. (1972), *The Phrase Phonology of English and French*, unpublished doctoral dissertation, MIT.

Selkirk, E. (1974), "French liaison and the $\overline{X}$ notation," *Linguistic Inquiry* 5, 573–590.

Selkirk, E. (1975), "Determiners, quantifiers and measure phrases in English," unpublished ditto, University of Massachusetts, Amherst.

Selkirk, E. (1976) "Some remarks on noun phrase structure," in this volume.

Selkirk, E. (forthcoming), *Phonology and Syntax: The Relation Between Sound and Structure*, MIT Press, Cambridge, Mass.

Siegel, D. (1970), "Non-sources for un-passives," in J. Kimball, ed., *Syntax and Semantics* II, Seminar Press, New York.

Siegel, D. (1974), *Topics in English Morphology*, unpublished doctoral dissertation, MIT, Cambridge, Mass.

Siegel, E. (1976), *Capturing the Adjective*, unpublished doctoral dissertation, University of Massachusetts, Amherst.

Steinberg, D. & L. A. Jakobovits, eds., (1971), *Semantics: An Interdisciplinary Reader in Philosophy, Linguistics, and Psychology*.

Steele, S. (1975), *The Auxiliary in Uto-Aztecan: Comparison and Reconstruction*, unpublished ms., Stanford University.

Sterba, V. (1972), "A grammar of conditions on transformations," unpublished mimeo, University of Massachusetts, Amherst.

Stockwell, R., P. Schachter & B. Partee (1973), *The Major Syntactic Structures of English*, Holt, Rinehart and Winston, New York.

Stillings, J. (1975), "The formulation of gapping in English as evidence for variable types in syntactic transformations," *Linguistic Analysis* 1, 247–274.

Sweet, H. (1900), *A New English Grammar: Logical and Historical*, Clarendon Press, Oxford.

Thomason, R. (1976), "Some extensions of Montague grammar," in Partee (1976).

Traugott, E. (1965), "Diachronic syntax and generative grammar," *Language* 41, 402–415.

Venneman, T. (1974), "Topics, subjects, and word order: from SXV to SVX via TVX," in J. Anderson & C. Jones, eds., *Historical Linguistics I*, Proceedings of the First International Conference on Historical Linguistics, North-Holland, Amsterdam.

Vergnaud, J.-R. (1973), *French Relative Clauses*, unpublished doctoral dissertation, MIT, Cambridge, Mass.

Vergnaud, J.-R. (1975), "La réduction du noeud S. dans les relatives et les comparatives," ditto, Centre National de la Recherche Scientifique, Laboratoire, d'Automatique Documentaire et Linguistique, France.

Visser, F. (1963), *An Historical Syntax of the English Language*, 1–3b, E. J. Brill, Leiden.

Voegelin, C. F. (1955), "On developing new typologies and revising old ones," *SJA* 11, 355–360.

Voegelin, C. F., A. K. Ramanijan, & F. M. Voegelin (1960), "Typology of density ranges I: introduction," *IJAL* 26, 198–205.

Voegelin, C. F. & F. M. Voegelin (1975), "Hopi /-ga/," *IJAL* 41, 381–398.

Wanner, E. & M. Maratsos (1974), "An augmented transition network model of relative clause comprehension," ditto, Harvard University.

Wasow, T. (1972), *Anaphoric Relations in English*, unpublished doctoral dissertation, MIT.

Wasow, T. (1975), "Anaphoric pronouns and bound variables," *Language* 51, 368–383.

Wasow, T. (1976) "Transformations and the lexicon," in this volume.

Wasow, T. (forthcoming), "McCawley on Generative Semantics: Review of *Grammar and Meaning* by James McCawley," *Linguistic Analysis* **2**, 279–301.

Wexler, K. & P. W. Culicover (1974), "The semantic basis for language acquisition," *Social Sciences Working Paper* **50**, University of California, Irvine.

Wexler, K., P. W. Culicover, & H. Hamburger (1975), "Learning-theoretic foundations of linguistic universals," *Theoretical Linguistics* **2**, 213–253.

Wexler, K., P. W. Culicover, & H. Hamburger (forthcoming), *Formal Principles of Language Acquisition*.

Wexler, K. & H. Hamburger (1973), "On the insufficiency of surface data for the learning of transformational languages," in Hintikka, Moravcsik, and Suppes, (1973).

Whorf, B. L. (1946), "The Hopi language, Toreva dialect," in H. Hoijer, ed., *Linguistic Structures of Native America*, Viking Fund Publications in Anthropology, New York.

Williams, E. (1975), "Small clauses in English," in J. Kimball, ed., *Syntax and Semantics,* **4**, Seminar Press, New York.

Williams, E. (forthcoming), "Discourse grammar," *Linguistic Inquiry* **8**, 101–140.

Woisetschlaeger, E. (1976), "Conditions on mixed terms," unpublished mimeo, MIT.

Woods, W. (1973), "An experimental parsing system for transition network grammars," in R. Rustin, ed., *Natural Language Processing*, Prentice-Hall, Englewood Cliffs, New Jersey.

Young, R. & W. Morgan (1943), *The Navaho Language* Education Division, U. S. Indian Service.

INDEX